The Politics and Process of
AMERICAN GOVERNMENT

The Politics and Process of
AMERICAN GOVERNMENT

★ ★

Robert S. Getz
State University of New York at Brockport

Frank B. Feigert
North Texas State University

Allyn and Bacon, Inc.   Boston   London   Sydney   Toronto

Production Editor: Nancy Doherty

LIBRARY OF CONGRESS CATALOGING IN PUBLICATION DATA

Getz, Robert S.
    The politics and process of American government.

    Includes bibliographies and index.
    1. United States—Politics and government.   I. Feigert, Frank B.   II. Title.
JK274.G43   320.973   81-3619
ISBN 0-205-06862-6   AACR2

        10 9 8 7 6 5 4 3 2 1   87 86 85 84 83 82
Printed in the United States of America.

CREDITS   Chapter 1: p. 2, photo © George W. Gardner; p. 4, photo © Dennis Brack 1980/Black Star; p. 5, photo by Tom Zimberoff/Sygma; p. 6, photo by Owen Franken/Sygma; p. 10, photo by Bulka-Siccoli-Wildenberg-Simon/Gamma-Liason; p. 11, photo by Owen Franken/Stock, Boston; p. 12, photo © Emilio Mercado/Jeroboam, Inc.; p. 13, photo by P. Ledru/Sygma.

Chapter 2: p. 16, photo by Talbot Lovering (Allyn and Bacon, Inc., staff photographer); p. 18, photo by Leonard Freed/© Magnum Photos, Inc.; p. 21, photo by Owen Franken/Sygma; p. 22, photo © Evan Johnson/Jeroboam, Inc.; p. 24, photo © Kent Reno/Jeroboam, Inc.; p. 25, photo by Bruce Davidson/© 1970 Magnum Photos, Inc.; p. 29, photo © Mark Godfrey/Magnum Photos, Inc.; p. 37, photo by Jean-Claude Lejeune/Stock, Boston; p. 40, photo by Frank Siteman/Stock, Boston; p. 46, photo by United Press International.

Chapter 3: p. 52, photo by Jean-Claude Lejeune/Stock, Boston; p. 54, photo © George W. Gardner; p. 57, photo by Henri Cartier-Bresson/© Magnum Photos, Inc.; p. 59, photo by Alex Webb/© Magnum Photos, Inc.; p. 60, photo on the left © Bob Adelman/Magnum Photos, Inc.; p. 60, photo on the right by United Press International; p. 65, photo by Paul S. Conklin; p. 66, Figure 3–1, Data from U.S. Bureau of the Census, *Statistical Abstract of the United States, 1977 and 1979,* Tables 472, 481, 525, pp. 283, 290, 329; p. 67, Figure 3–2, Data from U.S. Bureau of the Census, *Statistical Abstract of the United States, 1979,* Table 472, p. 283; p. 69, photo © Frank Siteman 1980/Stock, Boston; p. 70, Figure 3–3, Data from U.S. Bureau of the Census, *Statistical Abstract of the United States, 1979,* Table 522, pp. 326–327; p. 74, photo by Nicholas Saphieha/Stock, Boston; p. 75, Figure 3–4, Data from U.S. Bureau of the Census, *Statistical Abstract of the United States, 1979,* Table 509, p. 313; p. 76, photo by Joe Rychetnik/Photo Researchers; p. 78, photo by George Bellerose/Stock, Boston; p. 80, Figure 3–5, Data from U.S. Bureau of the Census, *Statistical Abstract of the United States, 1979,* Table 522, pp. 326–327.

(*Credits continued on page 589*)

this book is dedicated

 to our fathers—classmates, 1923—
 and to our families

Contents

Preface to the Instructor

We began this book shortly after Jimmy Carter took office and conclude in the first year of Ronald Reagan's presidency. It has become almost a cliche to say that we are now in, or have passed through, an unsettling era in American government. But there is usually truth in cliches. Five presidents in twenty years is not the norm. The resignations of a vice-president and a president are also without parallel. Now the partisan forces which shape our country appear to be undergoing change as well. From 1933 to 1981, the Congress had been Democratic in all but four years. Republicans held the White House for only sixteen years in that period. Ronald Reagan's 1980 victory was accompanied by Republican strength sufficient to capture the Senate. And those who are willing to vote, now slightly more than half of the eligibles, may very well have more surprises in store for us. Interest groups are also reshaping their influence upon the system. This is helped, in part, by changes in the laws which have regulated them and by widespread frustration with one or another set of policies.

As evidenced in the Reagan administration's dramatic departures from the policies of the previous forty-eight years, government policy decisions inevitably result in situations of winning and losing, with payoffs and losses that affect all of us. This theme is returned to throughout the book. It is both meaningful and inherently interesting to students; it is a useful vehicle for exploring the many achievements of our system, as well as its shortcomings; and it serves to keep students engaged in the learning process. But we have kept the theme light so that it never obscures the essential facts and substance of the political process.

We have made extensive use of contemporary examples to illustrate major points and concepts, and we have used boxed inserts, quotations, simple tables and charts, chapter summaries, a glossary of key terms, and end-of-chapter "issue" sections to develop a presentation that we believe will be well received by instructors and students. Our book can be distinguished from the many other fine American government texts by its use of issue sections, the integration of relevant sections of the Constitution into the body of the text, and our emphasis on giving expanded treatment to those topics that most instructors cover when teaching the introductory course, which we will discuss in a moment.

The innovative use of issue sections at the end of each chapter is a major feature of our book. Each issue provides an in-depth exploration of a topic which will remain contemporary for a number of years, such as:

★ Who Runs the States? (Chapter 3)

★ Equal Rights and Affirmative Action (Chapter 5)

★ Congressional Ethics (Chapter 10)

★ Is the President Too Powerful? (Chapter 12)

These sections provide case studies around which class discussions can be organized. In addition, they provide the spice of looking at controversial topics without falling into the trap of becoming a "political theme" text— most of which are essentially critical of American politics.

In recognition of the central importance of the Constitution, we have placed sections of the document into the appropriate chapters in the form of boxed inserts or paraphrased lists. This approach is convenient for the student, and it avoids the need to rely on the assumption that the reader will refer to the Constitution at the end of the book.

Finally, our long experience in teaching the introductory course convinced us that it is difficult, if not impossible, and perhaps inappropriate, to attempt to cover in one semester all of the chapters contained in many of the books currently on the market. The

prevailing tendency is to include from two to eight chapters on "policy making." In contrast, our approach to the important consideration of how policy is made is to include in most chapters discussions of the impact of the political processes and political actors on domestic and foreign policy making. Moreover, the last chapter in the book is a one chapter case study on energy policy, a problem that will not go away. Since the Arab oil embargo of 1973, we have become acutely aware of our nation's vulnerability in terms of energy availability and pricing. Virtually all the strands of American government and politics discussed in the book come together in addressing the question of how this, the world's largest democracy and industrial economy, will handle the energy problem that threatens our ability to survive into the next century.

By being judicious in our treatment of policy making, we have been able to devote two chapters each to the Congress and the president. Chapter 10, "Representatives and Representation," provides comprehensive treatment of such crucial topics as the impact of the personal backgrounds of the legislators and the environment of the "Hill" on congressional decision making. Chapter 13, "The Presidential Advisory System," includes discussions of the quality and power of the people who surround the president and the dangerous tendency of the staff to isolate the chief executive. This two chapter format allows us to devote the amount of attention to the legislature and the presidency that we think is warranted.

We owe a great deal to many people. We would especially like to thank former President Albert Brown of SUNY–Brockport who provided us with the necessary time to get the book underway. Our families have also undergone more than their fair share of unavailable husbands and fathers while we worked on this book.

We also would like to thank the editors of the Congressional Quarterly *Weekly Report* and the *Gallup Opinion Index* for their permission to make extensive use of materials from their publications.

We are indebted, for their assistance, to the people who helped produce this book. Fran Feigert prepared the index with her usual good humor. We are also grateful to a corps of typists who had to put up with the press of deadlines, not to mention our incomparable attempts at handwriting. Our special thanks go to: Anne Barton, Janice Brandon, Adele Catlin, Roxanne Gifaldi, Linda McIntre, Ernie Ragsdale, and Marla Summerville.

At Allyn and Bacon we have been ably assisted and spurred on by Al Levitt and Allen Workman. Our copyeditor, Laura Saunders, deserves a great deal of credit for the final form in which the book appears. Nancy Doherty, the production editor, was unusually helpful in her difficult role.

We are also grateful to the scholars who read and commented upon all or parts of the manuscript:

Jeff Conner, Metropolitan State College

John Kincaid, North Texas State University

Betty Zisk, Boston University

Walter Jones, Northeastern University

Ellis G. Sandoz, Louisanna State University

L. Gerston, San Jose University

David Garson, Tufts University

Franklin Patterson, University of Massachusetts, Boston

Roger Handberg, Florida Tech

Kenneth John Meier, Rice University

Richard Murray, University of Houston

David Vogler, Wheaton College

William Harader, Indiana State

Michael Smith, Tulane University

Paul Blanchard, East Kentucky University

Larry Elowitz, Georgia College

Grier Stephenson, North Carolina State/Franklin and Marshall

Philip DuBois, California State, Davis

Paul Holder, McLennan Community College

Scott Edwards, California State, Hayward

John C. Shea, West Chester State College

William Wagner, Foothill College

Theodore Pediliski, University of North Dakota

We are also grateful to the students and faculty at many colleges and universities who participated in the classroom testing of this book. Especially:

John Pesda, Camden County Junior College

Kendall Baker, University of Wyoming

Janna Merrick, St. Cloud State College

Don Maher, Lakewood Community College

James Jarvis, Wayne State University

We trust that their efforts have helped us to produce a current, comprehensive, and very readable American government book.

F.B.F.   R.S.G.

The Politics and Process of
AMERICAN GOVERNMENT

CHAPTER 1

Introduction

Politics and Government: Winners and Losers

More important than winning the election is governing the nation. That is the test . . .
    the acid, final test

ADLAI STEVENSON

*P*resident Reagan took the oath of office on January 20, 1981—a *winner*. His predecessor, Jimmy Carter, flew off for a vacation—a *loser*. Carter had not only lost the election; he had also failed in his last minutes in office to secure the release of fifty-two American hostages being held in Iran. In many ways, the events of that day symbolize one of the main themes of American government and politics, that of winning and losing.

While the new president could enjoy his new office and surroundings, the ex-president could take solace in his mission to Germany a few days later to greet the Americans who had just been released, largely as a result of special efforts he had made during his last few weeks in office. Further, he no longer had to deal so directly with some of the seemingly insolvable problems facing the president and all American citizens. Many of these are problems that regularly strain the workings of our governmental system, but these "system" problems can also suddenly become desperate issues in our daily lives, as everyone discovered one day early in the Reagan presidency.

A Country Faces Its Problems

If any one day could be taken as an example that shows the scope and complexity of the problems with which our government and society must cope, we might select March 30, 1981. At that time Mr. Reagan had been in office almost ten weeks. He had brought with him a Republican Senate—the first in almost thirty years—and was setting his sights on a Republican victory in the House in 1982. He had caught many people off guard with his sweeping proposals for budget cuts and for a series of tax cuts as well. Clearly he was the dominant figure in Washington, and

★ ★

*Starting off the decade of the 1980s, Ronald Reagan emerged from a large field
of candidates as the clear victor of first the Republican nomination and
finally the presidency.*

was establishing himself as a seasoned professional who could not be taken lightly. But, on that day, he almost became a loser.

★   Shots rang out at the entrance to the Washington Hilton. Mr. Reagan was seriously wounded in an assassination attempt that narrowly failed. His press secretary received a bullet in his brain, and a Secret Service agent and a Washington policeman were also shot. Thanks to immediate medical attention, all survived; the President quickly regained his health and high standing. He had won again. But this was not the first time Americans had

been threatened with losing a president through an assassination attempt. Presidents Lincoln, Garfield, McKinley, and Kennedy had all died in office from assassins' bullets, and others had been the targets of shooting attempts. Immediately the questions were raised: Does concentrated power in the presidency make us too vulnerable to a killer's bullet? How much protection can we offer a president in a free and open society? Should gun control receive careful reconsideration? What kind of law enforcement can control the violence that seems to permeate our society? We will be considering aspects of these

The eruption of Mt. St. Helens is the sort of unpredictable event that brings a sudden host of new problems to every level of government—local, state, and national.

problems in later chapters on the presidency and on civil rights.

★ On the same day, technicians at Three Mile Island near Harrisburg, Pennsylvania, were still wrestling with the problems caused two years earlier by the worst nuclear accident in United States history. Could the nuclear power plant ever be re-opened? Could it be made safe again without releasing dangerous radioactivity into the air? Who would bear the costs of the accident? Could similar or worse accidents be prevented? Was there a future for nuclear power in America? These

matters will concern us in later chapters on the federal system, on the bureaucracy, and on energy policy.

★ Americans were learning that gasoline and oil were exceptions to the economic law of supply and demand. Normally, as supplies increase, prices can be expected to level off or decrease. But, spurred on by President Reagan's total deregulation of oil prices, gasoline distributors were reporting record levels of supplies, stations were opened for long hours, and the price remained high. Was something wrong? Just two years earlier

Americans were enduring long lines at service stations, and various forms of gas rationing were either in use or under serious consideration. We were told that it would be necessary to reduce our consumption of foreign oil and we did so, by better than ten percent in one year alone. Yet, supplies expanded and prices escalated. Was it all a big hoax? Was there really an energy problem facing America? We will be discussing how people face such questions in the chapter on special interests and pressure groups, as well as in our final discussion of energy policy.

★ Soviet troops were massing on Poland's eastern border, continuing "maneuvers" which were taken both by the Poles and by the West as an exercise in intimidation—or worse. Polish labor leaders were attempting to work out a plan that would meet their own demands, placate the Polish government, and keep the Soviets from invading. In the U.S., President Reagan had just designated Vice-President Bush as the head of a "Crisis Management Team," to the discomfort of Secretary of State Alexander Haig. When the President was shot, Mr. Haig had announced, "I am in control here in the White House pending the return of the Vice-President. If something came up, I would check with him, of course." As things later developed, Mr. Bush was in control, from the airplane bringing him back to Washington. But for a short time, there was anxiety in Washington and elsewhere as to who was indeed in control of what. And, still

Cubans are the latest major immigrant group in our long history as a place of refuge.

unclear were Soviet intentions and who would decide among our possible responses if Poland were invaded. This kind of power issue will be considered later in the chapter on presidential staff and advisers.

★ Public officials in Texas and elsewhere were still trying to fathom the implications of a federal judge's order to completely revamp the state prison system so as to afford Fourteenth Amendment rights of due process and equal protection to convicted felons. Another order had stated that Texas must produce a workable bilingual education program so that the growing Hispanic minority could be educated in public schools. But, the new secretary of education had just taken a position that was seen by many as opposed to bilingual education. Had the judge overstepped his bounds? Did he, a lower-level appointed federal official, have the authority to issue directives to elected state officers? These matters will emerge in more detail later in chapters on the courts and on civil rights.

★ Interest groups for a variety of causes were reacting angrily to specific cuts proposed by President Reagan in his budget. Who would get hurt the most? Was it true, as some charged, that the poor and minorities would lose the most? Were the already-wealthy going to profit the most from his tax cuts? What about the middle-class? The chapter on interest groups and how they make their needs felt will explore these questions in more depth.

★ Atlanta police were still baffled by the string of more than twenty unsolved murders of young black males. Federal assistance had been offered by President Reagan, but the murders continued. Was this a single crazed killer at work? Or were the killings racially motivated? What can our government systems do in such

situations? Chapters on the federal system and on civil rights will provide part of the answers in this kind of case, but the long-range questions and problems still remain.

WHAT CAN GOVERNMENT DO?

In each of these cases there was a general demand that somebody should do something. And that somebody is ultimately our government in Washington. Even when a local issue is involved, the links within our economic and governmental system soon force a problem to be faced at the federal or national level. Who will pay for our constitutionally guaranteed programs for minorities, for the handicapped, or for various kinds of law enforcement? Though the branches of our government are constantly seeking a winning solution to such problems, they are not easily resolved in "either/or" terms; today's winning policy may become tomorrow's major governmental headache.

Indeed, while each of these problems was surfacing on March 30, 1981, Congress was responding to the President's initiative with direct action to cut the budget that affects virtually all federal programs.

In order for the government to spend less than it had the year before, programs were to be cut down in size and personnel reduced. In this "battle of the budget," we can see the persistent theme of winners and losers. Ironically, the list of programs to be cut included one that provided federal funds for medical trauma centers—such as the one which treated the President when he was shot. Basically, Congress was faced with a number of relatively unacceptable choices. While most agreed that the budget should be cut, it was seen as a question of "people" programs—education, welfare, unemployment benefits—versus an increased budget for the Pentagon. If some programs were winners, then others were clearly losers, at least in the short run.

A strong critic of government aid programs labelled them "socialistic."
For some reason, he forgot how many programs had benefited him.

Mr. President, as a senator from the state of Ohio, I receive almost daily letters from constituents in my state denouncing price controls and price supports for farm products, and all welfare legislation. During the last two days, since the Wheat Referendum, we have heard more talk in Washington to the effect that citizens are sick and tired of price supports and interference by the federal government in the daily lives of the people of our country.

In that connection I should like to tell a story about a young man who lived with his parents in a low-cost federal housing project in Hamilton County, Ohio.

He attended public school, rode the free school bus, enjoyed the free lunch program. Following graduation from high school, he entered the Army and upon discharge kept his National Service Life Insurance, as all of us who were in the armed services do, or should do. He then enrolled in an Ohio university, receiving regularly his GI check. Upon graduation, he married a Public Health nurse, bought a farm in southern Ohio with an FHA loan, and became a wheat farmer in my state. Later going into the feed and hardware business in addition to his farming, he secured help from the Small Business Administration when his business faltered. His first baby was born in the county hospital. This was built, in part, with Hill-Burton funds. Then he bought considerable additional acreage adjoining the farm, and obtained emergency feed from the government. He then put part of his land under the Eisenhower Soil Bank Program and used the payments from not growing crops to help pay part of his debts. His parents, elderly by now, were living comfortably in the smaller of his two farm homes, using their Social Security and Old Age Assistance checks. Though electricity

But the problems themselves were not likely to disappear. Who would pay for the outcomes in the long-run?

ARE THERE LIMITS TO GOVERNMENT? On the one hand, we have come to expect, over time, that government is the only institution capable of dealing with problems of a certain magnitude. Only Washington, for instance, could attempt to provide the needed disaster relief in 1980 after both Mt. St. Helens and Miami erupted, albeit in different ways. Only Washington has the resources to grapple with certain types of problems. But on the other *was at first lacking, the REA supplied the lines, and a loan from the Farmers Home Administration helped clear the land and secure the best from it. A Department of Agriculture agent suggested building a pond, and the government stocked it with fish for my constituent. The government guaranteed him a sale from his farm products. The county public library delivered books to his farm door. He, of course, banked his money in an institution which a government agency had insured up to $10,000 a depositor.*

As the community grew, he signed a petition seeking federal assistance in developing an industrial project to help the economy of his area. About that time he purchased business and real estate at the county seat aided by a Federal Housing Administration loan. He was elected to office of the local Chamber of Commerce. It was rumored, after all these years, that he joined a "cell" of the John Birch Society in the county seat.

He wrote me, as one of his two United States senators, protesting excessive government spending and high taxes and enclosed John Birch pamphlets, some containing outlandishly false statements, such as "take the United Nations out of the United States and the United States out of the United Nations," and the suggestion of an impeachment of Chief Justice Earl Warren, who, as we know, is one of the truly great men of our time. This man went on to say in his letter:

I believe in rugged individualism. People should stand on their own two feet, not expect government aid. I stand on my own two feet. I oppose all those socialistic trends you have been voting for and demand return to the free-enterprise system of our forefathers. I and my neighbors intend to vote against you next year.

Senator STEPHEN YOUNG of Ohio

Source: *Congressional Record*, 109 (May 23, 1963), p. 9294.

hand, the question is being asked more and more, can government effectively solve all the problems it addresses?

ARE WE TOO DEPENDENT ON GOVERNMENT? A major theme of many, both conservatives and now some liberals, is that we may have become too dependent on government. We may think that we can keep government minimal and "off our backs," but the ways in which we have come to rely upon government are significant.

While the author of the letter to the late Senator Young of Ohio (see insert) may

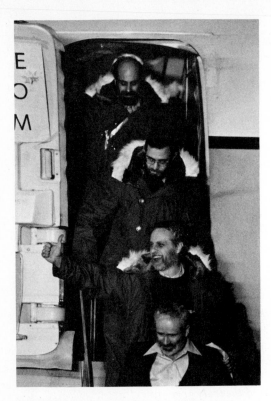

The Americans who had been held hostage in Iran are welcomed to freedom in what became a national celebration in the first days of the Reagan administration.

be an extreme example of a beneficiary of federal programs, most of us are unaware of how extensively our lives are influenced by Washington. Our food, housing, fuel—even our jobs—are potentially subject to federal regulations and standards.

Winners and Losers

We can look at these problems of government from several points of view, but one inevitable aspect of politics is that somebody emerges to govern over somebody else who is governed—that is, there is always a way in which someone wins and someone loses on any political issue. This may not be unique to government, but it is a familiar condition that can provide us a useful way of looking at how our government functions.

At the same time, looking at wins and losses calls for a great deal of caution; events rarely turn out as simple victories or defeats. As we saw before, a successful cut in taxes and government expenses can leave the government with a number of unpleasant headaches to work out. Victories and losses are highly relative.

WHO WINS? WHO LOSES?

In American government, or any government for that matter, winners and losers vary from issue to issue and institution to institution. It is easy to describe a spectrum of winning and losing that encompasses the average citizen.

EVERYBODY WINS! (OR, DO THEY?) Federal policies are usually couched in phrases such as "the general welfare." We are taught that we are all part of the same country, and that we should apply the Golden Rule in all of our dealings with others. However, many may have difficulty seeing the benefit for heavy taxpayers in knowing that some of their tax dollars are being used to benefit the unemployed and unemployable, the beneficiaries of many welfare programs.

However, one category of programs seems to have such broad social benefits that it appears to offer an outcome where everybody wins. This category is generally known as *public works,* or "pork-barrel" programs, in which we all get to share, directly or indirectly, in the largesse of the federal government.

Take, for instance, the problem of maintaining our rivers and harbors in a condition fit for commerce and recreation. The Army Corps of Engineers is charged with this aspect of pork-barrel spending. They attempt to develop projects which are both necessary and feasible. But in order to continue their own favored status, they will also work on projects that most appeal to senior members of Congress who control appropriations.

Does everybody win in this case? The public can benefit from navigable rivers as well as the power dams built under Corps supervision. But, there are questions about whether all the projects or the costs are always justified. Included are costs to our environment. Scenic wetlands may be bogged with silt from such projects, and the ecological balance of an area may be permanently damaged.

USUAL WINNERS. Federal officials constantly try to tell us that they are eminently fair, that most of us win and few of us ever lose. But there always seem to be individuals and groups who come out on top. To the rioters in Miami in 1980, the white policemen stood as symbols of this. They had been acquitted of beating a black businessman to death after a routine traffic violation. For others, the very wealthy, who can take advantage of tax loopholes, are the usual winners.

The political system has another set of typical winners, in a very real sense. These are the incumbents in elective office, who more often than not are able to secure re-election. As the campaign finance laws presently stand, there are a great many advantages to incumbency in the Congress. The ability to raise funds is typically greater for those already in office than for their challengers. Incumbents also receive an incalculable amount of free publicity from the simple fact that they hold office. They are constantly in the news, and they can become familiar to the public in a

The critical need for oil brings new demands to a governmental arena already laden with conflicting views of how best to maintain our coasts and waterways for the public benefit.

way that is difficult for their challengers to overcome. Thus, the system as it is structured can help incumbents stay in office as winners.

WIN SOME, LOSE SOME. Despite protests from office-holders that we are all the beneficiaries of a system looking out for our welfare, there are times when we must question this. The Vietnam war, fought without any apparent purpose other than upholding our honor and commitments abroad, is an example of this. For many of the families who lost more than 50,000 fathers, husbands, sons, and brothers, there is scant comfort in "honor" and "commitments."

On the other hand, we are a nation that has not seen sustained armed conflict within its borders for well over a century. For all our economic problems, we have an overall standard of living higher than that of most countries.

In short, the average American, who pays taxes, shops at the supermarket, and

The underemployed, along with the chronically unemployed, constitute a permanent underdog class in our society.

drives the family car (perhaps a little less now than just a few years ago), is both a beneficiary of the government and an occasional loser. Most of us fall into this category; sometimes we get ahead because of or in spite of the system, and sometimes we fall behind.

USUAL LOSERS. Although we are a nation founded on the premise of equality, there has never been any illusion that everyone is always equal. There is a continuing underdog class in the U.S. By every objective measure, blacks and Hispanics are the most frequent losers in our society, though they are not the only members of the economically and socially disadvantaged. Even worse, they often find themselves competing for the lowest paid jobs, when jobs are to be found at all.

In addition to those who are handicapped socially and economically, there is another group which in economic terms includes usual losers. These are people who work at jobs substantially below the level for which they are qualified. A term has been coined to describe them—the *underemployed.* Included in this group are women who graduated from college, yet find that they are only qualified to become secretaries. For some, underemployment is a consequence of lingering attitudes of discrimination. For others, it may be a consequence of short- or long-term structural problems in our economy.

EVERYBODY LOSES. Just as it is hard to imagine a game in which nobody loses, it is also difficult to conceive of a situation where nobody wins. Yet, there are several possibilities, all of which can have disastrous outcomes.

One is nuclear war. Survivors of a nuclear exchange would be little comforted knowing that they had "won." Mass-killing and destruction is a strictly no-win situation. Yet, our foreign and defense policies must take this possibility into constant account as we conduct our day-to-day affairs.

Another is the subject of the final chapter, the critical matter of energy and its

Our foreign and defense policies must account for events and personalities beyond our control, while a chilling outcome to escalation of hostilities remains nuclear war—where nobody wins.

availability. The United States has been called the "Saudi Arabia of coal," since we have several hundred years supply of this precious commodity. But, until we have solved innumerable technical and economic problems, we cannot fully take advantage of this resource and must remain dependent on other nations.

An immediate way we all lose on energy is at the gas pump, as prices are continually raised by both domestic and foreign oil producers. Thus far we have had no alternative except to pay. It also happens in other ways such as the costs for products which depend on oil for their manufacture and distri-

bution. Or, worse yet, imagine another Arab oil embargo, such as in 1973. Still worse, if possible, imagine if we exhausted not just our own but world supplies of oil and natural gas. There are very real technical limits to our ability to extract the last remaining sources of these invaluable fuels. Our economy is energy-dependent in a way that we can only barely comprehend. Should our present usable energy sources continue to dwindle, who will be the winner? What will be the economic, social, and political shape of the United States, one of the most advanced industrial nations in the world? Can anybody win?

Looking Ahead at the Issues

Government is frequently the only recourse for solving problems too large to be handled in other ways. As government has attempted to grapple with these problems, we have become increasingly dependent on it. Its actions make us winners and losers, whether for a relatively fixed period of time or only for the short run.

In succeeding chapters we will examine each of the major institutions of American government to see how each participates in the winner/loser decisions and how each institution can win and lose in its own power to make decisions. Further, we will attempt to show how this affects us as individuals, perhaps in ways we are not normally aware of. To this end, we have an "Issue" section at the end of each chapter. Consider the following, for example, and try to think, as you read through the book, how you are affected by:

★ Electoral college (Chapter 2)

★ Who runs the states (Chapter 3)

★ Selection of Supreme Court judges (Chapter 4)

★ Equal rights and affirmative action (Chapter 5)

★ Concorde SST (Chapter 6)

★ Decline of political parties (Chapter 7)

★ Rise of single-issue politics (Chapter 8)

★ Buying of elections (Chapter 9)

★ Congressional ethics (Chapter 10)

★ Ability of Congress to make policy (Chapter 11)

★ Power of the president (Chapter 12)

★ Presidential isolation (Chapter 13)

★ Reorganizing the bureaucracy (Chapter 14)

Some of these topics might appear, at first glance, to be remote from our daily lives, but they *do* have a bearing and impact on us and on whether we win or lose. Our final chapter draws together all the various institutions and processes of United States government and relates them to the making of foreign and domestic policy. The topic we have chosen to focus on is that of energy; for, as we have mentioned, this is a problem which will ultimately determine whether we, as individuals and as a nation, win or lose.

Suggested Readings

James B. Bryce, *The American Commonwealth,* 2 vols. (New York: Macmillan, 1889).

David Easton, *A Framework for Political Analysis* (Englewood Cliffs, N.J.: Prentice–Hall, 1965).

Murray Edelman, *The Symbolic Uses of Politics* (Urbana: University of Illinois Press, 1967).

Richard Hofstadter, *The Paranoid Style in American Politics* (New York: Knopf, 1965).

Max Lerner, *America as a Civilization: Life and Thought in the United States Today* (New York: Simon and Schuster, 1957).

Seymour Martin Lipset, *Political Man: The Social Bases of Politics* (Garden City, N.Y.: Doubleday, 1960).

David Schuman, *Preface to Politics* (Lexington, Mass.: D.C. Heath, 1973).

Alexis de Toqueville, *Democracy in America,* transl. by George Lawrence, ed. by J. P. Mayers and Max Lerner (New York: Harper & Row, 1966).

CHAPTER 2

The Constitution

★ ★

I have never been more struck by the good sense and practical judgment of the Americans than in the manner in which they elude the numberless difficulties resulting from their Federal Constitution.

ALEXIS DE TOCQUEVILLE

The Constitution means different things to different people; it has never been a single statement of unalterable truth, with one, single interpretation or meaning.

The Constitution as Symbol

First, it exists as a symbol of **legitimate government,** that is, as a reminder that the government exists by consent of the people. Perhaps you felt this if, like many other students, you took a school trip to Washington, D.C. At some point you were probably hustled into the National Archives to see the Declaration of Independence and the Constitution. The splendid way in which these documents are preserved and displayed probably lent a special meaning to what you were observing. Perhaps your teacher suggested that the Founding Fathers who wrote these documents were endowed with special gifts of foresight and intelligence.

There is a certain aura of mystery surrounding the Constitution, for indeed it is a symbol of and to our nation. Early in your education you probably learned something of the signers and how it was ratified. But even if you have forgotten the details by now, you learned and accepted the provisions of the Constitution. Every political system must show that its existence represents the will of those who are governed; even authoritarian systems try to do this. While the American public schools may formally transmit information about the political system, they also implicitly express values about the system itself, of which the schools are necessarily a part.[1]

Symbols such as the flag, the national anthem, and the Constitution all serve to reinforce the belief that the government is legitimate and represents a consensus on the part of its citizens. Our consensus is assumed by our

★ ★

Bryce, a perceptive observer of the American scene, recognized that the strength of the Constitution was its ability to meet the political needs of the time in which it was written and the combination of detail and generalities that has allowed it to survive to the present time without major overhaul.

The Constitution of 1789 deserves the veneration with which the Americans have come to regard it. It is true that many criticisms have been passed upon its arrangements, upon its omissions, upon the artificial character of the institutions it creates. . . . Yet, after all deductions, it ranks above every other written Constitution for the intrinsic excellence of its scheme, its adaptation to the circumstances of the people, the simplicity, brevity, and precision of its language, its judicious mixture of definiteness in principle with elasticity in details.

LORD JAMES BRYCE

Source: *The American Commonwealth*, vol. I (New York: MacMillan, 1913), p. 30.

Symbols such as the flag are used to represent belief in our political system.

The Constitution represents a balance between the need for rule of law and the rights and freedoms of the people.

On the one hand, the constitution legitimizes in morally unquestionable postulates the use of such bargaining weapons as groups possess: due process of law, freedom of expression, freedom of contract, and so on. On the other hand, it fixes as socially unquestionable fact the primacy of law and of a social order run in accordance with a code that perpetuates popular government and the current consensus on values: the rule of law, the power to regulate commerce, the police power, and so on.

MURRAY EDELMAN

Source: *The Symbolic Uses of Politics* (Urbana: University of Illinois Press, 1967), p. 19.

acceptance and obedience. The symbolic role of the Constitution is a reality: every political system, whether democratic or despotic, must have and use such symbols to be at all effective.[2] A careful reading of the Soviet Constitution of 1977, for instance, shows that it contains many provisions like those in our own constitution, and a good deal more. However, as we shall see, there is often a world of difference between symbols and the reality behind them.

The Constitution as Framework

SEPARATION OF POWERS

If a nation or any group of people is to be governed effectively, some plan must describe the basic governing institutions. Thus the Constitution is a framework that describes in broad outline the institutions and powers of our government.

Bear in mind that under the Articles of Confederation no one group was able to impose its authority absolutely. If anything, government under the Articles was hampered because there was no effective authority. Throughout this pre-Constitution period, various interests competed: prosperous and established farmers and merchants had economic interests that conflicted with those of less prosperous farmers and tradesmen. Under the Articles, existing interest groups were unable to resolve their difficulties with one another—or with competing groups in other countries—and were essentially at an impasse. It was evident that rules had to be made, or the country would be beset with confusion and inefficiency—and all interests would lose.

The contrasting experiences of an authoritarian rule under the English kings and Parliament followed by a more democratic rule under an ineffective Congress (operating under the Articles) laid the basis for what later evolved. It became clear to the Founders that it was necessary to establish a balanced government—one neither so strong that it could be arbitrary, nor so weak that it would be ineffective. It also became evident that no group should be allowed to gain a position of dominance—where it could control rule-making and win all that was to be won. Thus every group, at least in theory, should have a

The Constitution on major legislative powers

The Congress shall have power to lay and collect taxes, duties, imposts, and excises, to pay the debts and provide for the common defense and general welfare . . .

To borrow money on the credit of the United States;

To regulate commerce with foreign nations . . . ;

To coin money, regulate the value thereof . . . ;

To make all laws which shall be necessary and proper for carrying into execution the foregoing powers, and all other powers vested by this Constitution in the Government of the United States, or in any department or officer thereof.

more or less equal chance to win in any given situation. Points that could have been divisive were left unspecified, and the ultimate result is now one in which no single interest group or center of government power can dominate.

Hence the fundamental principle of our Constitution is that of **separation of powers.** In theory, if not always in practice, the legislative, executive, and judicial branches of government are distinct, with separate responsibilities and powers. Legislative powers, for example, are set forth in Article I, Section 8 of the Constitution. The authority for Congress (as well as the other branches) to act must be granted by the Constitution, however broadly the document is construed by the courts. This separation of powers works to limit the winning and losing of the various elements of the government so that none will be all-powerful.

The signers did not provide a lengthy list of powers for the president similar to the one they wrote for the Congress. Although a strong executive might evolve, they concluded that a potential center of power such as the presidency did not require too many specific duties. In Article II, there is provision for the president to command the armed forces, make treaties and certain appointments

(with the agreement of the Senate), receive ambassadors, and provide information to the Congress, including recommendations on legislation. The broadness of presidential powers is found in the opening words of Article II, "The executive power shall be vested in a President. . . ."

CHECKS AND BALANCES

Implicit in the concept of separation of powers is another concept, that of **checks and balances.** Under this principle, no branch of government can act entirely on its own. Thus, although the president may appoint ambassadors and department heads, he requires the consent of the Senate, which is normally given.[3] Treaties, also, must be ratified by two-thirds of those present and voting in the Senate. The president has to sign bills passed by Congress in order for them to become law. If he vetoes the bills, only a two-thirds vote in both houses can override it.

The Founding Fathers also set up checks within the legislative branch itself. They created two houses, each representing potentially different power centers. The House was to be popularly elected, but the

Senate's members were to be selected by the state legislatures, a form of indirect election. Most legislative matters require agreement between House and Senate, and inaction by either chamber acts as a temporary or long-term brake on action by the other. This was a deliberate act on the part of the framers, as they feared hasty and poorly-thought-out legislation by the popularly elected House. The composition of the Senate, guaranteeing two Senators to each state, also provides an internal balance of the small states against the larger ones and vice versa. Thus the Congress itself, while designed to act as a check on the executive and judiciary, also has a system of internal checks and balances.

The ability of the judiciary to say no is an effective check on the other branches. Though the Constitution does not clearly state that the judiciary can review the actions of the Congress or the president, this power is implied, since the power of the judiciary "shall extend to all cases, in law and equity, arising under this Constitution, the laws of the United States. . . ." Article III, which covers the judicial power, provides for a Supreme Court and allows the Congress to establish other courts. As we shall see in Chapter 4, the growth in power of the judiciary has come about in part because the courts have chosen to interpret and exercise their power of judicial review broadly.

What checks can be made on the judiciary? Is the Supreme Court really the final rule maker? Does it really have the final word on government actions? Are there no effective checks and balances on its powers?

One check exists in that the president, subject to Senate confirmation, appoints the judges to the Supreme Court and the lower courts. Thus, if the president believes the judiciary is becoming too liberal or conservative, he can attempt to balance or redirect the dominant ideology when a vacancy occurs. However, the opportunity to appoint a Supreme Court justice does not arise often, since vacancies occur only upon death or resignation of a member. President Nixon had the opportunity of nominating replacements for four vacant seats in his five-and-a-half years in the White House. If he had not resigned, he would have nominated the fifth, who was instead selected by President Ford. According to the Constitution, it is not possible to check or punish federal judges by lowering their salaries while in office. Another possible check is to impeach and remove a judge, but this is rare. It is also possible to check the courts by executive refusal to enforce their decisions—but this is also rare.

Separation of powers constitutes a fundamental principle of our Constitution and enables each branch to serve as a check and balance against the other two. Vice-President Bush (left) and President Reagan pay a courtesy call on Chief Justice Burger.

Other checks and balances are discussed later in this chapter, and again in later chapters. In addition to those checks and balances specifically named in the Constitution, there are others best described as **extra-constitutional,** or beyond the scope of the Constitution. This term does not mean that they are unconstitutional. Rather, the Constitution refers to "executive departments" without specifying what they should be, how they should operate, and what their powers should include. In Chapter 14, we will examine the executive departments and agencies in detail, and how they balance other units of government. Compared to the three main branches of government, there is little systematic control of the bureaucracy—the administrative and enforcing arm of the executive branch. Hence, there is a danger that the bureaucracy is checked only by restricted or reduced budgets and that it is not significantly counterbalanced by the rest of the formal government. In the sense of having the latitude for relatively independent action, the long-range winner in the checks-and-balances system is often the bureaucracy. Laws passed by Congress, exec-utive orders and policies of the president, and judicial decisions must all be enforced. If the bureaucracy fails to enforce them, or enforces them in a manner other than that intended, it may be the most powerful force among the institutions of government, and thus the winner of many long-range debates and conflicts. Whether the people win or lose in a situation such as this is debatable.

The bureaucracy can be checked, of course: presidential power of appointment—at least at the highest levels—and legislative power of the purse, as well as power to investigate bureaucratic operations, act as counterforces. When scandals developed in the General Services Administration—the house-keeping agency of the government, which acquires land, buildings, and supplies for day-to-day operations—President Carter appointed a new head to conduct a house-cleaning of the agency. The GSA and Congress conducted investigations that uncovered widespread corruption in the GSA. In a similar vein, when the CIA and FBI were alleged to have exceeded their authority in violating the rights of United States citizens, the Con-

Courts can deal only with problems brought to them. They cannot initiate investigations of abuses by other branches.

gress investigated, and regulations were changed to prevent similar abuses. Yet there is no assurance that either the president or the Congress can exercise any active supervision over the bureaucracy; instead, both branches must react to abuses—rather than maintain a thorough and ongoing review. In a similar manner, an agency action such as the denial of an airline route can be appealed in federal court, but here again we have only a reaction to a situation, since the courts can only deal with problems that are brought to them.

REPRESENTATIVE GOVERNMENT

The Constitution prescribes a representative government rather than direct democracy; that is, an office is held by someone who **represents** the wishes and interests of the people in a specific area (congressional district for the House, state for Senate, nation for the president). Originally, representation was very limited, and access to government for the masses was quite restricted. When the Constitution was ratified in 1789, and for 124 years afterward, the choice of representatives was limited solely to members of the House. Apparently the authors of the Constitution were of no mind to develop a system in which there was broad access to the legislative branch of government. Until the Seventeenth Amendment was ratified in 1913, members of the Senate were selected by state legislatures, which themselves were often dominated by wealthy commercial interests. Thus, access to the Senate was weighted in favor of those who were the economically advantaged—winners when compared to other members of society—and many considered the Senate to be a "rich men's club." Even though citizens of each state voted for the members of the state legislature, the choice of senators was obviously indirect and restricted.

WHO VOTES FOR PRESIDENT? We also had—and still have—indirect election of the president. It should come as no surprise that we do not vote directly for the president of the United States. Indeed, the chances of any of us knowing somebody who actually votes for president are very small, as only 538 people formally have this power. We will return to this point in the "Issue" section of this chapter, when we discuss the electoral college.

One may occasionally see impassioned letters to the editor from the political right and left suggesting that we have strayed from the ideals of our forefathers by moving toward a republic rather than staying a democracy. There is some doubt that we ever were intended to be a democracy in the original sense of that term. The term **republic** implies a form of representation in which citizens choose those who will represent their interests in the government. To suggest that the framers intended our government to be a democracy rather than a republic is an empty argument. Even at that time, restraints were placed on popular involvement by transportation and communication limitations. And today we have even greater limits given the sheer size of our nation.

Lately, much interest has been expressed in promoting greater popular participation in politics—perhaps because of a noticeable decline in the voting rate. Of the various techniques tried, that of phoning the president—introduced by Jimmy Carter in 1977—was novel and may have had several purposes: to enhance his own popularity and subsequent chances for re-election and to humanize government so that it does not seem as remote from the citizens. But its impact in translating the opinions of a very few citizens into policy is another thing entirely.

Democratic or Undemocratic?

As much as some admire, respect, and almost worship the Constitution, there are others who insist on debunking it. One argument concerns whether the authors of the Constitution intended to forge a democracy or a republic. One way to define **democracy** is in terms of direct participation in major decisions of the system. With few exceptions, there is little pretense at complete participation. Even in areas with New-England-style town meetings, these gatherings are usually only annual affairs. In fact it is difficult, if not impossible, to discuss democracy in this country, then or now, in terms other than that of voting for candidates or various referendums. For that matter, where there are traditions of direct participation such as town meetings, voting was once limited to men only—scarcely a democratic ideal in today's sense.

Because of large geographic areas and numbers of citizens, it is simply unrealistic to discuss direct popular involvement in government decision making. And there is no reason to assume that *democracy* and *republic* are antagonistic terms either in theory or in practice. Most concede that for any democracy to succeed, it must provide a meaningful choice to those voters who participate. In our system, the choice often comes down to choosing from two or more candidates for a particular public office. The voter hopes the differences between them are meaningful and not merely the products of advertising. The voter may ask whether the winner will truly represent the opinions of those who voted. Can the winner do so? If he or she can, is it necessarily

Citizen participation in politics is an indirect process of translating public opinion into policy by elected representatives.

in the best interests of the citizens to always have their opinions translated into policy by their elected representatives?

The original Constitution provided little opportunity for direct popular participation. Why was this the case? Some feel that the framers were not entirely pleased by the prospect of the common citizen participating in the running of the government. Restriction to indirect participation, except for the election of members of the House, could act as a check against popular passions that might force the government to take hasty and ill-considered actions.

Bear in mind that this was an era of popular passions. Those who think that the violence of the 1960s and early 1970s was new to the United States should study the history of this period more closely.[4] Radicals in Rhode Island controlled the state legislature from 1784 to 1787 and printed so much paper money that it became virtually valueless; those involved owed money on mortgages and fought to get out from under the burden of heavy debt. Shays' Rebellion in Massachusetts in 1786 was a similar debtor–creditor confrontation: farmers tried to prevent local courts from meeting to impose taxes on them. Trying to prevent future such civil disobedience—and aware that the government under the Articles of Confederation had been unable to help—the framers of the Constitution developed a strong central government, one relatively isolated from popular participation.

In order to understand this more fully, one may examine the framers themselves. One interesting and informed point of view is that of Charles Beard. His *Economic Interpretation of the Constitution of the United States* was a landmark in historical revisionism.[5] Essen-

tially, Beard suggests that those who went to Philadelphia were not a cross section of the common citizenry. Rather, the Founding Fathers were economically powerful and—as the major merchants, bankers, shippers, and large farmers of their day—anything but common. Beard argues that these wealthy men had interests to protect. The Articles of Confederation had proven inadequate for many reasons, not the least of which was financial. The Articles had not provided for common currency; shipment of goods in interstate commerce could be stopped by any state at its borders; and the national government had proven unable to control taxpayers' revolts. As a consequence, according to Beard, the Constitution was written in such a way that the framers' interests were not only protected but enhanced. By establishing a common currency, controlling interstate and foreign commerce, and providing for a strong central government backed up by a single army, the financial interests of the framers were secured. Further-

The Constitution's interstate commerce clause has played a key role in strengthening the powers of the central government.

more, by limiting popular participation to selecting members of the House of Representatives, popular opinion could not force the government into hasty action. Although several critics have refuted Beard's thesis, there is a certain sense to the thrust of his work.[6]

The strong central government brought about by the Constitution corrected many of the weaknesses of the Articles—thereby benefiting all. Not only were barriers to interstate commerce removed, not only did a common currency make it possible to have a uniform and stable means of exchange, but steps could be taken to enhance business and agriculture. The establishment of national roads, such as the opening of the Cumberland Gap, was possible only with a strong central government capable of dealing with interstate concerns from a national point of view.

It is possible, as Beard's critics showed, to take his point of view too far. To ascribe only one motivation—financial—to the authors of the Constitution would be as much in error as to worship them uncritically. We must take into account that there is a constellation of motivations possible in any human behavior. Economic concerns are not the only ones in operation—then or now. For that matter, if the Founding Fathers were solely bent on maintaining and improving their financial status, much more could have been written into the Constitution to have done just that.

COMPROMISE: THE NECESSITY OF RATIFICATION

The framers realized that their efforts would have to be ratified by the states and that it would be necessary to make compromises on many issues. Equal representation in the Senate and representation by population in the House calmed the fears of the smaller states that representation based solely on population would allow the large states to domi-

nate the government. The economy of the South depended heavily on the export of agricultural products, and the South fought for, and won, a provision outlawing export taxes. One compromise in particular stands out as an antidemocratic and antilibertarian measure—the **three-fifths compromise.** By this measure, slaves (referred to as "all other persons") were to be counted in the census differently from non-slaves. That is, a rough equation was devised whereby five slaves equaled three non-slaves for purposes of counting population—on which basis membership in the House of Representatives was to be determined. This compromise came about at the insistence of northern delegates, who feared that the southern plan of counting slaves as equal to whites would result in overrepresentation of the southern states. Southerners, on the other hand, did not want slaves counted as "full persons" for purposes of taxation based on population.

Provision was also made for continuing the slave trade for twenty-one years following the writing of the Constitution. Along with the three-fifths compromise, this is often cited by those who suggest that the original Constitution was antidemocratic. Just as often, this is rebutted by a simple argument. At the time of the Philadelphia convention, six states allowed slavery. In order to secure ratification, the approval of nine states was required; thus at least two of the slaveholding states were needed to ratify the document. As a practical matter, it was recognized that the approval of all thirteen states would probably be required to make the new document effective.

There was no formal published record of the proceedings in Philadelphia. That these debates were not disclosed has also been criticized by those who feel that the Constitution was antidemocratic; however, it soon became obvious that the framers could not do what they had been sent to the convention to accomplish. The original—and public—purpose

Representatives and direct taxes shall be apportioned among the several States which may be included within this Union, according to their respective numbers, which shall be determined by adding to the whole Number of Free Persons, including those bound to Service for a Term of Years, and excluding Indians not taxed, three fifths of all other persons. . . .

ARTICLE I, SECTION 2

The migration or importation of such persons as any of the States now existing shall think proper to admit shall not be prohibited by the Congress prior to the year one thousand eight hundred and eight, but a tax or duty may be imposed on such importation, not exceeding ten dollars for each person. . . .

ARTICLE I, SECTION 9

---

of the convention was to revise the Articles of Confederation, not to write a new document. Although the delegates could see that the Articles were unworkable and had led to a weak form of government, they knew that certain factions vigorously opposed a strong central government. For example, those who had participated in the various debtors' revolts, such as Shays' Rebellion, opposed a strong government that would force them to pay their debts. If the convention had permitted public meetings and published a daily record of its proceedings, the delegates might not have been allowed to continue.

The reality of the situation, as perceived by the delegates, was that there would be pressure either to dissolve the convention, or to force them to carry out their original charge—the revision of the Articles. If there was to be any form of government stronger than that which existed, it would be necessary to conduct the proceedings in secret.

Finally, one further point can be made concerning whether or not the Constitution is democratic. Critics of the document, then and now, point out that it is, in fact, a document for governance; that is, the Constitution structures and delegates certain types of powers

and allows the government a great deal of latitude in deciding how to act and on what issues. In Article I, Section 8, which defines the powers of Congress, we really have a statement of national powers that Congress implements. Although some concessions are made to individual liberties (the forbidding of bills of attainder, of *ex post facto* laws, of suspension of *habeas corpus*—all discussed in Chapter 5), the Constitution does not contain a clear statement of the limits of government as they affect the individual. If the rights and powers of government are described, what are the rights of its citizens? The authors of the Constitution could not have been unaware that this might present a problem. Provisions existed in each of their state constitutions severely limiting the power of the state. Most public officers were elected annually, and governors had little influence. Lengthy descriptions of individual rights were in these documents.

Thus, the framers of the federal Constitution had good reason to be aware of popular sentiment on questions of governmental power and individual rights. Yet, they chose to write a document which went against prevailing opinion on both issues. The absence

The Founding Fathers realized that the divisions of opinion throughout the thirteen states were so numerous that an open convention would collapse. As reported in 1888 by the British observer Lord James Bryce, secrecy seemed to be the price for success.

The debates were secret, and fortunately so, for criticism from without might have imperilled a work which seemed repeatedly on the point of breaking down, so great were the difficulties encountered from the divergent sentiments and interests of different parts of the country, as well as of the larger and smaller States. . . . they had in doing so to respect the fears and jealousies and apparently irreconcilable interests of thirteen separate commonwealths, to all of whose governments it was necessary to leave a sphere of action wide enough to satisfy a deep-rooted local sentiment, yet not so wide as to imperil national unity.

LORD JAMES BRYCE

Source: *The American Commonwealth*, vol. I (New York: Commonwealth Publishing, 1908), pp. 24–25.

of a Bill of Rights turned out to be a critical issue in the ratification battle. Only the promise that one would be written helped calm fears that the new government would not be tyrannical. In fact, the first ten amendments took effect in December 1791. Together they are known as the *Bill of Rights*. (We will discuss it in a later chapter.) Whether or not the absence of a Bill of Rights reflects an attitude of the delegates to the Constitutional Convention is another question. It could be argued that, after five months, they were simply weary, and submitted the best that they had done.

A Plan for Government

In discussing the Constitution, it is all too easy to forget the main result of the convention—a plan for a strong central government. Disenchanted with the Articles of Con-

federation, the delegates attempted to create a government strong enough to remedy the problems of the Articles, and yet still be acceptable to the states for ratification.

The states themselves were a particularly thorny problem in the writing of the Constitution; each had had unpleasant experiences under a central government before the American Revolution. By 1780, the various colonial charters had either been junked or rewritten as state constitutions with weak governments. Governors were mere figureheads, usually elected indirectly by the legislatures for one-year terms. The indirect election device, for which the framers have been so criticized, had ample precedent in the new states, which were themselves fiercely committed to "democracy," as it was then conceived.

Whatever powers existed for state governments to exercise were largely given to the legislatures. Since these bodies were also usually elected for one-year terms only, it was difficult for them to establish anything approaching long-term policies. It was necessary for the Founding Fathers to devise a Constitution that would appear to be not so much a strong but a limited government.

SEPARATION OF POWERS

The idea that the government is not a monolith that acts as a single, powerful force, with all of its agencies working in harmony, is implied in a fundamental precept of American government, the **separation of powers** between the legislative, executive, and judicial branches. This concept suggests that there are areas of distinct powers for each branch, a suggestion that is more myth than reality.

The powers of the government are essentially set forth in Article I, Section 8. In theory, these are legislative powers to be exercised by the Congress that are distinct from the powers of the president or the courts. Thus the power to establish a uniform national currency is theoretically a congressional rather than a presidential power. In the same vein, Congress has the power to borrow money and to regulate interstate and foreign commerce. Nowhere in the Constitution can we find the president mentioned as directly involved in these powers, for they are granted to the Congress alone. Or are they?

NECESSITY OF OVERLAP. In reality, a closer examination of the Constitution and of the way it has been put into practice reveals that there is no neat set of separate powers, one for each branch of government. In any of the so-called congressional powers, the president can and must become involved. That there are distinct powers we cannot disagree: Congress, and only Congress, can declare war; the Senate, and only the Senate, can approve treaties made by the president. However, this clear separation of powers has been sidestepped

quite often. For instance, the last time Congress passed a formal declaration of war was on December 8, 1941, the day after Pearl Harbor was attacked. Since then, we have committed troops to Korea, Lebanon, Vietnam, the Dominican Republic—and to recapturing the freighter *Mayaguez*. In each case, Congress either was not consulted at all or else consented only informally by funding the operations. Presidents have also avoided the constitutional provision that the Senate must approve treaties by not making treaties at all. Instead, the president simply signs an **"executive agreement"** with another head of state, never submitting the document to the Senate for approval or disapproval.

Appropriations bills can only be initiated by the Congress, a Constitutional provision which normally (at least until 1981) gives the Speaker of the House much of his power (Speaker Thomas P. O'Neill, Jr.).

The judicial power of the United States shall be vested in one Supreme Court, and in such inferior courts as the Congress may from time to time ordain and establish. The judges, both of the supreme and inferior courts, shall hold their offices during good behavior, and shall, at stated times, receive for their services a compensation which shall not be diminished during their continuance in office.

ARTICLE III, SECTION 1

The judicial power shall extend to all cases, in law and equity, arising under this Constitution, the laws of the United States. . . .

In all cases affecting ambassadors, other public ministers, and consuls, and those in which a State shall be a party, the Supreme Court shall have original jurisdiction. In all the other cases before mentioned the Supreme Court shall have appellate jurisdiction, both as to law and fact. . . .

ARTICLE III, SECTION 2

As for the role of the courts under the Constitution, there is little definitely stated. However, embodied in the seemingly simple language that describes the courts is a fairly clear statement of how the principle of separation of powers works (see insert). Under Article II the president can nominate individuals to sit on the federal courts. A simple majority of the Senate is required to confirm their appointment. Thus the president cannot attempt to control the courts without the collaboration of the Senate. In practice, most judicial nominations have been confirmed. However, to protect judges from political pressure, once they are on the bench, they serve as long as they show evidence of good behavior; and their pay cannot be reduced while they hold office. Neither Congress nor the president, acting alone or together, can express displeasure with court opinions by attempting to cut the salaries of federal judges.

Interestingly, this latter provision also applies to the president. Appropriations bills can be formally initiated only by Congress. To keep Congress from attempting to punish the president for actions that it disagrees with, the president's salary cannot be reduced while he holds office. It also cannot be increased for the term for which he was elected.

IMPEACHMENT. Removal of the president or a federal judge from office can only be accomplished through the difficult process of **impeachment** and trial. Impeachment is the bringing of formal charges before the House of Representatives. If a majority agrees that there is sufficient evidence to warrant a trial, the trial is then conducted in the Senate, with the Chief Justice of the United States presiding. As we can see in Table 2–1, there have been very few cases of impeachment in our history. Twelve persons have been successfully impeached by the House; only four (all judges) have been convicted by the Senate and removed from office. In the case of President Andrew Johnson, a change of one vote in the Senate would have provided the necessary two-thirds majority. President Nixon was not

NAME	OFFICE	DATE OF IMPEACHMENT BY HOUSE	RESULT IN SENATE
William Blount	U.S. Senator from Tennessee	January 29, 1797	Expelled from Senate after the impeachment; he was therefore acquitted.
John Pickering	U.S. District Judge from New Hampshire	December 30, 1803	Removed from office; known to be insane at time of trial.
Samuel Chase	Supreme Court Justice	March 2, 1804	Acquitted.
James H. Peck	U.S. District Judge from Missouri	April 24, 1830	Acquitted.
West H. Humphreys	U.S. District Judge from Tennessee	May 6, 1862	Convicted and removed from office.
Andrew Johnson	President of United States	February 24, 1862	Acquitted.
William Belknap	Secretary of War	March 2, 1876	Ultimately acquitted, but he had resigned a few hours before the House impeached him. It is thus questionable whether the Senate had the authority to try him.
Charles Swayne	U.S. District Judge from Florida	December 3, 1904	Acquitted.
Robert W. Archbald	Associate Justice, U.S. Commerce Court	July 11, 1912	Convicted and removed from office.
George English	U.S. District Judge from Illinois	April 1, 1926	Resigned six days before trial was scheduled to begin; charges were dropped.
Harold Louderback	U.S. District Judge from California	February 24, 1933	Acquitted.
Halsted Ritter	U.S. District Judge from Florida	March 2, 1936	Acquitted of six articles, but convicted of one, thereby removed from office.

Source: Committee on the Judiciary, U.S. House of Representatives, 93d Congress, *Impeachment: Selected Materials* (House Document 93–7).

impeached, since he resigned before the House vote. There seems little doubt that he would have been; many of his supporters deserted him after the last damaging tape was revealed, which indicated that he had had knowledge of the Watergate conspiracy six days after the break-in.

SUMMARY OF CHECKS AND BALANCES. We can summarize the separation-of-powers principle by the following outlines, which show how the branches interact. More detailed information follows in the chapters which deal with the courts, the presidency, and Congress.

Congressional control over the president
Approval or disapproval of:
- ★ Treaties
- ★ Appointments, such as ambassadors, judges, and executive department members
- ★ Organization and funding of the executive branch of the federal government
- ★ The president's legislative program
Investigation and review of:
- ★ Activities of the agencies under the president's control
- ★ Activities of the president, potentially resulting in impeachment and removal

Congressional control over the courts
- ★ Can refuse to increase salaries of judges
- ★ Can organize the court system
Empowered to:
- ★ Propose amendments to the Constitution to override court decisions (rarely used)
- ★ Pass legislation that both meets the objections of the courts and is constitutional
- ★ Control courts' appellate jurisdiction (rarely exercised)
- ★ Impeach and remove judges

Presidential control over Congress
- ★ Can veto legislation passed by Congress
- ★ Submits budget and legislative program, which may or may not have provisions acceptable to Congress
- ★ Nominates individuals to federal office, subject to Senate approval

Presidential control over courts
- ★ Nominates individuals to fill vacancies
- ★ Chooses whether or not to enforce court decisions

Court control over Congress
- ★ Declares congressional acts to be constitutional or unconstitutional
- ★ Interprets meaning of statutes

Court control over president
- ★ Declares presidential actions to be constitutional or unconstitutional
- ★ Interprets presidential actions as allowable or not under statutes enacted by Congress

SHARED POWERS OF THE BRANCHES

As the Constitution is written and as it has been interpreted, it is probably more accurate to discuss a *sharing of powers* rather than a clear separation of powers. Take, for instance, the legislative function. As some have interpreted it, this is exclusively a power of the Congress. Yet the Constitution requires that the president "from time to time give to the Congress information of the state of the Union, and recommend to their consideration such measures as he shall judge necessary and expedient" (Article II, Section 3). Although Congress has exclusive authority to legislate, it usually does so after presidents have outlined the legislative programs they want passed—this has become the annual **State of the Union Message.** Special messages on the various programs flesh out the proposed legislation in greater detail; these are usually drafted, in consultation with friendly members of Congress, by the executive branch. Then, and only then, does the formal legislative process required by the Constitution begin. Once the legislation is passed, the president, under the Constitution, has several options concerning whether or not to allow the bill to become law. In other words, the separation of powers actually requires a sharing of powers. This sharing is implied in the concept of checks and balances, since one branch can check another only if there is an area of shared authority.

DIVISION OF POWERS

Just as we may talk of a "separation" or "sharing" of powers between the three branches of government, we can also identify a **division of powers** between the national (federal) and state governments. That is, some programs can be carried out by the state governments alone; some can be achieved by the national government alone; and in some areas they share authority. Just as separation between the branches of the federal government is blurred, so is the division between the national and state governments. We will discuss this further in the next chapter.

FORMS OF GOVERNMENT

We can distinguish between three, basic, structural types of government. In the **unitary form,** all power is held by a central government. Any authority that exists at lower levels of government, such as in prov-

inces or states, is delegated by the central government and may be withdrawn at any time. This is essentially the form of government under which Great Britain operated at the time of the American Revolution, and under which it still continues to operate. It produces a strong central government. This unitary form was rejected by the framers for several reasons, among them the bitter taste left by their experience with England and the persistent opposition to it in the newly created states.

At the opposite end of the spectrum is the **confederation form,** in which the central government has only those powers that the states are willing to grant it. Such a government is essentially weak, since its central authority is seldom so strong that it can overrule its creators—the states. A current example might be some of the international arrangements in which we participate, such as the United Nations. The United Nations has never been such a strong central authority that it can enforce its actions and decisions unless that power is expressly granted by its members. Another example is the government of Canada, which is often unable to develop effective national policy on certain problems without the consent of its member provinces. In energy policy, for instance, the province of Alberta takes an independent approach, since it has extensive holdings in natural gas and oil and can ignore Ottawa's directives.

The third form is the one our own government takes: **federalism.** In fact it was supposedly created by the framers of our Constitution. In a sense, federalism is a compromise between the two other forms. Not only was it a compromise between two opposite forms of government, but it was also a reaction by the framers to the existing situation under the Articles of Confederation. Under the Constitution, neither the national nor the state governments are necessarily all powerful. The exception to this is in the area of **exclusive powers,** or those belonging only to ei-

John P. Roche argues that the Founding Fathers were a group of talented politicians who performed well under difficult circumstances and created a document that had substantial weaknesses, some of which were not resolved until the Civil War.

The Constitution . . . was a patch-work sewn together under the pressure of both time and events by a group of extremely talented democratic politicians. . . .

To conclude, the Constitution was neither a victory for abstract theory nor a great practical success. Well over half a million men had to die on the battlefields of the Civil War before certain constitutional principles could be defined—a baleful consideration which is somehow overlooked in our customary tributes to the farsighted genius of the Framers.

JOHN P. ROCHE

Source: "The Founding Fathers: A Reform Caucus in Action," *American Political Science Review* 55 (1961): 815–816.

ther the national government or to the state governments—but not to both. The exclusive powers of the federal government are basically those given to Congress in Article I, Section 8; exclusive powers of the states are harder to determine. (We will discuss exclusive and other types of powers in our next chapter.) Thus the Constitution provides for a form of government whereby the states are not mere administrative arms of the national government and in which the national government is not completely dominated by the states. The only time that the states were dominant, if ever, was in the ratification procedure, in which the states agreed to the Constitution in the first place.

Ratification of the New Constitution

The new constitution was not immediately popular in all the states. Nor, for that matter, was it acceptable to all the delegates at the Constitutional Convention, as only 39 of the 55 delegates present signed it. Thus the reluctance of some of the delegates, plus suspicions of both the secret convention and of a strong government, had to be overcome in order for it to take effect.

In order for the Constitution to be ratified, nine states of the original thirteen had to approve it. In reality, it would have been difficult for the new national government to be effective in any sense unless all the states approved it. Consider, for instance, a map of the United States at the time. By the time New Hampshire approved the Constitution and had become the ninth state to do so (see Figure 2–1, Table 2–2), there were still several geographical gaps in the new nation.

If New York, or Virginia, or North Carolina had failed to ratify the Constitution, the nation would have been physically divided. The shipment of goods from New Hampshire to Georgia, for instance, would have required using sea transportation, or en-

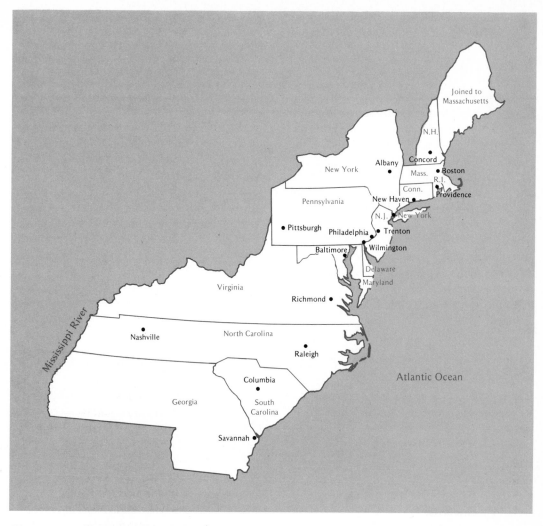

Figure 2–1 The original thirteen states.

tering territories not yet formally part of the United States, or crossing states that were presumably independent. It was therefore imperative to get all the states to approve.

The ratification debates focused on issues similar to those that had arisen at the Constitutional Convention. The colonists had doubts about *any* form of government—especially one that was centralized. As the votes in Table 2–2 demonstrate, these difficulties were not easily solved by any means. In New York, which was seen as a critical state, a special effort was undertaken to convince both the delegates to the state ratification convention and the public of the desirability of approving the new Constitution. Alexander Hamilton, John Jay, and James Madison contributed a series of newspaper articles written under the pseudonym "Publius." A collection of eighty-five essays, they are together known as

The Federalist and are regarded today as some of the most brilliant propaganda in American history.[7] These essays were designed to allay the fears of the delegates and the public regarding the Constitution. They are remarkable not only for their clarity and persuasiveness but also for what they reveal of the intentions of the framers. In their explanation of the origins and the development of the Constitution, they are unequaled.

With ratification by nine states an accomplished task, the document took effect on July 2, 1788. One of the promises demanded of the framers was that a Bill of Rights be added to the Constitution. The first ten amendments were passed by Congress in 1789 and ratified by three-fourths of the states before the end of 1791. This raises the next question: How can the Constitution be changed?

Changing the Constitution

A GENERAL DOCUMENT

In a sense, the Constitution can be considered simply a framework, a broad document with general statements of principle, with a minimum devoted to procedural requirements. The detailed procedures embodied in the Constitution concern how the president is to be elected, how legislation is to be passed, and so forth. Much, however, was left to future generations to work out.

One of the remarkable things about the Constitution is its relative brevity. By any standard it is unusually short, roughly six thousand words, or ten or so pages long. Many state constitutions, by contrast, run to well over one hundred pages. Why is this so?

The answer to this lies, for the most

★ ★ ★ *Table 2-2* ★

Ratification of the new constitution

STATE	SLAVE HOLDING?	DATE	VOTE
1. Delaware	yes	December 7, 1787	Unanimous
2. Pennsylvania	no	December 12, 1787	46–23
3. New Jersey	no	December 19, 1787	Unanimous
4. Georgia	yes	January 2, 1788	Unanimous
5. Connecticut	no	January 9, 1788	128–40
6. Massachusetts	no	February 6, 1788	187–168
7. Maryland	yes	April 28, 1788	63–11
8. South Carolina	yes	May 23, 1788	149–73
9. New Hampshire	no	June 21, 1788	57–46
RATIFIED			
10. Virginia	yes	June 25, 1788	89–79
11. New York	no	July 26, 1788	30–27
12. North Carolina	yes	November 21, 1789	184–77
13. Rhode Island	no	May 29, 1790	34–32

part, in its generality. By establishing broad principles, it became possible for future Congresses and presidents to work out legislation that could then be given a contemporary interpretation based on the meaning and intention of the Constitution. The Constitution has come to be changed through such informal interpretation as well as through formal change.

FORMAL CHANGE: THE AMENDMENT PROCESS

Recognizing that they were not casting the Constitution in stone—to stand unchanged forever—the framers incorporated into it provisions for formal change, known as the **amendment process.** This process represents a compromise between those who

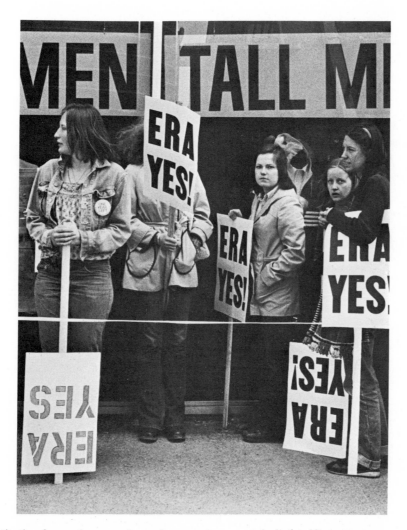

Constitutional amendments only rarely generate a great deal of public support or opposition.

wanted the Constitution to be rigid and unchangeable, and those who wanted to bring about rapid change. To guard against either possibility, the process works with comparative speed in the case of well-regarded amendments but with such slowness that ill-considered amendments are seldom passed.

NO LEGAL ROLE FOR THE PRESIDENT. The amendment process is one that involves only the Congress and the states; in a formal sense, the president is not involved in amending the Constitution. He may declare himself in favor of or opposed to a particular amendment, but his position carries no legal weight. Unlike his involvement in the normal legislative process, he is not directly or constitutionally involved.

PROPOSING THE AMENDMENT. A simple formula describes the formal amending process: two-thirds plus three-fourths (see Figure 2–2). For an amendment to become part of the Constitution, it must pass through two stages: **proposal** and **ratification.**

It takes two-thirds of either:

★   both houses of Congress to propose an amendment, or

★   state legislatures to petition Congress to call a convention. If Congress calls the convention, a majority of that convention may propose an amendment.

This second option has never been used, and perhaps for good reason. After all, what happened the last time a group of people met—supposedly to offer amendments to the Articles of Confederation? A whole new document was written.

The threat of the states' calling another convention has been a useful political tool in this century. Calls for constitutional conventions on specific subjects have prodded

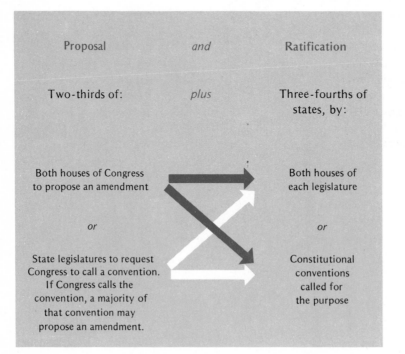

Figure 2–2   *The process for formally amending the Constitution.*

The state petitions for a convention to add a balanced budget amendment to the Constitution brought grave warnings from those who criticized this approach. One of the strongest statements came from Howard Jarvis, the Californian who led the successful "Proposition 13" movement to restrict spending by his state's government.

It would put the Constitution back on the drawing board, where every radical crackpot or special interest group would have a chance to write the supreme law of the land.

HOWARD JARVIS

Source: *Newsweek*, February 12, 1979, p. 28.

Congress to act on its own—usually out of fear that a convention could become a runaway and might conceivably attempt to rewrite the Constitution. Great pressure from the states persuaded Congress to act on the direct election of senators (Amendment XVII, 1913). The amendments for the repeal of Prohibition (XXI, 1933), a two-term limit on the presidency (XXII, 1951), and for presidential succession in case of disability (XXV, 1967) were all enacted following petitions from a handful of states calling for a convention. More recently, Congress enacted the federal revenue-sharing program in 1972 after more than a dozen states petitioned for a convention on that issue.

By the spring of 1981, 30 of the necessary 34 states had petitioned Congress to call a convention to propose a balanced federal budget amendment. There was some question whether all of the 30 had met the test of using the proper form for petitioning Congress. Uncertainty on this, as well as pressure from President Reagan to control government spending, had also led to Senate hearings in 1981 on a constitutional amendment which would require a balanced federal budget except in times of war. The outlook for the amendment appeared quite uncertain, but

given the public and presidential pressures on Congress, it would seem that advocates of the "balance-the-budget-amendment" may have lost the battle, but may eventually win the war.

RATIFYING THE AMENDMENT. It is clear that, no matter what dissatisfactions may exist with the Constitution, many senators and representatives would not want to risk the upheaval that could emerge from a constitutional convention. When amendments have been proposed—and for all practical purposes been approved by two-thirds of both House and Senate—they are submitted to the states for ratification. The method to be used for ratification is chosen by Congress and written into the amendment; sometimes a time limit for ratification is also specified. It takes three-fourths of the states to ratify the amendment, either by:

both houses of the state legislatures, or

constitutional conventions called for the purpose within each state.

The second method of ratification has been used only once, for the Twenty-first

Amendment, which **repealed** the Eighteenth Amendment—**Prohibition.** It was apparently decided that state legislatures would be too vulnerable to pressures from those against repeal of Prohibition.

The Eighteenth Amendment, ratified in 1919, prohibited the "manufacture, sale, or transportation of intoxicating liquors" in the United States. It had come about largely through the efforts of such organizations as the Women's Christian Temperance Union and the National Anti-Saloon League.[8] One of our great failures in social experimentation, it proved to be highly unpopular and quite unenforceable; in 1933, it was repealed by the Twenty-first Amendment.

In a sense, there is an important lesson in this brief case history: it demonstrates that constitutions should be written to outline general procedures and broad principles. When it is possible to amend a constitution too easily or too rapidly, it is then possible for the constitution to become a collection of interest-group proposals. Constitutions should be fundamental laws, on which all other laws for a particular political system are based. Imagine if the Constitution regulated the size of boxing rings, or specified the materials to be used in a highway system, or fixed maximum mortgage rates. Yet this is exactly what has been written into the constitutions of several states. Many desirable social goals can be achieved through legislation alone; but they do not require a place in the constitution, where they may be changed only with great difficulty.

Relatively few amendments have been ratified in the nearly two hundred years the Constitution has been in effect. Though more than five thousand have been suggested, only twenty-six have made it through the required process. At this writing, two additional amendments have been proposed by Congress and are now before the states for ratification. The first, the Equal Rights Amendment, would guarantee legal equality for women; the second would treat the District of Columbia more like a state, providing it two senators and appropriate representation in the House on the basis of population.

INFORMAL CHANGE: JUDICIAL INTERPRETATION

Of the two basic means by which the Constitution has been changed, the more frequent is judicial interpretation. This is not to say that the wording has been changed; it simply means that interpreters apply the Consti-

Public school integration was accomplished by judicial interpretation in the mid-twentieth century on groundwork laid by formal Constitutional amendment in the nineteenth century.

The amendment process is our substitute for revolution. The Civil War represented the one time in our history that both the formal and informal amendment process failed.

This country, with its institutions, belongs to the people who inhabit it. Whenever they shall grow weary of the existing government, they can exercise their constitutional right of amending it, or their revolutionary right to dismember or overthrow it.

ABRAHAM LINCOLN

Source: First Inaugural Address, March 4, 1861.

---

tution to a given case or situation. Probably the foremost interpreter of the Constitution is the Supreme Court, which uses the Constitution as its yardstick in hearing all its cases. Since it is a general document, there is no necessarily correct interpretation, and therein lies the possibility for interpretation. Such phrases as "necessary and proper" (to describe congressional power) and "executive power" (to describe the presidency) are ambiguous at best. When a specific case comes before the Supreme Court, its members interpret what the Constitution means—for that case, at that time.

The justices of the Supreme Court hear some cases in which one or more people challenge the *constitutionality* of a law or action. Although the specific circumstances are not likely to be covered by the Constitution or its amendments, the Court must decide, through **judicial interpretation,** whether the law or action in question is consistent with constitutional principles. For example, the Constitution has been informally changed by the Court's interpretation of the so-called **"necessary and proper" clause,** also known as the **elastic clause.** Found at the end of Article I, Section 8, this portion of the Constitution enumerates congressional (in reality, federal government) powers. Under this

clause, Congress is given the power "to make all Laws which shall be necessary and proper for carrying into Execution the foregoing Powers." The Supreme Court has therefore interpreted other, additional congressional powers as "constitutional," or consistent with constitutional principles.

Quite obviously, if the framers of the Constitution are people, so also are members of the Supreme Court. However much we may respect the Court and its members, they are also products of their backgrounds and their times. Take, for instance, the case of segregation of blacks. In 1896 the Court ruled that separate, but supposedly equal, facilities were constitutional.[9] In the late 1930s the Court struck down certain practices in higher education by ruling that the separate treatment was actually not equal.[10] In 1954, the justices declared that separation was inherently unequal and a violation of the equal protection clause of the Fourteenth Amendment.[11]

The **interstate commerce clause** has been one of the major vehicles for change, but only because the Supreme Court has chosen to interpret it by applying the elastic clause in a manner that reflects change in our society. Thus, in a broad range of cases—particularly those involving the elastic clause,

Hughes, later a member of the Supreme Court, expressed the reality that the most important mechanism for keeping the Constitution up-to-date and applicable to the needs of society is the informal amendment process that takes place when the Supreme Court determines whether a law is or is not constitutional.

We are under a Constitution, but the Constitution is what the judges say it is, and the judiciary is the safeguard of our liberty and our property under the Constitution.

CHARLES EVAN HUGHES

Source: Speech at Elmira, New York, May 3, 1907.

the interstate commerce clause, and the Fourteenth Amendment—the Constitution has been interpreted by the Court to apply to changing circumstances. By basing its decisions on constitutional principles, the Supreme Court has brought about a continuing informal change in the Constitution, without necessarily distorting the intent of the authors.

INFORMAL CHANGE: PRESIDENTIAL INTERPRETATION

The Constitution requires the president to take an oath that he will, to the best of his ability "preserve, protect, and defend the Constitution of the United States." The ways in which various presidents have chosen to do so are—like the ways justices of the Supreme Court have interpreted the Constitution—a product of their backgrounds and of the ways in which they have interpreted their office and the Constitution in reaction to events of their times. Some recent presidents have used a device not expressly prohibited by the Constitution, the executive agreement, to bypass the need for Senate approval of treaties.

PRESIDENTIAL DISCRETION. Other examples of **presidential interpretation** of the Constitution include personal definitions of "national security," "national interest," amnesties and pardons, and the like. An unprecedented example of this last power was President Ford's decision, apparently based on his own interpretation of the Constitution, to grant a pardon to Richard Nixon for federal crimes for which Nixon had not yet been accused. A pardon, by its very nature, cannot be granted until there is at least accusation—if not conviction and sentencing. In his proclamation of the pardon, President Ford stated:

The tranquility to which this nation has been restored by the events of recent weeks could be irreparably lost by the prospects of bringing to trial a former President of the United States.
The prospects of such trial will cause prolonged and divisive debate. . . .[12]

In other words, President Ford, it could be argued, interpreted his oath in such a manner that, by avoiding "divisive debate," he was protecting the Constitution. Presidential actions of any public sort are often rationalized as attempting to be within at least the spirit, if not always the letter, of the Constitution.

Thus, consciously or not, presidents interpret the Constitution and change it through their activities as chief executive.

INFORMAL CHANGE: CONGRESSIONAL INTERPRETATION

The Congress, like the courts and the presidency, can interpret the Constitution. One example of this **congressional interpretation** is the growth, in recent years, of what has come to be called the "congressional veto." Briefly, the **congressional veto** is a provision in a bill that permits Congress to disallow actions by an agency of the executive branch *before* they take effect. Suppose, for instance, that the congressional veto is written into a bill dealing with the Federal Communications Commission. The FCC could then have proposed regulations—or broadcasting license denials or renewals—reversed by the Congress within some specified time, such as thirty days. Such a power is not mentioned at all in the Constitution, nor has it been employed in traditional legislation. Yet if the president wants the bill so much that he doesn't veto it (or if the Congress overrides his veto on the bill), the congressional veto can stand.

Nothing is said in the Constitution about the internal organization of the Congress. Both House and Senate have developed intricate committee structures, in which many believe the real power in Congress is exercised. Neither are the duties of the speaker of the House of Representatives, often considered to be second only to the president in power and influence, described in the original Constitution. In the Presidential Succession Act of 1947, the speaker is named next in line of succession to the presidency, after the vice-president. Certainly, establishing such succession represents a modification of the Constitution. However, it could be argued that, like the president who daily interprets the Constitution, the Congress also interprets the Constitution every time it passes a law. In order for any law to go into effect, it is presumed to be constitutional, and thus within the bounds permitted by our governing document.

INFORMAL CHANGE: CUSTOM AND TRADITION

Beginning with the Magna Charta, the British constitution is often described as "a scattered series of documents held together by the glue of custom." For a good deal of the British fundamental law represents a developmental process. So it is with our Constitution. Although we do have a single physical document to which we can point, a large body of traditions and customs can also be considered part of constitutional law. For example, nothing at all is mentioned in the Constitution about political parties, their role in elections, or their function in government. Indeed, Madison, in *The Federalist*, warned about the danger of "factions" and argued that the Constitution would limit their influence. Whether by factions he meant what have become our political parties is the subject of some scholarly debate. Yet parties have taken root and our two-party system is considered by some to be a necessary ingredient of American political life. With rare exceptions, two major parties have dominated presidential, congressional, and most other partisan elections for more than a century.

The electoral college is probably the best-known example of the role of altering the Constitution—or at least altering the intent of its authors. The framers' intent was that the electoral college would be made up of individuals who would constitute an elite of sorts. After the election in which they were chosen, the members of the electoral college would then exercise their independence and select the candidates they personally wanted.

However, over time, each state political party has come to nominate slates of electors, all Democrats or all Republicans as the case might be. When a slate wins, members may, in theory, cast their votes for whomever they want; however, since parties control the nomination of electors, they select individuals who usually can be counted on to cast their ballots for the party's presidential and vice-presidential candidates. The electoral college gradually developed as a winner-take-all system in each state; thus in each state all electors pledged to Jimmy Carter "ran" against all the electors pledged to Gerald Ford in 1976. In short, the intent of the Constitution has been altered: the electoral college has lost the independence once envisioned for it. Instead, the winner-take-all system within each state usually means that the candidate who wins a state's popular vote is rubber-stamped by its electors.

★ Issue ★

The Electoral College

Defects in the electoral college were apparent almost from the start. The Constitution originally specified that, after the electors cast their ballots, the top two vote-getters would become president and vice-president, respectively. In 1800, when Thomas Jefferson was candidate for president, his running mate Aaron Burr received the same number of votes. This temporary deadlock had to be resolved by submitting the election of the presi-

★ ★ ★ *Table 2–3* ★
Presidents elected without popular majorities

YEAR	NAME	POPULAR VOTE	ELECTORAL VOTE
1824	J. Q. Adams	30.5%	32.2%
1844	Polk	49.6	61.8
1848	Taylor	47.4	56.2
1856	Buchanan	45.6	58.8
1860	Lincoln	39.8	59.4
1876	Hayes	48.0	50.1
1880	Garfield	48.3	58.0
1884	Cleveland	48.5	54.6
1888	Harrison	47.9	58.1
1892	Cleveland	46.0	62.4
1912	Wilson	41.9	81.9
1916	Wilson	49.3	52.2
1948	Truman	49.5	57.1
1960	Kennedy	49.7	56.4
1968	Nixon	43.4	55.9

dent to the House of Representatives and that of the vice-president to the Senate, as provided for in Article II of the Constitution. This defect, brought about by the fact that the authors of the Constitution had not considered the development of parties and slates of candidates, was remedied by the Twelfth Amendment, ratified in 1804. It provided that the votes in the electoral college should be cast "in distinct ballots" for the two offices.

WINNING WITHOUT A POPULAR MAJORITY. Another apparent defect soon emerged, one around which there has been much controversy—but little action—ever since. Specifically, it is possible through the indirect election method to elect a president who does not have a popular majority. We have on three occasions elected a president who was second in the popular vote: John Quincy Adams in 1824, Rutherford B. Hayes in 1876, and Benjamin Harrison in 1888. Uncertainties about how to count "unpledged" electors in 1960 also suggest that Kennedy may have finished second in the popular vote. As can be seen, in Table 2–3, we have elected presidents with less than a majority of the popular vote fifteen times, including those just mentioned.

The presence of third-party candidates has led to a less serious problem—the election of fifteen presidents who had more votes than the other candidates—a popular plurality—but failed to achieve a popular majority. Even in a two-party election it is possible for a candidate to be elected without a popular majority. In 1976, for example, we came very close to that possibility: a shift of less than 13,000 votes in Hawaii and Ohio would have made Ford the electoral college winner.[13]

There have been many proposals to abolish or modify the electoral college system. The reasons why none has succeeded boil down to the familiar question: Who wins and who loses? As things stand now, it might seem that the American people are the losers if a president is elected without a majority, or

comes in second in the popular vote but wins a majority in the electoral college. The barriers to change are discussed later in this section.

THE MECHANICS OF THE ELECTORAL COLLEGE

Basically the electoral college works in a fairly simple way. We do not vote for president but for slates of electors who are usually pledged to cast their ballot for the candidate of their party. The electoral college is administered at the state level, for all intents and purposes. Each state gets a number of electors equal to its representation in the House of Representatives and the Senate.

Since every state has two senators and at least one member of the House, each state is guaranteed a minimum of three electoral votes. A state with twenty-five representatives would have twenty-seven electoral votes, and so on. Furthermore, the District of Columbia, under the Twenty-third Amendment, is guaranteed as many electors—three—as the least populous state.

> 435 members of the House of Representatives
>
> 100 members of the Senate
>
>   3 electoral votes guaranteed to the District of Columbia
>   ___
>
> 538 electoral votes available

A majority, 270 votes, is needed to win the election.

Members of the House and Senate do not serve as electors themselves. Rather, political party committees at the state level appoint the requisite number of electors, who are pledged to vote for their party's candidate if the slate should win. If a state has three electoral votes, each party's state committee will designate three people to serve as electors. In some states, the names of the electors are actually on the ballot, while in others the ballot may simply read: "Electors pledged to vote for Jimmy Carter," or "Electors pledged to vote for Ronald Reagan." Thus a Republican slate of electors will oppose a Democratic slate of electors.

WINNER TAKE ALL. When all the popular votes for president (actually for electors) have been cast, they are tallied at the state level. Except in Maine, the candidate (actually the slate of electors) with the largest number of popular votes wins all the electoral votes of that state.[14] In other words, forty-nine states have a winner-take-all system. If we use Hawaii in 1976 as an example, Carter's slate of electors barely defeated Ford's slate of electors, but Carter received all of Hawaii's electoral votes.

AUTOMATIC VOTING. Several weeks after the popular vote, each winning slate of electors gathers in its state's capital, where the formal election is held. Usually there are no surprises; the electors are usually well-known members of the political party organization and are faithful in their devotion to the party and its candidate. However, no legal requirement forces electors to cast their ballots for the party's candidate; they are free to vote as they please. For example, President Ford carried the state of Washington by better than 60,000 votes. He was thus entitled to all of that state's nine electoral votes, and the media initially reported it this way. Nevertheless, one Republican elector cast his ballot for Ronald Reagan, who had opposed Ford for the Republican nomination. Thus, the final electoral vote was not 297 to 241 as most had

The president carries out the ceremonial function of interacting with the leaders of other governments. Here President Ford escorts Queen Elizabeth of England.

believed it would be, but 297 for Carter, 240 for Ford—and 1 for Reagan.

The results of each state's official balloting are forwarded to a joint session of Congress, where they are officially tallied and the winner is declared—finally. If no candidate wins a majority of votes in the electoral college, the vote for president takes place in the House of Representatives, and each state delegation casts one vote. The Senate, with each senator having one vote, chooses the vice-president.

A constitutional nightmare could develop if the vote were ever moved to the House. Would a state's delegation cast its ballot on a party-line basis? If they did, then a five-member House delegation, with a three to two Democratic majority, might cast its single ballot for the Democratic candidate. Or would they? What if the Republican nominee had carried that state in the popular vote? Would the Democrats do the partisan or the "honorable" thing? How would the other states resolve this problem?

THE DIFFICULTY OF REVISION

With all these problems with the electoral college, why has nothing been done so far? Part of the answer lies in the various proposed solutions—each of which raises new problems. Several major attempts have been made to correct the Constitution on the election of our president; the most recent attempt nearly passed in 1979.

★ ★ ★ *Table 2-4* ★

The influence of the smallest states under the electoral college

STATE	% U.S. POPULATION	% ELECTORAL COLLEGE VOTE	MULTIPLE OF VOTE*
STATES WITH ONE REPRESENTATIVE (OR THREE ELECTORAL VOTES)			
Alaska	0.18	0.56	3.1
Delaware	0.26	0.56	2.2
North Dakota	0.29	0.56	1.9
South Dakota	0.30	0.56	1.9
Vermont	0.23	0.56	2.4
Wyoming	0.21	0.56	2.7
STATES WITH TWO REPRESENTATIVES (OR FOUR ELECTORAL VOTES)			
Hawaii	0.43	0.74	1.7
Idaho	0.42	0.74	1.8
Maine	0.50	0.74	1.5
Montana	0.35	0.74	2.2
Nevada	0.34	0.74	2.2
New Hampshire	0.41	0.74	1.8
Rhode Island	0.42	0.74	1.8

*Computed by dividing the percent of electoral college vote by percent of U.S. population.

Why would anyone want to keep the present system? Remember that each state is guaranteed at least three electoral votes out of the 538 possible. Simple arithmetic can influence the actions of the states with the smallest population that have this minimum. As we see in Table 2–4, the smallest states are over-represented in the electoral college by factors of 1.5 to 3.1 times their actual proportion in the general population. Clearly, these states have an undue influence in the electoral college under the present scheme. Why then should they approve of a measure which would deprive them of this influence?

INFLUENCE OF LARGE STATES. Furthermore, at the opposite end of the scale, there is the question of whether those in the largest states would necessarily benefit by a direct election proposal. If one candidate carried New York and California by roughly 100,000 votes each but lost in Georgia by 250,000 votes, then obviously Georgia has greater influence in the election. Political party leaders in the largest states, under the present system, have a greater bargaining advantage—a large pot of many electoral votes—which can be used to make presidential candidates pay greater attention to them.

According to the 1980 census, the twelve states with the most population had 279 electoral votes, or a majority; presidential candidates are forced to pay greater attention to these states under the electoral college than they might in a direct popular election. This fact has not been lost on leaders of minority groups in these states, for their electoral potency may be stronger by retaining rather than restructuring the electoral college: minorities may hold the key to presidential victory by providing needed margins in these populous states.[15]

There are many other arguments that could be advanced for reform, but we come down to the essential element of amending the Constitution. It takes three-fourths of the states, or thirty-eight, to ratify an amendment, once it has passed both houses of Congress by a two-thirds margin. This fact can be presented in another way: only thirteen states are needed to block an amendment.

The issue is a simple one in some respects: if you were a party leader in any of the largest or smallest states, would you vote to reduce your own clout? Could you ask your party's members in the state legislature to diminish the influence your state already has? Would you voluntarily move from the position of a winner to that of a loser?

Summary

A POLITICAL DOCUMENT. The Constitution is a political document, broadly defining the structure of government. More than this, it also serves as the fundamental law of the United States government, and other laws must be tested against it for their constitutionality. This testing is done formally by the courts and informally by the president, the Congress, and customs and traditions that have developed. It is not an absolute document, but one changed gradually by both formal (amendments) and informal (interpretations and custom) means. Comparatively little formal amendment has taken place over the years, and reasons for this include: idealized attitudes of reverence toward it such that few dream of "tinkering with the Constitution"; the difficulty of the amending process; and the very general nature of the document, which permits it to be interpreted differently at different times.

A CONSERVATIVE DOCUMENT. Because it was a political document that sought to reconcile many different points of view, the Constitution has been seen as a very conservative approach to government. To some, at the time of ratification, it appeared to be radical in its implications for a strong centralized government. Yet the framers of the Constitution had cause to be afraid of the radicals in their own states, who stood to lose by approving the new Constitution.

The Constitution represents a series of compromises and thus is ambiguous on many issues of who wins and who loses. Who has the power? To do what? In this lies its proven strength, for it has been variously reinterpreted at different times to mean different things in different instances. This adaptability may help to explain its essential durability—with remarkably few formal amendments.

Terms to Remember

See the Glossary at the end of the book for definitions.

Amendment process

Checks and balances

Confederation government

Congressional interpretation

Congressional veto

Democracy

Division of powers

Elastic clause

Electoral college

Exclusive powers

Executive agreement

Extra-constitutional

Federalism (or federal government)

The Federalist

Impeachment

Interstate commerce clause

Judicial interpretation

Legitimate government

"Necessary and proper" clause

Presidential interpretation

Prohibition

Proposal

Ratification

Repeal

Representative government

Republic

Separation of powers

State of the Union Message

Three-fifths compromise

Unitary government

Notes

1. On this point there are many well-documented sources. See, for instance, David Easton and Jack Dennis, *Children in the Political System: Origins of Political Legitimacy* (New York: McGraw–Hill, 1967).

2. Seymour Martin Lipset, *Political Man: The Social Bases of Politics* (New York: Doubleday, 1960).

3. Donald G. Tannenbaum, "Senate Confirmation and Controversial Presidential

Nominations: From Truman to Nixon," a paper delivered at the annual meeting of the American Political Science Association, San Francisco, September 1975.

4. Jerome Skolnick, *The Politics of Protest* (New York: Simon and Schuster, 1969).

5. Charles Beard, *An Economic Interpretation of the Constitution of the United States* (New York: MacMillan, 1913).

6. Notably Robert Brown, *Charles Beard and the Constitution* (Princeton: Princeton University Press, 1956); and Forrest McDonald, *We the People: The Economic Origins of the Constitution* (Chicago: University of Chicago Press, 1958).

7. Among the several complete collections of *The Federalist* are those edited by Benjamin Fletcher Wright (Cambridge: Belknap Press of Harvard University Press, 1961); and Jacob E. Cooke (Middletown, Conn.: Wesleyan University Press, 1961).

8. See Herbert Asbury, *The Great Illusion* (New York: Doubleday, 1950); and Thomas M. Coffey, *The Long Thirst* (New York: Norton, 1975).

9. *Plessy v. Ferguson,* 163 U.S. 537 (1896).

10. *Missouri ex rel. Gaines v. Canada,* 305 U.S. 337 (1937); *Sweatt v. Painter,* 339 U.S. 629 (1950); *McLaurin v. Oklahoma State Regents,* 339 U.S. 637 (1950).

11. *Brown v. Board of Education of Topeka, Kansas,* 347 U.S. 483 (1954).

12. Congressional Quarterly, *Weekly Report* 37 (September 14, 1974), p. 2456.

13. Warren Weaver, Jr., "Electoral College vs. Direct Popular Vote," *New York Times,* April 13, 1977, p. D16.

14. Maine uses a district plan which gives one electoral vote to the winner of the popular vote in each congressional district and two electoral votes to the winner of the statewide popular plurality.

15. See, for instance, Judith Best, *The Case Against Direct Election of the President* (Ithaca, N.Y.: Cornell University Press, 1975), especially Chapter 4: "Inequalities in Voting Power."

Suggested Readings

Charles A. Beard, *An Economic Interpretation of the Constitution of the United States* (New York: Macmillan, 1956).

Catherine D. Bowen, *Miracle at Philadelphia* (New York: Bantam, 1968).

Robert E. Brown, *Charles Beard and the Constitution* (Princeton: Princeton University Press, 1956).

Jacob E. Cooke, ed., *The Federalist* (Cambridge: Harvard University Press, 1961).

Max Farrand, *The Framing of the Constitution of the United States* (New Haven: Yale University Press, 1926).

Carl J. Friedrich and Robert J. McCloskey, *From the Declaration of Independence to the Constitution* (New York: Bobbs–Merrill, 1954).

Forrest McDonald, *We the People: The Economic Origins of the Constitution* (Chicago: University of Chicago Press, 1958).

Saul K. Padover, ed., *The World of the Founding Fathers* (New York: Yoseloff, 1960).

Clinton Rossiter, *Seedtime of the American Republic: The Origin of the American Tradition of Political Liberty* (New York: Harcourt Brace, 1953).

Carl Van Doren, *The Great Rehearsal: The Story of the Making and Ratifying of the Constitution of the United States* (New York: Viking Press, 1948).

CHAPTER 3

Federalism

Federalism and the two-party system are not moral principles, but simply the accepted practices of the American People.

J. WILLIAM FULBRIGHT

Many believe that the greatest contribution of the Constitution was its creation of **federalism,** the division of powers between national and state governments. We find a certain irony in this, since the term *federalism* does not occur anywhere in the Constitution. Although the individual states were guaranteed a "republican" form of government by the framers, their specific powers were not clearly set forth—the framers assuming perhaps that the states' authority was understood or would evolve over time. Rather, they concentrated on describing the powers of the new central government and modified already accepted practices—although in some cases the modifications sharply changed earlier models. In short, since no authoritative definition of federalism is given in the Constitution, our working definition is based on the experience of nearly two hundred years of operating within it. Has this experience meant, as many claim, that the states have gradually lost out to the national government? Or are there benefits to the states, such as federal grants-in-aid, that are sometimes ignored?

Types of Government Powers

By examining the powers of the national and state governments, we can understand why federalism is defined as a division of powers. The national government has fairly well-defined powers, subject to interpretation of course, while those of the states are quite ambiguous.

EXCLUSIVE AND DENIED POWERS

Under the Constitution, there are certain powers that are exclusively those of the central government. Most of these are found under Article I, Section 8, which enumerates the powers of Congress. Only the federal government can, for example:

★ coin and regulate the value of currency

★ regulate interstate and foreign commerce

★ declare war

★ grant patents and copyrights

★ establish post offices

Further, although the executive power of the president is not clearly detailed in Article II, only he, and therefore the federal government, can:

★ make treaties

★ conduct relations with other nations

★ command the armed forces of the United States

This too-brief list of powers, which belong exclusively to the federal government, are, by implication and according to Article I, Section 10, **denied** to the states. This raises the question of so-called implied powers, to which we will return.

Do the states have any **exclusive powers?** This question has been the subject of continual debate, for there is no specific description or article dealing with state powers anywhere in the Constitution. Only certain powers can be exclusively exercised by the states, and they seem to be a very narrow set of powers. One of these, however, is extremely important: only the states can ratify amendments to the Constitution. Since it takes approval by three-fourths of the states, any thirteen states together can block ratifica-

Command of the country's armed forces is a power expressly granted to the federal government in the Constitution.

The powers not delegated to the United States by the Constitution, nor prohibited by it to the States, are reserved to the States respectively, or to the people.

tion of an amendment, either by failing to act or by defeating a proposed amendment in one or both houses of their state legislatures. This requirement—approval by a large proportion of the states—explains why, as we pointed out in the last chapter, the electoral college, with all of its problems, has yet to be scrapped or amended. For that matter, the Equal Rights Amendment (ERA), which guarantees legal equality to women, ran into difficulty not in the proposal or national phase but in the ratification or state phase. With the time limit for ratification running out, Congress in March 1979 extended the deadline by 39 months in order to allow proponents the opportunity to get three more state legislatures to ratify it. Will equal rights for women be set back if the ERA is not ratified? Who will be the losers in this highly emotional issue?

Other than ratification of constitutional amendments, no exclusive powers are allocated to the states, except those decided on a case-by-case basis in the federal courts. Does this make the states powerless losers before a federal juggernaut? The answer to this lies in what we refer to as *residual* and *implied powers.*

RESIDUAL AND IMPLIED POWERS

TENTH AMENDMENT: STATE POWERS. The **Tenth Amendment** was supposed to clarify the rights and powers of the states, but it was a masterpiece of constitutional ambiguity (see insert). Although this amendment can be taken to mean many things, it does not explicitly clarify the powers of the states. Indeed,

when Congress voted to propose this amendment, it took a very firm position in favor of a strong national government by voting down the word "expressly" before "delegated to the United States." If "expressly" had been used, as it had been in the Articles of Confederation, there would have been a sharp difference in the meaning. Madison spoke against using the word "because it was impossible to confine a government to the exercise of express powers; there must necessarily be admitted powers by implication."

STATE POWERS: RESERVED. Each state, therefore, has **residual** or **reserved powers.** As interpreted today, these powers usually involve the regulation of public safety, welfare, morals, health, and commerce within each state. An example of how states' residual powers are recognized in the Constitution may be seen in the Twenty-first Amendment, which repealed Prohibition. While there is no longer a national prohibition on the sale of intoxicating liquors, each state may impose such limits on itself, and one cannot bring alcohol into states with such laws.

IMPLIED NATIONAL POWERS. On the other hand, the problem areas under residual or reserved powers often involve national questions. For instance, neither a disease nor smog-laden air can be stopped by something as artificial as a state boundary. In such cases, the problem may raise questions of **implied powers,** or those which by implication belong to the national government. Debate has continued for years over the conflict between reserved powers (states' rights) and implied

The Congress shall have power . . . to make all laws necessary and proper for carrying into execution the foregoing powers, and all other powers vested by this Constitution in the Government of the United States, or in any department or officer thereof.

ARTICLE I, SECTION 8—the "elastic clause"

The judicial power of the United States shall be vested in one Supreme Court, and in such inferior courts as the Congress may from time to time ordain and establish.

ARTICLE III, SECTION 1

The judicial power shall extend to all cases, in law and equity, arising under this Constitution, the laws of the United States . . . to controversies to which the United States shall be a party;—to controversies between two or more States. . . .

ARTICLE III, SECTION 2

This Constitution, and the laws of the United States, which shall be made in pursuance thereof . . . shall be the supreme law of the land [*emphasis added*]; *and the judges in every State shall be bound thereby, anything in the Constitution or laws of any State to the contrary notwithstanding.*

ARTICLE VI—the "national supremacy" article

---

powers (national supremacy). However, the courts, interpreting the Constitution, have clearly made the doctrine of implied powers the source of consistent growth of the national government. Whether this growth is necessarily at the expense of the states—whether they are indeed "losers" and the national government is a "winner"—is problematic, as we shall see.

THE *McCULLOCH* CASE. Many of the implied powers of the national government are vested in the so-called *elastic clause,* as applied by the Congress in its legislation and as interpreted by the courts. Foremost among the cases that have tested this principle—and the one on which so many other cases have been based—is **McCulloch v. Maryland** (1819).[1]

Congress had chartered a national bank, and the State of Maryland had then attempted to tax this bank. Chief Justice John Marshall, who was probably more responsible than any single individual for the expansion of the federal government in its early days, wrote the decision in the McCulloch case, establishing two major principles. First, under the "necessary and proper" clause, the Supreme Court decided that Congress indeed had the power to establish a national bank. This power could be implied from its constitutional authorization to coin and regulate the value of currency. Thus, although nothing is explicitly written into the Constitution regarding national banks, Congress is free to use the "necessary and proper" clause to interpret the powers granted it by the Constitution.

In one sweeping statement, Marshall laid the basis for a broad interpretation of national powers.

Let the end be legitimate, let it be within the scope of the Constitution, and all means which are appropriate, which are plainly adapted to that end, which are not prohibited, but consist with the letter and spirit of the Constitution, are constitutional.

Chief Justice JOHN MARSHALL

Source: *McCulloch* v. *Maryland* (1819).

Second, Marshall faced the issue of federal versus state authority. He argued that Maryland could not tax the national bank, because it was a federal instrument, and wrote in his decision that "the power to tax is the power to destroy." If a state was free to tax an instrument or agency of the national government, it was also free, by extension, to destroy it. This Marshall could not allow. Thus, he interpreted the Constitution to mean that implied powers are derived from the elastic or "necessary and proper" clause.

When an individual state disagrees with an action of the United States government, and the matter goes to court, the dispute is settled in a federal court. Depending on the judgment and mood of the court, there is ample precedent—dating from *McCulloch* v. *Maryland*—for the state to lose and the national government to win.

CONCURRENT POWERS

We have suggested that winning and losing is sometimes more illusion than fact; this becomes even clearer when we look at those areas in which the states and the national government hold joint or **concurrent authority.** It has generally been conceded that the states' role lies in certain so-called **police powers,** which refer to the protection of the health, safety, welfare, and morals of the

The U.S. Mint, shown here, is part of the federal government. States are not authorized to issue money under the Constitution.

To those who feared that the new national government would be too powerful, Hamilton replied that the states would be protected by the stronger loyalties of the people to the state rather than to the central authority.

It will always be far easier for the State government to encroach upon the national authorities, than for the national government to encroach upon state authorities. The proof of this proposition turns upon the greater degree of influence which the state governments, if they administer their affairs with uprightness and prudence, will generally possess over the people. . . . the people of each state would be apt to feel a stronger bias towards their local governments, than toward the government of the Union. . . .

ALEXANDER HAMILTON

Source: *Federalist,* No. 17 (New York: Random House, 1941), pp. 102–103.

state's citizens. Some examples are health regulations, gambling laws, criminal codes, traffic ordinances, and building codes. When the national government began to develop police powers such as transportation safety rules (under the commerce clause) and taxed gambling under a generous interpretation of "taxing in the general welfare," it appeared that the states were losing power. On the contrary, this development led to national-state cooperation and has made it easier for the states to carry out many of their responsibilities.

An early expression of concurrent powers, which was defeated, occurred in the Virginia and Kentucky Resolutions of 1798. These resolutions proposed that the states could review actions by the national government to determine whether Washington had acted beyond the powers granted it under the Constitution. The specific issue then at hand involved the Alien and Sedition Acts, which made it a crime to criticize members of the government. These resolutions implied that the states were essentially equal to the na-

tional government and that any state could declare an unconstitutional statute null and void within its borders. Though quickly forgotten at the time, the acts were ruled invalid by the Supreme Court in 1958.[2]

In order for states to exist, they must be funded. In order to be funded, they must have powers of taxation. At present, states collect taxes in many ways; and the possibilities for additional taxation seem to keep increasing. States may tax income, estates, luxury items such as liquor and cigarettes (so-called *excise taxes*), gasoline, and the like. Although not all states tax these items, they have the option to do so. State and federal governments share taxation of these items, and are one visible area in which individuals are affected by concurrent powers. The federal government does not now impose general sales and property taxes; but because of the principle of concurrent taxation there is theoretically nothing standing in its way.

As federalism has developed, we have seen a move away from the belief that there

Alexander Hamilton theorized that citizens tend to feel more loyalty for their state than for a central government.

are truly distinct areas for the states and the federal government. A gradual blurring and overlapping of responsibilities and powers has taken place. Thus, federalism, like so many other constitutional principles, has changed over time. How and why has this happened?

Interpretations of Federalism

DUAL OR ORTHODOX FEDERALISM: STATES' RIGHTS

One interpretation of federalism, dominant for some time, was called **dual** (or **orthodox**) **federalism;** it is based on the concept of exclusive powers for both state and federal government. It held that there was a sharp line of division between the powers of the two levels of government. In theory, the national government was to have only those powers delegated to it by the Constitution. We have seen that "expressly delegated" was changed to simply "delegated" in the Tenth

Amendment before it was submitted to the states for ratification. Nonetheless—and despite the strong national flavor that federalism acquired under the decisions of Chief Justice Marshall—the concept of dual federalism held in the minds of many individuals for many years.

In its formative period, the national government tended *not* to legislate in as many areas as it does now. Grappling with the problems of launching a nation, developing procedures and legislation to handle its own exclusive powers, the new federal government had no excessive concern with problems that came to be viewed by some as proper for the states and the states alone. Thus it was possible for the states to see themselves as the proper repository for so-called *police powers;* this attitude is known as the *orthodox interpretation of federalism.* There is no provision in the Constitution specifying that the federal government must assume responsibility for all questions of health, safety, morals, and welfare. Nor does the Constitution stipulate that the

Believers in the doctrine of states' rights assumed states to have control over race relations within their own borders until court decisions in the 1950s and 1960s.

Alabama Governor George Wallace blocks school integration in 1963 to climax the struggle which states'-rights advocates ultimately lost to federal powers.

federal government should rule on or interfere with matters of education.

The states, left somewhat on their own throughout a good deal of the nineteenth and early twentieth centuries, gradually developed a doctrine of **states' rights.** This concept is based on the assumption of exclusive state rights, as opposed to the power of the federal government, and has been a constant source of problems in handling domestic affairs. For example, the states once assumed that they had exclusive control over education and race relations within their borders. In short, the relationship of national and state governments was "one of tension rather than collabora-

tion."[3] The federal government—whether acting in a "necessary and proper" manner or not—is often seen as growing at the expense of the states. Thus, it is often assumed that the exercise of federal or national power means the subjugation of the states to arbitrary rule from Washington. Those who favor states' rights have vehemently opposed the encroachment of the federal government into what they consider their exclusive powers.

SEGREGATION. Of course, those actually involved in state governments are seldom willing to concede authority to the federal government, whether that authority is theirs

Viewpoint:
Federalism and racial oppression

William Riker argues that while many minorities have benefited from federalism, the biggest winners in the past were segregationists. Segregationists were reinforced by court interpretations of federalism which became obstacles to national actions in this area.

The main beneficiary throughout American history has been the Southern whites, who have been given the freedom to oppress Negroes, first as slaves, and later as a depressed caste. Other minorities have from time to time also managed to obtain some of these benefits; e.g., special business interests have been allowed to regulate themselves. . . . But the significance of federal benefits to economic interests pale beside the significance to the Southern segregationist whites. The judgment to be passed on federalism in the United States is therefore a judgment on the values of segregation and racial oppression.

WILLIAM H. RIKER

Source: *Federalism: Origin, Operation, Significance* (Boston: Little, Brown, 1964).

to give up or not. Since politics often involves making allies and forming coalitions, officials who favor states' rights are seldom alone. As we shall see when we discuss interest groups (Chapter 6), a very common interest-group strategy is to line up others who will work together toward the same end. On the issue of states' rights, those who stood for "segregation, now and forever," commonly took the side of the states from the time of the Civil War onward. This represented a natural strategy for them. Given the violent and emotional history of several Southern states insofar as questions of race were concerned, segregationist groups saw nothing but harm emerging from federal interference and action. After all, it was the national government that had banned slavery and allowed blacks to become citizens. Furthermore, the national government had been responsible for the passage of the Civil Rights Act of 1891, although the provisions were not enforced for many years.

Since public education was long con-sidered to be an area of exclusive powers for the states, the 1954 Supreme Court decision in **Brown** v. **Board of Education of Topeka** was a perfect rallying point for those who favored states' rights.[4] Using the phrase "states' rights"—which had more potential for respect in other parts of the country than a declaration for segregation—they campaigned against integrated education. The unanimous decision by the Supreme Court against segregation in public schools surprised segregationists, but they recovered quickly. A court decision is one thing; implementing it is another. A series of events throughout the 1950s and early 1960s—court battles, national guardsmen, federal marshals, hostile crowds, Governor George Wallace blocking the schoolhouse door—symbolized the states-rights struggle on this one issue. These confrontations were hostile not only to integration but also to a central government that had presumably taken power into its hands at the expense of the states.

INTEREST GROUP BACKING.   Another example of the states rights struggle shows how interest groups can become involved in and further complicate state and national power struggles. Control of offshore oil sites was the subject of a major debate in the 1940s and early 1950s. The Congress twice passed a measure that gave control of these sites, known as tidelands oil, to the states, but President Truman vetoed the measure twice. The oil companies lobbied extensively on behalf of states' rights on this issue, although segregationists had given states' rights something of a bad name. Many organizations allied with one another to support the position of the states (see Table 3–1). Virtually every possible organization of state officials was represented, as was the Independent Petroleum Association of America. Obviously the organizations representing state officials took a position that would enhance the power of the states. But why did the oil companies take this position? One might expect them to want a uniform set of regulations under which to drill for and market oil.

STATES' RIGHTS AND OIL INTERESTS.   By securing state control of offshore oil leases, the companies believed that they could pick and choose drilling sites according to which states would require the least of them—if not actually help them with tax concessions and the like. The states stood to gain greater tax revenues, fees for drilling licenses, and the commercial and labor market development that follows oil company expansion.

After many attempts in Congress and the Supreme Court, the states won control of the tidelands oil reserves in 1953—an outcome promised by President Eisenhower during his campaign. The oil companies were clearly winners; the states were both winners and losers. Those states that saw oil companies rush to their offshore sites and then received increased revenues obviously won; but other states—those that joined the action on behalf of the principle of states' rights—had only the principle to console them if they did not grant the oil companies sufficient concessions.

It would seem that the federal govern-

★ ★ ★ *Table 3–1* ★
Pressure groups and the tidelands issue

GROUPS ORGANIZED ON BEHALF OF THE STATES-RIGHTS POSITION

Conference of Governors

Council of State Governments

Independent Petroleum Association of America

National Association of Attorneys-General

National Association of Secretaries of State

National Association of State Land Officials

National Institute of Municipal Law Officers

Southern States Industrial Council

United States Conference of Mayors

Source: *Congress and the Nation, 1945–1964*, vol. I (Washington, D.C.: Congressional Quarterly, 1965), p. 1402.

> The companies advocated state control of offshore oil sites because they believed the states would impose fewer regulations and it would be easier to control state agencies than federal agencies. They also feared direct competition by the federal government.

. . . the industry braced itself against this threat to its potential reserves. It feared the loss of existing investments and leases as well as the possibility of tougher royalty terms from a federal landlord. Very much in mind also was the thought that lands federally held might be leased or drilled (perhaps by the Navy) in a manner that would ultimately upset the delicate price-supply balance basic to the industry's control of oil. Publicly, oil leaders warned against this assault upon free enterprise and states' rights.

ROBERT ENGLER

The solicitude of the oil companies for states' rights is hardly based on convictions derived from political theory but rather on fears that Federal ownership may result in the cancellation or modification of state leases favorable to their interests, their knowledge that they can successfully cope with state oil regulatory agencies, and uncertainty concerning their ability to control a Federal agency.

ROBERT J. HARRIS

Sources: Robert Engler, *The Politics of Oil* (Chicago: University of Chicago Press, 1961), p. 288; Robert J. Harris, "States' Rights and Vested Interests," *Journal of Politics* (1954), p. 471.

ment was the loser in this case, since it gave up control of the tidelands. However, it was a federal Congress which passed the law in 1953, a federal executive—President Eisenhower—who signed the order, and a federal Supreme Court which upheld it. In other words, the states did not have an inherent right to control the offshore deposits; this right had to be granted by the various branches of the federal government.

A SURPRISE VICTORY. As recently as 1976, the federal government lost on a states-rights question. Congress passed a law in 1973 which included state and municipal employ-ees in federal minimum wage and overtime provisions. The Supreme Court held, however, that this was an intrusion upon the powers of state and local governments, and was therefore unconstitutional.[5] This case has revived the question of the validity of dual federalism, and we may expect further challenges by states on matters where their powers have been diminished by the national government.

The essential problem with orthodox or dual federalism is that it operates from a defensive posture, without an exclusive set of powers, powers reserved exclusively for the states and denied to the federal government. Members of Congress, operating from local power bases, often defend what they see as local prerogatives, such as education. Hence, federal intervention tends to be indirect—through loans and grants, for example. If the states object to federal action, the dispute must be settled in the federal arena—as the example of the tidelands case clearly illustrates. In short, orthodox or dual federalism implies that the national and state governments compete for power. Since the rules are made by one of the contestants, the competition is not very even. However, interpretation of these rules—by the Supreme Court—can change, and the national government does not always win.

COOPERATIVE FEDERALISM

The public is not often concerned with who has or should have the power or complex theories of dual federalism or states' rights. As this century has shown us, we are faced with many large-scale, concrete problems of a national nature that affect our daily lives. Under **cooperative federalism,** national and state governments arrive at joint solutions to common problems.

Only lately have we come to realize that we are all losers if we attempt to ignore or solve certain problems on a state-by-state basis. Many large-scale problems arise from social, technological, and demographic developments that have emerged since World War II. Among relatively recent concerns are government protection of civil and human rights, such as the simple right to live without worrying about the air we breathe, the water we drink, or the food we eat. Yet worry we must, for the multiple effects of environmental pollution are plainly evident. It seems that every day we learn of yet another disaster not limited by artificial state boundaries—and which requires a national solution.

Air pollution in Los Angeles, spread by prevailing winds, can quickly damage the Midwest and even the East. While California has led the nation in enacting clean air standards and auto emission controls—a positive example of states' rights—the federal government has usually not been far behind. In this case, California's standards are stricter than those of the federal government. In other states, the more permissive national standards are the only ones that must be observed.

Some believe that cooperative federalism is a convenient slogan for proponents of expanding the power of Washington, and it is difficult to deny that the power of the federal government has been increasing. But is it always at the expense of the states? As we shall see, there have been times when a branch of the federal government has acted because either the states or other branches have been passive or ineffectual. One example of this is the school desegregation case mentioned earlier, *Brown* v. *Board of Education of Topeka.* The Supreme Court acted when faced with a problem of overwhelming national significance. The area of civil rights had provided ample opportunity for the Congress to act, for the president to act, and for the states to act. Not all of these had been completely inactive on civil rights issues: laws were on the books but, without enforcement and penalties, they meant nothing. Thus the Supreme Court, with less to lose than others who depended on voter approval, could act when others could not or would not.

The essence of cooperative federalism is evident: too many problems are now completely unmanageable at the state level; the welfare of all states is now too interrelated to allow the independent attitudes of the past. When federal monies become available, states may or may not choose to participate in a program; however, state officials may be hard pressed to explain to constituents the sometimes valid reasons for ignoring federal aid. Another consideration is that the next time federal aid is offered, the state may have a harder time qualifying for it. In any case, *the states are not necessarily forced to give up any of their powers.* They may be persuaded to participate, especially if the federal government offers to pick up a substantial share of the bill. In short, cooperative federalism—mutual give-and-take—is probably the most pragmatic and productive direction for state and federal governments to take.

GRANTS-IN-AID. One principal means by which cooperative federalism has developed has been the **grants-in-aid programs.** In these programs, the national government offers to pay for a major share of the costs of one or several projects; these programs provide the state with enormous infusions of capital from federal agencies in Washington. The state is free to accept or reject participation in the programs and, indeed, must apply for federal subsidies under strict guidelines and conditions. Often the state government pays half the cost of the project and the federal government pays the other half. But for certain projects, such as the Interstate Highway System, there is a federal to state ratio of nine to one.

COSTS OF PARTICIPATION. Obviously the temptation to take federal dollars is very great. The states that participate in programs quite often find that a major part of their budgeted income depends on federal revenues allocated to them through grants-in-aid. On the other hand, these federal dollars are restricted to specific purposes, and the state's contribution

Federal money for school milk is an example of cooperative federalism via financial support to states.

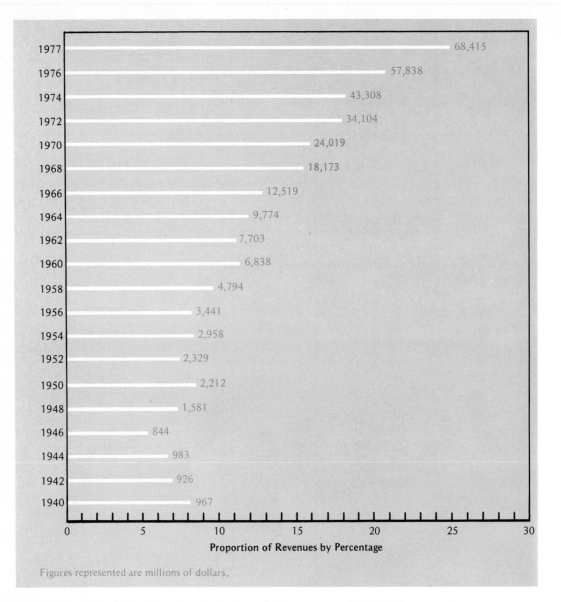

1977   68,415
1976   57,838
1974   43,308
1972   34,104
1970   24,019
1968   18,173
1966   12,519
1964   9,774
1962   7,703
1960   6,838
1958   4,794
1956   3,441
1954   2,958
1952   2,329
1950   2,212
1948   1,581
1946   844
1944   983
1942   926
1940   967

Proportion of Revenues by Percentage

Figures represented are millions of dollars.

Figure 3–1   Federal grants-in-aid as proportion of state revenues: 1940–1977. (Source: U.S. Bureau of the Census.)

must come out of the state budget. The effect of this two-edged sword on state budgets cannot be underestimated. Just as the total dollars in grants-in-aid and the federal contribution to total state revenues have increased dramatically, so has the cash outflow of the states increased.

It might appear that the states can only benefit from grants-in-aid, since they can undertake projects that were too expensive with-

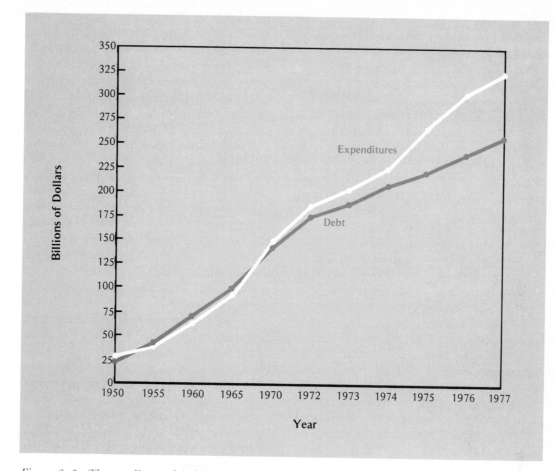

Figure 3–2 The spending and indebtedness of state and local governments: 1950–1977. (Source: U.S. Bureau of the Census.)

out federal dollars. Half-price specials can be as appealing to eager state officials as they are to the average consumer. However, if federal aid has increased, so has state spending. There is a crisis in state borrowing at the present time; though this crisis is not likely to disappear, it would be unreasonable to suggest that grants-in-aid are solely responsible for the increasing indebtedness of the state governments. It is, however, reasonable to say that they have played a role in this. The near-bankruptcy of New York City, which is a recurring event these days, may soon be fol-

lowed by bankruptcies in several states and major cities. Cleveland, for example, has already defaulted. City governments like these cannot market bonds because they are considered a poor risk. Of course, federal grants are not the only problems affecting state and local finances: for example, the shift of jobs and major industries to other areas also causes immediate loss of revenue. Federal assistance can temporarily relieve the burden but only postpones the problems.

There is a certain irony in the effect that grants-in-aid may have on a state's finances. Although in use for some time (the so-called land-grant universities in many states are beneficiaries of the Morrill Act of 1862, which set aside lands for universities and colleges devoted to the study of agriculture), the real spurt in financial grants-in-aid was during the Great Depression of the 1930s. The New Deal administration of Franklin Delano Roosevelt had to cope with many financial worries, not the least of which was widespread unemployment and the states' inability to pay for the minimal programs. Thus grants-in-aid were intended to help states pay for necessary and ongoing programs and bail them out of fiscal peril.

States' participation in federal programs can carry the costs of both decreased state power and expanded federal activity. We should remember that grants-in-aid have allowed federal extension into more and more state programs. Since he who pays the piper usually calls the tune, the grants have often had strings attached. We've already mentioned that states must provide matching funds. Furthermore, the states have had either to use existing state agencies or else to establish new ones for administering the grant programs. A state highway department is a good example of using an existing agency, since all states have departments that handle highway construction or maintenance. Many states, however, were unprepared to cope with environmental problems and had to create appropriate agencies to oversee efforts associated with their grants-in-aid in this area. The federal bureaucrats who administer these grants can then deal with individuals and agencies who have both authority and expertise at the state level. The state bureaucrats administering a federally funded program must submit to a minimum set of **performance standards,** agree to federal inspections, and deal with other guidelines that may be quite rigorous.

NATIONAL HIRING STANDARDS FOR GRANTS. In the 1970s, one vexing problem for many states was the development of plans under federal **hiring standards.** These required affirmative action and equal opportunity in the employment of women and minorities. If federal standards for certain programs, such as university research, required that affirmative action be used when hiring personnel, then it was up to the universities who accepted federal money to meet these standards. If the universities and colleges could not find the requisite numbers or percentages of minority members in each discipline, they risked losing federal funding. No matter how much some state education officials may have objected to such requirements, it was a simple case of either implementing these hiring practices or run the risk of losing the federal aid that made the research programs possible. In a sense, nationally mandated hiring requirements for federal grants-in-aid have been the velvet fist of civil rights programs. The power of the federal government in this area has also been applied at the local level: state agencies—which must apply similar affirmative action practices in hiring their own personnel—are used to enforce national standards.

The range of programs in which the federal government has become involved through grants-in-aid is astounding. For example, these programs include but are not limited to:

★ National Defense (emergency planning, civil defense, National Guard facilities)

★ Community Development and Housing (community action; model cities; public housing; urban renewal; urban planning; water, sewerage, and neighborhood facilities)

★ Education and Manpower (elementary and secondary education, vocational education, libraries and community services, manpower training, work incentive, employment security, emergency employment assistance)

Some states have legalized gambling to raise revenue because such activity can be heavily taxed.

★ Income Security (income maintenance, social services, food stamps, vocational rehabilitation, child nutrition and school milk)[6]

Other programs deal with health, veterans' benefits, commerce and transportation, natural resources and environment, and agriculture and rural development.

FEDERAL AID TO EDUCATION. As cooperative federalism has evolved, two areas have become especially controversial. In education there is a rich tradition in the United States of local control over local schools. Locally elected school board members select superintendents and principals and submit budgets and bonding questions to the voters. Although

turnout for these elections is rarely high, individuals still feel that they have some control over local matters. If we add to this the role schools play as a focus of community pride—whether in the fortunes of the high school football or basketball teams, the marching bands, or the numbers of students admitted to prestigious colleges—it is clear that schools are, for many communities, the very embodiment of localism and local sentiment.

Figure 3–3 shows the increasing costs of elementary and secondary education borne by the federal government. This money can be very welcome and may actually be necessary to finance new construction.

SCHOOL BUSSING. Federal involvement in local education is not always seen as desirable: Supreme Court decisions on desegrega-

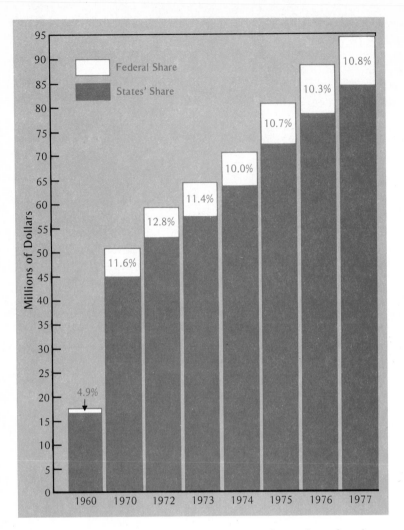

Figure 3–3 Federal and state spending on elementary and secondary education: 1960–1977. (Source: U.S. Bureau of the Census.)

tion have been far from popular in many communities—and not just in the South. As *Brown* v. *Board of Education* was gradually enforced from 1954 on, it became apparent that states and local communities would have to take certain positive steps to achieve integrated public education. One step has been to bus children to schools other than those in their neighborhoods. Although few white voices objected to bussing black children incredible distances to segregated schools, it was another thing entirely to bring them to

previously all-white schools—or to take white children to black schools. Bussing was one of the most emotionally charged issues of the 1970s: the burning of school buses in Pontiac, Michigan, and the attacks on busses and black children in South Boston, Massachusetts, were not isolated events. They clearly demonstrate that federal intervention in local school affairs is far from popular.

FEDERAL CONTROL OF CURRICULUM? Suspicion of federal funding for traditionally local affairs has only been enhanced by the effects of bussing and school desegregation attempts. There can be numerous strings attached to the federal dollar, such as requiring local school authorities to prove that they are eliminating segregation in schools and in hiring of teachers. Thus far, there has been little evidence of federal attempt to control curriculum, but many feel that local autonomy will soon be a thing of the past. If federally subsidized research shows, for instance, that one approach to the teaching of mathematics is more effective than another approach, might the availability of federal dollars be based on whether the approved method of instruction is chosen?

WELFARE AND FEDERALISM. The other issue—about which it seems no one has anything good to say—is welfare, a grab-bag term for a wide variety of programs. If we use the antiseptic government term of *income security,* welfare seems at first to have little threatening about it. However, we have heard a good deal about welfare cheating, a term guaranteed to arouse taxpayers and politicians alike. Certainly, cheating is something no one condones. How widespread it is is debated, with evidence laboriously gathered and emotionally presented on each side. Aside from determining who cheats how much, we also have to differentiate between programs. The costs of welfare, including unemployment taxes, have been spiraling, and many states are finding it harder and harder to fund their portion of federal welfare programs.

If, as Marshall stated (in *McCulloch* v. *Maryland*), the power to tax is the power to destroy, then it might be possible to extend his argument to the power of the federal government over the states. For the power to require appropriations and taxation can surely destroy, or at least bankrupt, a city or state that participates in such a program.[7] As an example, New York City's many near-bankruptcies hinge in large part on its enormous welfare burden. Having once chosen to participate in such joint programs, it became politically impossible to withdraw from them. Since New York City has had to tax its increasingly poorer base of citizens in order to participate in the programs, and since these taxes continue to escalate, the federal programs can be implicated in the financial collapse of New York City. Nor does the problem end with New York, for more and more states and cities are finding that the costs of welfare are greater than they can handle. It seemed, in 1976, that an unwritten requirement for the Democratic presidential nomination was that the candidate favor nationalizing welfare costs, in order to relieve the states of the terrible costs involved.

Changes in Cooperative Federalism

GENERAL REVENUE SHARING

To lessen the national controls that often go with federal dollars, a new program of relatively unrestricted aid went into effect in 1972. It was part of President Nixon's "New Federalism," in which he proposed to make major changes in the federal system. The other major program, an overhaul of the welfare system, was never passed by Congress. Basically, this program provides funds to be spent largely as states and local communities see fit. It was hoped that this approach, called **revenue sharing,** would provide greater autonomy to state and local officials.

POLITICAL ASPECTS. There are many political aspects to revenue sharing that cannot be overlooked. It may appear somewhat surprising that a conservative Republican president should sponsor such a program. Actually, the idea was not entirely new and can be traced to 1964, when it was proposed by Walter Heller, Lyndon Johnson's chairman of the Council of

In 1976, Congress extended the revenue-sharing program until mid–1980. A year earlier, Representative Henry J. Reuss (D., Wisc.) took a dim view of the spending priorities. He hoped for change, and he supported the program's continuation.

Reuss cited a fiscal-year 1973 listing of percentages of revenue sharing funds spent on various categories:

> *Education, 24%; Public Safety, 23%; Transportation, 15%; Health, 6%; Social Services, 3%; Housing and Community Development, 1%; Social Development, 0.5%; other, 27.5%.*

Aurora, Colorado, spent $536,000 of its allocation to build a golf course which only those with money to invest in expensive equipment will use. Corpus Christi, Texas, spent $100,000 to landscape an existing golf course. Still another recipient, Fairfield, Connecticut, used its share to improve a bridle path. Such frivolous but perfectly legal projects lend credence to the belief that revenue sharing entails at best a waste of federal funds and at worst a callous disregard for the needs of poorly housed, underfed, ill-educated poor and minority groups.

Rep. HENRY J. REUSS

Source: "Should We Abandon Revenue Sharing?", *Annals of the Academy of Political and Social Science,* 419 (1975): 88.

Economic Advisers.[8] However, other things occupied Johnson and his planners, notably the Vietnam War, and the proposal was deferred. The plan was also opposed by those who feared that the states would be too conservative in the ways in which they spent the funds. The eventual emergence of revenue sharing clearly shows a principal characteristic of the American political system as we know it—a history of proponents slowly building up support for a program before it is ever enacted.

Approximately $6.9 billion a year is now devoted to general revenue sharing, an amount some believe to be too little, too late. As with other programs, it is not a clear solution to any problem. Certainly, $6.9 billion where once there was nothing should not be

sneered at, and state and local officials have not turned any money back. But is it a gift horse, or a Trojan horse? The evidence is anything but clear.

ADVANTAGES AND DISADVANTAGES. On the one hand, the money from revenue sharing has provided state and local officials much more discretion in disposing of federal funds. They can not only savor the power involved in spending this money, but also feel less restricted by normally tight budgets. However, there are also disadvantages: rather than being used to shore up the already large grants-in-aid programs of federal assistance, the money was taken out of various existing programs, which then either died out or became underfunded. Who loses? It has frequently been alleged that the losers are those who would otherwise gain the most from federal assistance of one sort or another—specifically minorities and the poor, who are often the targets of federal grant programs.

Now states can use the funds largely according to their discretion. Local communities are more restricted but still have a wide range of activities on which to spend the available funds. Are they inclined to spend their money on so-called people's programs, or are they interested in concrete? Many public officials seem to have a building complex, and relish erecting buildings as monuments to their administrations. Others, aware of the popularity of cutting local taxes, may choose to spend their revenue-sharing dollars to replace revenues cut out of local tax rolls. Will social services for the aged, poor, and ill—the traditional losers—suffer? Will libraries receive less funding? The evidence is mixed, but one thing is clear: revenue sharing has not solved any specific problems and may have created new ones. Without federal guidelines regarding performance or hiring standards, the predictable losers are those who do not have strong political clout in local government. Even the winners, state and local officials who first pushed the idea, have begun to openly complain about the program, asking for adjustments in the amounts available and how it is administered.[9]

THE ROLE OF LOCAL GOVERNMENTS IN FEDERALISM

Federalism has usually been explained as a relationship between national and state governments only. This explanation excludes local governments, which are legally considered creations of the states. That is, a state can issue a charter for a county or a city. That charter is essentially a constitution, specifying just how far the community can go in using specified types of powers. In a sense, each state is a unitary government. The state assumes responsibility for the deeds or misdeeds of local governments and may actually have to withdraw or reshape local authority if necessary. One example of this was the forced resignation of Mayor Jimmy Walker of New York City, in 1932, which arose out of charges of financial misuse of the powers of his office. The governor, Franklin D. Roosevelt, held a hearing and intended to use his executive powers to remove Walker. In the face of this action, the mayor resigned. The various ways in which the state has stripped the mayor's office of fiscal power since 1975 also suggest the very real power of state over local officials.

LOCAL GOVERNMENTS AND FEDERALISM.

To use a concrete example, federalism has in the past usually been depicted as a ladder, with state and national governments comprising the two sides. Largely because of the grants-in-aid–revenue-sharing, the more appropriate picture of federalism is now of a three-legged stool.[10] That is, cities and counties have entered the federal system in a major way, though they remain the legal creations of states and are subject to state review. For instance, an urban renewal application is not usually made by a state on behalf of one of its cities. Instead, city officials consider the benefits and costs of tearing down decaying buildings and applying for federal aid to rebuild their downtown areas. Usually they consult their federal counterparts to ensure that the application is properly completed and that there is a reasonable chance of success. At the same time, they will consult state officials, seeking their approval; one reason the state becomes involved is that it is ultimately responsible for the fiscal integrity of the local government. It cannot afford to have scores of city and county governments go bankrupt and leave the state holding the bag. Another reason for state involvement is simply that state

Lobbyists for state and local governments are a significant influence on federal bureaucrats who decide where grants-in-aid will be allocated.

officials fear being left out. If politicians are human, bureaucrats are at least as human, and would not enjoy justifying their jobs should the state budget be cut. Of course, participation often is based on belief in the need for and wisdom of the programs.

IMPACT OF REVENUE SHARING. Revenue sharing has also increased the direct involvement of local communities in the federal system. Roughly one-third of all money sent to each state is kept at the state level; the balance goes to local governments—counties, towns, villages, and cities. Although guides for spending these funds exist, they still allow much latitude to local officials.[11] The building of playgrounds or the buying of snow-removal equipment are examples of local use of these funds. The often cumbersome process

of applying for a grant-in-aid can be bypassed, or an ongoing project can be supplemented with funds provided by revenue sharing.

LOCAL BACKGROUND OF FEDERAL OFFICIALS. As we saw in Table 3–1, there is no shortage of organizations for state and local officials. If the U.S. is a nation of "joiners" as some believe, then its officials are not immune to this impulse. These groups commonly have offices in Washington, where they constitute a significant lobby on behalf of state and local governments. Further, many federal officials have had previous experience at the state and local level and still have their own local contacts.[12] Thus, the scramble by local governments for federal funding has been encouraged by the amount of money available and the presence of federal officials susceptible to

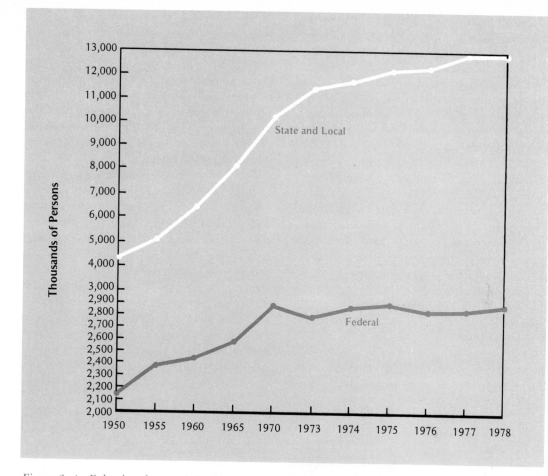

Figure 3–4   Federal and state civilian employment: 1950–1978. (Source: U.S. Bureau of the Census.)

pressure from their state and local counterparts.

THE ROLE OF THE STATES IN THE FEDERAL SYSTEM

STATE SPENDING.   A close look at the budgets of state governments reveals a dismaying fact: if there is incredible waste and duplication of effort at the national level—if national government is growing more and more expensive and falling heavily into debt—then it is still something of a model compared to state governments. State revenues, expenditures, and payrolls have been increasing at a rate that makes the federal government look efficient.

ARE THE STATES LOSERS?   It is widely acknowledged that the federal government has become more and more involved in local affairs. But national involvement has rarely come about at the point of a gun—as when federal marshals have enforced school integration; instead, it has largely been the result of the superior financial resources of Washington—usually when state and local officials wanted a share of the federal financial pie.

Yet no case can be made that the states have simply become administrative agencies for federal programs. While a good share of state budgets often goes to handling grants-in-aid programs—which were requested or approved by the states in the first place—there is still much state activity in areas in which the federal government has not legislated. State governments now receive roughly twenty-five percent of their state budgets from the national government. Considering how state budgets and payrolls have been expanded in recent years, especially in comparison to the national government, one is forced to ask where all that money is being spent. The states have seventy-five percent of their budgets free of federal government controls.

INNOVATIVE ROLE OF THE STATES. We have suggested that there are no clearly defined exclusive state powers. In theory, at least, there are no real constitutional limits that prevent the federal government from expanding its powers at the expense of the states. In practice, the states not only manage to survive, but manage to find more and more on which to spend their revenues. In part, this may be because of the unique role the states play in the federal system—they are the innovators and testers.[13]

At first glance, it might not be obvious to think of any particular state government as a hotbed of innovation. But given the number and diversity of states, and given the many different problems that arise, the states can individually legislate innovative programs in response to some problem or other. For instance, Oregon has developed imaginative legislation in response to environmental problems. After some debate, it passed a bill prohibiting nonreturnable bottles for beverages such as beer and soda. This is hardly what one might at first consider earthshaking, but the bill does directly address a serious prob-

Construction of modern docking facilities is an expensive undertaking that usually requires federal help but results in an improved employment and trade picture for a state.

lem of litter and waste in our society. Obviously, there were costs involved, and opponents to the bottle bill—representatives of the bottling and canning industries, as well as labor organizations representing their workers—worked hard in opposition to the bill because it threatened profits and payrolls. If these industries declined, the state's own revenues could be expected to decline as well, while the state's welfare programs might expand as more people joined the unemployment rolls. The law also requires administration—inspectors must oversee various production, wholesale, and retail outlets to ensure compliance. Although the affected industries consider themselves losers, a far larger proportion of the population benefits from this legislation. In this issue, as in others, Oregon served as a laboratory for one approach to environmental problems. Other states, in turn, began to imitate the concept, and consequently the federal government is considering making this legislation national policy. Thus the states can serve to test the novel and unfamiliar. If policies work on a small scale, they can be evaluated for application to national problems.

States can also act as safety valves, for people as well as policies. Quite obviously, not every law enacted in one state is worth passing on to other states and then to Congress. Indeed, we seem to have a history of hare-brained legislation that has passed, at one time or another, in various states. In Idaho, for example, it is unlawful for those engaged in "celestial [common-law] marriages" to vote. A since-repealed Indiana law defined the value of pi as 3.0, making life easier for its high school geometry students. Thus the states, acting individually, can test out some of the stranger ideas that seem to have merit. When they have proven their utter uselessness, they can be forgotten and repealed—with much less difficulty than if Congress tried to enact radical or experimental legislation on a national scale.

Although many public officials may seek higher office, very few can be elected to positions at the federal level. With 435 representatives, 100 senators, a president, and a vice-president, there are not as many federal elective offices as individuals who would like to fill them. By starting on a smaller scale, state and local officials can develop a feel for politics and public service; in turn, their performance can be judged by the voters. If there is enough substance, or appearance of substance, in their performance they may aspire with some hope of success to elective office in the national government. Considering the large available pool of those who want to enter politics at the state and local levels, this role of states—as a filter to test the performance of potential candidates—is probably one of the most important and least noted.

TESTING POLITICAL MOVEMENTS. Political movements are also tested in the states. We have a rich history of someone's putting forward one idea after another as an answer to all our problems. Many radical movements, both from the left and the right, have emerged at the state level; most have died aborning. Not all these ideas are worthless; occasionally they are incorporated into the mainstream of American politics. For example, between 1900 and 1925, states including Oregon and New York championed laws regulating the maximum length of the working day. Although sometimes thwarted by the Supreme Court, these states were the testing grounds for federal wage and hour laws.

The current wave of tax-relief proposals in the states, spurred on by the 1978 passage in California of "Proposition 13," a state constitutional amendment that cut property taxes drastically, has had some national impact. President Reagan and some members of Congress believe that the so-called "taxpayers revolt" represents a general demand for restraint in federal spending and taxation. Al-

The postal system is indisputably in the federal realm due to the chaos likely to result from multiple systems run by states.

though there is considerable doubt that the advocates of a constitutional convention to consider a balanced-budget amendment (see previous chapter) will be successful, federal taxing and spending policies are influenced by actions at the state level.

PRACTICAL LIMITS ON THE NATIONAL GOVERNMENT. Finally we come to the heart of the matter: the fact is, many of our problems are national in scope, but the federal purse is just so full. As states attempt to deal with these large-scale problems, they turn to the federal government for financial and technical assistance. But the Congress, the president, and the federal budget are simply incapable of dealing with all problems. Rather, most of our domestic affairs are handled by the states, under the rubric of "police powers." Since these cannot be clearly defined and cast in stone, the states must continue to develop responses to the perplexing problems they face. If the problems are too great for the states to handle, they may turn to the national government for assistance—but it may or may not be forthcoming. Whatever the outcome, the individual states are still actively working on the domestic problems facing our complex society. If coordination is to come, it generally comes from the federal government—but only when it has been determined that the problem is either too big for the states or that state action is improper and possibly unconstitutional.

★ Issue ★

Who Runs the States?

If you ask the average citizen who runs his or her state, the answer is likely to be "the state government" or "the governor." More cynical individuals might respond "big business" or "the unions." There might be a grain of truth in each answer, but there is yet another possibility. Were you to ask your governor, or a member of his or her administration, you might get the answer—spoken with a tinge of desperation or disappointment—"the federal government."

In this chapter, we have pointed out that there is no really clear-cut set of state powers. Certainly the powers of each state of-

Justice John Paul Stevens, considered a moderate-to-conservative member of the Supreme Court, questioned a decision which forbade the federal government from regulating minimum wages paid by state governments.

. . . the Federal Government may not interfere with a sovereign state's inherent right to pay a substandard wage to a janitor at the state capitol . . . [but may] . . . require the state to act impartially when it hires or fires the janitor, to withhold taxes from his pay check, to observe safety regulations when he is performing his job, to forbid him from dumping too much soft coal in the capitol furnace, from dumping untreated refuse in an adjacent waterway, from overloading a state-owned garbage truck or from driving either the truck or the governor's limousine over 55 miles an hour.

Justice JOHN PAUL STEVENS

Source: *National League of Cities* v. *Usery,* 426 U.S. 880.

ficer or institution are supposed to be defined by the state constitution and various state laws. Yet a world of difference often exists between formal laws and the ways in which the state actually operates. As we have shown, within a large gray area known as *cooperative federalism* the states and the national government collaborate on solutions to problems, often through the device of sharing costs.

THE FEDERAL DOLLAR

One of the most expensive programs in any state is that labeled *public assistance.* Included in this is the whole fabric of welfare programs designed to aid the unemployed, the disabled, and so forth. Both the cost and scope of these programs have increased dramatically over the years. As can be seen in Figure 3–5, their total costs increased more than ten times in the thirty-year period from 1950 to today. In that time, the state share has gone from more than one-half to less than one-third. While the share of these joint programs has varied, the absolute dollar outlay for the state has increased tenfold, as has the general cost of the programs. Inflation, however, has diminished the productivity of this increased spending. The costs to the states are in some cases mandated by a formula applied by the national government; when this is the case the states do not control their own finances.

When President Carter outlined his welfare reform package in August 1977, the response by state and local officials was predictably warm. Of course they welcomed an increased federal role in welfare or public assistance programs and decreased cost for themselves. Some would have welcomed a nationally equalized scale of payments in the various categories. New York City would not then, for example, be a "welfare haven" for those seeking to live off public assistance.

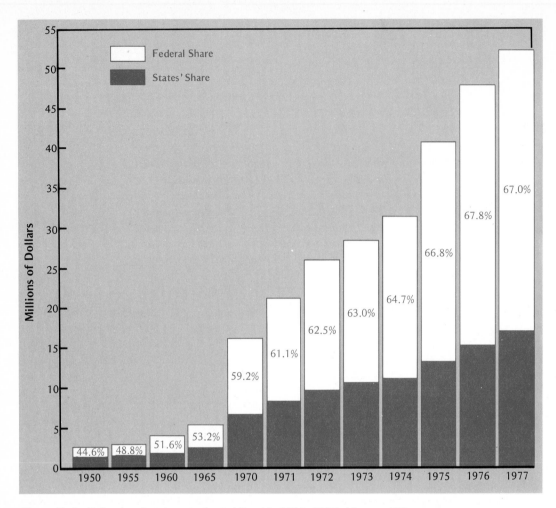

Figure 3–5 Federal and state costs for public aid: 1950–1977. (Source: U.S. Bureau of the Census.)

THE ROLE OF THE FEDERAL COURTS

Yet another way in which federal officials have become involved in state governments is through the federal courts. In our next chapter, we will point out the very political role played by federal judges in state affairs. Although this interference is not new to state officials, the media has recently paid at-tention to the fact that much state and local government activity is spent in following federal judicial orders.[14] In the last few years, for instance, federal courts in various parts of the nation have ordered:

★ bi-lingual education programs in public schools

★ public schools to admit children of illegal aliens

Viewpoint:
Can the federal courts run the states?

Although the federal courts already are overburdened by their normal responsibilities, the failure of cities, counties, and states to meet certain standards in operating public facilities has forced the courts to intervene.

Courts have taken over the operation of jails in St. Louis, Baltimore, New Orleans, Toledo, New York City, Boston, Jacksonville, Fla., Knoxville, Tenn., and Lubbock and Harris counties in Texas. They run prisons in Alabama, Mississippi, and Arkansas, state hospitals in Alabama, Louisiana and Mississippi and a school district in Boston.

MARTIN TOLCHIN

Source: "Intervention by Courts Arouses Deepening Controversy," *New York Times,* April 24, 1977, p. 1. © 1977 by The New York Times Company. Reprinted by permission.

★ use of school buses to achieve desegregation

★ desegregation of prison facilities

★ abandonment of electricshock therapy for patients in state hospitals without their consent or approval of their guardians

★ increases in state budgets for prisons and jail facilities

These rulings are the results of various suits brought against state and local governments and their agencies. If the court feels that an action is not likely to be corrected, it may not only issue orders directing changes but may actually assume control of the particular agency until the corrections are made.

In effect, the judges have stepped into a constitutional dilemma. On the one hand, the Tenth Amendment provides that the states are responsible for areas of governance not granted to the federal government. On the other hand, the courts are responsible—under Article III, Section 2—for all cases arising under the Constitution. When cases are brought because individuals believe their con-stitutional rights have been violated by mistreatment in a state hospital or prison, or when a case is brought alleging that a school district continues to have segregated facilities, then the federal courts may choose to act.

Little current evidence suggests that the federal courts are ready to put states' rights ahead of constitutional or human rights. In the future, the states may find that they are more and more under orders to act in a court-directed manner. Is this what was intended when the Tenth Amendment was ratified? How have the courts come to be so powerful in our society? We deal with this important question in the next chapter.

Although the issue of who runs state governments must remain unresolved for the time, it is apparent that state governments are often the losers when they challenge the national government; the states also lose some of their autonomy when the federal courts step in, as we have seen. And the courts may become more of a problem: the Supreme Court has ruled that judges cannot be held responsible for their actions—even if these actions were in error.[15]

Summary

One of our most remarkable contributions to the art of governance has been ascribed to our Constitution but cannot be found directly written into it. Federalism, instead, is the product of our experience; as our experiences have changed, so has our definition of the deceptively simple phrase *division of powers*.

These powers—exclusive and denied, residual and implied, concurrent or shared—show the complexities of governance. Increasingly, our nation has evolved so that most state powers are concurrent. The involvement of the national government, under the concept of cooperative federalism, has been steadily increasing; this has usually come about at the request of the states rather than in spite of their protests. The increasingly technological state of our economy, coupled with other social, political, and economic complexities, has forced state and local governments to recognize that they are often unequipped to deal with selected problems by themselves. The states often willingly seek federal aid and look upon it as a positive force, an opportunity to reach goals they would not be able to accomplish otherwise.

Nonetheless, the states still have a great many vital functions to perform, such as testing innovative policies and providing a training ground for national leaders. When the states fail to act responsibly, the power of Washington may be imposed upon them, as through the courts.

Terms to Remember

See the Glossary at the end of the book for definitions.

Brown v. *Board of Education* (1954)

Concurrent powers

Cooperative federalism

Denied powers

Dual (or orthodox) federalism

Exclusive powers

Federalism

Grants-in-aid

Hiring standards

Implied powers

McCulloch v. *Maryland* (1819)

Performance standards

Police powers

Residual powers

Revenue sharing

States' rights

Tenth Amendment

Notes

1. 4 *Wheaton* 316 (1819).
2. *Cooper* v. *Aaron*, 358 U.S. 1 (1958).
3. Richard E. Johnston and John T. Thompson, "The Burger Court and Federalism: A Revolution in Civil Rights?" *Western Political Quarterly*, 33 (August 1980), p. 200.
4. 347 U.S. 483 (1954).
5. *National League of Cities* v. *Usery*, 426

U.S. 833 (1976). See Johnston and Thompson, "The Burger Court and Federalism," for a discussion of the implications of this case.

6. A more complete listing, although still skeletal, can be found in any recent *Statistical Abstract of the United States*. For a description of all programs, see Office of Management and Budget, Executive Office of the President, *Catalog of Federal Domestic Assistance*. Both are annual publications.

7. Andrew Logan, "Around City Hall," *New Yorker* (February 28, 1970), p. 108. According to Logan, this approach to a suit against the federal government was apparently under consideration by the Corporation Counsel for the City of New York.

8. For a fuller treatment, see Walter W. Heller, *New Dimensions of Political Economy* (New York: Norton, 1967), especially Chapter 3.

9. An excellent study which takes these attitudes into account is Richard P. Nathan et al., *Monitoring Revenue-Sharing* (Washington D.C.: Brookings Institution, 1975).

10. This graphic picture of federalism is discussed in Roscoe Martin, *The Cities and the Federal System* (New York: Atherton, 1965).

11. See Nathan et al., *Monitoring Revenue-Sharing*.

12. On the background of our lawmakers, see Leroy Rieselbach, *Congressional Politics* (New York: McGraw–Hill, 1973). Older studies which support this conclusion include Heinz Eulau and John D. Sprague, *Lawyers and Politics: A Study in Professional Convergence* (Indianapolis: Bobbs–Merrill, 1964); and Donald Matthews, *U.S. Senators and Their World* (Chapel Hill: University of North Carolina Press, 1960).

13. Jack Walker, "The Diffusion of Innovations Among the American States," *American Political Science Review*, 48 (September 1969), pp. 880–899.

14. Some of the discussion which follows is based on Martin Tolchin, "Intervention by Courts Arouses Deepening Controversy." *New York Times*, April 24, 1977, pp. 1, 50.

15. *Bradley* v. *Fisher*, 13 Wall. 335 (1872).

Suggested Readings

William Anderson, *The Nation and the States: Rivals or Partners?* (Minneapolis: University of Minnesota Press, 1955).

Gordon E. Baker, *The Reapportionment Revolution: Representation, Political Power, and the Supreme Court* (New York: Random House, 1965).

Daniel J. Elazar, *American Federalism: A View from the States*, 2d ed. (New York: Crowell, 1972).

Suzanne Farkas, *Urban Lobbying: Mayors in the Federal Arena* (New York: New York University Press, 1971).

Walter W. Heller, *New Dimensions of Political Economy* (New York: Norton, 1967).

Roscoe Martin, *The Cities and the Federal System* (New York: Atherton, 1965).

Alpheus T. Mason, *The States Rights Debate: Anti-Federalism and the Constitution* (Englewood Cliffs, N.J.: Prentice–Hall, 1964).

Richard Nathan et al., *Monitoring Revenue-Sharing* (Washington D.C.: Brookings Institution, 1975).

Michael D. Reagan, *The New Federalism* (New York: Oxford University Press, 1972).

William H. Riker, *Federalism: Origin, Operation, Significance* (Boston: Little, Brown, 1964).

Aaron Wildavsky, *American Federalism in Perspective* (Boston: Little, Brown, 1967).

CHAPTER 4

The Court System

★ ★

We are the Supreme Court and we can do what we want.

Chief Justice WARREN BURGER

There is no such thing as justice—in or out of court.

CLARENCE DARROW

This president obeys the law." With these words President Nixon's lawyer announced that his client would respect the Supreme Court's order to surrender tapes that eventually revealed Nixon's role in the Watergate cover-up. Numerous editorials praising the strengths of our system greeted the announcement; it was generally accepted that even the president was not beyond the power of the courts. Why do we have this attitude of respect for the courts? How does the court system operate?

The courts are probably the least known and least understood part of the United States political system. Although they are generally held in high regard—most parents would be pleased if their children became judges—we often seem to know little specific information about the courts. The language of lawyers and courts is often confusing, laden with Latin phrases, *hereuntos,* and parties of the first and second parts. President Carter insisted that he would require government

regulations to be written in easily understood English, a step that would be nothing short of miraculous. But even if this were possible, it would probably take an army of lawyers and judges to determine exactly what the plain English means, and how the law and regulations should be applied.

Actually, very little is mysterious about the judicial system, whether we are discussing law, lawyers, or courts. It may be that we prefer to respect rather than try to understand it. If we fail to understand the system, we can become its victims—losers in a very real sense.

Basic Principles

FEDERAL COURT STRUCTURE

The Constitution established a Supreme Court and allowed for whatever system of lower courts the Congress saw fit to estab-

Cases are originally heard at the lowest-level court having jurisdiction over the dispute and may proceed through appeal all the way to the U.S. Supreme Court.

lish. Beyond this, there was no clear constitutional definition of how the courts were to be structured. Most of the federal courts were created by the First Congress, in the Judiciary Act of 1789, under the authority of Article III of the Constitution. This act also set limits on the jurisdiction of the federal courts. The original jurisdiction of the Supreme Court was established by the Constitution and cannot be altered by Congress; as we shall see, the Court itself seems to have altered its own jurisdiction.

Below the Supreme Court are two major layers of federal courts: the **United States Courts of Appeals,** created in 1891, and, under them, the **Federal District Courts,** created in 1789. The bulk of the workload is handled in the district courts, where more than 170,000 cases may be brought annually.

JUDICIAL DISTRICTS. To understand this a little more clearly, look at the maps in Figures 4–2 and 4–3. The country is divided into ninety-seven **U.S. Judicial Districts**—there is at least one federal district court for each state and one for each territory (Guam, Puerto Rico, and the Virgin Islands). Larger states may have more than one federal district court; Texas, for instance, has four. The number of judges assigned to each district varies from one to twenty-four, depending on the caseload. Cases are normally heard by a single judge; in exceptional cases three judges may

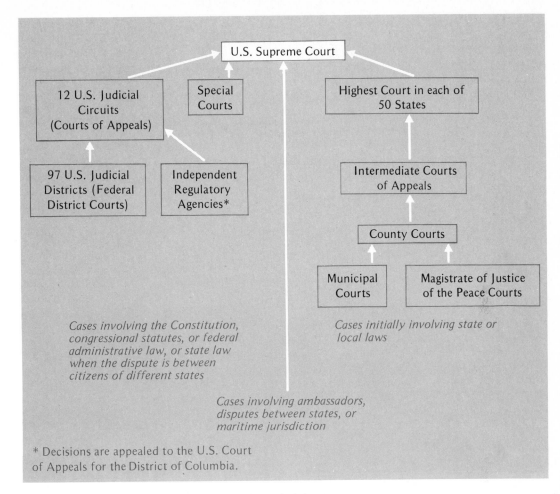

Figure 4–1 *Generalized court structure in the United States.*

conduct the trial. In the South, the heavy caseload arising from civil rights suits in the 1960s led to the assignment of additional judges to selected districts there. Caseload in the district courts was more than 170,000 in 1976, completely overwhelming the 400 judges. Two years later, 117 new judgeships were created.

JUDICIAL CIRCUITS. The nation is also divided into eleven **U.S. Judicial Circuits**—plus one exclusively for the District of Columbia. Appeals from the federal district courts go to these courts of appeals—as do appeals from certain executive agencies. These courts have between three and fifteen judges, also depending on caseload. In response to over 16,000 cases in 1976, Congress added 35 more circuit judges in 1978, bringing the total to 132. In 1980, Congress divided the old Fifth Circuit into two, creating the Eleventh. An appeal of a decision made by the U.S. Judicial

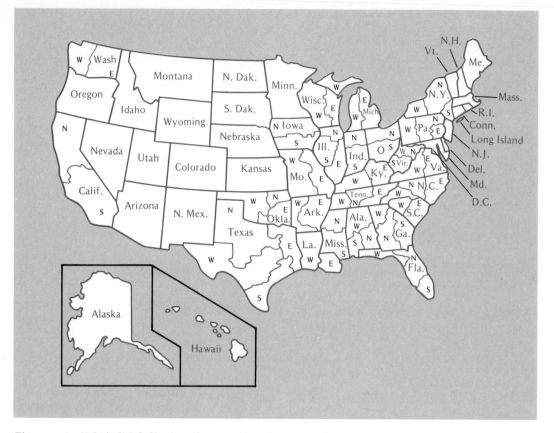

Figure 4–2 U.S. judicial districts. (Source: Administrative Office of the United States Courts.)

District Court in Oregon, for instance, would go to the U.S. Court of Appeals for the Ninth Judicial Circuit, which comprises the western coastal states. If the Federal Trade Commission made a decision on some product and that decision was appealed, it would go to the U.S. Court of Appeals for the District of Columbia.

SPECIAL FEDERAL COURTS. There is also a group of **special courts;** these function very much like the courts of appeals. The military justice system, for example, is headed by the **Court of Military Appeals,** created by Congress in 1950 to review the decisions of courts-martial. The **Court of Claims** has a unique purpose: as the federal government cannot be sued without its consent and it would be impossible for Congress to consider each case, this court was established. The decisions of the Court of Claims are rarely appealed; its monetary awards against the government must be backed up by a special appropriation from Congress. Respect for the Court of Claims decisions is demonstrated by the fact that these appropriations are usually made in a routine fashion. There is also a U.S. Court of Customs and Patent Appeals, which

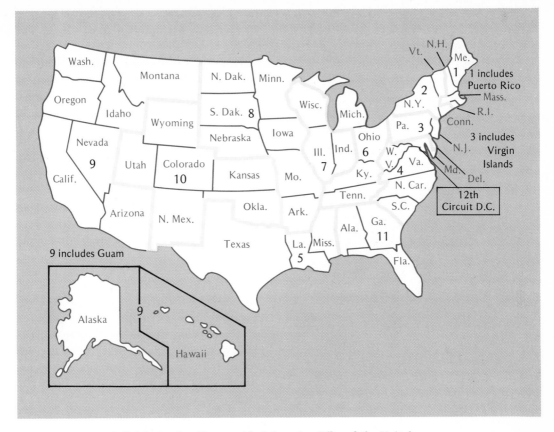

Figure 4-3 U.S. judicial circuits. (Source: Administrative Office of the United States Courts.)

reviews or hears appeals from the Customs Court, the Tariff Commission, and the Patent Office.

JURISDICTION

ORIGINAL JURISDICTION. **Original jurisdiction** is the right or authority of a court to try or hear a case for the first time. Federal district courts have original jurisdiction in cases involving a constitutional question or an interpretation of or challenge to a congressional law. The Supreme Court's original jurisdiction is granted by the Constitution only for very limited or special types of cases: essentially they involve ambassadors or other foreign diplomats, questions of maritime jurisdiction, or a disagreement between states.

APPELLATE JURISDICTION. **Appellate jurisdiction** is the ability to hear cases on appeal from lower courts. The Supreme Court has both appellate and original jurisdiction; the courts of appeals have appellate jurisdiction only. Normally, most federal cases start in a federal district court. If a party to the case

Archibald Cox upheld the public's confidence in judicial impartiality when appointed and then fired as Special Prosecutor by President Nixon during the Watergate scandal. Cox was succeeded by Leon Jaworski, who continued to press the case against the White House.

the President's associates. When Jaworski tried to force Nixon to turn over the subpoenaed tape recordings, the federal district court in the District of Columbia heard the case of *U.S. v. Nixon* and ordered the President to surrender the tapes. At this stage, the normal thing would have been for Nixon's lawyers to wait for nearly thirty days, the legal limit, and then file an appeal with the U.S. Court of Appeals for the District of Columbia. If Nixon lost there, his lawyers could appeal to the Supreme Court.

But Nixon's case was anything but normal: the President had been ordered by a federal court to surrender material that might show him to be guilty of criminal conduct. Jaworski—bear in mind that he was the winner at the district court level—petitioned the Supreme Court directly. He knew that the President's lawyers could drag the proceedings out for some time, so he chose to skip the court of appeals and go directly to the Supreme Court in hopes of obtaining a quick final decision. The Supreme Court heard the case and ruled, eight to zero, that the President had to surrender the subpoenaed tapes.[1]

COURT DISCRETION

At the lower levels of the federal courts, congressional statutes may require that a court accept certain kinds of cases. The Freedom of Information Act, for example, imposes such a requirement on the courts. The famous American aphorism that someone will "take a case clear to the Supreme Court," however, is plainly unrealistic: the Supreme Court is unique in that it may decide whether it will hear cases, based on their constitutional significance, and indeed it refuses many cases.

PRINCIPLES FOR ACCEPTING CASES. Many cases simply do not fall within federal jurisdiction. For a federal court to exercise **judi-**

wishes to appeal the decision (in other words, if the loser wishes to have the decision reversed), then it petitions a court of appeals. If the court of appeals hears the case, its decision can be appealed only one more time—to the Supreme Court.

We stress that this is the normal path for cases. In effect, the courts act as filters, for they can refuse to hear cases they consider unsuitable. A prominent exception to this normal path involved President Nixon. In 1973, while in charge of the Watergate case, Special Prosecutor Leon Jaworski sought to gain access to and control over some of the notorious Nixon tapes—White House conversations recorded on a system whose existence had been hidden from all except a very few of

cial discretion and decide to hear a case, it must be demonstrated that:

★ A federal question is involved. (An exception is a case between citizens of different states involving a question of state law).

★ The case is **justiciable** (there is a legal remedy).

★ The party bringing the suit is actually and substantially injured or can be injured if the case is not decided.

★ The question raised must not be hypothetical, but must be real, and one of the parties to the case must require a decision.

Cases come to the Supreme Court when one side of the case petitions the Court for review. Approximately 4,000 to 5,000 petitions are received each year, but the Court usually hears fewer than 300 of these. Some cases are accepted by the Supreme Court almost automatically. If, for instance, a lower federal court holds a law of Congress to be unconstitutional, the Supreme Court would probably be predisposed to settle the issue. If two conflicting decisions from lower federal courts involve the same point of law, the Supreme Court would probably find it necessary to accept an appeal. Without this action by the Court, contrary interpretations of the law or the Constitution could become confusing precedents for other cases.

The Supreme Court can also accept cases from state court systems, but only after all "state remedies" have been exhausted: an appeal to the Supreme Court can ordinarily be made only from the highest state court. Most Supreme Court cases originate in the state court systems; these cases are taken only if the court is satisfied that a federal issue is involved, such as the constitutionality of a state law or action. More than 900 state laws have been held unconstitutional by the Supreme Court, as compared with slightly more than 100 federal laws.

One factor that guides the Supreme Court in its decision to accept a case is its importance: does the case raise issues that extend beyond its immediate circumstances?

POLITICAL QUESTIONS

On some issues, mainly those it considers **political questions,** the Court has remained silent, usually by refusing to accept a case. These issues often involve the respective powers of the other branches of the federal government.[2] During the Vietnam War, no declaration of war was ever voted by Congress; but challenges to the authority of Presidents Johnson and Nixon to commit troops to action were rejected by the Supreme Court.

Even though certain issues are of the highest national importance and can be addressed only by the Supreme Court, its members sometimes avoid or postpone a review. These issues may eventually die down, as with the Vietnam-related cases after our withdrawal—or they may rise again in some other form.

NO DECISION IS A DECISION. One point should be emphasized here: when the Supreme Court refuses to hear a case, it is actually making a decision. By not deciding, it may be affirming or upholding the decision of a lower federal court or of a state court: Not deciding is still a decision. However, it does not result in a constitutional precedent, and that decision determines winners and losers as much as any full-fledged hearing and opinion on a case. Suppose, for instance, that homosexuals who worked for a certain city felt they were being denied equal employment opportunities and sought to have these practices ended by court order. If a lower court had previously decided that homosexuals lacked grounds for a complaint, then a Supreme

Viewpoint:
Chief Justice Vinson on the acceptance of cases
by the Supreme Court

To remain effective, the Supreme Court must continue to decide only those cases
which present questions whose resolution will have immediate impor-
tance far beyond the particular facts and parties involved. [Lawyers]
represent not only [their] clients, but tremendously important princi-
ples, upon which are based the plans, hopes and aspirations of a great
many people throughout the country.

Chief Justice FRED M. VINSON

Source: Address to the American Bar Association. Quoted in Anthony Lewis, *Gideon's Trumpet* (New York: Random House, 1964), p. 24.

Court refusal to hear the case would be a decision in favor of the city.

If the Court believes an issue is either too inflammatory or too political, it may reject an appeal. For instance, there was some debate about whether all the state ratifications of the proposed Equal Rights Amendment were valid, since some state legislatures later reversed themselves. Which action is valid—the state's ratification or its later reversal? The Supreme Court, in all likelihood, would prefer not to render an opinion on this type of question, and allow Congress to decide, if at all.

BAKER v. CARR. The Court was drawn into a major political question in the famous 1962 case of **Baker v. Carr**.[3] A suit was brought against the state of Tennessee to require it to redistrict the lower house of its state legislature according to population. The Tennessee constitution requires that state legislative districts be apportioned on the basis of population so that each district is about the same size; this had not been done for more than sixty years. As a result, urban areas, which had grown tremendously, still had the same numbers of representatives that they had had much earlier, and were underrepresented

in comparison with rural areas. Sixteen years before, in **Colegrove v. Green,** a case involving malapportionment in Illinois, the Court had stated that this was a political question. It had held that if legislative districts are not based on current population, relief could only come through the political process.[4]

However, waiting for state legislators to redistrict themselves—and perhaps remove themselves from office—had brought no results. Survival is as strong an instinct in politics as elsewhere, and few rural legislators were inclined to take the position that their seats really belonged to the large urban populations. To the surprise of many, the Supreme Court agreed to hear *Baker* v. *Carr*. It thus entered what one of its members, Justice Felix Frankfurter, had referred to as **"the political thicket"** in his opinion for the *Colegrove* case. Frankfurter held this same position in *Baker* v. *Carr*, fearing the consequences of the Court's becoming involved in such questions (see insert).

What was the "political" nature of this case? The Court's decision was that apportionment was a justiciable question and that a lower court could hear the case. If the Court could order the lower house of the Tennessee

*In a democratic society like ours, relief must come through an aroused popular
conscience that sears the conscience of the people's representatives.*

Justice FELIX FRANKFURTER

Source: *Baker v. Carr,* 369 U.S. 186, 270 (1962).

---

legislature reapportioned according to population, it could, in effect, order the states to structure their governments consistent with the "equal protection" clause of the Fourteenth Amendment. Not only was the federal government telling the states what to do, but one branch of the federal government (the judiciary) was issuing instructions to another branch of a state government (the legislative).

REYNOLDS v. *SIMS.* Having entered the "political thicket," as Frankfurter put it, the Supreme Court, two years later, rendered similar decisions on other cases involving reapportionment. In one of these, **Reynolds v. Sims,**[5] the Court held that both houses of a bicameral (two-house) state legislature must be apportioned on the basis of population (see insert).

The Court's next step was even more startling in its political implications, but it was both natural and inevitable. Membership in the House of Representatives is guaranteed, with an absolute minimum of one representative for each state. Every ten years the number of seats allocated to each state is determined according to the national census. However, the Constitution says nothing directly about how many people there must be in each congressional district. For that matter, nothing is directly said about the existence of congressional districts at all. But in one of the informal modifications of the Constitution achieved by custom, we elect our representatives to the House from districts within each

state. By law, there is one representative for each district.

The principle that governed the Supreme Court's *Baker* and *Reynolds* decisions is known as "one man, one vote." In other words, no one person's vote should be worth more than that of any other person. If one state legislative district should happen to have 10,000 people, and another should have 50,000 people, there is an obvious difference in the value of the vote.[6] Any single vote in the less populated district would effectively be worth five times that of any vote in the more populated district. The Court was faced the same year, 1964, with a logical but difficult extension of "one man, one vote"—in the House of Representatives.

WESBERRY v. *SANDERS.* Could the Supreme Court be so bold as to challenge the composition of a coordinate branch of the federal government? Earlier, the answer might have been no, but this was an unusual era: the Supreme Court had ignored its own actions in the *Colegrove* case of 1946, as well as Frankfurter's warning about the political thicket. In the Court plunged. It was shown that one congressional district in Georgia was about three times as large as another. This had come about because congressional district lines in Georgia were drawn by a state legislature dominated by rural interests. Rural legislators favored their own cause, and rural congressional districts had substantially fewer people in them than urban and suburban districts. The Court held, in *Wesberry* v. *Sanders,* that "as nearly as is practicable, one man's vote in a congressional election is to be worth as much as another's."[7]

The Court's decision created an uproar. Rural legislators, who could see their seats threatened by redistricting, were quite disconcerted. Yet the redistricting was to be done in their own states, not by the federal courts. Those doing the redistricting, or drawing the district lines, would no longer necessarily be dominated by rural interests. In effect, the Court had plunged into the political thicket and, except for some shouting, emerged unscathed.

Why didn't the Supreme Court apply the same "one man, one vote" principle to the Senate? The answer is simple. Article I, Section 3 of the Constitution guarantees two senators to each state—regardless of population; this apportionment was part of the Connecticut Compromise between the large and small states. The Supreme Court judges the constitutionality of actions, and the Constitution itself is the basis of the apportionment of Senate seats.

PRINCIPLES OF JUDICIAL ACTIVITY

JUDICIAL ACTIVISM AND JUDICIAL RESTRAINT. When the Court agreed to hear *Baker* v. *Carr,* it was not only ignoring Frankfurter's warning, but also engaging in **judicial activism;** that is, it was taking an active hand in the governance of this nation. The Supreme Court did not seek out the case, for no court can act except on cases that are brought before it. When courts engage in judicial activism, we associate this with social change and upheaval. In contrast to this is a period of **judicial restraint,** when courts refuse to hear cases or reverse previous decisions. In these conservative periods, the courts are less willing to make broad and far-reaching decisions.

THE WARREN COURT. The era in which the Supreme Court was headed by Chief Justice Earl Warren (1954–1969) is one of the most notable in our history. An earlier notable era, of course, was during John Marshall's tenure as Chief Justice (1801–1835); it was he who laid the groundwork for the doctrine of federal supremacy over the states.

As Chief Justice, Warren proved himself to be a visionary social thinker. One of his earliest decisions was delivered in 1954; he spoke for the Court in its unanimous decision on school desegregation—that "separate but equal" was not equal—discussed in the last chapter. *Brown* v. *Board of Education of Topeka* is widely recognized as a landmark, for it threw the weight of the federal government to the side of those seeking the application of the "equal protection of the laws" clause of the

Fourteenth Amendment to segregation and civil rights cases.[8] No longer would the Court allow skin color to determine who wins and who loses. It also heralded a period of judicial activism unlike anything since Marshall's term on the Court.

In a series of decisions for which he was variously applauded and vilified, Warren led the Court through a significant group of cases—*Brown* v. *Board, Baker* v. *Carr* and others; his actions can only be referred to as judicial activism, particularly in the areas of civil rights and civil liberties.

The Warren Court was accused of "legislating," or making the law, rather than confining itself to applying the law. This argument came from those profoundly disturbed by the liberal tenor of the Warren Court's decisions, which broadly interpreted the Bill of Rights and the Fourteenth Amendment. President Eisenhower was critical of the *Brown* v. *Board* decision, commenting, "you cannot legislate morality." Whether he was correct is another matter, but it is apparent that he was anything but happy with the Supreme Court and its Chief Justice. Eisenhower, however, had selected Warren to be Chief Justice in the first place. How could he have been so misled as to Warren's outlook?

SELECTION OF JUDGES

Under the terms of the Constitution, federal judges are nominated by the president and confirmed or rejected by the Senate. In most cases, approval is fairly routine. One reason for this is that the nominee's name is often cleared informally with senators before the nomination is announced. The president has usually solicited names of potential nominees from the American Bar Association or sought the association's approval of a list of nominees. As the national association to which most attorneys belong, the ABA has considerable prestige as a conservative organization. When the president selects a nominee, the

Justice Louis D. Brandeis was appointed by President Wilson in 1916.

Senate Judiciary Committee conducts hearings, normally a quiet, routine matter. After committee approval, the name is sent to the Senate floor, where approval is usually routine. Not including members of the present Supreme Court—through 1981—only ninety-six people, all men, had served on the Supreme Court. President Reagan's 1981 nomination of a woman, Sandra Day O'Connor, was a break in the males-only tradition. Another seven nominees declined their posts after confirmation; five had their names withdrawn; and twenty-four were rejected outright by the Senate.

PARTY AFFILIATION. The president must consider many factors when selecting nominees for the Supreme Court or other federal judgeships. It appears that political party affiliation is one of the most important, though

Byron White, a friend of President Kennedy and past chairman of the National Citizens for Kennedy organization, has a view of the selection process which, while realistic, may also be biased.

There is nothing odious about the preference for Democrats. Picking judges is a political process in the best sense of those words.

Associate Justice BYRON WHITE

Source: Remarks to the American Bar Association. Quoted by Victor S. Navasky, *Kennedy Justice* (New York: Atheneum, 1977), p. 256.

the public may not see the relevance of this criterion. Presidents have traditionally selected ninety percent of their nominees for federal judgeships from their own party— hardly an accident of fate. One reason is the strong American political tradition that to the victors belong the spoils. Thus, the president can select nominees from his party and keep the solid support of the party organization. Although there is not supposed to be such a thing as "Democratic justice" or "Republican justice," party members do like to see their own kind occupy positions of influence. Further, presidents may consider it more likely that judges of their own party will take a view of the law and its uses similar to theirs. The same thing applies to the creation of new federal judicial districts and new federal judgeships. In 1978, a Democratic Congress approved the addition of 152 new judgeships to federal district and appeals courts—to be nominated by Democrat Jimmy Carter.

A related consideration that presidents must take into account is known as **senatorial courtesy.** This means that a president normally defers to his party's senior senator from the state where the federal court appointment will be made; this courtesy is not limited to court appointments. The president and his staff will ask if there is a preference as to who should be nominated. If the senator has a preference, it is usually respected. If there is no preference, senatorial courtesy requires clearing the name of the person the president is considering with the same senator. If this senator is unhappy with a nomination—or has not been consulted—he can rise on the floor of the Senate and say that he feels the name under consideration to be "personally objectionable." Senators respect each other's objections, and this is normally a fatal blow to an appointment. Presidents therefore carefully respect the Senate and the tradition of senatorial courtesy.

LAW SCHOOL. Other factors enter into the selection of judges as well. In the composition of the Supreme Court, there has been a tendency to have at least one seat reserved to each of the most prestigious law schools—Harvard, Yale, and Columbia.

ETHNICITY. Following the appointment of Louis Brandeis by President Wilson in 1916, there was a tradition for more than fifty years of a "Jewish seat" on the Supreme Court.

After being nominated for Supreme Court Justice, G. Harrold Carswell's record had been sharply attacked as inadequate. In his defense, a Republican senator may have sealed his fate.

Even if he were mediocre, there are a lot of mediocre judges and people and lawyers. They are entitled to a little representation aren't they, and a little chance? We can't have all Brandeises, and Cardozos and Frankfurters and stuff like that there.

Senator ROMAN HRUSKA

Source: Quoted by Michael Barone, Grant Ujifusa, and Douglas Matthews, *The Almanac of American Politics 1976* (New York: E.P. Dutton & Co., 1975), p. 494.

Brandeis was joined by Benjamin Cardozo. Other Jewish members have been Felix Frankfurter, Arthur Goldberg, and Abe Fortas. If charges of impropriety had not been leveled against Fortas, which led to his resignation in 1969, he might still be on the bench. In 1967, Thurgood Marshall became the first black appointed to the Supreme Court—possibly the start of a new tradition.

PHILOSOPHY. Selections based on the dubious criteria of traditions and politics have little to do with judicial excellence; if they result in poor appointments, we all become losers. In addition to selecting members of his own party, the president also tries to select an individual who shares the same basic judicial philosophy—someone whose view of the law is like his own. However, occasional surprises occur: Warren no doubt surprised Eisenhower and other justices have revealed philosophies on the bench different from those with which they were originally credited. Byron White, a member of the present Court, was a close friend of President Kennedy, who nominated him. Yet White's performance has been much more conservative than anyone might have predicted.

REGION. Another factor that seems to matter is geographical region: not too many judges should come from a single area, such as the East or South. A revealing story with regard to this concerns President Nixon's attempts to appoint a southerner to the Supreme Court.

As part of his "Southern strategy" in the 1968 election campaign, Nixon promised that he would appoint a southerner at the first opportunity. No southerners had been nominated since Hugo Black joined the Court in 1937. When Fortas resigned in 1969, President Nixon nominated Clement Haynsworth of South Carolina, a federal appeals court judge. At first, nothing seemed wrong. In the course of the nomination hearings, however, questions were raised about his participation in judicial decisions in which he had a financial interest. After a major campaign the nomination was rejected. Many Republicans, including some of the leaders of the Senate, refused to support the President on this nomination.

Following this rejection, President Nixon still had the vacant Supreme Court seat to fill; and he still wanted to fulfill his promise to appoint a southerner. He selected, in 1970, another appeals court judge, this time a

Floridian originally from Georgia, G. Harrold Carswell. Having been through a major battle on the Haynsworth matter, the members of the Senate Judiciary Committee had little taste for a bitter fight. Civil rights groups and others raised questions about Carswell's alleged racism and his qualifications to serve as a judge. A major campaign was launched against Carswell, in which leading legal scholars analyzed various opinions Carswell had written while a judge (see insert). Once again, the Senate rejected Nixon's nominee, again with some Republican defections.[9] In 1971 Nixon was able to fulfill his promise to the South—by appointing Justice Lewis Powell, a Virginian.

The Courts and the Separation of Powers

EXECUTIVE PREROGATIVE

The immediate question raised by President Nixon after the Senate's rejection of Haynsworth and Carswell concerned the proper role of the president and the Senate in nominations and appointments.

What is centrally at issue . . . is the constitutional responsibility of the President to appoint members of the court. . . . *The fact remains under the Constitution, it is the duty of the President to appoint and of the Senate to advise and consent* [emphasis added].[10]

Nixon raised an interesting issue. What is the exact nature of the president's power of appointment? We can look at this question constitutionally, historically, and practically. In the constitutional sense, it would seem that Nixon was too inclined toward a rigid interpretation of his role according to the Constitution. Article II, Section 2, states, "the President shall nominate, and by and with the Advice and Consent of the Senate, shall appoint Ambassadors, other public Ministers and Consuls, Judges of the Supreme Court. . . ." The nomination power is strictly the president's under the Constitution. But the phrase "by and with the Advice and Consent of the Senate" suggests that his appointive powers are shared rather than exclusive. The argument advanced by Nixon received no significant support from his colleagues in the legal profession.

Historically it would also seem that he was incorrect: the Senate had outright rejected nine nominations for the Supreme Court before Haynsworth and Carswell; fifteen others had lapsed or been withdrawn. Historical practice suggests an informal change in the Constitution—a Senate veto power—even if the framers intended otherwise. For that matter, there have been many other rejections of presidential nominees for public positions.[11]

Nixon's anger at the Senate also seemed to ignore his own previous attitude toward the selection process. In 1968, President Johnson did not seek re-election. When he nominated Abe Fortas, who was already on the Court, to replace retiring Chief Justice Earl Warren, Nixon never spoke out against the campaign conducted by Senate Republicans who opposed the choice. When Fortas's nomination was held up in the Senate, it meant that Justice Warren would have to submit his resignation to Mr. Nixon, who was apparently enroute to an election victory. Republicans, with Nixon's blessing, provided him the opportunity of choosing the next Chief Justice, Warren E. Burger. Nixon's outburst against the Senate was more likely the result of frustration over the delay in implementing a 1968 campaign pledge that if elected, he would reverse the liberal leanings of the Court.[12]

RELIANCE ON THE EXECUTIVE

The courts can only make decisions; they do not have the authority to enforce them. For this, they must rely on the goodwill of the executive branch. Normally, the courts may expect that the executive branch of the government will take steps to enforce their decisions. Although President Eisenhower expressed displeasure with the decision of *Brown* v. *Board of Education,* he was obliged to deal with it and its consequences. One of these was the attempt, in 1957, to integrate Central High School in Little Rock, Arkansas; the order to integrate had been based on the Supreme Court's decision in the *Brown* case. Nine black children attempted to integrate the high school; they were barred by members of the Arkansas National Guard called out by Governor Orval Faubus. A federal court ordered the guardsmen to leave. When they were withdrawn and mob violence broke out, President Eisenhower called them to duty under federal control and augmented them with paratroopers from the regular army. In effect, it was the president who enforced the *Brown* decision.

The degree to which the courts must rely on the executive branch is further indicated by the well-known **Cherokee Indian case.** The Cherokee Indian tribe in Georgia had sought to prevent the confiscation of its lands, citing a 1794 treaty that protected them and their property; at stake, unfortunately, was gold on the Cherokee lands and the availability of property for whites. In 1832, the Supreme Court upheld the tribe's rights.[13] President Andrew Jackson, hardly a friend of the Indians, reportedly said: "John Marshall has made his decision; now let him enforce it." Of course, Marshall could not enforce it, and the Indians eventually lost their lands, beginning their trek to Oklahoma on the infamous "trail of tears."

COURTS VERSUS EXECUTIVE. Occasionally the Supreme Court must take action against the executive branch; it must then depend on goodwill and a tradition of acceptance for the decisions to be enforced. One memorable example of this involved the threat of a strike against the steel companies during the Korean War—though no formal state of war existed. President Truman believed the strike would have serious consequences for the war effort. He thus ordered the seizure of the steel mills and placed their operation under federal authority. In *Youngstown Sheet and Tube Co. v. Sawyer,* the Supreme Court ordered the steel mills to be returned to their rightful owners.[14] Without any dispute, President Truman complied with the Court's order.

COMPLIANCE TRADITION. This **tradition of compliance** is probably one of the strongest weapons the courts have. We have already mentioned the case of *U.S.* v. *Nixon,* in which suit was brought to force President Nixon to surrender certain tape recordings. Some had real concern that the President would not comply with a court order to surrender the tapes. His press secretary, Ron Ziegler, had stated that President Nixon would comply with a definitive court decision, but the question immediately arose as to what was meant by "definitive." Was it a unanimous decision? Or eight to one? Or seven to two? Or six to three? The debate ended when the Court held, eight to zero, that the claim of executive privilege (the right of the president to withhold information) could not be used to withhold evidence relevant to criminal charges unless there were overriding national security reasons. The Court found that Nixon's defense had failed to establish this point, and it ordered the surrender of the tapes.[15] Justice Rehnquist excused himself from the case. It was thought by some at the time that his reason involved his former work for Nixon as assistant attorney general—and a possible conflict of interest on this question. Judges are not required by law to excuse themselves from cases involving conflict of interest, but they frequently do so.

In other less well-known cases, this tradition of compliance has persisted—although the general acceptance of a decision may involve highly emotional issues. For instance, when the Supreme Court ruled that school prayers could not be required or made a part of the normal school day, strongly held values were at stake: many deeply religious people saw themselves and the nation as the losers. One response to such cases is to try to find a weakness in the decision and appeal a similar case based on that loophole. Another is to try to ignore the court decision entirely: in the school-prayer decision, some communities tried to overlook it—but were stopped by the tradition of compliance, upheld by influential people in the community.

The Court may recognize that its main source of power is, in fact, its own prestige, and may avoid cases in which it suspects that its decisions will not be enforced—a situation which would make it the loser.

President Franklin Roosevelt revolted against the Court's decisions in a markedly different way. The New Deal presidency of Roosevelt was noted for legislation that greatly extended executive power. Congress rushed through bill after bill, granting the president—and by implication the federal government—a body of sweeping powers. Taking a broad view of the elastic clause, Congress felt it had the necessary and proper powers to enact certain legislation in a time of economic crisis, the Great Depression. Not everyone was of the same opinion, however; case after case came before the Supreme Court, challenging Roosevelt and his New Deal programs. And in decision after decision, the Court struck down his programs as unconstitutional.

Roosevelt apparently wanted a few

John Marshalls on the Court—individuals willing to take a broader view of what was constitutional. By 1937, he had not made a single appointment to the Supreme Court. In his four years he had been faced only with justices appointed by his more conservative predecessors.

COURT PACKING. Roosevelt thus devised what is known as his "court-packing" plan. Since the Constitution does not specify the number of judges who will sit on the Supreme Court, and since Congress had altered that number several times in the past, Roosevelt proposed that he be allowed to nominate more judges. He would appoint one new judge for every Supreme Court justice over the age of seventy who had not retired after ten years on the bench. A limit would have been set of six additional judges; the Court would thereby have been increased from nine to fifteen members. He rationalized this as an improvement in the Court's efficiency, but he was clearly trying to pack the Court with judges more favorable to his programs. The plan was a transparent attempt to interfere with the Court and was defeated. However, Roosevelt achieved his aims, for the Court swung toward supporting his programs. Many believe that some justices feared conflict if they continued to oppose Roosevelt, and that continued opposition to the New Deal might cost them public support and lead to the success of the Roosevelt plan. The Court's swing had actually taken place before Congress defeated Roosevelt's plan. But by the end of his second term in 1940, through natural attrition, Roosevelt was able to appoint four new members and put his own stamp on the Court.

Who were the winners and losers in this situation? Roosevelt lost his battle to pack the Court but won his point about the Court's needing to be more responsive to changing times. The Court retained its nine members and proved that it was held in considerable respect by the press, the Congress, and popular opinion; it also proved that it was not unresponsive. If anything, the debate between Roosevelt and the Court showed that the principle of checks and balances has fine points found in human nature, not in the Constitution.

CONFLICT WITH THE CONGRESS

REVERSAL BY AMENDMENT? Just as the president may be disturbed by the Court's actions, the Congress can also react swiftly and loudly—if not always effectively. In recent years, certain Supreme Court decisions have produced strong reactions from members of Congress. As could be expected, a resounding outcry arose from the Court's decisions in the *Baker, Reynolds,* and *Wesberry* reapportionment cases. House members were especially irate because their friends in the state legislatures, who had always drawn congressional district lines, might no longer be dominant. Lower-house district lines had to be redrawn in many states because of *Wesberry.* Rurally dominated lower houses were declared unconstitutional by the *Baker* decision—as were rurally dominated upper houses by the *Reynolds* decision. Therefore the seats of many representatives were in jeopardy. Considerable discussion arose about a constitutional amendment that would allow apportionment on a basis other than population. Since the debate generated more heat than light, nothing came of it.

Another issue that vexed many members of Congress in the 1960s concerned the decisions on school prayers.[16] Many constituents sincerely supported school prayer; and various ways were tried to avoid compliance. Again there was talk of a constitutional amendment, but it did not get anywhere. In sum, an issue that directly affects members of Congress—through the disapproval of their constituents and by touching on deeply held values—may lead to attempts to reverse the decision. These attempts are seldom successful. One successful reversal is the Sixteenth Amendment, which authorized a direct personal income tax. This reversed a Court decision by including in the Constitution that which had previously been declared unconstitutional. But, short of reversal, what can Congress do?

PROTECTION FOR COURTS. Under the Constitution, Congress cannot punish federal judges by lowering their salaries while in office, a provision specifically included to protect federal courts from capricious treatment by Congress. In other words, the courts are protected from having to make politically popular decisions when their best instincts are otherwise. Judges also serve for life, unless removed for improper behavior; forced retirement or resignation is not possible under the Constitution.

CHANGING COURT JURISDICTION. One possibility, though rarely used, is for Congress to alter the Supreme Court's appellate jurisdiction. During the post–Civil War period of Reconstruction, Congress removed the Court's power to hear cases involving writs of **habeas corpus;** these are provisions for a court to order that a prisoner be handed over for either trial or release. In the late 1950s, an attempt to restrict the Court on criminal rights cases was narrowly defeated by the Senate. In 1964, the House passed a bill that would have removed the Court's jurisdiction in cases involving state legislative apportionment; however, the Senate never considered the bill and it died.

IMPEACHMENT AND REMOVAL. The only alternative open to Congress, short of these steps, is to impeach and remove a judge. In Table 2–1, we saw that this process has been tried several times. Only one member of the Supreme Court was ever impeached; in 1804, Justice Samuel Chase was charged with "mis-

Justice William O. Douglas was among the most prominent and controversial members of the liberal Warren Court.

conduct in trials impairing the confidence and respect for the courts." He was later acquitted of all charges by the Senate. Of the twelve impeachments voted by the House, nine have been against federal judges. Of these, five were acquitted by the Senate; three were convicted; and one resigned before Senate trial began. Over forty years have passed since the last impeachment charges were voted against any federal judge—or any other federal official, for that matter. It could be argued that the impeachment and removal provisions of the Constitution have fallen into disuse and are no longer effective.

Justice William O. Douglas, who served on the Supreme Court longer than any other member (1939–1975) was the object of two attempted impeachments. In 1953, he granted a temporary stay of execution to Julius and Ethel Rosenberg, who had been convicted of espionage and treason in passing nuclear secrets to the Russians. The attempted impeachment failed. Seventeen years later, in 1970, he became the center of another storm of controversy over his personal life, particularly the fact that he had remarried several times and his wives were considerably younger than he.[17] When Haynsworth and Carswell were both rejected for confirmation, a serious attempt was made to impeach Justice Douglas—by way of conservative vengeance.

Douglas was charged by Gerald Ford, then House Republican minority leader, with several instances of judicial and private misconduct. Although his penchant for marrying young women was not included in the formal charges, it seemed to many that this indicated his irresponsible attitudes. Essentially, Ford charged that Douglas had participated—and dissented—in a decision involving an obscenity charge against a publisher who had paid Douglas $350 for a magazine article. Douglas had also had an article appear in a magazine that published nude photographs, was a consultant to an organization described as "leftish," and assisted a foundation that donated funds to this same organization. These charges were referred to the House Judiciary Committee; eight months later, a subcommittee reported that the charges were either erroneous or based only on circumstantial evidence.

Ironically, when Justice Douglas resigned in 1975 for reasons of health, his letter was accepted by then President Ford, who duly noted that the retiring Douglas's "distinguished years of service are unequaled in all the history of the court."[18]

The decision in *Marbury* v. *Madison* firmly established the principle of judicial review over acts of Congress and the president. The reasoning appeared tortuous to some, and his decision caused a controversy which has never quite burned out. But, in one paragraph, Marshall laid the basis for judicial review which has never been contradicted.

It is, emphatically, the province and duty of the judicial department to say what the law is. Those who apply the rule to particular cases, must of necessity expound and interpret that rule. If two laws conflict with each other, the courts must decide on the operation of each. So, if a law be in opposition to the constitution; if both the law and constitution apply to a particular case, so that the court must either decide that case, conformable to the law, disregarding the constitution; or conformable to the constitution, disregarding the law; the court must determine which of these conflicting rules governs the case; this is of the very essence of judicial duty.

Chief Justice JOHN MARSHALL

Source: *Marbury* v. *Madison*, 1 Cranch 137.

Why the Power of the Courts?

JUDICIAL REVIEW

The courts have generally helped to build up their status with the public.[19] But there would not be the enormous volume of work for the courts if they did not have the power of **judicial review** over certain types of cases. In one major case, *Marbury* v. *Madison,* Chief Justice John Marshall laid the grounds for what many have come to see as the supremacy of the judicial branch over the legislative and executive branches.[20]

In the closing days of his administration, President John Adams had appointed a number of "midnight judges"—so called because they were members of his own political faction who were to fill positions created by a Congress that had already lost at the polls.

One of those appointed was William Marbury, who was named a justice of the peace in the District of Columbia. His commission was not received before President Adams left office, and James Madison, the new secretary of state, refused to give it to him. Marbury sued in the Supreme Court to compel the delivery of his commission. He was able to do so because the **Judiciary Act of 1789** had added to the constitutionally prescribed original jurisdiction of the Court, allowing cases of this nature to be brought directly to it.

Marshall agreed that Marbury was entitled to the commission and chastised Madison for not delivering it. However, he pointed out that Marbury's coming before the Court was only made possible by a section of the Judiciary Act of 1789—and Marshall declared that section of the act unconstitutional, for it enlarged the original jurisdiction of the Court under the Constitution. Since the Constitution is the highest law of the land and the document on which judges and courts base their decisions, it is not possible for Congress to alter the intent of the Constitution without amending it.

This piece of legal reasoning is a classic of its kind. At one and the same time, Marshall held that:

★ The courts have the power to review acts of Congress.

★ The courts can, by implication, review the actions of the executive branch.

Although Congress may not alter the intent of the framers of the Constitution, and although judicial review is not mentioned in the Constitution, courts and judges do have the implied right to make judgments based on Chief Justice Marshall's decision.

REVIEW OF STATE COURT ACTS. Having established the principle of judicial review of legislative and executive actions, the courts still had to resolve their position toward the states. The Constitution had provided for Supreme Court jurisdiction if a state was a party to a case involving the national government. Two cases quickly established the principles involved. In the case of **Martin** v. **Hunter's Lessee,**[21] Marshall declared that, if a federal or constitutional question was involved in suits between private parties, federal courts could review the decisions of state courts.[22] This finding was extended in **Cohens** v. **Virginia,** when the principle was hammered into place. If cases involve the Constitution, federal law, or treaties—even though a state may be a party to the action— federal courts are the appropriate place for review of state court decisions. If these questions are raised in a suit against a state, it is not an abridgement of the Eleventh Amendment, which limits suits by individuals against states.

Politics and the Courts

One reason why there is so much respect for our courts may be that they are perceived to be above politics. In the popular sense, politics is often considered to border on sin, if not actually partake of it. This view is naive and ignores the necessities and realities of government decisions. If we see politics as the process in which it is determined who wins and who loses, then politics is inevitable in our system, or in any system. It is also naive to believe that the courts are apolitical: in every sense of the word, they may very well be the *most* political of our institutions.

ACCEPTING CASES FOR REVIEW

One annual guessing game surrounding the courts, especially the Supreme Court, concerns which cases they will choose to hear. The courts do not have to accept all cases and they would be even more burdened than they already are if this were so. It is physically impossible for them to hear all appeals. In one of its periodic moods of judicial restraint, the Supreme Court may refuse to hear controversial cases.

Even if a case is accepted, a decision is not necessarily forthcoming: the Court can, for example, declare a case to be *moot*—that is, there is nothing truly to be decided. In 1974, the Court did just that in a case involving "reverse discrimination." The University of Washington Law School was charged with violating the "equal protection" clause of the Fourteenth Amendment by allowing special quotas for minority students. The white complainant, who had exceeded the qualifications set for minority students, had been denied admission to the law school. In the course of his suit, a lower court ordered him admitted, and the law school complied—but appealed the decision. The Supreme Court agreed to

Most cases are decided in the lower courts, where the constitutional requirement of trial by jury is most evident.

hear the case. Observers of the Court thought that, at last, a decision would be made on the question of reverse discrimination. Instead, the Court held the point to be moot, since the complainant was already in the law school—and would indeed graduate that year; in effect, there was no real complaint to be decided in this case.[23]

HEARING AND DECIDING CASES AS POLITICS

JURISDICTIONAL LIMITS. The Supreme Court can decide to hear cases only within certain rather clear-cut limits. For instance, it must have the jurisdiction to hear a case in the first place. If Congress places limits on the Court's appellate jurisdiction—without violat-

ing the Constitution—as it did following the Civil War, the Court simply cannot accept a case for review.

CERTIORARI. The main route by which cases reach the Supreme Court is through a **writ of certiorari;** this Latin term means "to be made more certain." When someone appeals for a review, a grant of the writ is an order that the record of the case—in the last court to have heard it—be sent forward. The Court cannot simply reach down to the lower courts, indiscriminately, and issue the writ: cases must be appealed to the Court by petition. One party or the other must request a review of the last decision made. If four or more justices feel that the issue warrants a hearing, and if they do not feel constrained by the possible political nature of the case, the Court may issue a writ of *certiorari*—in which event the case is scheduled to be heard. Given the press of business, the Court may join together two or more cases in which similar circumstances or principles are involved.

Since its decisions are made in secret, little is known of the internal politics of the Court.[24] Private conferences are held in which the justices discuss new cases under consideration for review and possible decisions on cases already heard. The decisions are written and circulated among the justices with great secrecy; the public seldom finds out what is contained in a draft opinion—or how one justice may have been persuaded by others to change his mind. The reported persuasion of the undecided by the majority in order to achieve a unanimous opinion in the case of *U.S.* v. *Nixon* is an example of this. Some justices felt unanimity was necessary, because they feared that the President would not surrender the tapes to Special Prosecutor Jaworski—and the tradition of compliance with and respect for the Court's decisions would therefore suffer.

BRIEFS.   Before they actually convene for the hearing, the justices have an opportunity to review the cases by reading **briefs** or written summaries of the legal and constitutional questions involved. The term *brief* is frequently a misnomer, for the summary can be quite lengthy. Each side submits a brief, setting forth the facts in question and citing the Constitution, statutory law, and the legal precedents of other decisions or common law that support its own position.

BRANDEIS BRIEFS.   Among the types of briefs the Court receives, two varieties may be used to illustrate the political nature of the Court. One of these is the **Brandeis brief,** so named after Louis Brandeis, who used this approach before he was appointed to the Supreme Court. In this type of brief, the argument is not restricted to normal references to Constitution, statute, precedent, and facts; instead, the consequences of a law or decision are examined. Probably the most famous example of this approach is the Court's use, verbatim, of large sections of the arguments presented by the plaintiff in the *Brown* v. *Board* case. Rather than limiting itself solely to whether or not the Constitution guarantees "equal protection" of the laws in cases involving public education, the Court went far beyond this and examined the sociological and psychological consequences of segregated education. This type of opinion and the brief on which it was based are often referred to as sociological law, as distinguished from constitutional, statutory, or common law.

AMICUS CURIAE BRIEFS.   The second variety is the **amicus curiae** brief—a written argument, submitted by one or more self-described "friends of the court." In theory, there are only two parties to a case, the plaintiff and the respondent; in reality, there are often many interested individuals and organizations who wish to make their position to the Court known and clear. What they offer may not all be new and may not contribute directly to the Court's decision in a substantive or legal sense. But their briefs are political statements about who is affected by the case and what they believe the decision should be. Imagine a case in which an environmental group sues a firm for dumping contaminants into a lake. An *amicus curiae* brief might be filed by the government, siding with the conservation group; other companies and industrial organizations might file on the side of the defendant. Thus briefs might be filed by organizations such as the Sierra Club and Friends of the Earth against the company; the United States Chamber of Commerce and the AFL–CIO might file on behalf of the company, since their interest in protecting profits and jobs might find them on the same side in this case. None of these organizations would be directly involved in the suit, but filing briefs on one side or another would let the Court know how they and other concerned groups felt about the case.[25] Chief Justice Burger has complained that too many *amicus* briefs are filed and contribute to the Court's workload. His complaint suggests that the briefs are, in fact, read, and may have some influence on final decisions.

The hearing of a case before the Supreme Court is one of the great spectacles that can be observed. Hearings are held in a magnificent courtroom and are quite different from cases as portrayed on television or in the movies. No jury is present; a time limit is set for oral presentations; and there is no examination of witnesses or introduction of surprise evidence. Attorneys for both sides are dressed formally. Justices can interrupt the attorneys at any time. Occasionally during the not-too-distant past, they have either dozed on the bench or shown their contempt for the argument by turning their backs and reading a newspaper. If the case is of unusual importance, observers may try to guess which way each justice will vote, based on the type of question each asks the attorneys.

CONFERENCES AND OPINION WRITING. After the formal hearing, the justices retire to discuss the case in secret. When ready to vote, they do so starting with the newest member and then according to increasing seniority—a custom that has apparently developed so that junior members will not be influenced by their senior colleagues. Then the Chief Justice will either write the opinion for his side of the case or assign the task to one of the associate justices who agreed with him; the senior justice on the opposing side will do the same. The assignment of an opinion can reflect internal Court politics as well as provide an indication of the importance of the case. When the Chief Justice decides to write the opinion for his side or to write a unanimous opinion—as in the *Brown* case—this signals the importance he attaches to it. Drafts of opinions for both

sides are circulated to other members of the Court, and comments are made by the other justices. Occasionally, the force and reasoning of a draft opinion may actually persuade a justice to change sides. It is said that Justice Oliver Wendell Holmes would simply comment "good law" on a draft opinion if he wished to give it his highest praise.

COMMON LAW. Judges participate in what is known as the **common law tradition** when they write decisions. This tradition, borrowed from the British, simply means that a decision, or judge-made law, may act as a *precedent* in later cases when similar questions arise. Thus the nature of a vote may be important to the future of similar cases. A unanimous decision implies that a reversal is unlikely in the foreseeable future; a strong majority such as eight to one or seven to two may also carry the same weight. In other cases, the decision may be split more evenly. Although there may be a single opinion written for each side, each justice may feel inclined to add his own opinion; it sometimes happens that a five to four decision is accompanied by eight or nine separate opinions. If a majority of five justices concurs—but each for different reasons—and four dissenting judges write four dissents, the legal principles governing the decision are anything but clear. Hence, the majority opinion would probably be challenged—in the form of a related case—very shortly. Lawyers are uncomfortable with these split opinions, especially when there are several sets of opinions offered, since no firm principle is established.

A LEGISLATIVE ROLE
FOR THE COURTS

Since the days of the New Deal, when Franklin Roosevelt felt so frustrated by the Supreme Court that he tried to pack it, the Court has become more and more active in civil rights and civil liberties. The scope of that activity is the subject of our next chapter.

This National Guard convoy prepares to enforce school desegregation in Boston, as ordered by the federal courts in 1975.

We can distinguish ebbs and flows in this activity: there was a great spurt of it in the days of Earl Warren and something of a retreat under Warren Burger.

Many critics of the Warren Court focussed on what they considered its attempts to legislate, rather than simply to make, decisions. Yet American law, which is descended directly from the English tradition, definitely includes judge-made, or common, law. Since it is impossible for legislatures to make laws governing all possible activities, situations will arise in which courts and judges must decide an issue for which there is no clear and definite rule. If they do not retreat from the decision by, say, refusing to hear the case, they must rely on previous cases, that is, on precedent or the common law, as well as on the Constitution and the statutes. In doing so, they must rely on their own best judgment. The Court has had to act to lend meaning to the Constitution—and to keep it alive through interpretation. If this is legislation, then the Court cannot avoid it.

★ Issue ★

The Selection of Federal and Supreme Court Judges

One little-known problem of our judicial system is the manner in which federal judges are selected. We have mentioned some of the criteria included in the president's choice of nominee. However, at the root of the selection process may be a genuine problem: the president alone is responsible for submitting a name to the Senate for confirmation. This problem was brought out forcefully in 1978, when a Democratic Congress approved the creation of 117 new judgeships for the district courts and 35 for the courts of appeals. The selection of 152 new judges, all to be nominated by President Carter and confirmed by the Senate, gave Carter an unusual opportunity to influence the federal court system. With all these positions to fill, Carter was clearly a "winner," but should any one person have such a major influence?

Federal justices hold their positions for life, or during periods of good behavior; very few have ever been removed from office. The average length of service on the Supreme Court has been fifteen years. In Table 4–1, we see that many members of the Supreme Court have served much longer. The problem exists because of the lengthy periods judges may remain on the bench and thus the influence that presidents may have through the appointment process.

Two members of the present Supreme Court have served more than twenty years. Presidents of the United States, under the Twenty-second Amendment, are restricted to two full elective terms. Actually, since that amendment was ratified in 1951, only Eisenhower has stayed in office that long. If President Nixon had not resigned, he would have been the second.

If we consider the length of service of most Supreme Court justices, any president making a successful nomination to the Court can have a significant impact on domestic policy. Presidents may leave office relatively quickly, but their appointments to the Supreme Court often stay on and on. From the data in Table 4–2, we can see that the oldest member of the Court was appointed by President Eisenhower, who himself left office before many of the readers of this book were born.

One of President Kennedy's two appointments is still serving. President Nixon appointed four members and would have had

★ ★ ★ *Table 4–1* ★
Length of service on the Supreme Court

TOTAL YEARS OF SERVICE	NUMBER OF JUDGES	% OF JUDGES
1–5	20	21
6–10	20	21
11–15	15	16
16–20	15	16
21–25	8	8
26–30	9	9
31–35	8	8
36+	1	1

This table does not include members of the present Supreme Court (listed in Table 4–2).

Source: Calculated from *Congress and the Nation* (Washington, D.C.: Congressional Quarterly, 1965–1973, vol. 1, pp. 1432–33; vol. 2, p. 340; vol. 3, p. 295.

the opportunity to nominate a fifth if he had not resigned from office. Herein lies the problem: should any single president, Democrat or Republican, be able to nominate a majority of the nation's highest court? We think not, for the influence of Court decisions can last for generations. We are, for example, still operating under some of the precedents laid down in the decisions of Chief Justice John Marshall, who left office only when he died in 1835.

BLOC VOTING. One indication of the influence a president can have through his Supreme Court appointments is exemplified in the voting patterns of the near-majority nominated by Nixon. Often voting as a bloc, these four justices—with one or more votes from the other justices—have been able to control the majority decision in several cases. The use of wiretaps by the government to gain evidence for criminal trials has long been restricted; however, the Supreme Court in 1974 held that it was not necessary to name every possible suspect in a warrant requesting a wire-tap. This opinion was reached by a six to three vote, with the four Nixon judges joined by Kennedy and Eisenhower appointees.[26]

It is not unreasonable to expect that Justice Rehnquist, who was only forty-seven when he took his seat, will survive and still be serving on the Court at the start of the next century, when he will be seventy-six. Rehnquist can reasonably be expected to outlast not only Presidents Nixon, Ford, and Carter, but also Reagan and several successors. Justice Hugo Black, who held his seat for thirty-four years, outlasted not only Franklin Roosevelt, who appointed him in 1937—

★ ★ ★ Table 4–2 ★
Members of the Supreme Court as of 1981

NAME	YEAR OF BIRTH	NOMINATED BY	DATE CONFIRMED	PRESIDENTS SERVED
William Brennan, Jr.	1906	Eisenhower	3/19/57	Eisenhower, Kennedy, Johnson, Nixon, Ford, Carter, Reagan
Byron White	1917	Kennedy	4/11/62	Kennedy, Johnson, Nixon, Ford, Carter, Reagan
Thurgood Marshall	1908	Johnson	8/30/67	Johnson, Nixon, Ford, Carter, Reagan
Warren Burger*	1907	Nixon	6/9/69	Nixon, Ford, Carter, Reagan
Harry Blackmun	1908	Nixon	5/12/70	Nixon, Ford, Carter, Reagan
Lewis Powell, Jr.	1907	Nixon	12/6/71	Nixon, Ford, Carter, Reagan
William H. Rehnquist	1924	Nixon	12/10/71	Nixon, Ford, Carter, Reagan
John Paul Stevens	1920	Ford	12/17/75	Ford, Carter, Reagan
Sandra Day O'Connor	1930	Reagan	9/22/81	Reagan

*Chief Justice

Source: *Congress and the Nation*, vol. III (Washington, D.C.: Congressional Quarterly, 1973), p. 295; Congressional Quarterly, *Weekly Reports, 33* (December 6, 1975), 2634, and (December 20, 1975), 2778.

but also Truman, Eisenhower, Kennedy, and Johnson. Justice Douglas, appointed by Roosevelt in 1939, outlasted these five presidents and Nixon as well.

On average, each president has made three appointments to the Supreme Court. Several presidents have actually appointed a majority of the Court; in Washington's case, this was unavoidable. The presidents who have appointed a majority to the Court are Washington, Jackson, Lincoln, Taft, Franklin Roosevelt, and Eisenhower. Indeed, at one point all of the Supreme Court justices were Franklin Roosevelt's appointees.

Should this situation be allowed to continue? If we refine our constitutional system, we might consider some limits and alternate methods of appointment when those limits have been reached.

For the sake of debate, we might start by suggesting that a constitutional amendment should limit the number of judges that could be appointed by any one president. For additional vacancies, another method of appointment might be considered—perhaps nomination by a majority of the House of Representatives and confirmation, as customary, by the Senate. This proposal would not necessarily bring greater wisdom from the Court, but it would limit the influence that any president could have on future generations through his appointments to the Court.

Summary

Courts, especially the Supreme Court, are among the most respected institutions in the United States. This respect may be based in part on a lack of knowledge about how they operate. This great respect for courts and their interpretations of the law is one reason why the executive branch of government enforces court decisions even when a decision rules against the President himself. In the population as a whole, the tradition of compliance with court decisions is deep-seated—even when these decisions run counter to strongly held cultural and social values.

The courts themselves are highly political and must rely on the executive branch of government to enforce their decisions. Occasional instances of conflict with the executive or legislative branches arise. In many cases, the courts have followed the doctrine of judicial restraint, choosing not to become involved in direct challenges to the authority of one or the other branch on whose goodwill they depend.

Periods of judicial activism are usually associated with much conflict with the other branches of government and with social unrest as well.

The ebbs and flows—from activism to restraint and back to activism—may very well assist the courts in perpetuating the tradition of compliance.

In many respects, the courts are at the heart of the political process in America, for they formally and explicitly decide who wins and who loses. Their decisions pertain not only to the immediate cases they decide upon but also to similar cases. Some critics feel that the Supreme Court is largely unchecked and has become too powerful, that it has taken for itself a legislative role not properly balanced by the legislative and executive branches of the government. Yet it can be argued that these branches themselves perform certain judicial functions. Though formal checks on the courts are minimal, Congress is allowed to restructure the federal judiciary below the Supreme Court and redefine the jurisdiction of all federal courts and even the Supreme Court—within the limits of the Constitution.

Terms to Remember

See the Glossary at the end of the book for definitions.

Amicus curiae brief	Court of Military Appeals	*Martin* v. *Hunter's Lessee*
Appellate jurisdiction	Federal district courts	Original jurisdiction
Baker v. *Carr*	*Habeas corpus*	Political question
Brandeis briefs	Judicial activism	"Political thicket"
Briefs	Judicial circuits	*Reynolds* v. *Sims*
Certiorari	Judicial discretion	Senatorial courtesy
Cherokee Indian case	Judicial districts	Special federal courts
Cohens v. *Virginia*	Judicial restraint	U.S. Courts of Appeals
Colegrove v. *Green*	Judicial review	*U.S.* v. *Nixon*
Common law	Judiciary Act of 1789	*Youngstown Sheet and Tube Co.* v. *Sawyer*
Compliance tradition	Justiciable	
Court of Claims	*Marbury* v. *Madison*	

Notes

1. *U.S.* v. *Nixon*, 418 U.S. 683 (1974). The reasoning behind his strategy can be found in Leon Jaworski's *The Right and the Power: The Prosecution of Watergate* (New York: Reader's Digest Press and Gulf Publishing Co., 1976).

2. See Philippa Strum, *The Supreme Court and Political Questions: A Study in Judicial Evasion* (University: University of Alabama Press, 1974).

3. 399 U.S. 186 (1962).

4. 328 U.S. 549 (1946). An interesting sidelight to *Colegrove* shows how the "political process" can be interpreted. The case had been brought before an election was to take place. It appears now that there was a majority on the Court, at that time, that would have established the Court's jurisdiction, long before the *Baker* case arose. However, the Court backed off, apparently because of the pending election.

5. 377 U.S. 533 (1964).

6. This is purely hypothetical data, yet stranger cases have been known. A useful guide to the malapportionment that existed before the *Baker*

decision is Paul T. David and Ralph Eisenberg, *Devaluation of the Urban and Suburban Vote* (Charlottesville, Va.: Bureau of Public Administration, vol. 1, 1961; vol. 2, 1962).

7. 376 U.S. 1 (1964).

8. U.S. 483 (1954).

9. An excellent and highly readable account of this episode is to be found in Richard Harris, *Decision* (New York: E.P. Dutton, 1971).

10. Quoted in *Congress and the Nation*, vol. III, 1969–1972 (Washington, D.C.: Congressional Quarterly, 1973). p. 297.

11. Congressional Quarterly, *Guide to the U.S. Supreme Court* (Washington, D.C.: Congressional Quarterly, 1979), p. 656.

12. See Richard Harris, *Justice: The Crisis of Law, Order and Freedom in America* (New York: E.P. Dutton, 1970).

13. *Worcester* v. *Georgia*, 6 Peters 515 (1832).

14. 343 U.S. 579 (1952).

15. *U.S.* v. *Nixon*, 418 U.S. 683 (1974).

16. *Engel* v. *Vitale,* 370 U.S. 421 (1962) and *Abingdon School District* v. *Schempp,* 374 U.S. 203 (1963).

17. In light of the revelations of 1976, when several members of Congress were accused of having clandestine affairs with members of their staffs, it could be argued that Douglas was more inclined to the honorable thing than at least some members of Congress.

18. Quoted in Congressional Quarterly *Weekly Report,* 33 (November 15, 1975), p. 2444.

19. See Charles L. Black, *The People and the Court* (New York: Macmillan, 1960).

20. 1 *Cranch* 137 (1803).

21. 1 *Wheaton* 304 (1816).

22. 6 *Wheaton* 264 (1821).

23. *DeFunis* v. *Odegaard,* 416 U.S. 312 (1974).

24. For every rule, there may be an exception. An example is the wholesale breaking of the rule of secrecy involving the Court's deliberative processes, as reported in Bob Woodward and Scott Armstrong, *The Brethren: Inside the Supreme Court* (New York: Simon and Schuster, 1979).

25. See Clement W. Vose, "Litigation as a Form of Pressure Activity," *Annals of the American Academy of Political and Social Science* 319 (1958), pp. 20–31.

26. *U.S.* v. *Kahn,* 415 U.S. 143 (1974).

Suggested Readings

Henry J. Abraham, *The Judicial Process,* 2d ed. (New York: Oxford University Press, 1968).

Henry R. Glick and Kenneth H. Vines, *State Court Systems* (Englewood Cliffs, N.J.: Prentice–Hall, 1973).

Sheldon Goldman and Thomas P. Jahnige, *The Federal Courts as a Political System* (New York: Harper and Row, 1971).

Herbert Jacob, *Justice in America: Courts, Lawyers, and the Judicial Process,* 2d ed. (Boston: Little, Brown, 1972).

Samuel Krislov, *The Supreme Court and the Political Process* (New York: Macmillan, 1965).

Leo Pfeffer, *This Honorable Court* (Boston: Beacon Press, 1965).

Richard Richardson and Kenneth Vines, *The Politics of Federal Courts* (Boston: Little, Brown, 1970).

John R. Schmidhauser and Larry Berg, *The Supreme Court and Congress: Conflict and Interaction, 1945–1968* (New York: The Free Press, 1972).

Earl Warren, *The Memoirs of Earl Warren* (Garden City, N.Y.: Doubleday, 1977).

Stephen Wasby, *The Impact of the United States Supreme Court* (Homewood, Il.: Dorsey Press, 1970).

Bob Woodward and Scott Armstrong, *The Brethren: Inside the Supreme Court* (New York: Simon and Schuster, 1979).

CHAPTER 5

Civil Rights and Civil Liberties

★ ★

There is danger that, if the Court does not temper its doctrinaire logic with a little practical wisdom, it will convert the constitutional Bill of Rights into a suicide pact.

Justice ROBERT JACKSON (1949)

We have talked long enough about equal rights in this country. We have talked for one hundred years or more. It is time now to write the next chapter and write it in the books of law.

LYNDON BAINES JOHNSON (1963)

In 1979, National Guardsmen and state police were sent to enforce a federal district court order that the schools of Cleveland be integrated. As the school busses rolled in Cleveland, angry mobs challenged them, cursing the black schoolchildren and fighting with the state troopers. Is it within the power of any court to force equality? And, if equality is to be the law of the land, who wins and who loses?

Since *Brown* v. *Board* we have experienced what some refer to as a "revolution in civil rights." **Civil rights,** or equal treatment under the law, is supposedly a hallmark of American democracy. Yet, is it? Are we really guaranteed equal justice, or is there only an ideal toward which we strive, however imperfectly? The 1980 acquittal of four white ex-policemen on trial for beating a black suspect to death suggests that treatment may not always be equal under the law. To pose this another way—is it more or less likely that the policemen would have been acquitted if they had been black and their alleged victim had been white?

We also deal in this chapter with **civil liberties,** our basic guaranteed freedoms under the Bill of Rights. Included in these are freedom of speech, press, petition, and so forth. Are these really guarantees, or are they merely promises that may or may not be kept? How far can they be pushed? What if there is a conflict between the rights of an accused person and freedom of the press? What is their cost to society? For instance, if accused criminals are given the right to remain silent, and to be represented by attorneys, what about the right of the people to safe and secure streets?

In short, it is one thing to state that we have "equal justice" and "guaranteed freedoms" as ideals; it is another thing entirely to

★ ★

assume that there are no conflicts involved in the pursuit of them. In the resolution of these conflicts, there are real winners and real losers, and determining which is which is not always easy. In this chapter we will deal first with civil rights, suggesting that we have not used an absolute standard of equal treatment under the law in our treatment of minorities. There are even occasions when majorities have been, or at least think themselves to have been, the objects of discrimination themselves. Following this, we will deal with civil liberties, and try to show that "guaranteed freedoms" really mean an imperfect attempt to satisfy expectations. The "Issue" section at the end of this chapter will pose questions about the unfinished business of this nation and how we win and lose even when court decisions supposedly put us on a "proper" course.

Civil Rights

We have all heard that a wealthy individual can receive a defense—and perhaps even avoid conviction—better than someone who is not wealthy. Is this equal justice in the United States? The spectacle of a vice-president pleading "no contest" on an income tax evasion charge relating to alleged bribery when he was governor of Maryland suggests to many that there is a double standard—one for the very rich and powerful, and one for those who are not.

It is important to realize that we refer here to a human standard of interpreting laws fairly—not an absolute standard of justice. Courts hear cases brought by human beings, and these cases are decided by human beings, who have less-than-perfect notions of what justice is or should be. To suggest that courts deal in perfect justice is to perpetuate a myth, for judges and juries make human interpretations of human laws. If justice is done, it may be a lucky by-product of the legal system.

As children, we were all exposed to this statement from the Declaration of Independence: "We hold these truths to be self-evident, that all men are created equal. . . ." We were taught that statement as fundamental truth, in part because these beautifully cadenced words were the beliefs of the Founding Fathers; in part because the ideas sound as if they are right and fair. Our current interpretation of this passage is that the signers meant that all people were entitled to *equal treatment* under the law, even though they might be quite unequal in their talents and abilities. After all, how many Thomas Jeffersons do we come across in everyday life?

This relatively recent idea, of equality of treatment, is the focus of this section on civil rights. We will start by tracing the roots of the civil rights struggle of black Americans, for theirs is the most extreme case of denial of civil rights. In their own attempts to secure equality they have, in a sense, "run interference" for other groups. We will then discuss equal treatment for other groups.

THE BLACK REVOLUTION: UP FROM SLAVERY

Unlike other immigrants to the United States, most blacks arrived here under unique circumstances—in chains. The Constitution recognized their status, even defining their position for purposes of determining how many members each state would be allowed in the House of Representatives (the Three-fifths Compromise). The Constitution allowed the slave trade to continue until 1808, and runaways were to be returned to their owners if they escaped to another state. In the infamous **Dred Scott decision** of 1857, the Supreme Court held that blacks could not become citizens or have any rights of citizenship.[1]

CIVIL WAR AMENDMENTS. Although the Emancipation Proclamation of 1863 suppos-

All persons born or naturalized in the United States, and subject to the juris-diction thereof, are citizens of the United States and of the State wherein they reside. No state shall make or enforce any law which shall abridge the privileges or immunities of citizens of the United States; nor shall any State deprive any person of life, liberty, or prop-erty, without due process of law; nor deny to any person within its jurisdiction the equal protection of the laws.

edly freed the slaves in areas under Confeder-ate control, the Civil War was still underway, and most slaveowners refused to recognize the proclamation. Following the war, three major amendments were proposed and ratified. The Thirteenth Amendment (1865) freed the slaves; the **Fourteenth** (1868) overturned the *Dred Scott* decision by making former slaves citizens; and the Fifteenth (1870) granted them the right to vote. However, there can be quite a gap between constitutional language and the realities of life, for blacks in the South were often prevented from voting by a variety of tactics, until relatively recently.

After the Civil War, the freeing of slaves was accomplished with relative ease; former slaveowners could do nothing in a legal manner to keep their former property tied to the plantation. However, Reconstruc-tion left many former slaves homeless and wandering, and some returned to their former plantations. Some had never left in the first place; these often became sharecroppers—ten-ant farmers who gave up a portion of the crops they raised as rent for the land they tilled. However, many studies have shown that the sharecropper's life often became a vicious cycle of borrowing and indebtedness, and often they were tied to the land as much as they had been in the days of slavery. For that matter, there are many migrants today, black, brown, and white, who are trapped in debt to a landowner or "labor contractor." In a sense they are as much slaves as the blacks before

the Civil War. They may not be "owned" by a landlord, but their indebtedness keeps them trapped from any realistic exercise of various freedoms we like to associate with living in America today.

NATIONALIZING RIGHTS THROUGH THE FOURTEENTH AMENDMENT. The most sig-nificant of the Civil War amendments was the Fourteenth, for it has provided the basis for many laws and countless court cases. There are two key phrases in this amendment: one refers to "due process of law," and the other to "equal protection of the laws." In these short phrases, we probably have the strongest arguments that can be used in court for guar-anteeing every individual's equal treatment before the law, and they provide the basis for federal court review of state laws and state court decisions.

DUE PROCESS AND EQUAL PROTECTION. As conceived in 1789, the Bill of Rights was a series of limits that applied only to Congress and the national government. The phrases are rather explicit in this regard, especially for a document which is often vague and ambigu-ous. Take, for instance, the opening words of the First Amendment: "Congress shall make no law . . ." as regards freedom of speech, religion, and the press. Nothing could be clearer in its intent. Chief Justice John Mar-shall, who favored a strong central govern-ment, also held in a decision that the Bill of

Rights served to limit only the national government, and not the state governments.[2] Although most states had lengthy bills of rights in their own constitutions, the Fourteenth Amendment clearly extended the force of the federal government, prohibiting the states from actions that might deny citizens equal treatment under the law. After all, state bills of rights had not been sufficient to stop terrorism and vigilante actions against former slaves during the late nineteenth and early twentieth centuries.

AN ERRATIC RECORD. As we have suggested, there can be a great difference between the written constitution and the realities of life—particularly with regard to civil rights. After the Civil War, repeated legislation was required to put teeth into the government's position on civil rights: Civil Rights Acts were passed by Congress in 1866, 1870, 1871, 1875, and 1891 to ensure that blacks were afforded equal treatment. But the Supreme Court at the time proved to be anything but receptive. In the Civil Rights Cases of 1883, the Court held that Congress could not regulate public accommodations, as such regulation would infringe on private rights.[3] Congress backed off—and gradually whittled down the guarantees offered by these acts.

PLESSY v. FERGUSON: LEGALLY SANCTIONED DISCRIMINATION. In **Plessy v. Ferguson** (1896) the Supreme Court upheld a state law requiring segregation in public transportation; if a state provided **"separate but equal"** facilities, segregation was constitutional.[4] With this decision, the Supreme Court essentially put the national government on the side of segregation. "Jim Crow" or enforced segregation became an official policy in all matters regarding public accommodations and education. If separate bathrooms and water fountains were provided for "colored only," then who could object? If blacks were sent to the back of the bus, then so what? Nowhere in the Fourteenth Amendment is there a statement of "separate but equal protection of the laws," yet the Supreme Court chose to interpret it this way.

Transportation, education, washroom facilities in public places, housing, and dining establishments were just a few of the areas of enforced segregation. In effect, segregation became the law of the land; the Supreme Court did little for many decades except to determine in particular cases whether separate facilities were actually equal to those for "whites only." But even with the Supreme Court's position, a good deal still could have been done by Congress, the executive branch, and the lower courts.

From the turn of the century through the post-World War II era, many different tactics were used to keep blacks "in their place," including whippings and lynchings. Blacks had to learn to step into the gutter—in both the literal and figurative senses—to avoid offending the dominant whites.

Not until the 1940s were there even occasional rays of hope. President Truman issued an executive order desegregating the armed forces, and previously all-black units were intermingled with white forces. However, the lack of blacks in the officer corps persisted for many years. In 1948, Hubert Humphrey demanded a strong civil rights plank in the Democratic Party's platform, and his concern for civil rights led to a convention walkout by several southern delegations and the formation of a splinter States' Rights Party led by Strom Thurmond, nominated to oppose Truman. That same year, Congress failed to pass a law that would have imposed a heavy penalty for lynching.

Some progress, however slow, was made in improving educational opportunities for blacks. In a series of related decisions, the Supreme Court held, in 1938, that a black could not be kept out of an all-white state law school in Missouri if no comparable but black

In 1954, the U.S. Supreme Court decided that separate educational facilities for blacks and whites are inherently unequal, a far-reaching new application of the Fourteenth Amendment.

sixty years—reversed *Plessy.* The wide-ranging Court opinion ruled that it is inherently impossible for separate facilities to be equal. Even if the facilities—schools, in this instance—are exactly alike in every detail, the mere fact that they are separate makes them unequal.

IMPACT OF *BROWN* DECISION. The impact of this decision was enormous, and went far beyond the issue of segregated public schools; the effects are still being felt. The Court decision implied that separate facilities in any area which is or can be regulated by the states are a violation of the equal protection clause of the Fourteenth Amendment. The impact on federal–state relations was very strong indeed. Because the federal government would no longer remain the passive protector (through the Supreme Court) of segregation, the decision provoked strong anti-federal government attitudes, and Washington was accused by segregationists of having violated virtually every moral and legal principle under the sun. Further, this decision also placed the whole area of equal rights for blacks and other minorities squarely in the public eye. It became both fashionable and necessary for the media to concentrate on events and circumstances which they had previously ignored.

SEGREGATION: A NATIONAL PROBLEM. Armed with the *Brown* decision, civil rights activists began to challenge the legality and constitutionality of many segregationist practices. If schools were segregated, this was often a consequence of housing patterns. Black ghettoes in the North as well as the South had created all-black schools. One rem-

in-state school existed. Even if such a facility was available, the "equal" provision had to be satisfied: in 1950, the Court ordered blacks admitted to the University of Texas law school, since the black law school in Texas offered an inferior education. That same year the University of Oklahoma was told by the Court that it could not require a black graduate student to sit at a separate table in a classroom, library, or dining hall. It said that by so doing, the university was depriving the student of a normal opportunity for an exchange of ideas—and thus his education could not be equal.[5]

REVERSING "SEPARATE BUT EQUAL." If there was a single turning point in the civil rights struggle for blacks, it was clearly the 1954 decision, ***Brown*** v. ***Board of Education of Topeka.***[6] In a nine to zero decision, the Supreme Court spoke through Chief Justice Earl Warren and finally—after almost

The Warren Court's opinion in *Brown v. Board of Education of Topeka* rested on the belief that segregation placed a lifelong stigma of inferiority on those discriminated against, and that this stigma could hinder total psychological and sociological development.

Today, education is perhaps the most important function of state and local governments. Compulsory school attendance laws and the great expenditures for education both demonstrate our recognition of the importance of education for our democratic society. . . . In these days, it is doubtful that any child may reasonably be expected to succeed in life if he is denied the opportunity of an education. Such an opportunity, where the state has undertaken to provide it, is a right which must be made available to all on equal terms. . . .

We conclude that in the field of public education the doctrine of "separate but equal" has no place. Separate educational facilities are inherently unequal [*emphasis added*].

BROWN V. BOARD OF EDUCATION

Source: *Brown v. Board of Education of Topeka*, 347 U.S. 483 (1954).

edy for this was court-ordered bussing of children in order to distribute blacks and whites more equally. At first, many non-southerners applauded this practice. After all, the school bus had often been used to perpetuate segregation in the South, and now it was being used for the opposite purpose. Central cities became ghettoes as white families moved or fled to the suburbs; these suburbs have been described as an "iron collar" around the neck of the cities. As schools became more and more segregated in the central cities, bussing would be ordered to bring about racial balance. This bussing would, in turn, provoke further moves to the suburbs and create a highly charged emotional situation. Whites, whose children were forced to leave neighborhood schools, felt they were losers in this process and fought bitterly to oppose it.

In 1968 Governor Wallace made bus-

sing one of his major presidential campaign issues and he received considerable support on this issue. More and more people—even those who favored desegregation—found themselves opposed to the use of bussing to achieve integrated schools. In many respects, forced bussing became a code word both for racism and reaction to the power of the federal government—in the North as well as the South.

Segregated housing exists for many complex, interrelated reasons, including poverty, unemployment, and underemployment of blacks; the practices of the banking and housing industries in denying mortgages to blacks; and white attitudes toward mixed neighborhoods. All of these have emerged as problems that require government intervention. As regards employment, one major problem has been the under-qualification of mi-

Characteristic of racial bitterness and alienation are the 1980 riots in Miami after a white jury acquitted white persons charged with killing a black motorcyclist.

norities—the result of a lack of education and marketable skills. Colleges and universities, under the prodding of federal officials and programs, have attempted to achieve a higher black enrollment so that more blacks can be college-educated and therefore acquire the necessary professional qualifications. This is necessarily a long-term solution to the complex cycle of unequal education, housing, employment, and income. Where qualified blacks are applying for high-level positions, attempts are being made to hire them as well as other minorities and women through programs described as "equal opportunity" and "affirmative action." We will return to these programs in the "Issue" section.

Here we must address ourselves to a fundamental question about civil rights—are we dealing with guarantees of equal treatment before the law, or with expectations? In an ideal world we would not have to worry about gross inequities in the treatment of citizens; in this same ideal world the guarantees would be the same as achieved realities. Instead, we find ourselves confronting inequitable situations as blacks and others are treated in less-than-equal fashions. Can government, this or any other, make guarantees and enforce them, or are there limits to what any government can ever achieve? The bitterness and alienation which characterizes the attitudes of many blacks, whites, Hispanics, and others, suggest that we have been dealing with a conflict between guarantees (as expressed in the Fourteenth Amendment) and the realities of life. These realities have led many to wonder if equal justice can ever be achieved.

CIVIL RIGHTS LEGISLATION

THE CIVIL RIGHTS COMMISSION. Just three years after *Brown*, the Civil Rights Act of 1957 signaled that the courts were not alone in their search for equal justice. Although the Act lacked any real enforcement provisions, it created the **Civil Rights Commission,** an agency which has come to be a bone in the throat of numerous individuals, both in and out of the government. The commission has few formal powers except to investigate allegations of discrimination and publish reports. But what the commission lacks in the power to correct abuses, it often seems to make up for in the attention it receives in the media and the government. Thus its power of publicity had often put it into the center of politics. Its findings also provided the basis for later legislation, such as the Civil Rights Acts of 1960 and 1964.

VOTING RIGHTS

POWER OF THE VOTE. President Johnson was often quoted as saying, "the first civil

★ ★ ★ *Table 5-1* ★
Major civil rights legislation

Civil Rights Act of 1957	Created Civil Rights Commission; allowed federal district courts to hear suits to protect the right to vote Authorized Department of Justice to seek court injunctions on behalf of those whose voting rights were jeopardized
Civil Rights Act of 1960	Extended powers of Civil Rights Commission Required preservation of voting records in federal election If a "pattern of practice" of denying right to vote existed, courts could appoint referees to make determinations in individual persons
Civil Rights Act of 1964	Outlawed discrimination in public accommodations (hotels, restaurants, etc.) Provided the financial basis for desegregating schools Outlawed discrimination in programs receiving federal aid Established equal employment opportunity regulations

The right of citizens of the United States to vote shall not be denied or abridged by the United States or by any State on account of race, color, or previous condition of servitude.

FIFTEENTH AMENDMENT (1870)

The Senate of the United States shall be composed of two Senators from each State, elected by the people thereof. . . .

SEVENTEENTH AMENDMENT (1913)

The right of citizens of the United States to vote shall not be denied or abridged by the United States or by any state on account of sex.

NINETEENTH AMENDMENT (1920)

The District constituting the seat of Government of the United States shall appoint . . . a number of electors . . . for the purpose of election of President and Vice-President. . . .

TWENTY-THIRD AMENDMENT (1961)

The right of citizens of the United States to vote . . . shall not be denied or abridged by the United States or any state by reason of failure to pay any poll tax or other tax.

TWENTY-FOURTH AMENDMENT (1964)

The right of citizens of the United States, who are eighteen years of age or older, to vote shall not be denied or abridged by the United States or any State on account of age.

TWENTY-SIXTH AMENDMENT (1971)

right is the right to vote." The Fifteenth Amendment was supposed to guarantee the right to vote to former slaves. Yet, in their struggle to achieve civil rights, blacks were again and again denied this right. Through this struggle blacks have brought the whole civil rights movement into focus, for all Americans. Johnson's point of view was that of a pragmatic politician, one who realized that representatives would be more inclined to vote as their constituents wanted if all constituents had a vote.

LIMITED INITIAL FRANCHISE. We should remember that this nation did not start with a full franchise, or right to vote. In several states, only free, white, property-owning males could vote. Not until the era of Andrew Jackson was the property-owning qualification dropped, and not until the Fifteenth Amendment was passed were blacks given the right to vote. Our nation has a history of formally extending the voting right through constitutional amendment (see insert) and then attempting to make that right a reality through legislation and judicial decisions. The franchise was extended when the right to vote was given to ex-slaves (Fifteenth Amendment), to women (Nineteenth Amendment), and to eighteen-year-olds (Twenty-sixth Amendment). Residents of Washington, D.C., were granted the right to vote for president by the Twenty-third Amendment. There was no direct election of senators until the Seventeenth Amendment was ratified. And not until 1964, with the ratification of the Twenty-fourth Amendment, was it possible for citizens in all states to vote without paying for the privilege through a poll tax.

RESTRICTIONS ON VOTING. Even though the Fifteenth Amendment gave blacks the right to vote, numerous tactics were employed to prevent them from casting ballots. Among these were terrorism and violence. The "night raiders" who burned crosses and engaged in lynchings sought to remind blacks of their inferior status. It would be nice to be able to say that all this is behind us, but there are still occasional instances of violence which show what we can do to our fellow humans to restrict their political and human rights.

Another tactic was the **"grandfather clause,"** a provision stating that one could vote only if one's grandfather had been eligible to vote before 1867. **Literacy tests,** or sometimes "constitutional understanding" tests were also used. These were notorious both for their difficulty and the unfair ways in which they were administered and graded. The **white primary,** a party election limited only to whites, was also widely employed before it was struck down by the Supreme Court in 1944.[7] And it took a constitutional amendment to abolish the **poll tax,** in which those who wanted to vote had to pay a tax in order to exercise this right.

THE VOTING RIGHTS ACT OF 1965. We have suggested that the black struggle for equal justice has brought into focus the general problem of equality for all. Nowhere is this more true than in the passage of the **Voting Rights Act of 1965.** A year earlier, the 1964 Civil Rights Act had addressed some of the problems of inequities in voter registration. But the provisions of this act were insufficient to

Discrimination based on age is being fought in areas such as hiring and advancement in jobs, retirement requirements, and the like.

bring about the changes needed. Hence, the 1965 Voting Rights Act was passed, with certain major provisions. These included:

★   suspension of literacy tests, if fewer than fifty percent of the voting-age residents of a state had registered to vote in 1964.

★   the appointment of voting examiners to oversee registration in any voting district where less than twenty-five percent of the persons of any race or color were registered.

★   a requirement for "preclearance" with the U.S. Department of Justice of any proposed changes in voting laws or procedures in any state that had less than fifty percent voting and used a literacy test.

The impact of the 1965 act was dramatic indeed. Vast numbers of blacks were registered for the first time, and in many states they began to approach political parity with whites (see Table 5–2). If President Johnson was right about the primacy of the vote, then more officials would be elected who would pay attention to the wishes of their constituents. And, more of these would be black, like their constituents. Since 1970, the number of black elected officials has tripled.[8] There are now more elected blacks in the South alone than there were in the entire country in 1970.

However, there is another side to the 1965 act, and that is in the way it was applied. There is no question but that it was applied only in the South. Yet many northern areas qualified to have those same examiners sent in. In New York City, for example, blacks and Puerto Ricans remain under-registered. Similarly, American Indians in Idaho and Eskimos in Alaska do not often appear on voter registration lists. Of course, only a limited number of federal examiners were available. If they had been sent to all the places needing their services—and not just to the South—their impact would have been diluted. One remaining step in the attempt to secure voting rights and equal treatment before the law is to admit the hypocrisy of applying the law unevenly.

FRANCHISE EXTENSIONS FOR OTHER GROUPS. The franchise has been broadened most widely by the **Nineteenth Amendment,** which gave women the right to vote. With this addition, the potential existed for doubling the number of voters, but this did not happen for some time. Before ratification, in 1916, more than 18.5 million people voted for president: after ratification, in 1920, the number increased to 26.7 million. In terms of actual numbers voting, not until 1936 was the pre-Nineteenth Amendment figure doubled.

★ ★ ★ *Table 5–2* ★
Southern voters registered: 1960–1976

STATE	1960			1976		
	% of WHITES REGISTERED	*% of* BLACKS REGISTERED	*GAP*	*% of* WHITES REGISTERED	*% of* BLACKS REGISTERED	*GAP*
Alabama	63.6%	13.7%	49.9%	79.3%	58.4%	20.9%
Arkansas	60.9	38.0	22.9	62.6	94.0	+31.4
Florida	69.3	39.4	29.9	61.3	61.1	0.2
Georgia	56.8	29.3	27.5	65.9	74.8	+ 8.9
Louisiana	76.9	31.1	45.8	78.4	63.0	15.4
Mississippi	63.9	5.2	58.7	80.0	60.7	19.3
North Carolina	92.1	39.1	53.0	69.2	54.8	14.4
South Carolina	57.1	13.7	43.4	58.4	56.5	1.9
Tennessee	73.0	59.1	13.9	73.7	66.4	7.3
Texas	42.5	35.5	7.0	69.1	65.0	4.1
Virginia	46.1	23.1	23.0	61.6	54.7	6.9

Source: U.S. Bureau of the Census, *Statistical Abstract of the United States,* 1977, Table 812, p. 507.

Legal restrictions aside, there were apparently strong social pressures against women exercising their franchise.

The last major change in the electorate that we are likely to witness is the **Twenty-sixth Amendment,** which gave the vote to eighteen-year-olds. Although this amendment had been brewing for years, it seems that the real impetus for it came about through a combination of forces. The Vietnam War had reminded us of a basic paradox: eighteen-year-olds could be called to fight for the country but they could not choose the officials who run it (see insert). The opportunity for change arose when the 1965 Voting Rights Act came up for renewal in 1970. This act included a provision for the eighteen-year-old vote—but the Supreme Court subsequently ruled that this provision could apply only to federal elections.[9] The Court ruling led to another paradox: that of eighteen-year-olds who could vote for president and vice-president but not the local board of education, county sheriff, or coroner. Facing such a ludicrous possibility— and an administrative nightmare for the states, which would have had to maintain two sets of voting lists—Congress introduced the Twenty-sixth Amendment. Quickly approved by Congress and sent to the states, the amendment was ratified in 1971—less than four months after Congress had finished its action.

Another major barrier to voting—for all citizens—was the **residency requirement.** Most states required minimum periods of residence for citizens to vote; typically, one year in the state, 180 days or 6 months in the county, and 30 days in the voting precinct. These provisions had accounted for a good deal of nonvoting in the United States, especially when we consider that roughly twenty percent of the population moves in any given year.[10] Under the 1970 Voting Rights Act, all that was required was a thirty-day residence period in order to vote for any federal office (president, vice-president, senator, representative).

UNFINISHED BUSINESS. From this brief review of the extension of the franchise we should not naively conclude that this most basic of civil rights has been secured; many questions still remain. What are the voting rights of prisoners, for instance? Many states do not now allow prisoners to vote. Should this be allowed to continue? Does this apply only to convicted felons?[11] What about those awaiting trial? For another example, not all states have a procedure for absentee voting. Should they? Under what federal authority can they be forced to do so?

We should remember one basic fact: voter participation in the U.S.—as a percentage of the total eligible population—has been declining recently, despite massive attempts at registering voters. The 1965 and 1970 Voting Rights Acts, along with the Twenty-sixth Amendment, made it legally possible for millions to vote who had never done so before.

A good deal of the decline may be traced to psychological factors—feelings of alienation, apathy or futility. However, we cannot blame all of the decline on these factors. Voting in America is still a complicated process, and millions of citizens never get to exercise their right to vote. In any case, nonvoters—for whatever reasons—are "losers" in the most profound sense.

MANY TARGETS OF DISCRIMINATION

The *Brown* decision triggered a revolution in civil rights for others besides blacks. While their problems finally received long-overdue attention, other groups—in the new spirit of the 1960s—began to coalesce and voice their own problems. It soon became evident that discrimination affects more of us than we would have liked to have believed: many groups are in the position of "losers" in society and have few opportunities to help themselves.

WHAT IS DISCRIMINATION? The basic problem consists of trying to define targets of discrimination. If we are all treated equally in the eyes of the law and if we are all entitled to equal protection of the laws, then theoretically there is no discrimination at all. But the discrepancy between theory and practice is enormous. As different groups raise their consciousness, their expectations rise also, and they may seek guarantees of equal justice.

RACIAL AND ANTI-ETHNIC BIASES. Orientals in our society are seldom treated as equals, and our history of dealing with the original Americans—the Indians—shows that

discrimination still persists. Thus, we can at least identify a racial context for discrimination. We can also distinguish an ethnic component as well: Hispanics—Cubans, Chicanos, and Puerto Ricans—have clearly felt discrimination in hiring and housing.

Others have demanded to be heard. It has not been long since signs were posted saying, "no Irish need apply," or advising Italian-Americans to seek employment elsewhere. The formation of the Italian-American Anti-Defamation League signaled a new awareness in that ethnic group; various suits were brought to challenge alleged discrimination against Italian-Americans. Jews, who had been the object of exclusionary quotas in jobs, housing, and education, have found in the last several years that federal programs do not consider them a minority although they constitute less than three percent of the total U.S. population. Some of their organizations began, in the 1970s, to protest minority definitions that seemed to indicate that they had been accepted into the mainstream of American life, while their own experiences seemed to deny this.

THE HANDICAPPED. Another group of Americans has organized to insist on equal treatment—the handicapped. Shortly after President Carter took office in 1977, the Department of Health, Education, and Welfare was besieged by representatives of various organizations of the handicapped, and they had an undeniable case. They could easily demonstrate that they had suffered many forms of discrimination: for years they were unable to enter public buildings that had stairs but no ramps for those on crutches or in wheelchairs, unable to use restrooms in public and private facilities that did not take their needs into account, and unable to ride public transit. Hence, they may have been denied jobs or other opportunities for which they otherwise qualified. They insisted that a

*The demand for civil rights triggered by the black experience spread in the 1960s
and 1970s to other groups who suffer from discrimination.*

whole range of compensatory actions be undertaken by the federal government.

WOMEN: A MAJORITY/MINORITY. There is yet one more target of discrimination, one which is according to the census a majority—women. Until quite recently, it was an accepted part of American social life that "a woman's place is in the home." Women were typically denied education, employment, or any position of power in the world outside their home. Unable to obtain credit except in their husbands' names, they were discriminated against economically—and in many other essential areas. Even now, how many women are on your college's faculty? How many have tenure, are full professors, or head their departments?

THE EQUAL RIGHTS AMENDMENT. As the self-awareness of other groups has increased in the last two decades, so has that of women. Various groups, led by the National Organization for Women (NOW), have emerged to demand equal treatment for all women. The single issue that most symbolized the struggle for women's rights is the proposed Twenty-seventh or **Equal Rights Amendment,** sent by Congress to the states in March 1972. The seven-year deadline for ratification was extended by thirty-nine months, until June 1982.

This amendment became the center of a major political debate in the 1970s. Not all women favored the amendment; many led the opposition to it in their state legislatures. The road to ratification has been difficult; only

Equality of rights under the law shall not be denied or abridged by the United States or by any state on account of sex.

thirty-five states had ratified when the deadline was extended.

There have been many questions associated with ERA, as it is known. Is it necessary? Doesn't the "equal protection" clause of the Fourteenth Amendment guarantee women full equality? And aren't women's rights protected by various acts of Congress such as the 1964 Civil Rights Act and the 1972 Equal Employment Opportunity Act? The history of lawsuits brought under these and other laws suggests that the apparently clear language forbidding discrimination on the grounds of sex is none too clear after all. Others fear that the ERA would harm women, such as in the disposition of courts to award them alimony in divorce cases, or their exemption from combat in the armed forces.

Some healthy side effects of the battle for and against the Equal Rights Amendment can be cited: in the action to secure ratification, more people of both sexes have probably participated in the discussion of women's liberation than ever before. In effect, they have not only had their consciousnesses raised toward women's rights but also toward the broader area of human rights for everyone. Furthermore, they have learned skills of political organization and communication that can be put to use on behalf of other human-rights issues. About twenty states have enacted their own version of ERA.

GAY RIGHTS. Among the emerging groups in the battle for equal rights have been homosexual communities of both sexes. They have lobbied extensively in legislatures, in the press, and in the courts. Their concerns have included equal opportunity in employment and housing. In many communities they have organized to enact ordinances to protect themselves and have demonstrated their political clout in helping to defeat candidates who oppose their point of view. However, their battle is far from over: several cities have held referendums to repeal such statutes; in most cases, the repeal efforts have been successful. Even where homosexuals have been able to make some gains, these have been highly emotional contests, frequently pitting the Constitution against the Bible—as opponents claim that homosexuals violate the laws of God.

Civil Liberties

Do we have guaranteed freedoms? How can we protect people from the government? We cannot assume that government always works in our best interests; many feared this danger when the Constitution was submitted to the states for ratification in 1787. The mere fact that the Bill of Rights was not included in the original Constitution raised suspicions. Although we would like to assume that the government always operates in our behalf, there may be times when we have grave doubts about its direction. Recent exposés of government wrongdoing include illegal wiretapping by the FBI, domestic activities by the CIA (which violate its charter to operate only abroad), and the attempt by Nixon's staff to use the Internal Revenue Service for political ends. Although some would protest that the innocent have nothing to fear—and only criminals have to worry about civil liberties—this is a naive attitude at best. What are the proper boundaries of government action relative to individuals?

FIRST AMENDMENT FREEDOMS

The **First Amendment** has often been called the cornerstone of our society. Broad in scope, it has been the source of many important cases that have come before the courts. Although it may seem simple on first reading, the courts have been asked to resolve many hidden questions.

FREEDOM OF RELIGION. It would appear that, when the First Amendment was drafted, there was fear the Congress might establish an official religion. Great Britain had shown that this was entirely possible when King Henry VIII named himself head of the Church of England. Many people had come to America in pursuit of religious liberty, fleeing persecution in Britain and on the Continent. Congress has never instituted an official religion, and any attempt to do so would clearly be unconstitutional.

But that is far from the end of it. As with the original Constitution, the amendments are susceptible to interpretation, and many cases have been brought into the federal courts to test the extent of this provision.

What do we mean by the "separation" between church and state? Is it simply that there will not be a single official religion? Or should it be extended to mean any aid to religious institutions is unconstitutional? If a local school district wishes to give released time to its students for religious instruction, is that released time a form of aid to the church? The way the Supreme Court rules on such a question often hinges on extremely fine legal points. In one case, the religious instruction was conducted on public school property; this was ruled to be an unconstitutional form of

aid to organized religion.[12] Four years later, a similar case arose in which the religious instruction did not take place on school grounds; the Court decided that this was constitutional.[13]

Whether religious schools can be subsidized by public funds raises another set of issues entirely; the Supreme Court has moved with painstaking care on this complicated problem. The issue is bound to be tested again and again in the future, for a very simple reason: parochial schools, caught in a financial crunch, are finding it harder to stay open. Many parochial schools have already closed, and their students have been forced to go to public schools. This places an increased burden on public facilities and local taxpayers. The Court will undoubtedly be asked to uphold at least limited public support in the near future, out of simple necessity.

NON-MAINSTREAM RELIGIONS. Many tests of the First Amendment concerning religious liberties involve religions that do not belong to the mainstream. In 1879, for instance, the Court ruled that bigamy, even though then acceptable in one branch of the Mormon faith, is not protected by the First Amendment if it is a crime in the state where the accused lives.[14] The Jehovah's Witnesses have forced the Court to consider a great many questions, including the right to not salute the flag in public schools.[15] Cases such as these involve conflicts between widely held social values and the religious practices of relatively small numbers of people. The Court has generally taken the position that the First Amendment does not distinguish between types of religion, and thus has offered a broader and broader definition of religious freedom. This may appear proper to some, at least until their own values are challenged.

WARTIME SERVICE. Among the deeply cherished social beliefs of Americans is the one that people should be willing to serve their

Congress shall make no law respecting an establishment of religion, or prohibiting the free exercise thereof; or abridging the freedom of speech, or of the press; or the right of the people peaceably to assemble, and to petition the Government for a redress of grievances.

country, especially in wartime. If necessary, they should be prepared to die. At various times we have had national drafts of young men into the armed forces. But what if a particular sect believes that bearing arms and killing others, even in defense of self or country, is contrary to the laws of God? Congress has provided for such instances by exempting "conscientious objectors" from armed duty, and allowing them to serve as noncombatants (often as medics), or in some alternate capacity, such as caring for the mentally ill. Nonetheless, there is still a public stigma in many places against those who refuse to carry arms.

SCHOOL PRAYER. One of the most sharply fought battles of recent years involves the question of school prayer. The Supreme Court probably reached the height of its unpopularity in the Warren Court era when it decided that compulsory and voluntary school prayers were unconstitutional.[16] Many bitterly opposed to the ruling believed these decisions were close to treason and would lead the country to atheism. Attempts at a constitutional amendment to overturn the Court's decisions were rapidly introduced in Congress—more than 150, as a matter of fact. In 1966, the Senate approved just such an amendment by a 49 to 37 vote. However, the number fell nine votes short of the necessary two-thirds majority and the amendment failed.

TAX-EXEMPT STATUS. Churches commonly enjoy freedom from taxation, including taxes on the property where their place of worship is located. To do otherwise would be "hostile" to religion, according to the Court; the Court insists that a property-tax exemption is simply an instance of "benevolent neutrality." The burden of these exemptions for local governments—and therefore for local schools—is often quite severe. Boston and New Orleans have a significant proportion of the taxable property within their city limits exempted from property tax. Someone must pick up the costs of supporting the local schools and government. In an interesting 1970 case, the Supreme Court held that states can exclude houses of worship from property taxes, but not that they must.[17] If a state wishes to tax the place of worship directly, there would seem to be room in the Court's decision to do so. But who would take the first step? When political careers are at stake, it would be an unusual legislator or governor who would risk his or her political popularity by proposing this.

FREEDOM OF SPEECH. If ever there was a general rule about our civil liberties, it would seem to be that no freedom is absolute. Although we believe that we have freedom of speech in the United States, there are limits on that freedom, and these limits are constantly tested.

In Holmes's comment (see insert), we see what is apparently the ultimate test underlying not only this but any other freedom. Every political system rests on one premise—its own survival. There is no guaranteed right

Justices Holmes and Black have both defended freedom of speech. Black's position is that there should be no restraint on discussion of political issues. Holmes suggests that some public debate could be restricted if the courts felt that the objective was the overthrow of the government by force.

The most stringent protection of free speech would not protect a man in falsely shouting fire in a theater and causing a panic. . . . The question in every case is whether the words used are used in such circumstances and are of such a nature as to create a clear and present danger that they will bring about substantive evils that Congress has a right to prevent.

Justice OLIVER WENDELL HOLMES

An unconditional right to say what one pleases about public affairs is what I consider to be the minimum guarantee of the First Amendment.

Justice HUGO BLACK

Sources: *Schenck* v. *United States,* 249 U.S. 47 (1919); *New York Times Company* v. *Sullivan,* 376 U.S. 254 (1964).

to revolutionary overthrow of a system. But when does revolution begin? With a single overt act, such as the storming of the Bastille, or the firing of the first shot at Bunker Hill? Or does it begin with plans, advocacy, and the spreading of seditious ideas?

As Americans, we tend to pride ourselves on certain guaranteed freedoms, such as freedom of speech. But we can be quite selective in determining who enjoys freedoms. Should they extend to all Americans? Or only to "right-thinking people"? In the effort to prevent social disorder and revolution, our government has taken certain measures that suggest that there are finite limits to our freedom of speech. The ink was barely dry on the Bill of Rights when, in 1798, Congress passed the Sedition Act. This act made it a crime to criticize the government, and some two dozen people were subsequently convicted under it.

One problem associated with freedom of speech is the character of people who hold office. If they tend to confuse themselves—as individuals—with the offices they hold, they may be more likely to try to repress their critics. As the Watergate scandal unfolded, we learned of a group in the White House known as the "plumbers." This group's purpose was to stop the leaking of confidential information from the Nixon White House; in their zeal, they engaged in unauthorized wiretaps and burglarized the office of the psychiatrist of one of their "enemies."

One test of freedom of speech has traditionally rested upon the gravity of the crisis faced by the nation. Holmes's doctrine of a **"clear and present danger"** was presented in the context of World War I, at which time any incitement to defy the draft apparently presented a clear and present danger to the

Sometimes there are cases in civil liberties which have a special irony. One such involved a New Hampshire resident who covered up a portion of his license plate which bore the state motto, "Live Free or Die." The Supreme Court, called upon to rule on this matter, set the record straight.

The right of freedom of thought protected by the First Amendment against state action includes both the right to speak freely and the right to refrain from speaking at all.

WOOLEY V. MAYNARD

Source: *Wooley v. Maynard,* 430 U.S. 705 (1977).

country. But the Court was careful to suggest that—in terms of limiting free speech—distinctions can be made between wartime and peacetime.[18] However, under the **Smith Act of 1940,** if one belongs to an organization that advocates overthrow of the government by force, it is possible for the government to take action.

In 1951, eleven leaders of the Communist Party were convicted of conspiring both to teach and advocate the overthrow of the government. In *Dennis v. United States,* a test of the Smith Act, their convictions were upheld by the Supreme Court.[19] Going beyond the clear and present danger doctrine, the Court essentially said that the government did not have to wait until the danger was imminent. However, in a rapid reversal, the Court just six years later (in *Yates v. United States*) changed its position substantially, holding that there is a difference between teaching what to believe and advocating that something be done.[20] Since then, the Court has gradually removed various restrictions on the Communist Party. In 1976, it appeared on the ballot in several states, a marked departure from the days when membership alone was sufficient grounds for prosecution.

The government has, in the past, attempted to limit freedom of speech through allegations of conspiracy. In the **McCarran Act of 1950,** Congress outlawed any conspiracy that attempts to establish foreign control over our government. The act, which does not draw any distinctions between peaceful and violent conspiracies, has been the basis for many lawsuits since. The 1968 Democratic National Convention in Chicago led to the trial of several who were allegedly conspiring together. Yet, in the trial of the "Chicago Seven" it was determined that some of the defendants had never met each other prior to the trial. The government's case was weakened by this revelation—as well as by many procedural errors in the trial itself, and the convictions were eventually overturned.

FREEDOM OF THE PRESS. Included under the First Amendment are matters relating to obscenity, criticism of the government, the publishing of information dangerous to national security, and the like. One point should be clarified: the term *press* has been broadened to mean not only the printed word but any form of communication, such as radio, television, and plays.

Definition and regulation of pornography comprise one of the most controversial applications of our First Amendment guarantee of freedom of the press.

OBSCENITY. The whole area of obscenity has continually vexed both the general public and members of the courts. What is obscene? An explicit display of sexual intercourse might be obscene to one person, entertaining to another, instructive to yet another, and so forth. And what about the language used? Are four-letter Anglo-Saxonisms acceptable among friends but obscene when they appear in print or in a play? If there is a rule, it is that there is no hard-and-fast rule at all. Definitions of obscenity are complex and constantly changing; and neither Congress nor the Supreme Court has been able to clarify the matter, despite determined efforts. Yet most Americans seem to want obscenity regulated.

Take magazine publishing, for instance. Many years ago, before it changed its policy, *Esquire* ran pictures that today would not draw a second glance. *Playboy,* with its Marilyn Monroe centerfold, achieved national prominence by showing the fresh-faced "girl next door" in the nude. Gradually poses became more and more explicit; nude men have now become commonplace subjects for camera studies. When did the attitude toward obscenity grow more permissive? Now it is quite possible—in some communities, if not all—to purchase magazines at newsstands that show members of both sexes, totally nude, engaged in sexual acts. Is this obscene?

THE ROTH DOCTRINE. In 1957, the Court established a standard that has found its way into a series of different cases. The standard, or the **Roth Doctrine,** establishes a test based on three criteria:[21]

1. Is the material "utterly without redeeming social importance"?

2. Does the material, taken as a whole, treat "sex in a manner appealing to a prurient interest . . ."?

3. Could this be determined by "the average person, applying **contemporary community standards . . .**"?

Having established this test, the Court promptly found itself facing a series of questions on how to apply the rules of social importance, prurience, and community standards. Although the Court normally does not consider evidence, the only way it could rule on certain cases was by viewing or reading the material in question. For nearly a decade, cases were brought before the Supreme Court for it to decide—on a book-by-book, magazine-by-magazine, or movie-by-movie basis—whether obscene material was present.[22]

In the increasingly difficult position in

Viewpoint:
HUSTLER and the First Amendment

No one is forced to buy *Hustler*. Many of those quoted here believe that the First Amendment should protect the individual—whether or not the publication offends someone's concept of decency or morality.

If you're going to have a principle, then you have to take the good with the bad.

> JASON EPSTEIN, editor, Random House

Since when has bad taste been a crime?

> JANN WENNER, editor, *Rolling Stone*

I am not sure that Hustler *is what Jefferson had in mind.*

> LEWIS LAPHAM, editor, *Harper's*

Flynt is not a dissident in our culture. He's a pillar of it.

> GLORIA STEINEM, editor, *Ms*

Source: Quoted in Richard Neville, "Has the First Amendment Met Its Match?" *New York Times Magazine* (March 6, 1977), p. 18. © 1977 by the New York Times Company. Reprinted by permission.

which it found itself, the Court once again tried in 1973 to find its way out of the dilemma by modifying the earlier Roth Doctrine, introducing local community standards, and a few additional tests.[23] The problem is still far from resolved. Whose community standards, and to be determined in what way? There is no evidence that a jury represents a fair sampling of any community. What if there were quite different standards in several adjoining communities? We have recently seen instances of just how difficult it is to apply local community standards: in some communities certain movies may be seen; in others, they may not. Certain magazines are obscene in one city but sold on the street in others. Federal officials can engage in harassment by focussing their activities on communities where convictions are more likely to be obtained. One example shows this rather clearly. The cast and producers of "Deep Throat," a hardcore

movie of the mid–1970s, were prosecuted and convicted in Memphis, Tennessee. Harry Reems, the male star of the movie, had never even visited Memphis, and the movie was not made there. But in their desire for convictions, prosecutors in Washington picked the place where they thought it most likely they could win. Since local prosecutors across the country are not actively seeking to obtain convictions, Washington officials look for prosecutors who are receptive and for communities where convictions are most likely.[24]

Who wins and who loses in a situation like this? Those who favor pornography are often engaged in it as a highly profitable business. Those who fear pornography and its easy availability believe it destroys traditional values and is harmful to children. But what if the right of freedom of speech conflicts with other rights? For instance, do children have a right to be protected from being forced to

> *. . . obscene materials would have to be assessed in terms of "community standards." This innocuous term concealed a trap, for the Court did not specify whether "community" meant the judicial district from which the jurors were selected and in which the trial was held, or an abstract concept encompassing what was morally acceptable to the average American. . . . Reems and 11 others were charged with conspiring to ship prints of* Deep Throat *to various parts of the country. The trial could be held at any point where an overt act of the alleged conspiracy took place. But why Memphis? "Because it's the buckle on the Bible Belt," said Harry Reems.*
>
> TED MORGAN

Source: "United States Versus the Prince of Porn," *New York Times Magazine,* March 6, 1977, p. 16. © 1977 by the New York Times Company. Reprinted by permission.

engage in sexual acts? Most states have severe penalties for child rape or molestation. Some pornography features children as young as five or six engaging in sexual acts. Obviously they cannot make an informed choice about participating. Others argue that, no matter how offensive the material may be, it is exceedingly dangerous to censor anything, as the First Amendment clearly protects the right to print and publish whatever one sees fit. For them, any form of censorship can lead to further censorship.

NATIONAL SECURITY. Closely linked to freedom of speech is the question of national security. This term has never been clearly defined once and for all. Are newspapers free to publish something that might endanger the nation's ability to survive? And how can anyone determine in advance that national security is at stake? There has been a tradition of voluntary cooperation by newspaper editors and publishers with national leaders in wartime, when the publication of classified information could have serious consequences.

THE PENTAGON PAPERS CASE. But what about peacetime? Or a time when our forces are in combat, but war has not been declared? The *New York Times* and *Washington Post* published installments from the **"Pentagon Papers"** in 1971. Taken from a top secret study of our involvement in Vietnam, the government moved to suppress their further publication on grounds that the national security was endangered. In a six-to-three decision, the Supreme Court ruled that the newspapers were free to publish the information.[25] But each of the nine justices wrote a separate opinion—hardly a situation in which a clear "rule of law" was established. If there is a rule from this and other related cases, including obscenity, it is that the government cannot exercise "prior restraint."[26] That is, the

In my view, it is unfortunate that some of my brethren are willing to hold that the publication of news may sometimes be enjoined. Such a holding would make a shambles of the First Amendment. . . . The press was to serve the governed, not the governors. The government's power to censor the press was abolished so that the press would remain forever free to censure the government.

Justice HUGO BLACK (in the majority)

To me it is hardly believable that a newspaper long regarded as a great institution in American life would fail to perform one of the basic and simple duties of every citizen with respect to the discovery or possession of stolen property or secret government documents. That duty, I had thought—perhaps naively—was a report forthwith, to responsible public officers. This duty rests on taxi drivers, justices, and the New York Times.

Chief Justice WARREN BURGER (in the minority)

Source: *New York Times Co.* v. *U.S.,* 403 U.S. 713 (1971).

---

action must be committed before the government can stop its continuance.

RIGHTS IN CONFLICT. What if rights are in conflict? For instance, there is a constitutional right to a fair trial under the Sixth Amendment. Can a reporter be required to give evidence, such as his notes, which would assist the defense? In 1978, Myron Farber, a reporter for the *New York Times,* was jailed in New Jersey for refusing to reveal his sources in a murder case. The Supreme Court refused to hear his appeal. Although he was later freed, it is apparent that there will be appeals in similar cases. Some members of Congress have suggested that we need a law which would protect the press from having to break the confidentiality of their sources. This so-called *shield law* is another example of a solution that might have undesirable consequences. For instance, if one Congress can give this right to reporters, then could another

Congress take it away and restrict freedom of the press even further?

CRIMINAL RIGHTS

NO BILLS OF ATTAINDER. The Constitution, in Article I, forbids Congress from certain acts. One of these is the passage of a **bill of attainder.** This is a legislative act that violates the separation-of-powers principle by punishing an individual or several persons without a trial. A test of this provision occurred in 1965, when the Supreme Court ruled that a law making it illegal for Communists to work for a labor union was in reality a thinly disguised bill of attainder.[27]

NO *EX POST FACTO* LAWS. The Congress also may not enact an *ex post facto* law. This means that a law cannot be passed which makes a certain action illegal after the action has already taken place. After the Civil War, for instance, Congress required oaths which would have excluded attorneys who had supported the Confederacy from practice in federal courts. The Supreme Court held this to be an unconstitutional *ex post facto* law.[28]

RIGHT TO COUNSEL. If the Warren Court was criticized for many things, not the least was its activity in the area of criminal rights. Some of these decisions involved the right to counsel, nominally guaranteed by the Sixth Amendment. This right had been secured for federal trials since 1938,[29] but its position concerning state criminal trials was less certain. In these, unless there were special circumstances, such as mental incompetence or a capital offense (one which might result in the death penalty), there was no requirement that counsel be provided to defendants who could not afford one.

This was significantly revised in the 1963 case of *Gideon* v. *Wainwright*.[30] A petty criminal, Gideon had been convicted of theft in a Florida court and had not been provided counsel. He petitioned the Supreme Court directly, declaring that his constitutional right to counsel had been violated. The Supreme Court accepted the case, and assigned Abe Fortas, who would later become a Supreme Court Justice, to represent Gideon. Fortas won the case on behalf of Gideon, and the states were required to provide lawyers for those "too poor to hire a lawyer" who were accused of felonies. This ruling was later extended to include misdemeanor cases as well.[31] In its decision, the Court relied not only on the Sixth Amendment but on the due process or "fairness" clause of the Fourteenth Amendment as well, further extending the scope of the Bill of Rights.

The Court soon extended the *Gideon* ruling even further. It ruled that if one is accused of a crime, then one must be informed of one's right to counsel and right to remain silent. If a confession is given without this warning, then it is not admissible in court.[32] This right to counsel was extended even further by the *Miranda* **decision** in 1966, in which the Court stated that a person must be told of the right to remain silent and the right to counsel, even though the investigation is not necessarily focussed on that person.[33] These decisions created an uproar from "law and order" proponents, who were convinced that the police would be handcuffed. Thus far, no evidence has been presented that the

★ ★ ★ *Table 5–3* ★

The Bill of Rights provisions in criminal cases

Fourth Amendment	Freedom "against unreasonable searches and seizures"; necessity of search warrants
Fifth Amendment	Freedom against double jeopardy; no requirement to testify against oneself; requirement for Grand Jury indictments
Sixth Amendment	Guarantee of a "speedy and public trial, by an impartial jury"; accused must be "informed of the nature and cause of the accusation"; right to confront accusers; right to counsel
Eighth Amendment	No excessive bail or fines; no "cruel and unusual punishments"

Ernesto Miranda, for whom the Miranda rule is named, was freed of criminal charges because police failed to tell him he had the right to remain silent and the right to call a lawyer.

police have been hampered in any significant way.

CAPITAL PUNISHMENT. One area that has received great attention lately is capital punishment. Is execution "cruel and unusual"? This punishment has typically been used only for crimes of murder, treason, kidnapping, and rape. The Supreme Court seems to be in a state of transition on this issue. At one point, capital punishment was not considered by the Court to be "cruel and unusual" in any respect. States were free to decide whether or not to execute criminals convicted of certain crimes. But in 1968 the Court ruled, in the case of **Witherspoon** v. **Illinois,** that one cannot be excluded from sitting on a jury because one is opposed to the death penalty.[34] The Court's ruling was made retroactive, and the executions of 435 prisoners on death row were suspended unless it could be shown that such exclusion of jurors had not occurred in each case.

Then, in 1972, the Court ruled in **Furman** v. **Georgia** that the death penalty for

certain crimes was unconstitutional if there were other options, since it was "cruel and unusual" punishment.[35] *Furman* was a case in which the politics of appointment clearly played a role: all four Nixon appointees were in the minority in the five-to-four decision. In addition, the opinion was divided, with each justice writing a separate opinion. It was apparent that the ruling would be challenged, and it was. The Court's decision in *Furman* had left open the possibility that mandatory death sentences might be acceptable. Congress and thirty-five states promptly revised their criminal codes to allow the death sentence for certain crimes—or provided guidelines for determining whether the death penalty was appropriate. In two 1976 cases, the Supreme Court arrived at the following rulings:

The punishment of death does not invariably violate the Constitution.[36]

A mandatory death penalty statute provides no standards to guide the jury in its inevitable exercise of the power to determine which first degree murderers shall live and which shall die.[37]

But, in 1980, the Court again backtracked. This time it indicated, in overturning a death penalty, that it might be willing to review convictions on a case-by-case basis, to determine if the state laws on capital cases were specific in describing a "wantonly vile" murder.[38] Much has yet to be resolved with regard to the death penalty. Since the 1976 Supreme Court rulings apply only to cases of murder, is capital punishment appropriate to other cases? Can treason, rape, and kidnappings be punished by death?

SEARCH AND SEIZURE. Other protections for criminals or those accused of crimes are specified by the Bill of Rights. The protection against "unreasonable searches and seizures" of the Fourth Amendment is directed against the infamous knock on the door in the middle of the night. A warrant must be secured in most cases, and it must be shown that there is reasonable or probable cause in order to get the warrant. The police cannot simply barge in because they suspect that you might be growing marijuana plants, for example. Collecting evidence by tapping telephones requires a warrant as well.

FIFTH AMENDMENT PROTECTIONS. There seems to be a popular assumption that if one "takes the Fifth," and refuses to testify against oneself, one is automatically guilty. However, this protection extends to and protects innocent individuals as well. Included in the protections of the Fifth Amendment is one against **double jeopardy;** that is, being tried twice for the same offense. Both national and state governments can conceivably try an individual for the same offense without violating this provision; however, the essential protection protects the individual from being repeat-

edly hauled into court by the same government until convicted. For example, after a Dade County (Miami) jury acquitted four ex-policemen in 1980 of killing a black man, the U.S. Department of Justice investigated the possibility of charging them with another crime—violating the Civil Rights Act of 1891 by depriving someone of life.

The **due process** clause in the Fifth Amendment, although subject to changing interpretations, provides in effect an umbrella for accused persons. At the heart of this clause is the assumption that prosecutors and courts will act in a fundamentally fair manner. The knowing use of perjured testimony against the accused would be a violation of the due process clause. Forcing a confession or using a jury known to be biased against the defendant would also be violations.

OTHER CIVIL LIBERTIES

In addition to the civil liberties we have discussed, there are others which affect us all that are not directly treated in the Bill of

The Second Amendment guarantees the right of the people to keep and bear arms.

The enumeration in the Constitution, of certain rights, shall not be construed to deny or disparage others retained by the people.

Rights. In this sense, they are like the "reserved powers" of the states, for they are not explicitly stated (see insert).

PRIVACY. In a way, the **Ninth Amendment** is one of the most vague and yet one of the most needed parts of the Bill of Rights. It would have been possible, in drafting the Bill of Rights, to have included many more civil liberties. But the Ninth offers room for considerable latitude in determining how free the people can be from their government. Consider, for instance, the right to privacy. Although the Fourth Amendment supposedly guarantees this through a freedom against "unreasonable searches and seizures," the explicit right to privacy is not otherwise guaranteed in the Bill of Rights. Justice Douglas argued that the right is implicit in the guarantees of the earlier amendments, but that the Ninth provides a further basis as well.

BIRTH CONTROL. We mentioned earlier the unequal status of women insofar as civil rights are concerned. It would seem a fundamental right of all people to use birth control devices if they desire to do so. Yet in Connecticut, it was formerly illegal to explain to someone the options available. In the 1965 case, *Griswold v. Connecticut,* the Supreme Court ruled seven to two that married couples have a fundamental right to privacy, and that this right was protected by the Ninth Amendment.[39]

ABORTION. An extension of the fundamental right to privacy concerns whether it includes the right to control one's own body. Until very recently, abortion was illegal in the United States, except under very strict and controlled conditions. Proponents of abortion, encouraged by the Court's position in *Griswold,* brought two cases to the Supreme Court for ruling. In 1973, anti-abortion statutes in two states were set aside as infringing on the right of each woman to the privacy of a decision over the control of her own body.[40] In these cases, the Fourteenth Amendment was applied as limiting the ability of a state to invade the privacy of a person's conscience and body. But the principle had been established in *Griswold.*

It might be added that the Court did not establish an unlimited right to abortions and that it has since backed away somewhat, allowing abortions only through the first twenty-four weeks of pregnancy, unless a compelling medical or psychiatric reason indicates that abortion is required. In deciding these cases, the Court has become the center of a major controversy over women's rights versus the right to life of the unborn fetus. In some respects, abortion was the hidden issue of the 1976 and 1980 presidential elections. It emerged again in 1981 when Congress considered legislation defining when human life begins. It now appears that this emotional issue may remain unresolved for years to come.

An unsettled picture exists regarding the right to privacy and electronic surveillance by government agencies. Should the government be free to wiretap under the Fourth Amendment? Under strict controls, in which law-enforcement agencies must show that there is "probable cause" to justify invading a person's privacy, the courts may issue warrants allowing eavesdropping on private conversations. Investigations in 1976 showed that the Central Intelligence Agency had frequently engaged in unauthorized wiretapping and had violated several statutes. Thus, as those who insisted on a Bill of Rights had claimed, we cannot expect government always to be benevolent and act in our own best interests. Court prosecutions do not always follow violations. Our only real protections may be a free press which publicizes governmental excesses and a Congress which suspiciously eyes the executive branch.

HABEAS CORPUS AND WARTIME LIMITATIONS. We referred earlier to **habeas corpus,** often considered a basic right in any free society. Briefly, it restrains law enforcement officials, and thereby the government, from holding prisoners without a charge. In other words, if a writ of *habeas corpus* is issued in a particular case, whoever has that prisoner in custody must bring him or her to court and show cause as to why the prisoner is being held. This is a strict limit on public officials who might be tempted to act like secret police, taking people into custody and hiding them away from the courts.

This right was considered to be so basic that, like the prohibitions on *ex post facto* laws and bills of attainder, it was written into the original Constitution, in Article I, not in the Bill of Rights. This once again suggests that the Founding Fathers were not unaware of the political and social environment in which they were operating. Though they were roundly criticized for omitting the Bill of Rights from the draft they sent to the states, and though they incorporated several apparently anti-democratic devices (such as indirect election of the president) into the Constitution, they acted vigorously to protect citizens against some governmental excesses.

Habeas corpus can be suspended by Congress in wartime. President Lincoln actu-

ally did this during the Civil War without proper authority; Congress later ratified the action he had already taken. Lincoln has been severely criticized for this, but it appears to be consistent with a fundamental premise we stated earlier: every state or nation sees as its first right that of self-preservation.

We might like to think of ourselves as an enlightened nation; yet in time of war, we have behaved in a way that is anything but enlightened. One example of this occurred during World War II. Following the attack on Pearl Harbor and our entry into the war, curfews were imposed on Japanese–Americans on the West Coast; by a unanimous vote this curfew was upheld by the Supreme Court.[41] Japanese–Americans were ordered to evacuate the states of California, Oregon, Washington, Idaho, Montana, Utah, and Nevada and were placed in detention camps under less than desirable conditions. The Supreme Court held that the evacuation was indeed constitutional.[42]

Because of pressing public necessity and the gravest imminent danger to the public safety, the majority of the Court held, some restrictions upon the liberties of a particular racial group, motivated not by racial prejudice but by military necessity, must be tolerated.[43]

Although the Supreme Court ruled that evacuation was acceptable, it found that the use of the camps was not.

Curfew and evacuation it could with difficulty accept; internment of loyal American citizens in concentration camps solely because of the accident of racial descent was too closely akin to what the Nazis were doing for the Court to acquiesce in, even under the claim of military necessity.[44]

But the fact remains that United States citizens were put in concentration camps, and most of them stayed there until the end of the war, while being slowly cleared for loyalty.

Equal Rights and Affirmative Action

While a majority of the nation apparently accepted the goals of the civil rights revolution, there were hidden points which only slowly emerged. Essentially they boil down to a single question—can attempts to correct inequalities create new inequalities? Or are we confusing equality of opportunity with inequality of ability through "reverse discrimination"?

EQUAL EMPLOYMENT OPPORTUNITY

The 1964 Civil Rights Act was a milestone in the development of equal opportunity in employment. An Equal Employment Opportunity Commission created by the Act was to determine whether discrimination took place in hirings. Specifically outlawed were considerations of race, color, religion, sex, or national origin in hiring and firing employees of government and private industry.

DISCRIMINATION IN COLLEGES.   Other agencies of the federal government got into the act as well. Using its power to withdraw tremendous amounts of federal funds as a weapon, the Department of Health, Education, and Welfare investigated numerous universities and colleges. To nobody's surprise, it was found that discriminatory employment practices were common. Women and blacks and other minorities were able to make strong cases—often forcefully denied by the universities—that they had been systematically denied promotions, tenure, and higher pay. HEW issued orders for each college to develop plans for **affirmative action,** with "realistic" dates of implementation. In the course of their investigations, it was also learned that women's sports had been systematically discriminated

against in terms of financing, program, staffing, and facilities. Steps were taken at many institutions to overcome this long-standing inequity.

QUOTAS.   Within a few years it was suggested that "reverse discrimination" was taking place. That is, claims were made that whites and males were being laid off and women or minorities were being hired to take their places. Discussions of "quotas" surrounded the 1968 and 1972 Democratic National Convention, and guidelines were developed to ensure that all groups of the population were adequately represented. In short, equality became a "hot" or newsworthy item. The issue of "reverse discrimination" was unavoidable and, in 1977, the Supreme Court agreed to hear one of the most significant cases in civil rights to emerge in our time. How would the Court handle it?

THE *BAKKE* CASE

BACKGROUND.   Allan Bakke, an engineer in his thirties, applied for admission to the medical school of the University of California at Davis in 1973 and 1974. On both occasions he was rejected. On learning that sixteen of one hundred spaces in each class were reserved for minority admissions, and that his entrance scores were higher than several of those who had been admitted, he filed suit for admission, claiming that he was unfairly discriminated against. A county court in California agreed, but did not order his admission. After appeals through the California state court system, the Supreme Court accepted the case, and heard oral arguments in October 1977.

The case drew immediate national publicity and attention. Some measure of the interest generated by the case is the fact that 120 *amicus curiae* briefs were filed by various groups and individuals representing some of the best-known and most powerful organizations in the United States. Of these, 32 were filed on behalf of Bakke and his complaint that he had been denied equal protection of the laws under the Fourteenth Amendment, 83 supported the university's minority admissions program, and 5 took various positions.[45]

As the Supreme Court entered its deliberations, public interest in the outcome mounted (see insert). Many legal experts as well as media representatives established an informal "*Bakke* watch" to be prepared for the eventual decision. When the decision came on June 28, 1978, it was both a bombshell and a dud, catching many by surprise.

THE *BAKKE* DECISION. In some ways, the decision reached by the Supreme Court illustrates the highly political nature both of the judicial process and of the law that is created

by the judiciary. In one way, at least, we are able to see the bitter divisions in the Court itself (see insert), since it divided five to four on each of the three issues to which it addressed itself.[46] The remarks of several of the justices show that they were as sharply divided on the issues associated with reverse discrimination as was the general public.

A specific question answered by the Court was whether Bakke was entitled to admission. On this, a bare majority agreed, and Bakke was ordered admitted. Bakke, in short order, enrolled in the medical school of the University of California at Davis.

But the case had wider implications: is race a proper criterion in medical school or university admissions policies? Four members of the Court found that this criterion is permissible—if the intent is to remedy past discrimination. Four others disagreed: they held that the 1964 Civil Rights Act does not allow racial discrimination in any form, either against blacks or against whites. Justice Powell, who cast the fifth and deciding vote, also agreed that race was an improper criterion,

Not only was the Supreme Court divided three ways in its five-to-four decision, but also a great deal of bitterness was apparent within the Court regarding its own decision.

It is more than a little ironic that, after several hundred years of class-based discrimination against Negroes, the Court is unwilling to hold that a class-based remedy for that discrimination is permissible.

Justice THURGOOD MARSHALL

In order to get beyond racism, we must first take account of race. There is no other way. And in order to treat some persons equally, we must treat them differently. We cannot—we dare not—let the Equal Protection Clause perpetuate racial supremacy.

Justice HARRY BLACKMUN

It is hardly necessary to state that only a majority can speak for the Court or determine what is the "central meaning" of any judgement of the Court.

Justice JOHN PAUL STEVENS

Source: *Regents of the University of California* v. *Allan Bakke,* 438 U.S. 265 (1978).

but his vote was based on the equal protection clause of the Fourteenth Amendment.

On the other hand, Justice Powell joined the first four justices on a third issue, one which leaves the question of reverse discrimination unresolved for the time being. Is it possible to consider race in admissions programs? Yes, ruled the Court. Although racial quotas are not permissible under the 1964 Civil Rights Act or under the Fourteenth Amendment, race can be considered in weighing whether or not a candidate is qualified for admission.

UNRESOLVED QUESTIONS

Allan Bakke won his case and was admitted to medical school. Although quotas are not permissible, race can be considered in university admissions programs. The sharp divisions within the Court, reflected in the three five-to-four decisions, left no clear rule of law that we can be sure will stand the test of time.

What is your opinion on the following questions? Take into consideration the 1964 Civil Rights Act, the Fourteenth Amendment, and the goal of society to establish full equality before the law for all citizens. The Court has held that private employers can voluntarily select minority workers for special training even if they have less seniority than white workers.[47] These questions center around just one issue—that of employment—but others could be asked on housing, the awarding of government grants, and so forth. Should race or sex be a consideration:

★ in hiring new employees?

★ in decisions on which employees to lay off when firings are necessary?

★ in promotions and guarantees of seniority or tenure?

These and related issues have yet to be resolved. No matter who wins, the losers will feel that our society and our government have embarked upon or perpetuated a system of inequality.

Summary

Although the original Constitution and the Bill of Rights supposedly state our basic freedoms, we have only slowly evolved toward becoming a society of freedom and equality. In the area of civil rights—or equality before the law—it took a Civil War and several constitutional amendments to establish legal equality for black Americans. Translating that legal equality into reality has been a painful process of social, political, and economic change. Highly instrumental in this change has been the Supreme Court—an institution that once helped preserve the bastions of segregation. We are still witnessing some of the changes brought about by the Court's momentous decision on behalf of civil rights for blacks in *Brown* v. *Board of Education of Topeka.*

We have also witnessed the slow development of equal legal rights for other minority groups and women. The first step toward legal equality for women was the Nineteenth Amendment, which gave them the right to vote; women are still pressing their claims for equal status in the worlds of economics and politics and bringing about long overdue changes in state and national laws. Rising self-consciousness among women, blacks, and other minorities can be expected to have a dramatic and beneficial effect on the shape of civil rights in years to come.

The necessity of protecting the individual against government was recognized in the original Constitution, which forbade *ex post facto* laws and bills of attainder and guaranteed the writ of *habeas corpus.* In the ongoing conflict between individuals and government in the area of civil liberties, the courts have had to resolve many complex and subtle questions that could not have been taken into account in either the Constitution or the Bill of Rights. Basic freedoms—for those accused and convicted of criminal offenses, for the average citizen, and for institutions such as the press—are constantly challenged.

An underlying issue before us all— whether we describe the government, its separate parts, or ourselves as individuals—is the extent to which a nation must ensure its security. If we are in a state of declared war, it is clear that steps must be taken that would otherwise be contrary to both the Constitution and fundamental human rights. In peacetime, however, human and civil rights are another issue entirely, an issue that is explored in the courts on a case-by-case and issue-by-issue basis.

Terms to Remember

See the Glossary at the end of the book for definitions.

Affirmative action	*Brown* v. *Board of Education*	Civil rights
Bill of attainder	Civil liberties	Civil Rights Commission

"Clear and present danger" doctrine

Contemporary community standards

Dennis v. *United States*

Double jeopardy

Dred Scott decision

Due process

Equal Rights Amendment

Ex post facto law

First Amendment freedoms

Fourteenth Amendment

Furman v. *Georgia*

Gideon v. *Wainwright*

"Grandfather clause"

Griswold v. *Connecticut*

Habeas corpus

Literacy tests

McCarran Act of 1950

Miranda decision

Nineteenth Amendment

Ninth Amendment

Pentagon Papers

Plessy v. *Ferguson*

Poll tax

Regents v. *Bakke*

Residency requirement

Roth Doctrine

"Separate but equal"

Smith Act of 1940

Twenty-sixth Amendment

Voting Rights Act of 1965

White primary

Witherspoon v. *Illinois*

Yates v. *United States*

Notes

1. *Dred Scott* v. *Sanford,* 19 Howard 393 (1857).

2. *Barron* v. *Baltimore,* 7 Peters 243 (1833).

3. 109 U.S. 3 (1883).

4. 163 U.S. 537 (1896).

5. *Missouri ex rel. Gaines* v. *Canada,* 305 U.S. 337 (1936); *Sweatt* v. *Painter,* 339 U.S. 629 (1950); and *McClurin* v. *Oklahoma State Regents,* 339 U.S. 637 (1950).

6. 347 U.S. 483 (1954). H. Frank Way, *Liberty in the Balance* (4th ed.; New York: McGraw-Hill Book Co., 1976), argues in Chapter One that the New Deal coalition, northern migration, and black organization were the turning point.

7. *Nixon* v. *Herndon,* 273 U.S. 536 (1927); *Nixon* v. *Condon,* 286 U.S. 73 (1932); *Grovey* v. *Townsend,* 296 U.S. 45 (1935); and *Smith* v. *Allwright,* 321 U.S. 649 (1944).

8. In 1979, there were 486 elected black law enforcement officials in the United States, compared to 213 in 1970. Most blacks elected to public office are from the South. In 1974 there were 1609 southern blacks holding elective office, and in 1979 there were 2,768. *Statistical Abstract of the United States,* 1980, Table 832, p. 512.

9. *Oregon* v. *Mitchell,* 400 U.S. 112 (1970). The Court's decision violated the principle, in Article I, Section 2, that qualifications for voting for Congress were to be based on state-determined qualifications for voting for the lower house of the state legislatures. And, two years later, the Court struck down a state requirement in Tennessee for one year's residence, on the grounds that no compelling state interest had been shown to require a residency of this length. *Dunn* v. *Blumstein,* 405 U.S. 330 (1972).

10. Philip E. Converse and Richard Niemi, "Non-Voting Among Young Adults in the United States," in William J. Crotty, Donald M. Freeman, and Douglas S. Gatlin (eds.), *Political Parties and Political Behavior,* 2d ed. (Boston: Allyn and Bacon, 1971), pp. 443–66.

11. *Richardson* v. *Ramirez,* 418 U.S. 24 (1974).

12. *McCollum* v. *Board of Education,* 333 U.S. 203 (1948).

13. *Zorach* v. *Clauson,* 343 U.S. 306 (1952).

14. *Reynolds* v. *United States,* 98 U.S. 145 (1879).

15. *West Virginia State Board of Education* v. *Barnette,* 319 U.S. 624 (1943).

16. *Engel* v. *Vitale,* 370 U.S. 421 (1962); *Abingdon School District* v. *Schemp,* 374 U.S. 203 (1963).

17. *Walz* v. *Tax Commission of the City of New York,* 397 U.S. 664 (1970).

18. *Schenck v. United States,* 249 U.S. 47 (1919).

19. 341 U.S. 494 (1951).

20. 354 U.S. 298 (1957).

21. *Roth v. United States,* 354 U.S. 476 (1957).

22. See Bob Woodward and Scott Armstrong, *The Brethren: Inside the Supreme Court* (New York: Simon and Schuster, 1979), especially pp. 192–204.

23. *Miller v. California,* 413 U.S. 15 (1973).

24. Tom Goldstein, "Survey Finds High Court Decision Fails to Spur Convictions on Smut," *New York Times,* March 20, 1977, p. 57; Ted Morgan, "United States Versus Princes of Porn," *New York Times Magazine,* March 6, 1977, pp. 16 *et seq.*

25. *New York Times Co. v. United States,* 403 U.S. 713 (1971).

26. *Near v. Minnesota,* 283 U.S. 697 (1931).

27. *United States v. Brown,* 381 U.S. 347 (1965).

28. *Cummings v. Missouri, Ex parte Garland,* 4 Wall. 277 (1867).

29. *Johnson v. Zerbst,* 304 U.S. 458 (1938).

30. 372 U.S. 335 (1963). An outstanding account of this case, which provides a superb insight into the workings of the Supreme Court, is Anthony Lewis, *Gideon's Trumpet* (New York: Random House, 1964).

31. *Argersinger v. Hamlin,* 407 U.S. 25 (1972).

32. *Escobedo v. Illinois,* 378 U.S. 478 (1964).

33. *Miranda v. Arizona,* 384 U.S. 436 (1966).

34. 391 U.S. 510 (1968).

35. 408 U.S. 238 (1972).

36. *Gregg v. Georgia,* 428 U.S. 153 (1976).

37. *Woodson v. North Carolina,* 428 U.S. 280 (1976).

38. *Godfrey v. Georgia,* 100 S.Ct. 1759 (1980).

39. 381 U.S. 479 (1965).

40. *Roe v. Wade,* 410 U.S. 113 (1973); *Doe v. Bolton,* 410 U.S. 179 (1973).

41. *Hirabayashi v. United States,* 320 U.S. 81 (1943).

42. *Korematsu v. United States,* 323 U.S. 214 (1944).

43. Leo Pfeffer, *This Honorable Court* (Boston: Beacon Press, 1965), p. 351.

44. Ibid.

45. Calculated from *Chronicle of Higher Education* (September 19, 1977), p. 4.

46. *Regents of the University of California v. Allan Bakke,* 438 U.S. 265 (1978). See also Allan P. Sindler, *Bakke, DeFunis, and Minority Admissions* (New York: Longman, Inc., 1978).

47. *Kaiser Aluminum v. Weber,* U.S. (1979).

Suggested Readings

Henry J. Abraham, *Freedom and the Court: Civil Rights and Civil Liberties in the United States* (New York: Oxford University Press, 1972).

Lucius J. Barker and Twiley W. Barker, Jr., *Freedom, Courts, and Politics: Studies in Civil Liberties,* 2d ed. (Englewood Cliffs, N.J.: Prentice–Hall, 1972).

William J. Brennan, Jr., *The Bill of Rights and the States* (Santa Barbara, Calif.: Center for the Study of Democratic Institutions, 1961).

Jonathan D. Casper, *The Politics of Civil Liberties* (New York: Harper and Row, 1972).

Richard Claude, *The Supreme Court and the Electoral Process* (Baltimore: Johns Hopkins University Press, 1970).

Learned Hand, *The Bill of Rights* (Cambridge: Harvard University Press, 1958).

Richard Harris, *Justice: The Crisis of Law, Order and Freedom in America* (New York: Dutton, 1970).

Samuel Krislov, *The Supreme Court and Political Freedom* (New York: The Free Press, 1968).

Leonard W. Levy, *Against the Law: The Nixon Court and Criminal Justice* (New York: Harper and Row, 1974).

Anthony Lewis, *Gideon's Trumpet* (New York: Random House, 1964).

Robert P. Wolff, ed., *The Rule of Law* (New York: Simon and Schuster, 1971).

CHAPTER 6

Interests and Pressures

A power has risen up in the government greater than the people themselves, consisting of many and various and powerful interests. . . .

JOHN C. CALHOUN

To discuss formal government and guaranteed civil rights and liberties is one thing. But who really runs the government? Is it the "powerful interests," who some say can buy and sell members of Congress, and maybe even the president? So goes one common argument. And it is sometimes difficult to deny. We often hear of corporate and union Political Action Committees giving campaign contributions to candidates. Does this mean that they are buying policy and becoming winners while the rest of us lose? Perhaps so, but there may even be limits on their power.

IS CONTROL POSSIBLE? To ask who really runs the government suggests that someone is in control. We cannot accept such a proposition on its face. If there is one essential characteristic of American government, it might be summarized by the following rule: authority and responsibility do not indicate who and what determines outcomes; decision making is decentralized and diffuse. From this rule we can draw a number of corollaries:

1. No one person or institution in government is ultimately responsible for the outcome of a single decision.

2. Although government institutions and officeholders lack responsibility, there is still an element of accountability. Presidents and members of Congress can be held accountable for their acts—in the media, in public opinion surveys, and at the polls.

3. Government is peculiarly susceptible to pressure at several points.

4. This pressure is seldom used for innovation, but rather to maintain a status quo.

5. If total responsibility does not rest in any one person, office, or institution, then intra-governmental

★ ★

pressures will exist. That is, there will be pressure from one part of the government on other parts.

Interest Groups

Let's see how the interest game is organized, who the players are, and what some rules of the game are. It is too easy to use phrases like "powerful interests" without really knowing who or what we are describing. Let's start with a basic premise—we all have interests. It can be as simple as a new stereo (interest as consumer), or making sure it does not get stolen from the dorm or apartment (interest as potential victim), or getting a job after graduation (interest as job seeker). That we should have interests is only natural. For our purposes we must determine if the

Coal miners are an example of a group with special interests to present to legislators and other policymakers, an activity known as lobbying.

interests are relevant to government, and whether there is organization with others to promote these interests.

INTERESTS RELEVANT TO GOVERNMENT

Since we have many roles as individuals, we also have many interests, but most are not **interests relevant** to the functioning of government. It will not make a whit of difference to the government if you decide not to purchase your stereo set. On the other hand, should you and many consumers decide not to purchase that set, then there may be severe dislocation in the electronics industry, involving the closing of factories and unemployment of thousands of workers. At that point the government will definitely find your action to be relevant. Or, if you and all other consumers decide to select a foreign-made stereo, then the same effects might result.

In other words, the interests you have, and the actions you take on them, short of criminal activity, are seldom relevant to the government, unless they are taken in concert with others.[1] Then, if government has an abiding interest in the results of your actions, it might be compelled to act. It may implement a program, or use any of its discretionary powers. For instance, if electronics workers are unemployed, existing programs of unemployment compensation would take effect automatically, as they already exist. If the problem is more widespread or of a longer duration, it might be necessary to use job-retraining under federal sponsorship. Should the problem arise because foreign-made goods have been "dumped" on our markets, negotiations might be started with the countries whose products are causing unemployment here. If necessary, the legislative and executive branches of government can limit the imports.

In some things the government has no deep and abiding interest. The government will not fall and the system will not crumble if you hold certain opinions, even if those opinions are relevant to the government. But, if you work with others to spread those opinions either directly or through your actions, then the government might have to pay attention after all.

ORGANIZED INTERESTS

ACCESS. There are some persons who, as individuals, enjoy what we call **access to government.** That is, decision-makers' doors will be open to them. Their opinions and actions are important, and those who work in government may find it important or necessary to listen to them. Their formal and informal positions are such that they need not organize themselves to gain attention. They may have helped certain officials get elected, or they may command information and influence of such magnitude that those in government will actually seek them out. President Carter's friend and confidant, Charles Kirbo, certainly did not need to shout to have his voice heard and his phone calls returned.[2]

LOBBYING. The use of access is generally referred to by the term *lobbying.* This description of the attempt to exercise pressure and influence upon lawmakers can conjure up images of representatives being bought and sold. Actually, it is a broad term, deriving from the fact that lawmakers were often met in the lobby of the House or Senate—hence, practitioners came to be known as *lobbyists.*

GROUP PURPOSES. Most pressures on government are generated through groups organized to promote one or more sets of interests, although these interests are not always relevant to the operation of the government. There are literally thousands of such groups

Viewpoint:
Harry Truman on lobbying and corruption

Looking back on his career before he became president, Mr. Truman suggested that the only people really corrupted by lobbying practices were those who wasted their money trying to buy influence.

In my first report to the Senate I condemned the action of lobbyists, whose attempts to buy and sell influence were weakening the public confidence in the integrity of government officials. . . . This made businessmen the dupes of peddlers of influence who approached them with stories of their close connections in Washington and with promises of contracts if they were paid a commission, usually five or ten per cent of the contract price. . . . The practice was difficult to expose and eliminate, however, because the businessmen who were duped by it hated to admit that their greed had led them to attempt what they thought was bribery of government procurement officers.

HARRY S. TRUMAN

Source: *Memoirs*, vol. 1 (Garden City, N.Y.: Doubleday, 1955), p. 177.

in the United States. These include labor unions, professional associations, and ideological organizations. Some class bias can be noted in such groups: people from poorer backgrounds seldom belong to formal organizations of any kind, and are less likely than others to bring pressure on the government through organized groups.

These groups are usually organized around a central purpose, such as acting on problems of a common nature. The problems may be purely social, so that the government need pay little if any attention. A local organization that encourages youngsters to participate in scouting or organized athletics is an example of this. The government may show no awareness of its existence, other than to send the usual laudatory messages at appropriate times. Or, the problems may be economic or political in nature, in which case there might be more need for the government to be aware. For instance, a group may organize to achieve greater savings in purchasing

through a cooperative buying plan. If there are no major disruptions in economic activity as a consequence, the government will pay little or no attention. On the other hand, a cooperative may be subject to government attention, inspection, and even regulation if it substantially disrupts the normal marketplace. Farmers' organizations of this nature, designed to market goods with greater efficiency, are the object of increasing government scrutiny, especially as some of them are acquiring an ever-larger share of the marketplace, to the point where they may become monopolies.

Avowedly political groups have developed in order to secure government attention and action. Locally, we seem to have a peculiar ability to organize ourselves to handle some problem, such as getting sidewalk crossing guards for school children. When we do this, the city or school district may have to listen to what we say. For problems at a state or national level, there are organizations which command great attention, too. Many of

Some selected organizations represented in Washington

American Academy:	for Cerebral Palsy; of Actuaries: of Environmental Engineers; of Orthotists and Prosthetists
American Association:	for Higher Education; of Advertising Agencies; of Blood Banks; of Chiropractors; of Community and Junior Colleges; of Homes for the Aging; of Retired Persons; of State Colleges and Universities; of State Highway and Transportation Officials; of University Professors; of University Women; of Workers for the Blind
American _____ Association:	Automobile; Bankers; Bar; Citizens Band Operators; Educational Research; Feed Manufacturers; Footwear Industries; Horse Protection; Hospital; Hotel and Motel; Humane; Imported Automobile Dealers; Land Development; Latvian; Leprosy; Library; Life Insurance; Medical
Association:	for Childhood Education; of American Colleges; of Auto and Truck Recyclers; of Bituminous Contractors; of Brass and Bronze Ingot Manufacturers; of Federal Investigators; of Interior Decor Specialists; of Local Transport Airlines; of Metropolitan Sewerage Agencies; of National Advertisers; of the United States Army; of Women Business Owners; of American Indian Affairs
Council of:	Better Business Bureaus; Defense and Space Industry Associations; National Organizations for Children and Youth; State Chambers of Commerce; State Planning Agencies; Urban Health Providers
National Association:	for Justice; for Mental Health; for Milk Marketing; for Retarded Citizens; for the Advancement of Colored People; of Alcoholic Beverage Importers; of Arab Americans; of Attorneys General; of Broadcasters; of Credit Unions; of Electric Companies; of Farmworker Organizations; of Food Chains; of Home Builders; of Insurance Agents; of Realtors; of Retail Grocers; of Truck Stop Operators

these are based in Washington, or at least maintain offices there. A quick sampling shows the variety of organized interests present in Washington (see Table 6–1).

Not all these organizations are deliberately formed to pressure the government, by any means. Some of them have interests which are only tangential to government, at best. Yet any of them would speak up on an issue it feels relevant to the interests of its members.

PRESSURE GROUPS. At this point we mention another definition, with a warning. We commonly understand the term *pressure group* to refer to an organization that wants to affect public policy to reflect the interests of its members. It organizes itself so as to make its members' desires known, whether at the local, state, or national level. However, we must add this *caveat:* there is nothing inherently wrong with pressure groups. Many terms used in politics are highly relative. Thus, to call a group a *pressure group* frequently carries the connotation of corruption. Thus, *we* belong to interest groups—those who oppose us belong to pressure groups. In fact, whether we are aware of it or not, we ourselves either belong to pressure groups, or else there are such groups which claim to represent us.

CATEGORIC GROUPS. There are also **categoric groups.** These are unorganized groups with no formal membership or leadership. They are simply categories by which we describe ourselves and others. Thus, men and women belong to separate groups, as do the races, and so forth. We can describe people by any number of attributes, such as age (under thirty and over thirty), income (low, medium, higher-than-mine), education (low, medium, high), and so forth. While it may be difficult to see these categories as having interests, their members can easily have interests relevant to government. For instance, women as a

categoric group can have a whole range of interests, such as developing equal opportunities, allowing abortion on demand, eliminating tax laws which discriminate against the single woman, and so forth.

Equally important, these very interests can be opposed by members of the same categoric group. The fight against the ERA was led by women just as often as women led the forces in favor of it. The point is an easy one—individual citizens can have interests deriving from their roles which are relevant to the government. And, organizations often develop to advance those interests, claiming to speak on behalf of all members of a categoric group. In the case of blacks there are such organizations as the National Association for the Advancement of Colored People (NAACP), the Congress of Racial Equality (CORE), the Urban League, and the Southern Christian Leadership Conference (SCLC). Each claims to speak and work on behalf of advancing the interests of all blacks, whether dues-paying members or not. The fact is that the category "black" is sufficient for these groups to claim legitimacy in speaking for blacks as a race.

PLURALISM

COMPETING INTERESTS. Thus we have a situation which political scientists refer to as *pluralism,* reflecting the many conflicting interests in society. Even organizations which claim to speak on behalf of whole categories, such as blacks, women, retired persons, and so forth, often compete with each other both for formal membership and effect on government policy.

COMPETITION WITHIN GROUPS. While the thrust of the civil rights movement of the 1960s was toward full integration, many local chapters of the black organizations just mentioned began to question whether full integra-

Leaders of four different black groups discussed their concerns with President Johnson: (left to right) Roy Wilkins of the NAACP; James Farmer of CORE; Martin Luther King, Jr., of SCLC; and Whitney Young of the Urban League.

tion was a desirable goal. To integrate fully would mean that there might be a loss of racial identity and pride—this at a time when black consciousness was just beginning to emerge publicly. If we honor Alex Haley's *Roots*,[3] for example, are we speeding toward integration, or moving in the opposite direction, toward racial separatism? Is integration compatible with maintaining ethnic awareness and identity? Another example might be the split existing among those who claim to speak for the elderly. On the one hand there are organizations which seek better retirement benefits and have worked to ensure that private pension funds are administered under strict government regulations. But there has been a new thrust in just the opposite direc-

tion, opposing mandatory retirement ages as discriminatory. If racism and sexism are discriminatory attitudes and policies, is it not possible that *ageism* is another evil? A good many workers do not look forward eagerly to retirement, and think that being forced to leave their jobs at a predetermined age is a denial of their right to work. These conflicts can exasperate and confuse government policy-makers, for whom there can be a damned-if-you-do and damned-if-you-don't payoff. This is another case of apparent winners sometimes being real losers, depending on one's point of view.

COMPETITION BETWEEN GROUPS. If there is pluralism *within* groups, there is also pluralism *between* groups. That is, policies advanced by one group frequently oppose policies advanced by another. What is in your best interest may not be in mine. If you believe that certain products are unsafe for consumption, and the Consumer Product Safety Commission or the Food and Drug Administration agrees, then the offending product may be banned. But opposing groups may show the product to be perfectly safe—in a series of tests which are "thoroughly objective," of course. Or, it may be argued that there is insufficient evidence to warrant removing the product from the shelves, or that a great many people will be needlessly put out of work. A series of slogans are usually trotted out at such times, and one can almost look forward to them, greeting them like old friends. "Entire Industry Threatened, Says Company Spokesman." "Children's Lives at Stake, Says Consumer Lobby." "Our Jobs on the Line, Says Union Head." The headlines are familiar enough to be brought out of the files and used with only minor modifications. "Government Ponders Problem" is usually the next headline, and for good reason, for the different interests must be considered and reconciled, if at all possible.

Such a situation arose in 1977, when the Food and Drug Administration (FDA) proposed to ban the manufacture and sale of saccharin as an artificial sweetener. Canadian tests had shown that mice developed bladder cancer after being fed a diet with large amounts of saccharin. Under the terms of federal legislation, the FDA was bound to prohibit the sale of any cancer-causing substance. However, the issue went far beyond those of us who used saccharin in our coffee instead of sugar. The soft drink industry, which had developed major product lines of "dietetic" beverages, was thrust into an immediate quandary. There was no other acceptable artificial sweetener available, since cyclamates had already been removed from the market for the same reason. Profitable product lines

would have only a short time to continue. Panic buying resulted in some areas of the country, and supermarkets and drug stores found it difficult to keep up with the demand. As the saccharin industry and soft drink suppliers began to object, they were joined by spokesmen for diabetics. Although this categoric group did not have a formal organization to represent them, members of the medical profession spoke on their behalf, pointing out the medical necessity of an alternative to sugar. It was incongruous, they suggested, for the FDA to remove a substance from the market because it posed a potential health hazard, if its removal created another and more immediate hazard for diabetics (making them losers, while the rest of the population supposedly won). Out came the headline again—"Government Ponders Problem." An interim solution was reached when Congress authorized the use of saccharin temporarily. In the meantime, it began to consider legislation which would allow the FDA greater discretion, and not force it to remove products from the shelves. In other words, there was no definite solution. Like so much in politics, there were conflicting interests, and compromises had to be reached and yet others studied.

THE NECESSITY OF COALITIONS. We often hear that "politics make strange bedfellows." Nowhere is this more evident than in interest group politics. Let's recount some of the more interesting **coalitions** that have arisen in recent years.

A major problem in recent years has been the proper disposal of waste. This can range from simple garbage, which can contaminate the water table, to deadly chemical and nuclear waste. In 1980, as attention focussed on Love Canal, near Buffalo, N.Y., it became apparent that the problem of chemical waste disposal was not limited to that area. Literally thousands of other similar sites were discovered. The problem of genetic mutations resulting from the dumping of hazardous chemical waste received increasing public and government attention. At the same time, nuclear waste disposal was becoming a major problem. As a result of the Three Mile Island plant breakdown in 1979, the public was sensitized to the potential of nuclear disaster. Included in this was the problem of how to dispose of the waste, even assuming the safety of the basic process (generating electricity, creating isotopes for medical purposes, and so forth).

Yet, there must be someplace to put all of our trash, no matter of what variety. To their surprise, municipal and corporate officials found that more and more areas simply rejected any attempt to dispose of trash, chemicals, or nuclear by-products in their vicinity. At least one corporation was forced to close a plant in Arizona that made exit signs using a radioactive product, because local officials would not allow it to continue disposing its waste there.

Rural areas rejected big-city garbage. When Rochester, N.Y., officials attempted to lease land-fills elsewhere in their home county, neighboring small towns objected, and quickly passed ordinances prohibiting Rochester's garbage from entering their towns. Met with opposition there, the officials turned to more rural neighboring counties. There they found not only formal government opposition, but physical opposition as well. People in these normally placid communities joined forces with environmental groups to obstruct roads leading to the new landfills. A tactic that had received much disdain during the Vietnam era was adopted by a strange alliance that would have been inconceivable shortly before.

COALITIONS TO WIN. Why does this happen? Why do such strange alliances form, and why do they use unfamiliar and otherwise distasteful tactics? The answer lies in our essential theme—winners and losers. No one loves to lose. And if important interests are at stake, then it is necessary to form and join such coalitions. In the case we just mentioned there were several such issues: peace, quiet, and safety in the rural dump zones which rejected Rochester's garbage. It seems that there are few more vital and emotional issues than the safety of one's family and children, or the sanctity of one's home and neighborhood.

TOBACCO AND MEDICINE. Pressure alliances are often formed in an attempt to affect government action in favor of one's interests. In 1964, there was a major attempt underway to pass a form of comprehensive medical insurance for the elderly. This program, known today as Medicare, was actively opposed by physicians and their local, state, and national organizations. Their battle cry was that this would inevitably lead to "socialized medicine." At the same time, legislation was pending to require the labelling of cigarettes as dangerous to one's health. The tobacco industry was up in arms about this proposal, since it represented a threat to profits and jobs.[4] The Surgeon General of the United States had recently compiled a report showing strong links between cigarette smoking and diseases including lung cancer, emphysema, and heart attacks. To go further and label cigarettes was seen as potentially disastrous to the industry. The two major interest groups involved at the national level, the American Medical Association and the American Tobacco Institute, joined forces on these two issues, each helping each other "lobby" against the pending legislation which would affect the other group. Thus, pluralism in this case led to cooperation instead of competition.

The only previous positive linkage between the two interests had been advertisements suggesting that "Nine out of Ten Doctors Prefer Camels." Indeed, there was every reason to think that the AMA would avoid an alliance with the tobacco industry. If doctors caution their patients not to smoke, why would they work with the tobacco interests? The answer is that each side believed it had vital interests at stake. Neither wanted to be a loser, and neither had sufficient resources to wage its battle alone. Thus, a tobacco spokesman, while persuading a member of Congress to vote against cigarette labelling, would also put in a good word for opposing Medicare as irresponsible and socialistic. Those representing the AMA would return the favor. They could suggest that the data were faulty and open to question, and that the proposed labelling would be an unwarranted intrusion of "big government" in the lives of its citizens. As a footnote we might add that each lost the battle, but has by no means lost the war. The medical profession has not been socialized by Medicare, and indeed seems quite interested in streamlining payments to physicians. Our cigarette packages are now labelled, but more low tar and nicotine brands are available. And tobacco growers receive federal price supports. Again, the status of winning and losing in politics is often more illusory than real.

BIPARTISANSHIP

WORKING WITH BOTH PARTIES. The essential tactic of pressure groups is a very old one, but it is absolutely necessary if they are to have any success. The rule that they follow is very much like that followed by members of Congress—you must have friends in both parties (bipartisanship). In other words, it is a poor lobbyist who works exclusively with Democrats or Republicans.

To ally oneself or one's interests with the fortunes of a single party is a major mistake. Members of the minority party can and often do vote with the majority on many issues. Even though the Democrats had a stranglehold on Congress from 1933 to 1953 and from 1955 to 1981, there was always the possibility that the Republicans might capture control of one or both houses. As it happened,

they won the Senate in the 1980 elections, and the chairmanships of all the committees. If interest groups had ignored the Republicans in preceding years, it would have been difficult to cultivate a whole new leadership.

SHOULD ISSUES ALWAYS BE PARTISAN? Many issues brought before Congress and the executive branch cannot be described as partisan; there is no necessarily Republican or Democratic view on many issues. Few issues consistently pit Democrats as one voting bloc against Republicans as the other. If a pressure group were to ally itself with one party, it would probably find an insufficient number of votes to support its position, even if it had chosen the apparent majority party.

We have outlined some ways in which we can have interests, and how they may be made relevant to government. There are, however, additional characteristics of pressure groups which we should acknowledge before considering them more fully.

Major Pressure Groups

Pressure groups often reflect economic organization in terms of the manufacture, distribution, and sale of commodities. We can discuss certain broad categories, such as business, agriculture, and labor. There are also many other groups that place demands on government.

BUSINESS GROUPS

UMBRELLA GROUPS. We often hear of major business organizations, and the influence they presumably wield. An umbrella organization (broad-ranging) for many of these is the U.S. Chamber of Commerce; it has local, county, and state chapters, and national headquarters are located in Washington. Its purpose is to help create a "favorable climate for business" in the United States. This is another way of saying that its members would like to be winners, with higher net profits. However, this very general purpose masks a good deal of both the competitive and oligopolistic characteristics of American business, for what is good for one company or business is not necessarily good for another. Hence, umbrella groups such as the Chamber of Commerce seldom take positions on specific issues which could split their diverse memberships.

OIL: BIG VERSUS LITTLE. For instance, the American Petroleum Institute, which represents the major oil companies, can take a general position on energy issues that represents its members. If the oil companies themselves are non-competitive, as many believe, then there will be little diversity within the oil industry. In truth, there is one form of competition that does exist. This is between the "Seven Sisters," as the major oil companies are known, and the independent oil producers. Now there is general agreement that the proper role for government is to promote the industry's goals. But if the goals of the two groups are dissimilar, then there may be substantial disagreement as to what the government should do, if anything. On at least one matter, however, there was general consensus—that federal regulation of marketing and pricing was harmful, and that controls should be lifted in order to encourage oil and gas exploration. The oil producers achieved their aim when President Carter started a phased deregulation and President Reagan lifted all remaining controls early in his administration.

COAL. Coal producers are caught in a similar bind. At a time when the government is encouraging greater use of coal to replace other fuels, the major coal companies applaud this goal. But should federal environmental policies be made less restrictive? There can be major disagreement within this industry as well, especially because the major oil companies have been buying out coal producers in order to increase their own profits.

In sum, there are numerous business and industrial groups, each with its own axe to grind, each seeking to become a winner. Most subscribe to a general policy that governmental regulation is bad, unless regulation of their competitors increases their own profits. Industry groups are not as powerful as they might be since this general policy is the only point on which they can get a consensus. On the other hand, they can be highly influential with the same government bureaucracies against which they protest, as John Kenneth Galbraith has pointed out.[5]

AGRICULTURAL GROUPS

BIG VERSUS LITTLE AGAIN. The same principles apply here to a certain extent. As the family farm falls prey to what is now called *agribusiness,* there is often considerable disparity between the goals of large and small farmers. This is reflected in the three major organizations: both the American Farm Bureau Federation and the National Grange are somewhat conservative and given to supporting Republicans, while the National Farmer's Union draws its membership from smaller and more militant farmers.

There is also organization of and disagreement between groups of farmers who grow different crops. These organizations, which cross-cut membership in the three groups just mentioned, can have very different aims. Dairymen might be interested in lowering the price of the feed grains, and making them readily available. But corn growers can be expected to want the best possible prices for their products, and might be willing to ship their produce abroad if a better price could be obtained there.

On one thing farmers usually agree—that their costs are too high, and their profit too low. This has been the subject of a constant love-hate relationship between farmers and Washington for years. Recently there has

Farmers and others engaged in agriculture lobby through large national organizations and through smaller groups representing a specific crop or activity, such as raising grain.

been a renewed tendency toward militancy, symbolized by the "farmers' strike" and "tractorcades" of 1978 and 1979. Using these and other devices, they attempted to draw public and government attention to the vital role they play in our lives. But, for all the media fanfare, the movement has so far had little impact. In the face of a threatened presidential veto in 1978, the House of Representatives easily rejected a bill favored by many farmers.

Lobbyists representing farm interests commonly concentrate on the Agriculture Committees of both House and Senate, and work closely with the Department of Agriculture as well. However, as with business interests, they also pay attention both to the con-

gressional committees dealing with labor and also the Department of Labor. Since these affect working conditions and pay rates, and farmers are seldom in a position to work their own farms without help, decisions on such matters can have a major effect on farm operations.

LABOR GROUPS

In the last fifty years there has been a tremendous growth and then leveling off in the numbers of persons who belong to unions. A great many industries have come to be covered by collective bargaining agreements, but there seems to be little growth underway at this time. More than three-fourths of all workers are still not unionized at present.

POLITICAL POWER. The focus of labor is extremely broad, dealing with such matters as wages, working conditions, and their own legitimacy. For instance, unions have had to go through major battles, both in and out of court, to win the right to organize and bargain on behalf of workers. Their rise in political power has been associated with the ways in which they can mobilize thousands of workers for elections, and canvass on behalf of candidates they support. They have also been major donors to political campaigns, principally to Democrats, but also to Republicans willing to support programs they favor.

Major union leaders are excellent examples of what we discussed earlier in terms of access based on position. The head of the AFL–CIO has seldom had difficulty obtaining an audience in the White House, whether the occupant was a Democrat or a Republican. Leaders of other national unions such as the United Mine Workers, United Auto Workers, the Teamsters, and the United Electrical Workers have also enjoyed access to the White House and to congressional leaders.

THE MEDIA AS
INTEREST GROUP

The media, taken as a whole, constitute one of the most potent groups in this country. We often hear of their influence on elections, but the way they pressure the government is both interesting and unique. The concerns of the media are several.

FIRST AMENDMENT QUESTIONS. One of these, of course, is to preserve their First Amendment freedom to seek out and publish news. We would normally let this pass, but recent history has shown that the media are quite sensitive on this issue, and with good

reason. Many recent court cases have challenged the freedom of the press. Reporters for newspapers, television, and radio have found themselves subject to judicial proceedings in which they are required to surrender their notes or their "outtakes," the films or tapes not actually used in broadcasts. The reasons for asking this of reporters usually involve questions of covering up allegedly criminal matters, such as the names of individuals engaged in the narcotics traffic. Sometimes members of the press have been accused of leaking classified information. One recent case against the *New York Times* and the *Washington Post* was brought because of their publication of the "Pentagon Papers," a classified government study.

GETTING THE STORY. Another concern of the media is that they have access to the news, and that they be fed as much information as possible. They want not only to be able to publish what they get, but also to have as much information available to them as possible. Reporters carefully cultivate sources of information. If these sources dry up with merely a "no comment" when approached by the press, there is the implication that something is wrong, and they may bring further pressure on members of the government. The reportage of the Watergate scandal, led by Bob Woodward and Carl Bernstein of the *Washington Post*,[6] showed probably better than any other example the occasional adversary roles of press and government.[7] As reporters dug deeper and deeper into the story of the cover-up, they were met with a more and more hostile response from the White House. The press was often blamed by those closest to Nixon as well as his bitter-end partisans for driving him from the White House.

RECIPROCAL NEEDS. However, there is a peculiar relationship between the press and members of the government: each needs the

Symbolizing both press and electronic media influence on government, Washington
Post *Watergate reporters Bob Woodward and Carl Bernstein watch
President Nixon on TV.*

other. Just as the press wants grist for its daily mill, the government and its various members want an aura of legitimacy. Some presidents have been quite open to the press, cultivating members of the working press as much as possible. Others have provided only information which made themselves look good.[8] Members of Congress routinely issue press releases and make radio and television tapes in the recording studio in the Capitol building, for release in their home districts or states, if not nationally. Executive department agencies also seek to make themselves look good, and try to provide as much information of this nature as possible. However, government-by-press-release, while making the jobs of reporters easier and less demanding, also has significant dangers for citizens, and we must sometimes rely on either good reporters or occasional leaks to get a major story into the open.

CITIZENS' LOBBIES

OFTEN TEMPORARY. From time to time hastily formed groups will petition the Congress or the president. These usually deal with temporary issues which have a significant portion of the public highly aroused. There are exceptions to this, of course, and we shall deal with them below.

In the course of the Vietnam War, numerous anti-war groups were formed.

These **citizens' lobbies** tended to have no real formal organization, and were often no more than letterhead groups that took advertisements in newspapers. Occasionally there would be a shift in tactics, as opposition to the war mounted. Demonstrations, parades, mass visits to congressmen, letter-writing campaigns, and even occasional passive resistance, such as refusing to pay taxes, were resorted to by more and more people. It is difficult to say what real effect this had on the government, and whether it really contributed to our getting out of Vietnam. For a time, government officials seemed even more resolved to stick it out. Perhaps they eventually reacted to what they saw as the likely electoral consequences of our staying involved; or perhaps the inability of South Vietnam to carry on on its own was the decisive factor. What was remarkable about the public pressure was that it was sustained and grew in intensity over a long period of time, despite the political naivete of many of its members.

Other issues have prompted mass attempts at bringing pressure on the government. One that arises from time to time is the attempt to institute effective gun control. Following the assassinations of Martin Luther King, Jr., and Senator Robert Kennedy in 1968, such an attempt was mounted. Letters were written, petitions signed, and personal appeals made. The absence of formal and politically knowledgeable leadership was soon apparent, however, when the anti-gun movement ran into its opposition, the National Rifle Association. This organization, long known as one of the most effective lobbies in Washington, has often boasted that it could have a million letters opposing any form of gun control arrive in Washington in one week. As it turns out, the Gun Control Act of 1968 was passed in the emotion following the two assassinations, but in substantially watered-down form. President Johnson and the temporary citizens' lobby had pushed strongly for the licensing of all gun owners,

and the registration of all firearms, but these proposals were not included in the bill that passed Congress. Discussion of effective legislation started again in 1981, following the shooting of President Reagan. However, it seems that no legislation will be enacted, partially because President Reagan opposes handgun controls.

SOME ARE WELL ORGANIZED. In addition to these temporary movements, a new form of citizens' lobby has appeared on the Washington scene. These well-funded and well-organized organizations seem to be anything but temporary. The most prominent among them have been Ralph Nader's **Public Interest Research Group** and **Common Cause**. Both are broad-based organizations, with voluntary donations of time and money from many thousands of members. The Nader approach for a long time was to consider the citizen as a consumer, and he sought effective controls on the manufacture and sale of unsafe automobiles and other products. Lately there has been an expansion into other issue areas as well. Common Cause has shown interest in several different issues, most of which involve some form of government reform. It has been a principal force in the reform of financing election campaigns, and for forcing full disclosure of the activities of formal pressure groups.

FOREIGN LOBBYING

SEEKING AID. So great are the power and resources of Washington that agents of foreign countries also pressure our government. One focus of the activity of the **foreign lobbyists** is the broad spectrum of foreign aid programs including direct grants of military aid, economic subsidies, and technical assistance. We are not discussing the formal diplomatic missions found in our nation's capital. Rather, besides the diplomatic corps there are many individuals, United States citizens and others, hired to do specific jobs by clients. They are subject to the Foreign Agents Registration Act of 1938, one which is really without parallel in other nations. The act requires that "every person who becomes an agent of a foreign principal shall, within ten days thereafter" file a statement with the Attorney General, outlining the existence and purpose of the relationship. However, there is no way to force such representatives to disclose their interests as they deal with members of Congress or of various executive departments.[9]

THE KOREAN CONNECTION. Several recent incidents show the influence that is possible. In 1976 wealthy Korean businessman, Tongsun Park, made large campaign donations to members of Congress and entertained them in lavish fashion. His interest in their re-election was more than that of just a good friend, for many who received campaign funds or gifts held key positions in congressional committees or their party's leadership. Why would Park have such an interest in American elections? In part the answer lies in the influence that these same persons wield in congressional votes, and influence on matters affecting South Korea was what Park most sorely needed.

The irony here is that the government of South Korea, which allegedly supplied the funds, is really a "client state" of ours, one which receives large grants. Further, the South Korean regime had not been noted for its democratic practices, and there is some question of whether we were subsidizing an authoritarian regime. In this incident it seemed that U.S. funds were going to the government of South Korea, which then channelled some to the Korean CIA, which in turn may have paid Tongsun Park to ensure that our Congress remained favorably disposed to continue support of the South Korean government.

Lobbying the Legislative Branch

Not all lobbyists[10] work through such methods, although other such incidents have come to light. Instead, most are engaged in very smooth public relations campaigns that seek to make things easier for their clients. Some of the most successful lobbyists are former members of Congress, and for good reason. Their expertise in knowing where the power is and who controls what decisions makes them essential to any well-conducted campaign.[11] What are the characteristics and tactics of our pressure groups?

DURABILITY

INSTITUTIONAL INTEREST GROUPS. First, we should acknowledge that any government is susceptible to interests, whether the political system is democratic or undemocratic. Interests need expression, and there are various ways of expressing them. Sometimes selected-issue interests may be dealt with while others go largely unheard. One way this might be done is through what are referred to as *institutional interest groups*.[12] These are formed for some purpose other than to affect public policy. They may actually be part of the government, such as the bureaucracy. Agencies also have interests and purposes and seek to express them in one way or another.

An example of such a bureaucratic or institutionalized interest group would be the army of a nation. The first function of any army, theoretically at least, is to be prepared to defend the nation if necessary. But there can be a hidden agenda in such a simple description. For instance, the word "prepared" is loaded with potential for bringing pressure on the rest of formal government. Most armed forces express their preparedness in terms of military hardware. It is not sufficient to be well-versed and schooled in the latest tactics if the opposing forces have arms which render those tactics useless. Therefore there will be strong pressures on the government to supply the latest arms. The Red Army in the Soviet Union, for instance, is not a passive beneficiary of whatever funds are allotted it. Rather, its leaders are capable of bringing strong pressures on the government to keep up with or surpass the United States. Our own armed forces react accordingly, demanding that the Soviets not be allowed to surpass us in the arms race. Suffice it to say that interests are always present in any government and that some of them will always be represented.

ASSOCIATIONAL GROUPS. If some interests are institutionalized, then there are others which may or may not be heard. Some of these find expression through groups more or less permanently organized. We refer to these as *associational interest groups.* That is, members specifically join, or associate with each other, in order to affect government decisions which are relevant to them and their purpose as an organization. Such groups tend to have formal organizations, with a dues-paying membership and elected leadership. They may have purposes other than keeping an eye on the government, but that remains one of their major functions.

UNIONS. The major unions of our country were originally organized to represent workers to employers, and negotiate for better working conditions and higher compensation and benefits. As they became aware of the power of the government, they brought pressure on it and developed ways of letting elected representatives know their interests. They also developed affiliated or subsidiary groups whose avowed purpose is to affect labor-related legislation and government decisions. Such an organization is the Committee on Political Education (COPE) of the AFL–CIO. Since the parent organization is forbidden by law from directly participating in elections, COPE acts as a convenient funnel for union-member funds, rewarding friends of big labor in the Congress as well as assisting in presidential campaigns. Other unions may not have organized a political arm quite as openly as has the AFL–CIO, but they are not without influence. A coalition of the United Auto Workers, Public Employees, and Oil, Gas and Chemical Workers unions is emerging as more liberal on social issues than the AFL–CIO. The ways in which the Teamsters Union has made its presence known are considerably less formal, but they have also shown increasing influence in recent years. When its leadership went golfing with President Richard Nixon, for instance, they may have accomplished more on the golf course than other unions have through complicated pressure techniques.[13] This is an instance of what we earlier called personal access. When the president of the United Auto Workers or the AFL–CIO decides to make a call on the White House, he usually has little difficulty getting in.

ACADEMIC ORGANIZATIONS. Other associations pay less attention to government, for their purposes are not always as germane to government processes and decisions. A great many academic organizations, for instance, are concerned primarily with advancing the professional goals of their members. The American Political Science Association, for example, is based in Washington, D.C., but it devotes limited attention to what government is doing or could do to benefit its membership, such as funding research and training programs. But the association does participate in a training program for newly elected members of Congress. These activities are relatively incidental to the association's formal purposes, such as publishing a major journal, running the annual convention, and helping its members find jobs. Nonetheless, the activities of the association help give it legitimacy as the formal spokesman for academic politi-

Merely having an organization is not enough to ensure that your cause will be heard. Scholar David Truman points out the necessity of earlier status in order to gain access.

Perhaps the most basic factor affecting access is the position of the group or its spokesman in the social structure. . . . The deference accorded a high-status group not only facilitates the acceptance of its propaganda but also eases its approach to government. Its petitions and claims may even in some instances appear less as demands or supplications and more as flattery of the official of whom a favor is asked.

DAVID B. TRUMAN

Source: *The Governmental Process: Political Interests and Public Opinion,* 2d ed. (New York: Alfred A. Knopf, Inc., 1971), p. 265.

---

cal scientists, and can thus help assure later access.

AD HOC GROUPS. Other organizations are more temporary, or **ad hoc.** These tend to arise in response to an issue of the moment. The group may last only a very short time, such as the neighborhood association which bands together immediately after a tragic accident to pressure the school board or city council for additional school crossing guards. When the issue is resolved, the organization disbands.

At the national level, an issue may generate lots of public heat. For instance, an attempt by the government to increase income taxes suddenly would bring organizations out of the woodwork. Some will have been groups of some long standing and durability. Yet others would be formed quickly, under a name such as the *Ad Hoc* Committee Against a Tax Increase. Such groups are organizations in only the loosest sense, and may be described as letterhead or paper organizations at best. An attempt would be made to raise funds from other "concerned citizens," but the

group may die aborning, with little hope for success or influence. Temporary organizations commonly have a good deal of fervor on their side, but little knowledge of how to achieve their ends. Unless they form coalitions with older and more experienced groups, or command certain resources, they are quite likely to meet failure more often than success.

An example might be the groups which came together in an attempt in 1976 to save the life of Gary Gilmore, the convicted murderer in Utah who wanted to be executed. Nobody on death row in any state had been executed for several years as a result of uncertainty regarding various Supreme Court decisions on the death penalty. When it appeared that Utah had finally passed a statute which would meet the Court's various objections to the death penalty, Gilmore asked to be shot. Groups were formed to save Gilmore's life over his own objections. Some of these joined older organizations, such as the American Civil Liberties Union, an organization which has long fought the death penalty as "cruel and unusual punishment" under the Eighth Amendment. Gilmore ultimately was the "winner"—he was shot—and the temporary groups disappeared, but the ACLU lived on as one of the more permanent and durable pressure groups in Washington and the rest of the nation. Gilmore served only as a temporary catalyst for the capital punishment issue. His death did not do away with it by any means, but only with those groups which had focussed on him alone.[14]

ORGANIZATIONAL TACTICS

The popular image of pressure-group tactics is that of "buying" members of the government. This view is quite shortsighted. Before we discuss other tactics, let us quickly examine the ways in which money can be used to influence government decisions, but in ways other than bribery.

MONEY AS AN INFLUENCE: BRIBERY. Bribery is an extreme. A bribe is a straight-out exchange of funds with the explicit understanding that thus-and-such an action will take place in return, like voting for or against a bill in Congress, or issuing a regulation someplace in the bureaucracy. This is what we have in mind when we talk about "government to the highest bidder," or "the best government money can buy," as suggested by Senator Edward Kennedy. The history of the United States is replete with such instances. The Teapot Dome Scandal of the Harding Administration is a sordid example of how government policy can be bought and sold. Huge sums of money can be exchanged in return for a proper vote, or a misappropriation of government lands to oil interests, as was the case in the Harding era.[15] It does take place, and there is no denying it. It seems there is no limit to the extent to which certain public officials can be bought (see insert). There is also no limit to the extent to which some journalists are willing to try to dig out such instances, and publicize them for all they are

worth.[16] After all, good news does not sell as many newspapers as does news of scandal in the highest places.

GREY AREAS. The buying of government decisions with explicit understandings is both illegal and morally repugnant to most. But there is a large grey area. What about campaign contributions? In recent years many companies and unions have formed **"Political Action Committees"** (PACs) in order to donate funds legally to candidates for various offices. Each PAC is restricted to a donation of $5,000 per candidate, but there are ways to raise that amount. For instance, if all the PACs in a given industry, and there may be a hundred or more, were to give that amount to a single candidate, could this affect that candidate if elected? The presumption is that it will certainly have some sort of an effect. At the very least, the newly elected officeholder would allow access to his office and advisers for that industry's lobbyists. And if he supports that industry's point of view, is this not really bribery? In cases like these, and there are many, it is often assumed that there has been bribery. But, it can be argued equally that the PACs were simply trying to get an audience for their point of view, or that they were supporting a legislator who had already shown a favorable predisposition to them.

SERVICES-IN-KIND. It is not uncommon for various interest groups to render **"services-in-kind"** for friendly members of Congress.[17] Campaign assistance can be provided, such as printing of handbills and posters, or the supplying of a few advance men to campaign trips. In this case, the service-in-kind must now be computed and added to the costs of the campaign, and duly reported. In the first case, however, there is no direct reporting requirement. For that matter, does reporting eliminate the potential for influence? Or, is talk of "influence" no longer necessary, since

The potential for corruption in politics is a favorite subject for political commentators. However, there is a different point of view, as expressed by a former Cabinet officer.

An honest politician is one who, when bought, stays bought.
                                            SIMON CAMERON, Secretary of War under Lincoln

the congressman has already proven to be a valuable friend of the pressure group involved, and is being paid for services rendered? Members of Congress have often received speaking fees as high as several thousand dollars, plus expenses. This might be readily supplied by any number of organizations which found it necessary to have a congressman or senator address them for perhaps an hour. This has now been largely eliminated since Congress placed a restriction of $8,625 per year on such outside service fees. But there is still the potential for monetary influence. What if a congressman wishes to return to his home district, and a friendly corporation just happens to have a company plane going that way?

In sum, there are many ways in which the almighty dollar can be used to influence a member of the government, or to keep a potentially less friendly opponent out of office. Those who participate most in the pressure system are already the "winners" of the system, and are therefore more likely to have the resources to continue winning. But, the key element remains the same—how does one secure an audience? The most precious elements available to anyone able either to make or affect government policy are information and time.

SUPPLYING INFORMATION. Popular misconceptions notwithstanding, we can probably boil down the secret of pressure techniques to a simple formula: the person who can supply the most useful and accurate information in the shortest time has the greatest chance of success.[18] A lobbyist must have a reputation for telling the truth or run the risk of ineffectiveness.

In its broadest sense, *lobbying* refers to any attempt to influence the actions of government. But this is really a sloppy definition, for there are numerous ways to bring pressure on government. If you, as an individual, without any prompting, write your representative or senator, are you lobbying? Or if you gather on the steps of the Capitol along with several thousand other persons to protest some action, is this lobbying? For the rest of this chapter, we shall deal with attempts which originate in interest groups and are carried out through their organizational efforts.

One reason why information is needed is that we have learned the folly of rushing legislation through Congress. When a bill is ill-considered and pushed through for one reason or another, the checks and balances internal to the Congress are simply not working properly. One major reason why the Congress was created as a bicameral or two-house legislature was a fear of precipitate action. But, the legislative process normally takes a great deal of time to winnow the thousands of bills that are introduced, find those that are truly worthwhile, and then proceed to modify them so that various interests will be reconciled. In this process, the lobbyist can be in-

The potential for corruption in politics is enhanced by the huge sums involved in government contracts for building weapons systems, public works projects, and the like.

valuable. Members of Congress have tremendous pressures on their time, what with handling demands from constituents, their party, the media, congressional leadership, and the like. When there is a concerted effort by one or more groups to pass a bill, or to block one, then this can signal the legislator or the leadership that the bill may deserve attention. Of course, not every bill can be considered, but the information that a group supplies through its lobbyists may mean that the bill will receive more serious consideration. And, since there are certain groups which are prestigious, their own particular interests may receive more attention than the interests of others. Thus, the fact of pressure group interest is of itself a piece of valuable information.

Information may also be supplied which shows the consequences of the proposed legislation, both financial and otherwise. If, for instance, a lobbyist for a farm group could show with hard scientific data that eliminating a certain pesticide in the name of environmental concerns would have a boomerang effect by allowing insects to com-

pletely destroy crops, there might be good reason for the legislator to pay close attention.

HELPING YOUR FRIENDS. One valuable technique available to pressure groups is to write legislation for friendly members of Congress to introduce. If a representative or senator is known to be predisposed toward a certain position, and staff members are pressed for time, there is nothing to be lost, and perhaps a good deal to be gained, by asking for sponsorship of a bill which has been carefully tailored to meet the legislator's leanings. All this will take place only after carefully asking the legislator to supply his or her own thoughts or to modify the legislation. Once the bill is introduced in Congress, members of the lobbyists' staff can arrange for expert testimony on the bill—favorable to their side, of course.

GENERATING PUBLIC SUPPORT. Another way in which pressure groups attempt to influence members of Congress is by showing that there is a great deal of popular support for a position. Since one of the first motivations

A number of the modern lobbies operating in Washington are of the highest quality. With plenty of money to spend, they spend it on qualified analysts and advocates and provide Congressional committees with lucid briefs and technical documentation in support of their positions. Nothing is more informative and helpful to a legislative committee than to hear the views of competent, well-matched advocates on the opposite sides of a legislative issue [*emphasis added*].

Congressman EMANUEL CELLER

Source: "Pressure Groups in Congress," in *Annals of the American Academy of Political and Social Science*, 319 (September, 1958), p. 7.

for many office-holders is to seek re-election, a flood of carefully timed mail arriving from the legislator's district or state may notify him or her that someone out there is paying attention.[19]

INSPIRED MAIL. Mail campaigns can range from the sublime to the ridiculous. When a legislator is not used to hearing from many constituents about pending legislation, a flood of **"inspired mail"** is pretty well apparent for what it is—inspired by a lobbyist. To suddenly receive thousands of letters a day, all dealing with the same bill, should certainly make the legislator more than a touch cynical. When pre-printed petitions or newspaper coupons are used, the source is only too obvious.

Some lobbyists pass the lessons they have learned on to their members in the legislator's district. For instance, handwritten letters normally receive the most attention, since it is assumed that if a person cares enough to write personally, then it might be important for re-election if there are a number of such letters. But if thousands of letters arrive on the same day, all handwritten, all dealing with the same bill, and perhaps all containing the same

wording, one would wonder why some members of Congress don't double over laughing at the transparency of the scheme. These problems aside, a letter-writing campaign can be useful to the group in another way, as its members, through this legislative activity, become committed to both the outcome and the group they belong to.

There is one technique never resorted to by a good lobbyist, and that is making threats, either direct or veiled, that a congressman will hurt his re-election chances if he does not vote in a particular manner on a bill.

Another tactic used by some of the larger and better-financed pressure groups is to rate each member of Congress, based on votes cast on selected legislation. A senator or representative who had always voted "correctly" on certain farm legislation according to the National Farmers Union would receive a score of 100, whereas an opponent of NFU interests who has always voted the "wrong" way would receive a score of 0. These scores can be used to inform constituents in the legislator's district or state, and are a way of letting members of Congress know that someone is watching. Whether a rating makes much difference probably depends on at least two factors. One is whether or not the legislator values the group's favorable appraisal or not. For some, a low rating by the AFL–CIO COPE might be taken as a positive sign in their home districts, whereas a congressman from a heavily unionized district might want a good rating from that pressure group. The other factor is simply one of funding, since the scores can be used for guidance in doling out campaign contributions under the old maxim, "reward your friends and punish your enemies."

TARGETS OF LEGISLATIVE LOBBYISTS

Lobbyists are not in the business of making converts. They concentrate their efforts where they have the greatest leverage. The labor lobbyist focusses on members in whose districts or states organized labor represents a large bloc of votes.

Lobbying, however, is a two-way street. Lobbyists are viewed by legislators as a testing ground for ideas and an important source of information in an arena in which the executive branch has most of the experts. In *The Washington Lobbyists,* Lester Milbrath concluded that "if we had no lobby groups and lobbyists, we would probably have to invent them to improve the functioning of the system."[20]

REGULATION OF LEGISLATIVE LOBBYING

DIFFICULTY OF REGULATION. When we use the term *lobbying* in its broadest sense, we obviously cannot talk about any broad form of regulation. The First Amendment guarantees that citizens can "petition the government for a redress of grievances." However, Congress regulates the activities of those who attempt to influence that body, through the **Federal**

Regulation of Lobbying Act (1946). The Supreme Court has upheld this act, narrowing the definition of lobbying to activities which involve direct contact with legislators or their staffs.[21] The Court held that the law applied only to groups and individuals who collected or received money for the "principal purpose" of influencing legislation. Many organizations and individuals do not register as lobbyists or file quarterly reports of their expenditures because they do not collect funds, but use their own monies. Some groups, like the National Association of Manufacturers, do not register because they claim that lobbying is not one of their principal purposes. Because of this narrow definition of *lobbying,* figures reported for lobbying expenditures represent only a small portion of what is actually spent to influence the legislative process.

Reported spending by various organizations averaged approximately $4.9 million in a twenty-year period, 1950–1969.[22] As Table 6–2 shows, there has been a significant jump in recent years. The difficulties experienced by various researchers, and various loopholes in the laws, suggest that these figures are only the tip of the iceberg.

The 1946 Federal Regulation of Lobbying Act is obviously inadequate; there is no real way of determining how much is spent, and for what purpose. Because the act lacks any real teeth, it is often easier for lobbyists to register with the Clerk of the House and the Secretary of the Senate, rather than risk violating an otherwise meaningless law. Pressure to revise the law mounted for some time and, in 1976, separate versions of a tougher law passed both houses of Congress. Hearings resumed in 1977 on the proposed law, attempting to reconcile the different versions. The bill's purpose was to force organizations into more complete disclosure, indicating in detail not only how they had been spending their money, but on what legislation. The bill died, however, the victim of intense lobbying by representatives of a great many organizations.

Included were both Ralph Nader and General Motors, proving once again that "politics make strange bedfellows."

EXECUTIVE LOBBYING OF THE CONGRESS

We have stressed the ways in which formal groups attempt to make their views known and enacted as law by the Congress. Another aspect of legislative lobbying concerns attempts by the executive branch to get legislation passed or blocked. Most agencies of any size maintain what are euphemistically known as "legislative liaison offices" on Capitol Hill. In reality, they are as much lobbyists as are representatives from more familiar interests in the private sector.

Many key bills introduced in any session are administration bills, attempts to legis-

★ ★ ★ *Table 6–2* ★
Spending by Washington lobbies

		AMOUNT REPORTED
CATEGORY		
Business		$3,287,562
Professional		732,633
Labor		1,886,794
Agriculture		672,839
Military and veteran		249,900
Miscellaneous		2,634,096
	TOTAL	$9,463,824
TOP TEN SPENDERS		
Common Cause		$ 934,835
International Union, UAW		460,992
American Postal Workers Union		393,399
AFL–CIO		240,800
American Trucking Association		226,157
American Nurses Association		218,354
United Savings and Loan League		204,221
Gas Supply Committee		195,537
Disabled American Veterans		193,168
The Committee of Publicly Owned Companies		180,493
	TOTAL	$3,247,956

Source: Adapted from Congressional Quarterly, *Weekly Report,* 32 (July 27, 1974), 1948, 1953.

Truman was known for his candor and sense of humor. When asked by
a reporter in 1948 if he would oppose lobbyists working for one of his
programs, Mr. Truman replied:

*We probably wouldn't call these people lobbyists. We would call them citizens
appearing in the public interest.*

HARRY S. TRUMAN

Source: *Public Papers of the Presidents of the United States: Harry S. Truman, 1948*
(Washington, D.C.: U.S. Government Printing Office, 1964), p. 955.

late into law parts of the president's program.
The president has become the agenda-setter
for Congress, with most major bills written in
whole or in part by the executive branch.
Presidents push for passage of their programs
in a variety of ways. They work with the congressional leadership of both parties and key
committee members; they use the status of
their position to encourage congressional
compliance; and they lobby directly or indirectly by organizing public support for their
proposals.

The size of the **executive lobbying**
corps is impressive and it includes parts of the
White House staff as well as agency liaisons.
In a newsletter to his constituents, one repre-
sentative complained that "the Executive
Branch is the most powerful lobby group in
Washington, using taxpayers' money to do
the job."[23]

COURTING CONGRESS. Agencies work hard
to build up supportive relationships with key
members of Congress, especially those on
committees that oversee their agency and appropriate funds. Such contacts are a two-way
street, with the agencies seeking support for
their programs and, in turn, supporting proposals desired by the legislators. One way
they do this is by appealing to the vanity of a

member of Congress. An agency may allow a
legislator to issue a press release containing
information of interest to constituents, even if
the member had little or nothing to do with it
in the first place. If a grant for sewer construction is approved by the Army Corps of Engineers and the Environmental Protection
Agency, each will notify the legislator to release the news to home district media. It is
nice to be the bearer of glad tidings.

MILITARY LOBBYING. The most successful
lobbyist in the executive branch is the Pentagon. With a budget of about $200 billion per
year, it has a lot at stake in Congress. At the
same time, it has powerful resources to muster
in its battle for congressional appropriations.
Along with defense industry personnel, the
military lavishes endless attention on Congress. At the tip of the military's lobbying iceberg sits the Pentagon's legislative liaison office, a multimillion-dollar operation directed
solely at congressional opinion. The comment
has been made that the Pentagon has Congress organized like a "Marine Corps landing," with generals, admirals, and top civilians "always ready to run up to the Hill
whenever a problem develops."[24]

The military has much to offer an interested legislator, and it offers its largesse

freely in return for positive consideration of its proposals. It hands out favors like free military flights to home districts, or larger favors like taxpayer-supported Army Engineer Corps projects in local areas. Finally, it offers the largest favors to the most important members of Congress on various military and appropriations committees—weapons contracts for home-state industries, or bases for home districts.

Such figures as the late L. Mendel Rivers (D., S.C.), chairman of the House Armed Services Committee, were well rewarded for their unflagging support of ever-increasing military appropriations bills. Rivers's former district in Charleston bristles with nearly a dozen important defense installations.[25] A common Washington joke for years was that if the Pentagon added one more soldier, sailor, or marine, Charleston would sink into the Atlantic. Of course, this is hardly a one-way process. Legislators campaign actively with the Pentagon and the executive branch for defense contracts for home-state corporations. In a typical report, journalist Richard Harwood wrote that Congressman John Brademas of South Bend, Indiana, "spends many hours promoting defense contracts for Studebaker and Bendix Corporation and frankly contends 'anyone who didn't do it wouldn't be here very long'."[26] Sometimes, however, both the Pentagon and district-promoting legislators can lose. A pared-down C–5A (cargo plane) program and President Carter's cancellation of the B–1 bomber are examples of how high-stakes games can produce big losers.

INSIDE INFORMATION. Another tactic used by the executive branch is the sharing of insider information, which can be a very powerful tool for slowly co-opting a member of Congress. Despite the presence of "watchdog" committees in Congress to keep an eye on government intelligence agencies, investigations have shown that some of these agencies have knowingly violated the law. Homes were illegally entered, mail was opened, and telephone wires were tapped. But, little effective was done, nor can we really expect that much will be done to curb these abuses. Why? Members of Congress have served on these committees, and have become privy to the secret activities or information possessed by the Central Intelligence and National Security Agencies. The abuses apparently took place without prior congressional knowledge or consent. But, in the process of learning other secrets, they have been co-opted into the scheme of things, insofar as those agencies are concerned. To protest one kind of activity might mean the loss of future intelligence information. Washington is every bit as much an "insider's town" as is any other city, perhaps more so. In an environment which values status and prestige, the sharing of the nation's vital secrets, and the knowledge by others that you are privy to certain secrets, creates an automatic bonus in social and political circles.

PRESIDENTIAL LOBBYING. While not all agencies can share top-secret information, they can and do attempt to play on a congressman's pride. Foremost among those who use such techniques is the **president** of the United States. In a power-oriented and status-conscious town like Washington, the president is the one person who is most able to make or break someone else, by the ways in which he distributes little tokens of recognition.

Two contrasting styles can be seen in the ways that Lyndon Johnson and Richard Nixon ran their congressional liaison. Nixon, who had been in the House and Senate only briefly, was never really an insider, and tended to treat members of Congress in a brusque and peremptory manner. He would issue invitations to dinner when necessary, but few, if any, members of Congress ever got close and personal treatment. The few times that this strategy was changed were when Nixon needed an extra few votes to get Congress to sustain a veto. In the midst of the impeachment inquiries, a number of legislators reported that they were invited to cruises on the presidential yacht.

Johnson, on the other hand, often acted like a long-lost cousin with members of Congress, and not only when he needed their votes. Invitations would come to visit him at the LBJ Ranch or at the White House for dinner, a chat, or a swim in the pool. A compulsive egotist, he constantly had photographers nearby, ready to take his picture with the visitor. The pictures were developed immediately, and carefully inscribed with a personal message, suitable for hanging on the walls of the legislator's office. Of course, it always made good cocktail conversation to drop that one had gone for a dip in the pool that afternoon with LBJ. Johnson often got his way or at least managed to neutralize his opposition in this manner. In short, flattery is a magic device, and the president is probably in the best position to use it. If there is an implication that he needs you and your advice, however distorted that inference may be, it is very hard to refuse.

Pressuring the Executive and Judicial Branches

It is not sufficient for a lobbyist to spend all of his time and efforts on the legislative branch of government. Given our system of checks and balances, it may be necessary to ensure that there is support in the bureaucracy for a certain position, or to try to pressure the judiciary for a favorable decision.

BUREAUCRACY AS AN OBJECT OF LOBBYING

HIDDEN LOBBYING. In many respects, this is one of the grey areas of our government. As we shall see in Chapter 14, dealing with the bureaucracy, we have an enormous enterprise going on in the federal government, one in which it is often difficult to fix either responsibility or authority. Since the members of the "permanent government" are often as faceless to the average individual as their agencies' responsibilities are amorphous, it is extremely difficult to know exactly what is going on.

Yet if a lobbyist wishes to work effectively it is often necessary to know which agencies are responsible for administering which sections of the law. It is one thing for Congress to pass a law, but quite another when the bureaucracy is given the job of administering it.

Although bureaucracies are primarily regarded as organizations which execute policies assigned to them by society, they must also be reckoned with as sources of influence upon social policies. The nature of this influence is twofold. First, members of bureaucracies can give shape to stated policies through the exercise of choice and judgment in administering them. Second, in attempting to affect the objectives and working conditions which society will authorize for their organizations, members of bureaucracies necessarily engage in pressure politics.[27]

One reason why this happens is the nature of congressional statutes. Although sometimes it is quite specific, Congress cannot anticipate every possible eventuality that will arise in implementing the law. Take, for instance, the Internal Revenue Code, probably the most lengthy and detailed piece of legislation on the books. It would appear that there is very little discretion allowed to the Internal Revenue Service in administering it. Yet the opposite is true. The forms which annually drive us crazy are designed by IRS. The many questions that arise concerning the law must be answered by IRS rulings. The specific questions which arise can be incredibly complex. If travel abroad for educational purposes is tax-deductible in certain instances, does that include travel for one's spouse and chil-

The auto industry has formed a major Washington lobby group for many years because of the important impact of government regulations and policies on that industry's economics.

dren? Exactly what expenses can be deducted when one moves to a new job? Should it include the costs of finding new housing? What are reasonable costs? On these and a great many questions the IRS must rule every day. Other agencies are also forced to deal with implementing legislation, though it is usually not as detailed as the Internal Revenue Code.

THE *FEDERAL REGISTER*. The bureaucracy is not given a totally free hand in devising the regulations necessary to properly administering a new law. They must issue their anticipated rules in advance, in the **Federal Register,** a publication issued each working day. This document is one of the most watched and carefully read in Washington, for it con-

tains the hundreds of proposed and adopted rules and other notices, major and minor, by which the government is administered day to day. Paid lobbyists, representing various interest groups in Washington, become expert at finding rules that might affect their employers' operations, so that they can plan a response. Regulations need not go unchallenged, and one may often request that a hearing take place to consider the potential effects of thus-and-such a regulation.

A TEMPORARY LOSS. An example might be the Medicare legislation we have earlier mentioned. The American Medical Association was strongly opposed to its passage in the first place. But, once passed, it had to live with the fact. This did not mean that it would roll over and play dead, by any means. Rather, once the law was passed, and the Department of Health, Education, and Welfare was given responsibility for administering it, AMA lobbyists had the potential for a field day. Having initially opposed the law as representing socialized medicine, it would be useless to refuse to cooperate. Instead, they had to find ways to turn the implementation of the law to their own best advantage. Could regulations be established which would make life easier on the member physicians of the AMA? What kinds of paperwork would be involved? How quickly could physicians get paid? Would the fees be reasonable and consistent with those charged patients who normally paid their own way? What would be the effects on nursing facilities, some of which were owned wholly or in part by physicians? All of these questions and others could be resolved in favor of physicians only if the AMA lobbyists carefully sought out those in charge of writing Medicare regulations and made sure that they heard the physicians' side of the story.

THREE-WAY LOBBYING. What we have here is a major part of the pressure group activity in Washington, but one that is often unseen by the general public. There is a **three-way relationship,** often noted by political scientists, between pressure groups, congressional committees, and executive departments and agencies. The committees nominally oversee certain agencies, in whose areas they are responsible for proposing and examining legislation. They conduct hearings, listening to agency and pressure-group representatives. If legislation passes, lobbyists can then turn their attention to the agency itself, keeping an eye out for ways in which the basic law may be modified in their favor, while keeping the heat on the agency to ensure that the law is administered "fairly" (which once again means in their own favor). As a result, the regulated often become the regulators. Members of their own association or industry may also serve at the highest levels of the regulating agency before going back to the private sector, a fact which improves their effectiveness in industry, if not always to the government and to the public.

REGULATING EXECUTIVE LOBBYING

The 1946 Federal Regulation of Lobbying Act does not cover contacts between members of the executive branch and paid representatives or lobbyists from pressure groups. That this area of influence has gone largely unregulated for so many years is a matter of great concern to those who would make our government more open and subject to public scrutiny.

HOW TO REGULATE THE UNSEEN? There is great potential for abuse of democratic institutions in the contacts between lobbyists and bureaucrats. Is there extensive bribery going on? It is hard to say, as there has been little evidence offered one way or the other. But, what about the simple day-to-day contacts

which can and must go on? If there is no way to force disclosure of such contacts, and the nature of the subject discussed, will the public's business continue to be carried out in a twilight zone? This topic was one reason why Congress, in 1976, was unable to pass a major act to reform lobbying. Professional lobbyists were not at all eager to have these activities covered, and they joined forces to oppose such disclosure requirements.

THE JUDICIARY AS AN OBJECT OF LOBBYING

The courts become involved in pressure politics by two devices—the *amicus curiae* brief, and so-called *test cases.*[28]

AMICUS BRIEFS. As you will recall, the **amicus curiae brief** is a written argument put forward by a so-called friend of the court. A brief is not only a summary of the available law and precedent which bears on the case. Attorneys for both sides can normally do this quite well without any help from their friends. However, some substantive value may be added to the case by *amicus* briefs. The government, for instance, through the Justice Department, was asked to submit an *amicus* brief in the Bakke case. The sponsorship of briefs is often revealing. The American Civil Liberties Union, for example, is keenly interested in cases involving the Bill of Rights, and has often submitted *amicus* briefs on cases in which it was not a direct participant. The mere fact that the ACLU has submitted a brief can act as a cue as to what members of this important pressure group feel. In fact, the Court may on occasion not only allow but actually request both briefs and oral arguments from *amici curiae*. In one ten-year period, friends of the court "submitted an average of sixty-six briefs and seven oral arguments in an average total of forty cases a term."[29]

The fact that judges occasionally solicit opinions from certain organizations or the government indicates that they do not operate in a vacuum and can be aware of the pressures on them. But the reaction may not always be as anticipated, and the occasional flooding of the Court with *amicus curiae* briefs can have a backlash.

TEST CASES. Another major approach to applying political pressure on the courts is through **test cases.** These are cases, carefully selected by an interest group, which embody the crux of an argument the group wishes to make or a principle it wants to establish; usually a test case is one a group believes likely to produce a favorable ruling as a result of the circumstances of the case. This was the principle used by the National Association for the Advancement of Colored People for more than fifty years:

By presenting test cases to the Supreme Court, the NAACP has won successive gains protecting the rights of Negroes in voting, housing, transportation, education, and service on juries. . . . [This] has depended on the development of individual test cases with a Negro as party in each.[30]

In short, what the NAACP and other organizations that use this approach have done is to sort through the many situations in which one or more of their members is currently at a legal disadvantage, and then make one of them a test of the apparent general principle.

Evaluating the Pressure System

There is no escaping the fact that we have many diverse interests. These are represented by pressure groups of varying durability and competence. Is this the evil system we hear about through occasional scandals? Or, is there something to be said in favor of the pressure system as it stands?

How well interest groups represent us is determined by many variables, such as the resources available, the skill and expertise involved, and the questions under consideration. Occasional scandals discredit the positive aspects of group pressure activity, and separating the illegal and unethical from the legal and ethical is too often like looking for a contact lens on the floor of an unlighted room.

It is possible to evaluate interest groups through an understanding of how they have come about. We already know the bare-bones outlines of the system of congressional representation. Under the Constitution, each state has two senators, and at least one representative; the number of representatives for each state is dependent on population, with the larger states sending more members to the House of Representatives.

SUPPLEMENTING FORMAL REPRESENTATION

So much for the basics. Now, let's remember that there is no fundamental logic to state boundaries, or the boundaries of congressional districts. Sometimes the boundary lines follow natural dividers, such as rivers or mountain ranges, but more often they do not. In the case of congressional districts, the lines are frequently drawn in an arbitrary manner for highly political reasons. These lines are drawn around people for purposes of representation. They have little or nothing to do with the interests that those people may have. There are interests, of course, which are distinctly regional, such as mining or tobacco farming, to mention just two. These can be dominant in a single district or state in the local political and economic life. However, the farmer living near a state border may have more in common with fellow farmers hundreds or even thousands of miles away than with an urban ghetto dweller in his state capital. Yet, two senators are supposed to represent both him and the ghetto dweller.

organizations can supplement the formal scheme of representation quite well, by informing members of Congress of the needs and desires of special groups.

KEEPING GOVERNMENT RESPONSIVE

For that matter, one great problem in dealing with the bureaucracy is how to keep it responsive to the citizenry. Since its members are not elected, they can be isolated from the realities and concerns which affect our daily lives. The same can also be said about the judiciary. Not only does the pressure system supplement the legislative scheme of representation, but it may also provide the only form of representation of our needs to the executive and judicial branches of government.

CONSERVATIVE BIAS

However, there is one characteristic which stands out in our pressure system, and it has both negative and positive aspects. If the system favors those with resources and expertise, can it favor innovation? Groups able to supply skilled lobbyists with large budgets and office staffs to engage in necessary research are usually groups which have developed a considerable stake in our political system as it is. In other words, those who are best represented in Washington may oppose any innovations or changes. That they can and do lose is borne out by history. But, given excellent resources, they may be able to wage an extended battle for the *status quo,* while temporary groups exhaust themselves and

In short, we have interests in which geography may be only incidental. Are your interests those of other members of your congressional district? Do you even know what areas are included in your district? Or do you share interests with others that have nothing at all to do with geography? Are you, like other students, interested in getting the most value for your educational dollar? Are there not students in other parts of your state or elsewhere in the country who feel alike? Of course there are. And that is where the pressure group system becomes a necessity.

In effect, the pressure system is a means of supplementing the formal system of representation. Members of Congress may search in vain for common threads of interest which hold their districts or states together. But, the needs of farmers in their districts become clearer when they are articulated by a farm organization. So it is with members of any other pressure group, be it labor, business, consumer, or what-have-you. Pressure their resources. And people who are not organized can go unrepresented in this manner.

The essentially conservative nature of the traditional pressure group system can protect us against hasty legislation and other governmental action. And the institutions of United States government are not in and of themselves readily adaptable to change. Hence, we have a political system in which it often appears that government institutions are slow and unresponsive. The pressure system can therefore slow the tortoise to a snail's pace.

★ Issue ★

Concorde: The Clash of Interests

ENVIRONMENTAL GROUPS

As the environmental movement has grown, it has spawned scores of national organizations and thousands of community and neighborhood groups. Their concerns have ranged from saving the whale from extinction to lessening noise pollution and stopping litter. The environmental movement has been diffuse, working on thousands of different problems, with varying degrees of success.

BACKLASH

As the costs of cleaning up the environment, or not polluting it further, were passed on to the consumer, a backlash developed. As a result, environmentalists have had to contend with an imposing array of well-financed organized interests, largely those of industry, which oppose the imposition of costly environmental controls. How successful can a "citizens' movement" be against such interests?

AN ECONOMIC INTEREST. One major fight in recent years has been against noise pollution. Rightly or wrongly, an object of the debate has been and continues to be the supersonic transport Concorde, jointly developed by the aircraft industries of Great Britain and France. Concorde was the only commercially available SST in the West, and a great deal of money was invested in it so that the two nations involved could keep their aircraft industries from collapsing. A great deal of prestige was also attached to Concorde by Britain and France, so there was an emotional investment as well. If the Concorde was to be a commercial success, it would have to be bought by several international airlines. For airlines to place their orders, they would have to know that they would receive approval to land the craft in certain critical cities, notably New York and Washington. Temporary approval was given to the airlines to land in the United States by Secretary of Transportation William Coleman.

CITIZENS' GROUPS. But a key element remained. After the Concorde began regular service in and out of Washington, D.C., tests began to show the amount of noise it produced to be quite high. And approval was still needed to land the plane at New York's Kennedy Airport, operated by the Port of New York Authority. The Authority declared that the plane produced an unacceptably high level of noise, and would make life intolerable for those who lived in the landing and takeoff paths of the Concorde. At the same time, the Authority was joined by several citizens' action groups in the affected areas. Like many such groups, they devised names both catchy and symbolic of their cause. These included

ROAR (Restore Our American Rights), Concorde Alert, and the Emergency Coalition to Stop the SST. They allied themselves with one government agency (the Port of New York Authority) against another (the U.S. Department of Transportation). The Port Authority is the creation of an interstate compact between New Jersey and New York, and its existence had to be approved by Congress. Thus, we had an agency which has often been criticized as unresponsive, joined by various citizens' groups, to fight the actions of an agency of the federal government.

FOREIGN LOBBIES. To further illustrate our earlier point that politics make strange bedfellows, our government was supported in its view by some well-financed and organized lobbies representing French and British interests. These lobbies had spent lavishly in attempts to convince the public and important officials in Congress and the state legislatures of Virginia and New Jersey of the fairness of their position.[31] They used some of the most prestigious law firms in Washington and several well-known and respected names to represent them. These included a former Secretary of State (William P. Rogers), a former head of the Environmental Protection Agency (William Ruckelshaus), and a former member of the House and Senate from New York (Charles Goodell).

APPEALS TO CONGRESS. Thus, we had an interesting battle, one which seemed to match uneven opponents against one another. And there was a perfect illustration of the various strategies possible. The case for and against the Concorde was made in the halls of the Congress. Some members of the House, representing areas of New York that would be most affected by noise from the Concorde, allied with the citizens' groups and lobbied their fellow members against allowing the Concorde to land. Several bills were introduced in Con-

gress which would have done just that, but none passed. High officials of the British and French governments, including British Prime Minister James Callaghan and French President Giscard d'Estaing, warned of reprisals if the Concorde was not granted landing rights. Pressures were put on the bureaucracy as well, in an attempt to get the Department of Transportation to certify that the Concorde would not create unusual noise.

APPEALS TO THE COURTS. Finally the federal courts joined the fight. A federal district court judge, in overruling the Port Authority, cited the supremacy of the national government over actions by state and local agencies. In his decision he pointed out that treaties made by the national government take precedence over local laws and administrative actions.

DECISION

The federal government acted. In late September 1977, the Transportation Department authorized Concorde landings not only in New York but in twelve other cities as well. Further protests by citizen action groups yielded little more than occasional headlines, and two months later the first Concorde landed in New York.

Had the Concorde lobby won? At first glance, it might appear so. New routes were opened and it became possible to think of producing enough planes so that the two governments might recover a major part of their costs in the plane's development. But there were still several unknown factors to be dealt with. The Transportation Department's authorization had made it clear that the cities where the Concorde might land could set their own noise standards—in effect, a compromise—and that stronger federal noise standards would apply to future models of the plane. Whether the anti-noise citizens' groups in New York would be joined by other groups in pressuring their local governments to keep the Concorde away from their airports remained to be seen, and to be fought out in each instance. If new standards were passed, those working on behalf of the Concorde could be expected to test the fairness of these standards in court. As we pointed out in our first chapter, "winning" and "losing" are sometimes questions of perception.

Summary

An important part of the American political process is the formal system of pressure groups, which are organized to represent a great variety of interests. These interests affect the legislative, judicial, and executive branches of government, and they commonly reflect more conservative than innovative economic views. Groups representing the disadvantaged in our society are themselves disadvantaged if they lack the resources necessary to make an effective case for their interests.

The resources of lobbyists are many, but the wise pressure group representative relies on one more than any other, and that is information. The ability to properly and correctly prepare and present a case which "objectively" shows the necessity of taking a certain position can be invaluable to harried public officials constantly in need of the best information available. The development of standing pressure groups which represent the interests of the "common man" has proven very useful, and the organizations involved have run up a string of impressive victories in consumer protection and government reform. However, as they become broader in their concerns, they risk the possibility of becoming less effective, spreading their already thin resources against a host of well-financed and staffed organizations, each representing a particular interest.

A hidden part of the pressure system is that involving the executive and judicial branches of government. The executive branch is both an object of intensive lobbying (by domestic as well as foreign interests) and the source of a good deal of lobbying. With its enormous control of information, and the resources it has to spend in the states and districts of members of Congress, it can appear a juggernaut. Yet there is little that can be done to regulate it. The judicial branch is often the object of pressure groups who bring cases when they have been unsuccessful in obtaining results from the other two branches of government.

On balance, it would seem that the pressure system, while far from perfect, is an essential element of our political and governmental system. Questions remain as to how to properly regulate it without infringing on First Amendment freedoms or limiting its utility.

Terms to Remember

See the Glossary at the end of the book for definitions.

Access to government	Associational interest groups	Citizens' lobbies
Ad hoc groups	Bipartisanship	Coalitions of groups
Amicus curiae briefs	Categoric groups	Common Cause

Executive lobbying

Federal Register

Federal Regulation of Lobbying Act of 1946

Foreign lobbying

Inspired mail

Institutional interest groups

Lobbying

Pluralism

Political Action Committees

Presidential lobbying

Public Interest Research Group

Pressure groups

Relevant interests

Services-in-kind

Test cases

Three-way lobbying

Umbrella groups

Notes

1. It might be added here that a working definition of *public opinion* is that "which the government finds it prudent to heed." V.O. Key, Jr., *Public Opinion and American Democracy* (New York: Alfred A. Knopf, 1961), p. 14.

2. See James T. Wooten, "Carter's Georgia Guru," *New York Times Magazine,* March 20, 1977, pp. 15ff.

3. Alex Haley, *Roots* (Garden City, N.Y.: Doubleday, 1976).

4. Lee Fritschler, *Smoking and Politics,* 2d ed. (New York: Prentice–Hall, 1975).

5. John Kenneth Galbraith, *Economics and the Public Purpose* (Boston: Houghton Mifflin, 1974).

6. See Bob Woodward and Carl Bernstein, *All the President's Men* (New York: Simon and Schuster, 1974); and Woodward and Bernstein, *The Final Days* (New York: Simon and Schuster, 1976).

7. On this point, see William L. Rivers, *The Adversaries: Politics and the Press* (Boston: Beacon Press, 1970).

8. James E. Pollard, *The Presidents and the Press: Truman to Johnson* (Washington, D.C.: Public Affairs Press, 1964).

9. For a concise review of the problem, see Congressional Quarterly, *Weekly Report,* 35 (April 16, 1977), pp. 695–705.

10. The term *lobbyist* has its origins in the practice of pressure group representatives waiting in the lobbies and corridors of Congress to speak to members of that body. It has now been extended to include all pressure group representations, whether to Congress or other branches of government.

11. Lester W. Milbrath, *The Washington Lobbyists* (Chicago: Rand McNally, 1963), especially pp. 72–76.

12. Gabriel W. Almond, "Introduction: A Functional Approach to Comparative Politics," in

Almond and James S. Coleman, eds., *The Politics of the Developing Areas* (Princeton: Princeton University Press, 1960), pp. 33–34.

13. A.H. Raskin, "Can Anybody Clean Up the Teamsters?," *New York Times Magazine,* November 7, 1976, pp. 31ff.

14. Abe Fortas, "The Case Against Capital Punishment," *New York Times Magazine,* January 23, 1977, pp. 8–9ff.

15. For a fine account, see Francis Russell, *The Shadow of Blooming Grove* (New York: McGraw–Hill, 1968).

16. See Robert N. Winter–Berger, *The Washington Pay-Off* (New York: Dell Publishing Co., 1972); and Drew Pearson and Jack Anderson, *The Case Against Congress* (New York: Simon and Schuster, 1968).

17. See Robert S. Getz, *Congressional Ethics* (New York: Van Nostrand, 1967).

18. See Milbrath, *The Washington Lobbyists,* on this point, especially Chapters 9 and 11.

19. David R. Mayhew, *Congress: The Electoral Connection* (New Haven: Yale University Press, 1974), pp. 13ff.

20. Milbrath, *The Washington Lobbyists,* p. 358. Also the following: Lewis Anthony Dexter, *How Organizations Are Represented in Washington* (Indianapolis: Bobbs–Merrill, 1969); and Thomas P. Murphy, *Pressures Upon Congress: Legislation by Lobbying* (Woodbury, N.Y.: Barrons Educational Series, 1973).

21. *United States* v. *Harris,* 347 U.S. 612 (1954).

22. *Guide to Congress,* 1st ed. (Washington, D.C.: Congressional Quarterly, Inc., 1971), p. 571.

23. Quoted in *Legislators and the Lobbyists* (Washington, D.C.: Congressional Quarterly Service, Inc., 1968), p. 9.

24. Adam Yarmolinsky, *The Military Establishment* (New York: Harper and Row, 1971), p. 42.

25. Ibid., p. 50.

26. Ibid., p. 40.

27. J. Leiper Freeman, "The Bureaucracy in Pressure Politics," in *Annals of the American Academy of Political and Social Science*, 319 (September 1958), p. 11.

28. The material for this section relies on the seminal article by Clement Vose, "Litigation as a Form of Pressure Group Activity." in *Annals* (September 1958), pp. 20–31.

29. Ibid., p. 27.

30. Ibid.

31. For a discussion of the Concorde lobby, see Congressional Quarterly, *Weekly Report*, 35 (April 16, 1977), pp. 698–699.

Suggested Readings

Richard J. Barber, *The American Corporation: Its Power, Its Money, Its Politics* (New York: Dutton, 1970).

Robert A. Caro, *The Power Broker: Robert Moses and the Fall of New York* (New York: Random House, 1974).

Robert Engler, *The Politics of Oil* (Chicago: University of Chicago Press, 1961).

Theodore Lowi, *The End of Liberalism: Ideology, Policy, and Public Authority* (New York: Norton, 1969).

Grant McConnell, *Private Power and American Democracy* (New York: Knopf, 1966).

Lester Milbrath, *The Washington Lobbyists* (Chicago: Rand McNally, 1963).

Mancur Olson, Jr., *The Logic of Collective Action: Public Goals and the Theory of Groups* (Cambridge: Harvard University Press, 1971).

Arnold M. Rose, *The Power Structure: Political Process in American Society* (New York: Oxford University Press, 1967).

E.E. Schattschneider, *The Semi-Sovereign People* (New York: Holt, Rinehart & Winston, 1960).

David B. Truman, *The Governmental Process: Political Interests and Public Opinion*, 2d ed. (New York: Knopf, 1971).

Adam Yarmolinsky, *The Military Establishment* (New York: Harper and Row, 1971).

CHAPTER 7

Political Parties

★★

. . . political parties created democracy and . . . modern democracy is unthinkable save in terms of parties.

E. E. SCHATTSCHNEIDER
Party Government

For more than a decade, observers have alternately predicted the death or the rebirth of party politics in the United States. The extraordinary growth of presidential power; the apparent weakness of the parties in Congress; the increasing body of voters who identify with neither party; the increasing influence of special interest groups; the widespread, if mistaken, belief among Americans that both parties are alike—all these have led to fears that 150 years of two-party politics may be coming to an end.

However, the infusion of young activists into the "system" during the 1968 and 1972 presidential races, the coming back together, at least temporarily, of the old Democratic coalition in 1976, the resurgence of the Republicans in the 1980 congressional races, and moves by both parties to reform the nominating process and campaign financing, have led some observers to see new strength in America's two-party system. Another positive note was the high turnout for some of the 1980 presidential primaries and party caucuses. (Non-primary states choose convention delegates in district meetings, or **caucuses,** open to all party members.)

The 1972 and 1976 presidential elections seemed to suggest that at least one party, the Republicans, was in deep trouble. President Nixon's landslide victory over George McGovern did not prevent Republicans from losing ground in the Senate and in governorship and state legislature races. His victory seemed to signal a further weakening of traditional Republican Party affiliations and party organizations. Even the Republican gain of twelve House seats in 1972 was more a reflection of redistricting and reapportionment than an indication of party strength.

Republicans faced another agonizing reappraisal after the 1976 elections. Democrat Jimmy Carter won a narrow popular-vote majority; however, the closeness of the presiden-

★ ★

tial race did not help Republicans capture House and Senate seats or control of the governorships.

But, the duration of winning and losing status is not certain. In 1978 the Republicans reversed their downward trend, picking up twelve House and three Senate seats, while capturing control of seven more state legislatures, raising their total to twelve. Ronald Reagan's resounding 1980 presidential victory was accompanied by a Republican gain of twelve seats in the Senate, giving the party control of that body for the first time since 1956. On the House side, the Democrats maintained control, but their net loss of thirty-three seats reduced their margin in the 97th Congress to 243–192. The fifty-one-seat Democratic majority was a shaky one because conservative Democrats voting with conservative Republicans gave the GOP a potential ideological edge on many issues.

A major disappointment for the Republicans was their failure to make more than modest gains in state legislature elections in spite of a massive national effort. The GOP gained control of only two more state legislatures and elected four more governors. The Republicans had hoped to do better in order to protect the party's interests during the re-apportionment battles of 1981, when many legislatures were forced to reshape congressional district boundaries based on the 1980 census figures (see Chapter 9).

The political score card of 1980 presented a generally encouraging picture to Republicans, as Table 7–1 indicates.

Democratic assumptions that the party could always do well at the congressional level, even in the face of an electoral disaster in the presidential race, was jolted by the 1980 results. However, it is too early to tell whether or not 1980 marked the beginning of a pro-conservative realignment by voters, or whether the outcome was more a reflection of public unhappiness with the state of the nation reflected in a massive anti-officeholder, anti-Carter, vote.

Looking at America's two great political parties today, one faces a variety of bewildering questions. Is the two-party political system still functional? Can the present political parties meet the needs of the American people? Can they plan and enact coherent programs at the national, state and local levels? Has the growth of presidential power irrevocably sapped their usefulness? Do we need a redefinition of purpose of parties? Or, "is the Party over"?

★ ★ ★ *Table 7–1* ★
Political score card: 1979–1981

	1979		1981	
	DEM.	*REP.*	*DEM.*	*REP.*
U.S. House of Representatives	276	159	243	192
U.S. Senate	59	41	47	53
Governors	31	19	27	23
Control of State Legislatures*	31	12	28	14
Divided State Legislatures	6		7	

*Control equals party majority in both houses. Nebraska has a one-house, nonpartisan legislature.

*Ranking Senate Republicans, led by Majority Leader Howard Baker (foreground),
gather after the resounding GOP victory in 1980.*

Political Parties—
American-Style

The purpose of **political parties** in the United States is to win elections. Our major parties are broad coalitions of various groups and interests, and their main purpose is to use the nomination and election processes to win control of the government. By organizing elections and providing voters with a choice of candidates and policies, the parties became the vehicle for giving meaning to "democracy." Another function of political parties is to provide a way for citizens to organize and accumulate political power. They are also the major way in which talent for public office is recruited. And, in a federal system of government based on division of powers, they provide a weak unifying thread which runs from the smallest town to the White House. In theory, parties should help educate the public about specific issues. In fact, most of this effort takes place during elections, and even then more "heat" than "light" is generated. The historical role of parties as communicators between the rank and file and those in leadership has increasingly been assumed by interest groups and structures organized around the mass media.

TWEEDLEDUM AND TWEEDLEDEE. Unlike European parties, which tend to represent very specific classes, interests, and programs and which form coalition governments after an election, the two large American parties form their coalitions before the election, a winner-take-all event. As a result, U.S. party politics is a politics of pragmatism—their goal is to do what is possible and appeal to the largest number of voters. This often makes the choice between Democrat and Republican appear to be a choice between Tweedledum and Tweedledee. But behind the American parties lurk the policies and interests of the groups that identify with them. The active minority within each party sticks to policies and a governing philosophy quite distinct from those of its opposite number.[1] However, policy differences are often masked because the two major parties are normally preoccupied with winning elections and managing the tensions of the groups that make up each party. Walter Dean Burnham calls this the secret to the parties' stability and also to their lack of concern with detailed policy when they capture office.[2]

UNDISCIPLINED OR RESPONSIBLE PARTIES?

In almost all other nations, a definition of party would include such phrases as "a group of people bound together by a common ideology (philosophy)" who "wish to put their philosophy into operation by gaining control of the government." But a glance at our system, particularly at the congressional level, reveals an influential Democratic conservative bloc within the predominantly liberal party. On the Republican side we see a small liberal group in a predominantly conservative party. When this ideological disparity is coupled with the fact that our major parties are loose coalitions of fifty state parties lacking an effective central organization, it is clear that we do not have national parties in the sense that characterizes the disciplined (party-line voting behavior) and centralized (party organization) parties of other nations.

UNDISCIPLINED AND DECENTRALIZED. Viewed from a national perspective, our two major parties are **undisciplined** and **decentral-**

Each major party is a loose coalition, not an organized ideological bloc. Republican candidates Ronald Reagan and George Bush acknowledge cheers at the 1980 GOP Convention where a disappointed liberal minority coalesced behind the party's presidential candidates.

ized; the focal point of organizational power exists at the state and county levels. While members of Congress often vote along party lines, they usually vote their perceptions of state or district attitudes when the two conflict. Assuming that a **responsible party model** means a party that has a unified program to which its officeholders are committed in theory and bound in practice, then we do not have responsible parties like those in Great Britain.[3]

RESPONSIBLE PARTY MODEL. The focal point of organizational power in the British parties is the central office; it controls campaign funds and can strip a member of the party label or prevent an individual from running as a member of the party. Party membership is based on common ideology, and elections are geared to a choice of competing platforms. The electorate can expect the party that controls the House of Commons to implement its policies, and voters can hold a party accountable for its success or failure to deliver on campaign promises. The majority party chooses its leader as Prime Minister, thus eliminating the paradox of one party controlling the legislative and the other controlling the executive, and each blaming the other for inaction, as is common in the United States. Prime Ministers can also expect party support for their major proposals, and in the absence of that support, the Prime Minister can dissolve Parliament and call new elections.

A responsible party system in the United States would require a clear conservative-versus-liberal division between the parties. It might lead to party membership like the dues-paying mass base of European parties. This would be in sharp contrast to our open-ended parties; an individual joins a party simply by **enrolling** as a Democrat or Republican at the time of initial **registration** to vote or at some later date. Membership requires no work for the party and no loss of freedom to vote for a split ticket or even for all

of the candidates of another party. But it does bestow the privilege of helping select the party's candidates by voting in primary elections.

American parties are collections of small numbers of leaders and elected officials at each level of government, a slightly larger core of workers who devote considerable time to the party, and a mass of party identifiers, most of whom (about sixty-three percent) limit their political activity to the act of voting. About eight percent of the population is active in a party or political organization. If we include all people who occasionally do work associated with party or campaign activity, the figure jumps to about twenty-five percent.[4]

Unlike individual interest groups, our parties are made up of people from differing social, occupational, and economic backgrounds. The prime function of interest groups is to articulate the particular interests of their members. But the parties are the vehicle for the pulling together or summarizing of these interests, particularly those groups most commonly identified with the party. The parties attempt this during the campaigns when they try to build winning majorities. However, the recent growth of **single-issue politics,** in which new groups form to lobby on behalf of just one issue, or established groups base their support of a candidate on his or her stand on one particular issue, has made the aggregation of interests almost impossible. This "politics of selfishness" has made it more and more difficult for the parties to translate promises into policies, particularly at the national level (see insert).

The parties appear to be losing out as the vacuum of specific policy is filled by bureaucrats and the spokespersons of specific interests. As the parties lose, their weakness works to the disadvantage of the usual losers, the unorganized. The organized, the usual winners, are served well by the interest-group process. But in the long run, rampant single-

Pressure groups stressing single-issue politics are fragmenting the political system and making it difficult for parties and officeholders to serve as summarizers of political demands. A former senator and a current member of the House comment on the problem. In the 1978 election, Rep. Abner Mikva of Illinois was a target of the National Rifle Association because he supported gun control. Former Senator Dick Clark (D., Iowa) was defeated in 1978. A group that had always supported him urged him to vote against the natural gas deregulation bill. Below, Clark describes the conversation that followed his refusal.

It could be that there are people out there who are Democrats on every issue, but when they see this [his vote on the issue], they become instant Republicans. When you get a single-issue voter, if the Democratic Party comes out for something he's against, then he simply says: "I'm not a Democrat anymore."

Rep. ABNER MIKVA

He said to me, "OK, if that's the case, we won't support you." I responded, "Look at my voting record as a whole. Don't make a decision like this based on a single vote." His reply was: "We don't give a damn about your over-all voting record. We're interested in this bill—period."

Senator DICK CLARK

Source: "Single Issue Politics," *Newsweek* (November 6, 1978), pp. 48, 54. Copyright 1978, by Newsweek, Inc. All rights reserved. Reprinted by permission.

issue politics may be undermining our system of representative government by depriving our officials of needed flexibility. In that case, we may be creating a situation in which everybody loses.

Finally, many of the roles parties fill are shared by other groups. But only the parties seek both to control the government and assume actual responsibility for organizing its parts. Interest groups and other social groupings may seek to influence the government, but not to control it.

The Two-Party System

One of the most striking features of American politics is the persistence of the two-party system. From the beginning of our history, the great majority of elections have been waged under two banners. No third party has ever come close to electing a president. In fact, only once (1912, Teddy Roosevelt) did a minor-party presidential candidate win more votes than one of his major-party rivals.

Two-partyism has been no less pronounced in Congress. Only three times (in 1854, 1858, and 1860) has the two-party hold on the House of Representatives fallen below ninety percent. In addition, most past minor-party members of Congress have belonged to regional parties which had gained major-party status in their own states and had successfully held important state offices.[5] The electoral failures of minor parties provide a stark contrast to the stability of the two major parties, as well as to the multi-party politics of many European democracies.

WHY TWO PARTIES? Two-party politics was not expected or desired by the Founding Fathers, and political scientists have had to explain why two-party politics developed such a tenacious hold on our country. While it is true that in the colonial period our political institutions were heavily influenced by the British parliamentary experience and Britain's developing two-party politics, a more significant factor can be found in the early history of the American colonies. Except for about seven thousand Dutch settlers in New York and a handful of Swedes in Delaware, virtually all three million settlers, not including slaves, who lived in the colonies at the time of independence were of English descent. In addition, they were largely from middle-class backgrounds, since the upper classes had little to gain by emigrating and the lower classes lacked the means. Religious conflict was minimized because the division between Puritan New England and the Anglican South was a regional one.

This common background left most Americans with a solid political consensus on questions that have torn other societies apart. The American Revolution, being a war for independence but not a true social revolution, did nothing to change this. Unlike in France, where class divisions led to a political conflict, the United States developed from scratch a politics of performance.

Even today, our problems tend to be agreed upon and the real question is simply: "Who can provide the best working solution?" This performance issue has always dominated the American scene. Officeholders are re-elected or replaced primarily according to each voter's view of their past or future performance in office. This frame of mind tends to divide the voters into only two camps, and the issue becomes, "Is the incumbent better than the probable alternative?"[6]

WINNER-TAKE-ALL. The earliest division pitted the pro-Constitution Federalists against the anti-Federalists, and although the formation of a two-party system came before the method of selecting officeholders was settled upon, the practice of electing national officeholders—senators, congressmen, and the president and vice-president—in a winner-take-all, single-member-single-ballot system has helped to sustain the system. For these offices, and for most state or local offices, the voters may choose only one person to represent their geographical unit (state, district, ward). Winner-take-all is a powerful inducement for competing groups to join forces. The classic example of winner-take-all is the majority requirement in the electoral college, which suggests that only large national parties can capture the presidency.

A British heritage, a homogeneous population, performance politics, and the winner-take-all electoral system all provided a strong basis for America's political system. Later, waves of immigrants changed the composition of our society radically, but they never displaced their predecessors. By the time they could play an effective role in politics, most had accepted the consensus and the two-party system that consensus had created. The only time that basic agreement was shattered—over slavery, in 1860—the two-party system collapsed before the nation itself split.

The Parties Develop

In searching for the roots of the Democratic and Republican parties, one theme emerges: major changes or party realignments have been the result of divisions within one or both of the dominant parties of a particular era, rather than the product of a successful challenge by a third party. However, the rise of a strong third party has sometimes signaled a realignment.

Organized political parties in the United States did not begin to form until the

The nation's first vice-president shared George Washington's fear of parties as a disruptive force.

There is nothing I dread so much as the division of the Republic into two great parties, each under its leader.[7]

JOHN ADAMS, while vice-president

Federalists and the anti-Federalists began to struggle over ratification of the 1787 Constitution. The anti-Federalists died out after the Constitution was adopted, and the Federalists, led by George Washington's Secretary of the Treasury Alexander Hamilton, formed the nucleus of America's first national party.

Though Washington sought to remain aloof from party spirit, parties began to form midway through his first term as disagreements over the policies of his administration emerged. Despite the warning he included in his farewell address against the "baneful effects of the spirit of party," Washington now is generally regarded as having been a Federalist during his second term, and John Adams, who succeeded him as president, favored the Federalists (see insert).

However, a real national party did not appear until Thomas Jefferson organized his own coalition and captured an electoral college majority in 1800. His party, the Jeffersonian Republicans (later called the Democratic–Republicans), was an alliance of convenience between rural America and the Sons of Tammany, the big-city political organization which controlled New York. It was an alliance destined to be seen again many times in our political history.

COMMON ANCESTOR. Against the Jeffersonian Republicans, the Federalists, who drew much support from affluent commercial interests, gradually withered away. Jefferson's party was left virtually alone in the field; it is the common ancestor of our two major parties today. From 1800 until the Civil War, Jefferson's party, under one name or another, was usually the majority party.

From 1812 to 1822, there was a period of one-party government at the national level. The Jeffersonian Republicans nurtured a widespread consensus on political means and political goals. There was general agreement that fundamental political decisions should be made within the party system. The actual shift to a two-party system resulted from divisions within the dominant party, and not from outside challenge. Factionalism with the Jeffersonian Republicans centered around the forces of Andrew Jackson ("Democrats") and Henry Clay ("Young Republicans"), and came to a head in the 1824 election. The Young Republicans became the National Republicans and, in the mid–1830s, evolved into the Whig party. Jackson's followers maintained the Democratic label.

It was during the Jacksonian era that a number of important developments in partisan institutions took place. We had our first national presidential campaigns (including parades, speeches, and candidate appearances), and the national political conventions emerged. Candidates for local and state offices began to adopt the national party labels, and jobs and other preference were used to link local party organizations to the White House.

During the 1840s, the Whigs, an unnatural coalition of northern industrialists and southern planters, again split into two camps. Members from the North advocated high protective duties advantageous to industry, while agrarian southerners took an anti-tariff position. After 1850, the slavery issue tore apart the Whigs and the Democrats.

In 1854, the Republican Party, founded by an anti-slavery coalition, captured almost intact the old Whig electorate in the North, as well as many northern Democrats. In turn, the former southern Whigs moved into the Democratic Party, totally shaking up America's two-party structure. A new emphasis was placed on sectional boundaries which previously had been ignored.

REPUBLICAN DOMINANCE.   After its first successful presidential election, the Republican Party of Lincoln became the largest party and the political voice of the dynamic North. It captured the Midwest, where most of the people feared the spread of slavery to the Great Plains.

The Republican Party retained its dominant status from the mid–1850s until the New Deal days of Franklin Roosevelt (1933–1945). Grover Cleveland (in 1884 and 1892) and Woodrow Wilson (in 1912 and 1916) were the only non–Republicans elected president during that period. Each won by the thinnest of margins.

By default, the Democrats after Reconstruction grasped the South in an iron grip. But unlike the Republicans, they retained some strongholds in other regions, especially the northern cities. Their urban politicians courted the lower classes, making a point of recruiting the new city dwellers who emi-

A delegate at the 1980 Republican Convention.

A delegate at the 1980 Democratic Convention.

Since Franklin Delano Roosevelt's 1932 presidential victory gave the Democrats control of the national government, Republicans have elected only war-hero Dwight D. Eisenhower, Richard M. Nixon, and Ronald Reagan. A Republican, Gerald R. Ford, succeeded Richard Nixon upon his resignation. With the exception of the 1952 election, even their victories did not result in Republican control of both houses of Congress. Republicans did capture brief control (1947–1949) of Congress as a result of the 1946 election.

It would be a mistake, however, to assume that Democratic dominance has meant that the interests of the lower and middle classes and minority groups control Washington. The interests of America's more prosperous citizens are represented by members of both parties, and the **conservative coalition** in Congress—a voting bloc of Republicans and southern Democrats—votes together on approximately twenty-five percent of all roll-call votes and wins about sixty percent of the time.

grated to the United States in great waves between 1880 and 1920.

ECONOMIC DISASTER AND DEMOCRATIC VICTORY.   Only an accident of fate shattered Republican dominance. Herbert Hoover happened to be president when the Great Depression of the 1930s began. The Republicans were blamed for the crisis. Masses of middle-class voters now held it responsible for their economic distress and deserted to the Democrats, as did blacks and other minority groups. Since that time, the Democrats have had about a three-to-two edge both in voters enrolled as party members and in the preferences of voters questioned for public opinion surveys. The Civil War had made sectionalism the determining factor in party allegiance, but the Depression returned economic status to its former place of importance.

CRITICAL ELECTIONS

Walter Dean Burnham identified the elections of 1800, 1828, 1860, 1896, and 1932 as "critical elections" signaling major realignments of the voters (see Figure 7–1). These elections were often preceded by third-party revolts and abnormally deep divisions on fundamental social, economic, and political issues such as slavery, the financial panic of 1893, or the Great Depression of 1929. The coalitions that made up the two major parties at the time of these elections did not adjust to the transformations taking place and the resulting social unrest and change. As a result, each critical election became a fundamental turning point in the course of American electoral politics, bringing about new alignments of coalitions and a reordered list of public policy priorities.[8]

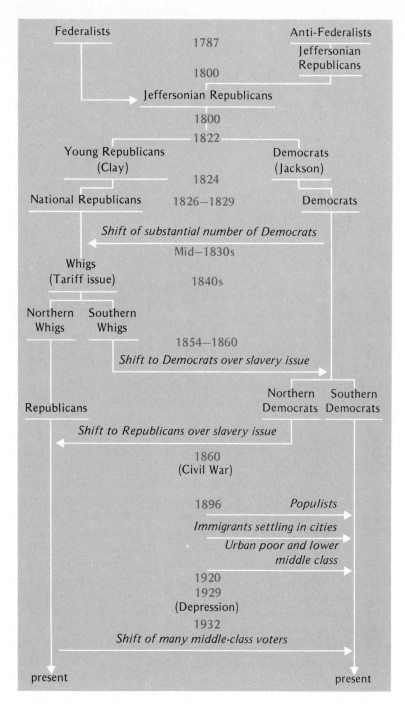

Figure 7-1 A schematic history of the major American political parties.

The two most recent critical elections, those in 1896 and 1932, provide excellent examples of fundamental change. The first reflected our nation's transition from an agricultural to an industrial society, and was triggered by the financial panic of 1893. The election broadened the base of the Democratic Party to the cities, and brought small farmers, the urban poor, and the lower middle class to its electoral base. The Republican Party, in turn, became the conservative force in American politics. The 1932 election reflected the nation's problems as a mature, industrial society, and capped the swing of large blocs of voters from the Republican to the Democratic ranks that had begun in 1924.[9] This election established the basic electorate and policies of the major parties as we know them today. The likelihood of another critical election occurring in the near future is discussed at the end of this chapter.

Third-Party Politics

Everything that has made two-party politics successful in America, from winner-take-all elections to a basic consensus on policy questions, has worked to inhibit third-party or minor-party movements. But if third parties have lacked success, they have not lacked energy. Scores of attempts have been made to establish alternatives to the two major parties. All have failed at the national level (see Table 7–2); however, the Farmer–Labor Party in Minnesota, and the Conservative and Liberal parties in New York, have had some success at the state and local levels. At the local level, there are a large number of parties that are not *Republican* or *Democrat*, carrying such labels as the *Citizen Coalition*, the *Good Government Alliance*, and so forth. Non-partisan elections are common in over two-thirds of U.S. cities with a mean population of 25,000. It is clear that political activity in this nation goes beyond the two major parties.

John Anderson's 1980 candidacy followed the American tradition of not electing a third-party candidate to the presidency.

Hundreds of minor-party candidates have run in presidential elections since 1832, but only nine have succeeded in carrying even one state and only eleven have received five or more percent of the vote. The most recent significant vote-getter was George Wallace, who ran under the American Independent Party (AIP) banner in 1968; he captured 13.5 percent of the vote and carried five states in the South. In 1976, the Independent Party candidate, Eugene McCarthy, was a factor in the close Carter–Ford race. In at least four states, his vote was greater than the margin by which President Ford defeated Carter.

The 1980 presidential candidacy of Representative John Anderson, a Republican from Illinois, falls outside the usual discussion of third parties because he ran as an "independent" candidate while remaining a Republican.

He received seven percent of the vote, but did not capture a single state.

Throughout the campaign, Jimmy Carter's campaign staff feared that Anderson would draw the support of enough liberal Democrats to cost Carter the election. However, if all Anderson's votes had gone to Carter, Reagan would still have carried a majority of states and more than enough electoral votes to capture the presidency. Without Anderson on the ballot, Carter probably would have carried a few more eastern states, including New York and Massachusetts.

Minor parties have usually fallen into two categories: **splinter parties** formed by short desertions from one of the major parties (Theodore Roosevelt's Progressive [Bull Moose] Party of 1912, the Dixiecrats of 1948, and George Wallace's American Independent Party), **single-issue parties** (or ideological

★ ★ ★ *Table 7–2* ★
The third party presidential vote: 1976 and 1980

CANDIDATE (PARTY)	1976		1980	
	POPULAR VOTE	%	*POPULAR VOTE*	%
Anderson (American)	160,000	0.2		
Graves (American)			6,539	0.0
John Anderson (Independent)			5,719,437	6.7
Camejo (Soc. Workers)	91,226	0.1		
Pulley (Soc. Workers)			6,032	0.0
Levin (Soc. Labor)	9,590	0.0		
Zeidler (Socialist)	6,022	0.0		
McReynolds (Socialist)			6,720	0.0
Wright (People's)	49,024	0.1		
Griswold (Workers World)			13,211	0.02
Hall (Communist)	59,114	0.1		
LaRouche (U.S. Labor)	40,045	0.1		
Bubar (Prohibition)	15,898	0.0		
MacBride (Libertarian)	172,750	0.2		
Clark (Libertarian)			920,859	1.0
McCormack (Right to Life)			32,319	0.04
McCarthy (Independent)	751,728	0.9		
Maddox (American IND)	170,780	0.2		
Rarick (American IND)			41,172	0.05
Bubar (National-Statesman)			7,100	0.0
Commoner (Citizens)			230,377	.2
Major Party Vote	79,976,200	98.1	79,385,632	91.99

Source: Congressional Quarterly, *Weekly Report*, 51 (December 18, 1976), pp. 3335–36; and *New York Times*, January 6, 1981, p. A14.

parties) such as the various Socialist parties who advocate public ownership of the means of production, or the Libertarian Party which wants to limit government to the fewest possible activities, such as defense and law enforcement.

At times it is difficult to distinguish between the two types of minor parties. For example, the American Independent Party mainly attracted southern Democrats who were unhappy with their party's civil rights policies, so the AIP could be called a *splinter party*. On the other hand, their focus on race issues puts them into the single-issue category.

IMPACT OF MINOR PARTIES. Although unsuccessful in their own right, minor parties have influenced a number of presidential elections and occasionally even reshaped a major party. In the election of 1844, the Liberty Party took the state of New York, giving the presidency to James K. Polk. In 1912, the Bull Moose Party split the Republican vote, providing a slim margin of victory for the Democrat, Woodrow Wilson. In the very close election of 1968, George Wallace received 13.5 percent of the vote, compared with Richard M. Nixon's (Republican) 43.4 percent and Hubert H. Humphrey's (Democrat) 42.7 percent. Wallace's greatest impact appears to have been in urban areas, where the average 9.5 percent of the vote that he received may have been fatal to Humphrey in such states as California, Illinois, Missouri, and New Jersey. Since many of his southern votes would have gone to Nixon, no one can say for sure whether the Wallace candidacy gave the election to the Republicans.

Minor parties have played a number of roles in American political history in addition to that of "spoiler." They have occasionally served to test public attitudes toward new, and usually radical (for the time), policies. As Wallace's American Independent Party

showed, they can provide a safety valve for the expression of fears and desires not normally acceptable within the two dominant parties. Third parties also leave a niche for dissent within the political system; without them there might be greater resort to organized violence.

One school of thought suggests that minor parties succeed while failing. In other words, the major parties act like sponges, absorbing the best proposals of the minor parties, or even the parties themselves. The impressive showing of the agrarian-based Populists in 1892 led to their absorption into the Democratic Party, a significant step in its own attempt to break out of its southern confines. Many of the planks of the Populists, Socialists, and Progressives became public policy during the Wilson presidency and later administrations, demonstrating that third parties can have considerable influence upon policy.

OTHER OBSTACLES TO THIRD-PARTY SUCCESS

The problems besetting most minor parties are reflected in the histories of the Socialist and the American Independent parties. The Socialists were the most successful of the parties of the "left," having captured at least two percent of the vote on six different occasions since 1900. The adoption of many of their proposals—unemployment compensation, social security, labor rights—by the Democrats and that party's identification with organized labor corroded their support to the point where the Socialists became almost invisible. Another problem is that the Socialists now are only one of a number of parties of the left (see Table 7–2) competing for the same core of voters. This same proliferation affects the parties of the "right."

Wallace's American Independent Party burst upon the scene in 1968 and made an impressive showing. It appealed to America's "forgotten man," the lower-middle-class white. The party, although composed mainly of southern Democratic defectors, put forward a national "ideology," attacking wealthy special interests on the one hand and the Great Society social policies of the 1960s on the other. Wallace advocated curbing the power of the federal government and returning to reliance on state and local government and personal initiative to handle the problems of civil rights and liberties, welfare, etc. Like a number of minor parties before it, it relied in part on the racial fears and economic insecurity of many Americans for its support.

The AIP was built around Wallace, and his near-fatal shooting during the 1972 Democratic primary campaign eliminated the party as a factor that year. In 1976, Wallace backed Carter, and the AIP split into two camps (American and AIP), ran separate candidates, and is no longer a viable force in politics.

IT TAKES MONEY TO WIN. All the minor parties face other substantial roadblocks to success. The winner-take-all (single-member district) electoral system makes any vote total short of a plurality virtually worthless. The politics of getting on the ballot is a further handicap to serious minor parties. They have to spend large portions of their limited funds in circulating petitions, complying with complex election laws, and sometimes, financing court battles to secure a place on the ballot. As a practical matter, the soaring costs of campaign spending make it extremely difficult for minor parties to campaign state-wide, let alone nation-wide. The 1974 campaign financing law provided the Democrats and Republicans $21.8 million each for the 1976 presidential election and $29.4 million each for the 1980 presidential election. Minor-party and independent candidates can qualify for post-election public financing if they receive at least five percent of the vote. John

Anderson has been the only minor-party or independent candidate to qualify thus far. These parties are caught in a vicious cycle: they are unable to raise the funds to attract a large following, and without a large following, they cannot raise sufficient funds. Since they tend to focus on the presidential race, they usually fail to develop the ongoing grass-roots organizations characteristic of the major parties.

Finally, it has been a rare moment when large numbers of Americans have been disenchanted enough to cast a protest vote. Considerable evidence supports the view that the competitive nature of our society translates directly into voting behavior: most people are simply reluctant to waste votes on a candidate who cannot win.

The problems of raising money and getting on the ballot and the wasted vote issue all plagued Anderson in 1980. He was able to get on the ballot in all fifty states and the District of Columbia, but it cost him dearly in terms of money and time. (See Chapter 9 for a discussion of ballot politics and Anderson's role in the 1980 election.)

In the absence of federal funding, Anderson faced a dilemma. He had difficulty attracting campaign funds and endorsements, and without the money necessary for a major media effort, he was unable to broaden his appeal. His organization turned to direct-mail fund raising, but it brought in less than half the anticipated $15 million. Lack of money was one reason that Anderson was unable to sustain his early momentum or demonstrate what the "Anderson Difference" really was.

As his standing in the polls declined, Anderson's campaign became increasingly vulnerable to the charge that he did not have any chance of winning and could only play a spoiler role, hurting Carter and helping Reagan. Undoubtedly this caused a portion of the electorate who were sympathetic to Anderson to choose between the two major party candidates.

In the face of every obstacle, third parties are encouraged by the rising number of independents and the various surveys (see Chapter 8) that indicate that the major reason for declining voter turnouts has been disenchantment with the candidates and the political system. They believe that someday third parties will be a real force in presidential politics.

State Politics and the Two-Party System

Though Republicans could take heart from the presidential successes of 1968, 1972, and 1980, their comparative failures in contests for lesser offices are an important reminder that state politics is another world.

PARTY COMPETITION? Even such givens as the two-party system do not necessarily extend to the state level. Political scientists have generally divided state party systems into **two party, modified one-party,** and **one-party** systems, with the designation determined by what percentage of the time over a period of years the contending parties elect their candidates to office. When he examined the races for governor and state legislatures, Austin Ranney concluded that only twenty-six states were two-party states in the 1960s.[10] Eleven were modified one-party Democratic (Fla., Hawaii, Ky., Md., Mo., N.C., N.M., Okla., Tenn., Va., W.Va.); seven were modified one-party Republican (Colo., Idaho, Kan., N.D., S.D., Vt., Wyo.); and seven were one-party Democratic (Ala., Ark., Ga., La., Miss., S.C., Tex.). The seven one-party states were all members of the Confederacy.

Whether or not state parties provide the voters with a party program worthy of the name is determined largely by the amount of two-party competitiveness in each state. The sectional, regional, and philosophic differences that give the so-called national parties a Noah's Ark look are usually not present in local and state party contests. Party commitment to certain policies is possible, but usually exists only where there is a strong two-party system and the majority can be turned out of office.

In one-party and modified one-party states, party government is a rarity. Instead, elected officials tend to rely on their own organizations and campaign as individuals with little reference to a party platform. In a number of states, one or a few economic interests attempt to control the state or whatever public policies impinge on their interests, thus overshadowing party politics.[11]

Austin Ranney points out the general importance of state parties by saying:

Whatever may be the future of inter-party competition, however, political parties will continue to be the states' principal agencies for making nominations, contesting elections, recruiting governmental leaders from the general populations, and so providing the vital link between the people and their government that democracy demands.[12]

One-Partyism in the South

The South always has been a special exception in state politics. As late as 1963, the eleven states of the South were fairly solid one-party Democratic in terms of presidential, gubernatorial, and state legislature races, in spite of the fact that since 1932 many attitudes among its white voters have been out of step with the sentiments of many non-southern Democratic officeholders at the federal level.

The key to the South's tenacious one-party politics was the region's preoccupation with the problems of race. "In its grand outlines the politics of the South revolves around the position of the Negro."[13] This is not to say that social and economic factors, such as one-crop agriculture, a slower rate of industrialization and urbanization, ethnic and religious homogeneity, nativism, and a strong sense of sectional history have not been contributing factors.

ONE-PARTY POLITICS AND CONGRESSIONAL POWER. The desire to protect the dominant regional social structure from national legislation provided the strongest motive for the South's one-party framework. The absence of serious second-party competition for House and Senate seats allowed the winners of the intra-party struggle to develop secure power bases and achieve continual electoral success. This, in turn, allowed the southern members of Congress to use the congressional seniority system to dominate the positions of power within both houses. In addition, the southern Democrats and members of the Republican Party have often formed the effective conservative coalition that allows them to be a majority on many key issues.

Serious Republican inroads in U.S. Congressional races did not begin until the mid-1960s. At one point in the early seventies, Republicans controlled 7 of 22 Senate and 35 of 108 House seats from the South. After the 1980 election Republican members from the region numbered 10 and 39 respectively.

PROBLEMS FOR REPUBLICANS. Many of the earlier Republican gains were based on "white backlash" votes against Democrats who took more moderate stands on civil rights issues, partially in response to the dramatic rise in black voting power. Democrats in the South have accommodated black voters and some black candidates and have capitalized on the great rise in participation among voting-age blacks following the Voting Rights Act of 1965. Race is no longer the overriding issue in the politics of the region.

The Democratic hold on southern loyalties in presidential races did not begin to decline until 1948, when southerners walked out of the Democratic convention because of the adoption of a liberal civil rights plank, and

formed a temporary third party. The real Republican breakthrough came in 1968, when Wallace and Nixon each won five states, leaving only Texas for Hubert Humphrey. In 1972, Richard Nixon made a clean sweep. White backlash was a factor in the Goldwater–Nixon–Wallace gains of 1964–1972. Jimmy Carter's 1976 sweep of all of the South except Virginia was aided by his being the first southerner (Johnson said he was a southwesterner) nominated by one of the two major parties since Zachary Taylor (1841–45). And while a majority of whites voted for Ford, enough shifted to Carter, so that, combined with overwhelming black support, Carter swept the southern states.

In 1980 Carter lost every state in the South except his home state, Georgia. Blacks held for Carter but apparently voted in reduced numbers. Many whites, probably most of those who had voted their southern pride in 1976, defected to Reagan, who long had been popular in the South.

The record in the region from 1968 through the last election suggests that at the presidential level at least, the South is now Republican country.

The Democratic decline at the presidential level reflects a growing southern dissatisfaction with the liberal policies of the party's presidential candidates. Disappointingly for the GOP, however, the Democrats are in firm control of the southern state legislatures; and, at that level, the states remain one-party or modified one-party Democratic states at best.

The Party Machinery: Decentralized Power

Neither major party is a monolithic beast. Each is more like the imaginary animal a child sometimes makes by sticking together a potato body, a carrot head, straw arms, and toothpick legs. When we talk about Democrats and Republicans, we are speaking of fragmented organizations whose component parts often have trouble operating in unison. Most important, we are speaking about people—party leaders, elected officials, activists who work for party causes or candidates, and people whose party attachment involves no more than registering and voting for the party's candidates.

The major American political parties are in truth three-headed political giants, tripartite systems of interactions which embrace all these individuals. As political structures they include a party organization, a party in office, and a party in the electorate.[14]

    In this section we will look at the extraordinarily decentralized party structures, in reality loose coalitions of state and local committees and national committees that reflect weakness at the top of the structure, or "politics without power."

    The federal system of government has vested significant powers in the states. These, in turn, have been subdivided into approximately 91,000 (usually semiautonomous) units of government and 850,000 elective political offices. Cooperation among the far-flung party units is hard to achieve, and campaigning is rarely a coordinated effort.

    Party organization at the national level is governed by custom rather than law. The **national committees** are composed, at a minimum, of one man and one woman from each state and territory. Officially, the committee members are designated by the national conventions of the parties, and the officers by the committee. In fact, the committee chairpersons are selected by the parties' presidential nominees.

POLITICS WITHOUT POWER. On paper, the national committees seem important, yet the total membership rarely meets more than once a year. Their professional staffs are left to engage in fund raising, publicity work, and the planning of the national conventions. The committees exercise no discipline and virtually no influence over the parties' congressional delegations and face a similar lack of real power with respect to the state and local party units. They play absolutely no role in the conduct of the internal affairs of the local party; they have nothing to do with selection of state and local candidates, determination of policy, designation of party officials, or the conduct of state primaries and conventions.

PRESIDENTIAL POWER AND THE DECLINE OF NATIONAL COMMITTEES

    The national committees are supposed to play a role in presidential elections, with the national chairperson acting as the candidate's campaign manager. But the national committees have not conducted the national campaigns. Instead, the candidates have formed their own campaign organizations.

    A recent study shows that presidents are very poor party leaders. In theory, they should head up the national organization that tries to elect candidates. Instead, a separate presidential machine develops around the incumbent, with the president often drawing off the most talented people from the national committee and using the committee as a "dumping ground" for hacks.[15] Richard Nixon assigned his 1972 campaign to his own organization, the Committee to Re-Elect the President. "CREEP" was the focal point for the secret cash funds, illegal solicitation of contributions, and "dirty tricks" revealed during the Watergate investigations.

    Shortly after taking office, President Ford said "Never again a CREEP," and during the 1976 campaign he made extensive use of the Republican National Committee as a campaign committee. However, the national chairman did not serve as his campaign manager. Carter's campaign was based primarily

The lack of power of the party organization at the national level is reflected in the remarks of an ex-president and a party executive.

Let's remember that there are no national parties in the United States. There are . . . state parties.

DWIGHT D. EISENHOWER

The [national] committee was comprised of people left over from the convention. They select a chairman, but there is a myth in the country that there is a national party structure.

WILLIAM WELSH, Executive Director
of the Democratic National Committee

Sources: Eisenhower was quoted by Louis W. Koeing, "More Power to the President (Not Less)," *New York Times Magazine,* January 3, 1965. ©1965 by the New York Times Company. Reprinted by permission. Welsh was quoted in Congressional Quarterly, *Weekly Report,* March 18, 1972, p. 583.

on personal organization, but the post-Watergate campaign finance reforms require all presidential campaign funds to be funneled through the national committees, restoring to them a function they had held in previous years. But presidents and congressional leaders of both parties appear to have no compelling reasons to encourage the development of strong national party leaders, and it may be asked whether the "national" parties can ever recover from the damage brought about by the enlargement of the presidency.

CAMPAIGN COMMITTEES IN CONGRESS. The congressional and senatorial campaign committees maintained by both major parties generally operate independently of the national party committees. They provide technical services such as research and broadcast facilities and provide funds to assist legislators who make frequent trips back home. Their most important function is to channel campaign contributions to incumbents and se-

lected challengers who have a good chance of capturing a seat for the party.

Personal Politics and Party Structure

The separation of the party organization from the politics of the nominating process weakens party organization at every level of government. Ordinarily, most people seeking their party's nomination run on their own in the party primary (see Chapter 9), with the party remaining neutral, at least in theory. Of course, the intelligent voter should be able to determine which candidate has the backing of which party leaders, but officially (and often by law) the party remains aloof. It pays for the party to stay uninvolved to avoid the embarrassment of backing a loser in the primary. The candidates develop their own personal organizations, and since the name of the game

Viewpoint:
Party crashers — A growing force in politics

Two successful 1978 candidates for the governorship of their states represent the declining importance of party loyalty in the race for nomination.

Forrest (Fob) James of Alabama left the Democratic Party in 1972, and for four years was a loyal Republican, serving in party posts. Knowing that he could not get elected as a Republican, he became a "born-again Democrat" in 1977 and began campaigning. James was aided by his great wealth, his status as a former football star, and the voters' receptivity to new faces not associated with the George Wallace era.

Lee Sherman Dreyfus of Wisconsin had neither money or fame going for him. His main asset was personality, and a situation to exploit. The party's candidate was closely tied to big business and the influence of the city of Milwaukee in state politics, the two major targets of Dreyfus's criticism. When he was asked about his very short tenure as a Republican, Dreyfus replied, "My mother always taught me it was polite to join a party before you take it over."

CONGRESSIONAL QUARTERLY

Source: *Weekly Report*, 36 (October 28, 1978), pp. 3107–08.

is winning, the successful contenders for the nomination would be foolish to disband their teams and turn over the general election campaign to the appropriate party organizations. Unless they put their own key people in charge of these groups, the party structures only can be complementary, though often important, auxiliaries to the candidate's personal organization.

AMATEUR HOUR. Although the parties do not officially back primary candidates, an assumption long held was that the contestants were no strangers to the party. However, the 1978 election saw nearly twenty relatively inexperienced candidates, who could be considered outsiders and political party crashers, win Senate and gubernatorial nominations over favored opponents closely tied to state or local party machines.

The post-1974 anti-politician mood, taxpayer resentment—the dominant issue in 1978, the weakening of party loyalty among the voters, and the fact that 1978 was the first time since 1970 that candidates could spend as much money as they could raise, combined to make it a good year for colorful and articulate amateurs. There is likely to be an extended period of party-crashing in American politics, a further symptom of the parties' loss of status in our political process.

At the national level, the presidential nominating conventions used to be considered the pinnacle of the party structure. As originally conceived, the conventions were to provide a place where state party leaders could choose the most acceptable candidate. But the rise of the primary system, beginning in the early 1900s, has led to the present-day situation in which, with few exceptions, the party's choice has been determined by the primaries. The only post–1948 departures from this rule are provided by the Ford–Reagan cliffhanger of 1976, and the strange events of 1968—which saw a non-primary contender, Hubert H. Humphrey, nominated by the Democrats after President Lyndon B. Johnson decided not to seek re-election, and Robert Kennedy, the frontrunner in the primaries, was assassinated. The national conventions have become an effort to create "a loose alliance out of fifty grand duchies and hundreds of petty baronies" to elect a president.[16]

The personal politics of the nominating process is both a cause and effect of party decentralization—some call it disorganization—at all levels of operations. Whether it is the "chicken" or the "egg," it is a fact, and also a reflection of the "winners and losers" focus of our politics.

Party at the State and Local Level

Party structure within each state is prescribed by law; however, these laws are so varied that they defy summary or classification. We can say that "the political party organization in the United States can best be described as a network of committees which interact and cooperate when it is to their advantage."[17] Figure 7–2 is descriptive of a general style for the fifty states.

STATE COMMITTEE. At the top of the state structure is the **state committee,** headed by the state chairperson. The chairperson usually maintains the party headquarters, coordinates party efforts within the state, and plays a major role in fund raising and campaign management. The chairperson also is the major contact with national headquarters. The chairperson of the state committee is normally the choice of the candidate for the highest executive position, the governor or candidate for governor, and the selection is rubber-stamped by the state committee.

The real source of power in state politics usually is found at the county level. The approximately 3,000 **county committees** are made up of members either selected by party voters in a primary, by those who hold office at the precinct (polling place) level in the party, or by the county chairperson. The wise county chairperson tries to designate members who will ensure his or her re-election by the committee.

COUNTY CHAIRPERSON. The county chairperson is the most powerful local party official. The chairperson may be elected by a county convention, the precinct leaders, an election open to all party voters, the candidates for office, or other party officials, or a popularly elected county committee. The chairperson's major functions are advising elected officials, influencing the distribution of patronage, candidate recruitment, and coordination of local campaigns.

Although **patronage** (appointment to the public payroll) has been severely limited by civil-service reforms, the county chairperson can still wield great influence in the granting of **preferments,** that is, rewards made administratively by the party in control of the county government. Preferments include contracts for official printing, construction of public buildings and handling of other building improvements, and the designation of lawyers as executors of individual estates unassigned at the time of death. Many of the party faithful are found on town, city, and county payrolls.

GRASS ROOTS. At the lowest level, or grass roots, are the city or town committees and the precinct leader, who is elected in a primary or precinct caucus, or as is often the case in cities, appointed. In urban areas, large populations have required the establishment of **ward committees,** which serve as a link between the many **precincts** and the city committee. Outside of the cities, precinct organization

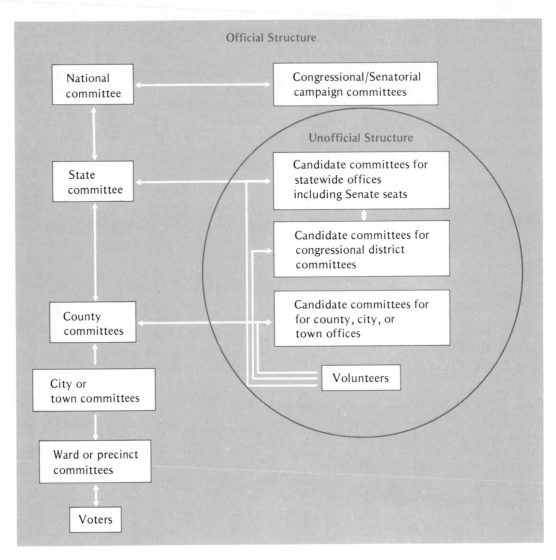

Figure 7–2 *American party structure.*

often is a one-person show. The 300,000 or more precinct leaders (for the two major parties) are, in theory, responsible for seeing that eligible residents who support their party are registered and vote. Precinct leaders also are responsible for polling the voters on issues, helping candidates solicit names for ballot petitions, recruiting campaign workers, and dealing with constituent problems.

Even though elections are usually won or lost in precincts, surveys have shown that many leaders do not actively carry out these responsibilities. The precinct leaders should be the basic link between the party and the electorate.

The committees are made up of the precinct leaders and other interested individuals allowed by law. Their role is to coordinate

Active neighborhood groups, like this one in San Francisco, can be an important base for political parties.

party activity in their geographic area, raise funds, recruit candidates, and assist in the election efforts of candidates for town, county, state, and national office.

GETTING INTO POLITICS. The grass-roots level provides the point of entry for most people who wish to become involved in party politics. City and town committees usually welcome workers with open arms, and it is not unusual for new people—including the eighteen-to-twenty-five-year-olds—to find local leaders asking them to serve as precinct committeemen (leaders). Our message is that in most communities the party is anxious to have young people become "actives," and volunteers are the lifeblood 'of any party or campaign organization.

Today, the precinct, ward, and county organizations provide the primary link between people who need services and officials who provide services. A homeowner who has a sewer problem or a group seeking the installation of a traffic light should be able to use local party officials to see to their needs. As a service organization, the local party can play an important role even without a coherent set of state or national party policies. Unfortunately, the bulk of the population lives in the nation's suburbs, where viable party organizations usually do not exist, but where these opportunities are the greatest.

Party structure becomes more complex when we include the informal groups that exist in some states such as the congressional district committees, state senatorial district committees, and state judicial district committees. Their primary purpose is to support the campaigns of candidates for particular elective offices. The committees are designed for candidates or officeholder party politics.

When we put the whole fragmented political structure back together again, do we end up with national parties? Or do we mistake for national parties the loose federation of state parties that come together every four years to choose a presidential candidate?

While party is an important determinant of voting behavior, neither the congressional party structure nor the president can keep a member in line when he believes that constituency, sectional, or philosophical considerations dictate his opposition to the party stand. A president with a party majority in both houses has no assurance that all, or most, of his legislative program will be enacted. It is the lack of discipline that makes our parties good vehicles for getting elected but weak organizations for governing along the lines of the responsible party models of other democratic societies.

Political Parties and Campaign Financing

As the Watergate scandal unfolded, most Americans read in their morning papers what their politicians already knew: that the national and state parties are only one element, perhaps a minor one, in the pyramid of individuals, organizations, and one-shot campaign committees which channel funds to candidates. Secret cash funds, vast sums of money laundered through Mexico, future ambassadorships sold to party contributors, hidden corporate contributions solicited and received—all represented just a part of the seamy underside of American campaign financing.

Little wonder. Astronomical sums of money are needed to run even the simplest modern campaign. Herbert E. Alexander, a leading authority on campaign financing, estimates that the total expenditure for the presidential general election in 1972 was more than $103 million, and congressional candidates and political committees spent $77 million.[18]

CAMPAIGN FINANCE REFORM. In 1974, however, Congress passed the most extensive reform of federal campaign financing practices in American history. (For a complete analysis of campaign financing see Chapter 9.) The Campaign Finance Reform Act was aimed at limiting the influence of big money contributors and preventing the kinds of abuses that came to light after the 1972 election.

With the 1976 campaigns already in progress, the Supreme Court created considerable confusion by declaring unconstitutional the provisions of the 1974 law that imposed spending limits on congressional campaigns and restricted the amount of personal money a candidate could spend on his or her own election. The court upheld the limits on how much individuals and political committees (including party committees) may contribute to candidates; public financing of presidential primary and general election campaigns; and the requirement for disclosure of contributions of more than one hundred dollars and campaign expenditures of more than ten dollars.

The Federal Election Commission, a six-member panel appointed by the president, supervises the administration of the 1974 law.

IMPACT OF REFORM. What did these "reforms" mean for the major parties? The failure to apply public financing to congressional elections gives a decided advantage to those already in office (see Chapter 9), and the public financing provisions for presidential elections discriminate against minor parties. Minor or independent parties do not receive any funding until after their first presidential campaign and then only if they get five percent of the general election vote and finish with a campaign debt after the first election. None of the minor parties that contested the 1976 race qualified for public funds prior to the 1980 election, and none, with the exception of Anderson, will qualify prior to the 1984 election. This will keep them in their position of perpetual losers while enshrining the Republican and Democratic parties in a permanently preferred position. The law makes the two major parties equally poor during presidential elections. They are limited to the federal subsidy and the private money that can be raised and spent by the national committees and certain monies ($4.6 million in 1980) that can be spent on their behalf by state, local, city, and congressional district committees. For the Republicans, this is a far cry from previous years: they traditionally

outspent the Democrats with the aid of wealthy givers. For example, campaign contributions in 1972 from officials of ten corporations (all major defense contractors) to Nixon totaled $1.76 million, while giving to McGovern came to $185,000.[19] This fact should serve as another reminder that both parties draw some support from the full range of socio-economic classes in our society.

While the law frees the candidates from the burdens of fund raising and should free them from private commitments to major contributors, the limits create budgeting problems for both parties, as was clear in 1976 as the campaign went into its final weeks. The limit for the presidential candidates may be unrealistically low. And, some observers felt that the relatively low voter turnout in 1976 could be equated with a lack of dollars available to mount stronger drives to get out the vote.

In response to complaints from state and local party organizations that the law cut them out of the presidential campaigns, Congress liberalized the rules in 1979. Party organizations now can purchase without limit campaign materials such as buttons, stickers, and brochures for volunteer activities to promote federal candidates. Certain kinds of voter registration and get-out-the-vote drives on behalf of presidential tickets have also been freed from expenditure limits.

Ironically, a change in the rules may hurt a party at one level and help it at other levels. From the point of view of fund raising by party organizations for use in congressional or state elections, as opposed to the efforts of candidates' organizations, the new finance law appears to hurt the Democrats more than the Republicans. Despite their image as the fat-cat party, Republican national committees are now receiving the vast majority of their funds in contributions of less than one hundred dollars, solicited by a sophisticated direct-mail operation. Democratic committees have relied on fund-raising dinners and large individual donations. The limits on individual contributions has forced the Democratic Party to move toward the direct solicitation of funds.

Federal Election Commission figures for 1977 and 1978 revealed a David-versus-Goliath situation, with the Republicans raising considerably more money than the Democrats using the direct-mail technique. Republican strategy for 1980 called for heavy party financing to become competitive and to overcome the advantages of **incumbents**—those holding office—which include the tendency of labor groups to give almost all their contributions to Democratic candidates and business and trade groups, formerly associated with the Republicans, to give almost half their money to Democratic officeholders who have been in a position to influence the allocation of resources. It was estimated that national-level Republican committees spent approximately $6 million to support congressional candidates, while Democratic committees spent just over $1 million.

The Parties: Are They Different?

If the parties are different, then they should draw their electoral support from different segments of the community; this is an assumption that receives some support from the sources of campaign funds of the two parties. Their political leaders should hold different views on many major policies, and, this difference in views should be reflected in the

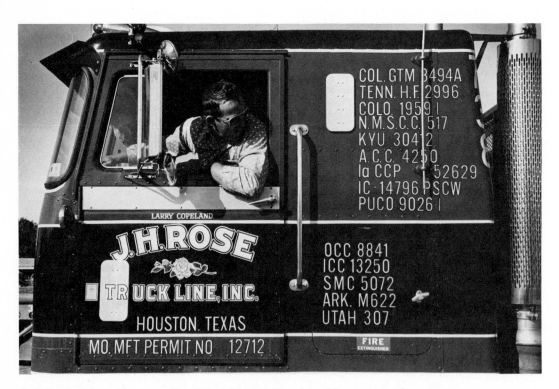

It is hard to draw a voter profile of Americans registered to either party, and there appears to be a substantial ideological gap between party leaders and rank-and-file voters.

voting behavior of elected officials who wear the party label.

PARTY IDENTIFICATION. Table 7–3 reveals what looks like a sad, but improving state of affairs for the Republican Party. They are heavily outnumbered by voters identifying with the Democratic Party, and since 1971, those claiming to be **Independents** outnumber Republicans. These figures were reflected in the Democratic dominance of both houses of Congress prior to 1981, and the party's success at the state level. However, they seem inconsistent with Republican presidential victories of 1952, 1956, 1968, 1972, and 1980, and the narrow Democratic wins of 1948, 1960, and 1976. Part of the explanation lies in the fact that certain elements of the Democratic coalition—the young, racial minorities, and people of lower educational, occupational, and income status—tend to have a poorer vote turnout. During a presidential

★ ★ ★ *Table 7–3* ★
Party identification: 1940–1980

YEAR	% OF VOTERS IDENTIFYING AS		
	DEMOCRAT	*REPUBLICAN*	*INDEPENDENT*
	18 YEARS AND OLDER		
1980	47	23	30
1977	49	20	31
1976	46	22	32
1975	45	22	33
1974	44	23	33
May–Sept. 1973*	43	24	33
Winter 1973	42	27	31
1972	43	28	29
1971	44	25	31
	21 YEARS AND OLDER		
1970	45	29	26
1969	42	28	30
1968	46	27	27
1966	48	27	25
1964	53	25	22
1960	47	30	23
1950	45	33	22
1940	42	38	20

*Falloff in Republican category and rise in Independent category during period of Watergate investigations.

Source: The Gallup Poll, Princeton, New Jersey 08540. Adapted from *Gallup Opinion Index*, Report No. 137, December 1976, p. 50, No. 149, December 1977, p. 30, and No. 183, December 1980, p. 64.

election, very visible issues and the candidates' personal appeal further blur party identification. Finally, the balance of power is in the hands of Independents, who, if they vote and split evenly, would give the election to the Democrats. But the term *Independent* is misleading, and a more sophisticated breakdown of party identification (see Table 8–6) indicates that many so-called Independents have a tendency to identify with one or the other party, and that only a minority of party identifiers can be classified as "strong" and relatively immune to crossing over and voting for the opposition candidate.

Kevin Phillips, in his now-famous book, *The Emerging Republican Majority* (1969), forecast a re-alignment of political forces which would create a new, conservative majority in America. As he saw it, this majority would be composed of the voters of the "Heartland" (Middle America), the South,

and the "Sun Belt" (which starts in Florida and winds its way across Texas and Arizona, all the way to Southern California).[20] The 1972 election suggested a "new majority," but only at the presidential level, and the 1976 results put the theory into limbo. However, Republican successes in 1980 gave encouragement to Phillips's concept. But, as we will discuss in the "Issue" section, it may not be realistic to speak of a majority party that can claim supremacy at both the congressional and presidential levels.

WHO ARE THE DEMOCRATS AND REPUBLICANS?

Any description of the **socio-economic characteristics** of the "typical" Democrat or Republican must be read with the following warning in mind: the descrip-

★ ★ ★ *Table 7–4* ★

Vote by parts of the Democratic coalition: 1952–1980

| YEAR | % OF TOTAL VOTE DEMOCRATS RECEIVED | % OF ENTIRE CATEGORY DEMOCRATS RECEIVED | | | | | | | |
		NON-WHITE	UNION FAMILIES	CATHOLICS	UNDER 30	GRADE SCHOOL ED.	CENTRAL CITIES	EAST	SOUTH
1952	44.6%	79%	61%	56%	51%	52%	51%	45%	51%
1956	42.2	61	57	51	43	50	55	40	49
1960	50.1	68	65	78	54	55	65	53	51
1964	61.3	94	73	76	64	66	74	68	52
1968	43.0	85	56	59	47*	52	58	50	31
1972	38	87	46	48	48	49	61	42	29
1976	50	85	63	57	53	58		51	54
1980	41	86	50	46	47	54		43	44

*In 1968 Wallace drew 15 percent of the under 30 vote and Nixon 38 percent.

Source: The Gallup Poll, Princeton, New Jersey, 08540. Adapted from *Gallup Opinion Index*, Report No. 183, December 1980, p. 74. The "Central Cities" category is from Robert Axelrod, "Communications," *American Political Science Review*, 68 (June 1974), p. 718.

tion is saying that a greater percentage of the people who identify with Party X have these characteristics than those who identify with Party Y.

Republicans tend to be older, better educated, and drawn from higher occupational and income levels than Democrats. They are predominantly white Protestants and live in suburban, small-town, and rural areas, particularly in the Midwest and West. Small business owners, managers, and other business executives are usually found in the GOP camp. Democrats tend to be better represented among younger voters. And the party is particularly strong among non-whites, Catholic and Jewish voters, and members of organized labor. Not surprisingly, Democratic strength is focused in the central cities, particularly in the East. The educational and income levels of party members generally are lower than those of members of the GOP. The socio-economic generalizations about the two parties are reflected in the common assumptions that the Democrats are the party of the "common man" and the Republicans are the party of "business interests." The Democratic coalition generally makes policy demands on elected and appointed officials that reflect liberal beliefs, as opposed to the conservative beliefs that characterize the mainstream of the Republican constituencies and party.

PARTY LEADERS

Voters "see a party as generally dedicated to the interests of a particular set of groups within society, or as committed to a broad range of policy objectives."[21] But the "winner-take-all" nature of our politics and the effort to capture the independent or "undecided" vote tend to make both parties sound alike in their public campaigning, and reinforce the widely held belief that there is no difference between the Democrats and Republicans. However, a 1956 survey of Democratic and Republican leaders' and followers' attitudes on twenty-four key domestic and foreign policy issues led to a very different conclusion (see insert).[22]

LEADERS ARE DIFFERENT. The survey showed that the leadership of each party is a distinct group of like-minded people who diverge sharply from their opposite numbers on many important issues. Generally, the Democrats are the more liberal, the Republicans, the more conservative. Though there are liberal and conservative elements within the ranks of both parties, the leadership groups are in greatest general disagreement on issues that touch most directly the forces that support them—the managerial, propertied, and high-status base of the Republicans; the labor, minority-group, lower-class, and intellectual base of the Democrats. For example, a basic constitutional and political issue that divides Democrats and Republicans in Congress, as well as conservatives and liberals within each party, is the role the federal government should play in domestic issues like combatting poverty, promoting civil liberties, or regulating the economy. Most Democrats favor a large federal role in dealing with these areas, while most Republicans advocate less government at that level and more reliance on state and local governments and individual initiative.

A survey conducted twenty years later asked party officials—national and state party committee members and state chairpersons—to rank, in order of importance, ten major problems. The results are shown in Table 7–5. The major differences between the two groups was the greater importance the Democrats placed on unemployment, freedom of speech, and equality for blacks, while their opposite numbers gave higher rankings to reducing the role of government and maintaining a strong defense.

The ideology of party leaders, activists, and officeholders is somewhat different from the philosophy expressed in party platforms or on the campaign trail, or from the ideology of the voters who simply are enrolled party members (the **rank and file**). The first of these might be called the private ideology of the party; the other two, its public ideology and the party's image among its followers.

The appeals of the platform and candidates attempt to attract wide support by offering something for everybody. They both reflect the prevailing public consensus and attempt to reshape the voters' image of what the party stands for. Although campaign appeals are useful for winning office, the private ideology is a better indicator of how the party will attempt to govern. A significant finding of the 1956 party survey was that the political beliefs which unite the leaders are not necessarily the same ones that unite the rank-and-file supporters. Republican voters were found to disagree far more with their own leaders than with Democratic Party leaders. For instance, they were found to be in considerable harmony with Democratic followers in support of the liberal regulatory and social programs of the Roosevelt and Truman eras, ideas that did not lose much of their popularity until the late 1960s.

A survey published in 1972 reinforced the McCloskey data. Democratic Party activists were more liberal than Republican activists, and they acknowledged a greater responsibility on the part of government to aid the poor and a greater concern with the income gap between the rich and the poor.[23]

The events of the 1970s, culminating

★ ★ ★ *Table 7–5* ★
The importance of ten national goals, as ranked by party officials: 1976

REPUBLICANS	DEMOCRATS
1. Curbing inflation	1. Reducing unemployment
2. Reducing role of government	2. Curbing inflation
3. Maintaining a strong military defense	3. Protecting freedom of speech
4. Developing energy sources	4. Developing energy sources
5. Reducing crime	5. Achieving equality for blacks
6. Reducing unemployment	6. Reducing crime
7. Protecting freedom of speech	7. Giving people more say in government decisions
8. Giving people more say in government decisions	8. Achieving equality for women
9. Achieving equality for blacks	9. Maintaining a strong military defense
10. Achieving equality for women	10. Reducing the role of government

Source: Survey by the *Washington Post* and the Harvard University Center for International Affairs. © *The Washington Post*, September 27, 1976, p. A2.

The results of a 1956 survey supported the assumption that Democratic leaders were more liberal than Republican leaders. This assumption is still valid.

Democratic leaders typically are more disposed to employ the nation's collective power to advance humanitarian and social welfare goals (e.g., social security, immigration, racial integration, a higher minimum wage, and public education). They are more critical of wealth and big business and more eager to bring them under regulation. . . .

The Republican leaders, while not uniformly differentiated from their opponents, subscribe in greater measure to the symbols and practices of individualism and national independence. They prefer to overcome humanity's misfortunes by relying upon personal effort, private incentives, frugality, hard work, responsibility, self-denial (for both men and government). . . .

Source: From a survey of convention delegates by McCloskey, Hoffman, and O'Hara, 1956. Herbert McCloskey, Paul J. Hoffman, and Rosemary O'Hara, "Issue Conflict and Consensus Among Party Leaders and Followers," *American Political Science Review*, 54 (June 1960), p. 426.

in the 1980 elections, suggest that the McCloskey et al. data on Democratic leaders are still accurate to a great extent. However, economic grievances in 1980 caused a considerable defection of Democratic voters to Reagan and to GOP congressional and senatorial candidates. Whether or not this will mean a permanent defection of many middle-class voters may depend on the success of Reagan economic policies and a possible moderation of the liberal stance of Democratic officeholders and candidates.

The potential ideological gap between leaders and followers is the result of a number of factors, including the low level of political participation of the public as contrasted with the leaders, who are usually well informed and highly partisan; they also have a political and psychological stake in the electoral struggle. In the case of both parties, most of the leadership comes from people with middle-

class, white-collar professional backgrounds. This suggests that the political stakes may be the main factor in differences between the two leadership groups. Neither party really challenges the dominance of business, a complaint heard more and more frequently by those seeking a reordering of our priorities. The rank and file of both parties is more diverse, contributing to a gap between the leaders and the led.

LOSER ON THE RIGHT. The lessons of 1964 and 1972 illustrate the problems a party faces when the private or campaign ideology differs significantly from the rank and file's view of the party. In 1964, Barry Goldwater was first in the hearts of Republican leaders in most parts of the country, but ran a poor fourth in a poll of party supporters. However, Goldwater captured the nomination, aided by confusion among the party's more moderate elements.

But he was too far to the right of center, and he was trounced by Lyndon Johnson.

LOSER ON THE LEFT. In 1972, the gap between the "new Democrats" and the old rank-and-file Democratic coalition resulted in a similar debacle for George McGovern. McGovern's outspoken liberal positions on defense spending (major cutbacks), economics, welfare, abortion, and drug control alienated many Democrats, especially organized labor. Unlike the situation with Goldwater (who had strong support from party leaders), McGovern's nomination was achieved by the new activists and his policy positions placed him outside the circle of political acceptability of both the leadership and the rank-and-file— this time too far to the left.

Since the 1972 election, the Democratic Party has been faced with a serious problem: the growing conservatism of many of the rank-and-file at the same time that liberal influence and control over the party organization at all levels has remained strong. Many of the working class who were part of the New Deal coalition are now middle class and consider themselves contributors to, rather than the beneficiaries of, current social and humanitarian programs, which they often characterize as taxing the many for the benefit of the few.

The issue-oriented newcomers to the ranks of party activists now find that they can control the party, but not the selection of candidates or the policies on which they campaign. Campaign finance laws and the media

The Democrats' internal struggle was highlighted in 1980 by the nomination contest between Senator Edward Kennedy (left) and President Jimmy Carter.

revolution have made candidates less and less dependent upon party structures and have also contributed to the decline of the parties.

Liberal Democratic leaders and activists could take little comfort in the 1978 election, which found many Democratic candidates defeating their Republican opponents by capitalizing on the issue that had been carefully developed by the GOP—national tax resentment. They campaigned in favor of tax cuts, but charged that the Republican plan to cut federal taxes by one-third would be inflationary. They understood that if the nation is moving in the conservative direction, it is a populist, anti-big-business sentiment.

This more conservative stance by the candidates, when coupled with the Carter administration's anti-inflation policies calling for cutbacks in many social programs, was little comfort to the liberals who had influence within the party disproportionate to their strength, and whose influence over policy is waning. And policy, after all, determines who wins and who loses in the struggle for limited resources.

The internal struggle in the Democratic Party was brought into full view in 1979 and 1980. The more liberal elements within the party, labor and minority groups in particular, encouraged and supported Senator Edward Kennedy's (D., Mass.) attempt to deny President Carter the renomination. The struggle culminated in Kennedy's unsuccessful effort to overturn the rule that bound delegates to vote on the first convention ballot for the candidate they represented during their home-state primaries and caucuses.

Even in defeat, the Kennedy forces enacted a heavy toll on Carter by forcing a more liberal platform on him than he wanted. Kennedy gave a rousing speech attacking Reagan and defending traditional Democratic liberalism based upon large federal expenditures to provide jobs, alleviate poverty, and restore urban areas, a liberalism that he believed Carter had abandoned. After Carter's

nomination, Kennedy joined Carter on the podium, but the distance between the two men was plain in Kennedy's weak handshake and lack of enthusiasm. We suggest that a repeat of the 1956 McCloskey study would reveal that a substantial gap now exists between Democratic leaders and many of the rank and file.

THE PARTY IN OFFICE

Once in office, do Democratic and Republican members of Congress support and oppose different policies? The answer to this question is yes, but we hedge the answer for the following reasons:

1. Party unity roll-call votes—votes in which a majority of Democrats oppose a majority of Republicans—account for approximately forty percent of the roll-call votes in Congress. Obviously, many issues do not divide the legislators along party lines, nor should they necessarily do so.

2. During the period of 1973–1979, party unity—based upon the percentage of time the member voted with his or her party majority on partisan issues—averaged 66 and 68 percent for Democrats and Republicans respectively.

3. The conservative coalition—an alliance of southern Democrats and most Republicans—appears on almost one quarter of the roll calls, and has won an average of 60 percent of the time from 1961–1979.

4. As a result of coalition politics, the minority party can and does win. In 1979, for example, there were 550 party-unity votes and the Republicans won 144 times.[24]

While both parties perform the important functions of organizing Congress—selecting leaders, staffing the committees, etc.—and one party provides linkage with the president, the party cannot force compliance with a position. And when a legislator believes that the party line and constituency attitudes are in conflict on a major issue, the member will vote constituency. However, other things being equal (see Chapter 10), party membership is the single most important determinant of congressional voting behavior.

As Table 7–6 shows, Democratic and Republican members of the House do vote differently on key issues, and their votes reflect their base of electoral support both in terms of votes and campaign financing. But the response time of the majority party to the felt needs of various segments of the society appears too slow to many critics. The backgrounds of our legislators, the nature of coalition and election politics, and the rules and procedures of Congress, make Congress a more conservative body than its Democratic majorities would suggest.

PARTY MAKES A DIFFERENCE. The relative conservativeness of Congress not withstanding, which party controls the White House and Congress does make an important difference. It is not a choice of Tweedledum or Tweedledee, and the intelligent voter should be aware of the general liberalism or conservatism that characterizes the parties' mainstream and the candidates who carry the banner. Recognizing regional and individual candidate differences—a southern Democrat may be conservative and certain Republicans are liberal—a vote should reflect which candidate will better represent the voter's interest.

★ ★ ★ *Table 7–6* ★

Party differences as reflected in selected House of Representatives votes: 1945–1976

YEAR	SELECTED LEGISLATION	% OF DEMOCRATS FOR	% OF REPUBLICANS FOR
1945	Full Employment Act	90%	36%
1954	Increase Unemployment Compensation	54	9
1961	Against Increase in Minimum Wage	34	86
1964	Anti-Poverty Program	84	13
1967	Enlarge Food Stamp Program	85	19
1968	Housing–Urban Development	79	63
1969	Increased Education Funds	84	55
1970	Extension of Voting Rights Act	71	34
1971	Hospital Construction	99	41
1972	Lockheed Loan	44	60
1973	Against Cut of Anti-Poverty Funds	91	50
1974	Regulation of Strip Mining	78	34
1975	Emergency Jobs for Unemployed	92	13
1976	Against Deregulation of Natural Gas	70	10

Source: 1945–1964 data from Robert A. Dahl, "Key Votes, 1945–1964," *Pluralistic Democracy in the United States* (Chicago: Rand McNally, 1967), pp. 228–242. 1967–1976 data from AFL–CIO Legislative Reports, *Labor Looks at the Congress,* issues for the 90th–94th Congress.

Party and candidate platforms usually represent a list of intentions that would be carried out, barring obstacles. But there are obstacles, and elected officials grouped as parties often do not have the internal cohesion to deliver on the programs to which the party appears to be committed. Our parties are not responsible in this; individual candidates are responsible to their constituents through the mechanism of elections. But, it can be argued that our parties reflect the federal structure of our nation, the diversity of our society, and the multiplicity of interests that support each. A responsible party model could be out of step with our society, which may be better served by the politics of compromise engaged in by our coalition politics in a Congress that pretends to be two-party politics.[25]

★ Issue ★

Is the Party Over?

For 150 years, American politics has basically been divided between two giant, sometimes shifting, coalitions. Most Americans have accepted the idea that politics is a choice between the candidates of one or the other of the two large, fragmented parties.

Events of the 1960s and early 1970s suggested that the system might be ripe for change. Protest movements among blacks, the poor, and the young, as reflected in the antiwar movement and women's liberation movement, placed strains upon the ability of the Democrats and Republicans to respond to change. In 1968, George Wallace had the traditional party leaders looking over their shoulders. Finally, the rise in the number of "Independents," the poor turnout for presidential and congressional elections, and the increasing number of voters looking to the issues and the candidates, rather than party label, for their voting cues, were other ominous signs to party regulars.

Has the great American political consensus broken down? Are the parties out of touch with the needs of the American people, or are Americans simply out of touch with the parties?

For decades, a few political analysts have been warning that unless the party system is significantly reformed, the future of the two-party system would be dim indeed. In 1950, for instance, a committee of the American Political Science Association wrote that

. . . the inadequacy of the party system in sustaining well-considered programs and providing broad public support for them may lead to grave consequences in an explosive way. . . [including a shift of] excessive responsibility to the president.[26]

In recent years, an increasing number of commentators have seconded such warnings. Two in particular, John G. Stewart, a staff member of the Democratic National Committee, and David Broder, political columnist for the *Washington Post,* have published books on the subject. Both stress that the party, as we know it, will surely die if it does not once again become an instrument for responding .to public needs through the passage of legislation.

In *One Last Chance: The Democratic Party 1974–76,* Stewart argues that much of what ails us today can be traced to a "widening gulf between what the people believe are their needs and what they see the government doing in response to these needs." Moreover, he links the declining confidence in public institutions to the decline of the parties.

. . . the parties in Congress and the states, if they are to be taken seriously by the president or anyone else, must address themselves in a more coherent fashion to the real problems, and they must assume greater responsibility to see that solutions are carried out.[27]

Both he and Broder point to the excessive shift of power to the president at the expense of the congressional parties. Broder states bluntly:

The governmental system is not working because the political parties are not working. The parties have been weakened by their failure to adapt to some of the social–technological changes taking place in America. But, even more, they are suffering from simple neglect; neglect by presidents and public officials, but, particularly, neglect by the voters.[28]

Broder and Stewart propose a number of reforms aimed at strengthening our present party system. These include: the direct election of the president, strengthening the congressional parties by giving more power to the party leaders and party caucuses, strengthening the nominating conventions, and using the party as the sole funnel for political money. But the problems extend to the state level and V.O. Key, for one, has argued that primary elections have stripped state parties of any chance to be responsible or to perform really important functions as organizations.

A RADICAL VIEW. A second, more radical school of thought argues that the major parties, tied to special interests, corporations, the defense establishment, and big labor, have lost all touch with the real needs of the majority of Americans. These writers claim that the parties have lost their real power to a presidential dictatorship, a new elite of "national managers" working in the government's vast bureaucracy, or the military-industrial complex. They discount party reforms because while there are differences between the parties, the differences do not make any difference. Michael Parenti, a political scientist, takes this view and argues that "Republicans

and Democrats are dedicated to strikingly similar definitions of the public interest, at great cost of the life chances of underprivileged people at home and abroad."[29] Only a restructuring of the party system can achieve the desired goals.

As we have suggested, there are no indications that reforms such as those proposed by Broder or Stewart, or the restructuring advocated by Parenti, will take place. On the contrary, the decline in the number of party identifiers and party loyalty reflected at the voting booths, the increasing independence of candidates who use the party label, but not the party organization, and the growth of power of the interest groups, have fragmented the political system, hurting both parties and contributing to their weakness. It has become increasingly difficult for the parties to carry out their important role as the "glue" of representative government, building coalitions and seeking agreements in an effort to legislate on major issues. Describing the situation, Senator Edward Kennedy (D., Mass.) said: "Representative government is in the worst shape I have seen it. The Senate and the House are awash in a sea of special-interest contributions and lobbying."[30]

One pollster observed: "Get out any ninth-grade civics book and see what political parties are supposed to do. The *ad hoc* interest groups have become the political parties of today."[31] Of course, serious scholars have long recognized that as American politics has become more complex, the parties have ceased to dominate the resources of electoral politics—money, organization, political and technical talent. But has this trend gone too far, and what does it mean for the role of parties and for us as citizens?

Although the role of party has diminished, the parties are deeply rooted in American law and as important symbols around which many people structure their political decisions. Many party organizations are alive and well, and parties appear destined to con-

Neither party commands its followers' loyalty to any great extent in presidential elections: many people still vote for the candidate, not the party.

tinue to play important roles in our politics. While the policy formulation role has declined at the national level, in many state and local situations party still has a great impact on policy.

When asked to rate the performance of our institutions of government—Congress, Supreme Court, president, parties—less than four percent of the people put the parties in first place. On the other hand, almost half of the same survey sample favored keeping the major parties as they are, while approximately forty percent would favor some reform. Only four percent would abolish the parties. Sixty-seven percent of the respondents favored keeping party labels on the ballot even though most people say it is better to vote for the man than the party.[32]

Most indicators point to continuation of coalition politics under the familiar labels at the national level. Short of the total inabil-

ity of the government to cope with the twin evils of the 1970s and 1980s, unemployment and inflation, the future looks fairly bleak for third parties.

It must be pointed out, however, that while the labels will be familiar, at least one of the major parties is in a state of flux. The Republicans are returning whole-heartedly to their conservative roots, but the Democrats are groping for a new definition of liberalism. Many Democratic voters no longer believe that the party reflects their views, and it may be that for the first time in half a century, the Democratic Party is out of step with a majority of the country.

The New Deal coalition of labor, ethnic and racial minorities, farmers, and intellectuals welded together by President Franklin D. Roosevelt (1933–1945) has been slowly crumbling for more than a decade, and the Democratic Party has done nothing to replace the coalition's social and economic reform policies that no longer capture the imagination of a majority of the voters. Commenting on this situation during the Democratic Convention, Senator Paul Tsongas of Massachusetts said,

We have gone a long way on the momentum of another era, and the engine is running down. There is a very keen sense that we better come up with something new or we are just not going to survive.[33]

But neither party has a hold on the electorate at the presidential level. The most realistic way of describing what exists today may be to call it a "one-and-a-half party system" in which both major parties exist in a weakened form. The Republican Party is the "half-party" because of its inability to capture control of Congress and its relatively weak position at the state legislature and governorship level. On the other hand, neither party dominates at the presidential level.[34] Divided government becomes the norm rather than the exception, and even when one party controls the Congress and the executive branch, President Jimmy Carter's problems with a Democratic Congress suggest how fragmented our politics has become. Of course, the "half-party" concept will no longer be valid if the Republicans are able to build upon their 1980 triumphs by taking control of the House and becoming more competitive at the state level.

Politics is a conflict process, a competition for resources often requiring compromise. Traditionally, parties were the vehicle for compromises among competing interests. While they apparently have lost their grip on this function, single-issue politics, or the politics of selfishness (as it has been called), is no substitute for representative government. Excessive direct democracy using the "group for every issue" strategy is making it increasingly hard to govern, particularly at the national level.

In the short run, members of those groups who successfully lobby for their policies are winners. And with the decline of the role of the party, particularly for the Democrats, the less affluent (the usual losers) find themselves more handicapped than usual. But, the emphasis on single-issue politics leaves little room for compromise, and our form of government cannot function effectively without a way of moderating its differences through compromise. Unless the parties can regain their health, we may all be losers.

Summary

In 1770, the British conservative, Edmund Burke, defined a political party as "a body of men united for promoting the national interest, upon some particular principle in which they are all agreed."[35] Certainly America's major parties do not fit that model. They are, instead, open-ended disparate coalitions which operate to win elections. Our parties are alive as vehicles for electing candidates, but, particularly at the national level, they have not been able to plan and enact coherent programs. While the growth of presidential power has been a negative factor for the parties, their programmatic failures are more a product of their decentralized and undisciplined nature, the diverse elements they represent, candidate independence, and the growing power of special interests.

Yet there are real differences between the two parties which the leadership of each tends to blur in order to gather more votes during campaigns. Behind the scenes, each party reflects its dominant constituencies, with Democrats being more liberal than Republicans and more inclined to use the federal government to deal with social and economic problems. And party differences are often reflected in the voting behavior of members of Congress. At the state and local level, the coherency of party programs and the ability of a party to govern are usually tied to the existence of two-party competition. In states without it, officials tend to function with minimal party help.

While not conforming to the responsible party model, the parties play essential roles in candidate recruitment, nomination, and campaigning—the organization of choice—that makes our democracy operable. The party is the vehicle for organizing the government and providing a link between the legislative and executive branches as well as attempting some nationwide coordination.

Minor parties are quite active during presidential campaigns, but the factors that encouraged the growth of the two-party system, particularly the winner-take-all system and the absorption of the most popular third-party ideas by the major parties, have operated against the continued success of minor parties. The high cost of campaigning and campaign finance law that discriminates against them are additional obstacles for new organizations. It appears that the future of the party system will be determined less by what new parties do and more by the ability of the Democrats and Republicans to adjust to changing conditions.

Terms to Remember

See the Glossary at the end of the book for definitions

Caucus

Conservative coalition

County committee

Decentralized party

Enrolled voter

Incumbent

Independent voter

Modified one-party system

National committee

One-party system

Patronage

Political party

Precinct

Preferments

Rank and file

Registered voter

Responsible party model

Single-issue parties

Single-issue politics

Socio-economic characteristics

Splinter parties

State committee

Two-party system

Undisciplined party

Ward committee

Notes

1. Herbert McCloskey, "Consensus and Ideology in American Politics," *American Political Science Review*, vol. 58 (June 1964), p. 373.

2. Walter Dean Burnham, *Critical Elections and the Mainsprings of American Politics* (New York: W.W. Norton, 1970), p. 177.

3. The major argument for the development of a "responsible" party model is found in "Toward a More Responsible Two-Party System," *American Political Science Review* suppl. vol. 44 (September 1950). For a dissenting view, see Julius Turner, "Responsible Parties: A Dissent from the Floor," *American Political Science Review*, vol. 45 (March 1951), pp. 143–152.

4. Lester W. Milbrath and M.L. Goel, *Political Participation*, 2d ed. (Chicago: Rand McNally, 1977), p. 22.

5. The best examples are the Populists in Kansas and Nebraska, 1890–1902; Farmer–Labor Party in Minnesota, 1922–1944; and the Progressives in Wisconsin, 1934–1936.

6. Much of the material on the roots of the two-party system is drawn from an unpublished manuscript by William G. Andrews, and is used with his permission.

7. Wilfred E. Binkley, *American Political Parties* (New York: Knopf, 1965), p. 19.

8. Burnham, *Critical Elections*, pp. 1–10, 91–174. Also see V.O. Key, "A Theory of Critical Elections," *Journal of Politics* (February 1955), pp. 3–18.

9. Burnham, *Critical Elections*, pp. 91–174.

10. Austin Ranney, "Parties in State Politics," in Herbert Jacob and Kenneth Vines, eds., *Politics in the American States*, 3rd ed. (Boston: Little, Brown, 1976), p. 62. The discussion of state parties as instruments for governing is drawn from this very perceptive essay.

11. L. Harmond Zeigler and Hendrick van Dalen, "Interest Groups in the States," in Jacob & Vines, *Politics in the American States*, 2d ed. (Boston: Little, Brown, 1971), pp. 122–160.

12. Ranney, "Parties in State Politics," p. 120.

13. V.O. Key, Jr., *Southern Politics* (New York: Alfred A. Knopf, Inc., 1949), p. 5.

14. Frank J. Sorauf, *Party Politics in America*, 3rd ed. (Boston: Little, Brown, 1976), p. 9.

15. Donald A. Robinson, "Are Presidents Leaders of Their Parties?," paper presented at the 1974 American Political Science Association meeting, Chicago, Illinois (Washington, D.C.: The American Political Science Association, 1974).

16. Clinton Rossiter, *Parties and Politics in America* (Ithaca: Cornell University Press, 1969), p. 153.

17. Frank B. Feigert and M. Margaret Conway, *Parties and Politics in America* (Boston: Allyn and Bacon, 1976), p. 138. Most of the material in this section is drawn from Chapter 5.

18. See Herbert E. Alexander, *Financing the 1972 Election* (Lexington, Mass.: D.C. Heath, 1976).

19. *Dollar Politics*, vol. 2 (Washington, D.C.: Congressional Quarterly, Inc., 1974), p. 38.

20. Kevin Phillips, *The Emerging Republican Majority* (New Rochelle, N. Y.: Arlington House, 1969).

21. V.O. Key, Jr., *Public Opinion and American Democracy* (New York: Alfred Knopf, 1961), p. 433.

22. Herbert McCloskey, Paul J. Hoffman, and Rosemary O'Hara, "Issue Conflict and Consensus Among Party Leaders and Followers," *American Political Science Review*, 54 (June 1960), pp. 406–427. The data contained in this section is drawn from the conclusions of the authors. The quotes in the insert are from p. 426.

23. Sidney Verba and Norman H. Nie, *Participation in America: Political Democracy and Social Equality* (New York: Harper & Row, 1972).

24. Congressional Quarterly, *Weekly Report*, 38 (January 19 & 26, 1980), pp. 145–147, 193–195. Party unity and conservative coalition scores are drawn from this source.

25. See Julius Turner, "A Dissent from the Floor," and Edward C. Banfield, "In Defense of the American Party System," both in Robert A. Goldwin, ed., *Political Parties U.S.A.* (Chicago: Rand McNally, 1964), pp. 22–39.

26. *American Political Science Review*, "Toward a More Responsible Two-Party System," suppl. vol. 44 (September 1950), pp. 93–95.

27. John G. Stewart, *One Last Chance: The Democratic Party 1974–76* (New York: Praeger Publishers, 1974), pp. 35–36.

28. David S. Broder, *The Party's Over: The Failure of Politics in America* (New York: Harper & Row, 1972), p. xxiii.

29. Michael Parenti, *Democracy for the Few* (New York: St. Martin's Press, 1974), p. 146.

30. Quoted in *Newsweek*, November 6, 1978, p. 48.

31. Congressional Quarterly, *Weekly Report*, vol. 45, no. 35, (February 12, 1977), p. 294.

32. Data is from Jack Dennis, "Trends in Public Support for the American Party System," *British Journal of Political Science*, 5 (April 1975), pp. 187–230.

33. *Newsweek*, August 18, 1980, p. 21.

34. Everett Carl Ladd, Jr. with Charles D. Hadley, *Transformations of the American Party System*, 2d ed. (New York: W.W. Norton, 1978), Chapter 5.

35. "Thoughts on the Cause of the Present Discontent," in *The Works of the Right Honourable Edmund Burke* (London: Bohn, 1854), vol. 1, p. 375.

Suggested Readings

Herbert E. Alexander, *Financing Politics: Money, Elections and Political Reforms*, 2d ed. (Washington, D.C.: Congressional Quarterly, 1980).

David S. Broder, *The Party's Over: The Failure of Politics in America* (New York: Harper & Row, 1972).

Walter Dean Burnham, *Critical Elections and the Mainsprings of American Politics* (New York: W.W. Norton, 1970).

Herbert Jacob and Kenneth Vines, eds., *Politics in the American States*, 3rd ed. (Boston: Little, Brown, 1976).

Everett Carl Ladd, Jr., *Transformations of the American Party System,* 2d ed. (New York: W.W. Norton, 1978).

Lester W. Milbrath and M.L. Goel, *Political Participation,* 2d ed. (Chicago: Rand McNally, 1977).

Kevin Phillips, *The Emerging Republican Majority* (New Rochelle, N.Y.: Arlington House, 1969).

John G. Stewart, *One Last Chance: The Democratic Party 1974–76* (New York: Praeger, 1974).

Sidney Verba and Norman H. Nie, *Participation in America: Political Democracy and Social Equality* (New York: Harper & Row, 1972).

CHAPTER 8

Public Opinion and Voting Behavior

Democracy is still upon its trial. The civic genius of its people is its only bulwark.

WILLIAM JAMES

On August 8, 1974, President Nixon told the nation that he had lost his base of support in Congress, concluding "therefore I shall resign the presidency effective at noon tomorrow." In an eighteen-month period, Nixon had seen his popularity in the polls plunge from sixty-eight percent right after the Vietnam peace settlement to twenty-four percent in August, 1974. The loss of forty-four points in that period of time was unprecedented.[1] While economic problems beset his administration, the Watergate scandal was his undoing. This scandal involved the attempted burglary and wiretapping of the Democratic National Committee headquarters in the Watergate Hotel. The planning and financing of the operation was directed by White House personnel, and President Nixon was implicated in the coverup.

Initially, the Gallup surveys reported that a majority of Americans chalked Watergate up to politics as usual. But, by August 1973, a majority believed that "corruption" in the administration had reached serious proportions. Support for Nixon's impeachment grew slowly; by the time he resigned, sixty-five percent favored his impeachment by the House and trial in the Senate; and fifty-seven percent replied affirmatively to the question, "Just from the way you feel now, do you think his actions are serious enough to warrant his being removed from the presidency, or not?"

LBJ'S DECLINE. Some six-and-one-half years earlier, President Johnson had announced that he would not seek re-election. Like Nixon, he had been a big winner in his previous election (Nixon received sixty-one percent in 1972, and Johnson sixty percent in 1964), but he was also subject to major shifts in public opinion. Under continuous fire for his han-

★ ★

dling of the Vietnam War, he had been seriously challenged in the New Hampshire primary by Senator Eugene McCarthy. After the primary, Senator Robert Kennedy entered the race and a Gallup Poll taken just before Johnson stepped aside showed Democrats favoring Kennedy over Johnson by a margin of three percent.[2]

Johnson and Nixon had at least one thing in common: each had lost public confidence. Whether Johnson could have been reelected is debatable, but could he have been an effective president? Richard Nixon had seen the evidence against him mount and the Congress respond, in part, to public opinion. Both cases suggest that the loss of public confidence is a significant, if not fatal, blow to political leaders.

Democratic political systems should be influenced by the opinions of their members. Is this the case in the United States? Do the opinions of the public matter when the government makes policy? If so, how are the messages sent? Even if the government wants to know, have the means been developed to interpret accurately what the people want?

Does voting make a difference? If so, who votes? Do we have an informed electorate? What role do the media play in informing the public? Does it unduly influence public opinion and voting behavior? Finally, to what extent *should* public opinion play a role in policy making?

Public Opinion

DEFINITION

"Public opinion" is a seemingly easy concept that nevertheless contains many shadings and meanings. For instance, what public? All voting-age citizens? Those who know something about an issue, event, or candidacy? Those who might be affected by a program? Is it public if it is unvoiced? How must it be expressed to be public?

A definition offered in Chapter 6 suggests some of the problems with which we deal when grappling with such a concept. Public opinion is that "which the government finds it prudent to heed."[3] Another definition

★ ★ ★ *Table 8–1* ★
Public awareness of Watergate

DATE	% OF PUBLIC WHO HAD HEARD OR READ ABOUT WATERGATE
June 17, 1972	Break-in and discovery
Sept. 22–25, 1972	52%
April 6–9, 1973	83
April 17–20, 1973	91
May 11–14, 1973	96
June 1–4, 1973	97
June 22–25, 1973	98

Source: The Gallup Poll, Princeton, New Jersey, 08540. *Gallup Opinion Index,* 111 (September 9, 1974), p. 7.

With his family present, President Richard Nixon addresses his supporters after bowing to public opinion by resigning from office in 1974.

is also useful; it is "the complex of preferences expressed by a significant number of persons on an issue of public importance."[4] We need not be concerned with opinions on such things as the latest fashions in dress, music, and Hollywood stars, which are totally irrelevant to government. In short, we focus only on those events, issues, situations, and persons which might require government action. Members of the government may find their attention drawn to these matters for reasons such as the scope of their jurisdiction (e.g., media criticism of an existing program); the potential for program expansion (and members of the government are human beings too—they are as adept at empire-building as was Caesar); or perhaps fears and hopes regarding election chances.

Take, for instance, the issue of congressional ethics. For most people, most of the time, it is probably an irrelevant issue, except to dismiss the notion by saying, "they're all crooks, anyway." But in the aftermath of Watergate a tough new ethics code was pushed through Congress, and many legislators were concerned about their chances at re-election if they did not vote for a crackdown (see insert).

TYPES OF PUBLICS

Public is a very broad term. Why seriously discuss "public reaction" to some issue or event, if only a small percentage of the population is aware of it? Thus, we com-

A former staff member in the Congress commented about the new ethics resolution, suggesting how members looked at it.

Once it reached the floor, a yes vote was inevitable. . . . Voting against it was like voting yourself a case of political syphilis.

Source: Quoted in Laurence Leamer, "Squaring Off in Washington: Tip O'Neill vs. Jimmy Carter," *New York*, 10 (May 16, 1977), p. 8.

monly differentiate among various types of publics—the mass, the attentive, the relevant, and the opinion-making.

MASS PUBLIC. The **mass public** comprises a majority of voting-age citizens. We often speak of informed and participating citizens in the United States, but this is usually more fictitious than real. Most of us, most of the time, on most issues, are part of the mass public. The mass public, in short, is a group so indifferent or passive that its members have little inclination to translate their opinions into government policy by communicating with government decision-makers.[5]

ATTENTIVE PUBLIC. On some issues, part of the mass public may nonetheless become very concerned, if they see an issue as somehow relevant to them; then this part joins a more select group, the **attentive public.** Perhaps ten percent of the people regularly constitute the attentive public. They are not opinion-makers, for they do not have access to the media; but they are well informed and provide a critical audience for the opinion-makers. Who are the members of the attentive public? Research shows that most of them are substantially above average in income, education, and most measures of social status. They may or may not have a personal stake in the issues to which they pay attention, but paying atten-

tion to politics and staying informed is a natural part of their way of life. It may be "to fill a need for knowledge, to satisfy their curiosity, to help solve problems, to fulfill the sense of duty that a good citizen must be informed."[6]

RELEVANT PUBLIC. Closely linked to this is the concept of a **relevant public.** These are individuals who have a personal interest in the outcome. That is, they have a deep and abiding interest in the issue and the way it is resolved. However, there is no necessary lack of attentiveness for one reason or another, and members of the relevant public could fall into the mass public just as easily. But, those who are always in the mass public, especially when some issues are clearly relevant to them, could be described as the "losers" in our society, for they are locked into a cycle of low education and inattentiveness, unable to see how the government affects their lives. Other members of the relevant public may be highly involved, whether well-educated or not.

OPINION-MAKING PUBLIC. Membership in the **opinion-making public,** perhaps one to two percent of the population, changes from issue to issue. Some opinion-makers, such as newscasters, editors, and politicians, may shape opinion on many issues. There are others, however, who are single-issue opinion-makers, such as speakers for particular causes

Members of the attentive public tend to possess above average incomes, education, and social status, and it is part of their life-style to keep themselves informed on current issues.

wagon until other problems, particularly the economy and government corruption, displaced environmental issues.

ELEMENTS OF OPINION

If we were simply to state that "public opinion on thus-and-such an issue is *X*," we would probably be falling into the same error as that made by many public figures and media personalities. Public opinion has many qualities, and it is difficult to assign a label and assume that it is fixed and unchangeable. Further, opinions are of interest to government because they may represent a need for new programs or changes in existing policies.[7]

or groups. When leading TV commentators, newspaper editorial writers, or key elected officials—the multi-issue opinion-makers—ignore a problem, there is little public discussion and the issue does not become a part of the political agenda. When opinion-makers are silent, legitimate public needs are generally ignored. The poor, especially, are likely to be the losers when this happens. Decision-makers then have a relatively free hand, and can respond to the pressures of the single-issue opinion-makers, who represent special interests with a stake in a particular question of public policy.

On questions of more general but relatively unpublicized concern, political leaders rarely take the lead in forming opinions or advocating policy. For example, environmental issues captured little attention in Congress until the Santa Barbara oil spill of 1969. After that event many legislators got on the band-

DIRECTION. The **direction of opinion** is of primary interest, for it signifies whether people are leaning toward or against certain positions or personalities. If eighty-five percent of the voting-age public feels positively about some given issue, this may be a real clue to the government that something should be done. Or if a large proportion of the public has no opinion at all, it could suggest either that policy-makers have a free hand, or that the issue can be safely ignored. Knowing only whether opinion on an issue is basically favorable or unfavorable is relatively useless, no matter how much public figures may like to cite surveys which show that clear majorities favor their own positions.

INTENSITY. One of the many factors of opinions rarely measured by the polls is the **intensity of opinions,** or how strongly they are held. Take that same eighty-five percent we mentioned as favoring a certain issue. While it may appear impressive, and television commentators may raise their eyebrows while mentioning the figure, it is virtually meaningless unless we know how strongly it is held. If for instance, most of the eighty-five percent answered the poll-taker with a "yes," but with a who-gives-a-damn shrug of the shoulders, then people are not very intense about the issue. Members of Congress can easily be deceived into believing that they have strong majorities on their side if the majority is there in numbers, but not in passion. Or, take the other side of the coin. If the remaining fifteen percent was violently opposed to that issue, and the eighty-five percent does not have a strong opinion, what should members of the government do?

The reason that intensity is so important when considering opinions is that it indicates a potential for action. Those who have less strong feelings are not very likely to act on them. President Carter found this out in 1980 when he sought re-election. Most Democrats liked Carter and preferred him to his challenger, former California Governor Ronald Reagan. But the Reagan forces had intensity of attitudes and opinions on their side, and turned out in larger numbers than did Democrats. In short, a weakly held opinion is less likely to be expressed or acted upon.

STABILITY. Are our political opinions likely to change, or are they fairly **stable attitudes?** One problem government decision-makers face is in determining how changeable our opinions are, for this provides a clue as to our response to new programs and candidacies. Our hypothetical eighty-five percent, for instance, might switch to opposing the program they once favored under the right circumstances. Or, they might have previously been on the other side. This quality or element of opinions is linked to the problem of intensity. Opinions which are strongly held, for instance, are not likely to be changed, or else

can change under only the most extreme of circumstances, if ever.

Take the 1980 Democratic race for the presidential nomination. Jimmy Carter was initially favored by only twenty-seven percent of the Democrats as against fifty-nine percent for Edward Kennedy. In a few months the tables were turned, and the President clearly led both in the polls and in the hunt for delegates (see Figure 8-1). Clearly, neither Carter nor Kennedy had a great deal of intensity or stability of attitude favoring or opposing them. Hence, the rapid shift could take place.

CARTER'S RISE AND FALL. The instability and volatility of public opinion on candidates is clearly demonstrated by the 1980 presidential election. Before either party held its national convention, President Carter held a lead of two to nine percent in the Gallup Poll as well as in other national surveys. Independent candidate John Anderson expected the support of roughly twenty percent of registered voters, and there was early talk of the electoral college's being unable to produce a winner with the needed 270 votes.

This likelihood seemed to increase in June, when Mr. Reagan began to pull even with the President and then go ahead, and Mr. Anderson was receiving the support of a quarter of those interviewed. Suddenly, in August, after the Republican convention and before the Democrats met to nominate Mr. Carter, Reagan was leading by a comfortable sixteen percent, and his lead seemed to be on the increase even further. Shortly after the Democrats nominated Carter and he received the lukewarm support of Senator Kennedy, the lead was an insignificant one percent in the Gallup Poll, and Mr. Anderson's support was evidently melting away, now down to fifteen percent. Would Carter pass Reagan again? News commentators had a field day with the "horserace" aspect of this election, as it seemed to be "too close to call" since the polls showed such a tight contest.[8]

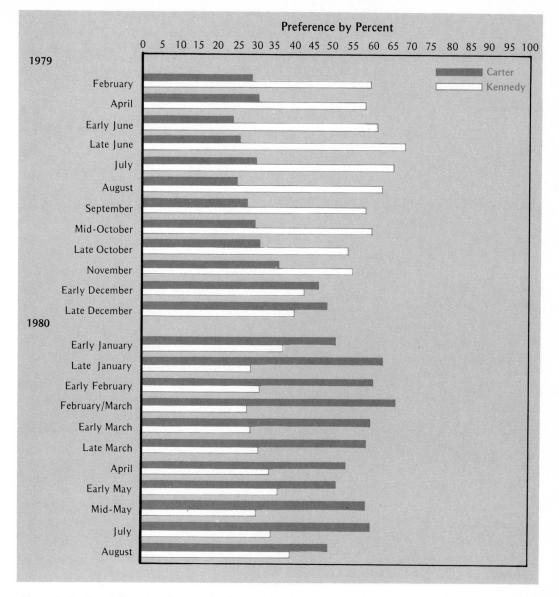

Figure 8–1 Instability of preferences in the Democratic Party: 1979–1980. (*Source:* Gallup Opinion Index.)

Even at the end, just before the election, as Mr. Anderson's chances of carrying even a single state seemed remote at best, many polls showed that the election was going to be very close. Yet, the final results showed a gap in excess of nine percentage points. Was this the fault of the polls, as some have suggested? Or, does this reflect the essential volatility of public opinion? We will discuss the accuracy of polling shortly, but suggest that these sudden

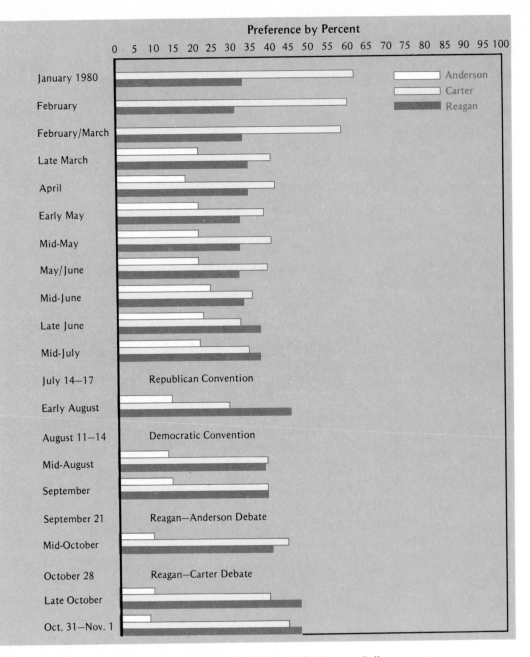

Figure 8–2 Reagan, Carter, and Anderson in the Gallup Poll. (Source: Gallup Opinion Index.)

changes in public appraisals of candidates are not at all uncommon.

Similar changes can occur with issues as well. A year before Mr. Carter took office, a Gallup Poll showed that the energy problem was not rated as one of the six most important problems facing the country.[9] In one of his first major addresses to the nation, the President struck hard at the problem, calling it the "moral equivalent of war," stressing the seriousness of the matter. (When Congress was in the process of gutting his program, it came to be known as M.E.O.W.) Initial polling showed a clear majority of those surveyed agreed with the President. But as the implications of his proposals became clear, support diminished as people saw that they might be losers, if they had to pay high taxes for "gas guzzlers," pay increased gasoline taxes if the rate of consumption did not slow down, and make other personal sacrifices. As his energy package was torn apart by Congress, President Carter threatened to mobilize public support—the army that was not there—in order to get Congress to approve his program. It seems that Congress may actually have been quite responsive to public opinion. How responsible it was is another story.

Finding out what voters think—between elections—is a challenge to every officeholder.

Measuring Public Opinion

George Gallup, the well-known pollster, has said:

In a democracy we demand that the views of the people be taken into account. This does not mean that leaders must follow the public's views slavishly; it does mean that they should have an accurate appraisal of public opinion and take some account of it in making their decisions.[10]

While we often question whether or not politicians and bureaucrats heed our views, the fact is that many of them constantly try to gauge our opinions. Congressmen are particularly sensitive to their constituency's views, although their perceptions may not always be accurate. Officials keep a constant eye on the media, to which they ascribe some special insight into the public mind. "Many officials treat the press and public opinion as synonymous."[11] Political polls are widely used. They are quoted in the press, leaked to reporters by candidates, and closely watched by officeholders.

THE BASICS OF SURVEY RESEARCH

There are contrasting sets of opinions regarding survey research. On the one hand there is a notion that surveys are impossible to do properly, that a few hundred or thousand people cannot reflect the true opinions of a nation as large as ours. Thus, Gallup's track record, for instance, is debunked as "lucky," and his detractors like to point to the error of 1948, when he predicted Dewey as the winner. On the other hand, for some there is a mystique about polling, suggesting that surveys are so scientific that they cannot be wrong. Both attitudes reflect ignorance as to how surveys are done, and their inherent strengths and weaknesses.

RANDOM SAMPLING. The essential element of any survey is the **sample.** Since it is usually impossible to interview or question all the people in a given population, it is necessary to draw a sample that reflects the most important characteristics of the population from which the sample is drawn. In the case of presidential elections, for instance, the population about which we wish to generalize would be voting-age citizens, and we would probably more narrowly define it as those who intend to vote. Samples may be drawn in various ways, but the principle underlying all good samples is one of randomness. Picking names out of a hat, or conducting street-corner interviews is anything but random, for there is no equal chance, as a **random sample** provides, of any one person's being selected. In national surveys, there is an attempt to get a broad geographical distribution, and well-planned surveys take this into account when drawing samples. Thus, the Gallup Poll normally draws its sample from some three hundred predetermined areas around the country, and the Harris Survey is conducted in a similar manner. Discretion as to whom one should interview is not left to the interviewer's biases or whims.

SAMPLE SIZE. It is also necessary to have a sample of a large enough size so that generalizations can be made safely. The commercial surveys with which most of us are familiar, such as the Gallup and Harris polls, typically have something like 1,500 respondents. This fact continually astonishes those who believe that surveys are either useless or supernatural, for how can such a small number adequately allow us to guess how the general voting-age population feels about issues and candidates? Suffice it to say that, properly done, such a **sample size** will allow the pollster to make a prediction that is accurate within two or three percentage points.

A CLASSIC MISTAKE. However, size alone cannot guarantee the accuracy of a sample. The classic example of this sort is the 1936 poll taken by the now-defunct *Literary Digest.* More than two million people responded to a postcard poll, and the magazine confidently predicted a victory for Governor Alf Landon of Kansas over FDR, by a margin of three to two. The margin was correct, but the predicted winner was not, and this in the largest "survey" taken. The chief problem in this poll was that the sample taken was anything but random. Names had been drawn from lists of people who owned automobiles, had telephones, and subscribed to that magazine. What the *Literary Digest* publishers did not realize was that people who fell into those categories were probably least likely to reflect the economic realities of the time—a Great Depression, when phones, autos, and magazines were luxuries for most people.

THE QUESTIONNAIRE. The **questionnaire** is another element used in surveys, and it is not the simplest thing in the world to draw up properly. For instance, how would you determine someone's party identification, if any? Good survey researchers have a large body of knowledge and experience on which to draw when determining wording, placement, and so forth. A properly written questionnaire should be neutral, and not suggest any "right" or "wrong" answers to the respondent.

CONGRESSIONAL SURVEYS. Policy-makers have been turning increasingly to the use of surveys to determine not only the chances of their own re-election, but how constituents feel about selected issues. One means used is the so-called *congressional* or **legislative poll**.[12] Members of Congress send out newsletters, with attached questions, seeking the opinions of their constituents on important issues. These surveys are typically flawed in every conceivable manner. The sample is often anything but random, as replies tend to come from members of the legislator's own party, hardly a representative group by any means. Those who answer, even if from the opposite party, usually tend to agree with the legislator anyway, as those who disagree are either unaware of his positions, or else feel that their opinions won't really count much. The response rate is often less than twenty percent, which is scarcely likely to be representative of the true distribution of attitudes in a district or state.

Even when there are responses in the tens of thousands—and congressmen love to flourish survey results that support their own positions—the results are likely to be anything but scientifically accurate. Finally, the questions usually provide cues as to what the congressman feels is an appropriate answer. ("Should we allow welfare cheats to bankrupt our nation?") Although some members of Congress may honestly feel that they are guided by these surveys, the real value is probably to provide cheap advertising for the legislator, by keeping "his name and policies before the public."[13]

THE ACCURACY OF POLLS. If we exclude the congressional poll, there is an excellent record of accuracy for the major commercial survey organizations, with the glaring exception of 1948. It should be borne in mind that they work on the basis of probability. Thus, if Gallup predicts that Candidate X will get fifty-five percent of the vote, he is doing so with a built-in allowance or **margin of error** of some three percent. What he is really saying is that the chances are ninety-five percent (or nineteen to one if you prefer gambler's odds) that X will get between fifty-two percent and fifty-eight percent of the vote. If X then gets exactly 55 percent, or 54.9 percent, or 55.1 percent, Gallup looks like a magician to those who revere the surveys. Yet, Gallup could not be at all certain that this would happen, as he was only nineteen-to-one sure that the results would fall within a given range.

The 1948 fiasco has been attributed to the fact that pollsters quit interviewing too soon, failing to take into account substantial late shifts in voter sentiment. Their samples were also overburdened with college-educated respondents, on the assumption that less educated people are often non-voters. But the turnout of the so-called non-voters was very heavy in 1948. The lessons of the election resulted in further sophistication of survey techniques.

Except for 1948, the Gallup Poll has indicated the winning candidate in presidential years, or the winning party in congressional years, in every election since 1936 (see Table 8–2). In 1948, the poll predicted that only 44.5 percent of the vote would go to the Democrat, Harry S. Truman. He actually won 49.9 percent of the vote. In the twenty-two other elections, however, the Poll's average deviation has been approximately two percentage points, and it has generally been declining.

THE EFFECTS OF SURVEYS

On complex economic, social, and foreign policy issues there is some doubt what impact the polls have on decision-makers. One could argue that politicians would be depressed if they paid too much attention to issue polls. A 1970 Gallup Poll found that

How accurate is the Gallup Poll?

YEAR	FINAL SURVEY*	FINAL RESULT*	DIFFERENCE	AVERAGE ERROR
1980	47.0% Reagan	50.8% Reagan	−3.8%	
1978	55.0 Democratic	54.6 Democratic	+0.4	
1976	48.0 Carter	50.1 Carter	−2.1	1.5%
1974	60.0 Democratic	58.9 Democratic	+1.1	
1972	62.0 Nixon	61.8 Nixon	+0.2	
1970	53.0 Democratic	54.3 Democratic	−1.3	
1968	43.0% Nixon	43.5% Nixon	−0.5%	
1966	52.5 Democratic	51.9 Democratic	+0.6	
1964	64.0 Johnson	61.3 Democratic	+2.7	1.6%
1962	55.5 Democratic	52.7 Democratic	+2.8	
1960	51.0 Kennedy	50.1 Kennedy	+0.9	
1958	57.0% Democratic	56.5% Democratic	+0.5%	
1956	59.5 Eisenhower	57.8 Eisenhower	+1.7	
1954	51.5 Democratic	52.7 Democratic	−1.2	1.7%
1952	51.0 Eisenhower	55.4 Eisenhower	−4.4	
1950	51.0 Democratic	50.3 Democratic	+0.7	
1948	44.5% Truman	49.9% Truman	−5.4%	
1946	58.0 Republican	54.3 Republican	−3.7	
1944	51.5 Roosevelt	53.3[1] Roosevelt	−1.8	
1942	52.0 Democratic	48.0[2] Democratic	+4.0	3.6%
1940	52.0 Roosevelt	55.0 Roosevelt	−3.0	
1938	54.0 Democratic	50.8 Democratic	+3.2	
1936	55.7 Roosevelt	62.5 Roosevelt	−6.8	

*Figures shown are winners' percentages of the two-party vote, except in 1946, 1968, 1976, and 1980.
1. Civilian vote 53.3% + FDR soldier vote 0.5% = 53.8%. Gallup's final survey was based on the civilian vote.
2. The final report said Democrats would control the House, which they did even though the Republicans won a majority of the popular vote.

Source: The Gallup Poll, Princeton, New Jersey, 08540. Adapted from *Gallup Opinion Index,* 183 (December 1980), p. 12.

only fifty-three percent of the sample knew the name of their representative. While sixty-two percent knew their representative's party, only twenty-five percent knew how he voted on any major bill.[14] Other surveys have highlighted the distressing reality that, as a nation, we are very poorly informed on international affairs.[15]

THE BANDWAGON EFFECT. Another potential effect of the surveys is on voting behavior. We must thus briefly anticipate the next section of this chapter. The **"bandwagon effect"** of surveys has often been mentioned by those who either fear or worship survey research. Candidates may be afraid that a poor initial showing in the polls will create a loser's image, and keep their potential supporters home. On the other side of the coin, those who are initially ahead in the polls may cite such surveys so that others will hop on their bandwagon. There is little evidence supporting the idea that the polls have a bandwagon effect, although it provides a convenient excuse to candidates who will not place the blame for losing on their own shoulders.[16] Candidates may occasionally manipulate the polls in order to show that they are ahead. In 1968, for instance, a supporter of President Johnson commissioned a survey designed to show that LBJ was clearly the preferred candidate. The "survey" was anything but representative, having been taken in a highly Democratic area.[17] There are times, it seems, when the desire to be a winner makes one forget the essentials of ethical behavior.

TIGHT ELECTIONS. Perhaps the Truman–Dewey, Johnson–Goldwater, and Nixon–Humphrey elections show that the key variable determining the influence of the polls is the effect they have on a candidate's strategy. During the 1968 campaign, for instance, a badly trailing Hubert Humphrey almost closed the gap. The polls showed him behind by fifteen percentage points in September and October. The image of him as a loser undercut his fund-raising efforts (a problem that beset McGovern in 1972). However, in the final weeks of the campaign, Humphrey attempted to emulate Truman (in 1948) by turning the underdog image to his advantage. It almost won him the election. Interestingly enough, Nixon, like Dewey in 1948, may have been lulled into a false sense of security, which was reflected in his sticking to a campaign of vague generalities.[18] And Carter's 1976 campaign theme of "you can trust me" may have initially served him well, but was fuzzy enough to cause many voters to switch to Ford in the last week of the campaign.

GAUGING OPINION: NON-SURVEY METHODS

Surveys are the most obvious means of judging where people stand on issues and candidates, but they are not the only means used. There are various ways by which political officeholders try to stay in touch. However, they do not always adequately reflect popular opinion, and lawmakers who allow themselves to be deceived into thinking otherwise may be fooling us as well.

NEWSPAPERS. It is common for legislators and their staffs to keep an eye on the newspapers from back home. These are read not only for their editorial content, but also for the letters to the editor. To assume that newspaper editorials mirror the thinking of the average citizen would be a serious mistake. Members of the press, especially those who write political editorials, are part of the opinion-making public. Consequently, they are or should be better informed on most issues than members of the mass public. It is possible to open almost any newspaper on any given day and find editorials dealing with issues of which the mass public is only dimly aware at best. If newspaper endorsements reflected the opinions of the average reader, we would seldom elect a Democratic president, since many editorial writers reflect a pro-Republican bias.

LETTERS TO THE EDITOR. An inaccurate and unrepresentative basis for judging opinions is the "Editor's Mailbag" section. National surveys show that most people have never written a letter to the editor.[19] And many letters deal with matters that are not political in nature. Letters commending the local school band for its performance in the state finals are all very well and good, but there is little in them to draw a legislator's attention—unless he wishes to dash off a telegram of congratulations, which might be useful come re-election time. Finally, many letter writers are not only unrepresentative of their neighbors, but also repeaters, writing frequently to the papers on some subject or other.

LETTERS TO LAWMAKERS. On the other hand, lawmakers may pay a great deal of attention to the mail which comes to their offices. When the usual information-request mail is sifted through, and pamphlets have been mailed out telling how to plan your septic tank, raise your children, or obtain social security benefits, there is a residuum of other personal appeals. There may be requests for flags flown over the Capitol, or appearances to make a speech. A good deal of congressional mail consists of appeals to straighten things out with the bureaucracy, such as seeing that an overdue tax refund is processed, or finding a missing social security check, or assisting in getting one's son transferred from the infantry (he can't shoot straight, anyway) to computer school, and the like.

For clues as to how his constituency is thinking on policy, the legislator usually has several staff members sort the mail and find out whether mail is running in favor of or against certain proposals. The letters may reflect some knowledge of the issue, and the lawmaker's stance, or they may be quite general. Staffs are sensitive to **"inspired mail"** and tend to discount it. Rarely does a legislator get a chance to personally read and reply to letters. Rather, a running count on both sides is kept by the legislative staff, and form replies are prepared on special machines, one of which can duplicate the representative's signature. Your "personal reply" is therefore usually quite impersonal in its handling, but at least lawmakers are usually told how constituents are reacting to policy proposals.

IMPORTANT CONSTITUENTS. Personal attention will be given to communications from persons who are personally close or important to the lawmaker. A wealthy campaign donor might not appreciate the stock reply: "Thank you for your letter. I will certainly consider its contents when I vote on this very serious matter." Those who have access to lawmakers can therefore have an unusual influence. Lawmakers also tend to hear most from those who already agree with them, and the important constituent may be one reason why this is so.[20]

HOME VISITS. Finally, lawmakers visit their districts from time to time. Their purposes vary, but most probably include the cultivation and building of political support.[21] Indeed, a good deal of time is spent with what is known as the *re-election constituency,* or the group the congressman believes votes for him.[22] When time is spent with constituents who want to discuss matters of public policy, there is a tendency to discuss past action (in which case the congressman has to defend his actions) rather than learn how constituents feel about votes not yet taken. Legislators also expose themselves most to those likely to agree with the positions they favor. Thus, meeting constituents is far from a perfect device for learning where they stand. There is some question as to the relevance of public opinion for policy making on most issues, regardless of what theorists of democracy may want.

Sources of Opinion: Political Socialization

When we are challenged by a new situation, issue, or candidacy, we are frequently able to offer an opinion on the subject. And, we can often do this without a great deal of information. How is this so?

DEFINITION

Many of our opinions are based on values which we have acquired over the years. The process of acquiring values relevant to dealing with others is frequently referred to as

Political socialization is a lifelong process of acquiring values relevant to the political process.

socialization; when values are acquired relevant to the political process, we call this **political socialization.** This process, highly important in any society, is how we learn basic attitudes toward the political system and how it functions. It is an ongoing process, and never ceases until we die. However, the greatest learning of political values probably takes place in early childhood.

THE FAMILY AS OPINION SOURCE

Children are seldom taught political values explicitly. It is most often a subconscious process: certain values are taught, and the process of transferral to the political arena is done subconsciously. Take, for instance, attitudes toward political authority. Studies have shown that children raised in homes where there is a benevolent father tend to see the president, and most political figures, as benevolent and well-meaning.[23] On the other hand, authoritarian practices, in which the child comes to see the parent as anything but Santa Claus, are likely to result in harsh attitudes toward political figures of authority such as the president.

LEARNING PARTY IDENTIFICATION. One of the more important learned political orientations is **party identification.** Children can be sensitive to the nuances of adult conversation. One study showed that sixty-three percent of fourth-graders identified with a political party, and considered themselves to be either Democrats or Republicans. This tended to be very close to the parties they associate with their parents.[24] Quite obviously, fourth-graders do not sit down, read and discuss the news of the day, and arrive at a thoughtful and rational selection of a political party. Ask yourself whether you identify with either major party, or as an Independent, and then think of your parents' preferences.

Children tend to assimilate political values and party identification from their parents.

When do you recall first thinking of yourself in this way? Or, if you do not care much for politics, does this reflect the environment in which you were raised?

RELEVANCE TO BEHAVIOR. Why is this important for the political system? In part it is because there are implications for adult behavior. If children learn subconsciously that they must be loyal to the political system, this is quite likely to carry over to adulthood. Attitudes toward political authority figures such as the president can also have implications for later experiences. Many commentators expressed fears, during the Watergate crisis, of a "political trauma" in the nation if President Nixon were found to be guilty in an impeachment and trial proceeding. Was there a trauma? Apparently we also learned other things as we grew up, including a cynical attitude toward politics in general. Rather than be traumatized, many of us simply transferred this cynicism to the president, and continued on our way.

IMPLICATIONS FOR WINNING AND LOSING. There are major payoffs, or lack of payoffs, for the children involved. Those who come from middle to upper-middle-class homes are most likely to acquire the information and attitudes which will be necessary to cope, as adults, with the political world. On the other hand, children raised in lower-class environments, unless they have some way of breaking the circle, will learn and know less about politics. Yet they are in a very real way the losers in today's society. Denied information and attitudes toward the political system (such as the desirability of participation) at an early age, they will be less likely as adults to emerge from a loser's position. In short, lower-class people have the greatest need for major changes in public policies, but are much less likely to participate in a way that will bring about those changes.

EDUCATION AS OPINION SOURCE

We often pretend that our schools are non-political, but they are intimately involved in the political process. In the types of training they offer, and the ways in which that training is imparted, they may be determining winners and losers for many years. This does not mean that high grades are the key to success in life, or that the only well-adjusted person you know is the class valedictorian. What it does suggest is that the schools are very much a part of the political socialization process.

LEARNING SYMBOLS. Recall some things you learned as a very young schoolchild. You learned to recite the Pledge of Allegiance, and to stand while doing it. The words may not have meant anything to you at first, but constant repetition may have had its effect, inasmuch as you now probably take the political system and formal government as legitimate. Symbols were also learned, such as the meaning of the American flag; the folklore and mythology of this nation were passed on in an unquestioning manner, as you memorized the Preamble for third-period Assembly. You may not have learned much that specifically dealt with the way our government operates, but a general set of positive feelings was more than likely acquired. This is not at all unusual, and indeed is part of the formal and informal purpose of schools in every nation of the world, a training for citizenship.

LEARNING SYSTEM RULES. Further, you learned something of the nature of citizenship. Rules of the game were explained, such as majority rule and minority rights. Class elections were held, initially with heads down (secrecy of the ballot—an important right!), and then later in high school with a ballot box or maybe even a voting machine. We learned not only about leading, but about following authority figures, whether it was the teacher or the class president.

PREPARATION FOR ADULT ROLES. Schools not only impart some of the attitudes and behaviors that are expected in adult life, but they also equip you for adult roles. Whether you took a general-education curriculum, or vocationally oriented courses, there was always the assumption that someday you would take your place in the adult world as a working member of society. Sex roles in politics may have been implicitly learned also. What offices in class and student government were usually held by women? How often were men elected secretary? Whether or not yours was a school that was racially integrated, you may have learned attitudes about other members of society, and their rights compared to your own. Those who attended poorer schools may have found themselves less able to cope with the demands of society, and that their status as losers has continued.

The system trains some to be winners, while others are unable to break out of a loser status. But, no matter what is taught, the schools are an important socialization force, following hard on the heels of our families, and are decidedly political in nature.

ADULT SOCIALIZATION

The process of learning about our government and the way it works does not end with passage to adulthood. As adults, we tend to become more aware of government, and may see that we have something to gain from it. This is probably reflected by the tendency of adults to vote at higher rates as they age (see Table 8–3). But, also as adults, we react to issues which we see as relevant to ourselves. If we own property, then property taxes and government spending become sub-

ject to our scrutiny (and probably to our complaints). Values and attitudes learned earlier in life are called into play, and are applied to the new situation.

GROUP INFLUENCES. If we have not already learned values which are seen as relevant, then we are subject to the socialization influences of those around us, including our family, friends, neighbors, and members of professional organizations. Family, co-workers, and fellow club members all help shape our opinions, mainly because of our desire to conform to their norms in order to win and maintain acceptance. Factors that enhance a group's persuasive effect include smallness of size, frequency of contact, sense of solidarity, and homogeneity (members sharing common characteristics).[25]

A person's race, sex, religion, and ethnic background may influence his or her opinion either individually or as a participant in a group whose membership is based on one of these characteristics. Such groups show varying cohesiveness, depending on the issue in-

★ ★ ★ *Table 8–3* ★
Voter turnout, by age group: 1968–1980

AGE GROUP	% OF TURNOUT			
	1968	*1972*	*1976*	*1980*
18–20 yrs.	33.6%	48.3%	38.0%	35.7%
21–24	51.1	50.7	45.6	43.1
25–34	62.5	59.7	55.4	54.6
35–44	70.8	66.3	63.3	64.4
45–54	75.1	70.9	67.9	67.5
55–64	74.7	70.7	69.7	71.3
65–74	71.5	68.1	66.4	69.3
75 +	56.3	55.6	54.8	57.6

Source: U.S. Bureau of the Census, *Current Population Reports*, Series P–20, no. 304 (December 1976), p. 3; and no. 359 (Advance Report, January 1981), p. 4.

volved, perhaps because their members are diverse in occupational, educational, and economic background. The issue of birth control, for instance, finds Catholics divided on questions relating to abortion laws. The Jewish population, on the other hand, generally takes a pro–Israel stance on Middle East questions. Other issues can divide people along ethnic lines.

Women's organizations such as NOW (National Organization for Women) further the political involvement of women. The 1970s might be labelled the "Decade of the Woman" as females sought elective and appointive offices from the lowest to almost the highest levels. Women have led the fight both for liberalization and repeal of abortion laws. Geography can also be a factor in developing political opinions; this is apparent in the regional strengths of the major parties.

When the norms, attitudes, and membership of our closest ties overlap with those of other groups, the probability of conflicting pressures is reduced. For instance, membership in the AFL–CIO, the American Medical Association, or the Chamber of Commerce each implies a certain class background which will correspond to the class setting of most of the individual's contacts.

Group membership can provide a powerful stimulus to political participation and the expression of one's opinions. Members of the gay community, for instance, were long reluctant to declare their sexual preference until organizations were formed which made it possible for them to do so. As more and more such organizations were formed, and members publicized their homosexuality, people of this inclination were persuaded to join, and bring pressure on the government to eliminate discrimination in matters of jobs and housing. The group, as a shaper of opinion, is usually most effective when it deals with a subject within its narrow realm of competence and, therefore, most relevant to its members.

Sources of Opinion:
The Mass Media

Are we manipulated? Are radio, television, newspapers, and magazines irresistible manipulators of public opinion? Are their presentations unbalanced and subjective? Attacks on the media during the Johnson and Nixon administrations, particularly over Vietnam and Watergate, have made these questions very important in contemporary America.

Most of the information upon which many people base their opinions is received directly from the mass media or indirectly from peers who pay attention to the media. However, with the exception of the three major TV networks (ABC, CBS, NBC), a few newspapers with nationwide distribution (*New York Times* and *Washington Post*), and magazines such as *Newsweek* and *Time,* most "mass" media are aimed at an audience that is geographic (local newspaper), economic (*Fortune* magazine), ethnic (foreign language press), or racial (*Ebony* magazine).

WIDE AUDIENCES

The media, particularly television, reach a huge audience. The 1970 census reported that eighty percent of the population read a daily newspaper and eighty-eight percent of American homes have one or more TV sets. The national Nielsen TV ratings report that on a typical 1973 evening 13,708,400 Americans watched "ABC News," 17,695,800 watched the "CBS Evening News," and 15,767,700 viewed the "NBC Nightly News." As impressive as these figures may be, their total does not equal the estimated 83–90 million people who watched the 1980 broadcast of the hit show "Dallas" in which we finally learned the answer to "Who Shot J.R.?" Newspapers with the largest 1980 daily circulation were the *Wall Street Journal*

Television, radio, and newspapers reach a huge audience, but the media's influence is greatest on the attentive public.

(1,599,559, plus another 1,604,708 in regional editions), the *New York Daily News* (1,607,040), the *Los Angeles Times* (1,013,565), the *New York Times* (841,890), the *Chicago Tribune* (780,636), and the *Washington Post* (578,831). *Time* magazine had a circulation of 4,314,279; while its rival, *Newsweek,* claimed 2,934,083 subscribers.[26]

LITTLE ON POLITICS

From these figures, one might expect each citizen to be faced with a wealth of political news stories and editorials. However, political coverage accounts for only a small portion of television or radio time. Newspapers subordinate it to their coverage of entertainment, guides to daily living, and sensational events. One study of the content of 130 daily newspapers revealed that coverage of national government news accounted for only 2.8 percent of the total space, whereas accounts of sporting events took up 11.6 percent of that space.[27] The relative slimness of political coverage reflects the commercial nature of a medium which must cater to what it believes to be the desires of its customers. Advertising revenue depends on circulation and program popularity. As a consequence, the industry tends to seek a common denominator in programming and newspaper content suitable for an audience which does not want the media to be very political. Political coverage is much more extensive in the national press—the *New York Times* and the *Washington Post*— which cater to the attentive as well as to the mass public. The national press and major TV/radio networks tend to be more liberal in their politics than the local-regional press or the local network affiliates. It was the national press and the major networks that came under attack during the Nixon administration.

SMALL AUDIENCE
FOR POLITICAL NEWS

It is part of American political folklore that the mass media have a great impact on the course of elections, legislation, and executive decisions, but it appears that no more than ten percent of adults read accounts of political events with attention and consistency. The influence of the media is probably greatest when the issue is one not ordinarily within the individual's sphere of experience. For example, organized labor may refine and expertly interpret for its members the flow of information on labor issues, but on topics such as foreign policy, pollution, and crime-in-the-street, the media provide most of the cues.[28]

Watergate is a case in point. George McGovern had tried in 1972 to make the Watergate break-in and corruption in government a major election issue, but few were interested until the press began to highlight it months later. The *Washington Post* received considerable recognition for uncovering much of the scandal, and the televised Senate and House hearings were witnessed by mass audiences. In 1974, a number of newspapers transcribed the Watergate tapes for their readers. Once Watergate had become a media issue, disenchantment with President Nixon cut across all regional and socio-economic categories. This apparent media power to shape opinion, especially on issues that are beyond the normal person's frame of reference, brings up questions about concentration of media ownership, and the objectivity of reporting.

CONCENTRATION OF
OWNERSHIP

The ownership of media in general, and the press in particular, is highly **concentrated.** Two or more daily newspapers compete in approximately 60 of the nation's 6,000 cities; and in 40 of the 60 cities, what competition exists is between morning and afternoon papers under the same ownership. Moreover, news and editorial opinion risk becoming standardized because one wire service, Associated Press (AP), sells news to papers controlling approximately 95 percent of the country's total circulation. Similarly, television presentation of the national and international news is dominated by the news bureaus of the three major networks, ABC, CBS, and NBC. Only radio has maintained considerable diversity of control, but it too is dependent upon AP and UPI (United Press International) wire services and the news bureaus of the major networks for other than local news.

OBJECTIVITY OF THE MEDIA

In the middle of his 1948 presidential campaign when most of the editorials and columns were unfavorable to his candidacy, Harry Truman observed that "whenever the press quits abusing me, I know I'm in the wrong pew."[29] Truman knew that the headlines he was receiving were working in his favor. His attitude contrasted with Nixon's running feud with the press, which can be traced back at least as far as the 1952 presidential campaign, when he was Dwight Eisenhower's running-mate. While the president can make headlines or news stories whenever he wants, Watergate demonstrated that media attention can be a two-edged sword.

Although the views of editorial writers and TV commentators are usually recognized as representing personal opinions, the average person is prone to accept the notion that the "facts" in a straight news story are **objective.** Newspeople know better. Bill D. Moyers, a former press secretary to President Johnson, once said: "Of all the myths of journalism, objectivity is the greatest." Ben Bagdikian, a reporter and critic of the media, said that in a real sense, "no reporter can be objective. If he could, he would go crazy because he can see

Viewpoint:
Nixon versus the press

The following exchange took place at a White House news conference on October 26, 1973. President Nixon was giving his overall appraisal of Watergate coverage—especially that of the TV networks.

Nixon: *I have never heard or seen such outrageous, vicious, distorted reporting in 27 years of public life.*

Robert Pierpont, CBS White House correspondent: *What is it about the television coverage of you in these past weeks that has so aroused your anger?*

Nixon: *Don't get the impression that you arouse my anger.*

Pierpont: *I have that impression.*

Nixon: *You see, one can only be angry with those he respects.*

Source: *New York Times,* October 27, 1973, p. 14.

---

more things than he can possibly report."[30] Both men meant that the selection of a story, the space or time allotted it, and the elements highlighted in it or excluded from it are subjective and at times politically motivated decisions.

WHAT TO COVER? Media bias stems in large part from the nature of modern journalism. Using TV as an example, the vast number of events from which to choose, the massive (but not particularly loyal or attentive) audience, and the emphasis on stories that provide interesting film footage all affect professional judgments on what to report and how to report it. The networks stress national and international news with high-interest and dramatic content, which often leads them to focus on conflict, adventure, and disagreement. Violence or the unusual naturally take precedence.

A MIDDLE-CLASS BIAS. Further, most broadcasters are part of our dominant middle-class culture. They view the U.S. and other societies within the perspectives shaped by the economic and social values of that culture.

Thus they generally see what goes wrong in Socialist countries more easily than what goes right, are more aware of propaganda in Russian pronouncements than American ones, consider protestors more militant than insistent lobbyists, and deem marijuana-smoking more of a social problem than alcohol consumption.[31]

Presentation of news provides a selective picture of reality. But the public is exposed to information from more than 900 television and 6,800 radio stations. This provides some counterweight to the decline in the number of daily newspapers and the increase in one-newspaper cities and towns.[32] Ordinarily, the combined media make divergent opinions available to the public.

Many Americans feel obliged to "keep up" with events, even if they do it in a superficial or haphazard manner. Media impact may actually be greatest between elections. Then, media information "strikes people at a time when their defenses are less effectively mobilized than they are during presidential campaigns."[33] During campaigns, media news must compete with entertainment as well as party loyalties, candidate preferences, and the contestants' claims. But although the long-run continuous, and cumulative influence of the media may be substantial, it would be an error to assume that we are politically "manipulated" by the mass media.[34] Rather, they provide the basic information (however selected), to which we react on the basis of previously-learned attitudes and values.

Voting Behavior

The only obvious way for most Americans to participate in politics is through voting. Despite the assumption that a democracy requires a citizenry that is not only informed and alert, but participates, we have a relatively slight political participation in our country. We suggest that levels of participation probably reflect and perhaps perpetuate

winning and losing status in the United States. There tends to be a strong association between levels of political participation and socio-economic status, as people with higher status tend to participate more. And, those in the lower classes probably have the most to gain from increased voting. In 1981, for instance, Congress slashed domestic welfare programs in trying to balance the budget. Obviously there were not enough legislators responsive to poor people in that session, due in large part to low turnout by this constituency.

VOTER TURNOUT

DECLINING TURNOUT. Approximately one-fourth of the population can be classified as relatively inactive, voting now and then and taking part in no other political activity.[35] The level of participation in presidential elections fell below fifty percent in 1920 and 1924, and stayed in the fifty to fifty-nine percent range between 1932 and 1952. The high

★ ★ ★ *Table 8-4* ★

Differences from the national average
in voting turnout for selected groups: 1964–1980

GROUP	1964	1968	1972	1976	1980
Whites	+1.4%	+1.3%	+1.5%	+1.7%	+1.7%
Northern	+5.4	+4.0	+4.5	+3.4	+3.2
Southern	−9.8	−5.9	−6.0	−2.1	−1.8
Blacks	−10.8	−10.2	−10.9	−10.5	−8.7
Northern	+2.7*	−3.0	−6.3	−7.0	−6.4
Southern	−25.3*	−16.2	−15.2	−13.5	−11.0
Hispanics	not avail.	not avail.	−25.5	−27.4	−29.3

*Includes other races

Source: Derived from U.S. Bureau of the Census, *Current Population Reports*, Series P-20, no. 359 (Advance Report, January 1981), Table A, p. 2.

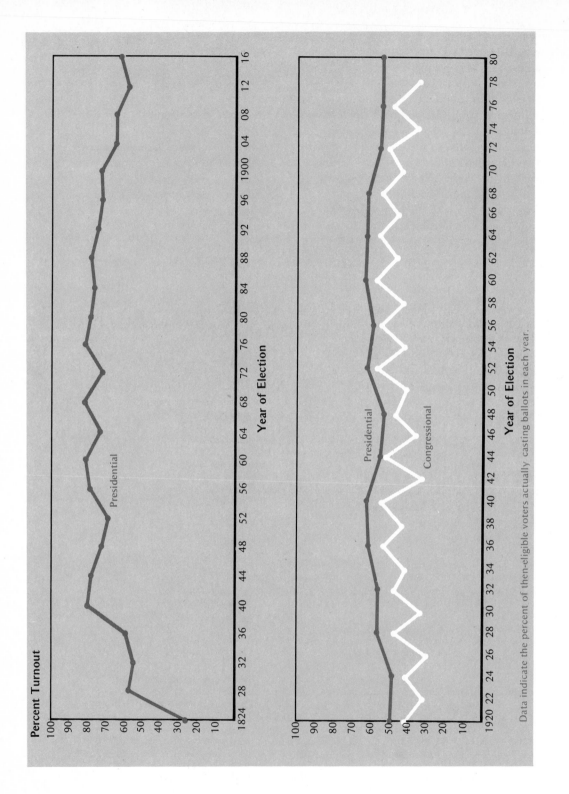

Percent Turnout

Presidential

Year of Election

Presidential

Congressional

Year of Election

Data indicate the percent of then-eligible voters actually casting ballots in each year.

water mark of **voter turnout** was in 1960, when 62.8 percent participated in the Kennedy–Nixon contest, and has steadily declined since. Balloting for U.S. representatives typically runs 3 to 4 percent behind the presidential vote. In a non-presidential year, the turnout is even lower, running about one-third in recent years.

MINORITY TURNOUT. To place the impression given by Figure 8–3 into perspective, it should be noted that the percentages are depressed by a consistently lower voter turnout in the South. In 1960, about 40 percent of voting age southerners went to the polls. In recent years though, the gap between southern turnout and that for the rest of the nation has been narrowing, for both whites and blacks. In part, we might add, this is due not only to increased participation rates for southerners but also to decreased rates for the rest of the country. However, there is evidence that the gap for citizens of Spanish origin is actually increasing. Despite major advances in voting rights legislation (see Chapters 5 and 9), there have been drops in voting rates for minorities as well as for the white majority.

In addition to blacks and those of Spanish origin—historically the losers in our affluent society—who else are the non-voters? A thumbnail sketch would include the following characteristics: those

★ of lower education

★ of lower income

★ of lower occupational status

★ under age 25 or over age 75

Figure 8–3

Voter turnout in presidential and congressional elections. (Sources: Walter Dean Burnham as cited in the Congressional Record; *U.S. Bureau of the Census; Martin Plissner and Warren Mitofsky,* Public Opinion.)

Voter turnout in the United States is low, compared to that in other democratic nations, and Americans increasingly refuse to register as members of a political party.

INDEPENDENT TURNOUT. One other group stands out and deserves special comment—those who call themselves Independents. It is a simple fact, borne out by numerous studies, that those who have a party identification tend to vote more often than do those who are Independents. And, the stronger the party identification, the more likely one is to vote. Over the last several presidential and congressional elections a declining proportion of the electorate has voted. It did not start with Watergate, though this may have contributed in part to voter alienation and disaffection. But it is also interesting that the percentage of people who refuse to identify with either party, and call themselves *Independents,* has been increasing dramatically at the same time that voter turnout has been decreasing.

WHY NON-VOTING? What are the reasons for non-voting? The Gallup Poll has looked at this question over the last several years. Non-registration has been and continues to be the largest single barrier to voting (see Table 8–5). No amount of election reform legislation can overcome simple problems of attitude, and non-registration may be a convenient excuse for those who simply do not care about the political system. Just adding those who admit that they did not like the candidates, had no particular reason, or are not interested in politics, we see that the percentages have shifted from twenty-seven percent (1968 and 1972) to thirty-two percent (1980). The sharpest increase was for those who are not registered, despite major changes in securing the franchise. This might say something about discontent and alienation.[36]

Generally, voting is highest in presidential election years. Too-frequent elections can also decrease voter turnout. Regular elections attract more voters than special elections; general elections draw more voters than primary contests; and partisan elections have higher turnouts than nonpartisan ones. Overall, American voter turnout compares unfavorably with the records of other democratic nations.

VOTER ORIENTATIONS

PARTY IDENTIFICATION. Democratic theory suggests that the voter should be well informed, and should gather information, weigh policy alternatives, and then choose a candidate consistent with his or her own philoso-

★ ★ ★ *Table 8–5* ★
Reasons given for not voting in presidential elections

REASON	1968	1972	1976	1980
Not registered	34%	28%	38%	42%
Didn't like candidates	12	10	14	17
No particular reason	8	13	10	10
Not interested in politics	7	4	10	5
Illness	15	11	7	8
Not an American citizen	**	**	4	5
New resident	10	8	4	4
Traveling, out of town	6	5	3	3
Working	3	7	2	3
No way to get to polls	**	**	2	1
Didn't get absentee ballot	2	1	1	**
Miscellaneous	3	13	5	2
Total	100%	100%	100%	100%

**Less than one percent

Source: The Gallup Poll, Princeton, New Jersey, 08540. *Gallup Opinion Index,* 183 (December 1980), p. 29.

phy. There has been considerable debate over the role that issues play in the electoral process. One thing is certain: the American electorate falls well short of any civics book model. There is agreement, however, that among issues, candidates, and party identification, the last has usually been the most important.

INCREASE IN INDEPENDENTS. The significance of party identification comes from the fact that the average voter usually depends upon the party system "to simplify, impose order on, and give meaning to his political world."[37] Is the importance of party identification and the strength of party allegiance weakening? In 1980, one-third of the electorate identified themselves as *Independents,* with most of the gain coming at the expense of the Republican Party. However, this decline of the GOP has not meant a corresponding gain for the Democrats. "Independent voters now constitute the largest bloc of voters among key groups, including young voters (18 to

29), persons with a college background, and the business and professional group."[38] When they vote, Independents may hold the balance of power in national elections. The figures in Table 8–6 suggest that it would be a mistake to view the rise of Independents as a short-run phenomenon. It may prove to be one of the most important developments in recent American politics.

As a result of the 1976 elections, the Democrats recaptured the White House, and continued their stranglehold on Congress. In 1978, capitalizing on low voter turnout and extensive organizational efforts, the Republicans made some unexpected but limited gains in contests for governorships and congressional seats. Loyal Republicans found solace in Ford's receiving roughly forty-nine percent of the 1976 vote, but his was largely a personal campaign, and he ran substantially ahead of many other Republicans. In the House elections for 1976, for instance, Republicans received about forty-four percent of the popular vote, winning about thirty-three

★ ★ ★ *Table 8–6* ★
Party identification: 1952–1980

	1952	1954	1956	1958	1960	1962	1964	1966	1968	1970	1972	1974	1976	1978	1980
Strong Republican	13%	13%	15%	13%	14%	11%	11%	10%	9%	9%	10%	8%	9%	8%	8%
Weak Republican	14	14	14	16	13	16	13	15	14	15	13	14	14	12	15
Independent	22	22	24	19	23	23	23	28	30	31	34	36	37	39	35
Weak Democrat	25	25	23	24	25	24	25	27	25	24	26	21	25	24	23
Strong Democrat	22	22	21	23	21	23	26	18	20	20	15	18	15	15	17
Apolitical*	4	4	3	5	4	3	2	2	2	1	2	3	1	3	1

*Individuals are classified as *apolitical* if they do not claim either party identification or independent status, or if they answered "don't know" when asked for their party identification by an interviewer.

Source: Data from Center for Political Studies, University of Michigan.

percent of House seats, a consequence of the districting which takes place at the state level. The future success of the Republican Party would seem, in the short run, to rest on further organizational efforts such as those which characterized their modest 1978 comeback. And, fundamental to this was the necessity to capture state legislative seats, since this is where, following the 1980 Census and reapportionment, redistricting took place. Finally, it should be pointed out that the victories of Nixon and Eisenhower were clearly personal rather than party triumphs, as their party failed to capture either the House or the Senate in each of those four elections. The 1980 Reagan victory may temporarily be classified as a personal triumph also, since his party captured the Senate, but not the House. Carter also badly trailed many other Democrats in 1976. This suggests that presidential candidates are being judged on qualities other than party label alone. Also, in 1980 we had the lowest proportion of eligible voter turnout since 1948, continuing a decline that started with the 1964 election. If fewer and fewer people vote in an election, and voting may be the only way many of us translate our opinions into policy, who loses?

CANDIDATE AND ISSUE ORIENTATIONS

Many voting studies focus on the presidential races; the contestants are highly visible and their general stand on issues well publicized. They have found a number of significant shifts among particular groups within the electorate during presidential contests. Such shifts lead to the following election classification:

★ **maintaining elections**—prevailing patterns of party loyalty persist (1940, 1944, 1948, 1964)

★ **deviating elections**—prevailing patterns of party loyalty remain intact but for some reasons the majority party does not win (1952, 1956, 1968, 1972)

★ **reinstating elections**—the majority party regains control after a deviating election (1960, 1976)

★ **realigning elections**—old loyalties are sufficiently disrupted to cause a reshuffling of majority and minority party status (1896, 1932)[39]

Classifying the 1980 election will have to await the perspective of the 1982 congressional and 1984 presidential elections. Obviously, deviating, reinstating, and realigning elections are significantly influenced by issues and candidates. But the far greater number of maintaining elections, in which party identification is the dominant orientation, says something else. In this century, not counting 1980, we can categorize ten presidential elections as maintaining, six as deviating, three as reinstating, and only one as realigning.

SOME RECENT ELECTIONS. The realigning election of 1932 was a response to the issues of the Great Depression. The maintaining election of 1948 focussed upon Democratic domestic policies and the candidate appeal of an aggressive and earthy Truman as opposed to a more patrician and confident Dewey. The deviating elections of 1952 and 1956 resulted from Eisenhower's popularity, which overwhelmed all issues or party identification, although he could not carry his party to a congressional majority. In the reinstating election of 1960, Kennedy's Catholicism was an issue contributing to the closeness of the contest. The Johnson–Goldwater election of 1964, although a maintaining election, was dominated by the issue of Goldwater's alleged extreme conservatism. Though neither candidate had widespread popular appeal, the conservatism issue led to a Johnson landslide. The deviating election of 1968 was basically an issue election. Neither candidate, Humphrey or Nixon, had charismatic qualities. How-

> *. . . the only difference I was aware of between Democrats and Republicans was that Republicans seemed to have lower handicaps and more sets of clubs while Democrats bet more—and paid off quicker.*
>
> DAN JENKINS

Source: *Dead Solid Perfect* (New York: Atheneum, 1974), p. 120.

ever, Vietnam, taxes, law and order, and race relations caused sufficient defections from the Democratic majority to give the election to Nixon. The contest was complicated by the third-party candidacy of George Wallace, with his emphasis on race and law and order. In 1972, fifty-seven percent of the nation's blue-collar workers went for Nixon and there was a significant drop-off in the Democratic vote cast by Catholics, from fifty-nine percent to forty-eight percent. Senator McGovern was seen as too liberal or permissive on law and order, drug abuse, welfare, national defense and other issues.[40] Again, it must be stressed that the American electorate has demonstrated a remarkable consistency in returning the majority party to Congress in spite of contradictory behavior when voting for presidential candidates. The 1972 trends were reversed handily in 1976. Jimmy Carter took fifty-eight percent of the blue-collar vote, along with fifty-seven percent from Catholics.[41] Thus, the Democratic Party was not only "reinstated," but so was a substantial portion of its normal support, which was lost again in 1980.

HOW DO WE VOTE? We commonly state that we vote on the basis of issues, and where the candidate stands on them. Only twenty-one percent recently stated that they rely on the candidate's image or personal qualities, while twelve percent vote according to party label.[42]

But the public's assessment of issues and specific government policies and programs is often ill-informed. Pollsters find most Americans willing to express an opinion—the "no opinion" category is usually no more than fifteen percent. But it is a disturbing fact that many people know little about the structure of their government, the length of congressional terms, or the names of their representatives and senators. On the other hand, certain public attitudes are well established and consistently held. These do influence policy direction, perhaps establishing the general boundaries within which political leaders can exercise their discretion.

One problem is trying to separate the influences of party, candidate, and issues on the voter. The fact that a voter may happen to have a party identification that agrees with his or her choice of candidate, and his or her assessment of issues, does not necessarily mean that party is the main factor. For that matter, party identification could come about because of previous choices as to candidates or issues. Starting in the mid–1960s, political scientists increasingly reported evidence of issue-based voting, including the possibility that voters were becoming increasingly well-informed, at least in terms of understanding party positions.[43] As a leading scholar has suggested,

. . . it is frequently true that loyalists of opposing parties who nonetheless share the same policy positions on a problem see their own party as the one more likely to do what they want on the issue. Strictly speaking, they cannot both be right, and often one of them is obviously misguided, yet . . . such misinformation is cumulated with genuine information to show how well informed and attentive to issues the public is![44]

SOCIAL FACTORS AND VOTING BEHAVIOR

Catholics, Jews, and blacks have historically demonstrated voting patterns that cannot be explained by reference to the usual socio-economic characteristics. This is particularly true in the case of Jewish and black voters, who have not reached the Catholics' level of assimilation into American politics. However, all three groups have in common a cohesiveness, which reflects their struggle against discrimination, and an identification with the Democratic Party.

RELIGION. Religion, like race, is hard to assess because of its association with other factors of socio-economic status. Jews, Catholics, and Protestants turn out to vote in descending order of rank, which is partly because the first two groups are more cohesive and make greater use of politics in an attempt to combat discrimination. They also tend to be proportionally more concentrated in urban areas.

The base of the Democratic Party outside the South, and particularly in the cities, has been immigrants and their descendants. Catholics were an essential element in this urban coalition, rebelling against the dominance of white Protestants or "old American stock." Catholics have in general stayed loyal to Democratic presidential candidates, with the exceptions of 1972 and 1980. Even upward social mobility and the move to the suburbs has not seriously diluted the Catholic vote.[45]

Jewish voting transcends socio-economic status even more than for Catholics. The Democrats' New Deal economic policies and their focus on urban problems particularly appeal to this most urban group of Americans, and to their economic liberalism. By whatever criteria one uses, as a group Jews must be rated considerably more liberal than Christians. One can attribute the Jewish attachment to the Democratic Party since the New Deal to their liberalism and internationalism.[46] Jewish internationalism continued after World War II, reinforced by the problems surrounding the establishment and maintenance of the state of Israel.

BLACK VOTERS. Pre–1932 election statistics show that the prevailing political identification among black voters was Republican—an attachment that was a consequence of the Civil War and the ensuing loyalty to the party of Lincoln. During the 1930s, however, black preference shifted strongly to the Democrats, without regard to individual socio-economic characteristics. They are now the group most overwhelmingly identified with the Democratic Party. This change was facilitated by the large migration of blacks from the rural South to the urban North, where they became a part of urban minorities to whom Franklin D. Roosevelt appealed. Their support for Democrats reached a high of ninety-four percent in the 1964 Johnson–Goldwater contest. And, without their support by a five-to-one margin, Carter would have lost in 1976, with only forty-six percent of the white vote.[47] However, there is one fact which must be stressed—despite legislation and enforcement to secure minority voting rights, recent declines in black voting do little to correct a "loser" status in a white-dominated society.

In addition, ethnic and religious groups tend to be attracted by candidates reflecting their own background. This is true whether we are talking about the Catholic response to John F. Kennedy, Jewish support for Republican Senator Jacob Javits, or the response of Polish voters to Polish candidates in Buffalo.[48]

CAN MINORITIES OR WOMEN WIN?

While more will be said about the rise and success of black and women candidates in the last few years, we conclude this discussion on a positive note. A study of survey results which ask whether or not individuals would vote for a woman, Negro, or Jew for president shows that positive responses increased from 1958 to 1972 as follows:[49]

	1958	1972
Woman	55%	70%
Negro	38%	69%
Jew	62%	86%

Of course, neither party has tested this shift by nominating a woman, black, or a Jew for president or vice-president. But in 1974, black candidates were elected to Lieutenant Governorships in California and Colorado, the highest state offices ever won by members of that race. A woman was elected governor of the state of Washington in 1976, joining another who was already governor of Connecticut, and who was re-elected in 1978.

What has changed in recent years is that not many people laugh when there is talk of electing a woman or a minority member president. Election to the nation's highest political office presents obstacles different from election to other political offices but the record at these lower levels reveals that changes are happening.

Kennedy's election in 1960 buried the idea that a Catholic could not win the presidency, and in 1976 Carter became the first southerner since the Civil War to be nominated by a major party and to capture the White House. What are the prospects for the election of a woman, a black, or a Jew? Politicians—a conservative breed by nature—believe that the initial breakthrough at the presidential level is more likely to come through the vehicle of a popular nominee choosing a woman, a black, or a Jew as a running-mate.

Just after the 1976 election, one Republican strategist said:

It is at least arguable that if President Ford had chosen Anne Armstrong (then Ambassador to Great Britain) as his running-mate instead of Bob Dole, he could have held the same vote and picked up enough more in a few close states to win the election.[50]

THE ERA OF WOMEN. Women are a "majority" minority, comprising more than half of the eligible voters. Some political analysts called 1974 "The Year of the Woman." Ella T. Grasso became the first woman to win a governorship (Connecticut) without succeeding her husband. North Carolina elected the first woman state supreme court justice in history. California elected the first woman mayor of a city of more than half a million people (San Jose). And Mary Ann Krupsak won the lieutenant governorship of New York. The female contingent in the House of Representatives rose from 16 to 18, and the number of women in state legislatures (443 in 1972) showed an approximate one hundred percent increase over the 443 in 1972.

More than 1,500 women fought their way through primaries, and 800 of them were major party nominees for posts ranging from city council to the U.S. Senate. These included 3 governorships (Conn., Md., Nev.), 4 lieutenant governorships, 3 U.S. Senate seats (Mo., Ore., S.C.), and 44 U.S. House races. The 44 who survived House primaries were the same number who entered primaries in 1970.

Women candidates received a boost from the reforms which opened up the 1972

Democratic National Convention, taking large numbers of women out of "lickin' and stickin'" volunteer work. The women's liberation movement encouraged women, while the National Women's Political Caucus (NWPC) aided women's efforts to lobby before state legislatures on behalf of the Equal Rights Amendment and liberalized abortion laws. The atmosphere of Watergate added to a general feeling among many women that it was time to make politics a "people's game" rather than a "man's game."

The NWPC provided campaign advice, helped raise funds, and sought out candidates with impressive professional, civic, and political backgrounds. Women ran as professionals, not as housewives looking for something to do. Led by former Representative Bella Abzug and Gloria Steinem, a network of mainly well-to-do and well-educated women raised funds for women candidates across the country.

Results have not been dramatic. Following the 1980 elections, there were only 19 women in the House, equalling the previous high. Of 31 challengers for House seats in 1980, only two were able to win. On the bright side, a woman was elected to the Senate in 1978, and she was the first ever to be elected without succeeding her husband. A second woman was elected in 1980. Hence, at this writing, women hold 19 out of 435 seats in the House, two out of 100 seats in the Senate, and none of 50 governorships.[51]

Republican Senator Nancy Kassebaum is one of the few women who is successful in national politics, although the tendency for women to enter and win elections is growing.

AN UPHILL STRUGGLE. Women still face an uphill struggle in American politics. In no political body does their representation come close to their majority status in the population. Typically, women running for office find fund-raising difficult, as they are not taken as "serious" candidates. Complicating the problem is that some women led the opposition to the Equal Rights Amendment, suggesting that male-dominant concepts are part of the thinking of many women.

BLACK CANDIDATES. Generally speaking, blacks are increasing in numbers and influence as political officeholders. Tables 8–7 and 8–8 show the increase which has taken place, broken down by years, general position, and region. A standing Black Caucus in the Congress attempts to speak with a united voice on issues central to blacks, but has had varying success at best in persuading several administrations of the validity of the views it holds. In 1978, the only black member of the Senate was defeated, following highly public divorce proceedings and various allegations of financial improprieties. No black holds office as governor, and blacks are generally in a very small minority in state legislatures as well. Nonetheless, more and more blacks are getting elected to a wide variety of offices, and their influence is bound to increase. For example, after the 1980 elections, four black Democrats became House committee chairmen.

JEWISH CANDIDATES. While constituting only three or four percent of the eligible voters, the number of Jewish members of Congress has risen from less than twenty in 1974 to twenty-seven after the 1980 elections. The

★ ★ ★ Table 8–7 ★★
A decade of progress—black elected officials: 1970–1979

YEAR	TOTAL	CONGRESS AND STATE LEGISLATURES	CITY AND COUNTY	LAW ENFORCEMENT	EDUCATION
1970	1,472	182	715	213	362
1971	1,860	216	905	274	465
1972	2,264	224	1,108	263	669
1973	2,621	256	1,264	334	767
1974	2,991	256	1,602	340	793
1975	3,503	299	1,878	387	939
1976	3,979	299	2,274	412	994
1977	4,311	316	2,497	447	994
1978	4,503	316	2,595	447	1,057
1979	4,584	315	2,647	454	1,138

Source: For 1970, 1971, U.S. Bureau of the Census, *Statistical Abstract of the United States*, 1977, Table no. 811, p. 507. For the remaining years, Ibid., 1970, Table no. 832. p. 512.

★ ★ ★ Table 8–8 ★★
Black elected officials by region: 1979

REGION	TOTAL	CONGRESS AND STATE LEGISLATURES	CITY AND COUNTY	LAW ENFORCEMENT	EDUCATION
Northeast	541	55	193	80	213
North–Central	985	89	542	105	249
South	2,768	147	1,828	233	560
West	290	24	84	68	114

Source: U.S. Bureau of the Census, *Statistical Abstract of the United States*, 1979, Table no. 832, p. 512.

Senate has six Jewish members. Jews have also been elected to various gubernatorial positions in recent years. In most cases, these elections have taken place in states with relatively small Jewish populations, suggesting a decline of anti-Semitism. Unlike women and blacks, Jews have been in the mainstream of U.S. politics a long time, and a presidential candidate from their ranks could benefit from the fact that both Kennedy and Carter were able to overcome religious obstacles to their elections.

OTHER MINORITIES. For many years, Hawaii was the only state where citizens of Chinese or Japanese ancestry had a reasonable chance of election. But not until 1974 did even that state elect a governor of Japanese ancestry. In addition to Hawaii's usual pattern of sending Oriental–Americans to the House and Senate, there are indications of modest changes elsewhere. In 1974 California elected the first Japanese–American from the mainland to the House. This was followed in 1976 by one to the Senate, and in 1978 by another House member.

Mexican–Americans, or Chicanos, have historically avoided political involvement, and typically have low voter registration and turnout. With rare exception, their involvement has been at the local level, notably in border states such as Texas and California. But, the 1974 election of two Chicanos, as the governors of Arizona and New Mexico, may provide the needed impetus for this minority to overcome national as well as local prejudices, and to learn the advantages and disadvantages of political involvement.

In the case of all of the minorities discussed, as well as with women, it will take a strong personality to overcome real prejudices or the obstacles that party leaders believe may exist. But we believe that in the next two or three decades one or both of our major parties will nominate and elect a member of one of these groups.

★ Issue ★

The Rise of Single-Issue Politics

A popular theme of political writers in the 1970s was that parties were in a state of decay. One reason for this was supposed to be that the parties no longer addressed themselves to the issues of the day, and people were frustrated with them.

But whether or not one believes that parties have ever been characterized by great concern with the issues—and there is considerable evidence for and against this—one thing had become clear: the parties were unable or unwilling to get involved in a broad range of very emotional issues, and something was needed to fill that vacuum.

That "something" is what we now call *single-issue politics,* or the tendency of some people to get involved in the political process out of their concern for a single issue. There is no doubting that it is one of the most sweeping political movements in our recent history. It is also one of the most upsetting to those who are normally involved in the political process. Where has it come from? Where is it taking us? What are its consequences?

BACKGROUND

At various points in our history, there have been broad political movements that have focussed on a single issue. A case in point, perhaps the strongest, was that of slavery. The parties were fiercely divided among themselves as to how best resolve the issue, and numerous groups in North and South formed to petition the Congress, and agitate in the press and in the streets. The horrible upshot of this highly emotional confrontation was the Civil War.

In this century we have seen other single-issue movements. During the Great Depression, for example, farmers organized themselves to get better prices, and their actions sometimes took quite violent forms. Veterans marched on Washington demanding better benefits, and did not leave until they were dispersed by the U.S. Cavalry, led by General Douglas MacArthur.

More recently, in the 1960s, the civil rights movement and anti-Vietnam War protests, while usually peaceful, were sometimes quite violent. But, despite whether or not physical violence was involved, these and other movements began to re-introduce an old theme into politics—are you *for* us, or *against* us? These and the movements of the 1970s followed another old political maxim—"reward your friends, and punish your enemies." That is, they would support members of Congress and other officeholders who had the "correct" point of view, and do everything possible to defeat those opposed.

THE PROBLEM

Politics in the United States has long been characterized by certain major assumptions. Among these is that people organize themselves into groups supporting particular policies. These groups, as we pointed out in Chapter 6, are typically of the "mainstream" variety, focussing on problems that affect business, labor, and agriculture. The groups have developed a certain political maturity, and each has had a certain success over the years. Among the reasons for their continuity and success is that they learned how to compromise and work with members of both political parties. The activities of these groups

are often professional in the fullest sense of the word; they have preferred to give a little to get a little, rather than risk all by confrontation and possible loss. To use an old cliché, they have been prepared to "fight" another day, and they have not tried to gain influence by making threats to officeholders that they will defeat them.

But however the membership of these groups might have felt about the issues, they typically have not and do not involve highly emotional values. Starting most recently with the civil rights movement and then the anti-Vietnam War groups, we have seen a rise in highly emotional issues, and a consequent rise in individuals who are prepared to either lead or follow to the bitter end on the basis of no-compromise. These movements cannot be accurately characterized as liberal or conservative by nature. But, it appears that more and more people are involved in highly emotional issues that affect them deeply.

Who are these people? There is no ready description, other than to call them political amateurs or novices. They may be rich or poor, young or old, Catholic, Protestant, or Jewish. They may or may not have followed electoral politics in the past, they may or may not be well informed on a broad variety of issues, but they care deeply about one issue; and they are prepared to judge political candidates and officeholders solely on their response to a certain issue.

ISSUE BASIS. What are these issues? For many of us, they are really not issues at all, but for others, they are the absolute basis for deciding how to vote. We cannot begin to mention more than a few, but they serve to indicate the concerns which have emerged:

★ *Abortion*—Do unborn babies have a "right to life," as anti-abortion crusaders feel? The very term implies the highly emotional and fervent content of the appeals made. Or, do women have an inalienable right to "control our own bodies," as some feminists have put it?

★ *Women's Rights*—Should the Equal Rights Amendment be ratified, guaranteeing legal equality of women? Who can oppose equality? Or, would this amendment to the Constitution give legal sanction to co-educational toilets and homosexual marriages, as opponents have charged?

★ *Gay Rights*—Do homosexuals of either sex have the same legal rights as heterosexuals? Should they have legal protection in seeking employment, including public employment, and especially in public school teaching?

★ *Gun Control*—Should the federal and state and local governments impose stricter requirements on the licensing of gun owners? Will this result in a decline in accidental deaths and injury? Or, is it true, as opponents claim, that "when guns are outlawed, only outlaws will have guns?"

★ *Motorcycle Helmets*—Should motorcyclists be required to wear safety helmets or is this an infringement of their personal liberties? Should the state take measures to protect all of its citizens, or should those citizens be free to decide that they do not want that protection?

★ *Farm Price Supports*—Should the federal government take steps to ensure that farmers get a "fair price" for their goods? Who can be against fairness? Or, will this result in higher consumer prices, and windfall profits for farmers?

This list could be further expanded, but we hope that the point is clear. These are issues which, for some parts of the population, invoke highly emotional responses. Not all such issues involve a polarizing of the public, with positions taken strongly on either side. But, those who are concerned with the issues may be prepared to take some form of action,

whether it be by vote, petition, or demonstration, which shows clearly that they want action, and want it now.

CONSEQUENCES

On some of these issues, and others like them, both parties feel free to take positions. For instance, until 1980 when the Republicans withdrew their support, both parties endorsed the Equal Rights Amendment. But, on other issues there need not necessarily be either a Democratic or a Republican response. Are motorcycle helmets at all related to the traditional view of politics and an appropriate role for government held by either party? To politicians in both parties, this may appear to be only a negligible issue.

But, on this and other issues, what may seem negligible to some is all-important to others. And since it is so important, they are not given to compromise, that old hallmark of politics. If one is against abortion, then allowing it only in the first twelve weeks is as unacceptable as allowing it in the first twenty-four weeks.

This rejection of compromise in any form is typical of those engaged in single-issue politics. They see their issue in simple either-or terms of black and white, good and evil. In dealing with elected members of the government, who are used to achieving compromises to satisfy the greatest possible numbers, they may run up against a stone wall of opposition. Or, government members may shy away from any form of resolution of the issue, caught in a dilemma of "darned if they do, darned if they don't." On other occasions, the remedies suggested may be extremely difficult to achieve. Opponents of abortion, for instance, have pushed for a constitutional amendment to overturn the Supreme Court's decisions in favor of abortion. Even if it were possible to frame an acceptable amendment, those supporting abortion might serve notice that they would work to defeat any official who voted for the amendment. Seeking alternatives, such as denying federal funding for abortions for those on welfare, will satisfy only the more politically sophisticated opponents, and then only temporarily. And, this can invoke the wrath of organizers for the poor, as well as feminists.

In this kind of atmosphere, politics-as-usual simply cannot satisfy those concerned with a single issue. But, in their focussing on a single issue, they may ignore the work that their legislators do on other issues. A case in point might be those legislators who are normally classified as *liberals*, such as ex-Senator Frank Church of Idaho. Yet, he and others like him routinely voted against any form of gun control, opposing their normal liberal allies. Why? Because he and the others had learned that gun-control opponents in their states would defeat them if they ever voted against their wishes, on that issue alone. Instead of taking such a risk, they would rather support their constituents' wishes, in order to fight and win other battles. Church lost in 1980, on other issues.

Can the political system sustain politics of this nature? Or, is it, as some maintain, a healthy sign that citizens are capable of becoming active on their own behalf? And what happens to traditional institutions such as parties, which have sustained themselves by building coalitions based on compromise? This could be just another temporary phenomenon, to disappear and re-emerge again at a later time. On the other hand, some feel that this is the beginning of a breakdown in the traditional political order, and that our system will never again be the same, as more people seek options to make themselves winners and not losers in the real issues which concern them.

Summary

Does public opinion affect political decisions? How well informed is the electorate? These were the crucial questions posed at the beginning of the chapter.

A democratic government must take the views of the people into account. The weight of evidence suggests that American decision-makers do try to keep their fingers on the pulse of citizen opinion, however poorly measured. On the other hand, it is clear that most people are poorly informed on most issues. Moreover, complex economic, social, or foreign affairs issues are probably little affected by public opinion. The public may view the economy as the most important national problem, but their opinions provide few guidelines on how to improve it. Yet, on a "gut" issue like corruption in government, loss of public trust can help bring down a leader, or even spur a new attempt at campaign finance reform. To put it neatly, public opinion creates the boundary lines of the field on which the game of politics is played.

We have seen that a large set of factors influences political attitudes and voting behavior; less educated, less affluent members of society have less information and participate less in political activity, including voting. Here we see an unfortunate paradox that hinders the achievement of "equality"—those who need the most help from the political process participate the least! Overall, American democratic politics caters to a relatively uninformed mass public whose voting turnout is low, a far cry from democratic theory. To balance this, the reader should remember that the two major parties share a consensus on fundamental principles. This tends to depress voter turnout because voters often look on the Democrats and Republicans as no better than "Tweedledum and Tweedledee."

Finally, opinions are formed on the basis of information received from the mass media, interpreted through long-held and deep-seated values. This is especially true when the issue is not part of an individual's everyday frame of reference. Media ownership is highly concentrated, and media objectivity open to criticism. Nevertheless, the media serve as our main continuing critic-reviewer of governmental policy and the performance of political leaders.

Terms to Remember

See the Glossary at the end of the book for definitions.

Adult socialization

Attentive public

Bandwagon effect

Candidate orientation

Concentration of media ownership

Congressional surveys

Deviating elections

Direction of attitudes

Inspired mail

Intensity of attitudes

Issue orientation

Literary Digest poll

Maintaining elections

Margin of error

Mass public

Media objectivity

Opinion-making public

Party identification

Political socialization

Public opinion

Questionnaire

Random sampling

Realigning elections

Re-election constituency

Reinstating elections

Relevant public

Sample

Sample size

Single-issue politics

Stability of attitudes

Voter turnout

Notes

1. *Gallup Opinion Index,* 111 (September 1974), pp. 4–20. This special report, entitled "Nixon Presidency," traces the rise and fall of his public image.

2. Ibid., 34 (April 1968), p. 5.

3. V.O. Key, Jr., *Public Opinion and American Democracy* (New York: Alfred A. Knopf, 1961), p. 14.

4. Bernard Hennessy, *Public Opinion,* 3rd ed. (North Scituate, Mass.: Duxbury Press, 1975), p. 5.

5. James N. Rosenau, *Public Opinion and Foreign Policy* (New York: Random House, 1961), pp. 19–26.

6. Lester W. Milbrath and M.L. Goel, *Political Participation: How and Why Do People Get Involved in Politics?* 2d ed. (Chicago: Rand McNally, 1977), p. 40.

7. For discussion of these and other opinion properties, see Key, *Public Opinion and American Democracy.*

8. *Gallup Opinion Index,* 183 (December 1980). See C. Anthony Broh, "Horse-Race Journalism: Reporting the Polls on the 1976 Election," *Public Opinion Quarterly,* 44 (Winter 1980), pp. 514–529.

9. *Gallup Opinion Index,* 127 (February 1976), p. 3.

10. George H. Gallup, "Polls and the Political Process: Past, Present, and Future," *Public Opinion Quarterly,* 29 (Winter 1965–66), p. 547.

11. Bernard C. Cohen, *The Press and Foreign Policy* (Princeton: Princeton University Press, 1963), pp. 233–234.

12. Leonard A. Marascuilo and Harriet Amster, "Survey of 1961–62 Congressional Polls," *Public Opinion Quarterly,* 28 (Fall 1964), pp. 497–506; "Congressional Use of Polls: A Symposium," *Public Opinion Quarterly,* 18 (Summer 1954), pp. 121–142; Walter Wilcox, "The Congressional Poll and Non-Poll," in Edward C. Dreyer and Walter A. Rosenbaum, eds., *Political Opinion and Electoral Behavior* (Belmont, Calif.: Wadsworth Publishing Co., 1966), pp. 390–400.

13. Wilcox, "The Congressional Poll and Non-Poll," pp. 391–392.

14. Quoted in David S. Broder, *The Party's Over: The Failure of Politics in America* (New York: Harper and Row, 1971), p. 184.

15. See Lloyd A. Free and Hadley Cantril, *The Political Beliefs of Americans* (New York: Simon and Schuster, 1968), pp. 59–61.

16. Joseph Klapper, *Bandwagon: A Review of the Literature* (New York: Office of Social Research, Columbia Broadcasting System, 1964), p. 18.

17. Leo Bogart, *Silent Politics: Polls and the Awareness of Public Opinion* (New York: Wiley, 1972), p. 32. See pp. 33–41 for further discussion of the misuse of polls in 1968.

18. William V. Shannon, "Score One for the Polls," *New York Times,* November 10, 1968, p. E2.

19. The Center for Political Studies at the University of Michigan has typically found two to seven percent of the public reporting that they had ever written a letter to the editor.

20. Raymond Bauer, Ithiel de Sola Pool, and Lewis A. Dexter, *American Business and Public Policy* (New York: Atherton Press, 1963).

21. Lewis Anthony Dexter, "The Representative and His District," *Human Organization,* 16 (Spring 1957), pp. 2–13.

22. Richard F. Fenno, Jr., "Congressmen in Their Constituencies: An Exploration," *American Political Science* Review, 71 (September 1977), pp. 883–917; and *Home Style: U.S. House Members in Their Constituencies* (Boston: Little, Brown, 1979).

23. Fred I. Greenstein, "The Benevolent Leader: Children's Images of Political Authority," *American Political Science Review,* 54 (December 1960), pp. 934–943; "More on Children's Images of the President," *Public Opinion Quarterly,* 25 (Winter 1961), pp. 648–654; "The Benevolent Leader Revisited: Children's Images of Political Leaders in Three Democracies," *American Political Science Review,* 69 (December 1975), pp. 1371–1398; John L. Sullivan and Daniel Richard Minns, "The Benevolent Leader Revisited: Substantive Finding or Methodological Artifact?" *American Journal of Political Science,* 20 (November 1976), pp. 763–772; and Greenstein's reply, "Item Wording and Other Interaction Effects on the Measurement of Political Orientations," *American Journal of Political Science,* 20 (November 1976), pp. 773–779.

24. Fred I. Greenstein, *Children and Politics* (New Haven: Yale University Press, 1965), pp. 71–73.

25. Robert E. Lane and David Sears, *Public Opinion* (Englewood Cliffs, N.J.: Prentice–Hall, Inc., 1964), pp. 39–49, provide an excellent resumé of the relevant sociological and psychological literature. See also Sidney Verba, *Small Groups and Political Behavior* (Princeton: Princeton University Press, 1961).

26. *Ayer Directory of Publications* (Philadelphia: Ayer Press, 1980).

27. Charles E. Swanson, "What They Read in 130 Daily Newspapers," *Journalism Quarterly,* (Fall 1965), pp. 411–421.

28. Robert E. Lane, *Political Life: Why People Get Involved in Politics* (New York: The Free Press of Glencoe, Inc., 1959), pp. 275–293.

29. Tom Wicker, "Mr. Truman, Mr. Nixon and the Press," *New York Times,* December 28, 1972, p. C31.

30. Quoted in "Is the Press Biased?" *Newsweek,* September 16, 1968, p. 67.

31. Herbert J. Gans, "How Well Does TV Present the News?" *New York Times Magazine,* January 11, 1970, pp. 32–43. The quotation is from p. 35.

32. James Reston, "Washington: Mr. Agnew and the Commentators," *New York Times,* November 21, 1969, p. 40.

33. Key, *Public Opinion and American Democracy,* p. 403. See also James N. Rosenau, *Citizenship Between Elections* (New York: The Free Press, 1974).

34. See Robert D. McClure and Thomas E. Patterson, *The Unseeing Eye* (New York: Putnam, 1976).

35. Sidney Verba and Norman H. Nie, *Participation in America: Political Democracy and Social Equality* (New York: Harper and Row, 1972), Chapter IV.

36. See Arthur H. Miller, "Political Issues and Trust in Government," *American Political Science Review,* 68 (September 1974), pp. 951–972.

37. Allan P. Sindler, *Political Parties in the United States* (New York: St. Martin's Press, 1966), p. 90.

38. *Gallup Opinion Index*, 112 (November 1974), p. 26.

39. See V.O. Key, Jr., "A Theory of Critical Elections," *Journal of Politics*, 17 (February 1955), pp. 3–18; and Walter Dean Burnham, *Critical Elections: Mainsprings of American Politics* (New York: W.W. Norton, 1970).

40. *Gallup Opinion Index*, 90 (December 1972), pp. 8–9.

41. *Gallup Opinion Index*, 137 (December 1976), pp. 1–3.

42. *Gallup Opinion Index*, 135 (October 1976), p. 9.

43. See, among others, Norman H. Nie, Sidney Verba, and John Petrocik, *The Changing American Voter* (Cambridge: Harvard University Press, 1976); John C. Pierce, "Party Identification and the Changing Role of Ideology in American Politics," *Midwest Journal of Political Science*, 14 (February 1970), pp. 25–42; and Gerald Pomper, "From Confusion to Clarity: Issues and American Voters, 1956–1968," *American Political Science Review*, 66 (June 1972), pp. 415–428.

44. Philip E. Converse, "Public Opinion and Voting Behavior," in Fred I. Greenstein and Nelson W. Polsby, eds., *Handbook of Political Science:*

Nongovernmental Politics, vol. 4 (Reading, Mass.: Addison Wesley Publishing Company, 1975), p.123.

45. Scott Greer, "Catholic Voters and the Democratic Party," *Public Opinion Quarterly*, 25 (Winter 1961), pp. 611–625. See also "How Different Groups Voted for President," *New York Times*, November 9, 1980, p. 28.

46. Lawrence H. Fuchs, "American Jews and the Presidential Vote," *American Political Science Review*, 49 (June 1955), pp. 385–401.

47. *Gallup Opinion Index*, 137 (December 1976), p. 1.

48. Walter A. Borowiec, "Perceptions of Ethnic Voters by Ethnic Politicians," *Ethnicity*, 1 (September 1974), pp. 267–278.

49. Myra Marx Ferru, "A Woman for President? Changing Responses: 1958–1972," *Public Opinion Quarterly*, 38 (Fall 1974), pp. 390–399.

50. Quoted in Warren Weaver, Jr., "South Opens a Door; When Can Jews, Blacks, Women Enter?," *New York Times*, November 7, 1976, p. E3. © 1976 by the New York Times Company. Reprinted by permission.

51. The Washington governor (Dixie Lee Rae) lost her 1980 bid for re-election. Ella Grasso of Connecticut resigned at the end of 1980, shortly before her death. Hence, as of 1982, there are no women governors.

Suggested Readings

Leo Bogart, *Silent Politics: Polls and the Awareness of Public Opinion* (New York: Wiley, 1972).

Walter Dean Burnham, *Critical Elections: Mainsprings of American Politics* (New York: Norton, 1970).

Angus Campbell, Philip E. Converse, Warren E. Miller, and Donald E. Stokes, *The American Voter* (New York: Wiley, 1960).

Robert D. Hess and Judith V. Torney, *The Development of Political Attitudes in Children* (Chicago: Aldine, 1967).

V.O. Key, Jr., *Public Opinion and American Democracy* (New York: Knopf, 1961).

Donald R. Matthews and James W. Prothro, *Negroes and the New Southern Politics* (New York: Harcourt Brace Jovanovich, 1966).

Lester W. Milbrath and M.L. Goel, *Political Participation: How and Why Do People Get Involved in Politics?*, 2d ed. (Chicago: Rand McNally, 1977).

Norman H. Nie, Sidney Verba, and John Petrocik, *The Changing American Voter* (Cambridge: Harvard University Press, 1976).

William L. Porter, *Assault on the Media—The Nixon Years* (Ann Arbor: University of Michigan Press, 1977).

James N. Rosenau, *Citizenship Between Elections* (New York: The Free Press, 1974).

Sidney Verba and Norman H. Nie, *Participation in America: Political Democracy and Social Equality* (New York: Harper and Row, 1972).

CHAPTER 9

The Contest for National Office

Whatever the future may hold, present conditions in the United States do enable the voters to influence, but not control, the government. . . . Elections in America ultimately provide only one, but the most vital, mandate.

GERALD POMPER
Elections in America

Shortly after dawn on the morning of November 4, 1980, President Jimmy Carter cast his vote in his home town of Plains, Georgia. Then he thanked a gathering of his neighbors for campaigning for him throughout the country. With tears welling in his eyes and a voice choked with emotion, he told them:

I've tried to honor your commitment to those other people. In the process, I've tried to honor my commitment to you. God bless you.[1]

Carter already knew something that his neighbors did not know, but would discover by that evening. The night before, his closest aides had told him that Ronald Reagan had an insurmountable ten-point lead in the surveys and that there was no hope that he would be elected for a second term.

Carter was the first Democratic incumbent president denied re-election since 1888, when Grover Cleveland was beaten by Republican Benjamin Harrison, even though Cleveland ran ahead in the popular vote. Unlike Cleveland, Carter ran far behind in the popular vote. In fact, since the Civil War, only two incumbent presidents—William Howard Taft in 1912 and Herbert Hoover in 1932—have been denied re-election by larger popular vote margins.

As for the victor, Ronald Wilson Reagan, it was a remarkable victory for one of the most underestimated men in American politics. Many people saw the former governor of California as a washed-up movie star who was too old, too simple, and too far right to be president. But, Reagan, who was only a few months shy of his 70th birthday when he was elected, became the oldest man ever elected president.

His victory culminated twelve years of trying to capture the nomination of his party. Reagan's time-for-a-change conservatism and

Less taxes, increased defense spending, and a gradual move toward balancing the budget appear contradictory. However, Ronald Reagan believed the contradiction could be handled by an attack on waste and fraud.

Lower tax rates, less spending, and a balanced budget are the keys to maintaining real growth and full employment as we end inflation by putting our monetary policy back on track.

Republican Party platform, 1980

Everybody agrees we need to reduce government spending, provide supply-side tax relief, increase defense spending, and provide incentives for energy.

Senator JOHN TOWER, Chairman,
Republican Platform Committee

One of the most critical elements of my economic program is the control of government spending. Waste, extravagance, abuse, and outright fraud in federal agencies and programs must be stopped.

RONALD REAGAN, Sept. 9, 1980, speech in Chicago

Sources: Congressional Quarterly, *Weekly Report* 38 (July 19, 1980), p. 2006; 38 (June 28, 1980), p. 1800; 38 (Sept. 20, 1980), p. 2768.

his "politics of nostalgia" promising a return to an America of plenty and power proved very attractive to voters, who took out their frustration about inflation, unemployment, and the decline in America's position as a world power, dramatized by the Iranian hostage crisis, on President Carter.

What process allowed a candidate who was unpopular among most of his party to capture the nomination? Was Ronald Reagan's fate in the contest for the Republican nomination unduly influenced by the outcome in the first two contests, the Iowa caucus and the New Hampshire primary? Are the presidential primaries a democratic means for selecting our candidates, or would a return to a system dominated by political leaders reaching their decision at the conventions actually be more representative?

Other questions raised in this chapter include: Is the advantage of those in office so great that the electoral system is less competitive than it should be? Does money have an undue influence on the process, converting a supposedly open system into one easily dominated by the best-financed candidates?

In addition to looking at these questions, this chapter discusses the process of congressional and presidential elections and the legal framework upon which they are based.

The Impact of Elections

In spite of inequities in our system, elections are a basic ingredient of democratic politics; they provide a key link between the behavior of the voter and the actions of government. True, initiatives lie with the politicians, not the voters; but elections are an indirect limit on the performance of any politician. The electorate controls the politician's job, exercising an after-the-fact sanction on actions. Successful politicians know that their policy positions can be important, and they develop a strong sense of what the voters consider the "limits of the arguable" to be. They avoid totally unpopular policies in favor of those for which mass support can be found. Of course, the meaning of elections depends not only on public actions but also on politicians' perceptions.

For example, a key issue in both the 1978 congressional election and the federal contests of 1980 was government spending in terms of priorities and the relation of spending to inflation (see insert). After the 1978 election, many politicians and observers read the results as a message from the people that "that government is best which costs the least."

And by 1980, President Carter was forced to advocate a **balanced budget** for 1981, one in which income and expenditures are equal, in an effort to fight inflation. He was forced to abandon this goal, however. Government was not costing less, and lawmakers were responding to a mainstream public outcry to cut back on social programs while increasing defense spending. Those groups hurt by the cutbacks—the poor, minorities, and urban dwellers—could not stem the shift to the right.

Elections are the major means of achieving control over the decision-making process, and the argument that elections are meaningless can be defended only if we assume that "the people" can and should directly control policy. Such direct control exists only in the realm of idealized theory, not political reality. However, "by their endorsement of particular contestants in the bargaining process, the voters can have the final word. The choice of governors can thereby become a choice of governmental policy."[2] And the laws regulating our system provide

After the 1980 California primary the three major Democratic candidates get together: California Governor Edmund G. Brown, Jr., President Jimmy Carter, and Massachusetts Senator Edward M. Kennedy.

unusual opportunities for the public's participation.

The Legal Framework of the Electoral System

The American method of choosing elected officials is unique. In other free-election nations, the role of the general electorate is restricted to a choice of candidates designated by the party machinery. In the United States, the electorate participates in a two-stage process–selection of candidates and general election.

FEDERAL REGULATIONS

CONSTITUTIONAL PROVISIONS. The Constitution stipulates who is eligible for elected federal office, and provides general guidelines for their selection. Its short list of qualifications is as follows: president—at least thirty-five years old, natural-born citizen, resident of the United States for fourteen years; senator—at least thirty years old, United States citizen for nine years, and an inhabitant of the state from which elected; representative—at least twenty-five years old, United States citizen for seven years, and an inhabitant of the state from which elected.

The Constitution established four, six, and two-year terms for the president, senator, and congressman respectively to prevent one "faction" from sweeping up all possible top political offices in one election. The time, place, and manner of holding elections for members of Congress was left to the discretion of the state legislatures with the provision that Congress could make or alter these regulations.

There is no constitutional requirement for the election of representatives by districts, but Congress imposed this rule in 1842. **Gerrymandering,** or the creation of oddly shaped districts to give one party an advantage over the other, has been a common problem since the nineteenth century.

The two-term limitation on holding the presidency and the issues of presidential disability and succession are dealt with in constitutional amendments. The other constitutional provision deals with the electoral college, already discussed in Chapter 2.

STATE REGULATIONS

Many citizens fail to vote, but are election laws and requirements a significant barrier keeping them from the polls? The constitutional amendments, civil rights acts, and court decisions discussed in Chapter 5 have extended suffrage to virtually all citizens over the age of eighteen. However, federal law does not prevent the states from establishing requirements of residency and registration.

RESIDENCY REQUIREMENTS. Residency requirements used to be the greatest barrier to voting, eliminating an estimated five million people in 1968. However, the Voting Rights Act of 1970 included a provision limiting to thirty days the residency requirement for presidential elections, and requiring the states to provide for absentee registration and voting. A person who moves from one voting place to another within thirty days before a presidential election may vote in the former election district. Later, the Court imposed the thirty-day rule for all federal elections. As a practical matter, these rules make it difficult for states to impose more than a thirty-day requirement for any election, because of the cost and complexity of establishing two separate ballots or machines on which to cast votes for federal and state/local offices.

Before these congressional and court actions, most states required the voter to live in the state for one year, the county for ninety days, and the polling district for thirty days prior to election time. Some jurisdictions imposed longer residency periods.

As of 1977, all but four states required voters to register in advance of election day by providing evidence of qualification. One state, New York, allows its residents to register by mail. Although the primary purpose of registration is to protect against vote fraud, there is evidence that it reduces voter turnout. And, the lower voter turnout among the minority poor may reflect failure to register. North Dakota (69%) has no registration requirement at all, Minnesota (73%) and Wisconsin (66%) permit registration at the polls on election day, and Maine (66%) permits registration on election day, but not at the polling place. The 1976 voter turnout in these four states, indicated by the figures in brackets, was considerably above the national average of 53 percent. It is estimated that nationwide use of election-day registration would increase turnout by 6 percent.

Unfortunately, President Carter's postcard and election-day registration proposal fared badly and were withdrawn in Congress because of partisan considerations, fear of encouraging vote fraud, and the satisfaction of incumbents with the present system.

While Supreme Court decisions and civil rights legislation have eliminated state preeminence in the area of registration and voting rights, the regulation of the nominating and election process remains a function of state and local governments. State law regulates parties, election finances (where not superseded by federal law), the selection of candidates by primaries or conventions, the form of the ballot, and the actual conduct of the elections.

THE POLITICS OF THE BALLOT. All states require a secret ballot. The two types of ballots generally used in the United States are the **party column,** or "Indiana," ballot and the **office block,** or "Massachusetts," ballot.

The first lists the names of candidates and offices in a column next to the party designation, an arrangement that encourages straight-ticket voting. Party officials prefer this ballot to the second type, which groups the candidates according to the position sought and requires the voter to make a separate mark for each position.

Position on the ballot can be important, then, particularly where the voter is asked to choose between relatively unknown candidates for lesser offices, particularly at the county and municipal level. Many jurisdictions require a system in which each party's candidates occupy the top row on an equal number of ballots. Where names are listed in alphabetical order, some jurisdictions require portions of the ballots to begin at different points of the alphabet. The concern for position reflects the feeling that some voters simply vote for the first name on the list. Party-column ballots increase straight-ticket voting, particularly among Independents.[3]

THE ANDERSON CASE. When John Anderson withdrew from the Republican nomination contest and announced that he would run in the general election as an Independent, his first obstacle was to get on the general election ballot in as many states as possible (see insert). As an Independent, he was not placed automatically on any state ballot, and he was forced to contend with a wide variety of state requirements. He added twelve lawyers to his staff to handle the political and legal aspects of the problem.

At one end of the spectrum is Tennessee, which requires a third-party or Independent candidate to collect only 300 signatures of registered voters. By contrast, North Carolina required 166,377 signatures by April 25. A few states have no provisions for "Independents," so Anderson had to call himself a third-party candidate. Moreover, some states have "sore loser" laws stating that an individ-

NAME OF PARTY	1 Presidential Electors (For President and Vice President)	2 United States Senator	3 / 4 Governor and Lieutenant Governor	5 Attorney General	6 Superintendent of Public Instruction	7 Reporter of Supreme Court and Court of Appeals	8 Representative in Congress 4th District	9 State Senator 18th District	10 / 11 / 12 State Representative 15th District (Vote for Three Only)	13 County Treasurer	14 County Coroner	15 County Surveyor	16 County Commissioner 1st District
Republican Ticket	1A RONALD REAGAN / GEORGE BUSH	2A DAN QUAYLE	3A BOB ORR / 4A JOHN M. MUTZ	5A LINLEY E. PEARSON	6A HAROLD H. NEGLEY	7A MARILOU WERTZLER	8A DAN R. COATS	9A JOHN R. SINKS	10A THOMAS E. FROSCHTENICHT / 11A PHYLLIS J. POND / 12A RICHARD L. WORDEN	13A LINDA K. BLOOM	14A ROLAND O. ARLBRAND	15A WILLIAM L. SWEET	16A RICHARD M. ELLENWOOD
Democratic Ticket	1B JIMMY CARTER / WALTER F. MONDALE	2B BIRCH BAYH	3B JOHN HILLENBRAND, II / 4B ROBERT E. PETERSON	5B BOB WEBSTER	6B JOHN LOUGHLIN	7B PHYLLIS SENEGAL	8B JOHN D. WALDA	9B	10B SAMUEL J. LETO, JR. / 11B DON McCLAIN / 12B GEORGE C. WOMAK, JR.	13B THERNER L. MILLER	14B ERNEST ANDERSON, JR.	15B	16B CHARLES L. MONTGOMERY
American Party of Indiana Ticket	1C PERCY L. GREAVES, JR. / FRANK VARNUM	2C	3C CLETUS R. ARTUST / SHIRLEY M. GEPHART / 4C	5C	6C LINDA KAY PATTERSON	7C	8C	9C	10C LARRY E. DAVIS / 11C BENJAMIN J. DIXON / 12C KENNETH LEE MANIFOLD	13C	14C	15C	16C
Libertarian Party Ticket	1D EDWARD E. CLARK / DAVID H. KOCH	2D	3D / 4D	5D	6D	7D	8D	9D	10D / 11D / 12D	13D	14D	15D	16D
Communist Party U.S.A. Ticket	1E GUS HALL / ANGELA Y. DAVIS	2E	3E / 4E	5E	6E	7E	8E	9E	10E / 11E / 12E	13E	14E	15E	16E
Socialist Workers Party Ticket	1F CLIFTON DeBERRY / MATILDE ZIMMERMAN	2F	3F / 4F	5F	6F	7F	8F	9F	10F / 11F / 12F	13F	14F	15F	16F
Independent Ticket	1G JOHN ANDERSON / PATRICK LUCEY	2G	3G / 4G	5G	6G	7G	8G	9G	10G / 11G / 12G	13G	14G	15G	16G
The Citizens Party Ticket	1H BARRY COMMONER / LADONNA HARRIS	2H	3H / 4H	5H	6H	7H	8H	9H	10H / 11H / 12H	13H	14H	15H	16H

Figure 9–1   Sample ballots: Above is a party column ballot; opposite is an office block ballot.

ual who ran and lost as a member of a party in the state's presidential primary, cannot get on the ballot as an Independent.

Anderson's legal staff challenged the early petition dates in the five states whose deadlines passed before he announced as an Independent (including North Carolina), and the "sore loser" laws. They were haunted by the memory of Eugene McCarthy's efforts in 1976. McCarthy managed to get on only twenty-five ballots, and it required a legal challenge in fifteen of them. Anderson was more successful, getting on all fifty-one ballots. This added credibility to his candidacy.

PRIMARIES.   Almost all states use direct primary elections to choose the candidates who will run in the general elections for federal offices and most state and local positions. A few states employ the pre-primary convention, in which a party convention or party commit-tees choose the individuals who will be the party's designee. This candidate then runs in a primary against people who do not have the party's endorsement. This process tells the voter who the party backs, unlike the usual primary, in which state laws prohibit official backing of any candidates. In any event, getting on the primary ballot is relatively simple, with most states requiring a petition signed by a modest number of registered voters. The primaries are financed by state funds and run by the regular election officials. Finally, presidential primaries—discussed later—are optional and are conducted under separate guidelines established by the states.

Our system is unlike that of most other nations, where candidate selection is in the hands of party leaders and activists. Primaries can be extremely important, particularly in areas where party competition is minimal, and where victory in the primary almost assures victory in the general election. But voter turn-

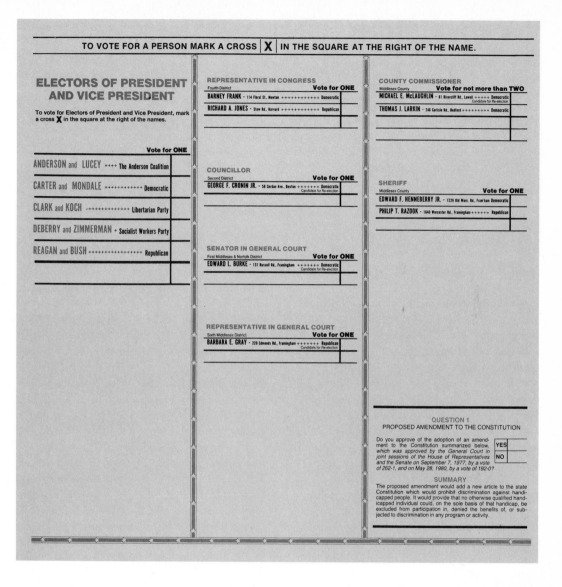

TO VOTE FOR A PERSON MARK A CROSS X **IN THE SQUARE AT THE RIGHT OF THE NAME.**

ELECTORS OF PRESIDENT AND VICE PRESIDENT

To vote for Electors of President and Vice President, mark a cross X in the square at the right of the names.

Vote for ONE

ANDERSON and LUCEY ++++ The Anderson Coalition

CARTER and MONDALE +++++++++++ Democratic

CLARK and KOCH ++++++++++++++ Libertarian Party

DEBERRY and ZIMMERMAN + Socialist Workers Party

REAGAN and BUSH +++++++++++++++++ Republican

REPRESENTATIVE IN CONGRESS
Fourth District **Vote for ONE**

BARNEY FRANK - 114 Floral St., Newton +++++++++++++ Democratic

RICHARD A. JONES - Stow Rd., Harvard +++++++++++++ Republican

COUNCILLOR
Second District **Vote for ONE**

GEORGE F. CRONIN JR. - 58 Cardan Ave., Boston +++++++ Democratic
Candidate for Re-election

SENATOR IN GENERAL COURT
First Middlesex & Norfolk District **Vote for ONE**

EDWARD L. BURKE - 137 Russell Rd., Framingham ++++++ Democratic
Candidate for Re-election

REPRESENTATIVE IN GENERAL COURT
Sixth Middlesex District **Vote for ONE**

BARBARA E. GRAY - 220 Edmands Rd., Framingham +++++++ Republican
Candidate for Re-election

COUNTY COMMISSIONER
Middlesex County **Vote for not more than TWO**

MICHAEL E. McLAUGHLIN - 61 Rivercliff Rd., Lowell +++++ Democratic
Candidate for Re-election

THOMAS J. LARKIN - 246 Carlisle Rd., Bedford +++++++++ Democratic

SHERIFF
Middlesex County **Vote for ONE**

EDWARD F. HENNEBERRY JR. - 1326 Old Ware. Rd., Fram'ham Democratic

PHILIP T. RAZOOK - 1640 Worcester Rd., Framingham ++++++ Republican

QUESTION 1
PROPOSED AMENDMENT TO THE CONSTITUTION

Do you approve of the adoption of an amendment to the Constitution summarized below, which was approved by the General Court in joint sessions of the House of Representatives and the Senate on September 7, 1977, by a vote of 262-1, and on May 28, 1980, by a vote of 192-0? | YES | NO |

SUMMARY

The proposed amendment would add a new article to the state Constitution which would prohibit discrimination against handicapped people. It would provide that no otherwise qualified handicapped individual could, on the sole basis of that handicap, be excluded from participation in, denied the benefits of, or subjected to discrimination in any program or activity.

---

out for primaries is usually low, and we believe it unfortunate that citizens deny themselves the opportunity to vote in these elections by failing to enroll as a member of a party. This act of identification does not diminish the individual's right to exercise a completely "independent" judgment during the general election.

OPEN AND CLOSED PRIMARIES. Most states employ the **closed primary,** in which voting in the party primary is restricted to party members. By contrast, a few states, Washington and Wisconsin for example, use the **open primary,** in which any registered voter can vote in the primary of his or her choice without having to reveal party affiliation. Washington goes so far as to hand the voter one ballot listing the candidates of all parties for all offices. In this **blanket primary,** a voter may choose a Democrat for one office and a Republican for another. However, the Demo-

Anderson complained in West Virginia about laws that are designed to keep Independent and third-party candidates off the ballot.

My voice simply can't be heard unless we first solve that riddle of gaining access to the ballot. We have laws in this state and other states around the country that are deliberate attempts to block access to the ballot of an independent candidate.

JOHN ANDERSON

Source: Congressional Quarterly, *Weekly Report* 38 (May 17, 1980), p. 1315.

cratic Party prohibits open primaries at the presidential level.

Party officials dislike the open primary because it demeans the meaning of party membership. They also argue that if the party is to be held accountable for the actions of its candidates, then only party members should engage in the selection process. The open primary also is very vulnerable to **raiding**— the practice of crossing over to vote in the opposition party's primary with the hope of electing the weakest candidate to oppose your party's choice.

We have argued that elections are a basic ingredient of democratic politics; however, voter turnout in primaries and general elections for the presidency and congressional seats continues to decline at an alarming rate. Some reasons for this were discussed in Chapter 8. An additional factor may be the public's disenchantment with the use or abuse of campaign money.

Money and Elections: Costs, Source, and Impacts

Running for Congress or the presidency is a very expensive undertaking, with the donors of campaign funds often expecting something in return. Testifying in 1973 before a Senate subcommittee considering the public financing of federal elections, John Gardner, chairman of Common Cause, said that the advantage of incumbency (in terms of raising funds) "raises grave doubts as to whether we presently have a competitive system of representation." Fred Wertheimer, the group's legislative director, added: "In Congress today we have neither a Democratic nor Republican Party. Rather we have an incumbency party which operates a monopoly."[4]

Surveys have shown that, as a group, incumbents are able to raise funds twice as easily as their challengers, and outspend them by approximately a two-to-one margin. Money is not the only advantage of incumbency (see later discussion), but it provides a big edge. Only 31 of the 392 incumbents entered in the 1980 House races were defeated; however, 9 of the 25 Senate incumbents lost in the general election. These figures represented an unusually high loss rate for incumbents. Most of the losers were Democrats to fall before the Reagan–led Republican tide.

THE HIGH COST OF WINNING AND LOSING

Estimates of the costs of running for office at all levels of government in presidential years increased from $140 million in 1952, to $500 million in 1976. The price tag for the pre-convention and general election phases of the presidential contest soared from $91 million in 1968 to $160 million in 1976.[5] The escalation of presidential general election costs (see Table 9–1) was checked by passage of the Federal Elections Campaign Act of 1974, which provided for public financing for the major party candidates.

CONGRESSIONAL RACES.   Table 9–2 tells the tale of skyrocketing costs of congressional races. Candidates who survived the primaries

in 1978 spent 44 percent more on House and 42 percent more on Senate races than in 1976. When the more than $41 million spent by people who lost in the primaries is added in, the total for 1978 is $195 million. By contrast, the 1976 Parliamentary elections in Great Britain cost a little more than $3 million.

Table 9–2 shows the dramatic rise in costs of congressional contests. Average expenditures continue to rise for every category—incumbent, challenger, **open-seat** (nonincumbent) **contests**—in elections for the House and Senate. House incumbents have

★ ★ ★ *Table 9–1* ★
Presidential general election campaign costs: 1932–1980

	REPUBLICAN	DEMOCRATIC
1932	$ 2.9 million	$ 2.2* million
1936	8.9	5.2*
1940	3.5	2.8*
1944	2.8	2.2*
1948	2.1	2.7*
1952	6.6*	5.0
1956	7.8*	5.1
1960	10.1	9.8*
1964	16.0	8.6*
1968	25.4*	11.6
1972	62.0*[1]	50.0[1]
1976	21.8[2]	21.8*[2]
1980	29.4*[2]	29.4[2]

* Indicates winner

1. Figures are approximate and reflect new disclosure laws that went into effect on April 7, 1972. Republican expenditures include secret funds contributed to the Nixon campaign that came to light as the result of court action.

2. Legal limit imposed by 1974 law. 1976 and 1980 figures do not include money that can be spent on behalf of campaign-related activities by party organizations. Actual spending in 1976 totaled 29.5 million for each candidate and was estimated at 38.5 million in 1980.

Source: 1932–1968 figures are from Herbert E. Alexander. *Political Financing* (Minn.: Burgess Publishing Co., 1972), p. 6. For 1972 figures see *Dollar Politics*.

widened their expenditure gap over challengers, and in the Senate, most incumbents outspent their rivals by huge margins. The heavy expenditures in open-seat contests in the House occur where the out-party believes it has a reasonable chance of wresting control from the in-party.

Expensive House campaigns often have the following common characteristics: one or both candidates face primary opposition; the campaigns are lengthy; the elections are close, with the winner receiving fifty-five percent or less of the vote; and, seats are open and party control is likely to switch.

There were 74 districts in 1978 where the race was "close," and the average combined campaign cost was $448,000, more than twice the national average. The average combined cost in the 58 open seats was approximately twice the national average. And, there has been a substantial increase in the number of races in which the combined costs reached or exceeded the quarter-million-dollar mark, a figure that used to be considered unusually high. The figure rose from 24 races in 1972 to 63 in 1976, and it reached 129 in 1978, or nearly one-third of the House contests.[6]

It is more difficult to generalize about Senate races. For example, the 1978 campaigns in Illinois, Massachusetts, and Michigan involved high costs and close outcomes. Mississippi and New Jersey had open-seat races where the expenses exceeded two and three million dollars respectively. On the other hand, a number of incumbents spent large sums on races where there was little or no opposition.

HIGH SPENDING AND WINNING. Do the big spenders always win? Although the answer is no, Table 9–3 demonstrates that in 1978, 366 of the 435 House seats were won by the candidates who spent the most. Waging a well-financed campaign has its advantages, but there is a point at which additional spending results in few benefits. Of the 19 House candidates who spent more than $400,000, 11 lost. Of the losers, 9 lost to opponents who spent less. A new House spending record was set in a 1978 New York race where the combined expenditure was $1,716,112, the loser

★ ★ ★ *Table 9–2* ★

Average expenditures by candidates for Congress: 1976 and 1978

	HOUSE		SENATE	
	1976	*1978*	*1976 (33 RACES)*	*1978 (35 RACES)*
Democrats	$ 74,757	$108,501	$1,150,000 (combined average)	$ 730,453
Republicans	71,945	107,611		1,151,407
Incumbents	79,836	111,246		1,341,942
Challengers	48,945	54,430		351,940
Open seats	114,868	159,466		508,000

Figures do not include expenditures by candidates who lost in primaries.

Source: Congressional Quarterly, *Weekly Report* 35 (October 29, 1976), p. 2301; and *Election '80* (Washington, D.C.: Congressional Quarterly Inc., 1980), p. 132.

accounting for $1,136,112 of the total. The 1974 and 1976 records had been approximately $537,000 and $1,700,000.

Very expensive Senate races are not unusual; however, the $1 million plus general election spending club jumped from 10 in 1976 to 21 in 1978. The old record of $3 million set in 1976 was surpassed in 1978 when incumbent Republican Jesse Helms of North Carolina spent $7.5 million. The popular conservative received most of the money in contributions of $100 or less solicited by mail. His opponent spent only $261,982 and received 45.5 percent of the vote. Ten of the 21 candidates lost their races, including 3 incumbents. However, spending large sums against incumbents did not usually pay off.[7]

SENIORITY AND CAMPAIGN COSTS. The advantages of incumbency discussed later in the chapter apparently allow most House incumbents to spend less after their initial election. The following figures are the average costs for 1978 for the pre-1974 through "Class of 1978" representatives:[8]

First elected in 1978 (1st term)	$229,000
First elected in 1976 (2nd term)	143,000
First elected in 1974 (3rd term)	127,000
First elected before 1974	87,000

INFLATION. The campaign price tag is rising considerably faster than the inflation figures.

The costs of public opinion polling doubled between 1972 and 1976, and television advertising rates went up 64 percent during the same period. Of course, newspaper rates, transportation costs, etc. have also risen. In addition, the campaign financing regulations, discussed in the next section, have added to the financial burden by forcing candidates to seek small contributions, often through costly direct mail campaigns, to overcome the problems created by the $1,000 per election campaign contribution limit on individual donors.

FEDERAL CAMPAIGN REGULATIONS

Federal attempts to prevent campaign finance abuse date back to the 1925 Corrupt Practices Act, which limited expenditures for House and Senate races to $2,500 and $10,000 respectively. Although more generous allowances were made for larger states and districts, the limits were absurdly low and easily evaded. Subsequent legislation amending the act limited spending by any political committee to $3 million a year but did not prevent the establishment of many committees, each able to spend the legal limit. Individual contributions were limited to $5,000 to each candidate or nationally affiliated party committee, but given the number of candidates and committees, wealthy people could

★ ★ ★ *Table 9–3* ★
Spending by 1978 House winners

	INCUMBENTS	CHALLENGERS	OPEN SEATS	TOTAL
Spent more	312	11	43	366
Spent less	46	8	15	69
Total	358	19	58	435

Source: *Election '80* (Washington, D.C.: Congressional Quarterly Inc., 1980), p. 133. Reprinted by permission.

legally contribute huge sums of money. Corporations and labor unions were prohibited from directly contributing to campaigns, but they could and did circumvent the law by establishing political action committees (PACs) whose operating expenses are paid by the parent organization and who collect and distribute "voluntary" contributions. Most of the 1925 Act and its amendments did not apply to primaries and it rarely was enforced. President Lyndon Johnson called it "more loophole than law."

Three important changes were made in 1971. A law was enacted that included a tax check-off that gave taxpayers the opportunity to contribute $1 of their tax obligation to a fund to subsidize presidential general election campaigns. The check-off system raised about $90 million prior to the 1976 election. The success of the tax check-off aided the advocates of the full public-financing approach enacted in 1974.

DISCLOSURE. The major thrust of the Federal Elections Campaign Act of 1971 was the requirement of **disclosure**—the reporting of all receipts, expenditures, and debts involved in the primary and general election campaigns. Political committees must register with the government and file periodic reports that include the names, addresses, and dollar amounts for any contribution of more than $100 (the 1974 act reduced this to $10; it will be discussed later in this chapter), the details of any expenditures of more than $100, and a statement of political debts incurred as the result of the campaign. Disclosure, and the extension of the concept to the primaries, gave us the first opportunity to get a total picture of campaign spending.

The act also took the restrictions off all contributions except the amounts that a candidate or the immediate families could contribute to their own campaigns. But, candidates for federal office were limited in the amount of money they could spend on advertising—television, radio, newspaper, campaign handouts—to ten cents per voting-age person. This reflected the concern that a very well-financed candidate could use a media

Democratic President Jimmy Carter and Republican candidate Ronald Reagan shake hands after their televised debate in the 1980 contest.

blitz—particularly TV—to overwhelm the opposition.

MEDIA AND CAMPAIGNS. TV came into its own as a political tool in 1960 with the famous Kennedy–Nixon debates and in the 1968 presidential campaign when Nixon spent $12.1 and $6.1 million respectively on radio and television. The use of radio and television also rose significantly in Senate races. House candidates tend to make less use of the electronic media, particularly TV, because it can be inefficient, requiring them to buy coverage they don't want because it reaches people outside their district.

Many campaign consultants are media experts, specializing in selling an "image" of a candidate and/or transforming relative unknowns into household words. The broadcast media are the easiest means of reaching the voters in a national or statewide race. But do they have a sufficient impact to warrant such huge campaign expenditures? The answer to this question is "yes" if the individual must overcome relative obscurity. For example, the 1970 Ohio Democratic Senate primary involved two non-incumbents: Cleveland industrialist Howard Metzenbaum, unknown to most of the population, and former astronaut and national hero John Glenn. The "unknown" overcame Glenn through a media blitz whose price tag for TV alone may have been $500,000, most of which the candidate paid for himself. By contrast, Glenn had difficulty raising money because most potential contributors thought he was a "shoo-in." He only spent $31,000 on his media efforts.[9]

The deluge of electronic electioneering in the 1970 congressional campaigns brought this reaction from Senator Gaylord Nelson (D., Wis.):

A two-dimensional, 18-inch high candidate presented with all the candor of a laundry product or a dancing dog act does little to assure a concerned public of the relevance and responsiveness of the political process in this country.[10]

Ray Price, an adviser in the 1968 Nixon campaign, wrote one of the most candid appraisals of what a media campaign is all about. The memo concentrated on "selling" an image of a new Nixon.

[Talking about voter reaction] . . . we have to be very clear on this point: that the response is to the image, not to the man, since 99 percent of the voters have no contact with the man. It's not what's there that counts, it's what is projected. . . . It's not the man we have to change, but rather the received impressions. And this impression often depends more on the medium than it does on the candidate himself.[11]

Finally, a 1974 study of the impact of broadcast campaigning on election results concluded that "in elections other than those for the president, campaign broadcasting appears capable of making a significant difference, and this is particularly true for primaries." But the study found that the most important election factor remains incumbency.[12]

In summary, the nation entered the 1972 election with a full disclosure requirement and a limit on media spending, but no restrictions on contributions or total campaign expenditures. The advantages of incumbency had not been damaged and only the efforts of the citizens' lobby group, Common Cause (which detailed the spiraling costs and incumbency advantages in congressional races and pushed for overall reform), and the Watergate scandal led to further campaign finance reform.

WATERGATE REVELATIONS. On June 17, 1972, five men were arrested attempting to break into the Washington headquarters of the Democratic National Committee, which was housed in the Watergate apartment and office complex. They were carrying electronic

Public Financing

Presidential General Election—Full financing $20 million to major-party candidates. (Actual figures: 1976, $21.8 million; 1980, $29.4 million.) Minor-party candidates' funds based on votes party's candidate received in last election.[+]

Presidential Primaries—Up to $5 million per candidate in matching funds if candidate raised $100,000 (at least $5,000 in each of 20 states in contributions of $250 or less). Government will match additional contributions of up to $250.

Conventions—Public funding optional.

Spending Limits

Presidential Primaries—$10 million per candidate for *all* primaries. (Actual figures: 1976, $10.9 million; 1980, $14.7 million.)[+]

Presidential Nominating Convention—$2 million for major party.

Senate Primaries—$100,000 or 8 cents per eligible voter.[*]

Senate General Elections—$150,000 or 12 cents per eligible voter.[*]

House Primaries—$70,000.[*]

House General Elections—$70,000.[*]

Contribution Limits

Candidate and Family
  Presidential race: $50,000.
  Senate race: $35,000.[*]
  House race: $25,000.[*]

Figure 9–2 The Federal Election Campaign Act of 1974 and amendments highlights.

eavesdropping equipment and were led by James W. McCord, Jr., a former CIA agent and then director of security for the Committee for the Re-Election of the President (CREEP). The operation was financed from a secret Nixon campaign fund. In retrospect, the attempted break-in appears absurd, particularly in light of the expected easy victory of President Nixon. The actual motives still remain a mystery. But whatever the motives, subsequent investigations of the Watergate break-in revealed a sordid tale of secret campaign financing.

The monetary aspects of the Nixon campaign were handled by the Finance Committee to Re-Elect the President, which was totally outside the control of the Republican Party organization. The committee was a White House creation, whose only loyalty was to the President. White House and CREEP officials had more money available than they could legitimately use. As the later

Individuals
    To congressional candidate: $1,000 per election.
    To presidential candidate: $1,000.
    To national party committee: $20,000.
    To any other political committee: $5,000.
    Total per calendar year: $25,000.
National Political Committees (national committee and House or Senate campaign committee)
    2 cents per voter in presidential general election (National Committee only).
    $17,500 direct aid to senatorial candidate or candidate for at-large House seat and $29,440 or 2 cents per voter in coordinated spending.++
    $20,000 direct aid to House candidate ($5,000 per National Committee for primary and general election) and $14,720 in coordinated funds.
State Party
    $5,000 per election for Congress.
    $5,000 overall to presidential candidate.
    2 cents per voter in coordinated spending for Senate candidates.
Other Political Committees
    Multi-Candidate (contributes to 5 or more)—$5,000 per election to Congress.
    Other (contributes to less than 5)—$1,000 per election to Congress.

  * Declared unconstitutional.
  + Limits apply if presidential candidate accepts public financing.
 ++ Coordinated spending involves the party paying for services the candidate requests, usually polling or television ad production, but the party has a say in how the money is spent.

Figure 9–2   continued

Senate Watergate investigation revealed, these campaign monies were used instead to finance the break-in at Watergate; pay the salary of the head of the campaign "dirty tricks" effort; and finance a group of "plumbers" who broke into the office of Dr. Lewis Fielding, Daniel Ellsberg's psychiatrist, while Ellsberg was standing trial for his part in the publication of the Pentagon Papers.

Among major financial revelations was the corporate "giving" (actually armtwisting) campaign headed by Herbert W. Kalmbach, one of Nixon's personal attorneys. He "collected" more than $10 million from U.S. corporations, the bulk of it prior to April 7, 1972, when the reporting of such campaign funds became law. Most of the money was extracted from corporate executives in an elaborate industry-by-industry canvassing effort. Some of these funds were given not only secretly, but illegally, eventually leading to indictments and convictions.

One massive illegal set of contributions came from the 40,000 member American Milk Producers Incorporated. Eyebrows were raised when AMPI and two other major dairy cooperatives contributed $250,000 only six months after the Nixon administration had raised milk price-support subsidies. The Nixon milk fund proved just one link in a giant (still only partially known) chain of secret or ethically questionable fund raising.

FAT-CATS. The 1972 election marked the end of large individual contributions by "fat-cats," contributors giving $10,000 or more to individual candidates. While the full story of Nixon's 1972 election campaign may never be brought completely to light, we do know that filed reports indicate fifty people contributed $50,000 or more. The individual high was $300,000; the reported total, $4,360,096. However, in an unreported, pre–April 1972 contribution, W. Clement Stone, Chairman of the Combined Insurance Companies of America, gave the Nixon campaign $2 million. McGovern had only 13 individuals in the $50,000 plus category. They donated a total of $2.4 million. The largest single reported contribution was $274,430 by Stewart Mott of New York.[13]

THE FEDERAL ELECTION CAMPAIGN ACT OF 1974. The Watergate revelations and the efforts of Common Cause led to the passage of the **Federal Election Campaign Act of 1974.** Although members of Congress declined to extend the concept of public funding to their own races, the act was the most far reaching campaign reform in our history. In addition to strict disclosure requirements, it imposed spending limits on all federal election contests, established contribution limits on candidates, individuals, and organizations, and provided for partial public funding of presidential primaries and full public funding of the presidential general election (see Fig-

ure 9–2). Unfortunately, in 1976 the Supreme Court struck down the spending limits and candidate personal contribution limits that applied to congressional contests as violations of the First Amendment. The restrictions that apply to presidential campaigns were upheld on the grounds that the limitations were a trade-off for public financing that was an option the candidates could accept or reject.[14] The act established a bipartisan, six-member **Federal Election Commission.** The commission administers the finance laws and enforces compliance. For example, it investigates and determines whether or not a candidate or organization has violated the regulations, and it can rule on whether or not certain outlays count as campaign expenses.

The new law allows individuals to contribute up to $1,000 and organizations up to $5,000 to congressional candidates per election (primary and general). Even using the committee route, individuals face an overall $25,000 limit per year on contributions to all federal candidates and organizations. The $1,000 and $5,000 limits apply to giving to presidential candidates, but the matching funds and overall spending limits imposed on those who accept the partial public financing greatly restrict large contributions to the presidential candidates. To a large extent, the presidential elections have gone off the auction block. Refinements in the law actually resulted in an overall general election spending limit in 1980 of $38.5 million from the following sources: public funding—$29.4 million; national committees—$4.6 million; state and lower level committees—$4.5 million.

Minor parties complained that the new public-financing rules discriminate against them, keeping them in their position of usual losers. To qualify, a third-party independent candidate must have received five percent of the vote in the previous presidential election. They can receive some federal funds retroactively if they reach the five percent threshold.

Another complaint was that the spending limits were too low and the lack of money for "get out and vote" drives contributed to the low voter turnout in 1976. In response, the law now allows state and local party organizations to spend unlimited amounts on registration and voting drives. However, turnout has continued to decline, with only 53 percent of the nation's voting-age population going to the polls in 1980.

PARTISAN COMPLAINTS. The Republican Party was used to receiving substantially more money from the big donors than were the Democrats. The GOP was generally opposed to public financing of presidential elections, as they were the usual winners in the contest for dollars. They were also very unhappy with the 1974 law's original restriction on congressional campaign spending and individual contribution limits, on the grounds that the only means many challengers have to defeat incumbents is to outspend them. The Supreme Court decision quieted some GOP concerns, and the party has taken much greater advantage of the law's rather generous party contribution limits than have the Democrats, particularly in terms of **coordinated spending,** in which the party pays for services the candidate requests, such as polling or television ad production, but has a say on how the money is spent.

The GOP also has been the beneficiary of the creation of a number of conservative political action committees that have taken advantage of another part of the Court's 1976 decision that a candidate's supporters may spend an unlimited amount of money to aid him as long as there is no contact with the candidate or his campaign (independent expenditures). The most prominent of these organizations, the National Conservative Political Action Committee (NCPAC) reportedly put $1.7 million into the 1980 presidential race.

CAMPAIGN MONEY: WHERE DOES IT COME FROM?

The 1974 law, as modified by the Supreme Court, has created a whole new ballgame, affecting not only the sources of political money, but also the campaign strategy in the pre-convention phase of the presidential contests.

The results of the 1974 law were predictable. The big givers are restricted by the contribution limits, particularly as they apply to presidential primaries and the now publicly funded presidential general elections. At the same time, political action committees have multiplied, particularly among business, professional, and agricultural groups, many of which had sought political influence through the large contributions of individual members, particularly to Republican candidates. The PACs can now concentrate their spending on congressional races, escalating spending at that level. Also, rich congressional candidates are virtually unrestrained in their personal spending. The individual contribution limits have forced the Republicans to rely heavily on fund raising by the party and, in a reversal of form, Republicans now rely heavily on direct-mail appeals to small givers, those who contribute from $1 to $100.

CONGRESSIONAL CAMPAIGN MONEY. Figure 9–3 indicates that the contributions of Political Action Committees are growing in importance, and now rank second only to the "other" category, which is made up largely of candidates' contributions to their own campaigns, loans to their own campaigns, and loans from other sources. Apparently, loans are becoming a more and more significant factor. Of course, the post–1974 elimination of the large individual contributors forces reliance upon PACs and loans. As the treasurer for one successful 1976 Senate candidate put it: ". . . a thousand dollars in today's market

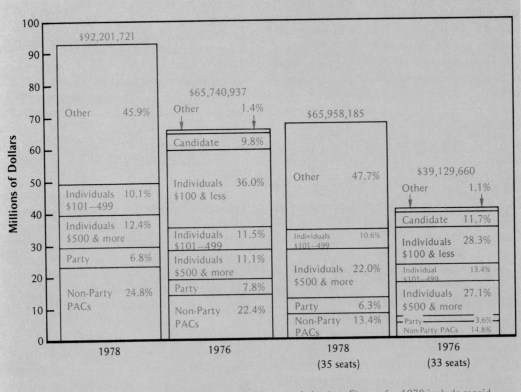

Figure 9–3 *The source of receipts for congressional candidates: 1976 and 1978.*
(*Source:* Election '80.)

is ridiculous. There are people giving us a thousand who in the old days would have given us fifty thousand."[15]

If the 1980 efforts of the Republicans set a trend, we can anticipate a further reliance upon the political parties as a source of funds. The limitations outlined in Figure 9–2 allowed national party committees to spend as much as $34,720 for any House seat and $502,524 for a Senate seat from California,

the Senate ceiling being based upon a state's population. In the California case, a Senate candidate could benefit from a comparable amount of coordinated spending by state committees (an unlikely event as few state committees have that kind of money). The National Republican Senatorial Committee contributed over one-half million dollars to Paul Gann during his unsuccessful attempt to defeat Senator Alan Cranston of California.

PACs. As indicated earlier, the impetus for the growth of PACs initially came because they were a vehicle for getting around the prohibition against direct giving by unions and corporations, and the original personal contribution limits. The new 1974 rules led to a phenomenal increase in their number. In 1974 there were 457 PACs registered in Washington; by 1978, this number was 1,938. And, as Table 9-4 indicates, PAC contributions have grown from $12.5 million for the 1974 election to $35.1 million for the 1978 election cycle (January 1, 1977–December 31, 1978). However, the total represented less than half the money spent on politically related activities such as independent expenditures.

In the 1980 elections, NCPAC targeted six liberal Democratic senators for defeat, and spent $1.2 million in "independent" funds on these contests. The group also made direct contributions of another $250,000 to 112 other candidates. Four of the six senators were defeated, and 58 of the candidates receiving direct contributions won. While the group was a factor in some of the races, the results in other contests were predictable even without NCPAC's efforts.

NCPAC targeted another twenty incumbent senators for defeat in 1982, including Edward Kennedy and a few moderate Republicans. The Chairman, John Dolan said that, "NCPAC doesn't question the integrity of these twenty senators. We feel they are simply wrong."[16] Being wrong means voting against conservative causes.

Labor contributions go almost exclusively to Democratic candidates. However, incumbency, rather than party, has had a greater influence on the giving of the other categories, creating a less lopsided balance in favor of Republicans than would be expected from the corporate and trade memberships (including agriculture), and health organizations. Of the 1978 contributions, $20 million went to incumbents, with the rest divided among challengers and candidates for open seats. Only $50,000 went to presidential candidates.

THE WHY OF GIVING. The motives of the givers of small sums are usually party loyalty, identification with the candidate, or a desire to be involved. But what motivates the "big" giver? Jesse Unruh, while Speaker of the California Assembly, said, "Most people who put

★ ★ ★ *Table 9-4* ★
Campaign contributions by political action committees: 1974–1978

	NUMBER OF PACs			CONTRIBUTIONS		
CATEGORY	*1974*	*1976*	*1978*	*1974*	*1976*	*1978*
Labor	160	225	211	$ 6.2 million	$ 8.2 million	$10.3 million
Corporate	99	412	697	$ 2.5	$ 7.1	$ 9.8
Trade-membership-health	198	332	399	**	$ 6.4	$11.5
Other	**	**	**	**	$ .9	$ 3.5
Totals				$12.5	$22.6	$35.1

Source: Congressional Quarterly, *Weekly Report* 34 (October 23, 1976), p. 3033; *Weekly Report* 36 (January 21, 1978), pp. 118–119; and Congressional Quarterly, *Election '80,* pp. 137–138.

A PAC representative suggests that being a "friend" of the group is the key to getting contributions. A member of the House, however, questions the group–legislator relationship.

We're not that interested in whether the man's a liberal, conservative, Democrat or Republican. We're just interested in whether he is friendly or has an open mind on the issues we're concerned with.

JOHN M. KINNAIRD, American Trucking Associations

I know it is true in most cases when members say they can accept money from a PAC and then turn around and vote against them. But, I think there's still sort of an unspoken quid pro quo of some kind. Whether it's lending an ear, or more than lending an ear, I don't know.

Rep. DON J. PEASE (D., Idaho)

Source: Quoted in Congressional Quarterly, *Weekly Report* 38 (May 17, 1980), pp. 1345 and 1346.

money into political campaigns aren't contributors, they're investors."[17] In some cases, the contributor is not seeking a specific act, but is buying access to the decision-making process. They expect to receive, and usually do receive, preferred treatment when they seek the assistance of the beneficiaries of their generosity.

Creating "friends" in high places is part of the American political game and, the key to PAC giving often is incumbency and the committee or sub-committee assignment of the individual legislators. The point is, of course, that contributions to members of Congress—chairmen or others—are made in anticipation of favorable consideration of group goals. Backing usual winners is a time-proven method of providing an advantage to the contributors (see insert).

THE INCUMBENCY PROBLEM. A number of conclusions can be drawn from the data already presented. First, and we will return to this later, incumbents have done things for the groups and can continue to use their past ex-

perience to aid the groups. The power of incumbency can overcome normal ideological ties. Second, the power of incumbency in the eyes of the PACs has hurt Republican chances in the past and forced the GOP to seek funds from a different source—the small givers. Third, the high cost of congressional campaigns and the large number of candidates who make personal financial sacrifices suggest that the real impact of money on politics may be in preventing some people from running at all, from having the opportunity to be winners or losers. And, cost usually works to the advantage of incumbents, most of whom enjoy ready access to campaign funds. Most incumbents agree that the 1974 laws have increased their advantage in running for re-election because the limits on individual contributions make it more difficult for challengers to amass large campaign treasuries to help offset the advantages of incumbency.[18]

PUBLIC FINANCING OF CONGRESSIONAL CAMPAIGNS. In terms of congressional campaigns, we are almost back to square one.

There are no restrictions on media spending, overall spending limits, or use of personal funds by candidates. While the ceiling on individual contributions gives some headaches to fund raisers, the groups have taken up the slack, and they have considerably more money to spend on congressional races now that we have public financing of the presidential race.

Congress rejected partial public financing of congressional campaigns as part of the 1974 act, and subsequent efforts have met strenuous opposition. Republicans are particularly concerned that public financing would protect incumbents by preventing challengers from using as much money as possible in their campaigns in an attempt to overcome incumbency advantages with the power of the dollar. And, since incumbents already enjoy a fund-raising advantage, prospects for change are dim. As one journalist pointed out after the 1974 debate:

Public funding would have meant that virtually every Congressman would have had an amply financed opponent in both the primary and the general election every time he came up for re-election. That is something that members of Congress well-established in their states and districts can easily do without.[19]

DOLLARS AND THE PRESIDENTIAL NOMINATION. Partial public financing of campaigns for the presidential nomination was designed to clean up the contest by restricting the giving by wealthy individuals and interest groups, and to provide an opportunity for all candidates to put together a campaign treasury. However, the law has had unanticipated side effects, such as requiring the serious candidates to begin raising funds earlier, forcing campaign strategists to focus on the early caucus and primary contests, and making candidates play games to keep within the state spending limits, which are based upon population.

For the 1980 primary races, the spending limit was set at $14.7 million; candidates were eligible for up to one-half that amount ($7.36 million) in federal funds. Only John B. Connally, the Texas Republican, rejected matching funds and was free to spend as much as he could raise. The state spending limits ranged from $294,400 for New Hampshire and 18 other jurisdictions, to $3.9 million for California. Connally outspent all other candidates prior to his withdrawal on March 9th, spending between $10 and $12 million dollars and winning one delegate.

The two eventual nominees, Ronald Reagan and Jimmy Carter, raised over $7 and $5 million dollars respectively by the end of 1979 and spent most of it during that year in preparation for the races. The two runners-up, George Bush (R.) and Senator Ted Kennedy (D., Mass.) were third and fourth in the 1979 spending derby. By contrast, John Anderson raised only half a million dollars, and the other contenders in both parties lagged behind in the dollar contest.

THE MATCHING FUNDS PARADOX. Once the nominating season starts—the Iowa caucus was held on January 21, and New Hampshire kicked off the primaries on February 26—it is essential that a candidate do well if he or she hopes to attract campaign dollars, especially the individual contributions of no more than $1,000. And, since matching funds are only given for contributions of $250 or less, a broad popular support is needed. Also, if a candidate draws less than ten percent of the vote in two consecutive primaries, he becomes ineligible to receive matching funds thirty days after the second primary. To requalify, a candidate must get twenty percent of the vote in a later primary, a particularly difficult task for a candidate who has lost momentum and hasn't the funds that might reestablish it. The early 1980 withdrawals of Governor Edmund G. Brown of California and two Republican contenders, Senator Robert Dole of Kansas and Representative

Philip M. Crane of Illinois, were caused, in part, by matching-fund problems.

The new rules appear to be a two-edged sword. On the one hand, it can be argued that under the old unlimited spending rules, lesser-known or less-popular candidates might put together an adequate treasury from the contributions of "fat-cats" and special interests. Yet, campaign finance expert Herbert E. Alexander made a good point when he wrote:

A vital part of the (1976) Carter success story is the FECA. Without stringent contribution limits, better-known candidates who had connections with wealthy contributors could have swamped Carter; and without federal subsidies, Carter would have lacked the money to consolidate his early lead.[20]

THE FOCUS ON THE EARLY CONTESTS. The key, then, is to raise enough money to be able to make a strong showing in the late January to end of March races, with the hope of sustaining a lead with the limited financial resources on hand or still available. The early contests are usually far more important than the later ones, and candidates find it difficult to make a maximum effort in the April through June contests (see insert).

Finally, the psychological effect of a good or poor showing in New Hampshire forced the 1980 candidates to circumvent that state's spending limit of $294,400. Candidates stayed overnight in neighboring states and put New Hampshire staff members and campaign workers on the payrolls of their national headquarters. Since Boston television services most of New Hampshire, advertising time on the Boston stations was purchased and charged against the Massachusetts limit of $1,001,667.

Obviously, the partial public financing of the primaries, and the full public financing of the presidential general election, which will be discussed in the next section, have had a major impact on campaign strategy.

Nominating and Electing a President

Once every four years our nation goes through its "quadrennial madness"—nominating presidential candidates and electing a president. However, we must generalize about primary and general election campaigns, as each has its own character, shaped by the personalities and events of the time.

At one point the parties tried to choose their presidential candidates in congressional caucuses, and later in mixed caucuses. The caucus, however, proved unable to unify a badly factionalized party. So, following the 1831 example of the Antimasonic Party, the major parties adopted the convention as the device for selecting their presidential tickets. Although periodically attacked as unrepresentative, the national conventions remain to this day the official device for candidate selection. In reality though, we have a hybrid system, with the real choice of candidates usually made prior to the conventions.

PRESIDENTIAL PRIMARIES AND CAUCUSES

Progressive reformers pushed the presidential primary at the turn of the century; the first primary was held in Florida in 1904. After a long period of rising and then falling popularity, the growth in primaries began to swell after 1968, when 17 were held. The number reached 23 in 1972, 30 in 1976, and 37 in 1980. In 1968, only 41 percent of the delegates were chosen by primaries, but by 1980, 76 percent of the Republican delegates and 71 percent of the Democrats were elected in primaries or bound to reflect the results of their respective state primaries.

The major reason for the increase in primaries was the recognition that in the recent past the contest for the nomination was

Viewpoint:
Focus on the early primaries

Partial public financing of the pre-convention races has had a major impact on candidate strategy.

Spending limits combined with proportional representation and the mix of primaries have taken a lot of strategy out of the campaign. It makes early stages far more important. You can't pick and choose.

RICK STEARNS, Edward M. Kennedy campaign

It's impossible to run a good campaign in thirty-five primaries if you take matching funds. It means you can't make the maximum effort in the middle and late primaries.

CHARLES BLACK, Ronald Reagan's one-time national political director

Source: Quoted in Congressional Quarterly, *Weekly Report* 5 (February 2, 1980), p. 282.

decided during the pre-convention campaigns, as was the case in 1960 (Kennedy), 1964 (Goldwater), 1968 (Nixon), 1972 (McGovern), 1976 (Carter), and 1980 (Carter and Reagan). The absence of primaries in a major state may deny interested voters a meaningful voice in the process. However, how "meaningful" the voice is may be a factor of how early the primary is held.

States and territories without primaries elect their delegates through a multi-tier caucus process, which usually begins with open, but sparsely attended meetings at the precinct level, with the actual selection of delegates taking place later at district or state conventions. However, the apportionment of delegates reflects the candidate's success in the initial caucus votes.

TYPES OF PRIMARIES. There are two basic types of presidential primaries. The first, and most popular, is the **presidential preference primary,** in which voters indicate their choice for the nomination. The second is the **delegate selection primary,** in which the

voters elect delegates to the national conventions. Actually, most states use various combinations of the two methods. However, the most common approach is to combine presidential preference with delegate selection.

Party rules vary: the Democrats require all delegates—primary and caucus—to declare as preferring a particular candidate or as uncommitted; the Republicans do not require that a choice be made. Democratic delegates are bound for one convention ballot to support the candidate they are committed to. Republicans require only those delegates bound to a candidate by state law to vote for that candidate.

Another significant difference is that the Democrats require proportional representation on the basis of presidential preference with delegate apportionment reflecting the percentage of the vote each candidate received in the primary or caucus. Republicans allow winner-take-all. Also, the Democratic Party allows only Democrats to participate in its presidential primaries and caucuses, while the Republicans allow crossovers—the voting

Candidate Reagan wore many hats, an approach that helps members of different societal groups identify with the candidate.

open to any registered voter—if state law permits.

RULES MAKE A DIFFERENCE. Rules are not neutral; they determine outcomes. For example, John Anderson was popular among Independents and many liberal Democrats who were unhappy with their choice of either Carter or Kennedy. His showing in the early 1980 Republican contests was bolstered by the fact that sixteen Republican primaries were open (crossover) and another five allowed party members and Independents to cast ballots. Kennedy, in turn, refused to bow out of the race after Carter won enough delegates to clinch the nomination. He vowed a convention floor fight to overturn the one-ballot-bound rule in an effort to free the delegates and have an open convention. He was unsuccessful.

The winner-take-all provision on the Republican side had an impact on the 1976 race, in which President Gerald R. Ford barely defeated Ronald Reagan. Ford did very well in the early primaries, but Reagan finished strong, thanks in part to victories in a number of later primaries, including winner-take-all contests in California, Georgia, and Indiana.

PRIMARY STRATEGY. Serious contenders for the nomination now enter almost all the primaries and caucus contests, and begin their quest a year before the races begin. As indicated earlier, the politics of campaign fund raising and the importance of doing well in the early caucuses and primaries mean that much of the organizational building and campaign planning around the country must be done before the candidates turn their attention to the Iowa caucus in January and the late February and early March contests in northern New England.

During the last two presidential elections, the field had narrowed by early April. In 1976, the Republican contest was a Ford–Reagan affair; however, the Democrats had a crowded field, but six candidates dropped out early. In mid–May, Edmund Brown and Senator Frank Church of Idaho entered the race, and between them they defeated Carter in six out of eight primaries in which one or both were entered. But it was a case of too little, too late.

CAMPAIGNING FROM THE WHITE HOUSE. In 1980, the parties reversed roles. The Dem-

ocratic contest was a Carter–Kennedy struggle. Growing dissatisfaction among major parts of the Democratic coalition—labor and minorities in particular—with Carter's performance in office, encouraged Kennedy to announce his candidacy against the president from his own party. In the fall of 1979, most observers thought Kennedy would capture the nomination, and a Lou Harris poll had him ahead by 60 to 36 percent. Events intervened however, and on November 4th, Iranian militants took over the U.S. Embassy in Tehran and seized 53 hostages. That same evening, Senator Kennedy gave a very poor performance on a nationally broadcast CBS interview conducted by Roger Mudd.

The press began persecuting Kennedy again about the 1969 incident at Chappaquiddick, Massachusetts, in which his car went off a bridge and a female passenger drowned. Questions about his character hounded him throughout the campaign. At the same time, the nation instinctively rallied around the President and supported his cautious handling of the Iranian crisis. By mid–December, Carter passed Kennedy in the polls, and pulled far ahead in January in the midst of handling another crisis, the Soviet invasion of Afghanistan.

Carter withdrew from the Iowa caucus debates, claiming he wished to avoid political appearances while he was monitoring the international crisis. Throughout the primary season he maintained this position, refusing to debate his rival and benefitting during the early contests from Kennedy's inability to shift the spotlight from international issues and get the voters to focus on the economic problems of inflation and unemployment.

Kennedy could not recover from losses in Iowa, New Hampshire, and the Maine caucuses. And Carter's devastating victory over him in Illinois on March 18 gave Carter the momentum to withstand Kennedy's victories in the industrial north where the President was vulnerable. Kennedy won five of the last

World events intervene in national elections. For instance, President Carter was embarrassed by the failure of an American military operation to rescue the hostages in Iran.

eight primaries, but again, it was too little, too late. Carter won 24 of the 34 preference primaries.

THE REPUBLICAN STORY. The Republicans started with a crowded field in 1980. Lack of success in the early contests forced three contenders out of the field by mid–March. In fact, after New Hampshire it was a two-way race between Reagan and George Bush, with John Anderson using the post–New Hampshire primaries to build support for his eventual independent candidacy. Bush stopped campaigning in late May. The contest had been between Reagan, with a solid base of 35 to 40 percent of his party behind him, and Bush, who had an exceptionally fine campaign organization.

IMPACT OF THE MEDIA. Who determines the winner of early contests, the voters or the media? In 1972, Edmund S. Muskie beat George McGovern in New Hampshire by ten percentage points. Because Muskie was a heavy favorite, the media turned it into a McGovern victory. In 1976, Carter's win in Iowa propelled him to center stage, and his 23,373 votes (28.4%) to 18,710 (22.7%) margin over his nearest rival in a more than ten-person New Hampshire field, made him a clear cut media winner. Reagan had cause to complain when his 1.4 percent loss to Ford in 1976 made him a "big" loser because he did not do as well as anticipated.

In a sense, George Bush was a 1980 media event. Reagan did not participate in a televised debate before the Iowa caucus and,

This commentary by Congressional Quarterly stresses the importance of the media in determining the choice of presidential nominees.

In the last decade, the media have moved to fill the void caused by the decline of party organizations. They have largely assumed the party role of establishing important battlegrounds, defining the viable candidates and interpreting the results—a particularly important function in the early stages of the process.

CONGRESSIONAL QUARTERLY

Source: *Weekly Report* 38 (February 2, 1980), p. 282.

in fact, he only spent twenty hours to Bush's thirty days campaigning in the state. Perhaps it was overconfidence. Bush beat Reagan 31.5 to 29.4 percent, but his "upset victory" earned him the title of "front-runner."

Reagan recovered quickly and campaigned hard in New Hampshire. He pulled even with Bush and the polls projected a very close vote. But four days before the election, Bush rejected pleas that a Bush–Reagan debate be expanded to include the other Republican candidates. This didn't sit well with the voters, and one pro–Reagan political operative said: "I've been in this business for twenty-five years and that was the clearest case I've ever seen of a candidate blowing himself out of the water."[21]

Bush made the additional mistake of returning home to Houston after the debate and not campaigning during the last three days. Reagan buried Bush by a two-to-one margin. Although Bush was able to stay in the race because of his fine organization, the contest for the Republican nomination was as good as over.

Has the media taken over from the party? Does the impact of the media help distort the presidential nominating contests as less democratic than they were supposed to be (see insert)?

IS THE NOMINATING PROCESS DEMOCRATIC?

The Democratic contests in 1976 and 1980 and the Republican race in 1980 were decided early. The Ford–Reagan issue in 1976 was not settled until the convention, but it can be argued that Ford's early victories were the key to his surviving Reagan's second-half change. If the voters in Iowa, New Hampshire, and the other states that have had the wisdom or luck to get an early date, are the key to success, doesn't their vote carry disproportionate weight? Conversely, the votes cast in the April, May, and June contests may be virtually meaningless.

To put it numerically, the votes of approximately 100,000 members of each party in Iowa and 111,000 and 147,000 Democrats and Republicans respectively in New Hampshire, had considerably more impact—to put it conservatively—than the votes of 5.7 million Democrats and 3.9 million Republicans in the June 3, 1980, California primary. California shared that date with eight other states, including such populous places as New Jersey and Ohio.

Possible reforms of the presidential primary system, such as holding them all on one date or having a set date for the primaries within a region, could decrease the "bandwagon" effect of the media. On the other hand, such changes would alter campaign strategy. They would probably drive long-shot, but reasonably well-financed candidates—like Kennedy in 1960 and Carter in 1976—from the races as they could not count on a gradual buildup of support resulting from a good showing or two. It would put a time strain on serious candidates that might require campaigns for the nomination to start earlier than they do now. And, the reforms could prevent a candidate, such as Reagan in 1976, from taking advantage of the present schedule to mount a late but serious challenge to the front-runner.

DIRECT NATIONAL PRIMARY

A major argument supporting a **direct national presidential primary** is that all the members of a party could have a voice in the choice of candidates. Realistically though, there is no certainty that the turnout in such a primary would be any more impressive than it is in existing primaries. And, assuming the continuation of public funding, a one-shot national primary, a crowded field such as the Democrats had in 1976, and the Republicans had in 1980, could (a run-off would have been required in 1976) require a run-off primary. In a real sense, the survivor would have faced two national campaigns before the general election, taxing his stamina and the patience of the voters.

Some supporters of the direct national primary suggest that television offers an answer to the physical burden of campaigning throughout the country, but the costs of television time and the elimination of face-to-face

contact create other problems. And political realities suggest that the prospects for adoption of a national primary are very dim.

Perhaps the old-style convention, with the delegates chosen by party leaders and activists, guaranteed that more of the voting population would have a voice in the choice of their party's nominee. Of course, party leaders would be the vehicle through which choice would be expressed. But, the assumption here is that leaders would have a good grasp of the dominant opinion within their constituencies. State and local party leaders are concerned, first and foremost, with how a presidential candidate will affect state and local contests.

Although the last Republican convention withmore than one ballot was 1948, and the last multi-ballot Democratic convention was 1952, conventions still serve useful purposes. And, the Ford–Reagan race in 1976 was decided at the Kansas City convention by a handful of uncommitted delegates. This suggests that conventions still could play a major role in the choice of the nominees.

THE NATIONAL CONVENTIONS

The national conventions held every four years can be considered the pinnacle of the party structure. They were instituted to choose the presidential and vice-presidential candidates and write the party platforms that theoretically provide policy guidelines for the next four years. But their real business is to create "even a loose alliance out of fifty grand duchies and hundreds of petty baronies" to elect a president.[22] They provide a temporary unifying mechanism to a decentralized system. By temporarily drawing together thousands of state and local party organizations, conventions provide forums for efforts to achieve a wide measure of consensus on candidates and policies. Without this temporary consensus, there might be no way to efficiently organize the competition for the highest national offices.

DECLINE OF CONVENTIONS. As originally conceived, the conventions were to provide a place where state party leaders could choose the most acceptable candidates. The party leaders controlled delegate selection and dominated the delegates' decisions at the conventions, giving the rank-and-file little voice in the selection of presidential candidates. But, the twin forces of the spread of the primaries and the impact of electronic media have reduced the nominating function of the conventions. One has to go back to the 103 ballots of the Democratic Convention of 1924 to find the sort of conflict that was common in earlier times.

The TV viewer sees only the fanfare, demonstrations, real and staged, and nominating and seconding speeches, sometimes for favorite sons who are not really contenders. They do not witness the crucial work of the convention before—the credentials committee settling disputes that may arise between contending delegations from the same state, the work of the platform committee in creating key compromises with which leading candidates will feel comfortable, or the maneuvering involved in the selection of a vice-presidential nominee.

PLATFORMS. The **party platform** as an expression of the intentions of the party is accorded little honor in the myths surrounding our politics. Yet, since campaigns are mainly battles for the votes of marginal (undecided) voters, the platform becomes an important political instrument. Although party platforms serve primarily as campaign instruments, fulfillment of platform pledges is common although not required. "Legislative or executive action directly fulfills more than half of the planks, and some definite action is taken in nearly three-fourths of the cases."[23]

The 1980 GOP and Democratic platforms differed sharply on such major issues as the economy, abortion, education, health, and the Equal Rights Amendment. The Republicans keyed their economic planks to major tax cuts and a reduction of government spending, while the Democrats called for very limited tax cuts and a $12 billion anti-recession jobs program. On abortion, the Republicans called for a constitutional amendment banning the procedure, a concept opposed by the Democrats. On ERA, the Republican position was not to become involved, leaving the ratification issue to the state legislators. The Democratic platform supported ratification, a boycott against holding national or regional party meetings in states that had not ratified the ERA, and withholding party funds from candidates opposed to the ERA. And, Republicans called for the elimination of the Department of Education and the ending of most federal regulation in that area, while their opposite numbers advocated an increase in the federal role.

The business of nominating and voting for the presidential candidate takes place on the third day of the convention; but, depending upon the particular political situation, the most dramatic moments of the convention may take place in the headquarters of the serious candidates and the caucus rooms of the large uncommitted delegations. Representatives of the leading candidates—Ford and Reagan for example—busily attempt to hold or form a majority, or if behind, desperately try to gain defectors and prevent a first-ballot nomination. In 1980, the key struggle was Kennedy's futile attempt to alter the rules to permit an "open" convention. The theory is that if the front-runner does not win on the first few ballots, he will suffer a significant erosion of strength, which can lead to another candidate's victory.

CHOOSING A V.P. The last day of the convention is devoted to the choice of the vice-presidential candidate. Recent conventions have merely ratified the presidential nominee's choice for his running mate. The vice-presidential choice usually reflects an attempt to produce a geographic balance on the ticket so that the two candidates can exploit their popularity in different sections of the nation.

What appears to be a routine matter can turn into a suspenseful event. In 1976, Jimmy Carter conducted a well-publicized talent search for a running mate, but kept his choice of Senator Walter F. Mondale of Minnesota a reasonably well-guarded secret. On the Republican side, Reagan tried to force Ford's hand before the nomination by announcing who his vice-presidential running mate would be and urging the convention to adopt a rule requiring the contenders to announce their choice in advance of the presidential nominating ballots. The convention rejected his plea. Ford eventually surprised the delegates when he selected Senator Robert Dole of Kansas to join him on the ticket.

While the Carter–Mondale ticket remained intact in 1980, the real drama of the Republican convention in Detroit revolved around the possibility that Gerald R. Ford would take the second spot on the Reagan ticket, an action that would have made him the first former president to run for vice-president.

Based upon private polls that suggested that Ford was the only Republican who would improve Reagan's prospects for victory, a group of influential Republicans arranged for negotiations between themselves and members of Reagan's team at the convention. Reagan and Ford met a number of times, and rumors mounted that Ford would be the nominee. However, Ford expressed, both to Reagan and during interviews with Walter Cronkite and Barbara Walters (see insert), a reluctance to operate within the normally limited scope of a vice-president, suggesting that he would have to be more of a White House Chief of Staff. His general description of his concept of a meaningful vice-presidency would have made him, in effect, a co-president with Reagan.

The negotiations broke down, and after midnight on July 17, Reagan appeared at the convention, announced that George Bush was his choice, and that Ford believed that he could be of more value campaigning than as a member of the ticket.

DELEGATE SELECTION. The composition of the 3,331 (1,666 needed to nominate) Democrats and 1,994 (998 needed to nominate) Republicans who went to New York City and Detroit in 1980 was, in part, a product of the reforms that followed the riot-torn 1968 Democratic Convention in Chicago. Amid the cries of war protestors, battles raged over the racial and sexual imbalance of delegations and the **unit rule,** long before abandoned by the Republicans, that required all delegates to cast their votes for the candidate supported by a majority of the state's delegation.

The convention ordered the establishment of a commission to study reform of the party structure and delegate selection. As a result, the unit rule was abolished at every stage of delegate selection, and state parties were required to "take affirmative steps to encourage participation" of blacks, Chicanos, young people, and women. Delegations were to include representatives of minorities and young persons in "reasonable proportions" to their representation in the party as a whole in that state. Winner-take-all primaries were scrapped with exceptions previously mentioned, and the concept of proportionate allocation of delegates was applied to the non-primary states where selection had to take place at open party caucuses at the congressional district level.

The sun had set on the old idea of state party leaders controlling hand-picked delegations, and the composition and independence of the post–1968 delegations reflected this fact.

In 1968, the Democratic delegations

In interviews with Walter Cronkite and Barbara Walters, Gerald Ford suggested a greatly expanded role for the vice-president that might have made the position acceptable to him.

I would not go to Washington and be a figurehead vice-president. If I go to Washington I have to be there in the belief that I would play a meaningful role.

CRONKITE interview, CBS, July 17, 1980

[Ford did not want the job unless his role would be] non-ceremonial, constructive and responsive. [Such an arrangement would require a] far different structure [from the duties performed by past vice-presidents.]

WALTERS interview, ABC, July 17, 1980

Source: Congressional Quarterly, *Weekly Report* 38 (July 19, 1980), pp. 1982–1983.

---

in Chicago had included only 13 percent women, 5.5 percent blacks, and 4 percent under thirty years of age. In 1972, the proportions rose to 38 percent women, 15 percent blacks, and 21 percent youths, and fell off to 34, 11, and 13 percent respectively in 1976. Five percent of the delegates were classified "other," including Spanish-speaking and American Indian. The Republicans also took steps to encourage a more diverse representation, and in 1972 and 1976, approximately 30 percent of their delegates were women, and 9 percent came from the 25-years-old-and-under group.[24]

The "reasonable" guideline for delegate selection had been interpreted as imposing a quota system on the state parties, and it created deep divisions in the party. The old line organized labor (AFL–CIO) and traditional party leaders were embittered by the rules and their loss of a virtual monopoly of power in state and local party organizations and delegate selection. The new powers in the Democratic Party are the women, blacks, Latinos, and the aggressive liberal labor unions, particularly the United Auto Workers,

the Communication Workers of America, and The American Federation of State, County and Municipal Workers.

THE GENERAL ELECTION CAMPAIGNS

One unique feature of American politics is the difference in the strategy employed in winning primaries and winning a general election. The primaries are basically intramural battles and the contenders take strong, even belligerent stands on the issues in an effort to distinguish themselves from their opponents. In the general election, the two survivors must appeal to the broadest possible constituency, hoping to hold party adherents in line, encouraging defections from the opposite party, and focusing on the forty percent of the population who now declare themselves to be *Independents* (see Chapters 7 and 8). The tendency is to make broad, issue-straddling appeals.

Perhaps the best example of a candidate trapped by his primary campaign image is provided by George McGovern. In 1972, he captured the nomination largely through the campaign efforts and voting support of people (primarily young) whose loyalties were stirred by his very liberal and outspoken stands on such issues as foreign policy, disarmament, abortion, and legalization of drugs such as marijuana. This "radical" image hurt him in the election campaign, alienating some of the traditional elements of the party coalition and many Independents. When he moved toward a more moderate, middle-of-the road approach during the campaign in an effort to build unity, he disillusioned numbers of his primary race supporters.

Of course, a change in time makes a difference. In the 1976 Democratic primaries, most of the candidates "ran against Washington" in an attempt to capitalize on mistrust of big government. Jimmy Carter was in the best position to do this because, unlike most of his opponents, he had no prior experience at the national level. Not surprisingly, the theme of mistrust carried over into the election campaign. Four years later, Jimmy Carter was "Washington," and had to defend "his" government from his opponent's attacks during the general election.

POLITICAL REALITIES. Each campaign has its own character, shaped by the candidates and the political, social, and economic climate of the times. However, there are a number of political "truths" or assumptions that influence campaign decisions. These are:

1. Voter turnout is unpredictable; therefore, it is necessary for party organizations and other groups (interest groups or temporary campaign groups) to try to get a candidate's supporters out to vote.

2. Interest groups and party organization can be appealed to on the basis of policy commitments and promises of access to decision-making.

3. The existing electoral college mechanism forces an emphasis upon winning at least some of the large two-party states.

4. Neither party can take the vote of any particular region for granted. However, the time and cost demands of a campaign suggest that the emphasis be placed on the competitive two-party states, taking some states, like predominantly Republican Kansas or Democratic Massachusetts, for granted.

5. Effective use of the media is essential, and media costs, particularly TV, require a careful husbanding of resources.

6. The Republican candidate, although representing the minority party (see Chapters 7 and 8), has an excellent chance of winning the presidency (Eisenhower, 1953–1959, Nixon–Ford, 1969–1977, and Reagan, 1981–). The need to appeal to the approximately forty percent of the voters who declare themselves to be independent, as opposed to a forty and twenty percent Democratic and Republican identification respectively, moderates the level of partisan campaign rhetoric.

PROS AND CONS OF INCUMBENCY. In addition to a financial advantage, an incumbent president can make things happen, while the challenger can only say what he or she would do if elected. While Jimmy Carter talked about expanding America's wilderness preserves in 1976, President Ford signed a bill that expanded the preserves. During the 1980 campaign, President Carter timed several key announcements, such as the August 28th release of his "economic blueprint for the 80's," promising tax relief for lower- and middle-income groups as well as tax and investment incentives for business.

The other side of the coin is that incumbents tend to be blamed for the domestic state of the nation and/or international problems. The burdens of incumbency—the Vietnam War—led to Lyndon B. Johnson's decision not to run in 1968, and being in the White House was a major problem for Carter in 1980.

In the case of Ford, he was not an "elected" president, and the Watergate affair had an impact on the outcome. Nevertheless, the keystone of Ford's campaign was his "incumbency," perhaps even to a greater extent than the campaigns of Lyndon Johnson in 1964 and Richard Nixon in 1972. A Republican campaign document advised the President to:

. . . resist his natural impulse to campaign and instead to stay put in the White House. He lacked the style to win on the hustings; his best bet was to appear presidential while Carter got into trouble on the road.[25]

This strategy almost worked; Ford nearly pulled off a political miracle, almost overcoming Carter's huge initial lead and losing by less than two percent of the vote.

THE TV DEBATES. The impact of the three nationally televised Ford–Carter debates will be argued for years to come. It was assumed that the lesson of the Nixon–Kennedy debates of 1960 was that an incumbent or the better known candidate (Nixon was then vice-president) would never again engage in public debates with an opponent. However, the public opinion polls taken at the conclusion of the Democratic Convention placed Carter a whopping thirty-three percentage points ahead of the President. By the end of the Republican Convention this lead had fallen to a wide, but more realistic, twelve points. In a calculated gamble, Ford challenged Carter to debate him in the series sponsored by the League of Women Voters. He assumed that he had little to lose and that he could take advantage of his prestige and the information available to him as the president. Carter was

eager to debate in an attempt to dispel the charge that he was ambiguous on most issues.

Almost seventy percent of all registered voters watched the debates, but different polls of viewers, taken after each encounter, presented conflicting opinions of who won or lost, with the possible exception of the second debate. If there was a critical point in the debates—and the Ford momentum had been building up to the second debate on October 6—it came when Ford said that "there is no Soviet domination of Eastern Europe and there never will be under a Ford administration." Carter replied:

I would like to see Mr. Ford convince the Polish Americans and the Czech Americans and the Hungarian Americans . . . that those countries don't live under the domination and supervision of the Soviet Union behind the Iron Curtain.

Ford's slip of the tongue placed in question his competency in foreign affairs, an area in which the incumbent should always have a clear advantage. His campaign stalled as he spent much of the next week or ten days explaining away this statement to the public in general and Americans of Eastern European heritage in particular.

It appears that the 1976 debates set a precedent, and in 1980 Carter said he would debate Reagan and Anderson on separate occasions. Reagan and Anderson pushed for three-way debates, but Carter, fearing a drawing off of Democratic votes by Anderson, refused and argued that a three-way debate would amount to two Republicans against one Democrat. Reagan and Anderson accepted a League of Women Voters' invitation to debate on September 21 in Baltimore. Both men made pointed reference to Carter's absence.

The League eliminated a barrier to Carter's participation when Anderson's support in the polls dipped below fifteen percent, a threshold they had established for his partic-

At home in front of television cameras, Jerry Falwell (foreground) is an effective leader of the "Moral Majority" which supports conservative candidates for national office.

four years ago?" was effective. After the debate, the Carter campaign seemed to lose momentum.

THE MEANING OF THE 1976 AND 1980 ELECTIONS

The election of 1976 confirmed a number of trends that had been developing since the 1960s. First, the South has changed. Although Carter's victories in the South were a product of a solid black vote, a majority of whites voted for Ford. However, enough whites responded to Carter's being a southerner to carry the region. But over and above that fact, the South has become a biracial voting area no longer dominated by the white vote. The 1980 election proved that the Democratic Party could not assume that the South has returned to the fold, as Carter's place of residence had almost no impact the second time around.

Second, and of significance nationwide, is that the black voters have become a major force in American presidential politics. In 1976 Carter received five of every six votes cast by blacks, but he was the choice of only a minority (forty-six percent) of white Americans. His narrow victories in many states was attributable to the solidarity of the black vote. In 1980, blacks and Hispanics gave Carter eighty percent of their vote, a decline from 1976, but their support could not offset other defections from the Democratic coalition.

A third lesson of both campaigns is that dependence on a big-city strategy in the future will be a risky business. City populations have declined, and the winner in the more populous states must do well in the sub-

ipation in the debates. Carter agreed to meet Reagan in a debate held in Cleveland on October 28th. The polls had shown Carter closing the gap on Reagan, and the President viewed the debates as an opportunity to raise voter fears that Reagan, as a hawkish right-winger, would be a threat to world peace. For his part, Reagan welcomed an opportunity to refute this, appear presidential, and attack Carter's alleged mismanagement of the economy.

The effect of the debate was difficult to gauge, but most polls showed that viewers believed Reagan had won by a narrow margin. Neither candidate made a major gaffe like Ford's "Eastern Europe" remark, and Reagan's stage presence, affable manner, and responses appeared to dispel the warmonger image. And, his oft-repeated question to the viewers, "Are you better off than you were

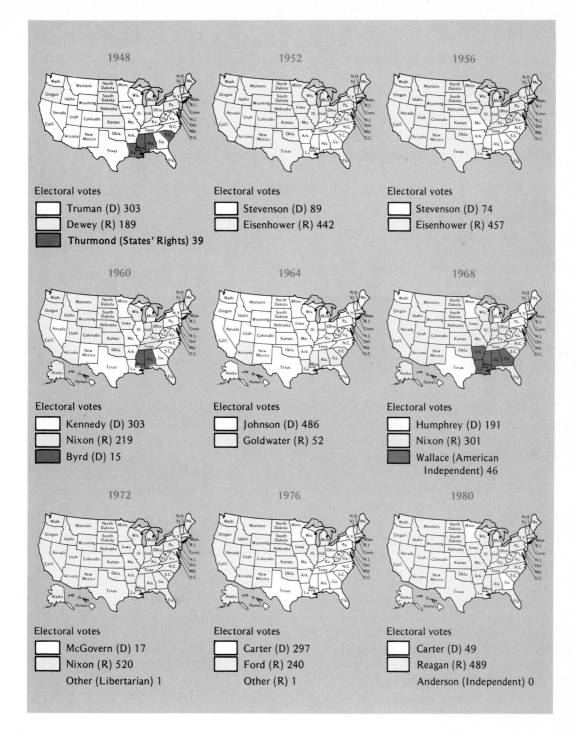

Figure 9–4 The results of presidential elections: 1948–1980.

urbs, in particular, small towns and rural areas. A striking example is provided by Chicago which in 1976 gave two-thirds of its vote to Carter who lost the state by 3 percentage points. In 1960, Chicago provided better than one-third of the total state vote in Illinois. In 1976 it contributed only 25 percent.[26]

Fourth, a look at the electoral map (see Figure 9–4) can present a distorted picture of an election. On the surface, the 1976 map suggested that the outcome of the contest was determined by sectional decisions, with Carter elected by the South and East. But, the outcome was a national decision that divided the voters within states, not among states. In only 20 of the 50 states and the District of Columbia was the margin of victory more than 10 percent. Nationally, a shift in 1 voter in 100—one percentage point—would have sent Ford back to the White House. A shift in 2 votes in 100 either way would have meant a very comfortable electoral college victory for Ford and/or a landslide for Carter. No less than 18 states had contests that fell within this narrow range. On the other hand, no such electoral map confusion existed in 1980, when Reagan carried 44 states, 489 electoral votes, and 51 percent of the vote, compared with 41 percent for Carter and 7 percent for Anderson. In only 10 states was the victory margin 2 percent or less, and Reagan won 9 of these contests.

Fifth, and of vital importance to the Democratic Party, is the fragility of the Democratic coalition. Both elections demonstrated that economic issues are the key to holding on to the votes of the working class, and the religious minorities. This is particularly true because the groups that were the beneficiaries of the New Deal policies of the 1930s and 1940s now see themselves as benefactors whose taxes pay for welfare programs for the less advantaged, many of whom are the still-loyal blacks and Hispanics.

Labor, which deserted the party in 1972, gave more than 60 percent of its vote to Carter, but support from Catholics, Jews and the young fell below expectations. But, in 1980, the bottom fell out, and for the first time since the 1930s polls reported that the Republican Party was looked at as the group best able to deal with the economy. This attitude was reflected in the presidential and congressional races.

Post-election surveys—often polling place exit interviews—revealed that Carter received only 5 percent more of the vote of members of union families than Reagan and that the Jewish vote split 42 to 35 to 13 percent for Carter, Reagan, and Anderson respectively. The President got only 67 percent of the votes of Democrats compared with 79 percent in 1976, and he also was hurt by the failure of many Democrats to vote, a reflection of their unhappiness with Carter and their reluctance to vote for Reagan.[27]

While the surveys focused upon the presidential contest, the breakdown of the coalition seriously affected many congressional races. It undercut the long held Democratic assumption that the party is so strong at the congressional level that it can withstand the burden of an overwhelming defeat by the head of the ticket.

As we suggested in Chapter 7, the Democratic Party must regroup and redefine its liberal position. It is too early to tell whether or not a realignment of the parties is in the making. Perhaps 1980 represented a disalignment. On the other hand, the 1980 results did indicate a continuation of the drift to the right characterized by a growing dissatisfaction with large government outlays for social-economic programs, particularly those designed to aid the disadvantaged. Finally, the election did little to undercut the dominance of the two major parties. The viability of John Anderson's challenge appeared to be heavily dependent upon the unpopularity of Carter, rather than on a widespread belief that neither major-party candidate could lead the nation.

Congressional Campaigns

Are the advantages of incumbent representatives and senators so great that, in general, the contest for congressional seats is not really competitive? Since 1896, fifty percent of the winners in House elections have won by at least a sixty to forty margin, the equivalent of a landslide. In 1980, 252 of the 435 contests were non-competitive. It is not unusual for ten to fifteen percent of the major party candidates to face no opposition in the general elections from another major-party candidate.

Turnover in the House of Representatives seldom exceeds twenty percent. But in

★ ★ ★ *Table 9–5* ★
The re-election success of incumbents: 1946–1980

	SENATE					HOUSE			
YEAR	SEEKING RE-ELECTION	DEFEATED PRIMARY	DEFEATED GENERAL	PERCENT RE-ELECTED	YEAR	SEEKING RE-ELECTION	DEFEATED PRIMARY	DEFEATED GENERAL	PERCENT RE-ELECTED
1946	30	6	7	56.7	1946	398	18	52	82.4
1948	25	2	8	60.0	1948	400	15	68	79.2
1950	32	5	5	68.8	1950	400	6	32	90.5
1952	31	2	9	64.5	1952	389	9	26	91.0
1954	32	2	6	75.0	1954	407	6	22	93.1
1956	29	0	4	86.2	1956	411	6	16	94.6
1958	28	0	10	64.3	1958	396	3	37	89.9
1960	29	0	1	96.6	1960	405	5	25	92.6
1962	35	1	5	82.9	1962	402	12	22	91.5
1964	33	1	4	84.8	1964	397	8	45	86.6
1966	32	3	1	87.5	1966	411	8	41	88.1
1968	28	4	4	71.4	1968	409	4	9	96.8
1970	31	1	6	77.4	1970	401	10	12	94.5
1972	27	2	5	74.1	1972	390	12	13	93.6
1974	27	2	2	85.2	1974	391	8	40	87.7
1976	25	0	9	64.0	1976	384	3	13	95.8
1978	25	3	7	60.0	1978	382	5	19	93.7
1980	29	4	9	55.2	1980	398	6	31	90.7

Note: Number seeking re-election is the total number of seats up for election less those where the incumbent was retiring or running for another office or where a vacancy existed.

Source: Congressional Quarterly, *Weekly Report* 38 (April 5, 1980), p. 908. 1980 figures from 38 (November 8, 1980), pp. 3302, 3318–21. Reprinted by permission.

1974, new faces accounted for twenty-one percent of the membership. There were a large number of retirements, and in the first election after "Watergate," Republican incumbents were hit particularly hard. The defeat of ten incumbent senators in 1978 and 1980 contributed to the largest freshmen classes for the upper chamber since 1958.

Table 9-5 documents the exceptional track record of incumbents in both primary and general elections. Retirements have become a significant element in the turnover in both houses, contributing to the relative newness of the members. More than half the legislators in each chamber were first elected in 1974 or in subsequent elections.

Every race has a character of its own determined by the nature of the candidates, state or local conditions, whether or not it is a presidential election year, or the general political climate which may be operating against incumbents—as was the case with the "Watergate" backlash of 1974. Challengers must weigh all these factors (as well as the advantages held by incumbents) before deciding to invest the time, money, and emotion that go into a congressional race.

THE PROBLEM OF GETTING NOMINATED

Securing party nomination has moved from self-announcement or selection by an informal party caucus to our present-day primary system. But primary challenges are seldom very challenging. Turnout in most primaries is very low, often attracting less than thirty percent of the eligible voters.

INCUMBENCY ADVANTAGES. Incumbents enjoy a great edge in the primaries because they are known to the voters, have better access to information about issues and voter attitudes, and can use their existing contacts

and campaign organizations to great advantage. Their proven vote-getting abilities and congressional voting records are used to acquire funds and the support of non-party groups. In races where the incumbent appears to be "safe," the out-party usually takes little interest in candidate recruitment. In these contests "political parties and their leadership permit the self-recruitment of poorly prepared, inexperienced, and naive candidates."[28]

In the few primaries where challengers unseat incumbents, they usually manage to outspend their opponents. In primaries where there is no incumbent or the incumbent appears to be vulnerable, primary costs can be high; and in Senate races, it can be astronomical. For example, in 1978 four Democratic contenders for the Senate spent over $1 million in unsuccessful primary races.

THE GENERAL ELECTION CAMPAIGN

The advantages of incumbents generally carry over into the general election. Usually, the challenger must start from scratch. In addition, if the state or national party organization views the district as safe for the present officeholder, the challenger will receive little or no campaign assistance—monetary or otherwise—from his party (see insert). The incumbent, on the other hand, is likely to receive campaign assistance from party committees at all levels. The overall result is that many House seats go virtually unchallenged. On the Senate side, most seats are seriously contested, and non-incumbents are rarely left to flounder. But even in these statewide races, incumbents are better organized and financed and are usually heavy favorites to win.

The national party organizations prepare a target list of seats held by the other party where there is a reasonable hope of turnover, and campaign assistance is directed

Viewpoint:
Odds on favorite—To lose

This selection discusses the way parties leave challengers on their own when they are in races against heavily favored incumbents or in a non-incumbent race where the other party dominates the district.

The candidate was destined for defeat the day he announced and filed his petitions for his party's nomination for election to the U.S. House of Representatives. No nominee of his party has received more than forty-two percent of the vote in the congressional election in that district for over thirty years. . . .

The leaders of the party, used to losing this particular contest, provided but perfunctory encouragement. Realizing full well the hopelessness of this effort, barring a miracle, they were reluctant to discourage a candidate who, for whatever reason, was willing to enter the fray.

Source: Robert J. Huckshorn and Robert C. Spencer, *The Politics of Defeat* (Amherst: University of Mass. Press, 1971), p. 1

mainly towards these marginal contests. Challengers who decide to run hopeless races in "safe" districts or states ordinarily do so because of one or more of the following reasons: a strong belief that the democratic system requires challenges to incumbents; loyalty to the party; and desire to gain exposure for programmatic or ideological positions.

COATTAILS. During presidential election years, all other races are affected by the contest for the White House. When a strong presidential candidate carries a majority of his party into the House or adds to his party's strength in the Senate, it is said that some of his partisans have ridden into office on his coattails—the **coattail effect.** This was the case in 1932 when Franklin Roosevelt won and transformed the Democrats into America's majority party. But in only three of the last eight presidential elections (1948, 1964 and 1980) has there been a strong coattail effect. In 1964, a reverse-coattail phenomenon was in operation, with voter shifts being

chalked up more to abandonment of Barry Goldwater than to a positive feeling for Lyndon B. Johnson, and many observers believed that the same thing happened in 1980.

Another phenomenon is the off-year losses ordinarily suffered by the president's party. Since 1934, when the Democrats picked up strength in both houses, the only exceptions to the rule have been 1962 and 1970, when the incumbent president's party gained seats in the Senate. The pattern of the last forty-two years suggests that the off-year loss phenomenon is stronger than presidential coattails. A reason for this may be that the off-year elections attract more "negative" voters who are dissatisfied with the majority party's performance and vote accordingly.

The fear of the coattail effect is one reason for congressional resistance to proposals for a four-year term for House members that would coincide with the presidential terms. And, while advocates of a strong presidency see the idea as a means of making Congress more responsive to executive leadership, backers of congressional independence favor the present two-year term or a four-year term with House elections coming during the non-presidential election years.

The discussion of the presidential and congressional campaigns has highlighted the high cost of winning office. Our "Issue" section focusses upon the possible abuse of the dollar as a political tool.

★ Issue ★

Are American Elections Won or Bought?

Does money win elections? Obviously, money rarely loses an election unless a candidate so badly misuses it that he leaves a bad taste in the mouths of the voters. But, as one scholar points out:

. . . money isn't everything. Issues, organization, leadership, skill, control of information, the prestige of the office, and the advantages of incumbency count heavily. In the end, people, not dollars cast the vote.[29]

Still, there are very few elections that can be won without a minimum campaign chest. "Money translates into messages that candidates send to prospective voters, and candidates must be able to deliver a sufficient number of messages if free elections are not to be a mockery."[30]

How much inequality can money buy? Does personal wealth, corporate wealth, and special-interest wealth own America by buying up its politicians? Do you need your own money to run for office?

A case can be made that the effects of personal wealth have been overrated at the presidential level. Thomas Dewey, Harry Truman, Hubert Humphrey, Richard Nixon, and George McGovern, among other presidential candidates, were not wealthy when they first ran for the White House (though some presidents have become wealthy before leaving it). And, the post–1974 regulations have removed the direct expenditure of personal wealth from the presidential, but not the congressional contests. At either level, however, the candidate of great personal wealth may have considerable advantages beyond personal seed money to invest in his or her own campaign. The wealthy usually have wealthy friends, some of whom can drop everything to devote their prestigious efforts to their friend's campaign.

SPECIAL INTEREST DOMINATION? The key question may be whether or not American democracy, through the medium of money, screens out capable individuals who are unwilling to "talk turkey" with important interests, and find themselves consequently unable to attract the financial support necessary for a political campaign. Would Standard Oil, ITT, or the AFL–CIO be willing to put up the money to support a candidate not committed or willing to make commitments to certain policies? The answer is fairly obvious. Does this mean, then, that money sets the limits beyond which ideas, the heart of a democratic process, cannot stray? Are certain people simply locked out of our politics because they can't buy their way onto TV and into the hearts of America?

The crucial point may not be how much money a candidate inherits from his parents or makes in business, but what effect the appeal to vested interests for funds has on any person, rich or poor. If funding sources are people or interests who wish preferential treatment from the government, how can a winner enter office not "locked-in" to certain commitments which may have nothing to do with the public interest or the reasons ordinary Americans voted the candidate into office? Testifying before a Senate hearing, Senator Russell Long (D., La.) commented on how the "needs" of a campaign can alter a candidate's perspective:

I have seen men start out running for Governor with the firm intention of promising nothing. Coming down the stretch, I have seen them making commitments that it made me sick to see. They did it because they could not pay for radio and television. . . .[31]

Moreover, if both candidates in a campaign must go the same funding route, then what real choice is offered to the voter? Do voters simply find themselves voting for one unknown powerful minority of interests rather than another? Does money restrict real choice in American elections?

As we have seen, the reforms of 1974 that limit large individual contributions to all races, restrict the use of personal money by presidential candidates, and provide partial public financing for presidential primaries and full public financing for the general elections, have taken the presidential races off the auction block. Unfortunately, special interest groups have diverted the dollars that used to be spent on presidential elections to the congressional races.

Although the biggest spender does not always win the election, particularly when challenging an incumbent, does that actually prove that the power of monied interests are less than we might expect? It may, in fact, only prove that we are engaging in a "politics of dollar overkill," with outlays going beyond the point of diminishing returns. Candidates who have the funds spend lavishly out of uncertainty, to convince all concerned that they are serious, or to put on a "good show" to stimulate their campaign workers.

One U.S. Senator said: "The trouble is that you never know the basic minimum that you need. You have to overspend just to make sure that you reach that point."[32] Another commented: "If a candidate feels he can get his story across it takes a lot of pressure off. If I spent $200,000 on television and my opponent spent $400,000, I think I could beat him. But if I spent $100,000 and he spent $300,000 it might be a different story."[33]

DO WE SPEND TOO MUCH? Overall, do we spend too much money on political campaigning? In terms of the total amount of money spent by governments at all levels or as share of our gross national product, the answer is no. The $300 million spent in 1968 was 1/1000 of government spending and .0003 of the GNP. And it was only $30 million more than Proctor and Gamble's advertising budget for 1968.[34] The answer is a probable yes in terms of the effectiveness of the dollars spent and a definite yes if it keeps good people out of electoral contests and makes losers of the American people.

While the reforms of 1974 took the presidential elections off the auction block, it appears that congressional races went on the block. The Supreme Court's 1976 decision gives full reign to personally wealthy congressional candidates. Special interests now lavish their dollars on contenders for House and Senate seats. The solutions to this problem may be some form of public funding of these contests. Alexander Heard writes: ". . . it is clear that under some conditions the use of funds can be decisive. And under others no amount of money spent by the loser could alter the outcome. . . . Financial outlays cannot guarantee victory in elections."[35] But the absence of financial resources prevents some candidates from having the opportunity to be winners or losers.

Summary

The electoral process itself has been the subject of considerable debate, but the electoral college and the hybrid system of primaries and conventions by which we choose presidential nominees appear to be in no real danger of being abandoned.

Our sketch of some of the factors influencing congressional and presidential campaigns recognizes that each campaign is a unique event, shaped by the personalities involved and the political environment in which the race is contested. The early 1970s witnessed the fuller realization of political involvement and power by minorities, and women in particular, and lends encouragement to those seeking to make the system more representative. On the other hand, a theme running through the entire chapter is "the power of incumbency."

Incumbents have the advantages of name familiarity, more information on issues, and past opportunities to serve individual and group interests; as a result of these advantages they have a much easier time raising funds for their campaigns. The advantages of incumbency and the high cost of many congressional contests and all presidential races raise grave doubts about the competitiveness of the system and the obligations that the winners carry into office. For those who contribute large sums of money to campaigns usually are buying access and/or hope for favorable consideration of certain policy questions. The Federal Election Campaign Act of 1974, as modified by the Supreme Court, restricts the costs of presidential elections, but the failure of Congress to extend public financing to its own races leaves the money advantages of incumbency largely intact.

One lesson of the 1974 reform is that reform often has surprising side effects. Public financing of presidential campaigns has altered primary strategy, perhaps making the primary/caucus system unrepresentative. And, the incumbent edge may have been enlarged by the limit placed on general election spending.

Terms to Remember

See the Glossary at the end of the book for definitions.

Balanced budget

Blanket primary

Closed primary

Coattail effect

Coordinated spending

Delegate selection primary

Direct national primary

Disclosure rule

Federal Election Campaign Act of 1974

Federal Election Commission

Gerrymandering

Office block ballot

Open primary

Open-seat races

Party column ballot

Party platform

Presidential preference primary

Raiding

Unit rule

Notes

1. Quoted in *Newsweek,* November 17, 1980, p. 29. See pp. 27–32 for an excellent analysis of the election. Also see Congressional Quarterly, *Weekly Report,* 38 (November 8, 1980), pp. 3296–3299.

2. Gerald M. Pomper, *Elections in America* (New York: Dodd, Mead & Company, Inc., 1968), p. 67. Also see John W. Kingdon, "Politicians' Beliefs About Voters," *American Political Science Review,* 61 (March, 1967), pp. 137–145.

3. Angus Campbell, Philip E. Converse, Warren E. Miller, and Ronald E. Stokes, *The American Voter* (New York: Wiley, 1960), p. 285.

4. Congressional Quarterly, *Weekly Report,* 31 (December 1, 1973), p. 3130. For Gardner, see 31 (September 22, 1973), p. 2515.

5. See Herbert E. Alexander, *Financing the 1964 Election* (Princeton, N.J.: Citizens' Research Foundation, 1966), p. 13; Herbert E. Alexander, *Financing the 1972 Election,* p. 77; Herbert E. Alexander, *Financing Politics* (Washington, D.C.: Congressional Quarterly, 1976).

6. *Election '80* (Washington, D.C.: Congressional Quarterly, 1980), p. 134.

7. Ibid., p. 133.

8. Ibid., p. 134.

9. *Dollar Politics,* vol. 1 (Washington, D.C.: Congressional Quarterly, 1971), pp. 22, 30.

10. Quoted in *Dollar Politics,* vol. 2 (Washington, D.C.: Congressional Quarterly, 1974), p. 20.

11. Joe McGinnis, *The Selling of the President 1968* (New York: Trident Press, 1969), p. 204.

12. Gary C. Jacobson, "The Impact of Broadcast Campaigning on Electoral Outcomes," paper presented at the 1974 Annual Meeting of the American Political Science Association, August 29–September 2, 1974, pp. 48–50.

13. *Dollar Politics,* vol. 2, p. 69.

14. *Buckley* v. *Valeo,* 424 U.S. 1936 (1976).

15. Congressional Quarterly, *Weekly Report,* 34 (October 23, 1976), p. 3033.

16. *Newsweek,* November 24, 1980, p. 48. For a discussion of party campaign spending and figures, see Congressional Quarterly, *Weekly Report* 38 (November 1, 1980), p. 3234–39.

17. CBS–TV Interview, April 27, 1972.

18. Survey by Peter D. Hart cited in Congressional Quarterly, *Weekly Report,* 35 (October 29, 1977), p. 2300.

19. David E. Rosenbaum, "Reform, Yes, But Congress Protected Its Flanks," *New York Times,* October 6, 1974, p. E2.

20. Quoted in *Election '80,* p. 127.

21. Dan Campbell, "Primaries Went According to Form—Or Did They?," *Rochester Democrat and Chronicle,* June 8, 1980, p. A14.

22. Clinton Rossiter, *Parties and Politics in America* (Ithaca: Cornell University Press, 1969), p. 153.

23. Gerald Pomper, *Nominating the President* (Evanston, Ill.: Northwestern University Press, 1963), p. 202. For a narration of convention politics, see Theodore H. White, *The Making of the President, 1960* (New York: Atheneum Publishers, 1961).

24. *The Party Reformed: Final Report of the Commission on Party Structure and Delegate Selection* (Washington, D.C.: Democratic National Committee, July 7, 1972), pp. 7–8. Figures for the Republicans are from Congressional Quarterly, *Weekly Report,* 33 (August 16, 1975), p. 1807. Democratic 1976 figures are from *Weekly Report,* 34 (July 17, 1976), pp. 1874–75.

25. Cited in *Time,* November 15, 1976, p. 37.

26. Gerald Pomper and colleagues, *The Election of 1976* (New York: David McKay Co., 1977), p. 73. Much of our analysis of the 1976 election and what it suggests for the future is drawn from Chapter 3 of this excellent book of essays.

27. *Newsweek,* November 27, 1980, pp. 31–32, and Congressional Quarterly, *Weekly Report,* 38 (November 8, 1980), pp. 3296–98.

28. Robert J. Huckshorn and Robert C. Spencer, *The Politics of Defeat* (Amherst: University of Massachusetts Press, 1971), p. 43.

29. Herbert E. Alexander, *Political Financing* (Minneapolis: Burgess Publishing, 1972), p. 14.

30. Stephen Hess, *Presidential Campaign* (Washington, D.C.: The Brookings Institution, 1972), pp. 80–81. Hess's discussion of money goes beyond presidential campaigns and extends to congressional races.

31. Delmar D. Dunn, *Financing Presidential Campaigns,* (Washington, D.C.: The Brookings Institution, 1972), p. 24. This study also discusses money in the context of congressional campaigns.

32. Ibid., p. 5. Also see Alexander, *Political Financing,* pp. 16–17.

33. Ibid., p. 10.

34. Alexander, *Political Financing,* pp. 38–

39. Also see David W. Adamany, *Campaign Finance in America* (N. Scituate, Mass.: Duxbury Press, 1972), p. 12.

35. *The Costs of Democracy* (Chapel Hill: University of North Carolina Press, 1960), p. 16.

Suggested Readings

David Adamany, *Campaign Finance in America* (N. Scituate, Mass.: Duxbury Press, 1972).

Herbert E. Alexander, *Financing Politics* (Washington, D.C.: Congressional Quarterly, 1976).

Angus Campbell, Philip E. Converse, Warren E. Miller, and Donald E. Stokes, *The American Voter* (New York: Wiley, 1960).

Delmar D. Dunn, *Financing Presidential Campaigns* (Washington, D.C.: Brookings Institution, 1972).

Alexander Heard, *The Costs of Democracy* (Chapel Hill: University of North Carolina Press, 1960).

William R. Keech and Donald R. Matthews, *The Party's Choice* (Washington, D.C.: Brookings Institution, 1976).

Joe McGinnis, *The Selling of the President 1968* (New York: Trident Press, 1969).

Gerald Pomper and colleagues, *The Election of 1980* (New York: David McKay, 1977).

Stephen J. Wayne, *The Road to the White House* (New York: St. Martin's Press, 1980).

Theodore H. White, *The Making of the President, 1972* (New York: Atheneum, 1973).

Theodore H. White, *The Making of the President, 1968* (New York: Atheneum, 1969).

Theodore H. White, *The Making of the President, 1964* (New York: Atheneum, 1965).

Theodore H. White, *The Making of the President, 1960* (New York: Atheneum, 1961).

CHAPTER 10

Congress: Representatives and Representation

★ ★

Legislation is . . . a business in which you do something, then wait and see who hollers, and then relieve the hollering as best you can to see who else hollers.

T.V. SMITH
Social Forces

In 1976 the House Committee on Standards of Official Conduct (Ethics Committee) took its first action against a member in its eight-year history when it "reprimanded" Robert L. F. Sikes (D., Fla.). Sikes had become a millionaire during his service on the House Appropriations Committee's Subcommittee on Military Construction, which he chaired. Subsequently it was revealed that he had profited from investments in a bank that he persuaded the Navy to build on a Florida base. He also pushed legislation that permitted development of land in which he had a secret interest. Though congressional rules do not prohibit investments that conflict with official duties, Sikes was guilty of failing to follow the House rule that requires the listing of investments (disclosure) on an annual financial statement that is available for public inspection.

When Congress convened in January 1977, the Appropriations Committee voted to allow Sikes to keep his chairmanship. The Democratic caucus, however, voted to strip him of his post, and Sikes did not seek re-election in 1978.

The reaction to the Sikes case by long-time House and Senate staff aides (see insert) suggested some of the complexities of the representative function, particularly the demands to vote for "good" or "bad" projects for the state or district. For some, it is only a small step from voting bad projects for constituents to voting questionable projects for favored friends, or themselves.[1] In the category of "friends" we would have to include the special interest groups, from within and without the legislators' **constituencies,** whose substantial campaign contributions are a major source of their access and influence.

Early in his first term, Jimmy Carter discovered congressional sensitivity when he announced his intention not to approve the

★ ★

Viewpoint:
Congressional aides on the realities of representation

The aides who work for members of Congress get a first-hand look at pressures on legislators to push any policy, good or bad, which gets results for constituents or special interests back home. Here is how they see the legislator's dilemma.

There's no real oversight (of the executive branch) because they (legislators) can't live without the boodle from the agencies they're supposed to be watching. Their constituents don't judge them on how well they supervise the Department of the Interior, but only on the number of land-reclamation projects they get for their state.

Senate aide

There are pressures from back home that say "get everything you can for the state," whether it's good or not, whether they deserve it or not. What sort of ethics do you expect when they're voting hundreds of millions of dollars like that day after day?

Senate aide

Many of the old-timers see Mr. Sikes as being punished not for making money, but for doing favors for others. And that's their stock-in-trade. They all know that back in the home district there's someone younger, handsomer, and more energetic who wants their job, and the only advantage they've got is that they can do favors.

House aide

Source: Anthony Marro, "Congressional Ethics and the Need for Basic Reform," *New York Times*, January 30, 1977, p. E5. © 1977 by the New York Times Co. Reprinted by permission.

funding of eighteen water projects because they were unsupportable on economic, environmental, and/or safety grounds. He had not consulted the legislators whose states and districts would be affected, and they, and many of their colleagues, were enraged. The House refused to go along with Carter and passed a public-works jobs' bill that required the spending of the appropriated money for the projects. In the face of a threatened presidential veto, the Senate eliminated funds for nine projects and reduced funding for four others, and the House accepted the compromise. It can be argued that the President won in this case, but at the price of strained relations with Congress.

This chapter explores the background of members of Congress, and the nature of the representative function including voting behavior; it ends with a discussion of congressional ethics. It seeks to provide some answers to the following: Is Congress an unrepresentative body? What is the impact of constituency on voting behavior? Does the desire for re-election distort the activities of the legislators and contribute to the slowness of congressional reaction to the need for programmatic change? Does the congressional environment

foster an abuse of office? What is the significance of the new codes of ethics? Questions
concerning the rules and procedures of Congress, majority rule, and the ability of the institution to make public policy are taken up in
the next chapter.

Congressional Power

In 1907, Woodrow Wilson, while still
a political scientist at Princeton University,
described the president's authority over Congress in these words: "The President is at liberty, both in law and conscience, to be as big
a man as he can."[2] He believed that if the
president confronted Congress with accomplished facts, it could not resist his will, particularly in the area of foreign policy. Yet
when he became president, Congress proved
far more difficult than he had imagined. In the
end, the Senate's rejection of the Versailles
Treaty, which he negotiated after World War
I, shattered his career and his health. He had
made a spectacular miscalculation. Both before and since Wilson, presidents have had to
learn to live with the fact that while the president proposes, Congress disposes, more often
than not by failure to enact presidential measures. Table 10–1 gives the "Presidential
Boxscore" (1954–1975). It shows that in
only five of the twenty-two years have presidents seen at least half of their legislative proposals approved by Congress. Moreover, this
does not include the fact that Congress often
returns legislation to the chief executive substantially altered or containing provisions
with which he is not happy.

Beginning in 1976, the Congressional
Quarterly abandoned the boxscore; now it
lists only a presidential success rate based on
legislation that is voted on in the House and
Senate. Since many bills never get out of committee, and this accounted for low boxscore
percentages, this approach gives presidents

*Most presidents have learned that a power resides
in the halls of the United States Congress that
can make or break administration policy
initiatives.*

much higher, but somewhat misleading,
scores. For example, Ford's 1975 twenty-
seven percent boxscore rating is in contrast
with a presidential success score of sixty-one
percent.

Congress is one of the world's oldest
representative assemblies which has maintained its constitutional powers intact. In few
other places in the world does a national legislature play as active and decisive a role as
Congress does in the formulation of public
policy. Yet the governing role Congress plays
changes over time. For example, the president
and his staff have become the authors of most
of the nation's key legislation. In a real sense,
the president is the agenda-setter for Con-

gress. But the legislators are still the lawmakers, with the power to confer or withhold consent, to grant or refuse the purse, and to oversee the administration.

THE POWER "NOT TO ACT." The criticism and praise that inaction brings on Congress is discussed in the next chapter. At this point, however, we must point out that criticism and

★ ★ ★ *Table 10–1* ★
Presidential boxscore: 1954–1975

YEAR	PRESIDENT	PROPOSALS SUBMITTED	NUMBER APPROVED BY CONGRESS	% APPROVED
1954	Eisenhower	232	150	65
1955	Eisenhower	207	96	46
1956	Eisenhower	225	103	46
1957	Eisenhower	206	76	37
1958	Eisenhower	234	110	47
1959	Eisenhower	228	93	41
1960	Eisenhower	183	56	31
1961	Kennedy	355	172	48
1962	Kennedy	298	133	45
1963	Kennedy	401	109	27
1964	Johnson	217	125	58
1965	Johnson	469	323	69
1966	Johnson	371	207	56
1967	Johnson	431	205	48
1968	Johnson	414	227	55
1969	Nixon	171	55	32
1970	Nixon	210	97	46
1971	Nixon	202	40	20
1972	Nixon	116	51	44
1973	Nixon	183	57	31
1974	Nixon	97	33	34
1974	Ford	64	23	36
1975	Ford	156	42	27

The boxscore includes only the specific presidential legislative requests contained in the president's messages to Congress and other public statements during a calendar year. Measures endorsed by the president but not specifically requested by him, nominations, and routine budget requests are not included. The boxscore was discontinued in 1975.

Source: Figures for 1954–1971, Congressional Quarterly, *Weekly Report,* 30 (February 19, 1972), p. 386. For 1972, see Congressional Quarterly, *Almanac,* 1972, p. 76. For 1973, 1974, and 1975, see *Weekly Report* 32 (February 16, 1974), p. 331; 33 (February 22, 1975), p. 369; 34 (March 20, 1976), p. 649.

praise, not surprisingly, are based upon whose policies win and whose policies lose. The legislator often is a middle man or broker in a clash of warring interests between groups who expect to "win" on certain policies. The legislator's attitude toward these contestants is shaped by interests that are a product of his or her own background and the overriding interest in winning re-election. This suggests that the contestants who have the best odds are those whose interests most nearly resemble those of the individual legislators and/or the majority of the members of Congress.

Members of Congress and the Legislative Career

Is our national representative assembly made up of individuals drawn from a cross-section of the American public? The answer is no. The average member of Congress is atypical in social position and family background. *He* is white, Protestant, native-born, college-educated, and from an upper middle-class background. Though drawn from the upwardly mobile groups of the society, most legislators do not trace their backgrounds to what we would call the upper class—people of long established "old wealth." But they started life with certain advantages and capitalized upon them.

LAWYERS AND BUSINESSMEN. Politically, the United States has always been a country of lawyers. The predominance of lawyers in Congress today can best be explained by the fact that a lawyer's role as advocate is a natural preparation for a future political life. In addition, participation in public affairs is professionally beneficial to lawyers and their firms. Even at the national level, many congressmen retain ties with their firms and engage in legal work. And, it is important to remember that

most lawyers in Congress have longstanding relationships with business. The "agricultural" category could be merged with "business," as most lawmakers listing this profession were in agriculture-related business.

The figures for the 96th Congress continued the recent trend in the dramatic drop in the number of people listing "Public Service/Politics" as a prior occupation. Four years before, 440 members placed themselves in this category, but only 86 did so in 1977. Legislators are free to list more than one occupation, and their failure to identify with politics should not be taken as a sign that "amateurism" is the rule of the day. We suspect the omissions were a reflection of the "running-against-Washington" and "anti-professional politician" themes of the 1976 and 1978 campaigns. In fact, a higher percentage of freshmen in the 95th Congress had held prior elective office than had the newcomers in the 94th Congress.

RELIGIOUS BACKGROUND. Sociological studies have shown that a majority of the upper and upper-middle classes identify with the Presbyterian, Episcopal, and Methodist denominations, and these are the groups that members of Congress are most likely to come from. Table 10–2, however, indicates that a few countertrends are developing. The number of women and blacks in Congress is slowly increasing, and the average age of House members is falling relatively rapidly. The year 1975 marked the first time since World War II that the average age in either chamber dropped below fifty. In that year eighty-seven members of Congress were under forty, an increase of more than fifty percent from the previous Congress.

Still, it is obvious that women, racial and ethnic minorities, non–Christians, and individuals in lower-level occupational skills are comparative strangers on Capitol Hill. In 1979, only seventeen blacks, seventeen women, four Asian-Americans, and five Hispanic-Americans served in Congress.

The 1980 election did little to change the picture. One less black was elected, and women made only marginal gains, adding two to their number. One, however, was Paula Hawkins (R., Fla.), who was elected to the Senate. The youth movement continued, with eight representatives under thirty years old winning. The number of lawyers declined,

★ ★ ★ *Table 10–2* ★
Characteristics of members of two Congresses

	91ST CONGRESS (1969–1970)			96TH CONGRESS (1979–1980)		
	SENATE	*HOUSE*	*TOTAL*	*SENATE*	*HOUSE*	*TOTAL*
AVERAGE AGE	56.5	52.2	**	52.7	48.8	49.5
Number of women	1	10	11	1	16	17
Number of blacks	1	9	10	0	17	17
PRIOR OCCUPATIONS[1]						
Agriculture	16	34	50	6	19	25
Business or banking	25	159	184	29	127	156
Educator	14	59	73	7	57	64
Engineer	0	0	0	0	2	2
Journalism	8	39	47	2	11	13
Labor leader	0	0	0	0	4	4
Law	68	242	310	65	205	270
Law enforcement	0	0	0	0	5	5
Medicine	0	0	0	1	6	7
Public service/politics	97	364	461	12	41	53
Clergyman	0	0	0	1	6	7
Scientist	0	0	0	2	2	4
Veteran	69	320	389			
RELIGION						
Protestant		400[2]			362	
Roman Catholic		109			129	
Jewish		19			30	

1. In 1969, Congressional Quarterly only used occupations listed by ten or more members. Members can list more than one occupation.

2. Protestant figures are an approximation because of a number of members listing "Unitarian" and an occasional "none listed."

Source: Adapted from Congressional Quarterly, *Weekly Report,* 27 (January 3, 1969), pp. 45–46; and 35 (January 20, 1979), pp. 80–81.

but the number of members with business and agricultural backgrounds rose.

Our legislators, though atypical in terms of the total population, are typical members of the politically active segment of our society. As we already know, high socio-economic status and high levels of political participation go hand-in-hand.

THE IMPACT OF SOCIAL CHARACTERISTICS

The formal constitutional qualifications for election to Congress are minimal—representatives must be twenty-five years of age and a citizen for seven years; senators must be thirty and a citizen for nine years; both must reside in the states they represent. However, the previously cited informal socio-economic characteristics substantially limit the field. About twenty years ago, in *U.S. Senators and Their World*, Professor Donald Matthews concluded that perhaps only five percent of the American people met the informal requirements for membership in the Senate.[3] While contemporary statistics would show a somewhat more open political arena, the conclusions drawn from Table 10-2 and our discussion in the last chapter of the costs of campaigning suggest that the winners and the losers in our political contests share common socio-economic characteristics.

The social background of most of the legislators suggests the general conclusion that there is a difference between "them" and "us," and that a class pattern of representation exists. But this appears to be a natural result of our attitudes of wanting our leaders to have "class." Professor Matthews concluded:

As long as the system of stratification in a society is generally accepted, one must expect people to look for political leadership toward those who have met the current definition of success and hence are worthy individuals.

Voters seem to prefer candidates who are not like themselves but who are what they would like to be.[4]

BACKGROUND AND BEHAVIOR. Connections between an individual's social background and legislative behavior are difficult to establish. But it is fair to say that most individuals, lawmakers included, find it difficult to see how the world works through the eyes of a stranger. Those elected to Congress usually share middle-class and upper-class educational, occupational, and social experiences. Despite frequent disagreements over policy, they function in a world of shared interests that contribute to the ways they view such matters as civil rights, economic programs, or foreign affairs. Their middle-class and upper-class values may be slower to react to need for change and this may help explain why Congress has generally failed to take the legislative initiative in handling certain national problems such as poverty, inflation, and unemployment.[5] If they were all replaced by steel-workers, welfare mothers, sharecroppers, and unemployed workers, no matter what policies emerged, Americans would be governed by a whole new set of experiences and interests.

Those unrepresented or underrepresented groups in the congressional population are a collection of potential losers. They often lack political clout because of their small number (American Indians), lower voter turnout (the poor in general), or lack of unity on issues (women). Their influence may be reduced further by the political climate of the times as represented by the "tax revolt" that has been so characteristic of the last few years and has been a factor in the scaling down of welfare and urban aid programs.

Background is important and influential, but not conclusive because many other factors affect legislative outcomes. Before 1981, Democrats dominated Congress, and most of them had "liberal" voting records. But, Congress was not as productive in turning out liberal legislation as some people desired. The structure of power in Congress—the committee system, seniority, and legislative rules and procedures—create an arena in which it is easier to defeat legislation than it is to pass it, making it more difficult to respond to the various social needs (see Chapter 11). Finally, conservatism is encouraged by the activities that legislators find most useful to engage in in an effort to get re-elected.

THE FINANCIAL REWARDS OF OFFICE

The occupational insecurity of elective office has been overstressed. In fact, Congress offers long-term career opportunities despite the always present possibility of involuntary retirement imposed by the **electorate** (voters). Membership in both houses is reasonably stable, and few elective or corporate institutions in the United States have the low turnover of personnel that has characterized the post–1932 Congress. The advantages of incumbency and the lack of competitiveness in many contests make a congressional "career" a reality for many officeholders. As a result, "careerism" has a major impact upon policy outcomes, the organization of Congress, the growth of certain norms or **folkways** which are unwritten rules of behavior, and attitudes toward reform.

CONGRESSIONAL PAY AND ALLOWANCES. What causes the famed "Potomac fever" which infects legislators with the desire to seek re-election time after time? One natural place to look for part of the answer is the financial rewards of office. Members of Congress created a small storm of protest when they did not reject a presidentially recommended $12,900 raise for themselves that went into effect in 1977 as part of pay increases for members of all three branches.

Their new salary of $57,500 is supplemented by annual cost-of-living increases (which they can reject). Other fringe benefits include cheap health and life insurance, health care, government contribution to a retirement plan, cut-rate merchandise, a $3,000 tax break for having to maintain two residences, exemption from D.C., Maryland, and Virginia income taxes, a wide range of "freebees" such as junkets abroad, thirty-three free round trips to the home district, and free recreational facilities. They get free office space, and allowances for telephone and telegraph service in Washington, stationery, virtually unlimited **franking privileges** (the free use of the mails to communicate with constituents), money for rental of district or state offices, and a $7,000 personal-expense allowance. In addition, contacts made in the course of a Washington career can lead to lucrative jobs later in life, and the earnings of the members average an increase of more than thirty percent when they leave office.

On the other hand, the extra expenses of office include unreimbursed travel expenses above the travel allowance, maintaining two residences, entertaining constituents, and being expected to make contributions to many worthwhile organizations. Of course, some members, particularly senators, have large independent incomes; but, for others, the congressional pay scale may leave them living well, but also well above their means. Many lawmakers turned to speaking engagements and to writing to supplement their incomes, and some claimed this was the only way they could make ends meet. As we will discuss in the "Issue" section, large fees for these activities, paid by groups with vested interests in congressional decisions, led to ethical problems.

Comparative statistics for the period from 1969 to 1976 suggest that the pay raise was overdue. Congressional pay had risen by approximately 6 percent. The pay of executives in 318 private corporations had gone up

Viewpoint:
Senator Hathaway on the 1977 congressional pay raise

The Senator suggests that good people will not run for a low-paying post. Perhaps he is suggesting that low pay would make officials more dependent upon the favors of outside interests.

I realize that this is not a popular position with many voters, but it is a necessary one given present-day economic realities and their impact on our federal government's ability to attract and retain the very highest caliber of public servants for all three branches of government.

Senator WILLIAM D. HATHAWAY (D., Maine)

Source: Quoted in Congressional Quarterly *Weekly Report* 35 (February 12, 1977), p. 269.

52.5 percent, high level (GS11–18) federal employees had a 49 percent increase, and average hourly earnings in the nation rose 70 percent. But, the Consumer Price Index jumped by 60 percent, eating up much of the "paper" raises.[6]

RICH MAN'S CLUB? Is Congress a rich man's club? We know that salary represents only a part of the picture, and that senators, given their visibility and scope of responsibility, have greater opportunities to make money than most of their colleagues in the House. For example, the Ethics Code of 1977 placed a restriction of $8,625 on outside "earned" income (the result of work as opposed to investment dividends); it took effect for the House in 1979 but was suspended in the Senate until 1983. Since then senators, as a group, have earned three to five times more money from speechmaking, writing, or media appearances than have members of the House. Data released in 1979 indicated that probably one-third of the 100 senators have a net worth of $1 million or more, and two-thirds of the senators have outside incomes of $20,000 or more. Approximately 30 House members are

millionaires, and nearly 100 have outside incomes of $20,000 or more. But the House is the poorer chamber, as the proportion of wealthy members is much lower than in the Senate.[7]

In 1977 the *Washington Post* published data from a survey of the personal financial situation of senators. Some senators, particularly first-termers adjusting to the new life, were having a hard time making ends meet. Gary Hart (D., Colorado), for example, needed over $20,000 from speaking engagements and $5,000 from a constituents' fund (prohibited after 1977) to stay even. Under the new code, members without stock or real estate investments could be hard put. As Hart said:

You're always sending flowers for a funeral, or wedding presents, or bar mitzvah gifts for the kids of somebody who worked on the campaign. It's nickels here and dimes here and there, but you end up spending a couple of thousand a year on it.[8]

MONEY-MAKING OPPORTUNITIES. In contrast to Hart's position, the survey's most significant point was the ability of senators to make great improvements in their financial positions while serving in the Senate. Being in Congress, and in the Senate in particular, has in the past provided the opportunity to earn big fees that could be reinvested, and to raise and convert to personal use excess campaign contributions (now outlawed, as explained in Chapter 9). While new provisions have eliminated certain opportunities, members of Congress serve on committees that make important economic decisions, and appear to be in a position to make good use of the information they acquire through one source or another. The new code notwithstanding, Congress will probably remain a "land of opportunity."

The money-making opportunities provide one form of personal incentive for the lawmakers to keep winning. Do these opportunities make a difference to you or your family? The answer is yes if the financial interests of the congressmen influence their policy decisions. For example, if you are employed by a defense contractor who loses out because a decision on a particular weapon may have been affected by the stockholdings of committee members—you too are a loser.

AN ENVIRONMENT OF PRIVILEGE AND POWER

A sense of excitement fills the halls of the House and Senate office buildings, and the members of Congress are involved with the making of important policy. The job is an exciting and interesting one, and the atmosphere on Capitol Hill can encourage an individual to develop an overblown sense of importance.

The "Hill" is a city within a city, providing for almost every human need. There are beauty parlors, barber shops, health spas, banks, car washes, and a range of restaurants that are available to the members, and usually to congressional employees and the families of members. Plants, plant care, and paintings are provided for the offices, receptions are catered, and a carpentry shop attends to the particular needs of the lawmakers.

LOBBYISTS AND THE GOOD LIFE. Lobbyists for special interests seek the sympathetic ear of members, and often court their favor by providing free transportation on company planes or free vacations at resorts or hunting lodges. A major scandal appeared in the making in December 1975 when a vice-president of Gulf Oil Corporation admitted that the company had distributed more than $5 million of illegal corporate funds to the campaigns of dozens of legislators. Neither house pressed the investigation and all acknowledged recipients claimed they had no knowledge that the contributions were illegal. Six months later, the Justice Department announced it was gathering evidence concerning a mysterious South Korean businessman, Tongsun Park, who was alleged to be behind the distribution of $500,000 to $1 million in cash and gifts to more than twenty-six past or present members of Congress and other officials. Park's alleged mission was to promote a "favorable legislative climate" for South Korea in Washington.

A federal grand jury had indicted Park on conspiracy, bribery, offering illegal gratuities, and mail fraud, and the jury named former representative Richard T. Hanna (D., Cal., 1963–74) as an unindicted co-conspirator. Park and Hanna were alleged to have worked together in a scheme to get large commissions from sales of U.S. rice to South Korea and to use large portions of the money in an "influence purchasing effort" centered on the U.S. Congress during the period from 1967 through 1975. The indictment also contained a list of twenty-five present or former members of Congress (five senators and twenty representatives) who had received money from Park, mainly in the form of campaign contributions. Most of those listed had

Tongsun Park testifies before the House Ethics Committee in regard to whether his contributions to President Nixon's re-election constituted an influence-buying bid by the South Korean government.

The most famous congressional "affair of the heart" took place in 1976. Shock waves went through Congress when it was revealed that Wayne L. Hayes (D., Ohio), chairman of the powerful House Administration Committee, had kept a mistress on the public payroll. The lady in question, Elizabeth Ray, blew the whistle, and her charges were followed by the claims of a number of other women that accommodating their bosses' sexual demands was the price for job advancement. A threatened House investigation forced Hays's resignation, and the Administration Committee was stripped of its authority over congressional office allowances and other perquisites.

While stories of indiscretion make interesting reading, the misdeeds of some should not be taken as a condemnation of all legislators. Our point here is that people who have power are pursued and are sometimes the pursuers. People, men or women, are attracted to those in power, and abuse of office is not confined to members of either sex. Capitol Hill is a heady, temptation-filled environment. And as in most groups, some individuals will go astray.

acknowledged the receipt of these funds during the preceding months as press attention focussed on Koreagate.

Park was eventually granted immunity in return for his testimony and all charges against him were dismissed in 1979. Hanna pleaded guilty to conspiracy and served a little more than a year in jail. The only other trials resulting from Koreagate led to the acquittal of one former member; perjury charges against another ex-legislator were dropped.

A Congressional Quarterly survey of the 1973–1975 period turned up few recorded votes that affected Korea, and most of these were "pro–Korean" by a substantial margin, reflecting the votes of many legislators who were not alleged to have had contacts with Park. The twenty-five members listed did not vote the pro–Korean position consistently.[9]

THE SHOCK OF LOSING.   Arthur Levin's article "Down and Out on Capitol Hill," about the dismay of some of the losers in the 1974 election, provides additional insights into the drive for re-election. Beyond the excitement and the sense of importance that comes from being at the center of interesting events, a major loss to many of the vanquished was the minor flatteries of office which follow in the wake of power and status. "The day after you win, everybody's asking your opinion on absolutely everything. The media and the public

This former congressman may be suggesting that the interest in re-election for some members is exclusively psychological or material well-being.

All members of Congress have a primary interest in getting re-elected. Some members have no other interest.

Rep. FRANK E. SMITH (D., Miss.)

Source: *Congressman from Mississippi* (New York: Random House, 1964), p 127.

think I know what's going on, but I don't," one congressman commented reflectively.

The legislators will also become nostalgic about other side benefits that made them feel so important. They will recall those bargain-priced meals in the House dining rooms, the paddleball games in the Rayburn gym, the special elevators reserved only for them. Gone from their lives are the aides and secretaries, the briefing sessions, and the tight schedules. And no one will call them "Mr. Congressman" any more.[10]

It is also true that the longer a legislator stays in office, the more painful a return home may be. A Washington-oriented lifestyle is developed by officials and their families. Ties with constituents tend to erode and the distance weakens friendships. The full-time nature of serving in Congress has made Washington home. The prospect of returning to a quieter, duller life may seem unpleasant. It is not surprising, then, that many ex-congressmen attempt to stay in the Capital in government jobs or as lobbyists for special interests.

THE NATURE OF THE REPRESENTATIVE FUNCTION

Who or what does a member of Congress actually represent? There are two major theories: in one, the **trustee theory,** the legislator represents the national interest according to his or her own best judgment; in the other, the **delegate theory,** the lawmaker responds to the particular demands or sentiments of the home district or state. A classic example of the way in which these two "constituencies" can cross occurs when the Defense Department announces closing of bases because they are no longer necessary to the national defense. Rather than adopt the national view of "the most defense per dollar," members of Congress from constituencies affected by the closings mount a massive effort to have individual installations exempted. As a result, congressmen with clout are able to save some installations. In terms of the "big picture," a base may be expendable, but to a particular district it means jobs and revenue. No legislator can ignore these needs.

A third role is that of the **politico** or **broker,** in which the lawmaker tries to strike a balance between competing interests in their constituencies or between national and local needs. Almost half of the congressmen admit to perceiving themselves as "politicos."[11] However, they all play all of the roles, depending on the nature of the issue at hand. In fact, legislators' positions on issues are determined largely by the nature of their districts and their perceptions of constituency attitudes. Depending on the breadth of an issue, the constituency may be the voters in general or a **policy constituency**—that is, a group particularly affected by, or interested in, a proposal. When an issue is perceived to be of considerable importance to a constituency, the legislator will usually vote according to what he or she believes is the dominant opinion of the constituency. When the issue does not fall into this category, there is freedom to respond to cues provided by party leaders, committee chairmen, members of the state's delegation, interest groups, the president, or personal inclination.

WHO IS WATCHING? Legislators tend to think they are more visible than they really are. Except in a few emotionally charged areas like civil rights, research indicates that they have basically inaccurate ideas of their constituencies' attitudes. In turn, the average voter has very little knowledge about what his or her representative or senator does in office. Members of Congress hear more often from people who agree with them than those who do not. When they return to their home districts to "feel the pulse of the people," they tend to gravitate towards selected individuals who reinforce their own views—often opinion leaders in the state or district who can later be counted on to provide campaign resources. One member's assistant referred to his boss's communication list as the "thought leadership" of the district.[12]

A catalog of "thought" or "opinion" leaders within a district would include all or some of the following: media industry people; church leaders; key educators; interest group leaders; top people in various civic organizations; and, political leaders. These individuals have greater access to the legislators. This fact, and the low level of attention paid by the average citizen, improves the chances of particular policy constituencies of being on the winning side of the legislator's choices. Many decisions appear to involve only winners because there are no groups which recognize

that they would be hurt by a particular decision. For example, a bill including a change in licensing procedure may benefit one or two shipping lines by giving them a monopoly on a particular route. In the long run, however, shippers of produce and consumers of goods may pay higher prices because of their lack of attentiveness.

The flexibility of choice among representational roles, encouraged by low visibility and lack of party discipline, is reinforced by the fact that "few bills are centrally important to a majority of congressmen."[13] Those that are *centrally important* are usually bills for which there is a strong constituent interest in the outcome; therefore, legislators believe that voting the wrong way on the bill could affect the outcome of the next election. This flexibility allows for **bargaining,** the real name of the game in Congress, where party label does not guarantee a particular voting pattern and the obstacles to passage of legislation are many. Bargaining could not take place if legislators were locked into one or another representational style.

It is important to understand that legislative activities occupy only a part of a member's time. Casework and the constant activities associated with re-election compete for the available hours. And members are dependent upon the congressional staff to assist them in performing their duties.

CASEWORK AND CONSTITUENCY SERVICES

The rapid expansion of the federal bureaucracy has also expanded the legislator's role as an intermediary between constituents and the national government. **Casework** receives high priority in most congressional offices. Requests for congressional intervention run the gamut from getting an emergency military leave for a son or husband to helping secure defense contracts or TV licenses. In addition, legislators and their staffs spend

Viewpoint:
What is a congressman?

While former Congressman Patrick's tone seems somewhat facetious, his comments suggest that "small favors" casework imposes heavily on a legislator's time.

A Congressman has become an expanded messenger boy, an employment agency, getter-outer of the Navy, Army, and Marines, a wardheeler, a wound healer, trouble shooter, law explainer, bill finder, issue translator, resolution interpreter, controversy-oil-pourer, glad hand extender, business promoter, Veterans Affairs adjuster, ex-servicemen's champion, watchdog for the underdog, sympathizer for the upperdog, kisser of babies, recoverer of lost baggage, soberer of delegates, adjuster for traffic violations and voters straying into the coils of the law, binderup of broken hearts, financial wet nurse, a good samaritan, contributor to good causes, cornerstone layer, public building and bridge dedicator and ship christener.

Rep. LUTHER PATRICK

Source: *Congressional Record*, May 13, 1963, daily edition, p. A2978.

considerable time meeting individuals or delegations from their home districts and responding to mail asking for government publications, opinions on legislation, or other information. The importance of constituents is reflected in the fact that the staffs of representatives spend the bulk of their time handling casework, answering mail, and meeting with people from home. While their bosses spend two-thirds of their time on such legislative activities as being on the House floor, attending committee meetings, and doing legislative research, the staff devotes only about fourteen percent of its time in support of these activities.[14]

On the Senate side, generalizations about staff activity are more difficult. Senate staffs are larger, and this allows a division of labor: certain individuals devote their time to constituency matters while others are more involved with legislative activities. The electoral payoff for helping an individual constituent is probably greater for representatives than for senators, who may have to deal more often with the problem of "policy constituencies"—groups such as a particular industry, etc.

CASEWORK AND RE-ELECTION. Casework gives the legislator an opportunity for "credit claiming" or creating an illusion of power. Gerald R. Ford, while a member of the House, expressed a view widely shared by veteran members when he told the 1963 freshman congressmen:

You will find that your constituents will evaluate your merit or lack of it, based on how well or how badly you handle the cases which they submit to you. I won't pass judgment on whether this is right or wrong. I am simply saying that as a matter of fact this is true.[15]

The time devoted to casework comes at the expense of Congress' major role: law-

Members of Congress divide their time between casework—essential to re-election—and other duties such as writing and researching new legislation. Shown is Representative Les Aspin of Wisconsin.

making. Office staff preoccupation with casework leaves little room for legislative research, and this in turn makes individual legislators more dependent upon committee members and committee staff for information and voting cues. And, it can be argued that the emphasis on casework makes Congress more dependent upon the information received from the army of very specialized experts who work in the agencies of the executive branch.

THE ELECTORAL CONNECTION

"It seems fair to characterize the modern Congress as an assembly of professional politicians spinning out political careers," comments Professor David R. Mayhew.[16]

Re-election, he claims, is a legislator's principal motivation. This desire to be re-elected establishes an important accountability relationship with the voters. It also leads to incredible levels of posturing and self-advertisement rather than the production of legislation. And, legislators who fear a loss tend to act conservatively and to take a cautious approach to change. They assume that what worked last time will work the next time around.

ADVERTISING. In Mayhew's view, the major activities of members of Congress are advertising, credit claiming, and position taking. Lawmakers try desperately to get their names before their constituency. They want to create a favorable image through the time-honored baby-kissing route. They visit the state or district, make "non-political" speeches, send newsletters, or write newspaper columns. They may, in a single day of touring, eat spaghetti, knishes, strudel, and shish-kebab to show their sympathy for the various ethnic groups they represent. The franking privilege, that allows them to send out mail at public cost, facilitates this process of self-advertisement. This "free" mailing right costs the public approximately $50 million.

CREDIT CLAIMING.   Credit claiming involves getting people to believe that you are personally responsible for causing the government to do something desirable for your constituency. The "something desirable" may be a dam in the district, the awarding of a Pentagon contract to your hometown, the passage of a bill that creates a new wildlife sanctuary supported by your local Audubon Society, or any one of the many items that come under the heading of casework—the handling of individual voter problems.

Lawmakers place their emphasis on these **particularized benefits**—actions that favor specific individuals, groups, or geographical constituencies. Assignment to House committees such as Post Office and Civil Service, or Interior and Insular Affairs, is sought by some lawmakers, because members on these can get special attention for their own particular constituencies, "thereby insuring their re-election."[17] A member of the House Public Works Committee was quoted as saying:

The announcements for projects are an important part of this. . . . And the folks back home are funny about this—if your name is associated with it, you get all the credit whether you got it through or not.[18]

Committee chairmen, and other powerful members of Congress, whose opinions can help or wreak havoc on projected agency budgets, are particularly successful at this sort of pork-barrel favoritism. Senator Warren Magnuson of Washington was referred to as "the Senator for Boeing" for his often-successful efforts on behalf of the giant aircraft company based in Seattle. Lyndon Johnson, both as senator and president, was notoriously successful in getting Pentagon money flowing into Texas electronic firms, creating a whole new center of corporate wealth in America. Such examples could be repeated endlessly.

POSITION TAKING.   Position taking involves making public statements on issues of interest to the constituency. It involves speaking rather than doing. As Mayhew comments, "the electoral requirement is not that he makes pleasing things happen but that he makes pleasing judgmental statements."[19] Senators, because of their greater visibility through the media, have more opportunities to make good use of position taking. Members of the House are more inclined to credit claiming through getting particularized benefits for their constituents.

Particularized benefits aside, the blunt fact is that Congressmen have less of a stake in winning victories than they normally appear to have. . . . We can all point to a good many instances in which congressmen seem to have gotten into trouble by being on the wrong side in a roll call vote, but who can think of one where a member got into trouble by being on the losing side?[20]

It appears, on the other hand, that there is little relationship between passing broad-based major legislation and re-election. This allows congressmen to live in what Mayhew calls a "cocoon of good feeling," stressing particular benefits, while only being moderately interested in the contents or passage of much of the legislative agenda. However, emphasis on re-election does not have to be inconsistent with the desire to produce good public policy. Careerism and the "electoral

Using staff for election activities is supposed to be illegal, but this staff member points out how it is rather than how it is supposed to be.

Everyone who's running has guys in his state office working on politics during his campaign—and not just during the campaign, but all year round, every year, all the time, for crying out loud.

Congressional aide

Source: Quoted in Spencer Rich, "Staff Election Role Troubles Hill," *Washington Post,* February 4, 1976, p. 88.

connection" do not eliminate this desire in the average members; they just help explain the slow pace and conservative attitude toward change and innovation that characterizes the legislative process. In spite of these factors, Congress has been responsible on its own, or at presidential request, for many far-reaching laws.

STAFF RESOURCES

The effectiveness of members of Congress cannot be considered apart from the personnel and research services provided to help them carry out their role. Each member of the House is allowed a basic clerk-hire allowance of almost $300,000. On the House side, there is a limit of 20 staff but senators can hire more people limited only by the dollar amount of their allowance, calculated on the basis of their state's population ranging from approximately $500,000 for Delaware to $900,000 for California. The size of congressional office staffs varies greatly, with the average in the House being 12; on the Senate side, 24 is the norm, with a high of about 50 for the senators from California. Members of both houses use some of their staff to man home offices in the district or state.[21]

STAFF ACTIVITIES. As we have noted, House staffers spend most of their time on constituent-related activities such as casework or legislative solutions to problems raised by individual constituents. The volume of mail that they handle is staggering; it averages 75,000 letters per year per office, or more than 1,400 per week. Senators also receive an abundance of mail, but their larger staffs can devote proportionately less time to it.

A second time-consuming duty is the generally accepted—but often criticized—use of personal staff in both houses for campaign-related functions carried out on government time and property. This is not legal; however, subterfuges are many, such as transferring staff to the district office on a temporary basis so they can more easily campaign on their own time. Often the line between official activity and campaign work is not very clear. So another role of staff is to help the boss get reelected.

The size of senatorial staffs permits a division of labor that can encourage serious staff activity on legislative matters such as research and the development of policy positions. But this is a generalization, and some senators do not use their people in legislative roles, preferring to use the professional staffs of the committees.

Professional committee staffs are a modern phenomenon. First created by the Legislative Reorganization Act of 1946, they represented an effort to get away from excessive dependence upon experts in the executive agencies. Both houses employ more than 1,000 committee staffers. Originally, the staff was to be non-partisan, but this idea was quickly abandoned. Now most committee people are appointed and work for the majority party members; however, the minority is guaranteed a proportionate share of the staff.

Use of committee staff varies from legislator to legislator, but they are employed most heavily by the committee and sub-committee chairmen and the ranking minority members. With most senators having this status, and with reforms in the House (see Chapter 11) leading to a wider distribution of chairmanships, committee staff are becoming more important to more members. However, the most recent surveys indicate that the average representative relied on himself or herself and the office staff for most legislative research and preparation for committee hearings and floor debates.

STAFF AND DECISION MAKING. Members of Congress do not suffer from a lack of sources of information. Aside from their own efforts and the information gathered by their office staffs, committee staffs, the Congressional Research Service of the Library of Congress, the Congressional Budget Office, and the General Accounting Office, they receive solicited and unsolicited information from the executive branch, lobbyists, and the media. The most important cue-givers on how to vote or what position to take are fellow legislators, particularly members from the state delegation in the case of the House, or from the region, party leaders, and varying from issue to issue, the constituency, members of a particular committee, the president, or lobbyists. Effective personal and/or committee staff work is often necessary to sort out the information

As a majority leader, Senator Howard Baker serves as an important cue-giver to Republicans in the Senate.

and the cues, reconcile executive branch information with that provided by other sources, and process and organize them in such a way that the lawmakers can make intelligent decisions. In a very real sense, the staff provides the ammunition and the legislator pulls the trigger.

FOLKWAYS AND DISCIPLINE

The representative function takes place in an atmosphere that is shaped, in part, by "folkways"—unwritten, but generally accepted, norms of conduct. In both chambers the folkways include the carrying by each member of a fair share of the committee work load; development of a legislative specialty; reciprocity or the willingness to bargain; observance of the rules of courtesy; and institutional loyalty.[22] Another folkway, the lengthy apprenticeship—the unspoken expectation that a freshman senator will silently observe and learn the trade—has eroded. Numerous senators have used the office as a springboard for a presidential race, and more and more states are sending people to the Senate who are expected to "make waves." On the House side, the structure and organization of power (see Chapter 11) dictates a long apprenticeship, but 1975 saw an impressive break with the norms when the freshmen insisted on a major role in the reform of the committee assignment and chairman selection processes.

Without these folkways, Congress would lose some of its institutional stability. However, not all congressmen conform to tradition. Some deliberately choose to be political mavericks or "outsiders." The choice of the "outsider" role may be based on an evaluation of how constituents expect their representative to act. For instance, Wisconsin has always prized independent legislators, and Senator William Proxmire's choice of a maverick role reflects this.[23]

In spite of some erosion, the folkways are by no means dead. Members of Congress who wish to go against club rules still do this at their own risk. The member who loses club protection in such a close-knit body is probably as good as dead in terms of legislative effectiveness, although the voters may re-elect him or her. The structure of Congress, the complexities of the rules and procedures, and the ample opportunities for defeating measures (see Chapter 11) make it crucial for a legislator to have the good will of colleagues. Without it, the structure operates against the member and reduces the ability to perform as a broker, an obtainer of particularized benefits, or as a spokesperson for broader issues. One may remain an electoral winner but become a policy loser.

The Constitution makes each house the judge of "the elections, returns, and qualifications" of its own members and gives it authority to punish its members for "disorderly behavior," and by a two-thirds vote expel a member. **Expulsion** of a seated member is the most severe penalty, and prior to 1980 this prerogative had been exercised only once by the House since 1861, when three representatives were removed for siding with the South. A number of other members resigned rather than face expulsion for various corrupt activities. On the Senate side, the Civil War led to 22 expulsions, and the only non-Civil-War-related expulsion dates back to 1797. A number of senators have resigned before final action, the last case coming in 1906.

ABSCAM. The issue of expulsion was given contemporary importance in February 1980 when it was revealed that the FBI had undertaken a massive and highly secret undercover operation, "Abscam," in which agents—posing as businessmen and wealthy Arab sheiks—had implicated six members of the House and one senator in criminal wrongdoing involving taking bribes in return for promises of legislative favors or influence peddling. In each instance, conviction could have led to expulsion proceedings.

On October 2, 1980, the House expelled Michael (Ozzie) Meyers (D., Pa.), the first of the legislators to be convicted. And John W. Jenrette Jr. resigned after his conviction to avoid a similar action. Both ran for re-election and were defeated. The voters eliminated the need for House action in three other cases by denying one member renomination and defeating two others during the general election. A sixth representative, Raymond F. Lederer (D., Pa.), was re-elected, but his subsequent conviction led to his resignation.

The one senator charged, Harrison A. Williams Jr. (D., N.J.) was not up for re-election in 1980. He was convicted in the spring of 1981 and the Senate recommended his expulsion that fall.

Censure—a formal condemnation by majority vote—is the more common sanction. The Senate has censured eight members and "denounced" one. The House has censured sixteen members and "reprimanded" one.[24] The other action of a judicial nature that the House or Senate can take against one of their own, or a potential member, is **exclusion.** This is the refusal to administer the oath of office to an individual because that person does not fulfill the constitutionally mandated requirements, or because of election fraud. The other judicial functions Congress has are the power of impeachment, discussed in Chapter 12, and the power to cite individuals for contempt of Congress, usually for failure to provide information to committees.

The party organizations in Congress also exercise a disciplinary role. Since "seniority" and appointment to committee and sub-committee chairmanships are allocated by the parties, members occasionally lose their privileges or positions because of unethical behavior or breach of party loyalty, such as supporting the presidential candidate of the opposition party.

DISCIPLINE AND INSTITUTIONAL LOYALTY. With the formal party disciplinary powers providing the setting, we now turn to the cases involving "institutional loyalty." In 1954, Senator Joseph R. McCarthy (R., Wis.) was censured by the Senate for abuse of his fellow legislators. Even though there were stronger conflict-of-interest grounds (conflict between official conduct and private economic affairs) for censuring him, the investigating committee chose to punish him for a violation of courtesy. In 1967, Senator Thomas J. Dodd (D., Conn.) was censured for diverting funds from testimonial dinners and campaign contributions to his personal use. The committee investigating Dodd stopped treating him like a friendly witness and made him a "defendant" immediately after he accused the committee of bias, particularly the Republican members—a dreadful breach of courtesy.

THE POWELL CASE. Finally, the decision of the House in 1967 to exclude—refuse to administer the oath and seat—Adam Clayton Powell (D., NY) can be traced in large part to his "violation" of institutional loyalty by bringing discredit upon the House. Powell's troubles began in 1962 when the press accused him of having a non-working relative, his wife, on his office payroll. He replied by breaching an unwritten folkway of Congress: never criticize the personal ethics of your fellow members. He claimed that "everyone else was doing" just what he had done and that he was being picked on merely because he was black. Four years later he received a great deal of bad publicity for refusing to pay a libel judgment against him, thus placing him in contempt of the law. He was again punished for bringing discredit upon the legislators, who are particularly sensitive about adding to the negative image of the politician.

Powell was disciplined not so much for what he had done but for how he had done it. In the eyes of his peers, he was guilty of gross violation of institutional loyalty and courtesy. What a majority of the members of the House ignored was that the severity of his punishment involved other factors, such as partisanship, emotionalism, and racism.[25] The exclusion was a cheap form of expulsion, which would have required a two-thirds vote that Powell's opponents could not have mustered. In *Powell* v. *McCormack* (1968), the Supreme Court ruled that Powell's exclusion had been unconstitutional, as he held the qualifications for office and there had been no claim of election fraud.[26] Powell had been re-elected shortly after his exclusion but refused to take his seat because he had been fined by the House and stripped of his chairmanship and seniority by his party.

Congressional Voting Behavior

THE IMPACT OF CONSTITUENCY

In his fascinating study, *How Congressmen Decide,* Professor Aage R. Clausen argues that in Congress there are few "highly complex and politically sophisticated orientations to policy questions that set congressmen apart from their fellow citizens." Rather, legislators' decisions are heavily influenced by their general policy positions which are a product of "enduring personal policy views, their perceptions of constituency interests and views, their relations with interest groups, and their party loyalties."[27] These factors usually are stable over time.

Clausen focused on five broad policy areas: social welfare, civil liberties, agricultural assistance, international involvement, and government management (which includes the regulation of the economy, natural resources, and tax and fiscal policy). His conclusion:

Tell me where a congressman lives and what party he belongs to, and I will tell you what his policy position is on each of the four domestic policy dimensions![28]

While qualifying his statement to take individual exceptions into account, Clausen found that policy differences among members of a state party delegation, all dealing with similar environments, were minimal on domestic issues. Clausen's analysis might lead us to conclude that a legislator's attitudes are shaped primarily by constituency and party even when particular issues are not that visible to the folks back home. So, constituency indeed may exert as significant a conscious or subconscious influence on the lawmaker as does his or her background.

In the area of civil liberties and international involvement, constituency influence is much stronger than party influence. In other domestic areas, constituency influence has to share the stage, with party being increasingly important as one moves into the less localized issues of social welfare and government management (areas in which the business-versus-labor or rich-versus-poor issues generally divide the parties). Clausen's findings dispute the idea that the president is the sole shaper of congressional attitudes in foreign affairs.[29] On international involvement, Clausen believes that a "policy constituency," made up of the specialized public that follows foreign affairs issues, has more influence on a legislator's attitudes than does the president, but the president exerts more "pull" in this area than the other forces.[30]

Of course, every winner claims that he or she is going to Washington to "represent all of the people." But the background of the legislators, the nature of the dominant groups within the constituency, the forces that divide people into different parties, factions, and philosophies, and the fact that the resources important for re-election may be concentrated in the hands of a few dominant interest groups or individuals, all make it inevitable that the lawmakers will represent some constituents better than others, and some, perhaps not at all.

FUNCTIONAL REPRESENTATIVES. Fortunately, this reality is mitigated somewhat by **functional representation** that exists alongside geographical representation. The concept of functional representation suggests that citizens may be represented by someone other than their district's or state's legislators, and that this representation is based upon occupational, ethnic, racial, religious, or other characteristics. For example, a union member from a district where organized labor has little clout, will still be indirectly represented in Congress. An interest group like the AFL–CIO becomes the person's shadow voice in the national legislature. In a sense then, he or she is "represented" on issues central to labor by legislators in whose states or districts organized labor is an important policy constituency. Of course, this concept can be carried only so far. Certain groups, American Indians and migrant workers, for example, remain virtually unrepresented. They cannot benefit from functional representation either because their numbers do not give them significant voting power within any constituencies, and/or their life-styles (migrant workers) tend to prevent their voting. While party and constituent interests often mesh, they occasionally conflict with each other. Statistical studies of congressional voting behavior bear this out, and enable us to add to the insights provided by the Clausen study. In addition, they share none of the leverage provided by the factors we have just discussed. They are, in short, usually losers.

WHO WINS? Clausen's findings, our knowledge of interest group strategies, and the politics of campaign financing combine to suggest whose policy interests are more likely to win or lose. The personal policy views of the legislators generally coincide with those of the dominant interests within their constituencies, and these interests are a major source of campaign support. Where an issue is classified as "centrally important," and where dominant interests and the legislator's perception of general constituency attitudes are in conflict, the vote cast usually will reflect the broader constituency's position. Since most issues are not very visible, legislators can be sensitive to the needs of special interests from outside their constituencies who have access because of one or more of the following reasons: the group provides campaign contributions to the individual or the party; the group is part of the party's base of support—labor for the Democrats or business for the Republicans; and the group shares common attitudes with the lawmakers. Interest groups also benefit from the general willingness of the members of Congress to go along with the allocating of particularized benefits important to individual members.

THE IMPACT OF PARTY

Despite the party organization in Congress, the undisciplined and decentralized nature of American political parties is often seen in congressional voting behavior. Although party affiliation may be the single most important indicator of voting patterns, many votes do not divide the parties, and others reflect a **conservative voting coalition** of Republicans and southern Democrats squaring off against northern Democrats.[31] Surprisingly, though, most votes are bipartisan. In the 96th Congress (1979–1980), only 1,020 of the 2,304 recorded votes, or forty percent, were party unity votes, pitting a majority of voting Democrats against a majority of voting Republicans.[32] But when forced to make a choice on an important, visible issue, a member will often place constituency opinion above party loyalty. The most significant breakdowns in party unity occur on the major domestic issues that tend to divide congressmen along rural–urban or liberal–conservative lines. Legislation on civil rights, organized labor, immigration, or agriculture tends to bring the conservative coalition to life.

MINORITY-PARTY POWER. The power of the conservative coalition is indicated in Table 10–3. Translating percentages into numbers, the coalition appeared on 204 of the roll calls in 1980 and won 147 times. Among their 1980 victories were additional restrictions on the use of federal funds for abortions, the resumption of draft registration for men, and the prevention of the Justice Department from seeking court-ordered school bussing. The conservative coalition's success rate highlights an important fact: members of the minority party can be on the winning side of many important "partisan" votes.

PARTY UNITY. Party unity scores are another measure of the impact of party on voting behavior. They represent the percentage of party unity roll calls on which a member votes in agreement or opposition to a majority of his/ her party. Table 10–4 shows that southern Democrats in both chambers had the lowest support scores. The division of the GOP into northern and southern is not a specific enough breakdown, but eastern and far western Republicans generally have the highest opposition scores in their party, with southern and midwestern Republicans being most loyal. The party unity scores were consistent with the figures for the 1970–1978 period, in which the highest and lowest scores for either party were 70 and 57 percent.

★ ★ ★ Table 10–3 ★

Conservative coalition votes and victories

YEAR	% OF RECORDED VOTES ON WHICH COALITION APPEARED	% OF VOTES WON BY COALITION
1961	28%	55%
1962	14	62
1963	17	50
1964	15	51
1965	24	33
1966	25	45
1967	20	63
1968	24	73
1969	27	68
1970	22	66
1971	30	83
1972	27	69
1973	23	61
1974	24	59
1975	28	52
1976	24	59
1977	26	68
1978	21	52
1979	20	70
1980	18	72

Source: Congressional Quarterly, *Weekly Report* 39 (January 10, 1981), p. 84. Adapted by permission of Congressional Quarterly Inc.

Viewed from the perspective of the electoral connection, the parties in Congress are more useful for what they are not than for what they are. Lack of party discipline leaves members free to take positions that serve their advantage; while party structure serves for

organization and communication (see Chapter 11).[33]

VOTING INTELLIGENTLY. Finally, the volume and scope of the legislation that confronts the lawmakers makes it impossible for

★ ★ ★ *Table 10-4* ★

Party unity and opposition in the 96th Congress: 1979–1980

GENERAL SUPPORT AND OPPOSITION

	% SUPPORT		% OPPOSITION	
	1979	*1980*	*1979*	*1980*
Senate				
Democrats	68%	64%	22%	20%
Republicans	66	65	25	23
House				
Democrats	68	69	23	20
Republicans	73	71	19	19
Senate and House (combined)				
Democrats	69	68	23	20
Republicans	72	70	20	20

SECTIONAL SUPPORT AND OPPOSITION

	% SUPPORT		% OPPOSITION	
	1979	*1980*	*1979*	*1980*
Senate				
Northern Democrats	74%	69%	17%	15%
Southern Democrats	56	54	34	31
Northern Republicans	64	64	27	25
Southern Republicans	73	74	17	16
House				
Northern Democrats	75	74	16	15
Southern Democrats	55	57	37	32
Northern Republicans	71	69	20	21
Southern Republicans	80	79	14	14

Source: Adapted from Congressional Quarterly, *Weekly Report* 38 (January 19, 1980), p. 145; and 39 (January 10, 1981), p. 80. Adapted by permission of Congressional Quarterly Inc.

North Carolina Senator Jesse Helms discusses foreign policy at the 1980 Republican platform meetings.

each member to have knowledge in depth about more than a few of the measures that he or she is asked to vote upon. As discussed in the next chapter, part of this problem is eliminated by the committee system and the specialization it promotes. Members of Congress believe that committee reports, staff research, and the information and voting cues provided by the sources we have mentioned, enable them to vote intelligently, even without being present for the debates on the floor of their chamber. Their assumption that if they had more information they would agree with their particular cue-givers, allows them to cast "rational" votes on the basis of no first-hand information.[34] Nonetheless, the House is now using a closed circuit television system and a basic computer setup which allows the members to monitor the action on the floor from their comfortable offices, and retrieve information from a data bank.

The Democrats' failure to effectively use their large majorities (289 of 435 seats in the House and 61 of 100 in the Senate) to pass more legislation in 1975 provoked this comment from Rep. Morris K. Udall (D., Ariz.).

If you're looking for a story from me that more competent leaders might be able to produce more, I don't think John the Baptist could produce, or that you could resurrect Henry Clay and Lyndon Johnson (as Senate majority leader) and make this Congress produce more. They might have done a little bit more because they had a more activist view of what the leadership role is.

Rep. MORRIS UDALL

Source: Congressional Quarterly, *Weekly Report* 33 (June 28, 1975), p. 1333.

★ **Issue** ★

Congressional Ethics

We have argued that the congressional career presents the officeholder with many temptations for abuse of office, and history shows that Congress has been reluctant to use its disciplinary powers. However, the pay raise controversy of 1977, coming on the heels of a series of scandals, Loreagate, and the February 1980 revelation that the FBI had undertaken a massive and highly secret undercover operation, "Abscam," in which agents—posing as businessmen and wealthy Arab sheiks—had implicated eight members of Congress in criminal wrongdoing involving bribes in return for legislative favors or influence peddling, focussed renewed interest upon the issue of congressional ethics.

In March and April of 1977, the House and Senate adopted tough new ethics codes that were pushed by the respective floor leaders. House Speaker Thomas P. O'Neill,

Jr. (D., Mass.) had promised the adoption of the code as a follow-up to the congressional pay raise. He told his colleagues:

. . . the issue before us is not unofficial office accounts, honorariums, outside income, earned or unearned. The issue is credibility, restoring public confidence in this Congress.[35]

On the Senate side, majority leader Robert C. Byrd (D., W. Va.), fought for passage of the code because of "the necessity of the times" and the "climate created by the errant actions of a minority of public officials," which demanded that the Senate take action to restore the public's confidence in Congress.[36]

THE IMAGE PROBLEM. Public respect for congressional performance had received a boost during the decline of President Nixon and the impeachment proceedings. However, it received a setback during the stand-off between the large Democratic majority and President Ford which resulted in government by stalemate during 1975–76. And, the public's perception of legislators' personal conduct has been badly damaged by the scandals and foot dragging by both chambers in investigating the misconduct charges. Between 1944 and May 1981, approximately fifty members of Congress have been indicted on criminal charges and all but eleven pleaded guilty or were convicted.

In fairness, it must be said that Congress's problem stems, in part, from the tendency of many people to lump all 535 members together, forgetting that the overwhelming majority of legislators perform their public service in an honest way. But, while cases of criminal activity are few in number, they are highly publicized.

Two other factors can be blamed on the members. One is the well-documented reluctance of legislators to investigate and punish their colleagues. The House and Senate committees charged with this responsibility were created in 1965 and 1968 respectively, but had a history of pre–1979 avoidance of cases that was consistent with Congress's historical preference for gathering around offenders to shield them from embarrassment, to rely and defer to the judicial system in criminal cases, and to allow the voters to determine whether or not an offender should be returned to office. When Congress has acted, it usually has been in response to public pressure generated by the exposure of wrongdoing by the media. And, part of Congress's reluctance to take the lead in this area has been because the publicity given to the actions of a few members casts doubt on the integrity of all. Fortunately, there is evidence that the committees now are taking a more active approach.

Third, and perhaps most important, are the constant questions raised about the use of the legal advantages of office, such as the franking privilege, expense accounts, and foreign travel. There also is considerable criticism of large campaign contributions, and outside income derived from speaking and writing fees or service on boards of directors. While these activities are not illegal, they often raise questions about ethics, particularly when the sources of contributions and outside income typically come from special interest groups concerned with legislation before Congress.[37]

RULES OF CONDUCT. Prior to the establishment of the new codes, both houses had codes of ethics that read like the Ten Commandments. They included such general admonitions as avoiding activities that conflict with official duties, and giving a full day's labor for a full day's pay. Legislators are also covered by some provisions of the **conflict-of-interest** (a situation in which an official's conduct of his office conflicts with his private economic affairs) statutes which prohibit their receiving compensation for services rendered in relation to matters affecting the government, and they cannot practice law before the U.S. Court of Claims (claims against the government). Some critics have argued that Congress used a double standard by applying some portions of the code to the executive branch and not to itself. For example, executive officials cannot act in an official capacity on matters in which they have a private interest. But the application of this provision would ignore the part of the representative function that makes the members the intermediaries for their constituents in dealing with executive agencies, and in furthering their interests in particular legislation. Members of Congress consider and act upon measures that influence all sectors of the economy; and this makes it difficult for them to avoid all possible or actual conflicts between their legislative duties and their private interests. And, members often have a community of interest with the constituents by their participation in a predominant economic enterprise of the district or state. For example, a legislator may have agricultural interests that would be directly affected by a bill, but a decision not to take part in deliberation and voting on the bill probably would conflict with the duty to represent a predominantly agricultural constituency.

Congress's pre–1977 major response to its ethical problems came in the form of **disclosure** rules, which in the Senate provided very little information to the public. Senators had to file public reports that listed the source and amount of any gift of more than $50 (cash or value) and each honorarium of $300 or more. They were required to file a detailed report of their income, assets, and debts, and a copy of their income tax returns with the Comptroller General. However, these reports were secret and would only be turned over to the Ethics Committee if requested in the course of an investigation. Representatives, on the other hand, filed annual reports open to public inspection listing sources of income. The theory behind disclosure was that the public could judge whether or not a representative's financial situation might create conflicts of interest. But, the regulation's high threshold of $5,000—a representative did not have to report most income or investments of a value of less than $5,000 or exact dollar amounts above that figure—and the lack of detailed information on amounts of money or extent of holdings created real loopholes.

Codes of ethics, conflict-of-interest statutes, and disclosure not withstanding, Congress was still faced with a long list of practices that lent themselves to unethical behavior or the appearance of unethical behavior, and led to a climate of public distrust.

THE NEW ETHICS CODES. The 1977 codes eliminated or reduced the potential impact of a number of questionable practices. Unofficial

office accounts, financed by constituent and/or group contributions, were eliminated, and foreign travel by defeated or retiring—"lame-duck"—members has been restricted. The acceptance of gifts totalling more than $100 from anyone with an interest in legislation is prohibited. Senate rules virtually prohibit the practice of law, and the earned income limit in the House has forced most representatives to abandon their legal work. Finally, the codes provide for extensive financial disclosure of sources and amounts of income, holdings, gifts (including transportation, lodging, food, etc.), real and personal property, debts, and business transactions. For the Senate, meaningful public disclosure is a dramatic change from the former rule.

The 1976 Federal Election Campaign Act limited to $25,000 annually what a member of Congress can earn from **honoraria**—money received for speaking engagements and writing articles—unless the excess is to cover expenses or is donated to charity. The House uses a $750 ceiling for each honorarium, and the Senate uses $2,000.

LOOPHOLES. A number of problems remain and will continue to tarnish Congress's image unless remedial action is taken. The disclosure rules require a listing of the "category of value" owned by the member, spouse, and dependents. One category represents a "range" of wealth, such as "between $15,001 and $50,000," "between $100,001 and $250,000," and "over $250,000" for **unearned income**—interest, dividends, royalties, capital gains, etc. The categories for real and personal property are similar. However, the top category in the House is "over $250,000," while in the more affluent Senate, the top category is "over $5 million."

A classic example of the "categories of value" problem was the example of Rep. Fred Richmond (D., NY). He did all that the law required when he reported his 1978 holdings

Is the Congressman suggesting that the prohibition may make legislators more dependent upon special interests than before?

> *[The provision will] create a Congress of two kinds of people. Some will have large unearned income and the rest will need their political jobs in order to feed and clothe and educate their families. Whether this will be a more ethical Congress, only time will tell, but I think not.*
>
> Rep. OTIS G. PIKE (D., NY)

Source: Quoted in Congressional Quarterly, *Weekly Report* 35 (March 5, 1977), p. 388.

in a particular concern as "over $250,000." However, the stock market value at that time was about $16.5 million, or $16.25 million more than he had to disclose.[38]

OUTSIDE INCOME CONTROVERSY.   The most controversial part of the codes is the limit (effective January 1, 1979) on "outside" earned income to fifteen percent of official salary, which at the salary of $57,500 amounted to $8,625 per year. "Earned" income refers to money made through honoraria—the days of the speaking gravy train are over—or professional practice, legal or otherwise. The limit does not apply to "unearned income"—such as dividends from stocks and bonds—or income from a family-controlled business. Speaker O'Neill had argued that the outside income provision was the "heart and soul" of the package, but he acknowledged that it would require sacrifices by many members.

In March 1979, the Senate placed a four-year delay on the implementation of the earned income limitation. The action was a sudden move that took place with only six senators on the floor and five minutes of debate. Some members were outraged, and a sec-

ond vote took place on March 31, 1979. The attempt to reimpose the limit, sponsored by Gary Hart (D., Colo.), was rejected 44 to 54. Tad Stevens (R., Alaska) said that the limits made senators "financial eunuchs" and compromised their independence. On the other side, the president of Common Cause called the action "the Senate's version of 'take the money and run and the public be damned.'"[39]

CONFLICT OF INTEREST.   While the problem of excessive campaign funding, discussed in Chapter 9, can only be met by spending limits—struck down by the Supreme Court in 1976—or the proposed public financing, we believe that the institution and the people were the losers when Congress failed to come to grips with the conflict-of-interest situations created by "unearned" income from investments. The ethical question concerning stockholdings is the propriety of members having a financial interest in companies that can profit from the actions of their committees and subcommittees. For example, a member serving on a committee dealing with energy who has substantial holdings in oil company

Senator Herman Talmadge owned a large farm while chairing the Agriculture Committee. The Senator contributed personal knowledge of the subject yet was in a classic conflict of interest posture financially.

stocks may have to decide between the public interest and personal financial interests.

The problem is a real one. In 1979, no less than six members of the Senate Finance Committee, the body that writes important energy-tax legislation, had oil holdings. The Chairman, Russell D. Long (D., La.), owned $1.2 million worth of oil and gas property and earned $100,000 from these sources in 1978. In the House, 18 of the 43 members of the Agricultural Committee owned farms or other farm interest, and the Senate Agricultural Committee included three members with farm holdings. The Chairman, Herman E. Talmadge (D., Ga.), owned a 1,388-acre farm valued at between $1 million and $2 million.[40]

Community of interest with constituents, the pre-office financial situation of the

members, and the logic of assigning people to committees where their prior experience can be put to use, make some conflict of interest inevitable. Nor do we suggest that we should only elect princes or paupers. But the long history of conflict between investments and committee assignments calls into question the motivations behind important decisions. We do not believe that it would be unreasonable to require that a member sell holdings that conflict with committee assignments. At the very least, the codes should prohibit members of Congress from making investments while in office that create conflict-of-interest situations. Investments can create a direct relationship between legislators and special interests and make their attitudes one and the same. The end result can affect you because the connection may determine winners and losers in the legislative struggle. These post-election actions are avoidable and should not be tolerated. In the absence of the suggested change there will be more situations similar to the one that came to light in the Sikes Case.

Questions of ethics are woven into the entire legislative process. But, the recent reform, if further supplemented, may lead to a public realization that Cabell Phillips of the *New York Times* was correct when in 1967 he said:

Congress is neither as doltish as the cartoonists portray it nor as noble as it portrays itself. While it has its quota of knaves and fools it has a fair share of knights. And sandwiched between these upper and nether crusts is a broad and representative slice of upper-middle-class America.[41]

Summary

Members of Congress are no story-book group of public-spirited citizens; they have a good deal to gain from going to Washington. The relatively low turnover in Congress means politics is a potentially good career. As a result, a primary consideration, for many members of both houses, is always re-election; this, in turn, dominates their activities and encourages a conservative approach to innovation and change. Even many long-time members constantly "run scared."

Issues of crucial national significance to certain groups may not be "centrally important" to most members. And, the career aspects of service in Congress removes the press of time for the accomplishment of certain ends. Unlike the president, who views his role from the constraints of a four-to-eight-year period, many senators look forward to careers of eighteen or more years, and representatives often serve for eight or more terms. The background of the legislators and the "electoral connection" are important elements in Congress's success or lack of success as an instrument of change and in determining the winners and losers of the struggle over policy.

Even though Congress is not a cross-section of the public, members of Congress cannot and do not ignore the views of the constituents who have elected them to office. When an issue is perceived as centrally important to the district or state, this perception becomes the most important one, overriding the cues from party, colleagues, the president, or personal preferences. Members make a serious effort to discover constituents' preferences, but there is evidence to suggest that they hear most often from those who agree with them and that legislators have a tendency to equate the voters' attitudes with their own. In general, each member provides fairly good representation for the dominant interests within his or her constituency. And, the attention paid to constituency casework reflects the importance of this activity to the electoral connection.

The review of congressional voting behavior reveals an important fact—the members of the minority party often can be on the winning side. The success of the conservative coalition has a great impact on congressional ability to enact legislation.

Terms to Remember

See the Glossary at the end of the book for definitions.

Bargaining	Disclosure rule	Honorarium
Casework	Electorate	Particularized benefits
Censure	Exclusion	Policy constituency
Conflict-of-interest	Expulsion	Political broker
Conservative coalition	Folkways	Trustee theory
Constituency	Franking privilege	Unearned income
Delegate theory	Functional representation	

Notes

1. Anthony Marro, "Congressional Ethics and the Need for Basic Reform," *New York Times,* January 30, 1977, p. E5.

2. Woodrow Wilson, *Constitutional Government in the United States* (New York: Columbia University Press, 1908), p. 70. Wilson's lectures were given in 1907.

3. Donald R. Matthews, *U.S. Senators and Their World* (Chapel Hill: University of North Carolina Press, 1960), pp. 44–46.

4. Ibid., p. 45. Also see David J. Vogler, *The Politics of Congress,* 2d ed. (Boston: Allyn and Bacon, 1977), pp. 57–64.

5. Leroy N. Rieselbach, *Congressional Politics* (New York: McGraw-Hill Book Co., 1973), p. 34.

6. Congressional Quarterly, *Weekly Report,* 35 (February 12, 1977), p. 269.

7. For financial information, see Congressional Quarterly, *Weekly Report,* 35 (September 1, 1979), pp. 1823–1892.

8. Quoted in T.R. Reid, "Rich Man's Club," *Washington Post,* March 14, 1977, pp. A1, A4.

9. The most convenient coverage of Koreagate is in the Congressional Quarterly, *Weekly Report,* for 1977 and 1978.

10. *The Washington Monthly,* January 1975, pp. 21–32. Quotes are from p. 30.

11. Roger Davidson, *The Role of the Congressman* (New York: Pegasus, 1969), p. 119.

12. Quoted in David R. Mayhew, *Congress: The Electoral Connection* (New Haven: Yale University Press, 1974), p. 40. Also see Lewis Anthony Dexter, "The Representative and His District," *Human Organization,* 16 (Spring 1957); and Warren E. Miller and Donald E. Stokes, "Constituency Influence in Congress," *American Political Science Review,* 57 (March 1963), pp. 45–56.

13. Lewis A. Froman, Jr., *The Congressional Process* (Boston: Little, Brown, 1967), p. 20.

14. Malcolm E. Jewell and Samuel C. Patterson, *The Legislative Process in the United States* (New York: Random House, 1977), p. 211.

15. Donald G. Tacheron and Morris K. Udall, *The Job of the Congressman* (Indianapolis: Bobbs-Merrill, 1966), p. 68.

16. Mayhew, *Congress: The Electoral Connection,* pp. 14–15. The discussion of congressional activities is drawn from pp. 49–73.

17. Richard F. Fenno, Jr., *Congressmen in Committees* (Boston: Little, Brown, 1973), pp. 6–9.

18. James T. Murphy, "Partisanship and the House Public Works Committee," paper presented at the Annual Convention of the American Political Science Association, 1968, p. 10. Quoted in Mayhew, *Congress: The Electoral Connection,* p. 55.

19. Mayhew, *Congress: The Electoral Connection,* p. 62.

20. Ibid., pp. 117–118.

21. Jewell and Patterson, *The Legislative Process,* pp. 211–212. Discussion of staff is drawn from this source and Vogler, *The Politics of Congress,* 2d ed., pp. 130–137.

22. Matthews, *U.S. Senators and Their World,* pp. 92–117. Matthews confined his observations to the Senate, but the folkways apply to both houses.

23. Ralph K. Huitt, "The Outsider in the Senate: An Alternative Role," *American Political Science Review* 55 (September 1967), pp. 566–575.

24. For a discussion of these remedies see, Robert S. Getz, *Congressional Ethics: The Conflict of Interest Issue* (New York: Van Nostrand Reinhold, 1967), p. 84–116.

25. Ibid., pp. 102–103, 188–195.

26. 395 U.S. 486 (1969).

27. Aage R. Clausen, *How Congressmen Decide* (New York: St. Martin's Press, 1973), Chapter 1. The quotations are from pp. viii, 4, and 9.

28. Ibid., pp. 189–190.

29. Ibid., pp. 148–149.

30. Ibid., pp. 225–226.

31. For purposes of the "conservative coalition," the following states are considered to be "southern": Alabama, Arkansas, Florida, Georgia, Kentucky, Louisiana, Mississippi, North Carolina, Oklahoma, South Carolina, Tennessee, Texas, and Virginia. All others are "northern."

32. Congressional Quarterly, *Weekly Report,* 39 (January 10, 1981), p. 79.

33. Mayhew, *Congress: The Electoral Connection,* pp. 97–100.

34. Donald M. Matthews and James A. Stimson, "Decision Making by U.S. Representatives: A Preliminary Model," in Sidney Ulmer, ed., *Political Decision-Making* (New York: Van Nostrand Reinhold, 1970), pp. 14–39.

35. Quoted in Congressional Quarterly, *Weekly Report,* 35 (March 5, 1977), p. 388. See pp. 387–391 for details of the House code.

36. Quoted in Congressional Quarterly, *Weekly Report,* 35 (April 2, 1977), p. 591. For

details of the code, see pp. 596–599.

37. For an excellent summary, see Congressional Quarterly, *Weekly Report,* 38 (February 9, 1980), pp. 323–342.

38. For a comprehensive review of disclosure see Congressional Quarterly, *Weekly Report,* 37 (September 1, 1979), pp. 1823–1892. The Richmond example is from p. 1830.

39. Congressional Quarterly, *Weekly Report,* 37 (March 10, 1979), p. 399.

40. Congressional Quarterly, *Weekly Report,* 37 (September 1, 1979), pp. 1824–1825.

41. Quoted by Larry L. King, "Dear Congressman: Is Doddism Dead?" *New York Times Magazine,* April 16, 1967, p. 26.

Suggested Readings

Aage R. Clausen, *How Congressmen Decide* (New York: St. Martin's Press, 1973).

Roger Davidson, *The Role of the Congressman* (New York: Pegasus, 1969).

Richard F. Fenno, Jr., *Home Style: House Members in Their Districts* (Boston: Little, Brown, 1978).

Richard F. Fenno, Jr., *Congressmen in Committees* (Boston: Little, Brown, 1973).

Harrison W. Fox, Jr., and Susan Webb Hammond, *Congressional Staffs: The Invisible Force in American Lawmaking* (New York: The Free Press, 1977).

Lewis A. Froman, Jr., *The Congressional Process* (Boston: Little, Brown, 1967).

Robert S. Getz, *Congressional Ethics: The Conflict of Interest Issue* (New York: Van Nostrand Reinhold, 1967).

Donald Matthews, *U.S. Senators and Their World* (Chapel Hill: University of North Carolina Press, 1960).

David R. Mayhew, *Congress: The Electoral Connection* (New Haven: Yale University Press, 1974).

Donald G. Tacheron and Morris K. Udall, *The Job of the Congressman* (Indianapolis: Bobbs-Merrill, 1966).

CHAPTER 11

Congress: Structure and Process

*. . . if that government is best that governs least, then Congress is one of the most
perfect instruments of government ever devised.*

ROBERT BENDINER
Obstacle Course on Capitol Hill

On February 8, 1978, the House dealt a decisive blow to the consumer movement by defeating (189 to 227) legislation to create a federal Agency for Consumer Protection (ACP). President Carter had made the creation of the ACP a priority on his legislative agenda, and the defeat was caused, in part, by the defection of some Democrats who had supported the plan in previous years.

The vote was a victory for the U.S. Chamber of Commerce, the National Association of Manufacturers, and other business groups that had waged a lobbying campaign against the ACP idea. House Speaker Thomas P. O'Neill Jr. (D., Mass.) said, "I have been around here for 25 years—. . . I have never seen such extensive lobbying." Business spokespeople countered that their success was a product of public opposition to a growing federal bureaucracy and the fact that the American people "are weary of too much gov-

ernment in their lives—too much protection, too much of what other people think is good for them."[1] They had argued for four years that a new agency would only harass business people, and that it would interfere with the work of existing regulatory agencies such as the Federal Trade Commission. In 1978 they broadened the attack by making the issue freedom from government. And they did not hesitate to point out that one of President Carter's campaign pledges had been to trim the bureaucracy.

Throughout the struggle, consumer and labor groups, led by the Consumer Federation of America and consumer advocate Ralph Nader's Congress Watch, argued that the nation's "powerless consumers" needed an agency to protect their interests in fact, not just in theory. They also had evidence that public opinion was in favor of an ACP.

The 1978 action marked the third

★ ★

time that the proposal had been blocked. Its legislative history was one of frustration, minority rule, and presidential-congressional tensions.

In 1974, the House passed its version of the bill to create the ACP by a lopsided margin of 293 to 94. However, a bitter two-month filibuster in the Senate killed the effort. During the debate, President Nixon had threatened to veto the bill; after his resignation, President Ford took a public stance of "neutrality," but Nader accused Ford's aides of openly lobbying against the measure. In the end, a minority of thirty-four senators forced the Senate to table the bill.

The 1974 congressional elections returned an expanded Democratic majority to both houses. In 1975 Congress approved the creation of an Agency for Consumer Protection, but the bill had passed in the House by the close vote of 208 to 199. President Ford had indicated that he would veto the bill, and with no chance of getting the necessary two-thirds in the House to override the expected veto, the agency's advocates let the bill die rather than send it to a conference committee to work out the differences in the House and Senate versions.

Unlike Nixon and Ford, Carter favored the ACP bill, and consumer advocates assumed that a Democrat in the White House would mean passage of the bill. However, the industry lobbying campaign was effective, and as 1977 drew to a close, Democratic leaders in both chambers avoided bringing the proposal to the floor because they were not confident about its passage. Their fears were justified.

The frustrating road traveled by the various ACP bills raises some important questions about Congress, over and above the issue of representativeness discussed in the last chapter. Are its rules (like the unlimited debate rule in the Senate) "neutral," or do they reinforce the privileged positions of key club "officers"—committee chairmen, floor leaders, and others? Can the rules defeat a really determined majority? Is "majority rule" a joke in our major representative body, made meaningless by the intricacies and power arrangements of the committee system? These questions are part of another, larger question. Can we rely on Congress to make public policy? Can such a disparate, unwieldy body cope fairly with the pressing needs of a giant industrial nation? And even with Congress and the White House in the hands of the same party, can and/or should Congress react positively to presidential initiatives?

Congress Versus the President: A Perspective

Congress's power "not to act" provoked much criticism from political scientists, journalists, and its "liberal" members, particularly from the late 1940s through 1968. Most of the professional literature about Congress during this period was written by individuals who considered themselves liberals, and who felt that the rules and procedures of the legislative process, as used by the congressional leadership, were barriers to the enactment of progressive policies of the president. Those critics believed that American economic stability depended upon a strong, liberal, presidency. Naturally, they supported centralizing the power in the executive branch. Their position reflected a powerful faith in the presidency and confidence in the benefits of large national bureaucracies. Only Congress seemed to stand in the way of this vision.

CONGRESS AS VILLAIN. As a result, Congress was characterized as "obstructionist" and "unrepresentative," bent on hamstringing a series of liberal or middle-of-the-road presidents. Among the most popular targets of this wrath were the method used to select committee chairmen, the powers of that office, the

seniority. He called the Senate "archaic, outmoded, obsolete as a meaningful democratic institution."[3] In 1965, Bolling argued that it would take major reforms to make Congress responsive to the needs of the time and move it away from being "the least responsible organ of government. . . ."[4]

MYTH VERSUS REALITY

Several excellent studies of the internal workings of both houses cast some doubt upon the 1960s' claims that Congress was run by a small, elite group of elderly men. One work argued that in the Senate power was widely distributed, making the Senate more of a collection of equals than a body divided into the leaders and the led.[5] On the House side, two studies claimed that bargaining, accommodation, and acceptance of committee norms, rather than an image of heavy-handed leadership by committee chairmen, was the rule. The great power of some individual committee chairmen was attributed to skill, knowledge, and sensitivity to the personal and political needs of committee members.[6]

CONGRESS AS HERO. In the late 1960s and early 1970s, the presidency was captured by conservative Republicans and the liberal critics of Congress suddenly fell silent. It was as if they had gone to sleep one night and awakened the next morning to find themselves in bed with a stranger. They came to recognize that the conservative scholar, James Burnham, was correct when he warned in 1969 against the dangerous imbalance in the relationship between the branches of government and a drift toward executive domination.[7]

committee assignment procedure, and the unlimited debate (filibuster) rule in the Senate, all of which enabled Congress, allegedly dominated by southern conservatives, to maintain the status quo and to prevent liberal victories in the contests for resources.[2]

The critics suggested that the primary roles of the legislature should be those of legitimizing executive proposals by enacting them into law, overseeing the administration, and representing their constituents. They argued for congressional "reforms" to overcome the previously mentioned obstacles.

The critics occasionally received reinforcement from within Congress itself. Two outspoken members were Representative Richard Bolling (D., Mo.) and former Senator Joseph S. Clark (D., Pa.). In 1967 Clark attacked what he called the "Senate establishment," a group of influential and primarily southern senators who gained power through

Certainly, the Senate's role in curtailing our involvement in Vietnam, though not exactly an impressive showing, was applauded by liberals. In addition, congressional opposition to the Nixon White House, investigation of the Watergate scandals, and refusal to dismantle certain social welfare programs pleased liberals.

The liberal switch in sides in the institutional struggle between the Congress and the president was not an example of fickleness. It was a recognition that the chief executive shared few policy interests with them and could not be relied upon to be a key force in liberal attempts to win legislative victories. On the other hand, conservatives now could play the game on both fronts, depending on both the White House and the conservative coalition in Congress, whose power was reinforced by the rules of the legislative game. But, to the surprise of many, in the early 1970s, Congress began to take steps to make long-needed changes in its rules and procedures.

REFORM FROM WITHIN

Members of Congress have been increasingly sensitive to the institution's poor public image and the widespread public belief that Congress's problems are directly tied to "archaic" and "undemocratic" practices. In the late 1960s and the 1970s, a number of senior legislators retired, died, or were defeated, providing a rare opportunity for change. The 1974 elections sent ninety-two freshmen to the House of Representatives, including seventy-five Democrats, and most have been re-elected. The new group was younger and more liberal, and they led the drive for reforms. The results: the committee selection procedure for House Democrats was significantly altered; chairmen were individually interviewed by the freshmen; and the Democrats refused to reappoint three of the chairmen. The "revolt" toppled a few chair-

men who were "despotic," insensitive to others, or failing to provide leadership, and put the remaining chairmen on notice that they must be more responsive to the party leadership and to the other Democrats in the House. While some journalists were quick to talk about the decline of the chairmen, it was inevitable that new power centers would develop to replace the old ones. In fact, changes in House committees in 1975 led to a shift in power to a larger number of subcommittee chairpersons at the middle-level in seniority. They are the winners in the recent changes.

AN INDEPENDENT CONGRESS

Major changes in the House were not accompanied by similar moves in the Senate, where the leaders and the led are more accommodating to each other. There, evolution—the defeat and retirement of many of the old guard—rather than revolution, changed the players. Moreover, it remains to be seen whether the "new order" in Congress will be better able to use its power to produce policy than the "old order." The 1976 election appeared to signal an end to eight years of stalemate between Congress and the president. But Jimmy Carter did not fare well, and he faced a legislature that valued its newly rediscovered institutional independence, and legislators who prized their own independence, as contrasted to the days of very strong leaders in both houses.

Reform can be a two-edged sword, and the diffusing of power means that Congress has made itself less able to act. President Ford, for example, found that he did not have a small group of powerful chairmen to bargain with, and this made political compromise between the two branches extremely difficult. President Carter encountered the same dilemma, and his problems were reduced only slightly by having Congress controlled by his own party.

During the early 1970s, Congress took

Viewpoint:
Revolt in the House

Here James Reston refers to the January 1975 action by the Democratic caucus which stripped three chairmen of their posts. The system of voting by secret ballot for chairmanships, started in 1971, allows the party to circumvent the seniority tradition.

The House is in revolt, not against the whole seniority system but against what Woodrow Wilson called the "petty barons" or "lord proprietors" at the head of the committees, who "exercise an almost despotic sway within their own shires." . . . The House will never be quite the same. The reformers in the House, with the help of the new members who were swept into office in last November's election, have demonstrated that they can change the system.

JAMES RESTON

Source: *New York Times*, January 17, 1975, p. 33. © 1975 by the New York Times Company. Reprinted by permission.

steps (to be discussed later) to harness presidential war-making powers and to try to recapture the control of the purse. It also gained stature at the expense of the presidency during the Watergate scandal. President Carter hardly had the chair warm in the Oval Office when he felt congressional wrath over his proposal to cut funding for water projects, reluctance to buy the details of his energy proposals, and disappointment among many congressional Democrats because of the modest nature of his social welfare programs. The Assistant Majority Leader in the House, John Brademas (D., Ind.), put it this way:

. . . the members are products of the decade of Watergate, civil rights, and Vietnam, so they're not going to be led around by the nose by either the Congressional leaders or by the President of the United States.[8]

Disappointment turned to disillusionment for liberal Democrats when Carter announced his budget plans for **fiscal year 1980**; they called for cutbacks in many social programs in an effort to reduce the federal deficit. (The fiscal, or budgetary, year for the government runs from October 1 through September 30.) Republican conservatives applauded the President and smilingly suggested that he would find more support among them than in his own party. Liberal unhappiness was compounded when Carter called for a $16 billion cut in his proposed 1981 budget in an effort to fight inflation. Programs aiding the poor and the cities bore the brunt of the cuts.

WHY MAKE REFORMS? Before we assume that changing the rules will affect dramatically the ability of Congress to respond to the nation's needs with timely legislation, another word of caution is in order. Congressional reformers always argue that their proposals are offered in the name of efficiency; but both proponents and opponents of reform are usually motivated by their policy orientations and desires for power within Congress.

Legislators do not seek reform in order to make the Congress more responsive to executive leadership. They have their own interests at heart, primarily the attempt to exercise more control over the decision-making process—to determine who wins and loses. So the question remains: can a body of 535 persons, divided by chamber, party, region, philosophy, and party-factionalism be expected to produce clear and specific policy? Or, as critics have argued, is Congress at ease only in opposition, not in developing positive programs of its own? As Senator Robert C. Byrd (D., W.Va.) put it, "No Congress of 535 individual voices can effectively lead the nation."[9]

The Organization and Structure of Power

Any list of the roles or functions Congress should or does perform would include lawmaking, **administrative oversight** (evaluating the performance of the bureaucracy and seeing that the laws Congress has passed are administered as intended), and representation of particular organized interests as well as the individual constituent. These functions are interrelated, and often take place at the same time.

HOUSE–SENATE DIFFERENCES. In both houses of Congress, power is decentralized. Where the houses differ in their methods, their sizes and the constituencies their members represent are usually the cause for this. The House, with 435 members, operates under rather rigid rules. Debate is strictly governed by guidelines set by the Rules Committee. An individual member is not likely to take part in the general debate on a bill unless he or she has cleared it in advance with the floor managers of the bill. For the one hundred senators, greater informality is the order of the day. Unlimited debate and flexible scheduling is the norm. Power is more widely distributed, the apprenticeship period is shorter, and the difference between the leaders and the led is less meaningful in the Senate than in the

House. The House, with over four times as many members, has only seven more standing (permanent) committees (twenty-two) than the Senate (fifteen). As a consequence, Senate committees are smaller and it is not unusual for a senator to become a subcommittee chairman shortly after taking office.[10]

Senators share power more evenly because each senator represents a sovereign state and therefore has more prestige than does a House member. Senators also receive more press coverage and are more widely known to their constituents. As representatives of an entire state, it is difficult for senators to ignore broad social welfare or civil rights issues. While there are many conservative senators, it may be fair to generalize that the nature of senatorial constituencies makes that body relatively more "liberal" than the House of Representatives.

PARTY AND LEADERSHIP

A distinction must be made between the role of the party in organizing Congress, and the ability of the party to muster a party-line vote in either house (discussed in Chapter 10). With respect to internal personnel questions, party discipline is very strong; it is exercised primarily through the party caucuses, or conferences (meetings of all party members) in each house. The main function of the caucus is not policy making, but the selection of party leaders and the approval or rejection of the recommendations of the "committee on committees" concerning committee assignments and the designation of committee chairmen.

PARTY LEADERS. The major party post in the lower chamber is the **Speaker of the House**—the presiding officer of the House and the leader of the majority party. While technically elected by the entire House, the speaker is really chosen by the caucus of the majority party. Before 1910, the speaker controlled committee assignments and procedures for selecting chairmen, served as chairman of the powerful Rules Committee, and had unlimited power to recognize speakers. In 1910, these powers were curbed; but the office is still the most potentially powerful in Congress. The modern view of this position has been influenced greatly by Sam Rayburn of Texas, who served as speaker from 1940 to 1947, 1949 to 1953, and 1955 to 1961. Rayburn ran a centralized, highly personal operation, and had a reputation as a legislative wizard. His great power got a wry once-over in the following poem:

I love Speaker Rayburn, his heart is so warm,
And if I love him he'll do me no harm.
So I shan't sass the Speaker one little bitty,
And then I'll wind up on a major committee.[11]

The presiding officer of the Senate is the Vice-President of the United States. He is customarily regarded as the intruder, that is, a member of the executive branch who has no right to participate in debate, and he may vote only in case of a tie. Moreover, he may be a member of the minority party, as were Vice-Presidents Agnew, Ford, and Rockefeller. The vice-president rarely presides, his place being taken by the **President Pro Tempore,** a largely honorific position given to the elder senator of the majority party. Other positions of party leadership are the **majority and minority floor leaders** and assistant floor leaders, or **"whips,"** in both houses.

With the exception of the Democratic whip in the House, who is appointed by the majority leader, all of these positions are filled by election within the party caucuses or conferences.

In the Senate, the real leadership is exercised by the majority leader. He is chairman of the caucus, head of the policy committee, and potentially the most influential participant in the committee-assignment procedure. His influence is conditioned, to an extent, by the relative equality of the members of his chamber. When his party controls the presidency, he is the president's spokesman to the Congress; when the White House is in the hands of the other party, as was the case when Lyndon Johnson was majority leader, he is more powerful as a part of the bargaining process.

Again, the influence of the majority leader depends on personal style and the individual's view of the role. Lyndon Johnson (1955–1961) ran a highly personal operation, controlling the flow of information and attempting to lead at all times. Mike Mansfield of Montana (1961–1977) was less aggressive and did not take the position that the leader's role has to be a constant struggle to develop consensus and to structure each issue in such a way as to get a maximum number of senators to support it. The Mansfield approach may be best suited to the post–World War II Senate that has moved from decentralized power in the hands of leaders and committee chairmen to an individualized situation "in which significant legislative power is spread among virtually all senators of both parties."[12] The selection of Senator Robert C. Byrd (D., W.Va.) as majority leader in 1977 reflected senatorial preference for a leader who would pay attention to necessary housekeeping duties rather than concentrate on "majority building."

Howard H. Baker, Jr., (R., Tenn.) became the majority leader in the wake of the Republican takeover of the Senate in 1981. Baker, a candidate for his party's nomination in 1980, is more policy-oriented than Byrd, and is counted on to be a bridge between some of the very conservative Republicans and their more moderate GOP colleagues.

The majority floor leader in the House is the prime mover of his party's measures and a leading negotiator with the factions within his own party and with the opposition. The minority leaders in both houses are primarily concerned with directing the floor strategy of their party when attempting to defeat or amend the legislation proposed by the majority. In general, majority or minority floor leaders in both chambers try to structure situations so that as many members as possible will be able to stand with the party. In carrying out this role, each is assisted by the party whip organizations, whose four functions are: to transmit information from the leadership to the rank and file; to assist the leader in deter-

★ ★ ★ *Table 11–1* ★

Standing committees of the 97th Congress: 1981–1982

SENATE	HOUSE
Agriculture, Nutrition, and Forestry	Agriculture
Appropriations	Appropriations
Armed Services	Armed Services
Banking, Housing, and Urban Affairs	Banking, Finance and Urban Affairs
Budget	Budget
Commerce, Science, and Transportation	District of Columbia
Energy and Natural Resources	Education and Labor
Environment and Public Works	Foreign Affairs
Ethics*	Government Operations
Finance	House Administration
Foreign Relations	Interior and Insular Affairs
Government Affairs	Interstate and Foreign Commerce
Judiciary	Judiciary
Labor and Human Resources	Merchant Marine and Fisheries
Rules and Administration	Post Office and Civil Service
Veterans' Affairs	Public Works and Transportation
	Rules
	Science and Technology
	Small Business
	Standards of Official Conduct
	Veterans' Affairs
	Ways and Means

*Although Ethics is not considered a standing committee, it is included because of its permanent nature.

mining members' attitudes and voting intentions; to assist efforts to bring members in line with the leadership position; and to maximize attendance for key votes of party members who intend to vote "right." Obviously, some of the roles of leaders and whip organizations reflect the fact that party membership often is not a predictor of voting behavior.

THE COMMITTEE SYSTEM

Congressional government is primarily government by committee. The committee system is far more important in the internal organization of Congress than is the party system. Any bill introduced is first referred to a committee. Whether or not that bill ever reaches the floor of Congress depends, in the overwhelming majority of cases, upon the committee itself. For example, the shape of the 1977 energy legislation was determined, in part, by the attitudes of the seventeen-member Energy and Power Subcommittee of the House Interstate and Foreign Commerce Committee. The congressmen were badly divided on the major energy issues, and not necessarily along party lines.

TYPES OF COMMITTEES. There are fifteen Senate and twenty-two House **standing** (permanent) **committees.** Each is assigned an area, such as agriculture, the military, or foreign affairs, over which it has almost exclusive jurisdiction. Its permanent jurisdiction and the stability of its membership allows a committee to develop some of the expertise so sorely lacking in many congressional activities. Specialization is encouraged by the division of most committees into a number of regular subcommittees.

In addition to the standing committees, **special** or **select committees** are created to study and investigate a particular problem. Such groups are temporary, lasting only for the two-year life of the Congress that

creates them, unless renewed by the succeeding Congress, and they usually do not have the power to report out legislation. The Senate Watergate Committee (Select Presidential Campaign Activities) and the special Senate Committee to investigate the Central Intelligence Agency (1975) are recent examples. Some select committees take on a permanence similar to the standing committees. The Senate's Select Small Business Committee is a classic example, serving the needs of particular economic interests not handled by a standing committee. The Senate's Ethics and Intelligence committees are other examples of "permanent" select committees.

Finally, Congress also makes use of **joint committees,** whose primary purpose is to study particular subjects and report back to both houses. Both select and joint committee recommendations may lead to legislation coming out of the standing committees.

SUBCOMMITTEES: THE CENTERS OF POWER

During the 96th Congress (1979–80) there were 51 committees of all kinds and 253 subcommittees, broken down as follows:

★ 20 Senate committees, with 101 subcommittees

★ 27 House committees, with 147 subcommittees

★ 4 joint committees, with 5 subcommittees

Prior to the Legislative Reorganization Act of 1946 there were 81 standing committees and 174 subcommittees. The act cut the number of standing committees in half, and with adjustments over time, there now are 37 standing committees.

NEED FOR SUBCOMMITTEES. The growth in the number and power of subcommittees has been in response to a number of factors, both practical and political. Subcommittees are a logical focal point for the increased specialization that Congress requires to deal with complex problems and to respond to the concentration of expertise and information in the executive agencies. They also provide an opportunity for individual legislators to occupy leadership positions, a scarce commodity if confined to full committee chairmanships or congressional party leadership posts. A subcommittee chairmanship, or for that matter, assignment to a subcommittee with jurisdiction over matters particularly relevant to their constituency, provides legislators a policy turf from which to wield influence, engage in "credit claiming," and build a record to help win the next election.

POWER IN THE SENATE. The smaller size of the Senate provides almost instantaneous leadership for all members of the majority party. New minority party members often find themselves as the ranking minority member of one or more subcommittees. In 1977 the Senate limited members to service on no more than three committees and eight subcommittees, and the chairmanship of no more than four committees and subcommittees (senators do not chair more than one committee). While 11 assignments appear to spread a senator thin, it represents a considerable reduc-

tion from the average of 18 for the senators in 1975–76. Some served or chaired many more, with Jacob K. Javits (R.,N.Y.) leading the way by serving on 31 and Howard W. Cannon (D.,Nev.) following close behind, by chairing one committee and 9 subcommittees. The change obviously meant a further distribution of leadership roles among senators.

POWER IN THE HOUSE. The impact of size on the distribution of power is apparent when we contrast the House with the Senate. Representatives are assigned to only two committees—one if they serve on Ways and Means or Appropriations (the money committees), or Rules, which controls the flow of House business. The large size of House committees is not compensated for by an abundance of subcommittees. For example, Table 11–2 indicates that almost all the Democrats on the Senate Appropriations Committee chaired subcommittees, while on the House side, only slightly more than a third had that opportunity.

Reforms adopted by the Democrats during the 1971–75 period helped to ease somewhat the long apprenticeship—often ten years or more—that representatives served before attaining positions of influence. No House member can be chairman of more than one legislative subcommittee, and committee chairmen are required to involve all Demo-

★ ★ ★ *Table 11–2* ★

Power distribution on appropriations committees in the 96th Congress: 1979–1980

	SENATE	HOUSE
Members	25	55
Party line-up	17D, 11R	36D, 18R
Number of subcommittees	13	13
Number of members with subcommittee chairmanships	13*	13*

*Including chairman of full committee

Source: Congressional Quarterly, *Weekly Report*, supplement, 37 (April 14, 1979).

crats on their committees in the decisions concerning subcommittee jurisdiction, budgets, the selection of subcommittee chairmen, and the equitable distribution of assignments. And, senior representatives are limited to membership on no more than two of a committee's subcommittees.

The impact of these reforms was to give younger and middle-level members more opportunities and to shorten the apprenticeship to an average of six to seven years.[13] And, the changes resulted in an increase in legislative activity at the subcommittee level. In 1975, an influential member of the House complained:

We're going the way of the Senate. We've spread the action by giving subcommittees more power and by making it possible for members to play more active roles on them. But there's nothing to this point to coordinate what all these bodies are doing and to place some checks on their growing independence.[14]

VOTING CUES. Members of Congress must often vote on the basis of very little information. Consequently they frequently look to the members of the committee reporting out a bill, particularly those from their own party, for voting cues. The more complex the subject, the more the other members depend on the "experts" within the committee, who often have what appears to be a monopoly on information. While a few committees regularly disregard the recommendations of their subcommittees, most of the full committees usually ratify the recommendations of their subcommittees. This dependence, combined with the prerogatives of the committees and subcommittees, frequently places great power in the hands of small groups of legislators.

CHANGES IN COMMITTEE ASSIGNMENTS AND SENIORITY

The assignment process is supposed to provide a means for selecting among competing candidates for committee vacancies, accommodating the requests of veteran legislators for transfer from one committee to another, and matching prior experience with assignments in order to get expertise on each committee. In the Senate, the Democrats use the Steering Committee, chaired by their Leader, to make committee assignment recommendations, while the Republicans use a Committee on Committees. In the House, the Democratic Steering and Policy Committee, a leadership group, and the Republican Committee on Committees make the assignment recommendations. In each case, the recommending body submits the list to caucuses of all the members of the party of the particular house for their approval.

PRINCIPLES OF ASSIGNMENT. Committees are so important in the power structure of Congress that assignment to them is a milestone event in the life of a freshman legislator. Three general principles guide committee assignments. The first is that the majority party in each chamber can name the chairman and a majority of the members of each committee, though an attempt usually is made to retain a committee membership ratio which reflects party ratios in the entire chamber. The second principle is that assignments are permanent, continuing from one Congress to the next, unless a member wishes to transfer into a vacant position on another committee. An exception can occur if an election results in a major change in party ratios. Then the majority party's demands can only be met by forcing the transfer of the least-senior member of the minority party from one of the coveted committee's seats.

The third principle is **seniority**, the practice of naming the member of the majority party with the longest consecutive service on a committee as chairman. Seniority also plays a key role in the selection of subcommittee chairpersons and in subcommittee assignments. Seniority, in terms of length of service in the Congress, also influences the disposition of requests for transfer from committee to committee. In recent years, however, automatic deference to seniority has given way to a more flexible system. In 1971, both parties in the House adopted the rule that seniority does not have to be followed by committees when nominating chairmen or ranking minority members. The Republicans have an automatic secret vote in the caucus on each ranking minority member nominee, and the Democrats' rules require a secret vote on chairmanships if requested by one-fifth of the members; however, automatic secret ballots have become the normal practice. Up to the 1981 majority changeover, Senate Republicans have allowed the members of their party on each committee to choose the ranking minority member, but this has not led to any departure from the principal of seniority. A secret request of twenty percent of the Democratic senators requires a secret ballot to confirm the appointment of a chairman. Secrecy prevents possible reprisal if the effort to remove a chairman fails.

ASSIGNMENT AND RE-ELECTION. In general, the criteria by which new members are assigned to a committee are their desires, previous experience, and, most importantly, the hope that the assignment will assist them in being re-elected. For example, a representative from a predominantly agricultural district can be very visible and effective if assigned to the Committee on Agriculture. An urban representative would be unhappy with the same assignment.

While freshman representatives, particularly those from competitive districts, seem most concerned with the electoral connection, the desire to help the constituents and achieve re-election also motivates some requests for transfer. Other assignment request motivations of new or veteran congressmen include the desire for influence in the House—appointment to the exclusive committees, or an interest in helping to shape pol-

icy in a particular field—education, health, etc.[15]

The assignment procedure is far from automatic. Competition for certain seats may be greatly affected by the composition of the selecting group. Who you know may be more important than what you know. And, another factor is the attempt at achieving regional or state distribution which may lead to the choice of one legislator over another on the basis that the loser is from a state that already has a number of people on the sought-after committee.

THE SENIORITY CONTROVERSY

There are two types of seniority in Congress: one reflects a member's total years of service in his or her house, and the other refers to length of uninterrupted service on a committee. The first determines a legislator's place in line for various amenities, including office space, location of seat (in the Senate), etc. The second, because of its use in determining committee chairmanships and subcommittee chairmanships and assignments, has been the focus of controversy since the late 1940s.

ATTACK ON SENIORITY. The critics of the system have attacked it on the following grounds: it rewards longevity with power and suppresses younger, and perhaps more able legislators; it gives disproportionate power to southern senators and representatives; and, it keeps in power chairmen who abuse their office. The system itself is a party custom, rather than a rule of either house, and can be modified.

The "reward for longevity" argument was well put by former Congressman Donald W. Riegle, Jr., (D.,Mich.) in *O Congress* when he complained about the long apprenticeship (see insert).

It would be extremely difficult to make

The high-visibility issues of 1979—tighter budgets, lower taxes, and no-frills government—were reflected in the "ins" and "outs" of shopping for committee assignments. As usual, the D.C. committee had little "constituency" appeal, and no one enjoys investigating their colleagues, a responsibility of the Ethics Committee.

Judiciary is Out.
Commerce is In. So is Government Operations.
District of Columbia is—as usual—Out.
Budget is Very, Very In.
And Ethics is so far Out it's not on anybody's list this year.

Source: Congressional Quarterly, *Weekly Report,* 37 (January 27, 1979), p. 155.

a case that *seniority* equals *senility*. However, it is true that chairmen on both sides of the Hill are older than the average member. In 1979 the average age of chairmen in the Senate was 70 and in the House, 62, while the average senator was 53, and the average representative was 49. All but 4 of the standing committee chairmen in the Senate had been in that body for 18 or more years, and 15 of the 22 House chairmen had served at least 20 years. Another 16 Democrats in the House had served at least 20 years but they did not hold chairmanships, either because they had shifted committees—broken consecutive service—or were on committees with senior colleagues who were blessed with safe districts and good health.[16]

DEFENSE OF SENIORITY. Defenders of the system point out that it provides a virtually automatic way of dealing with a hot potato.

Committee assignments and rank are of crucial importance in the ambitious legislator's career. If these were subject to power plays and maneuvering, much congressional time and energy would be exhausted in organizing, and Congress would be less able to play an active role in representing the diversity of the nation in policy formation. Moreover, the system usually provides competent chairmen.[17]

The seniority system certainly does force the executive branch to deal with strong committee chairmen, probably strengthening Congress in its ability to resist presidential power.

From the point of view of "liberal" members of Congress, the southern problem associated with seniority was a real one, but it is being eliminated by the death, defeat, or retirement of senior senators and representatives from that region. The Republican capture of the Senate in 1981 has eliminated the issue for liberal Democrats. And, Republican chairmen from the South are not out of step with the rest of their party.

SENIORITY AND THE SOUTH. Prior to the 1970s, southern and conservative domination of Congress through the seniority system rested on the limited party competition in the South. In these "conservative" areas, the

Here Donald Riegel is suggesting an extreme, though possible, situation.
The turnover in the House since 1974 is leading to a shorter
apprenticeship. But, he is correct that unless a more senior member is
passed over for ideological reasons, including party disloyalty, or an
unwillingness to deal fairly with his fellow committee members, the
"ablest" person may have to wait in line for a long time.

*A man can come to Congress when he's thirty-five, serve here twenty years, at
age fifty-five, be the ablest man on his committee. But because he has to
wait for all the members ahead of him to retire or die, he may have to
wait another twenty years—until he's seventy-five—before he becomes a
chairman. The practical and psychological implications of this are
obvious.*

Rep. DONALD W. RIEGLE, Jr. (D., Mich.)

Source: From *O Congress* (New York: Doubleday, 1973), p. 141.

incumbents, often unopposed, were able to build a record of continuous service while some of their colleagues from more hotly contested states and districts fell by the wayside. Southern dominance was greatly enhanced by heavy Democratic losses in the 1946 election, which hurt the party everywhere but in the South, and by the Legislative Reorganization Act of 1946, which reduced the number of congressional committees by half. The returning southerners were able to add to their committee strength on Agriculture, Appropriations, Armed Services, Finance, Foreign Affairs, and Judiciary in the Senate, and Agriculture, Appropriations, Armed Services, Banking–Currency, Rules, and Ways and Means in the House.

What particularly aggravated the liberals in the Democratic Party was that these "party leaders," individually and as a group, usually had party unity scores (based on the percentage of time a legislator votes with the party on issues that divide the two parties) below fifty percent. In 1975–76, none of the six southern chairmen in the Senate had a party unity score of better than forty percent. In the House, only three of nine scored better than fifty percent. Obviously, the supposedly liberal party was being handicapped by defections from the ranks of its senior, conservative members (see Chapter 10).

During the period from 1947 through 1968, an average of sixty percent of the standing committees in both houses were chaired by people from the South.[18] By 1979, southerners chaired only three of fifteen Senate standing committees and six of twenty-two in the House. Before long, the South may be complaining that it is underrepresented in these important positions. As southern chairmen were replaced by non-southern Democrats with more liberal voting records, the demands for further reform or even abandonment of the system quieted. Some former critics saw themselves as beneficiaries or soon-to-be beneficiaries of seniority, and they did not want to abandon a procedure that now served their interests. This explains why both

*Senators Russell Long and Harry Byrd were part of a longstanding southern bloc
which held disproportionate Congressional power due to seniority customs
in committee assignment.*

houses have tinkered with seniority, but continue to be guided by it except in rare instances. And, the distribution of power also has lessened the impact of seniority (see insert). The changeover in 1981 to Republican control of the Senate, and the possibility of a change of power in the House, should not threaten the present seniority system.

Ignoring the question of which group has or will benefit from the seniority system, seniority is a force that slows the impact of electoral coalitions by delaying the transfer of leadership in Congress. Elections infuse new blood into the legislative branch, but equally important, they often suggest that the time has come to tackle new problems or try different approaches to solve old ones. But, the senior-

ity system can buy time for those who resist change, and it can determine who wins and loses on legislative policy.

COMMITTEE CHAIRMEN

Obviously, there would not be any great fuss over the chairmanships if the posts did not confer power on the occupants. In the Legislative Reorganization Act of 1970, a number of committee procedures were changed, limiting the power of chairmen to delay action; to call hearings abruptly, preventing the testimony of witnesses to whom the chair is hostile; or to operate in an arbitrary fashion behind closed doors. Commit-

Southern dominance of Senate committees has been eliminated through death, retirement, and defeat. Non-southerners have inherited most of the leadership positions and reforms have reduced the power of chairmen.

No longer is the Senate run as the private preserve of elderly conservative Southern Democrats. Many of the old-time Southern power barons have been replaced by sons of the New South, and those that remain have had their wings clipped. The power in the dominant Democratic Party in the Senate has shifted to Northern Liberals.

DAVID E. ROSENBAUM

Source: "The Senate's Revolution Is Without An R," *New York Times*, February 2, 1975, Sect. 4, p. 3. © 1975 by the New York Times Company. Reprinted by permission.

tees now must make public all roll-call votes taken in committee. Hearings and meetings are to be open to the public—unless the committee decides to close them. Hearings may be broadcast or televised if a majority of the committee approves. Moreover, with few exceptions, committee hearings must be announced at least one week in advance. However, the act contained loopholes, and many of the restrictions on chairmen depend upon majority sentiment in the committees to apply them.

These anti-secrecy provisions have been surprisingly effective. The number of secret meetings has continued to decline, and most of the closed sessions involve national security matters or the mark-up of appropriations bills. In 1975, the open-meeting concept was extended to cover House–Senate conference committee meetings to resolve differences in legislation passed by the two houses.

POWERS OF CHAIRMEN. In addition, each committee has a set of rules which appears to guarantee democracy within the body, subjecting the powers of the chairmen to majority rule. But, chairs of full and subcommittees

still exercise considerable control over scheduling hearings and meetings, committee agendas, and committee resources such as staff and budget. They serve on the conference committees that resolve House and Senate differences on bills and appoint the other members. They also serve as the floor manager or appoint the manager to handle bills from their committee that reach the floor of their chamber. And, through their formal powers and informal influence among other leaders, they are in a position to further the interests of members of their committees.

It should be remembered that the power of many chairmen has been built upon their expertise and personal skill in handling the needs of their committee members. The late Daniel Berman often pointed out how paradoxical it was that the powers of the chairmen were continually criticized in Congress, though the committees had the weapons at hand to alter their rules. He suggested that the all-powerful chairman was a convenient target on which to pin many of Congress's legislative failures.[19]

But certain chairmen were deemed to be insensitive to their colleagues, and ran their committees in an arbitrary or dictatorial fashion. Others were considered inept or too conservative, and for one or more of these reasons, the Democrats ousted three chairmen in 1975 during the previously mentioned revolt in the House.

Not since 1925 had as many as two chairmen been dethroned by the majority party. The action put all House chairmen on notice that they must be more responsive to the mainstream leadership of the party and less dictatorial in the use of their powers. And, it meant a considerable loss of power for the overthrown bloc. After the vote, Henry Reuss of Wisconsin said, "From now on the sword of Damocles hangeth over every chairman."[20]

In January 1979, the congressional seniority system in the House took another beating when three junior Democrats defeated more senior colleagues in elections for subcommittee chairmanships. The choices are made by the majority party members on each committee. Unlike the cases of the full committee chairmen ousted in 1975, the issues did not involve autocratic attitudes or a lack of party loyalty on the part of the three individuals who were expecting to become chairman for the first time. The upsets were based on the fact that the heavy concentration of liberal young Democrats on the two committees involved—Commerce and Governmental Operations—felt that the less senior members who were elected held views closer to theirs than did the more senior members. Younger members of the House, particularly those elected since 1974, feel less bound by seniority and are likely to put winning policy victories ahead of tradition.[21]

Congressional Roles

THE POWER OF THE PURSE

When not attending to constituents, Congress must deal with the other half of the political equation—the workings of the national government. One of its greatest weapons in maintaining control over national policy is its constitutionally exclusive powers to raise and appropriate money. Simply put, Congress holds, or attempts to hold, the purse strings. Even when it authorizes money for a long-term program, there is no guarantee that it will make yearly appropriations. Economic conditions, the changing winds of congressional opinion, or even new national priorities may lead to drastic cutbacks or termination of federal programs.

It is important to keep in mind the distinction between **authorization** and **appropriation.** For example, if Congress passes a $5 billion farm support program in 1982, with outlays of $2, $2, and $1 billion over the following three years, this is just an authorization to spend, and does not provide the money. The budget for the Department of Agriculture that is submitted by the president during each of the three years will request the stipulated amounts, assuming, of course, that priorities and conditions do not change. Each year Congress may or may not include all or some of the authorized monies in the appropriation bills providing Agriculture's budget.

This power of the purse involves three types of laws: laws levying taxes, laws authorizing the incurrence of debt, and laws appropriating funds. The first two areas are the responsibility of the House Ways and Means and Senate Finance Committees; the third, the Appropriations Committees of both houses. The Constitution requires tax bills to originate in the House and by custom, the president's budget requests are considered by the House Appropriations Committee before moving on to the Senate. The House body usually was more conservative and the Senate Appropriations Committee tended to be a "court of appeals," seldom lowering and usually increasing House figures. However, the current Republican control of the Senate has reversed these roles.

October 1   Fiscal year begins.

November 10   President submits Current Services Budget (an estimate of the budget outlays needed to carry on existing programs for the next fiscal year, given certain economic assumptions).

December 31   The Joint Economic Committee reports its analysis of the Current Services Budget to the budget committees.

January (last week)   President submits his budget (fifteen days after Congress convenes).

February   House and Senate budget committees hold hearings and begin work on the First Budget Resolution.

March 15   All House and Senate committees and joint committees submit budget estimates and views regarding spending in their policy areas to the House and Senate budget committees.

April 1   The Congressional Budget Office submits its report on fiscal policy and national priorities (including programming at alternative budget levels) to the House and Senate budget committees.

April 15   Budget committees report First Budget Resolution (on or before April 15).

Figure 11–1   The congressional budget process. (Source: Adapted from David J. Vogler, The Politics of Congress, *2d ed.)*

The complexity of the separate budget proposals for each executive department or agency has made the membership of both houses particularly dependent on their respective appropriations committees. A study of the appropriations for thirty-six bureaus (subunits of departments) from 1947 to 1962, revealed that the House accepted committee recommendations 89.9 percent of the time and the Senate supported them 88.5 percent of the time.[22] Conservative dominance of the powerful money committees made them a logical target for the reforms of 1974–75.

PROBLEMS OF CONTROL. Despite the official monetary control Congress holds, it has had great difficulty staying on top of federal spending, and many legislators felt that the power of the purse had slipped into the hands of the president.[23] They had to work with a

May 15   Deadline for all committees to report legislation authorizing new budget authority.

May 15   Deadline for Congress to complete action on First Budget Resolution.

June, July, and August   Congress enacts appropriations and spending bills; the Congressional Budget Office issues periodic scorekeeping reports that compare congressional spending with the First Budget Resolution.

August   House and Senate budget committees prepare Second Budget Resolution and report it to their respective chambers.

September (7th day after Labor Day)   Deadline for Congress to complete action on bills providing budget authority.

September 15   Congress completes action on Second Budget Resolution. The second resolution confirms or revises the target levels of spending, income, and debt limit contained in the first resolution. After this date, Congress can't consider any bill, amendment, or conference report that would result in an increase in spending ceilings contained in the Second Budget Resolution or a reduction in revenues contained in that resolution.

September 25   Congress completes action on reconciliation bills or resolutions that implement the Second Budget Resolution.

October 1   New fiscal year begins.

Figure 11–1   continued

budget that expressed the president's view of proper spending ceilings, and Congress had no expert body to attempt to match the Office of Management and Budget (OMB), the president's fiscal policy "right-arm" (see Chapter 14). Congress was frustrated by the president's ability to **impound**—refuse to spend—appropriated funds, and by its own fragmented and decentralized process which saw a lack of coordination between authoriza-tion of programs and the ability to pay for them, and the separate consideration of bud-gets for each major governmental function or operation. Finally, the fiscal year of July 1 to June 30 forced Congress to consider the next fiscal year's budget in a hasty fashion.

The Congressional Budget and Im-poundment Act of 1974 represented a major step in Congress's attempt to recapture con-trol of the process by giving the legislature

Social services are largely funded by federal programs whose purse strings are ultimately held by the Congress.

machinery for coordinating spending and revenue programs and for setting budget priorities. The act also was motivated by the Democrats who wished to disprove Nixon's charge that they were reckless spendthrifts.[24]

REFORM OF THE BUDGET PROCESS. Major revisions in the new system included the following: a new fiscal year more in line with congressional operations—October 1 to September 30; creation of a Congressional Budget Office (CBO) to provide economic information and analysis—a counterbalance to OMB; and the establishment of Budget Committees in both houses. The process (see Figure 11–1) includes a November submission by the president of estimates of budget outlays necessary for the next fiscal year, two more months of lead time than in the past. And, presidential impoundments may be vetoed by either house. Both houses must approve any presidential request to eliminate a project that Congress has funded.

Critics of the new system thought it would flounder because congressional committees must now submit budget estimates and their priorities to their respective Budget Committees who prepare the First Budget Resolution setting targets for revenue raising and spending in each of the major categories of the budget and determining the budget deficit. May 15th is the deadline for committees to report out bills that will require new monies (budget authority). Put more simply, members of Congress now have to determine how much they want to spend and for what within a framework of an overall ceiling and ceilings for each category such as defense, health, education, agriculture, etc. In the past, the legislators sought to make winners out of their favored constituencies without regard to the amounts their colleagues wanted to spend in their favored areas. If targets are overrun during the summer, Congress must reconcile the differences between spending and revenue that will be raised by tax bills. The Second Budget Resolution updates the first one and formally binds all committee action to conform to these budget levels.

Reforms notwithstanding, Congress knows that it has little control over three-fourths of federal spending. The "uncontrollable" part of the budget results from "entitlement" programs, so called because the recipients are "entitled" to benefits. Examples of programs in this category are Social Security, Medicare, interest on public debt, and retired military personnel pay. However, Reagan's proposals to adjust some of the Social Security regulations and benefits may signal that this program, and other entitlement programs, may no longer be untouchable.

POLITICAL HOT POTATO. Due to the reforms, the budget should be more of a product of Congress than in the past. Prior to the FY 1982 budget, the members tended to increase the ceilings in some areas rather than make the hard political choices to cut back on programs. However, Congress was given renewed reason to doubt how much control it really had over the budget in the face of President Reagan's cutbacks for fiscal year 1982. Capitalizing on his mandate to reduce "Big Government," Reagan steamrolled his budget through the supposedly Democratic-"controlled" House. And it was smooth sailing in the Republican-dominated Senate.

Reagan's victories on the first budget resolution (May) and a reconciliation bill (June), whereby Congress ordered its committees to make changes in the law to meet the target of a $35 billion spending cut, were made possible by the support of 63 House Democrats on the first issue and 29 on reconciliation. Some Democrats seemed afraid of the electoral dangers of not giving the President's economic plans a chance. This feeling carried over to the 1981 passage of a 33-month, 25 percent reduction in individual income tax rates. The budget made deep cuts into social programs such as food stamps, housing subsidies, and student loans, that have been fashioned by Democratic Congresses since 1933.

Reconciliation is rarely used and is intended to be a last resort at the end of the budget process to bring spending and budget targets into line. The successful Republican

strategy to use a one-vote reconciliation package early in the 1981 process meant that the usual lengthy committee hearings and program-by-program action on the floor of both houses was avoided. The Democrats had counted on these stages to reduce the cuts in many social programs. The lack of hearings and deliberations caused members of both parties to be concerned about the distortion of the process, and Congress's future budgetary role.

OVERSEEING THE ADMINISTRATION

The legislative power to authorize programs, create agencies, and appropriate funds for them suggests that Congress should have some control over the administration of its creations. Yet, legislative **oversight** has become increasingly difficult in the face of an ever-expanding bureaucracy. Most observers believe that legislative oversight should be used for the following purposes: to see that programs and policies are carried out efficiently and in accordance with the intent of Congress; to provide data on the effects of policies; and to hold executive agencies accountable for the expenditure of appropriated funds. There is general agreement, on the other hand, that Congress should not direct or supervise the administration excessively and thus interfere with the executive function.

Oversight activities can focus on very narrow questions or pursue broad questions about the scope and direction of important policy. The House Armed Services Committee, for example, has often been accused of being a real estate committee that concerns itself with the location of facilities while deferring to the House Appropriations Committee the review of substantive policy issues regarding the military establishment. Examples of broader oversight concerns include past hearings on hunger, manpower, spending practices of the Department of Defense, and the ongoing hearings in both houses concerning the effort to exercise more effective control over the nation's intelligence agencies.

Another device of oversight is the **congressional veto,** which has been included in over one hundred bills in the last decade. The veto gives Congress the authority to disapprove of regulations written by an executive agency or independent regulatory agency as a result of agency implementation of the legislation. The executive branch dislikes the congressional veto and resists efforts by Congress to vote itself broad veto powers (see Chapter 14). Thus far, a majority of Congress is hesitant to pass a general congressional veto authorizing disapproval of any executive agency regulation. With over 10,000 new regulations being made each year, they are reluctant to have their committees assume the burden of review.

OVERSIGHT PROBLEMS. Congress is hampered in its oversight function, much of which takes place in committee and subcommittee hearings, by the fact that every executive unit may be looked at by six or more congressional committees, including one or more subject matter committees, the appropriations committees of both houses, and the permanent watchdog groups, the Government Operations and Affairs Committees. And, what members get out of a hearing often is a product of what they ask. If a legislator is content that a program benefits the constituency—they are winners—he or she will not be too interested in questions of efficiency. Finally, the president can have his officials claim **executive privilege** on his behalf and refuse to testify on sensitive matters, another serious barrier to effective oversight.

THE POWER OF INVESTIGATION

Although the day-to-day hearings of the standing committees may be called inves-

tigations, the term is usually reserved for special probes undertaken by standing, special, and select committees. These investigations have dealt with such topics as corruption in public office (including the Watergate investigation), stock exchange practices, price fixing among drug manufacturers, union corruption, and subversive activities. The scope of Congress's investigating power is limited only by the requirement that some valid legislation may result from the inquiry. Given the range of current legislation, it is difficult to imagine an area that could be excluded.

The emotionally and politically charged nature of some topics has resulted in a tremendous amount of publicity for these investigations. The Watergate Committee's probe brought down Richard Nixon, made a folk hero out of its chairman, former Senator Sam Ervin, Jr. (D., N.C.), and propelled Howard Baker of Tennessee into the forefront of Republican politics. The 1975 and 1976 House and Senate investigations of our intelligence agencies (see Chapter 14) led to a major overhaul of congressional oversight of the CIA, the FBI, and other parts of the intelligence community.

Occasionally, investigators have been overzealous and probes have become grand inquisitions. Witnesses have been bullied and have often raised the constitutional question: what limits are there on Congress's power to compel private citizens to answer questions? The Supreme Court has ruled that the First Amendment is not a barrier to a question that is within the scope of a committee's legislative purpose, but a witness can take the Fifth Amendment, refusing to answer on the grounds of self incrimination.[25] Unfortunately, even the most idealistic use of the Fifth Amendment may make a loser out of the witness because many people assume that the witness has something to hide. The social penalties even may include loss of job. On the other hand, the Court has ruled that Congress cannot expose for the sake of exposure and

President Richard Nixon consults Attorney General John Mitchell after two successive Nixon nominees to the Supreme Court were rejected by the Senate.

that a committee's questions must be relevant to its legislative purpose.[26]

ADVICE AND CONSENT

The Constitution assigns to the Senate two important roles that the House does not share—the power to approve or reject treaties, and to judge the suitability of presidential appointments. Although the president has exclusive constitutional authority to negotiate treaties, they do not become effective unless ratified by two-thirds of the senators voting. The Senate has approved most treaties unconditionally and the bulk of the rest "with reservations." However, ratification is not always a sure bet; the most famous rejection came after

World War I, when the Senate refused to ratify the Treaty of Versailles.

The most important Senate review duty is that of cabinet appointments—rarely rejected—and nominations to non-cabinet policy-making posts such as commissioners of regulatory agencies or federal judgeships. This category has been the source of most of the struggles between the president and the Senate. The most famous appointment fights of recent times came when President Nixon attempted to fill the Supreme Court seat vacated by Abe Fortas. As already discussed in Chapter 2, in November 1969, the Senate rejected Clement F. Haynsworth, Jr., of South Carolina. In April 1970, it refused to confirm G. Harrold Carswell of Florida. In the Carswell case, an angry President Nixon claimed that the Senate was overstepping its constitutional authority by attempting to substitute its judgment for his. He claimed that the rejection effort, headed by liberals and civil rights groups on the basis of the nominee's alleged segregationist attitudes and mediocre record as a judge, was an example of vicious regional discrimination. The vacant seat was finally filled by the unanimous confirmation of Harry A. Blackmun of Minnesota.

A conflict with the Senate over key appointments damages presidential prestige, and possibly party solidarity. The relatively few examples of Senate disapproval of key appointees reflects the wise and often-used precaution of clearing the appointment with the Senate leadership prior to any public announcement of the nomination.

CONGRESS AND FOREIGN POLICY

The constitutional division of powers in foreign affairs is an open invitation to conflict. The president is commander-in-chief of the armed forces, makes appointments, negotiates treaties, and has the power to recognize foreign governments. He is, in short, the sole official organ of United States foreign policy. The power to ratify treaties and approve appointments is vested in the Senate; and both houses share the power to declare war. Moreover, the billions of dollars needed to carry on modern warfare gives Congress at least a nominal voice in war policy. Nevertheless, Congress's constitutional right to declare war has not been applied in a meaningful way since our entry into World War I. In fact, during and since World War II, many major arrangements between our nation and foreign governments have been concluded by **executive agreements** rather than treaties. Such an executive agreement is binding upon the country even though it has not been subjected to Senate ratification. Though an executive

agreement is theoretically valid only during the term of office of its initiator, it is unlikely to be scrapped by a succeeding president.

By using the overarching label of *national security*, control over congressional access to military and civilian intelligence agencies, and its enlarged powers, the executive branch often has been able to turn the Congress into a foreign policy rubber stamp. Whether it was simply the extension of an American military base into a new part of the world, or the actual running of the Vietnam War for over a decade, the executive branch pretty much had its own way.

THE VIETNAM EXPERIENCE. Since World War II, American forces have engaged in two major wars, in Korea and Vietnam; both were called **police actions** because no declaration of war was ever made by Congress. In these presidential wars, the commander-in-chief committed our forces and simply presented the Congress with an accomplished fact. In the case of Vietnam, President Johnson did a good deal more than that. He stampeded Congress into the famous August 1964 Tonkin Gulf Resolution (". . . the Congress approves and supports the determination of the President, as Commander-in-Chief, to take all necessary measures to repel any armed attack against the forces of the United States and to prevent further aggression.") The resolution conveniently confirmed Johnson's free hand in the conduct of the war. To accomplish this, he and his advisers had fed Congress false or deceptive military intelligence about alleged North Vietnamese attacks on two U.S. destroyers in the Gulf of Tonkin. One of the attacks may not even have taken place, and the other took place under, at best, questionable circumstances.

These incidents provided the Johnson administration with a pretext for rallying congressional support. Such conscious deception of Congress continued throughout the course of the Vietnam conflict. When the Congress finally began to take feeble steps to regain control over the situation by prohibiting the funding of air operations over Cambodia or the introduction of American ground troops into Laos, the administration just went its own way in secrecy. If discovered, presidential spokesmen claimed that each forbidden action was aimed at ending U.S. involvement in the area or saving American lives, and was consequently consistent with congressional wishes.

Frustration led the Senate to pass the National Commitments Resolution on June 25, 1969. It was designed to reassert a congressional voice in decisions committing the United States to the defense of foreign nations. Presidential action was to be dependent upon the approval of both Houses of Congress. This action expressed the "sense" of the Senate, although it did not bind the president.

WAR POWERS ACT. In the summer of 1973 Congress overrode Nixon's veto of a War Powers Act. The measure requires the president to report in writing to Congress the reasons for committing armed forces to combat abroad, and requires the withdrawal from combat of the forces within sixty to ninety days unless Congress authorizes a longer involvement. Some critics complained that the bill simply ratified Congress's loss of power to make war. They said it made official what presidents had previously done through an implied power—made war on their own initiative. But most lawmakers felt that Congress had moved, however minimally, to reassert its control over warmaking. They felt that the balance of power in this area still remained with the chief executive; but that the scales were tipped less heavily in his favor.

The War Powers Act also states that whenever possible, the president should consult with Congress "before introducing United States Armed Forces into hostilities or into situations where imminent involvement in hostilities is clearly indicated by the circumstances. . . ." Prior to the April 24, 1980 attempt to rescue the hostages held in Iran, President Carter did not consult with Congress. Neither did President Ford, when he used force to "free" the merchant vessel *Mayaguez* after it was seized for a brief period by the Cambodian Navy. The potential seriousness of the 1980 incident may suggest that the critics were correct.

Post–Vietnam Congresses have been more active in efforts to avoid armed conflicts. In 1976 Congress prohibited further U.S. aid or involvement in the Civil War in Angola, and it debated for a month before agreeing to allow 200 American civilians to be stationed in the Sinai Desert to man electronic gear to monitor the Egyptian–Israeli accord. But, the handling of the Iranian hostage crisis of 1979–81 and the verbal American response to the Soviet invasion of Afghanistan in 1980 were left, of necessity, to the president. However, it was up to Congress to provide additional defense spending, aid to friendly nations in the Middle East, legislation to reduce dependence on imported oil, and to reinstate the draft registration. Congress rejected registration for women and, after lengthy debate, approved registration of males ages 18 through 20. However, Reagan's 1981 decision to send weapons and U.S. military advisers to aid the government of El Salvador's efforts to put down a revolution raised the fear among many people that our nation was taking the first small steps into another Vietnam.

TRADE AND AID. Congress can have a significant impact on foreign policy through its control of foreign trade and foreign aid bills. In 1974 it attached conditions relating to free-access rights for Soviet Jews to leave the USSR to a bill giving trade preferences to the Russians. The Russians rejected the conditions and U.S.–Soviet relations suffered a setback. And, in 1974 and 1975, Congress cut off military aid to Turkey because of that nation's invasion of Cyprus and reluctance to negotiate with Greece. President Ford and the State Department argued to no avail that this action threatened the defense posture of NATO.

The Senate's historic 1978 struggle over ratification of the Panama Canal treaties may signal that advice and consent in this area is becoming more meaningful. Congressional-presidential conflict over treaties and executive agreements is treated in more detail in Chapter 12.

Foreign policy has been the subject of a power conflict between the institutions of Congress and the presidency. For individual legislators, particularly senators, the contests have often provided an opportunity for beneficial "position taking," allowing them to win the support of particular groups while not being held accountable for the final outcome. Prior to the election of 1978, it was difficult to find contemporary examples of members of Congress whose winning or losing at the polls could be attributed to their foreign policy positions. However, the fallout from the Panama Canal debates did hurt some 1978 Senate incumbents, and the 1979 debates over the recognition of the Republic of China and dropping of the treaty with Taiwan were potentially dangerous for a few senators up for re-election in 1980. Perhaps Congress's more active role in foreign policy will prove to be a much more individually risky business than it has been in the past.

JUDICIAL FUNCTIONS

Congress's judicial functions include:

★   The impeachment process

★   The disciplining of its own members by expulsion, exclusion, or censure

★   The resolution of election disputes

arising from irregularities, claims of fraud, or violation of election laws

★   The citing of nonmembers for contempt of Congress, usually for refusing to testify before congressional committees

The consideration of Articles of Impeachment against Richard Nixon was headed off by his resignation (see Chapter 12), but a resolution of impeachment would have required a majority vote of the House of Representatives. Such a resolution is similar to an indictment, saying that there are sufficient grounds for a trial. The trial itself is conducted in the Senate, where a two-thirds vote of those present is required for conviction and removal from office. Only twelve persons so far have been impeached, and only four (all judges) have been convicted. In the turbulent period after the Civil War, President Andrew Johnson was impeached and subjected to a politically motivated Senate trial. Though he was charged with misconduct in office, his real offense was disagreement with Congress. He was saved from conviction by a single vote.

ELECTION DISPUTES.   On occasion, the results of congressional elections are challenged by the losers, usually on the grounds of vote fraud or counting irregularities. Following the 1976 elections, the results of eight House contests were challenged. Seven challenges were dismissed, but in the eighth case, the first-term member resigned his seat just prior to a committee recommendation to have a new primary and election. He was defeated in the primary and subsequently pleaded guilty to fraud and went to prison for a year.

Perhaps the most interesting case of this sort took place in 1974, when Democrat John A. Durkin appeared to have defeated Republican Louis C. Wyman by a ten-vote margin, making the New Hampshire senatorial race the closest one on record. After a recount and the challenging of some absentee ballots,

Wyman was certified by the state as having won by two votes. The Senate wrestled with the case for seven months, with partisan divisions preventing any resolution. Finally, New Hampshire decided on a special election, and Durkin won.

A Bill Becomes a Law—Maybe!

During the 96th Congress, 1979–80, 10,171 bills were introduced. Only 348 of these were enacted.[27] In other words, only 3.4 percent of the proposals survived. This batting average looks worse than it is as numerous bills represent duplication of effort and many others are introduced with little or no expectation of committee consideration. They are meant to satisfy the desires of constituents or to pad legislators' records of legislative activity. Many are private bills dealing with individual claims against the government. Interest groups also write bills for members of Congress to introduce. But, the low level of output is also due, in part, to a complicated lawmaking process that provides many opportunities for intentional delay. At each stage of this process bargaining takes place, with the supporters of a bill challenged to maintain a majority. Yet, the opposition must win the vote at only one point along the line to defeat a bill. This is called the power of the **single negative**.

COMMITTEE ACTION

Every bill must be introduced (sponsored) by a member of Congress, although many of the most significant are written in executive agencies. Bills are referred to the appropriate committee by the Clerk of the House or the Secretary of the Senate. However, most bills are **pigeonholed**—not scheduled for hearings. A bill that is to receive serious consideration is usually referred to a subcommittee where a hearing takes place. Most hearings are open; and interested individuals, including lobbyists and other legislators, may ask or be invited to testify for or against the bill.

At the conclusion of the hearings, the bill is considered section by section in an executive session of the whole committee. During this stage in the process the most important bargains are made in an effort to achieve consensus. A congressional axiom holds that "bills should be written in committee, not on the floor." The committee may kill the bill, approve it with amendments, or draft a new bill for submission to its chamber.

The lifespan of each Congress is two years, and a bill that does not run the entire course from introduction to becoming a law during the two year period "dies." However, we saw at the beginning of the chapter that the consumer protection agency issue was before Congress for eight years. Major bills often spend more than two years in committee. The work of one Congress is not lost when time runs out on a proposal. Its proponents can, and often do, reintroduce the measure in the next Congress, and the bill usually is referred to the same committee where the members can make use of the previous research and deliberations.

With the exception of tax legislation that must originate in the House, bills may be introduced first in one house or simultaneously in both houses. For reasons of strategy, a bill's advocates may think that the best approach is to introduce the proposal in that house where they think it has the best chance. This was true with most civil rights legislation, where passage in the House was easier and the bargaining from a position of relative strength—passage in one house—could take place in the Senate. But, for the purpose of tracing the obstacle course, we will trace the path of a bill that is introduced at approximately the same time in both houses.

REACHING THE FLOOR

THE RULES COMMITTEE. If a bill clears the committee in the House it is placed on one of the House calendars and debate is scheduled by the House Rules Committee. Legislation on specific subjects from certain House committees is "privileged," that is, it may be scheduled for consideration on the House floor without seeking a special rule from the House Rules Committee.[28] However, even privileged legislation usually goes through the Rules Committee because no other body can specify the number of hours of general debate to be allowed on the floor, waive possible points of order, or report a bill out under a **closed rule** which specifies that parts or all of the bill are immune from amendment on the floor. In addition, the Rules Committee can delay or block legislation by refusing to schedule hearings, holding prolonged hearings on the subject matter of the bill, or refusing to report the bill out of committee. In 1975 the House Democrats gave the speaker (when the speaker is a Democrat) the power to appoint the Democratic members of the Rules Committee in an effort to make the committee focus on its original role as a traffic cop. In theory, it is supposed to work on behalf of the leadership to see to it that the most important legislation reaches the floor in an orderly fashion.

The Rules Committee was a center of congressional controversy for many years. Its liberal critics contended that conservative members turned it into a policymaking body. They pointed to its powers to withhold essential rules or to cripple a bill's chances by prohibiting the amendment of controversial sections. However, a study of the committee revealed that it denied very few requests for hearings and rarely refused to grant the desired rule after a hearing. The study cut through the surface criticisms and pointed out that the committee's real power is its ability to bargain in advance with the standing committees about the form of a bill in exchange for a favorable rule.[29]

Representative Margaret Heckler of Massachusetts makes a point at hearings in the House.

The process in the Senate, which has no equivalent of the Rules Committee, is less complicated. Bills are placed on the Senate calendar and scheduled for floor debate by the majority leadership, usually in conjunction with the minority leader. Reported bills rarely are held up from floor action. When the committees in both houses report out a bill, it is accompanied by a written report, and often by a minority report. These reports provide a major voting cue to non-committee members, and they help explain why visitors to the House or Senate galleries may find only a handful of members taking part in a debate. Committee business and other activities take place while the houses are in session. A quorum need be present only at the start of business or when a member uses the delaying tactic of demanding a quorum call.

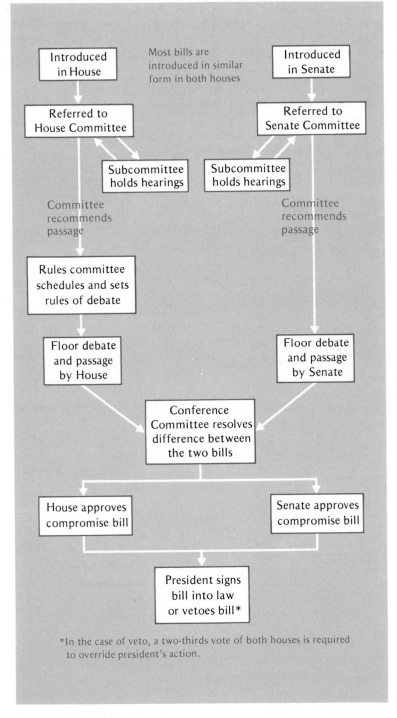

Figure 11–2 How a bill becomes a law.

Legislators believe that committee reports plus information and voting cues from the party leadership, committee leaders, interest groups, the president, and selected colleagues enable them to vote intelligently without being present during certain debates. Behind this lies the legislators' assumption that, if they had more information, they would agree with the cue-givers. As a result, they may well cast "rational" votes on the basis of no first-hand information (see Chapter 10).

FLOOR CONSIDERATION

LIMITED DEBATE IN THE HOUSE. General floor debate in the House is usually conducted in the **Committee of the Whole,** a parliamentary arrangement that allows business to proceed with only a one-hundred-member quorum. Debate time is limited—usually two hours—and divided equally between proponents and opponents. A member cannot take part in the general debate unless he has made prior arrangements with the bill's floor managers. After the debate, the bill is then subject to amendments—five minutes pro and con—which if defeated at this point, cannot be voted on again. Afterwards, the Committee of the Whole dissolves itself into the House, and reports the bill and the approved amendments, which are subsequently considered and voted upon. Finally, the whole bill as amended is voted on.

If a bill has not been introduced simultaneously in both houses, it is reported to the second chamber and referred to committee where it runs risks similar to those it faced in the house of origin.

UNLIMITED DEBATE IN THE SENATE. All business on the floor of the Senate is subject to unlimited debate, which is usually terminated by request of the leadership. Nevertheless, any senator can try to use the unlimited debate rule to prevent a measure from coming to a vote. This action is called a **filibuster.** In the late 1950s and 1960s, the Senate's southern Democratic minority adopted this method as its final recourse against civil rights legislation which it found abhorrent. "Senator Strom Thurmond of South Carolina still talks with pride of the August day in 1957 when he held the floor for 22 hours and 18 minutes, sustained only by three glasses of milk and a pitcher of orange juice."[30]

The impact of the filibuster cannot be judged by the number of times it has been employed. The mere threat of its use must always be considered in committee deliberation on controversial legislation. Even liberals, once strong opponents of the filibuster, began using it in the 1970s to kill the projected supersonic transport plane, the SST, and an antibussing bill.

Before 1917, there was no way of ending a filibuster. In that year, the Senate adopted the **cloture rule,** agreeing that any objection to ending debate could be overridden by a two-thirds vote of the members present. Between 1917 and the 1975 change in the rule, cloture was attempted 103 times, but succeeded only 21 times. Successful clotures were invoked prior to passage of the Civil Rights Act of 1964, the Voting Rights Act of 1965, the Open Housing Act of 1968, and the Voter Registration Act of 1973. A successful cloture led to the passage of the Election Campaign Reform Act of 1974.[31]

Nevertheless, the difficulty of getting a two-thirds vote and the association of the filibuster with southern conservatives had long made it a particular target of liberal attack. Congressional critics have been especially angered by it because it allows an intense minority to thwart the will of the majority. In March 1975, after years of failed attempts at reform, the Senate finally pushed through a new cloture rule—over a determined filibuster by conservatives. Only three-fifths of the entire Senate is now required to stop a filibuster. Since the adoption of the new rule, approximately one-half of attempts at cloture have been successful, a great improvement over the record of the past.

In the Senate it is easier to amend a bill on the floor than in the House. Amendments do not have to be **germane**—relate to the main subject of the bill. Each can amount to a separate bill unrelated to the main bill, but attached to it as a rider. The **non-germane amendment** (rider) often is a clever way to introduce a measure and avoid a hostile committee in one or both houses. For example, if it is attached to an important bill that has been passed by the House, the rider will have to clear only the hurdle of the conference committee. Opponents of the rider may not be willing to risk defeat of the main bill because of their opposition to the rider. The expanded bill makes them winners and losers.

CONFERENCE COMMITTEES

Assuming both houses pass a bill, but with major differences in their versions, one house will ask for a conference. The conferees will be appointed by the leadership of each chamber. Those designated are almost always members of the standing committees that handled the legislation. The rules of both houses limit **conference committee** negotiations to areas of disagreement. No new sections can be incorporated into the bills and no section already mutually agreed upon can be revised. Few bills are stranded in conference, and the two chambers seldom fail to approve the conference reports, which are privileged and cannot be amended on the floor. This gives enormous power to the conference committees.

PRESIDENTIAL VETO

After passage by both houses, the bill is transmitted to the president for his signature or veto. If he does not sign or veto the bill within ten workdays, it becomes law without his signature—a means of demonstrating dissatisfaction without actual rejection. In the fall of even-numbered (election) years, Congress's final adjournment prior to the expiration of the ten workday period allows a presidential failure to act to result in a **pocket veto** that kills the bill.

A presidential veto may be overridden by a two-thirds vote of both houses. However, as with the filibuster, a two-thirds majority in favor of a controversial piece of legislation is extremely difficult to muster. With this in mind, legislative leaders attempt to structure measures that will be acceptable to the chief executive. On the other hand, the president is faced with the black and white choice of accepting or rejecting each bill in its entirety. In some cases, a veto is a message to Congress that says, "Revise the bill, send it back, and I will sign it." Any bill which survives this Capitol Hill obstacle course becomes a law.

The complex rules that make up the obstacle course on Capitol Hill are not neutral. They play an important part in shaping policy. The independence of committees, the limited debate in the House, and unlimited debate in the Senate are examples of factors that influence the strategy of proponents and opponents of legislation. And, those legislators who are masters of the rules of the game have a greater opportunity to determine which bills win and which lose.

★ Issue ★

Can Congress Make Policy?

In the fall of 1974, President Ford worried about a "veto-proof" Congress and a possible "legislative dictatorship." The results of the

elections, which gave the Democrats better than two-thirds of the seats in the House and almost two-thirds of the Senate, suggested

The growing independence of members of Congress, particularly those elected since 1974 who have less regard for the old traditions, and the departure of long-term powerful chairmen has made it more difficult for congressional "leaders" to lead.

There've been no lack of attempts at leadership, but it's difficult for any sheriff to find a posse to head if everybody is going off in his own direction.

Rep. ALAN STILLMAN (R., Texas)

Source: Quoted in *Congressional Quarterly, Weekly Report, 33,* (June 28, 1975), p. 1345

that the President had grounds for concern. Two years later, the "Democratic" Congress had been able to override only eight of thirty-two vetoes and its failure to produce a real alternative to Ford's energy proposals underlined the difficulty that Congress has in making policy dealing with a complex subject matter. Rep. Sam Gibbons (D., Fla.) remarked, "Really, the people overestimate the capability of Congress." And he and other members wondered aloud whether Congress was structurally and temperamentally suited to devise long-range national energy policy.

The battle over energy and other key issues between Carter and Congress demonstrated that Ford's problem was not a matter of a Republican-versus-a-Democratic-legislature. On the contrary, the energy issue shows that congressional responses to presidential initiative or congressional attempts to originate legislation to deal with major public concerns often become entangled in a complex battle of interests, including jurisdictional power struggles among committees. And, ironically, the reforms that have "democratized" Congress have created a leadership problem. There may be no congressional leaders who can effectively "lead" the members (*see* insert).

The events of recent years raise questions about Congress's future policy role. And, when it comes to Congress, efficiency and effectiveness are, one might say, in the eye of the beholder—especially when the beholder is someone with a strong view of how politics in America should function.

CONGRESS'S ROLES

There are perhaps four major roles which Congress may or may not, should or should not play, depending upon which political observer you choose to question. These are: Congress as negator; Congress as incubator; Congress as conflict resolver; and Congress as watering trough for the rich and powerful.

CONGRESS AS NEGATOR. In 1964, Robert Bendiner wrote a book that was critical of the legislative process. In it he said:

A United States Congressman has two principal functions: to make laws and to keep laws from being made. The first of these he and his colleagues perform only with sweat, patience, and a remarkable skill in the handling of creaking machinery; but the second they perform daily, with ease and infinite variety. Indeed, if that government is best that governs least, then Congress is one of the most perfect instruments of government ever devised.[32]

Bendiner was writing from the perspective of a liberal frustrated by Congress's failure to respond to liberal presidential initiatives. Seventeen years, three conservative presidents, and a number of procedural and power distribution reforms later, Bendiner and others could still voice their dismay at Congress's inability to respond quickly and effectively to the nation's needs. But remember that evaluations of Congress depend upon the biases of the observers. From a conservative's perspective, the legislature's negative powers were a positive factor before the Nixon, Ford, and Reagan presidencies, and a negative factor during their terms in office.

When Congress acts as a negator, it is making policy by refusing to alter the status quo. On an issue-by-issue basis, this role makes winners out of those who do not want change, and losers of those who seek change.

CONGRESS AS INCUBATOR. Defenders of the congressional contribution to policymaking reject the widespread notion that the president is the initiator of legislative ideas, that policy innovation begins with a presidential message to Congress. They point to James Sundquist's startling study of the ancestry of legislative programs proposed by a number of administrations. He concluded that most of President Kennedy's proposals were developed by Democratic senators in the 1950s, and that President Johnson's program was "incubated" in Congress, slowly picking up support, before it was "hatched" by the president.[33]

Unfortunately, they point out, long-term congressional initiatives are invariably upstaged by the president, who, after checking the political waters via a congressional toe, seizes Congress's legislation as his own.

Yet a number of headline-catching presidential policy proposals of recent years were actually germinated in congressional soil. From Medicare to revenue sharing, we can find their seeds in congressional initiatives.

CONGRESS AS CONFLICT RESOLVER. The president enjoys an undeniable advantage over Congress. He can orchestrate a policy— present what appears to be a coherent program after using behind-the-scenes compromises and bargaining to smooth out conflict within the executive branch. Then, of course, his "coherent" proposals are received by a body divided by party, intra-party, regional, and philosophical differences that give it a chaotic appearance in contrast with the president's order. Congressional defenders say that the much-criticized high mortality rate of legislation is a product of Congress's role as a conflict resolver and consensus builder. Taking civil rights legislation as an example, Roger H. Davidson and John F. Bibby point out that the Kennedy–Johnson administration was not widely criticized for taking two years to draft and submit to Congress a comprehensive civil rights bill; yet, the Senate was condemned for its eighty-seven day filibuster prior to the passage of the Civil Rights Act of 1964.

This bill, like most that emerge from the tortuous legislative halls, was too weak to satisfy some and too strong to satisfy others. But it did represent a broad area of agreement on probably the most controversial domestic issue of our time. The conflict had been blunted; a temporary consensus had been reached.[34]

Congress, its defenders claim, uses its decentralized power to provide the public with many points at which it can exert its own pressure on the legislative system. As a result, Congress has a healthy way of feeling the pulse of the nation, of achieving a sort of lowest common denominator on issues of great importance to all Americans. Its very disunity, in fact, helps to unify the country behind public policy that is enacted into law.

CONGRESS AS WATERING TROUGH. To some critics, no matter what positive light is thrown on Congress, its actions nonetheless appear insensitive to the needs of most citizens. Whether Congress can or cannot make policy effectively, they claim, makes little difference for the majority of Americans. In either case, the goal of Congress is serving the needs of the organized, especially the needs of organized corporate power. It is hardly surprising, they say, that congressmen, who are "representative" only of a small percentage of Americans, should tend to service (whether well or badly) only that percentage, while, at best, throwing breadcrumbs to the rest of America. Even where Congress moves to deal with a problem like hunger which plagues so many poorer and less organized citizens, critics claim that they do so mainly for show, never bothering either to effectively legislate against it, or even oversee implementation of the weak legislation they do pass.

We would argue that this condemnation of Congress is an oversimplified exaggeration. Certain interests are better represented than others, but, the "electoral connection" requires at least a partial resolution of the problems that afflict large numbers of people. The winners and losers vary from era to era and issue to issue. Certainly the labor legislation of the 1930s and 1940s that gave unions power, welfare legislation such as social security and minimum wage, and more recently, Medicare and the windfall profits tax on the oil industry were passed over the strenuous objections of the "monied interests."

The "watering trough" is longer than some critics care to admit, but obviously, it is not long enough. The under- or unrepresented suffer, and members of Congress are representative but not visionary. But, the "electoral connection" was reflected in the general public's lack of support after the mid–1960s for the extensive social legislation embodied in Lyndon Johnson's Great Society programs, many of which were aimed at bringing the poor into the mainstream of society. And, the results of the 1980 election were interpreted as a public endorsement of the concept of reduced government spending for social programs.

THE QUESTION

Can Congress make policy? One response is that Congress constantly makes policy by rejecting proposals—many of them originating in the executive branch—modifying other proposals, and occasionally pulling together its own full-blown alternative to presidential initiatives. A more detailed response depends upon what type of policy is under consideration. For, despite the decentralizing forces of undisciplined parties, and ideological, regional, and constituency differences, the reports of Congress's demise as a policy-making institution are exaggerated.

Policies can be classified as *distributive, regulatory*, or *redistributive*, depending upon their relative impact on society.[35] Some policies, such as tax and energy legislation, fall into all three categories. **Distributive policies** generally give some good, resource, or service to individuals or groups such as agricultural subsidies, defense contracts, public works (dams, post offices, etc.), or tax loopholes. The term *distributive* carries the same meaning as Professor Mayhew's *particularized benefits* discussed in the last chapter. In the area of distributive policies we find each group seeking its own rewards and not opposing others seeking their share of the pie. The politics of distribution are characterized by bargaining or "non-interference," and Congress, particularly its committees and subcommittees, dominate the policy-making process. Congress has little difficulty making distributive policy. And, for the most part, the president stays out of this arena.

Regulatory policies, such as Medi-

Distributive policies, such as industrial contracts, are the easiest for Congress to pass because different groups support each other's benefits in return for support on their own.

care, national health insurance, trade policies, or campaign finance regulation, tend to limit one group for the benefits of others and/or reduce or expand alternatives of private individuals. Unlike distributive policies, regulation usually involves an overall policy that affects wide segments of the public. It often pits competing interests against each other, as is the case in the conflict over energy policy, or the consumer versus the private insurance industry in the contest over national health insurance. Congress has a major role to play in formulating regulatory policies, but it does so with difficulty. The president often plays a major role as initiator, coordinator of the interests during the bill drafting and congressional consideration stage, and as a public advocate.

It is in the area of **redistributive pol-**

icies that the presidential dominance, or attempted dominance, is most evident. These policies affect large groups—often in terms of social class, race, big and small business, or "haves" and "have-nots." Programs to relieve unemployment, poverty and welfare legislation, or civil rights bills are considered redistributive because they take something of value from one group and give it to another group. In the case of poverty and welfare it is a redistribution of federal dollars that obviously means there is going to be less money for other purposes. In the case of civil rights, the attempted redistribution involves power.

The struggle over redistributive policies usually is intense and does not lend itself readily to congressional bargaining. The policies involve basic decisions which will have long-range impact, and their formulation is dominated by the executive branch and its superior informational sources. Congress is not asked to draft redistributive policies, but to ratify them. Of course, this does not mean that Congress must follow blindly, as the history of tax reform, poverty programs, and energy policy will attest to. Redistributive policy is the area in which key legislative decisions are made by the entire membership in floor votes rather than in committee, an arena which adds to the legislature's difficulty in making policy in this area.

Finally, our discussion has indicated that the executive branch, with its informational advantages, has dominated foreign and defense policy making. In recent years the legislature has attempted to redress the balance in this area, but it will be unable to play a major role as long as the primary source of foreign policy and defense intelligence is in the executive bureaucracy.

In summary, the answer to the question—Can Congress make policy?—varies from issue to issue. And, we can question the idea that we would be better served by a Congress that responded more readily to presidential leadership. An independent, decentralized legislature—slow to react to the need for change—may be a necessary counterforce to the centralized executive led by the very visible president.

Summary

The legislative process is a small group process, and the focal point of power is the committees of Congress. As we have seen, the obstacle course on Capitol Hill is a tortuous one, with failure at any one point—the power of the single negative—meaning defeat for a proposal. Much of Congress's power, in fact, is the power not to act. But, the new budgetary process, the War Powers Act, and congressional resistance to presidential domination of foreign policy provide us with ample evidence that there now is a more balanced relationship between Congress and the president.

Past critics of Congress focused upon rules and procedures that they argued kept the power in the hands of a conservative minority at the expense of the majority and progressive presidents. With the more conservative administrations of Nixon and Ford, and the large Democratic, and predominantly liberal majorities, the critics looked with new favor on Congress. But, Nixon and Ford engaged in a politics of stalemate with the legislators, and the Carter administration found that it was difficult to "lead" a Congress that enjoys its independence and vigor. If policy delays continued, did the fault lie with such old targets of criticism as the seniority system and the distribution of power?

There has been considerable democratization within Congress. The seniority system no longer is an ironclad protection for chairmen, the filibuster rule has been modified, and the distribution of power on committees has been broadened in both houses. But, resistance to far-reaching reforms of committee jurisdiction has continued because efficiency would be at the expense of power, and those who are winners under present arrangements do not want to become losers.

The absence of strong party discipline, the fragmentation of power through the committee system, and the opportunities for delay and defeat that face a bill make it very difficult for Congress to make policy effectively. These factors, when combined with congressional "careerism" and constituency interests, call into question what role Congress is actually suited to play in America today.

Terms to Remember

See the Glossary at the end of the book for definitions.

Administrative oversight

Appropriation

Authorization

Closed rule

Cloture rule

Committee of the Whole

Conference committee

Congressional veto

Distributive policy

Executive agreement

Executive privilege

Filibuster

Fiscal year

Germane

Impoundment

Joint committee

Majority leader

Minority leader

Non-germane amendment

Oversight

Pigeonholing

Pocket veto

Police action

President Pro Tempore

Redistributive policy

Regulatory policy

Seniority

Single negative

Speaker of the House

Special or select committee

Standing committee

Whips

Notes

1. Congressional Quarterly, *Weekly Report*, 36 (February 11, 1978), p. 323.

2. Examples of the literature would include: American Political Science Association, *The Reorganization of Congress* (Washington, D.C.: Public Affairs Press, 1945); James MacGregor Burns, *Congress on Trial* (New York: Harper & Row, 1964); George B. Galloway, *Congress at the Crossroads* (New York: Thomas Y. Crowell Company, 1946); James MacGregor Burns, *The Deadlock of Democracy* (Englewood Cliffs, N.J.: Prentice-Hall, 1963).

3. Joseph S. Clark, *The Senate Establishment* (New York: Hill & Wang, 1967), p. 15.

4. Richard Bolling, *Power in the House* (New York: Dalton, 1965), p. 269.

5. Randall B. Ripley, *Power in the Senate* (New York: St. Martin's Press, 1969), pp. 215–232. Also see Ralph K. Huitt, "The Internal Distribution of Influence: The Senate," in David B. Truman, ed., *The Congress and America's Future* (Englewood Cliffs, N.J.: Prentice-Hall, 1965), pp. 77–101; and

Nelson W. Polsby, *Congress and the Presidency* (Englewood Cliffs, N.J.: Prentice-Hall, 1969), p. 36.

6. Richard F. Fenno, Jr., "The House Appropriations Committee as a Political System," *American Political Science Review*, 56 (June 1962), pp. 310–324. Also Fenno, *Congressmen in Committees* (Boston: Little, Brown, 1973); John F. Manley, "Wilbur D. Mills: A Study in Congressional Influence," *American Political Science Review*, 63 (June 1969), pp. 442–464.

7. *Congress and the American Tradition* (Chicago: Regency Press, 1959).

8. Quoted in Martin Tolchin, "Carter Has Acted As If Patronage Doesn't Count," *New York Times*, May 22, 1977, p. E3.

9. Quoted in "Ford's Fingers Are in the Dike, So Congress Has a Free Hand," by James M. Naughton, *New York Times*, January 19, 1975, p. 1, Sect. 4.

10. See Chapter 1 of Lewis A. Froman, Jr., *The Congressional Process* (Boston: Little, Brown, 1967) for a more extensive discussion of House–Senate differences.

11. Quoted in Arthur Krock, "In the Nation," *New York Times*, April 8, 1958, p. 28. © 1958 by the New York Times Company. Reprinted by permission.

12. Randall B. Ripley, *Power in the Senate*, p. 53.

13. Material on subcommittees is from David J. Vogler, *The Politics of Congress*, 2d ed. (Boston: Allyn and Bacon, 1977), pp. 149–155.

14. Quoted in Bruce F. Freed, "House Reforms Enhance Subcommittees' Power," Congressional Quarterly, *Weekly Report*, 33 (November 8, 1975), p. 2407.

15. Richard F. Fenno, *Congressmen in Committees*, Chapter 1.

16. Congressional Quarterly, *Weekly Report*, 37 (January 13, 1979), pp. 43–55.

17. George Goodwin, Jr., "The Seniority System in Congress," *American Political Science Review*, 53 (1959), pp. 412–436.

18. George Goodwin, Jr., *The Little Legislatures: Committees of Congress* (Amherst: University of Massachusetts Press, 1970), p. 131.

19. *In Congress Assembled* (New York: Macmillan, 1964), Chapter 6.

20. *New York Times*, January 23, 1975, p. 24.

21. Congressional Quarterly, *Weekly Report*, 37 (February 3, 1979), pp. 183–87.

22. Richard F. Fenno, Jr., *The Power of the Purse* (Boston: Little, Brown, 1966), pp. 450, 597.

23. See Louis Fisher, *Presidential Spending Powers* (Princeton: Princeton University Press, 1975).

24. Vogler, *The Politics of Congress*, pp. 188–197 provides an excellent summary of the new process.

25. *Barenblatt* v. *United States*, 360 U.S. 109 (1959).

26. *Watkins* v. *United States*, 354 U.S. 178 (1957).

27. Congressional Quarterly, *Weekly Report*, 38 (December 20, 1980), p. 3595.

28. Committees whose legislation may be privileged are House Administration, Interior and Insular Affairs, Public Works, Veterans Affairs, Ways and Means, and Rules itself.

29. James A. Robinson, *The House Rules Committee* (Indianapolis: Bobbs–Merrill, 1963).

30. David E. Rosenbaum, "The Filibuster Change Falls Far Short of Revolution," *New York Times*, March 9, 1975, Section 4, p. 5.

31. For a list of all cloture votes through 1974, see Congressional Quarterly, *Weekly Report*, 33 (March 1, 1975), pp. 452–453.

32. *Obstacle Course on Capitol Hill* (New York: McGraw-Hill, 1964), p. 15.

33. *Politics and Policy: The Eisenhower, Kennedy, and Johnson Years* (Washington, D.C.: The Brookings Institution, 1968), pp. 396–415.

34. *On Capitol Hill*, 2nd ed. (Hinsdale, Ill.: Dryden Press, 1971), p. 10.

35. The classification scheme is from Theodore Lowi, "American Business, Public Policy, Case Studies and Political Theory," *World Politics* (July 1964), pp. 677–715. Much of the discussion of the various policy areas is from Vogler, *The Politics of Congress*, Chapter 6.

Suggested Readings

Robert Bendiner, *Obstacle Course on Capitol Hill* (New York: McGraw–Hill, 1964).

Roger H. Davidson and John F. Bibby, *On Capitol Hill* (Hinsdale, Ill.: Dryden Press, 1971).

Richard F. Fenno, Jr., *Congressmen in Committees* (Boston: Little, Brown, 1978).

Richard F. Fenno, Jr., *The Power of the Purse* (Boston: Little, Brown, 1966).

George Goodwin, Jr., *The Little Legislatures: Committees of Congress* (Amherst: University of Massachusetts Press, 1970).

Joseph P. Harris, *Congressional Control of Administration* (Garden City, N.Y.: Doubleday, 1964).

T. R. Reid, *Congressional Odyssey* (San Francisco: W. H. Freeman, 1980).

Randall B. Ripley, *Power in the Senate* (New York: St. Martin's Press, 1969).

James A. Robinson, *The House Rules Committee* (Indianapolis: Bobbs–Merrill, 1963).

David J. Vogler, *The Politics of Congress,* 3rd ed. (Boston: Allyn and Bacon, 1980).

CHAPTER 12

The President: Roles and Powers

On July 27, 29, and 30, 1974, the House Judiciary Committee approved three articles of impeachment and a formal resolution recommending that the House of Representatives impeach Richard Nixon for obstruction of justice, abuse of power, and contempt of Congress. Each article outlined the offenses and ended with the following words:

In all of this, Richard M. Nixon has acted in a manner contrary to his trust as president and subversive of constitutional government, to the great prejudice of the cause of law and justice, and to the manifest injury of the people of the United States.

Wherefore, Richard M. Nixon by such conduct, warrants impeachment and trial, and removal from office.[1]

President Nixon avoided impeachment by resigning from the office on August 8, 1974, effective the following day, twenty-one months after his re-election by a record sixty-one percent of the popular vote. He had begun his fifth year (1973) as president in triumph, having ended direct American involvement in Vietnam, secured the release of American prisoners of war, and strengthened ties with the Soviet Union and China. But scandal and embarrassment rocked his administration, and Watergate was his undoing. Watergate confirmed the words of Emmet John Hughes, author of *The Living Presidency,* who wrote:

Beyond all tricks of history and quirks of Presidents, there would appear to be one unchallengeable truth: the dependence of Presidential authority on popular support. . . . And the judgments of all historians of the Presidency concur that the loss of the people's trust is the one mortal disaster from which there can be no real recovery.[2]

The rise and fall of Richard Nixon, surrounded as it was by the emotionalism of

★ ★

Watergate, tended to cloud consideration of perhaps the most important question concerning the structure and function of our national government: What is the proper scope of presidential power? The issue had been raised in the late 1960s as liberals reacted to Lyndon Johnson's foreign policy and began to lose faith in the presidency as the seat of virtue and the source of progressive direction and leadership. With Nixon's coming to office in 1969, the former advocates of more power to the presidency fell silent and most of the literature on the chief executive concentrated on the president's dangerously personalized and "imperial" power in foreign affairs, the isolation of the president from the "real" world, and the fear that the imperial presidency might extend to domestic affairs.[3]

While criticism of the presidency reached its peak during the Nixon years, the Kennedy and Johnson administrations came under fire for their dominance of information, secrecy, and presidential war making. The new dimension added by the Nixon administration was the heavy-handed use of **executive privilege** (the right to withhold information from Congress and the Courts), and fiscal devices such as **impoundment** (the refusal to spend appropriated funds) in an attempt to scuttle social welfare programs, or to prevent, in the name of anti-inflationary measures, expenditures for water pollution control, rural electrification, or highway construction. Nixon was also guilty of making frequent use of national security as a justification for infringement of the Bill of Rights by permitting actions such as the burglary of Daniel Ellsberg's (of Pentagon Papers fame) psychiatrist's office by the White House "plumbers." Probes have revealed that the Kennedy and Johnson administrations were guilty of other excesses under the guise of protecting national security.

The shift in scholarly, journalistic, and public attitudes toward the presidency was dramatic, particularly in view of the "Super-man" image of presidents, largely shaped by Franklin D. Roosevelt (1933–1945), and given credibility by American Government textbooks. At least three generations of students had learned that the presidency is "the great engine of democracy," that the president alone can be the real architect of policy, and that if "the right man is placed in the White House, all will be well, and somehow, whoever is in the White House is the right man."[4]

What is the price that was, and perhaps still is paid for this "Superman" image? The imagined presidency is one of pomp and prestige, with an underestimation of the limitations—constitutional, statutory, and political—on the president's power. The president's unlimited power to propose legislation and to define possible solutions, his exclusive claim to a national constituency, and his unrivaled access to the media, all add to the image of great power. However, when anticipated results do not materialize, there is an appearance of failure that is frequently the result of the president's inability to do what the public expects of him. And, the president's standing is not only his problem, it can be our problem.

If excessive expectations result in a loss of public credibility, is the president the only loser, and are there winners? Certainly a weakened chief executive strengthens the other branches of government in the struggle for power. From the perspective of the citizen, joining the president in the loss column depends upon the issues involved. If we look to him as the political figure that offers the public a chance to "win" on a national scale over regional or special interests, a decline in popularity hurts this effort. But, from a more parochial point of view, if we look to Congress to protect a particular interest we are involved with, certain tax advantages, for example, a weakened president is to our advantage.

Another offshoot of the "Superman" problem is that it can inflate a president's view of his own infallibility and encourage isolation from his critics, a problem discussed in greater detail in the following chapter.

Finally, the indiscretions of one or more presidents may be associated with the presidency or the growth of power, and its misuse by an individual can lead to calls for drastic surgery on the institution. Fortunately for the institution, Gerald R. Ford's major accomplishment of his two-and-a-half years in office was to return the presidency to a position of respect among the American people. And, despite claims that he was an ineffective leader, President Jimmy Carter was able to handily defeat the 1980 primary challenge of Senator Edward M. Kennedy (D., Mass.), partly because of the public perception of his inherent honesty and decency.

This chapter explores the nature of presidential power—its scope and limits, and who wins and loses in the push and pull of power between the president and the other branches. Have the checks and balances of the Constitution provided the anticipated check on executive power? Is the presidency too powerful in some or all areas of policy making? Or is it possible that the presidency is not powerful enough, particularly in the area of domestic affairs? Can the president be a major agent for change? Is abuse of power a natural outgrowth of the expansion of power or is the key element in the equation the president and not the office? Finally, are there flaws in the process of replacing presidents and vice-presidents (Twenty-fifth Amendment) and is the impeachment process an adequate protection against corruption and the abuse of power?

The Constitutional Bases of Presidential Power

The presidency, as created by the Constitutional Convention, represented a compromise between the fear of a too-powerful executive that carried over from the Revo-

lutionary War period and was reflected in most of the state constitutions (Massachusetts and New York being the exceptions), and the framers' recognition that an effective but responsible chief executive was required. The difficulties of the Articles of Confederation period demonstrated the weakness of a government without strong executive guidance. The impetus to create a strong but responsible presidency was encouraged by the attitude of distrust of the masses, generally held by the framers, and reflected in a belief that popularly elected legislatures were too radical. Responsibility would be ensured by the separation of powers and checks and balances designed to prevent the dominance of any one branch of the government.

At the heart of the contemporary controversy over presidential power is the question of whether or not the presidency has ceased to be accountable to the Constitution and been converted into a "plebiscitary" presidency, an office only accountable every four years to the electorate, and not to the other branches of government.[5]

CONSTITUTIONAL POWERS. The powers granted to the chief executive by the Constitution are sometimes specific but more often rather general. The general language permits an expansion of the powers by judicial interpretation as well as an expansion or reduction in power depending upon how each president views the nature of the office. Powers expanded tend never to be reduced.

Article II assigns the following powers to the chief executive:

★ The executive power is vested in the president.

★ He is commander in chief of the armed services and of the militia of the states when called into federal service.

★ He may grant reprieves and pardons for offenses against the United States.

This critic calls for radical surgery on the presidency. But would the public really be the winner if the office was weakened substantially?

The American Presidency has become a greater risk than it's worth. The time has come to seriously consider the substitution of cabinet government or some form of shared executive power. . . . The only way to defuse the presidency and minimize the risk of a knave, a simpleton, or a despot exercising supreme authority, without check or consultation, is to divide the power and spread the responsibility. Constitutional change is not beyond our capacity.

BARBARA W. TUCHMAN

★ He has the power, with the advice and consent of the Senate, to make treaties.

★ He has the power, with the advice and consent of the Senate, to appoint ambassadors, other public ministers, judges of the Supreme Court, and all other officers of the United States.

★ He may, on extraordinary occasions, convene either or both houses of Congress, and if they cannot reach a decision on the time of adjournment, he may adjourn them.

★ He receives ambassadors and other public ministers.

★ He commissions all officers of the United States.

★ He shall take care that the laws be faithfully executed.

Article II also assigns a number of responsibilities to the president:

★ He shall from time to time inform the Congress on the state of the Union.

★ He shall recommend to Congress legislation that he thinks is necessary and expedient.

Obviously, the Constitution establishes only the general outlines of presidential power. It does not catalog all executive powers, nor does it guarantee that the president will see to it that all laws are faithfully executed. For example, political considerations often determine how resolute the chief executive is in enforcing laws such as civil rights legislation and laws regulating business practices. What the Constitution did do was to set "the limits of permissibility" within which various presidents could operate. In fact, *executive power* is a term of uncertain content.

Perceptions of the Presidency

TYPES OF PRESIDENTS. In *Presidential Power*, Richard E. Neustadt wrote that the "X" factor that sets one incumbent apart from the other is his personality and his conception of the roles of the office.[6] Each president has

President Taft's restrictive view of his powers does not fit the contemporary scene. His successors, and particularly the post–1932 presidents, have taken a broad view of their implied powers.

The true view of the Executive function is, as I conceive it, that the President can exercise no power which cannot be fairly and reasonably traced to some specific grant of power or justly implied and included within such express grant as proper and necessary to exercise. Such specific grant must be either in the Federal Constitution or in an act of Congress passed persuant thereof. There is no undefined residium of power which he can exercise because it seems to him to be in the public interest.

WILLIAM HOWARD TAFT

Source: *Our Chief Magistrate and His Powers* (New York: Columbia University Press, 1925), pp. 138–140.

placed his own stamp on his administration; allowing for individual variations, incumbents can be classified as "literalists" (weak), "middle-ground," or "strong" presidents. The literalist chief executives—James Madison (1809–1816), James Buchanan (1857–1860), and William Howard Taft (1909–1912), for example, adhered strictly to the word and letter of the Constitution and assumed that legislative power was popular power and, for that reason, should take precedence.

At the other end of the scale have been the strong presidents who have placed their emphasis upon their political skills and have liberally interpreted their constitutional powers. The key figures in the evolution of the strong presidency have usually served in office during times of crisis, and each added some precedents and practices which their successors built upon. Among the strong presidents, the architects were George Washington (1789–1796), Thomas Jefferson (1801–1808), Andrew Jackson (1829–1836), Abraham Lincoln (1861–1865), Theodore Roosevelt (1901–1908), Woodrow Wilson (1913–1920),

and Franklin D. Roosevelt (1933–1945). Examples of middle-ground presidents are provided later.

ARCHITECTS OF THE MODERN PRESIDENCY

George Washington launched the office on a high note of success and defended the presidency from congressional interference. When the House of Representatives called for the instructions and papers bearing on John Jay's mission, which resulted in the Jay Treaty, a controversial 1795 trade agreement with Great Britain, Washington refused to show the papers on the grounds that secrecy was necessary and that the treaty did not require the House's concurrence. This action set the precedent for the exercise of executive privilege.

IMPLIED POWERS. Thomas Jefferson was the first president to be the real head of his party. Because his party was the dominant one, he

T.R.'s broad view of presidential power set the stage for the modern concept of the strong presidency. Contrast his attitude with Taft's.

[The chief executive is a] steward of the people bound actively and affirmatively to do all he could for the people. . . . [And he acts] for the common wellbeing of all of our people, whenever in whatever manner was necessary, unless prevented by direct constitutional or legislative prohibition.

THEODORE ROOSEVELT

Source: *Roosevelt: An Autobiography* (New York: Charles Scribner's Sons, 1925), p. 357.

was able to employ this role to create a semblance of responsible party government at the national level. His expansion of the nation's territory through the "Louisiana Purchase" gave legitimacy to the idea of **implied powers,** as the authority for the transaction could not be traced to a specific grant of power in the Constitution. An implied power is one that can be claimed as a logical outgrowth of a specific power granted to a part of the government. In the case of Jefferson, his action was based upon his treaty-making power.

The next truly strong incumbent was Andrew Jackson (1829–1836), who set a precedent when he protested the Senate's attempt to interfere with his authority over the action of the Secretary of the Treasury in a matter relating to bank deposits. Jackson told the Senate that "the entire executive power is vested in the president of the United States" and that any power granted to the executive branch or its parts is power granted to the president.[7]

WAR POWERS. Abraham Lincoln's most significant contribution was the development of the war powers of the president as a result of the crisis of the Civil War. With the Congress not in session, he declared the existence of a state of war on April 15, 1861, and took steps necessary to raise an army. His legal position was that the war power was an implied power, an outgrowth of his responsibilities as commander-in-chief, and that he was the one who must assure that laws are faithfully executed. He claimed that the president had the **prerogative** to take whatever action he deemed necessary to preserve and protect the welfare of the nation, including "unconstitutional" actions such as going directly to the Treasury for funds. No other president has publicly talked of operating under the prerogative theory, but modern-day chief executives have adopted Theodore Roosevelt's **stewardship theory** (see insert for definition) of presidential discretion within constitutional constraints as their operational model.

CRISES EQUAL POWER. The World War presidencies of Woodrow Wilson and Franklin D. Roosevelt added a new dimension to the war powers, largely through an immense delegation of authority to the president by the Congress. A series of statutes empowered

Presidential war powers significantly expanded in this century to include a high degree of control over the country's economy as well as raising and equipping the armed forces.

Wilson to license operations dealing with the manufacture, transportation, and distribution of necessities: he was authorized, in other words, to seize companies and control prices. To carry out these duties, President Wilson was permitted to create the administrative agencies needed to carry out his expanded responsibilities. Similarly, Roosevelt, as the World War II leader, was given legislative authority to manage much of the domestic economy. His powers included all of those wielded by Wilson in addition to rationing, broad price fixing, and rent control.

Of course, even before the war, Roosevelt had seen an expansion of presidential power during the Depression years, 1933–40. Most of the present-day independent regulatory agencies that control wide segments of the economy were created during those years.

And, with the Jackson view in mind, the new powers given to the executive branch were new powers placed in the hands of the chief executive. The expansion of powers was not reversed as the economic crisis came to an end, but became a permanent part of the executive role.

MIDDLE-GROUND PRESIDENTS. The middle-ground presidential style, attributed to Grover Cleveland (1885–1889 and 1893–1897) and Dwight D. Eisenhower (1953–1961), suggests that the primary tactics of the president are defensive and reactive. Through the use of the veto, or a reluctance to implement the action of others, primarily Congress, a president can maintain what he believes is a suitable balance. He is mainly a chief administrator, who does not step into the fray until the other institutions of society, public or private, have failed to take the necessary action. For example, Eisenhower allowed a disastrous steel strike in the winter of 1958–59 to drag on for months before he used his authority under the Taft–Hartley Act to order a cooling-off period and a reopening of the mills. In contrast, John Kennedy involved the Department of Labor in the steelworkers-management negotiations in the fall of 1961 in an effort to ensure that there would be no strike when the contract ran out.

We have had no weak presidents since 1932, and even Eisenhower, if his *middle-ground* label is accurate, was a strong president in terms of the tools and powers that were available to him. The ongoing reappraisal of his presidency suggests that his foreign policies put him closer to the strong category in that area. Labelling is a tricky business, and domestic and foreign policy dimensions may be unrelated in terms of a president being classified as weak or strong. And, through historical precedent, court interpretation, congressional delegation of responsibilities and authority, and public expectations, each occupier of the White House must lead. The obligations go with the office. The approach to meeting the obligations varies from president to president.

ANALYZING PRESIDENTIAL BEHAVIOR. In recent years there have been a number of interesting attempts to analyze presidential behavior from a psychological point of view, looking to the childhood and other experiences of the incumbents. James David Barber suggests that presidential performance can be predicted based on whether or not the incumbent is active or passive in the approach to the office and powers and positive or negative in his view of his environment and his own activity. The active presidents are aggressive and tend to use their powers to shape events; passive presidents are motivated more by a sense of duty and are reluctant employers of powers, using them to react to situations. Presidents classified as positive enjoy politics, are optimistic, and appear to be open in their dealings with other political actors. The negative types do not enjoy politics and may consider that they are operating in a hostile environment. By combining these factors, Barber categorizes presidents as active-positive (Truman, Kennedy, and Ford), active-negative (Johnson, Nixon), passive-positive (Taft, Harding), or passive-negative (Eisenhower, Coolidge). For example, he suggested that Nixon's prior experiences would reveal themselves in a pattern of behavior characterized by suspiciousness and decision making in isolation from others, including his own aides. And, Barber predicted that Carter would prove to be an active-positive.[8] However, Carter's record suggests that a passive-negative label may be more appropriate.

The Expansion of Presidential Power: A Reaction to Events

The delegation of power by Congress to the president cannot be explained simply in terms of strong presidents, particularly in light of the incumbency of so-called weak or literalist presidents. In *President and Congress*, Louis Fisher suggests that the delegation of power is best understood in terms of Congress's traditional recognition of certain qualities of the office. The full-time Congress is a twentieth century phenomenon, and in the days of congressional sessions that lasted only a few months, the legislature saw that the continuity of the presidency, and the flexibility of timing that certain actions demanded, made the president the appropriate instrument of power. For example, in 1794 and 1798, Congress gave the chief executive discretion in applying embargo powers and suspending commerce with France. Presidential discretion to transfer appropriated funds from one category to another is a modern extension of the principle. The appropriateness of the president's role as the channel of communication with foreign nations, and his broadened authority during domestic emergencies and in wartime, are also deeply rooted in our history.[9]

The concept of the president as the "national representative" elected by all of the people made popular by Andrew Jackson, has, at times, prompted Congress to delegate power in areas where the legislators viewed congressional dominance as carrying high political risks. For example, external pressures that built up at the end of the nineteenth century crippled Congress's ability to make the budget and the president became the protector of the purse. The official transfer of budget making to the executive came in 1921, and Congress has only recently tried to regain some control over its power of the purse (see Chapter 11). It was politically convenient for legislators to have the president decide on budget priorities, and then be able to impress constituents by their efforts to have cuts restored. In this case, an institutional loss of power was assumed to be a benefit to the members.

DOMESTIC AND INTERNATIONAL CRISES

The Depression years (1929–40) found Congress unable to cope with the economic crisis; the economic legislation it passed was very general in content giving the executive branch the responsibility for providing the details. The president was given the authority to create the executive machinery necessary to handle the expanded functions. The president became the coordinator of economic policy.

World War II saw the United States become the dominant force in the affairs of the Western world and assume the now-questioned role of "world policeman," particularly in terms of containing communism. Because he is a world leader in a nuclear age, the president's role as commander-in-chief has assumed frightening dimensions and the interrelatedness of foreign and domestic policy has led to a spillover of potential power into the domestic political arena.

In response to the need for more centralized approaches to the complex issues of our times, the post–World War II era saw a reluctant Congress placing more responsibility in the presidency and establishing the executive machinery necessary to handle the duties. The creation of the National Security Council in 1947, the Employment Act of 1946 (which requires the president to give a yearly state of the economy report to Congress and to recommend means of stimulating the economy), the Taft–Hartley Act of 1947 (which empowers the president to seek an eighty day back-to-work order to temporarily halt ruinous strikes), and the creation of the Department of Housing and Urban Development in 1965 are all examples of the trend. Many past presidential assumptions of power have become set by statute as a regular requirement of office. Taft–Hartley was passed over Truman's veto, and provides an example of the fact that much presidential power comes from Congress—even if the president doesn't want it.

THE COMPLETED PRESIDENCY. By the time that Harry S. Truman's (1945–1953) first term in office was nearing its end, the outlines of today's presidency had been completed. By and large, each chief executive since then has found the same implements of power at his command. Whether or not the incumbent takes the approach of a clerk watching over these powers or a leader putting them to positive use is based upon his personal conception of the office. And the

The Democratic Speaker was putting a Democratic President on notice that he would be, and should be, facing a powerful Congress.

With the War Powers Act and the new budget process, Congress is proving that it is capable of operating on an equal footing with the executive. Common sense and the Constitution demand that Pennsylvania Avenue remain a two-way street.

THOMAS P. O'NEILL, JR.

Source: Quoted in Congressional Quarterly, *Weekly Report* 35 (February 26, 1977), p. 361.

---

desire to lead is often frustrated by the fragmentation of political power that faces the president as he undertakes the varied roles that have been given to him by the Constitution, statutes, and the practical necessities of our times.

Despite the overall trend toward expanding presidential power, history indicates that there has been a pendulum effect in the relationship between the Congress and the presidency. The Jackson, Lincoln, and Wilson years were followed by periods of congressional assertiveness. And, since the 1970s, Congress has been trying to swing the pendulum its way again. Congress's increased impact on foreign affairs, and its attempts to regain control over the power of the purse (see Chapter 11) are symptoms of an aggressiveness that does not appear to be a temporary phenomenon. Both Nixon and Ford were frustrated by an aggressive legislative branch controlled by the Democratic Party, and Carter achieved few domestic policy victories although his party dominated both houses. The record of all three suggests that the norm is becoming a strong president–strong Congress model (see insert).

Unfortunately for the presidency, the growth of presidential powers and responsibility has become a two-edged sword. As we suggested earlier, powers are no guarantee of power. They provide the occupant of the White House with an opportunity to lead and to claim credit for victories. But, the public's continued overestimation of presidential power—the ability to control decisions—means that he takes the blame for failures that may be beyond his control.

Presidential Roles

In his book, *The Vantage Point,* Lyndon Johnson described some of his thoughts as Richard Nixon took the oath of office:

As I watched the ceremony, I reflected—as I have done so many times in the last several years—on how inadequate any man is for the office of the American presidency. The magnitude of the job dwarfs every man who aspires to it. Every man who occupies the position has to strain to the utmost of his ability to fill it.[10]

CONFLICT IN ROLES. The magnitude of the job is the product of the president performing

The president wears many hats, a phenomenon that confused this foreign observer. Perhaps the numerous roles also confuse the chief executive.

Whenever there has been a national crisis (real or supposed) during my stay in America, I have found myself worried by the interventions and appearances of the president. Who, I always want to know, is speaking? The head of state? The commander-in-chief? The head of a temporary administration? The temporary head of a political party? It is never quite clear, at least, I am never clear. All right: "Hail to the chief." But what chief, I ask, and chief of what?

HENRY FAIRLIE

Source: "Thoughts on the Presidency," in *The Public Interest*, Fall 1967.

many roles that blend, overlap, and at times conflict with each other. He is chief of state, chief executive, party chief, chief legislator, chief diplomat, and commander-in-chief. For example, when President Kennedy appeared to drag his feet on proposing major civil rights legislation, it reflected a conflict between his chief of state (national representative) role and the realities of his problems as the head of a party whose majority in Congress was undercut by the southern wing of the party that opposed civil rights measures. And, a major effort in the area of civil rights could have jeopardized his effectiveness as a legislative leader attempting to push through his overall program.

Although the comments (see insert) of the British scholar, Henry Fairlie, refer to times of crisis, the confusion of roles that he refers to is a chronic condition of the American presidency. In carrying out his roles, the president is assisted by the presidential bureaucracy of the Executive Office of the President (see Chapter 13), which includes the White House Office, often the locale of his closest advisers. The bureaucrats of the many departments and agencies that make up the regular bureaucracy are also a source of assist-

ance, and sometimes resistance (see Chapter 14).

CHIEF OF STATE

The distinctive character of the presidency is a result of a combination in one office of the symbolism associated with ruling monarchs and the political powers of their prime ministers. And most important is the fact that a successful performance of the symbolic role of chief of state has a significant impact upon a president's ability to carry out his other functions.

Constitutionally, the symbolic role of the president is given only brief mention, limited to a reference to "receiving ambassadors and other public ministers." Although Alexander Hamilton believed that this role would be more a matter of dignity than authority, George Washington's conduct of the office started the national habit of looking upon the president as the embodiment of the dignity and authority of the government.[11]

SYMBOLISM. Obviously, the president is a very public person, whose symbolic and polit-

At his first news conference as president, Ronald Reagan steps to the podium.

ical roles constantly overlap. Whether he is receiving foreign dignitaries, addressing Congress, holding periodic press conferences, or using the media to inform the United States (and the world) of his position on domestic or foreign matters, the president personifies the nation and may add or detract from its and his own esteem. The following examples are only the more dramatic ones—only a few items from a very crowded calendar. For example, each week the president receives a stream of callers to the White House who represent the full spectrum of the many special interests of our society; he helps to highlight an endless list of special days and weeks of the year, dedicates public works, and attends charitable, political, and sporting events. All of the examples cited are time-consuming and some

appear to be frivolous, but they have all become a part of the responsibilities and opportunities to create a favorable image.

The very public nature of the presidency is a product of the media revolution, the expanding role of the national government, and the ever-present domestic or foreign crises or mini-crises that have made Washington the center of political activity and the major source of news for the major networks and the nationally oriented newspapers and magazines. At the center of this activity stands the president, whose every political and private act seems to be captured by the reporters and photographers.

The president has unprecedented access to the media, and a popular incumbent has an unrivaled opportunity to exert influence upon the people and attempt to bring the force of public opinion to bear on the other branches of government. On the other hand, the "spotlight" is a two-edged sword, as the experiences of Johnson, Nixon, and Carter demonstrated.

POMP AND CIRCUMSTANCE. For six years the nation was faced with the contradiction of the pomp and circumstance of the Nixon presidency, including the ridiculously outfitted White House Police and the Key Biscayne and San Clemente White Houses, side by side with the president's attempts to relate to the average person through his devotion to sports and the liberal use of sports terminology such as "game plan" etc., in his public announcements. Watergate destroyed Nixon's ability to make use of the chief-of-state role, but prior to his downfall, there was an aura of unreality about the man.

FORD'S CONTRIBUTION. Gerald Ford managed to pick up the pieces and recapture, in his own way, the essence of the chief-of-state role. During his "accidental presidency" he proved to be the steady and decent individual

The President's comment reflected an appreciation of the fact that the powers, privileges, and deference that go with the office can isolate the occupant from the realities faced by the average citizen.

It requires a conscious and sustained effort to bridge the gap between those who make the decisions and the average families who are most directly affected by those decisions.

JIMMY CARTER

Source: Quoted in Congressional Quarterly, *Weekly Report* 35 (February 19, 1977), p. 324.

that was necessary to give the nation the belief that it had a future after the chaos of the previous two years. Although his popularity rating in the Gallup polls—a judgment of performance—was not high, falling to thirty-nine percent in January 1976 and only rising to forty-five percent before the convention, the people's judgment of his character rather than his performance was a major element in his almost miraculous comeback during the campaign. Of course, some of his support was based upon hesitancy about the unknown quantity—Jimmy Carter—but part of it was his ability to cut through some of the royal trappings of the presidency and come across as a hard-working, honest, and down-to-earth individual. In a post-election remark, Carter noted that Ford had "restored confidence in the White House," and in his inaugural address Carter thanked him for "healing the country."

THE CARTER APPROACH. During the 1976 campaign it appeared that everyone—the presidential and congressional candidates—was running against big government, the pomp of office, and the separation between the leaders and the led. Carter's campaign style of informality and openness, including his celebrated or "infamous" interview in *Playboy* maga-

zine,[12] and his devotion to religious and family ideals, were carried over into office and reflected in his personal actions and in his demand to his staff to "de-pomp" the presidency.

Carter's first years stressed symbolism. He began by walking back to the White House after his inauguration and quickly followed this up by ending chauffeured limousine service for White House staffers, suggesting that Cabinet officers also give up this benefit, dressing in a sweater for his TV "fireside" chat, visiting executive departments for informal discussions with the employees, cutting back on the presidential fleet of planes, selling the presidential yacht, imposing a strict code of ethics on his appointees, and demanding a cutback in paperwork and a return to "plain English."

Jimmy Carter's attention to the symbolic aspect of the chief-of-state role, and his attempt to stay close to the people, proved to be good politics, at least in the electoral sense. The politics of symbolism did not lead to policy victories, and by October 1977, more than half the people gave him a poor to fair rating for his performance in office. Of the last five presidents, only Ford had a lower performance rating at a comparable time in office. With the exception of a burst of public approval after the September 1978 Egyptian–Israeli peace treaty, Carter's performance rating remained quite low, only thirty-two percent just prior to the November 1980 takeover of the American Embassy in Iran. The Iranian and Afghanistan crisis gave Carter a great boost in the polls, and approval stayed above the fifty percent mark until the inevitable decline took place in March.

As we discussed in Chapter 9, the foreign policy crises were an important factor in Carter's ability to defeat Ted Kennedy for the Democratic nomination. However, another factor was the President's ability to maintain the people's belief that he was a decent, hard-working man. Personal trust became more important than performance ratings. Symbolism, the Boy Scout image, was more important than able leadership.

REAGAN AND THE OLD VALUES. The value of symbolism did not escape Ronald Reagan as he based his campaign on the "politics of nostalgia." He promised a return to an America of plenty and power that he remembered from his youth, and he stressed the old values of self-reliance and freedom from Big Government. He benefited from an enthusiastic anti-Carter vote and became the most conservative president elected since Herbert Hoover in 1928.

CHIEF EXECUTIVE

The president's executive power and responsibility to "take care that laws be faithfully executed" are implemented through the tremendous bureaucracy which he heads. In theory, the approximately 2.8 million civilian employees of the national government are responsible and responsive to the chief executive. While the growth of the structure has been an unavoidable companion to the expansion of the federal role and the need of the president for staff assistance, this expansion

has in turn created control problems for the chief executive (see Chapters 13 and 14). It can be argued that all important executive functions should be conducted under presidential direction because it is the president who is responsible to the electorate, but there are numerous constitutional, statutory, political, and practical barriers to his being able to control his administration effectively.

PROBLEMS OF CONTROL. The first major task facing a new president-elect is that of creating an administration. This is begun in the interval between election day and the swearing-in ceremonies, and as was the case with Carter and Reagan, it is often not completed until months after taking office. An incoming president inherits a vast bureaucracy of career civil servants who have served under a number of presidential administrations, and who have independent power bases among members of Congress and the constituency their agency serves. In other words, the president often becomes a victim of the fragmentation of the political process—the "bureaucracy becomes a funnel into which political support is channeled from numerous sources, and for this reason it becomes in many instances the most powerful limitation upon the president."[13]

Career bureaucrats view each new incumbent with some skepticism, anticipating with some apprehension the task of adjusting to a new presidential style and to new superiors. This bureaucratic lag imposes a trial period upon the president, during which time the bureaucrats determine how much leeway they will have to interpret executive orders in a manner compatible with their previous methods of operation.[14]

Before leaving office, President Truman reflected on the problems that former army general Eisenhower would have: "He'll sit here and he'll say, 'Do this! Do that!' And nothing will happen. Poor Ike—it won't be a bit like the army. He'll find it very frustrating."[15] Ten years later, in the fall of 1962, President Kennedy was confronted with a serious example of what Truman was talking about. During the Cuban Missile Crisis he discovered that a spring 1962 order to negotiate for the removal of U.S. missiles on the Turkish–Russian border had been left unaccomplished because of Turkish objections.[16]

BUILDING A TEAM. The president has to fill approximately 2,000 key positions that are outside the civil service system, but many of these jobs are filled by individuals who work their way up through the career systems that have been developed within a number of federal agencies. Although the president theoretically makes all appointments, in most instances he is merely ratifying a choice made within a particular agency. The president's major task in building his administration is to find people to appoint (subject to Senate confirmation) to the cabinet and subcabinet positions. The cabinet, ambassadorial, and the occasional Supreme Court appointments receive the most publicity. However, some of the 2,000 upper-level federal positions that the president fills, such as posts in the White House staff, are not subject to the Senate's advice and consent.

The real significance of the Senate's power is the practice of clearing major appointments with the appropriate committee before any public announcement of the designee's name. In this way, the Senate imposes some limit on the president's freedom of choice.

Appointees who are squarely within the executive branch are subject to removal at the president's discretion. In 1926 the Supreme Court held that with respect to agents of his own power appointed by the president, "his removal power is susceptible to no constitutional limitation or by Congress." For example, Carter fired the one holdover Democrat on the Civil Service Commission, despite

his having time left in his term. However, in 1935 the Court refused to uphold President Roosevelt's firing of a commissioner of the Federal Trade Commission, holding that the FTC was an administrative body created by Congress to carry into effect legislative policies embodied in statutes; Congress could therefore prescribe that commissioners be removed only for cause.[17] The "immunity" of the commissioners of the independent regulatory agencies does not protect them from presidential pressure to resign.

Perhaps the greatest legal barrier to the president's structuring of his administration is that he may ordinarily make appointments only to existing offices, as the creation of agencies is a congressional function. Congress usually has given the chief executive limited power to reorganize the executive branch by redistributing functions and overhauling structures. However, reorganization is subject to congressional approval.

The American people tend to associate the whole bureaucracy with the president, and when a high ranking public official speaks, the assumption is that he or she is expressing the chief executive's views. The president must rely upon the cabinet officers and members of the Executive Office of the President (see Chapter 13) in the effort to win the struggle to exercise control over the vast governmental apparatus. And when these advisers appear to be going off in contradictory policy directions, as was the case during the first year-and-a-half of the Carter administration, the president appears to be disorganized and his standing with the public and other politicians suffers.

The preceding array of limits should not obscure the fact that an efficient administration is an invaluable asset to the chief executive. The ultimate success of presidentially sponsored legislation that is enacted by Congress depends on proper implementation by executive agencies. Although the president must compete with Congress and groups of constituents for the loyalty of his own administrators, he can occasionally use his influence with a particular agency as a bargaining weapon in his negotiations with other political participants. For example, his intrusion into the matter of defense contracts can carry considerable weight with a member of Congress who the president is trying to persuade to back a particular bill. And, as the chapter on Congress pointed out, executive-branch lobbying plays a significant role in the legislative process.

ABUSE OF THE CHIEF EXECUTIVE'S POWER

EXECUTIVE PRIVILEGE. The Nixon years, culminating in the Watergate scandal, focussed attention on the abuse of executive powers. One area of conflict involved the scope of a president's inherent right to withhold from Congress or the courts requested information by invoking executive privilege. Historically, executive privilege has been used most often by members of the administration, under presidential orders, to deny information to Congress on the grounds of national security or the need for the privacy of communications to run an efficient operation. The extension of the concept by Nixon to cover conversations between his staff and third parties was considered in Congress to be unwarranted.

As the Watergate investigation progressed, President Nixon used "executive privilege" as grounds for refusing to allow his staff to testify, and then backed off. However, when the existence of the Watergate tapes was revealed during the hearings, the Senate Watergate Committee and special Watergate prosecutor Archibald Cox went into federal court to force the release of the tapes. Cox's persistence resulted in his being fired, but Leon Jaworski, his replacement, pursued the matter. The President then agreed to release some subpoenaed tapes, but two were missing; others, it was argued, were edited; and one had an eighteen-minute gap. Jaworski

continued to press for additional material, and in July 1974 Federal Judge John J. Sirica directed Nixon to turn over to him sixty-four tapes for use in the Watergate cover-up trial. Nixon refused and the case reached the Supreme Court. In July 1974, the Court ruled that to the extent that confidentiality related to the president's ability to discharge his powers effectively, executive privilege had a constitutional basis. However, the Court upheld the order to turn over the tapes saying that:

We conclude that when the grounds for asserting privilege as to subpoenaed materials sought for use in a criminal trial is based only on the generalized interests in confidentiality, it cannot prevail over the fundamental demands of due process of law and the fair administration of criminal justice.[18]

In most respects, the Court's decision strengthened the presidential weapon of executive privilege by giving judicial recognition to its constitutional base.

MISUSE OF AGENCIES. A more generalized abuse or misuse of the powers associated with the chief executive role was President Nixon's use or attempted use of executive agencies to engage in or plan unethical and illegal activities in violation of individual rights and government decencies. The abuses included the use of the FBI to conduct lawless wiretaps; interfering with the FBI, the Justice Department, and the Central Intelligence Agency in their lawful operations; authorizing and allowing the creation and work of the White House "plumbers" unit that made an illegal entry into the office of Daniel Ellsburg's psychiatrist to steal documents related to the Pentagon Papers Case; and attempting to use the Internal Revenue Service to harass certain citizens—particularly those on his "enemies list"—through discriminatory tax investigations. Finally, the illegal actions of his White House staff were done with his full knowledge.

Post–Watergate revelations indicate

that the misuse of government agencies was not a Nixon phenomenon. It is alleged that Lyndon Johnson used the FBI to make illicit wiretaps during the 1964 presidential campaign, including bugs on the phone lines of Dr. Martin Luther King and Robert Kennedy. Johnson, according to some reports, used the agency to gather intelligence on political friends and foes in and out of Congress.[19] The various congressional committees that began to look into the activities of the "intelligence community" in 1975 found that the abuse of power extended into the administrations of other presidents.

The statements of many Watergate figures made it clear that the chief executive sets the moral tone for his administration, and that serious problems arise when loyalty to the man replaces loyalty to the rule of law. In 1928, Supreme Court Justice Louis D. Brandeis wrote:

In a government of laws, existence of the government will be imperiled if it fails to observe the law scrupulously . . . If the government becomes a law-breaker, it breeds contempt for law. . . .[20]

PARTY CHIEF

Unlike the heads of some other governments, the president usually does not enjoy the advantage of leading a strong party organization that can be counted upon to enact his legislative program. As titular head of a decentralized party over whose members he has no institutionalized means of forcing compliance to his views, he is in reality often only the leader of one wing of his party. He must therefore constantly cultivate the support of members of the opposition party, particularly when the issues divide both parties along rural-urban or liberal-conservative lines. The last two Republican presidents before Reagan—Nixon (1969–1974) and Ford (1974–1977)—worked under the additional burden of divided government, with the op-

position party controlling Congress. President Eisenhower (1953–1960) had a Republican Congress only during his first two years in office. And President Carter found that having majorities in both houses of Congress did not often give him a significant advantage in his struggle to win legislative victories. Louis Koenig summarizes the situation by saying, "The major American party does well as a vehicle of power and badly as a vehicle of policy."[21]

Ronald Reagan may fare better than most of his predecessors with his party in control of the Senate and with the Republicans and conservative Democrats in the House providing a potential policy majority on many issues. This optimism reflects the assumption that the Republican Party is less diverse and more united than are the Democrats.

PARTY AND VOTING. Although our chief executive cannot use his party as effectively as can the British Prime Minister to stabilize his impact upon policy making and translate platform planks into policy, it is worth repeating that party is still the single most important predictor of roll-call vote patterns. However, the substantial deviations from party positions that do occur are best explained in terms of differences among constituencies. The most significant breakdowns in party discipline occur on major domestic issues, and they are among the most visible and important confrontations, involving as they often do key parts of the president's legislative program.

ROLE CONFLICT. The chief executive's position as party leader is complicated further by the conflict that often exists between his partisan role and his role as leader of the entire nation, particularly when the conflict between the two roles results from the diversity of ideological, sectional, and economic interests that are found within each of the two major parties. President Johnson's War on Poverty and his strong civil-rights position could not

A president cannot really be above politics. Eisenhower's and Nixon's attempts at non-partisanship reflected their status as minority-party presidents.

No President, it seems to me, can escape politics. He has not only been chosen by the Nation—he has been chosen by his party.

JOHN F. KENNEDY

In the general derogatory sense . . . I do not like politics . . . . the word "politics" as you use it, I think the answer to that one, would be, no. I have no great liking for that.

DWIGHT D. EISENHOWER

I ask everyone . . . to join our majority, not on the basis of the party label you wear in your lapel. . . .

RICHARD M. NIXON

Sources: *Congressional Record,* January 18, 1960, pp. 1, 2; In Neustadt, *Presidential Power: The Politics of Leadership* (New York: Wiley, 1976), p. 166; Renomination speech, August 23, 1972.

help but alienate the powerful southern wing of his party. President Nixon's use of the impoundment and veto powers to thwart certain social programs created opposition among urban–liberal congressmen of both parties. It is virtually impossible for an active president to formulate a legislative program tailored to please the diverse elements within his own party; Carter was criticized first for not moving aggressively enough on unemployment and social welfare programs, and then, from liberal Democrats, for his anti-inflation budget that cut funds to these areas. And, Reagan's deep budget cuts caused discomfort even among some moderate and conservative Republicans. If a president becomes overly partisan, he loses the support of members of the opposition party that he often needs.

Regardless of the limits of the role, most presidents attempt to fill it. They choose the National Chairperson, the National Committee reports to them, and an eligible incumbent can expect to be renominated by his party. Presidents stay in close contact with the floor leaders of their party in Congress, and, the undisciplined nature of our parties notwithstanding, the occupant of the White House usually has the support of most of his partisans on the majority of legislative issues on which he takes a position.

One aspect of President Eisenhower's appeal in the eyes of the public was his desire and seeming ability to put himself above politics, but the experiences of President Nixon have given rise to the question of whether or not being "above" politics is good for the president or the nation. A serious question in terms of the presidency and the parties themselves is that an "above-politics" stance by the president and the reliance upon party leaders in Congress to provide partisan leadership has made the president less accountable for his actions. And, Thomas Cronin suggests that presidents have been isolated from a broad scope of opinions and from reality by their too-heavy reliance on their own staff and

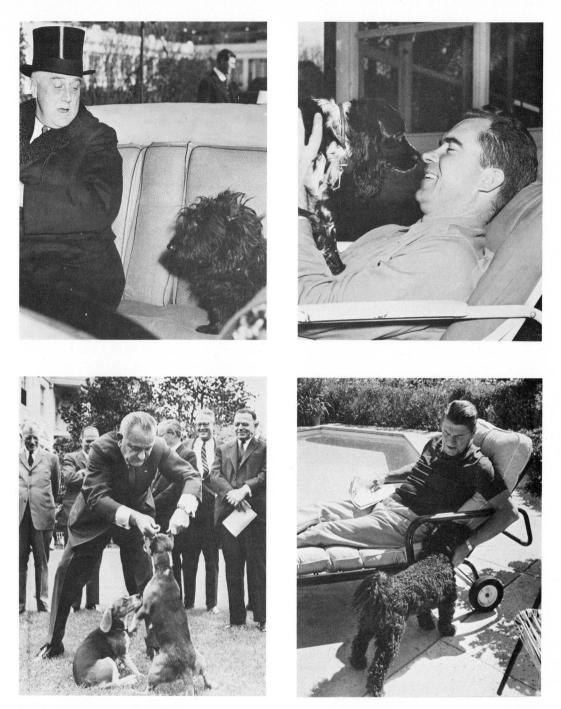

Presidential pets help the public see the human side of the office-holder: Franklin Roosevelt with Fala (top left); Checkers with Vice-President Nixon (top right); Lyndon Johnson's famous beagles getting their ears pulled (bottom left); Ronald Reagan with Muffin, one of his three dogs.

neglect of the communication channels provided by more close contact with their party and its leadership.[22]

LEGISLATIVE LEADER

Although most books about the presidency contain a chapter devoted to the role of chief legislator, the title itself is somewhat misleading; for even though the authorship of much legislation must be credited to the executive branch, actually, the president proposes and Congress disposes. The lawmaking function—the heart of the legislative role—is a congressional function. It is more accurate to think of the president as chief initiator rather than chief legislator, particularly in view of the weakness of his position as party leader, and the nature of the parties in Congress.

PRESIDENT'S AGENDA. Presidential success measured in terms of bills proposed and bills passed is not impressive. The "Presidential Boxscore" has gone above the fifty-percent-approved mark only five times since 1954 (see Table 10–1). But, the power that resides in the role of legislative leader comes from the fact that presidents have become the agenda setters for Congress. His program, usually outlined in a series of messages, establishes his priorities, tells the legislature what its largest customer wants, indicates the proposals behind which the prestige of the presidential office will be placed, and indicates what the president might veto. Although the boxscore may indicate a mediocre "win–loss" record, the president's priorities usually determine what policies have a chance of winning.

Given the diffusion of power in Congress and the division of that body by party, intra-party, regional, and philosophical differences, the executive branch is in a superior position to articulate or orchestrate a program for the legislature's reaction. What fails to appear on the presidential agenda has less chance of passage because of the president's influence with many members of his own party and some members of the opposition. Nixon was able to employ the "conservative coalition" of Republicans and southern Democrats to support his position on many bills; and Reagan relied on conservative Democrats in the House to help pass his programs. While presidential support is no guarantee of passage, presidential opposition is ordinarily a guarantee that the obstacle course will be difficult.

PRESIDENTIAL LOBBYING. When the president "lobbies" for or against a bill he can call into play a range of weapons that run the gamut from an appeal to personal loyalty to the carrot of defense contracts. He may speak privately with many members of Congress, usually in his office or over a meal. He can argue the merits of his position, appeal to party loyalty, and perhaps use promises of campaign support to convert people to his side. In addition, he can activate the lobbying resources of the agencies to bring pressure to bear on opponents or the undecided.

Unlike his predecessor, Ronald Reagan is an excellent lobbyist and he relishes the role and his interaction with members of Congress. A constant stream of lawmakers were invited to the White House during the administration's first 100 days to discuss economic policy. Reagan clearly was the lead player in the successful effort to get his budget passed, and when he was shot on March 30, 1981, one of the fears of the GOP was that his incapacitation would cost them their best communicator and salesman. However, his quick recovery allowed him to give a nationally televised economic address to a joint session of Congress on April 28; and during the week before the House budget vote he saw sixty Democrats during oval office visits arranged by his excellent congressional liaison office (see Chapter 13).

CARTER AND CONGRESS. The effective use of the tools of presidential power depend upon the skills of each incumbent. Neither the 1968 nor the 1972 elections gave Nixon a Republican Congress, and this restricted his, and then Ford's, ability to influence the passage of their policies. Both were most successful in the negative sense, when using the veto to prevent laws they opposed.

Jimmy Carter had to deal with a resurgent Congress, but one of his own party. The results of the 1976 election suggested that there would be opportunities for many legislative victories for the president; but a combination of his approach to the office, and conflict with members of his own party over his anti-inflation policies and budget priorities led to a mediocre record of domestic legislative victories from 1977 through 1980. In part, his problems were caused by an initial attempt to ignore some traditional rules of the political game, such as using patronage to gain loyalty, and consulting with legislators on public-works projects—mistakes not repeated by Reagan. Carter also was handicapped by his attempt to cut back on programs long supported by liberal Democrats and used by them as the cornerstones of their election victories. He and his staff misread the difficulties of translating personal popularity into legislative victory. Their over-confidence was reflected in underestimation of the power of organized interests such as the gas and oil lobbies, the independence of the Democratic Congress, and the overestimation of the power of unorganized support.

VETO POWER. If the president finds a bill passed by Congress to be unacceptable he

★ ★ ★ *Table 12–1* ★
Presidential vetoes: 1914–1980

PRESIDENT	REGULAR VETOES	REGULAR VETOES OVERRIDDEN	POCKET VETOES	TOTAL
Wilson	33	6	11	44
Harding	5	0	1	6
Coolidge	20	4	30	50
Hoover	21	3	16	37
Roosevelt	372	9	261	633
Truman	180	12	70	250
Eisenhower	73	2	108	181
Kennedy	12	0	9	21
Johnson	16	0	14	30
Nixon	24	5	19	43
Ford	50	12	16	66
Carter	13	2	18	31

Source: R. D. Hupman (compiler), Office of the Secretary of the Senate, *Presidential Vetoes*, 1789–1961 (Washington, D.C.: U.S. Government Printing Office, 1961), p. iv. Data for Presidents Kennedy and Johnson are from the Congressional Almanacs, 1962–1968. Data for Nixon, Ford, and Carter are from Congressional Quarterly, *Weekly Reports and Almanacs*.

may veto it and return it to the Congress, where a two-thirds majority in each House is required to override the veto. If he wishes to indicate reluctant acceptance of a bill, he can leave it unsigned—knowing, of course, that it will automatically become law in ten days (excluding Sundays), unless Congress happens to adjourn before the ten days have elapsed, in which case the president's failure to sign the measure kills it. This is known as a **pocket veto.**

The use of the veto varies widely from president to president, as Table 12–1 indicates. Overrides are infrequent because a controversial piece of legislation rarely achieves much more than a majority vote when originally passed and sent to the president. President Nixon's success rate in having his vetoes sustained did not decline until the last few months of his administration, when the extent of his Watergate involvement was becoming clear and the move for impeachment had achieved some momentum. His successor, President Ford, inherited the office during a pre-election period of anti-executive feeling, and then he was faced by huge Democratic majorities in both houses. However, Ford made frequent use of the veto and Congress failed in most of its override attempts. In fact, Ford's administration was referred to as "Government by Veto." A president who is at all effective as a party leader can usually get the votes of one-third of at least one house from his party alone. The infrequency of overrides makes the veto a very powerful weapon in the struggle for power between the executive and the legislature.

While President Carter hoped to avoid the use of the veto, Table 12–1 shows that having the Congress and the White House in the hands of the same party does not eliminate the use of this weapon. In fact, Carter vetoed more public bills during his first two years than did Kennedy in three years and Johnson in five. Legislators respond to a different set of constituency pressures from the Chief Execu-

tive, but the experiences of Kennedy, Johnson, and Carter suggest that compromise is more likely than when the government is not divided as it was from 1969 through 1976.

In some instances, a presidential veto contains a message, implicit or explicit, that a few changes in a bill will make it acceptable. More often than not, modifications are made and the president signs the new version. In this situation the veto becomes an instrument to force compromise. For example, members of Congress were faced with a choice of win some benefits for their constituencies or lose all benefits when Carter vetoed a public works bill because of water projects he opposed, and a defense bill because he thought expenditures on a nuclear aircraft carrier were not needed. They chose to "compromise" by repassing the bills with the offending items eliminated.

IMPOUNDMENT. Another weapon used by chief executives since the 1920s is impoundment of funds. There is no constitutional requirement that the president must spend what Congress appropriates. Historically, most impoundments have really been deferrals, with the funds released at a later time. This was the case during much of the 1960s, when impoundment was used as a weapon to fight inflation. Impoundments were also used to cut programs back to presidentially approved spending levels. But under Nixon, impoundment was often permanent and employed as a form of veto over programs that he opposed, particularly in the area of social welfare.

Although President Nixon was sure of his authority to impound (see insert), a series of lower federal court decisions looked at the intent of Congress when they appropriated funds and ordered the release of certain monies. Congress passed the Congressional Budget and Impoundment Control Act of 1974 (see Chapter 11) making presidential withholding of funds subject to congressional approval. Then, early in 1975 an impound-

Viewpoint:
Richard Nixon on impoundment

Impoundment was a convenient form of veto not subject to override. But, Nixon's views on impoundment were successfully challenged by Congress and in the courts.

The constitutional right for the President of the United States to impound funds . . . is absolutely clear. . . . I will not spend money if the Congress overspends, and I will not be for programs that will raise taxes and put a bigger burden on the already overburdened American taxpayer.

RICHARD M. NIXON

Source: January 31, 1973, news conference.

---

ment case reached the Supreme Court. It ruled that $9 billion in water pollution funds had been improperly withheld by Nixon because the legislation authorizing the program had not given him that authority. The bill had clearly intended that the money be spent. The case did not deal with the question of whether a president has an implied power to impound funds.[23]

The unrestricted power to impound funds had put the president in a position to make losers of legislators and interest groups who thought they had won, to one extent or another, the struggle for resources. In the case of the water pollution funds, members of Congress had taken credit for securing the money, communities made plans to spend it, and contractors and workers counted on the profits and wages. The impoundment took place prior to the 1974 law's going into effect; however, for the people concerned, the Court provided a happy ending.

CHIEF DIPLOMAT

No field of activity has added so much power to the modern presidency as has the area of foreign relations, which encompasses the roles of chief diplomat and commander-in-chief. The two roles are intertwined, as the threat of force is an element in diplomatic negotiations; however, for purposes of our discussion, they are treated separately.

The Constitution authorizes the president to appoint ambassadors, receive foreign ambassadors, and make treaties with the advice and consent of two-thirds of the Senate. There is no specific conferral of the power to make foreign policy, but it is implied, and over time, certain forces have operated to make the president, in the words of the Supreme Court, the sole official organ of United States foreign policy.[24]

Presidential power has grown in response to modern technological advances that have made the globe smaller and dictated speedy responses in an era of airpower and push-button warfare. Intelligence gathering and analyzing functions have become increasingly important and led to the creation of a national security complex. With the preponderance of expertise residing in the executive branch and with much of the information necessary for decision making being classified, Congress has reluctantly recognized the need for centralizing decision-making responsibility. The president has become the chief risk-taker, with the responsibility for making decisions that may result in irreversible mistakes.

Beginning with the presidency of John F. Kennedy in 1960, the occupants of the oval office have acted as their own secretaries of state or shared this function with their special assistants for national security affairs—Walt Rostow under Johnson and Henry A. Kissinger in Nixon's and part of Ford's administration. The official heads of the State Department became "mechanics" in a sense, and the potential for conflict surfaced during the Nixon years and led to Kissinger's occupying the special assistant and secretary of state roles between 1973 and 1976. In Carter's administration, Secretary of State Cyrus Vance struggled with National Security Adviser Zbigniew Brzezinski for the role of number one foreign policy adviser. Vance submitted his resignation when the decision was made to carry out the ill-fated, April 1980 raid to free the hostages from the American Embassy in Tehran. After the raid, he announced his departure and was replaced by Senator Edmund Muskie, a Democrat from Maine.

Reagan's appointment of Alexander M. Haig, Jr., whose prior assignments included being Kissinger's assistant, White House chief of staff in the final days of Nixon's administration, and NATO commander, suggested a return to prominence of the secretary-of-state post. It appeared that the new administration did not intend to have a repetition of the secretary–national security adviser conflict of previous years. Unfortunately, it took less than two months for a conflict to surface between Haig and the President's closest advisers who objected to his prima donna attitude, public saber-rattling, and attempts to enlarge his areas of responsibility.

The problem received wide attention when Haig publicly voiced his unhappiness over Reagan's designation of Vice-President George Bush as the head of the administration's "crisis-management" team. Haig then received additional unwanted publicity when he "misinterpreted" the Constitution while briefing reporters at the White House on the day of the Reagan assassination attempt. In response to a question about who was making decisions in the White House, Haig suggested that the order of succession was the vice-president and the secretary of state, rather than the correct order which places the speaker of the House and the president *pro tempore* of the Senate ahead of the secretary of state. Haig said he was in charge because Bush was in Texas. He added to the impression that he was power hungry by ignoring the fact that Secretary of Defense Casper Weinberger was in charge of emergency military commands in the absence of Reagan and Bush.

In spite of public presidential reassurances, Haig's difficulties raised serious doubts about his longevity as part of the Reagan team.

PRESIDENTIAL DOMINANCE. From 1945 until the mid–1960s, Congress contributed to presidential dominance by its commitment to **bipartisan foreign policy.** Translated into political terms, this meant that foreign policy, particularly as it related to our response to real or imagined threats from communist powers, was immune from the partisan and public criticism and debate that other political decisions are subjected to. For example, our Southeast Asian policy, born in the early 1950s, did not include the type of public debate that Congress could have conducted. Instead, decision making was done quietly and the legislators usually adopted the approach of showing the rest of the world a picture of bipartisan support of the chief diplomat.

Arguments that dissent is unpatriotic and damaging to our position lost their credibility during the Vietnam War. The investigations and hearings on our involvement in Vietnam, the widespread congressional criticism of the Vietnam policy, and more recent examples such as the War Powers Bill of 1973, investigations of the intelligence agencies, the Panama Canal treaty debates, and probes into the Tehran rescue mission are clear indicators of a reassertion of the congressional role in foreign policy and a new trend in congressional–executive relations.

Ironically, it was former Senator J. William Fulbright (D., Ark.), who from 1966 through 1974 was a leading critic of the "imperial" presidency in foreign affairs, who said in the late 1950s that "for the existing requirements of American foreign policy we have hobbled the President by too niggardly a grant of power."[25] But, the contemporary cry of "less power to the president" has not removed the chief executive from his place as the major force in the foreign policy arena. During the Nixon administration, the President and his chief foreign policy adviser, Henry Kissinger, were credited with the softening of relations between the U.S. and the Soviet Union and the opening of diplomatic relations with China. President Nixon's dramatic 1972 trip to the People's Republic of China was a classic example of personal diplomacy and added to Nixon's popularity and margin of victory in the 1972 campaign.

Carter took the lead in setting the tone and direction of foreign policy, and directed the delicate Middle East negotiations, highlighted by the 1978 Camp David meeting between President Anwar Sadat of Egypt and Menachem Begin, Prime Minister of Israel. American responses to the Iranian crisis and the Soviet invasion of Afghanistan were orchestrated by the chief executive. And the American response to the El Salvador situation was a Reagan team decision.

The president has the sole power to recognize foreign governments. The most famous refusal to use this power was our nation's failure to recognize the Soviet Union until 1933, sixteen years after the Russian

Revolution. International complication kept us from full recognition of China, whose government had been in power since 1949. But, on December 15, 1978, Carter announced the formal recognition of The People's Republic of China, effective January 1, 1979.

TREATY MAKING: PRESIDENTIAL–CONGRESSIONAL CONFLICT

Presidential–congressional conflict over foreign policy has become more visible in recent years with the passage of the War Powers bill, close congressional consideration of the use of American personnel for peace-keeping purposes, and legislative resistance to certain administration-backed foreign aid and trade programs (see Chapter 11). Members of Congress also have been vocal in their opposition to presidential decisions on the development or deployment of such weapons systems as the B–1 bomber and the neutron bomb.

EXECUTIVE AGREEMENTS. Aside from the previously discussed question of war making, the Congress in general, and the Senate in particular, have been frustrated by the undermining of the Senate's treaty-ratification role by the extensive use of **executive agreements.** These are made solely under the authority of the president and have the full force of law.

Senatorial frustration with the bypassing of its role in treaty making reached a high point in 1953, when John W. Bricker (R., Ohio) introduced a constitutional amendment which would have stated that treaties and executive agreements could not become law unless approved by Congress. Such a restriction would have severely limited the president's flexibility in dealing with other nations. When it was brought to the floor in 1954, it

At the White House to sign a peace treaty in which President Jimmy Carter's
diplomacy was instrumental are Egypt's President Anwar Sadat (left) and
Israel's Prime Minister Menachem Begin (right).

came within one vote of the necessary two-thirds majority.

Bricker's attack did not halt the widespread use of executive agreements, which can run into the hundreds each year. Among some of the more controversial subjects handled by executive agreements have been the 1972 U.S.–Soviet agreement to limit offensive land- and submarine-based intercontinental missiles, and the 1974 agreement to provide Egypt and Israel with nuclear technology for "peaceful" purposes.

Executive agreements have allowed presidents to avoid potential losses on the floor of the Senate or extended debates that could alienate supporters they might need for other legislative struggles.

Many of the major foreign policy arrangements, such as regional defense organi-zations like NATO and SEATO, and arms limitation agreements, involve treaties that require Senate ratification. Unfortunately, from a senatorial viewpoint, the most signifi-cant treaties are negotiated amid much public fanfare and reach the Senate after the other parties have signed the documents. This creates an after-the-fact situation in which it would be very embarrassing for the country if ratification were not forthcoming.

PANAMA AND SALT II. Occasionally, the Senate refuses to assume that its function is merely to approve what has been done al-ready. In September 1977, President Carter and the Panamanian ruler, Brig. General Omar Torrijos Herrera, signed two controver-sial treaties that would give Panama control over the Canal by the year 2000 while giving the United States the right to maintain the waterway's neutrality indefinitely. President Carter urged support of the pact as an example of fairness in dealing with other nations and as a vehicle for setting the tone for inter-American relations in the future. But many Republican and some Democratic senators, as well as conservative groups, voiced very strong opposition to the treaties claiming they amounted to a "giveaway" of American property, warning of the danger of communist takeover in Panama and the resultant threat to American security, and criticizing the vagueness of the documents' wording about our right to act against any aggression or threat directed at the Canal.

With presidential and national prestige on the line, the Democratic leadership in the Senate was forced to inform the president that there were not enough votes to secure ratification in 1977.

The struggle resumed in 1978, emotions ran high, and there was intensive lobbying by a well-financed coalition of conservative organizations After thirty-eight days of repetitive debate, the Senate approved both treaties by a vote of 68 to 32, one more than the 67 needed for ratification. Carter had staked his administration's ability to conduct foreign policy on their ratification, and the outcome was considered a major victory for him.[26]

Carter suffered a setback in 1980, when he was forced to recommend that the Senate defer action on SALT II Treaty (Strategic Arms Limitation Talks). SALT I had limited only the number of long-range nuclear missiles that the United States and the U.S.S.R. would keep in their arsenal. It expired in 1977, but both parties agreed to keep within the limits while a broader SALT II was negotiated. The Nixon, Ford, and Carter administrations worked on SALT II, and agreement was reached in 1979. However, critics claimed that the provisions of the treaty would not provide for American nuclear equality, and that the provisions guaranteeing compliance were inadequate.

The invasion of Afghanistan was a major blow to SALT II backers; however, it provided Carter with an excuse for postponing debate. In fact, before the invasion the treaty had little chance of coming close to the required two-thirds approval in the Senate.

FOREIGN POLICY VERSUS DOMESTIC PROBLEMS

In *The State of the Presidency,* Thomas E. Cronin notes that presidents spend from one-half to two-thirds of their time on foreign policy and national security matters.[27] Without denying the importance of these areas or the tie between international affairs and domestic economic problems, a significant factor contributing to this preoccupation is that the president has more freedom of action and less frustrations in shaping foreign policy. He does not have to deal with a multitude of competing domestic interest groups and an often-reluctant bureaucracy (see Chapter 14), nor is the division of power with Congress as equal as it is in the domestic area. Presidential trips abroad; summit conferences; statements of high ideals such as President Carter's 1977 letter to the Soviet dissident Andrei Sakharov and his criticism of former Ugandan President Idi Amin, or the appearance of strength in the face of foreign crisis, Iran and Afghanistan; all these are rewarded, at least temporarily, in the popularity polls, even when the action fails (though Carter's actions caused disquiet among foreign policy experts). Carter found, as have presidents before him, that domestic struggles in Congress were not unduly influenced by foreign policy successes. However, the president does not usually lose in this situation as popularity among the public can be an important ingredient in the next presidential election. Ideally, an incumbent chief executive would like a

A traditional use of trips abroad is to strengthen support at home. For instance, President Nixon's stature was enhanced by his impressive trip to China in 1972.

major foreign policy triumph in the election year.

Unfortunately for Carter, a foreign policy failure contributed to his defeat in 1980. As we suggested in Chapter 9, the seizure of 53 Americans by Iranian militants on November 4, 1979, substantially contributed to the President's success in defeating Senator Kennedy's attempt to deny him renomination. However, the political benefits of the situation lasted only for a few months, and as the crisis dragged on for 444 days, the nation's frustrations about the failure to secure freedom for the hostages were focussed on the President and contributed to his defeat.

Actually, President Carter's halt of oil exports from Iran, the withholding of military supplies already bought and paid for by the Iranians, and the freezing of all Iranian assets in the United States, represented the only direct actions our government could take short

of some military action. This last resort seemed unsuitable in terms of the risks it would place the hostages in. However, after five-and-one-half months of attempting to deal with what often appeared to be a headless government, Carter ordered the aborted rescue mission.

In many respects, the Carter administration was held hostage by the crisis. A settlement was not reached until the last hours of Carter's presidency, and the hostages were released a few minutes after Reagan was sworn in as our fortieth president. In return for the hostages, Iranian assets of 8 to 9 billion dollars were unfrozen. However, only about $2.8 billion was available to Iran, while the remainder was held in accounts in Algerian banks to pay off loans made by American banks to Iranian borrowers and to settle claims against Iran.

Presidential influence on the shaping or implementation of domestic programs usually is relatively weak. Frustration over his domestic program led Johnson to exclaim: "Power? The only power I've got is nuclear . . . and I can't use it." Kennedy, commenting about the architectural remodeling of Lafayette Square across from the White House, told an aide: "Let's stay with it. Hell, this may be the only thing I'll ever really get done."[28]

Although Carter's situation was better than that of Nixon and Ford, who faced opposition Congresses, Carter had to deal with a legislative branch in which reform (see Chapter 11) had created a wide dispersion of power. There were no strong leaders of the stature of Lyndon Johnson (Senate Majority Leader, 1953–1961) or Sam Rayburn (Speaker of the House, 1940–1947, 49–53,

The adviser recognizes that the opportunities for the president to win are greater in the foreign policy area because he controls that situation to a much greater extent than domestic issues.

In foreign policy, you get drama, triumph, resolution—crisis and resolution—so that in foreign policy Nixon can give the sense of leadership. But in domestic policy, there you have to deal with the whole jungle of human problems.

LEONARD GARMENT

Source: Quoted by Theodore H. White, *The Making of the President 1972* (New York: Atheneum, 1973), p. 52.

55–61) to pull the Democrats together. Even though Speaker of the House O'Neill proved to be an effective leader, the situation in the Senate made it difficult for the President and his majority party in Congress to walk to the beat of the same drummer.

Unlike recent chief executives, Reagan devoted most of his attention during his first year in office to domestic politics. His campaign promises were founded on the economy, and the almost counter-revolutionary, anti-New Deal nature of his proposals demanded his active participation in the struggle to enact them into law.

COMMANDER-IN-CHIEF

Civilian control of the military is firmly stated in the Constitution and divided between the Congress and the president. While the president is commander-in-chief, the whole Congress is given the power to declare war and control the funding of the armed forces through taxing and appropriations, and the Senate approves appointments and promotions of officers—usually a mere formality. Also, Congress can make rules for the regulation of the armed forces, a power that pro-

vided the basis for restricting operations in Indochina; and it has the powers contained in the War Powers Act.

Alexander Hamilton considered the division of powers as a protection against presidential abuse and said about the commander-in-chief role:

It would amount to nothing more than the supreme command and direction of the military and naval forces . . . , while that of the British King extends to the declaring of war and to the raising and regulating of fleets and armies—all which, by the Constitution under consideration, would appertain to the legislature.[29]

PRESIDENTIAL WAR MAKING. History has proven Hamilton to be right about "supreme command and direction" but wrong about the ability of the chief executive to institute military hostilities. George Washington actually led American troops for a brief period during the Whiskey Rebellion of 1794, but none of his successors have followed suit. While most strategy decisions are left in the hands of the generals and admirals, Lincoln took an active planning role during the Civil War, as did Franklin D. Roosevelt during World War II. President Truman made the decision to use the atomic bomb in 1945 and to send U.S. forces into Korea in 1950. During the Vietnam conflict, Lyndon Johnson made decisions to escalate the conflict in 1964 and both he and Richard Nixon took responsibility for the on-again–off-again bombing campaigns against North Vietnam and in support of troops of the Cambodian government. Harry Truman's phrase, "the buck stops here," seems to apply quite often when the conflict is an undeclared war, and the effects of a military decision can have a major effect on our relations with other nations.

Despite the hot debates over the legitimacy of presidential power to wage war in Vietnam without a congressional declaration of war, history was on the side of the chief executive. In 1964 Congress overwhelmingly passed the Tonkin Gulf resolution; it appeared to give President Johnson, and later Nixon, a blank check in preventing aggression in Vietnam or against any member of the Southeast Asia Collective Defense Treaty (SEATO). Johnson had gone to Congress in a political move to share the burden of responsibility, and when Congress repealed the resolution in 1970, Nixon did not try to block their action. In reply to the argument that the presidents exceeded their authority, Professor Louis Koenig wrote:

Just as Jefferson sent naval frigates to fight the Barbary pirates, as McKinley dispatched troops to China to subdue the Boxer Rebellion, as Kennedy flung a naval blockade around Cuba, and as Johnson sent marines to the Dominican Republic, Johnson as Commander-in-Chief could wage war in Vietnam.[30]

In fact, Congress has declared war in only five of our nation's eleven major conflicts with other nations.[31] During the Vietnam conflict, congressional frustration was at a high point. The Senate debated and eventually passed the National Commitments Resolution of 1969 (see Chapter 11) that was opposed by Nixon on the grounds that he, as

president, had the sole constitutional power to send forces abroad without congressional approval and that he could conceive of no conditions under which a declaration of war would be appropriate. An exasperated Senator Fulbright replied:

Declarations of war, we are told, are inappropriate to limited wars . . . and unthinkable in the event of an all-out nuclear war . . . with both limited and general wars accounted for, I do not know what kinds of war are left for Congress to declare.[32]

THE WAR POWERS ACT. Although the War Powers Act of 1973 places some curbs on presidential war making by requiring a withdrawal of forces from combat within sixty days unless Congress authorizes continued action, the president still can use "his planes" (see insert) to initiate a conflict that could expand beyond a limited military action and turn into a situation in which a congressional resolution to disengage might have little meaning. Congress became painfully aware of this when Cambodian forces seized the U.S. merchant vessel *Mayaguez* in June 1975. President Ford reacted by dispatching marines to recapture the ship and rescue the crew, at a cost of 41 marines and $9.5 million. The Cambodians released the crew before the attack and congressional criticism focused on presidential "overreaction" and the lack of real prior consultation with Congress. President Carter's decision to attempt to rescue the hostages in Iran also was reached without consultation with congressional leaders, as the act seems to require.

The ability to place the nation in a state of war, limited or otherwise, remains the most dangerous personal power of the modern presidency; perhaps it is most effectively checked by the power of public opinion, as reflected in the media and Congress's renewed vigor in the foreign policy area. Public opinion was a factor in forcing our disengagement in Vietnam, and presidents are aware of the

Here, Lyndon Johnson's reply suggests the enormous personal power
that is held by the president as commander-in-chief.

*An exchange in 1968 between President Johnson and an airman as the
President was walking toward his plane.*

*Airman: Sir . . . Mr. President . . . your plane is over there on the other
side, sir.*

*President: Son, I want to tell you something—just so you never forget. . . . All
of them—those over here and those over there—are my planes.*

Source: Quoted in Emmet John Hughes, *The Living Presidency* (New York: Coward,
McCann & Geoghegan, 1973), p. 17.

people's distaste for the "policeman for the
world" role our country has played.[33]

DOMESTIC DISORDERS.   As part of his power
as commander-in-chief, the president can
employ the regular armed forces or activate
state National Guard units to see that the federal laws are enforced within the boundaries
of the United States. Dramatic examples of
this power were the use of troops to enforce
school integration in Little Rock, Arkansas
(1957), the University of Mississippi (1962),
and the University of Alabama (1963), and to
quell the Detroit Riots of 1967.

The present standards for employment
of forces against domestic disorder within a
state provide that the president can act under
the following three circumstances:

1. On call of the state legislature

2. On call of the governor

3. To enforce federal law when the
president believes that the local authorities
have lost the ability or desire to enforce
them

This third provision gives the president what
is tantamount to complete discretionary
power: he may act after issuing a proclamation

ordering the immediate end to obstruction of
the law and the enforcement of all legal and
constitutional rights. During the period of use
of troops to put down domestic disorders, a
qualified form of martial law is usually
imposed. Unlike what obtains under complete
martial law, during which time all offenders
can be tried by military courts, local
authorities are expected to cooperate with the
military, and offenders are turned over to the
civilian courts for trial.

Again we have a power that enables
the president to win when confronting
resistance at the state level, but the victories
are won at some cost. When the federal
system breaks down and there is a resort to
force, the president alienates those against
whom the force is employed. Eisenhower's
action in 1957 came at a time when the
Republican Party was making headway in
the South. The party suffered, and the president lost points with southern legislators.
Kennedy's confrontations in 1962 and 1963
also further undercut his already weak support
from Dixie members of Congress.

BROADENING   OF   PRESIDENTIAL   WAR
POWERS. A broad war power has been
developed   through   the   marriage   of   the

commander-in-chief clause and the president's responsibility to "take care that the laws are faithfully executed." Lincoln, Wilson, and Franklin D. Roosevelt were the main architects of this doctrine; the last two extended the war powers, with the cooperation of Congress, to control of the nation's economy in periods of crisis. During World War II the president ordered price controls, rationing, and seized industrial plants. All of these actions were upheld by the Supreme Court. With rare exception, the Congress and the Supreme Court have not seriously challenged presidential actions during actual military conflicts involving the nation's survival. The Court has imposed some limitations upon the commander-in-chief power, but has been unwilling to guarantee civil liberties during wartime, apparently preferring to wait until the crisis passes before telling the president that some legal boundary has been overstepped.

An extreme application of the concept of war powers involved a presidential executive order of February 19, 1942, which ordered the removal of persons of Japanese ancestry, including Japanese–Americans, from the West Coast into what amounted to imprisonment in relocation camps further inland. In a series of cases the Court avoided coming to grips with the obvious constitutional issues and based its decisions affirming the actions upon a broad reading of the executive's powers.[34] When the Court did order the release of these Americans, it was on the basis of a technicality rather than constitutional rights.

In 1952 the Supreme Court ruled that President Truman's Korean War seizure of most of the nation's steel plants in an effort to end a strike was unconstitutional.[35] The six justices in the majority each wrote separate opinions and the case is not a strong precedent. Truman weakened his position by refusing to use the Taft–Hartley Act that provided a mechanism for ordering strikers back to work for an eighty-day cooling-off period.

We have suggested that the roles played by the president are interrelated, and we can ask whether or not the commander-in-chief hat is a heavy one to wear. From the White House perspective, the problem is the public's tendency to associate wars with the officeholder. Harry Truman saw his domestic legislative agenda thwarted in 1951 and 1952 as Congress held him accountable for the unexpectedly drawn out Korean conflict. Public dissent over the Vietnam War was instrumental in Johnson's decision not to run again in 1968, and Nixon's 1970 decisions, particularly the move into Cambodia, created major opposition. On the other hand, he was able to take credit for the wind-down of the conflict. The post–World War II experience suggests that the extraordinary powers as commander-in-chief have led to personal and domestic policy losses for the president.

The Two-Term Limit, Disability, Succession, and Impeachment

The Twenty-second Amendment (1951) limits a president to two terms in office or one term in the case of a vice-president who becomes president and serves for more than two years of his predecessor's term. Lyndon Johnson became president on November 22, 1963, more than two years into John F. Kennedy's term. He was elected in 1964 and could have been a candidate in 1968 had he chosen to run. Ford would have been limited to one full term because he served more than two years of Nixon's second term.

The amendment was a reaction to Franklin Roosevelt's election to four consecutive terms (1933–1945), and it became effective during the presidency of Dwight

Eisenhower. Ironically, the amendment, which was strongly backed by Republicans reacting to twenty years of Democratic chief executives, had its initial impact on a Republican incumbent who urged its repeal.

TWO TERMS: PRO AND CON

The two-term limit can be looked at as a denial of the people's right to return to office a popular and successful president, and it could be disruptive in terms of national crisis when continuity of leadership might be both necessary and desirable. It may also undercut presidential power, particularly during the last two years of the second term when the so-called "lame duck" cannot use his availability for renomination as a lever to keep other officeholders in step with his policy goals. Eisenhower has been the only case in point, as the assassination of Kennedy, the withdrawal of Johnson, the resignation of Nixon, and the defeat of Carter have prevented a further test of this theory. Lyndon Johnson's power eroded very quickly within weeks after his March 1968 announcement that he would not seek renomination, and he was frustrated at every turn during his last ten months in office.[36] But his problems were the product of many factors and cannot be attributed solely to his announcement.

Another aspect of the two-term limit is that a second-term incumbent may feel that he is freed from the need to bargain with the various pressure groups in the society and other political leaders and thereby becomes isolated by cutting off his life-lines to reality. In the case of Richard Nixon, it appears that his large electoral victory in 1972 and the knowledge that he had only four years left to accomplish his goals contributed to his uncompromising approach on economic and social programs and to too much reliance on his White House staff.

Proponents of the Twenty-second

Amendment believe that the possible unwanted side effects are outweighed by preventing any one individual from controlling the powers of the office for an excessively long period and dangerously personalizing the presidency. And, a new president means a new staff of advisers and the infusion of some new ideas into the decision-making process.

THE SIX-YEAR TERM. The proposal for a single six-year term could increase the danger of isolation as well as make the president a "lame duck" as soon as he takes the oath of office. He would be free to try to do whatever he wanted and at the same time be severely handicapped in dealing with the other participants in the political arena.

A president immunized from political considerations, is a president who need not listen to people, respond to majority sentiment, or pay attention to views that may be diverse, intense and perhaps at variance with his own.[37]

On the other hand, the virtue of the six-year term is that the incumbent's policy considerations would be free, from the outset, of the burden of shaping decisions with a view to the next election. And, given the vast power of the presidency, the "lame duck" argument may be overdrawn.

SUCCESSION

The Constitution provides that in the case of death, resignation, or disability of the president, the "Powers and Duties" of the office "shall devolve on the Vice-President." It was unclear whether these words meant that a vice-president would be the president or merely an acting president. However, the first of eight men to become chief executive as a result of the death of the incumbent, John Tyler who succeeded William Harrison in 1841, settled the matter by declaring that he was the president. His precedent was incorporated into the language of the Twentieth, Twenty-second, and Twenty-fifth Amendments.

The Presidential Succession Act of 1947 placed the speaker of the House and the president *pro tempore* of the Senate next in the line of succession after the vice-president. Should there be a need to go beyond these officials, the line of succession would go into the Cabinet in the order of the establishment of the various departments. When Franklin Roosevelt died in 1945, Harry Truman served for almost a complete term without a vice-president. Lyndon Johnson did not have a vice-president from November 22, 1963, until January 1965, and in that instance the next two people in line were John McCormack, then age 72, and Senator Carl Hayden, then 86.

The Twenty-fifth Amendment went into effect in 1967 and it was designed to deal with three problems: unhappiness over the laws relating to the order of succession to the presidency; filling the vice-presidency in the event of a vacancy in that office; and, how to determine if the president is disabled and unable to serve.

Criticism of the 1947 law centered on the possible succession of officials whose constituency was limited to a district or a state and whose elections had little or nothing to do with their qualifications for the highest office in the land. It was assumed that the Twenty-fifth Amendment would reduce if not eliminate this problem by having the president fill vice-presidential vacancies by nominating a replacement who takes office upon confirmation by a majority vote of the House and Senate. However, the vice-presidency remained vacant for fifty-seven days while Congress held hearings and debated the Ford nomination, and for 131 days before it confirmed Nelson Rockefeller.

When Congress passed the Twenty-fifth Amendment and the states ratified it, few if any people conceived of the possibility of the events of 1974 which found the nation's top two leaders not elected by the people. The amendment came into play twice, when Spiro Agnew resigned as vice-president and when Gerald Ford, his replacement, succeeded Richard Nixon, again creating a vacancy that was filled by Nelson Rockefeller.

DISABILITY. The disability issue was ignored by our Founding Fathers. Two presidents have been disabled for extended periods: Garfield lingered for eight days after being shot in 1881. And after Wilson had a stroke in 1919, his illness continued throughout the remainder of his term. For two years it was said that Mrs. Wilson and Colonel House, Wilson's adviser, ran the country. The issue of disability was raised again when President Eisenhower suffered three serious illnesses, including a heart attack in 1955 that required four months of reduced activity. Eisenhower, Kennedy, and Johnson had private agreements with their vice-presidents about the assumption of the duties of the office upon the president's request or if it was clear that the president was incapacitated. In fact, the decision on inability was left to each president.

The Twenty-fifth Amendment provides that the vice-president becomes acting president if the president notifies Congress in writing that he cannot perform his duties. In the case of a president not recognizing his own disability, the vice-president and a majority of the Cabinet officers can declare him to be disabled, and the vice-president becomes acting president. In either situation, when the president informs Congress that the disability no longer exists, he resumes his office, unless the vice-president and a majority of the Cabinet officers claim that he is not recovered. Within three weeks Congress would have to decide the issue, with a two-thirds vote of both houses required to prevent the president from resuming his duties.

IMPEACHMENT. Under the Constitution, the Congress can impeach civilian executive and

Viewpoint:
The importance of the power to impeach

Impeachment is the ultimate solution to abuse of power. This Founding
Father would have disagreed with Nixon that impeachment would have
torn the nation apart.

No point is of more importance than that the right of impeachment should be
continued. Shall any man be above justice? Above all shall that man be
above it, who [as president] can commit the most extensive injustice?
GEORGE MASON at the Constitutional Convention

Source: Quoted in Arthur M. Schlesinger, Jr., *The Imperial Presidency* (Boston: Houghton Mifflin, 1973), p. 415.

judicial officers of the federal government.[38] The House of Representatives serves as a grand jury, investigating charges, and it is empowered to bring impeachment proceedings against the individual by a majority vote. If the House votes articles of impeachment for "Treason, Bribery or other high crimes and Misdemeanors," the Chief Justice of the Supreme Court presides over a trial conducted by the Senate, and conviction and removal from office requires a two-thirds vote.

The Founding Fathers were agreed that the power to impeach, particularly as a remedy against a president, was both necessary and an instrument of last resort. James Madison stated that impeachment was to be reserved for "great and dangerous offenses" and it clearly was not to be used in cases of legitimate disagreement over policy or over constitutional interpretation.[39]

Prior to 1973 only one president, Andrew Johnson, had been subjected to an impeachment inquiry. The politically motivated proceedings grew out of Johnson's efforts to carry out Lincoln's post–Civil War policies of Reconstruction that were conciliatory toward the South. Radical Republicans in Congress favored harsher policies and used the president's firing of his Secretary of War as an excuse to charge him with misconduct in office for violation of the Tenure of Office Act.

Johnson was impeached by the House, but was saved from conviction in the Senate by a single vote. Not until October 24, 1973 did the House of Representatives again undertake impeachment proceedings against a president of the United States. Impeachment, it should be remembered, is like a grand jury indictment, and affirmative action on the part of the House indicates a belief that enough evidence exists to warrant trial by the Senate.

Congressional reluctance to use the impeachment power is understandable. The Johnson case demonstrated the possibilities of the power being used for partisan reasons; there were differences of opinion over whether or not an impeachable offense had to be for a specific violation of the Constitution or of specific laws, and removing the official elected by all of the people is a drastic step. Finally, could the nation stand the turmoil of an impeachment?

The sad chronology of the Watergate affair that led to the resignation of Richard Nixon was illustrative of congressional caution and answered some of the questions about the impeachment process. Throughout the eighteen months that Watergate received national attention, the president and others suggested that the country ran grave risks of being torn apart by an impeachment and trial. But the nation survived the Andrew Johnson

June 17, 1972   Break-in at the Democratic National Committee Headquarters in the Watergate Office Building.

February 7, 1973   Senate votes to create the Watergate Committee.

April 30, 1973   Key members of the White House staff resign. The President accepts responsibility but says he was not personally involved in the break-in or cover-up.

May 7, 1973   Watergate hearings begin.

July 16, 1973   Existence of tapes revealed.

October 20, 1973   President fires special prosecutor Archibald Cox for refusal to compromise on his efforts to secure the Watergate tapes. Deputy Attorney General William B. Ruckelshaus also is removed for refusal to fire Cox. Attorney General Elliot Richardson resigns.

October 23, 1973   Impeachment resolutions introduced in the House.

May 9, 1974   House Judiciary Committee begins official impeachment inquiry.

July 24, 1974   Supreme Court orders Nixon to turn over sixty-four tapes.

July 27-30, 1974   Judiciary Committee votes in favor of reporting out three articles of impeachment.

August 5, 1974   Nixon releases three tapes that clearly indicate his involvement in the cover-up.

August 8, 1974   President announces that he will resign the following day.

September 8, 1974   President Ford pardons Richard Nixon.

Figure 12–1   A selected Watergate chronology.

impeachment, and it was not shaken to its foundations by the Nixon affair. "The genius of impeachment lay in the fact that it could punish the man without punishing the office."[40] The powers of the office have remained intact with the slight modification that executive privilege cannot be used to withhold evidence in a criminal case unless a clear national security argument can be made. And, the preoccupation with Watergate and the delays in policy making were the price that had to be paid for the principle that ours is a government of laws, not men.

NIXON'S CASE. The article of impeachment relating to "abuse of power" indicates that the majority felt that impeachment does not have to be based upon a violation of a specific law. A number of Nixon's defenders on the Judiciary Committee voted against the resolutions on the ground that it had not been proven that the president had violated the Constitution or any law, and therefore was not guilty of an impeachable offense. They were left "holding the bag" after the release of tapes on August 5, 1974 showed that Nixon was guilty of obstruction of justice.

The House Judiciary Committee proceeded slowly and came under attack for alleged foot-dragging. It took six months of investigations before the hearing began, but during this period, the withholding of original tapes and the selected release of edited transcripts meant that there were differences of opinion on the facts relating to the president's involvement. Was he guilty of negligence, irresponsibility, or deception? Are these impeachable offenses? Was there sufficient evidence that he had knowingly violated the law? With these questions to be considered, caution was dictated, and it was essential that the verdict of history not be that Richard Nixon was "railroaded" or "hounded" out of office by a partisan majority. The post-resignation analyses generally agree that the process worked well and that Congress is qualified

President Gerald Ford officially pardoned former President Richard Nixon of corruption charges that clouded the public's respect for the office.

and able to play its proper role in the impeachment process. Although the House never got the chance to vote on the impeachment resolutions, and the Senate did not conduct a trial, the probability of impeachment resulted in the president's resignation.

Nixon's resignation closed off the impeachment proceedings but led to two more related disputes. By avoiding impeachment, Nixon retained his rights under the Former Presidents Act (1950) to a $60,000-a-year pension, an office staff, and up to $96,000 a year for staff salaries. But under provisions of the Presidential Transition Act, President Ford had recommended an $850,000 six-month transitional allowance for the former President. Congress cut the figure to $100,000 and reduced and set the post-transitional pension and staff allowance package at $100,000 per year. The cloud under which Nixon left office, widespread displeasure over President Ford's pardoning of Nixon, and Nixon's acceptance of the pardon without a forthright admission of guilt, led to congressional refusal to approve huge transitional appropriations.

THE NIXON PARDON. Finally, President Ford came under attack when he issued the pardon on September 8, 1974. It gave Nixon a "full, free and absolute pardon for all offenses against the United States which he . . . has committed or may have committed."[41] The pardon freed Nixon from probable indictment and conviction for obstruction of justice, as well as other possible violations uncovered during the Watergate probe. The pardon provided immunity for the leader at a time when some of his lieutenants had already been convicted and were in jail, and others were standing trial.

Ford's power to pardon was rooted in a constitutional grant of authority, but the propriety and wisdom of issuing the pardon before the former chief executive had been indicted was questioned. It appeared that the judicial process had been short-circuited, and Ford's action ended his short honeymoon with the Congress and the public; it was subsequently viewed by some Republicans as adding to their difficulties in the November 1974 elections.

Who won and who lost as a result of the Nixon affair? Obviously, Nixon was a loser, and Ford suffered some loss of popularity, and perhaps votes, because of the pardon. But, the careful approach taken by the House of Representatives raised, at least temporarily, the prestige of that body, and the presidency itself was shown to be a healthy institution, bigger than a single occupant of the office. Finally, the nation may have been a winner if the long-range product of the Nixon years is a better balance of power between the Congress and the president.

★ Issue ★

Is the President Too Powerful?

Since the mid–1960s many students of the presidency have been concerned with the question of excessive power in the hands of the chief executive, particularly the very personal power of putting the nation into a war, declared or undeclared. Disenchantment with this presidential power was spurred by unhappiness with our Vietnam policy and then became a general complaint as President Nixon was accused of using his office to reverse a trend that had been underway since the 1930s—the growth of the national government as the chief instrument for domestic public policy and services. But to incumbents, the massive power of the office has appeared to be more illusory than real.

Reflecting on his position, Harry Truman remarked:

I sit here all day trying to persuade people to do the things they ought to have sense enough to do without my persuading them. . . . That's all the powers of the president amount to.[42]

And John F. Kennedy expressed his frustration over the failure to achieve passage of most of his legislative program. In an interview he said:

The fact is, I think the Congress looks more powerful sitting here than it did when I was there in Congress. . . . When you are in Congress you are one of a hundred in the Senate or one of 435 in the House, so that the power is so divided. But from here I look at a Congress, and I look at the collective power of the Congress . . . and it is a substantial power.[43]

PRESIDENTIAL FRUSTRATION

The modern occupants of the White House probably would reverse the question posed in this issue and ask, "Is the president powerful enough?" Presidential frustration is partly a product of the fixed four-year term of office that sets the pace and the rhythm of the office and puts "special pressure on the president to get great deeds done quickly. . . . This pressure brings a perspective on history and a sense of urgency in the White House that finds no match elsewhere in the national government."[44] Lyndon Johnson addressed this point in his memoirs:

The President and the Congress run on separate clocks. . . . Consequently, the Presidency is geared to force decisions and actions. . . . In contrast . . . a careful Congressman can make a home for life on Capitol Hill. While the President must live with crisis and deadlines, a Congressman can cultivate the art of delay and refrain from commitment.[45]

While most scholars and journalists agree that an imperial presidency has developed in the area of foreign affairs, some of these same writers question the adequacy of presidential power to exercise effective leadership in the domestic sphere. Arthur M. Schlesinger, Jr., makes the point that while the president exerts considerable influence over the pattern and level of economic activity, he has less discretion in economic management than any other chief executive of a democratic state. As an example, Schlesinger points to the paradox of Congress's lack of capacity to act quickly and its refusal to grant standby power to the president to adjust tax rates in response to economic conditions.

Professor Philippa Strum acknowl-edges that presidential–congressional relations in foreign affairs have become unbalanced, but she makes the same point in reference to domestic matters. However, in the second area, she states that Congress is too powerful. In this case, the villains are the congressional committees in general and the powerful chairmen in particular who can prevent the entire Congress from voting on presidential proposals. Professor Strum would like to put the question of correctness of the president's ideas to the full membership of both houses by requiring every committee to report out all major bills reported to it.

A reduction in the power of congressional committees without a reduction in the power of Congress to vote down presidential requests would mean a far better balance between president and Congress in the area of domestic affairs.[46]

The events of the last few years do not suggest that Congress has any intention of adopting the Strum proposal.

Jimmy Carter, dealing with a Congress of his own party, was unable to secure passage of many of his major programs, and he had to resort to the veto more often than he had anticipated. Certainly he would have been justified in asserting that there was no imperial presidency in domestic affairs. And, he found it difficult, as had his predecessors, to push his view of the national interest in opposition to the special interest politics that dominate the congressional scene. Unlike the situation posed by Strum, Gerald Ford, a president who lacked an electoral mandate and who faced serious economic conditions as well as a largely hostile Congress, was able to use the veto to impose his own conservative views on a wide range of domestic policies and programs. The imbalance in this case appeared to be too much power for the president born out of congressional inability to override vetoes. The presidential-congressional conflict during the period from 1968 through 1976 suggests

The public may feel both threatened by presidential power and disappointed by apparent weakness when he cannot deliver on his policy promises.

A prime paradox of the modern presidency is that it is always too strong, always too weak. A president will always have too much power for the realization of that cherished ideal—government by the people—yet never enough to solve all the problems we expect him to solve.

THOMAS E. CRONIN

Source: *The State of the Presidency* (Boston: Little, Brown, 1975), p. 2.

---

that the nation pays a heavy price for the luxury of divided government—Congress in the hands of one party and the White House in the hands of the other.

ACCOUNTABILITY IN FOREIGN AFFAIRS

How can the president be made more accountable for his actions in foreign affairs? Writing in 1973, Emmet John Hughes concluded that some cosmetic surgery was called for, including the following requirements:

★ The submission to Congress, or some part of it, of the substance of any executive agreement of a military nature that the president proposes to sign with any foreign power

★ Observance of some formal liaison with congressional leaders that would involve them in private deliberations of major foreign policy decisions

★ Return of the Department of State to its former role as the main instrument of foreign policy formation

Hughes considered this last point to be the most important one, saying:

Disconcerting or distasteful as this might be to modern presidential ways, it would give back the day-to-day burden of foreign affairs to men who know they must answer the calls or the critiques of Congress. And it would bring into the oval office the voices of some who are likely to care less about the immediate luck of the presidents than about the long life of the nation.[47]

Congress's resurgence in the 1970s and 1980s suggests an attempt to create a new balance in the foreign policy area. While a president can still put us into war, resolute exercise of its constitutional powers by Congress, and the power of public opinion may be the only practical and reasonable checks on the "imperial" presidency.

Whether the issue is the power of the "imperial" presidency created by wars abroad, or the threatened extension of this power to the domestic scene, the lessons of Vietnam and Watergate suggest that the proper balance of power is determined in part by public opinion and its expression through the other branches of government. Watergate and a weakened president provided the opportunity for a healthy redressing of the congressional-presidential balance without what might have been a foolhardy and uncalled for attempt to rush the presidency into the operating room for major surgery.

The most radical surgery was proposed in 1973 by Barbara W. Tuchman, who would replace the presidency with a six-member directorate serving as a unit for six years with each member serving a one-year term as chairman.[48] While not believing that a parliamentary system or his suggestion would be adopted, George Reedy proposed that the House of Representatives elect a "chief of government" who would serve at the pleasure of the House. This would allow for the removal of a president who had lost public confidence, rather than saddle the nation with an unpopular leader until the next election.[49] But, the steadying influence of Ford, Carter's rejection of the pomp of the imperial presidency, and Congress's renewed vigor have quieted, for the time, demands for a major restructuring of the office.

Is the president too powerful? This question will be asked about each incumbent. To quote Hughes once more:

What politically matters and historically decides will be what the citizenry, and their chosen representatives, accept or reject, welcome or question, and give or withhold. These are the crucial contingencies: whether they are too distracted to have a will of their own about their own world, whether they are pleased to leave all concern and judgment to supposedly higher authority, and whether they are uncritical enough to ascribe this authority to any man who may happen to be president.[50]

Summary

The president is given a broad and vague grant of executive power by the Constitution, and the scope of the powers and duties of the office have been interpreted differently by the various incumbents. However, the modern presidents come into an office of great power, and the so-called *strong* presidency is now a given; the differences between chief executives has become a matter of how strong they choose to be. Much of the growth of the power of the presidency has been born out of crises, the practical necessity for the legislature to delegate authority and responsibility, and political considerations that find the congressmen more comfortable at times with the ball in the president's court.

But the image of the all-powerful president is misleading. The chief executive plays many roles that sometimes conflict with each other, and he is checked in the conduct of his office by constitutional, statutory, and political roadblocks. For example, the inherited bureaucracy makes him a competitor for the loyalty of his own bureaucrats, and the undisciplined parties make the leadership of the majority party no guarantee of success in enacting policies. Constitutional checks and balances such as the Senate's advice and consent to treaties and personnel appointments, and Congress's power to declare war and power of the purse are barriers to unbridled executive power.

While it is true that some of the checks and balances appeared to wither in the face of executive agreements, presidential impoundment of funds, and presidential warmaking through the use of the powers of commander-in-chief, Congress has taken corrective measures in the last two areas to redress the balance of power and has given notice that it does not intend to retreat to a position of subservience. The decision of Lyndon Johnson to step aside after 1968 and the trials and tribulations of Richard Nixon demonstrated the power of public opinion as a "check and balance."

As the power of the presidency grew, so did the potential for the abuse of power, probably less because of the nature of the office and more because of the atrophy of the checks and balances and the failures of Congress to exercise sufficient oversight, particularly of the intelligence agencies. President Nixon, and probably some of his predecessors, abused these powers under the guise of protecting national security. The questions of right or wrong, abuse or legitimate exercise of authority, are often matters of judgment, and some men occupying the White House are more likely to choose the improper course than others. Public opinion, a watchful and purposeful Congress, and, as a last resort, the impeachment process, can prevent a president from being a czar.

But the president of the United States remains the single most powerful political force in our system. He sets the political agenda for Congress, which by its present nature, cannot orchestrate a program. He must lead and he sets the priorities. When the executive and the legislative branches do not or cannot cooperate, the result is frustration, the inability of the nation to act on pressing problems of the present or prevent future ones, and the failure of both to be successful agents of change. The Watergate era taught us that the president can be prevented from being a Czar, and there are no indications that the present or future incumbents will be transformed into puppets. Students of the presidency, however, can still ask the question, "Is the president too powerful?"

Terms to Remember

See the Glossary at the end of the book for definitions.

Bipartisan foreign policy

Executive agreement

Executive privilege

Implied powers

Impoundment

Pocket veto

Prerogative theory

Stewardship theory

Notes

1. For text of articles, see Congressional Quarterly, *Weekly Report*, 32 (August 3, 1974), pp. 2020–2021.

2. Emmet John Hughes, *The Living Presidency*, (New York: Coward, McCann & Geoghegan, 1973), p. 69. Copyright © 1973 by Emmet John Hughes.

3. For a review of the literature see William G. Andrews, "The Presidency, Congress, and Constitutional Theory," in Aaron Wildavsky, ed., *The Presidency*, 2d ed. (Boston: Little, Brown, 1975).

4. Thomas E. Cronin, "Superman, Our Textbook President," *The Washington Monthly*, (October 1970), pp. 47–54. Quote is from p. 50. Also see Cronin, *The State of the Presidency* (Boston: Little, Brown, 1975).

5. This is the central question raised in Arthur M. Schlesinger, Jr., *The Imperial Presidency* (Boston: Houghton Mifflin, 1973), p. 377.

6. *Presidential Power: The Politics of Leadership* (New York: Wiley, Science Editions, 1962).

7. James D. Richardson, *A Compilation of*

the *Messages and Papers of the Presidents, 1789–1887* (Washington, D.C.: U.S. Government Printing Office, 1897), vol. 3, pp. 69–93.

8. *The Presidential Character: Predicting Performance in the White House* (Englewood Cliffs, N.J.: Prentice–Hall, 1972). For comments on Nixon's isolation see pp. 423–424. Also see Barber, "An American Redemption: The Presidential Character from Nixon to Ford to Carter," *The Washington Monthly*, (April 1977), pp. 6–38.

9. Louis Fisher, *President and Congress: Power and Policy* (New York: The Free Press, 1972), pp. 55–84. Also see Fisher, *Presidential Spending Power* (Princeton: Princeton University Press, 1975).

10. Lyndon B. Johnson, *The Vantage Point* (New York: Holt, Rinehart & Winston, 1971), p. 565.

11. See *The Federalist*, No. 69.

12. *Playboy*, (November 1976), pp. 63–86. The interview was a thoughtful probe of Carter's attitudes on life in general, religion, politics, etc. Controversy focussed on his choice of *Playboy*, his use of a phrase to describe illicit sexual activity, and his admission that "I've committed adultery in my heart many times."

13. Peter Woll, *American Bureaucracy* (New York: W.W. Norton, 1963), p. 165.

14. See Laurin Henry, *Presidential Transitions* (Washington, D.C.: The Brookings Institution, 1960).

15. Richard E. Neustadt, *Presidential Power: The Politics of Leadership* (New York: Wiley, 1976), p. 9.

16. Robert F. Kennedy, *Thirteen Days* (New York: W.W. Norton, 1969), pp. 94–95.

17. *Meyers v. United States*, 272 U.S. 52 (1926); and *Humphrey's Executor v. United States*, 295 U.S. 602 (1935).

18. *U.S. v. Nixon*, 418 U.S. 683, 713 (1974).

19. See James Reston, "A Pattern Long Developing," *New York Times*, January 28, 1975, p. 33; and Nicholas M. Horrick, "The F.B.I. as Private Presidential Police Force," *New York Times*, February 9, 1975, Sect. 4, p. 5.

20. Quoted in Anthony Lewis, "The Sentences: A Message on True Law and Order," *New York Times*, February 23, 1975, Sect. 4, p. 1.

21. Louis Koenig, *The Chief Executive*, rev. ed. (New York: Harcourt, Brace & World, 1964), p. 87. In 1953 and 1954, Republicans controlled both houses.

22. Thomas E. Cronin, "Putting the President Back into Politics," *The Washington Monthly*, (September 1973), pp. 7–12.

23. *New York Times*, February 19, 1975, p. 1.

24. *United States v. Curtiss Wright Export Corporation*, 229 U.S. 304 (1936).

25. Quoted in Eleanor Lansing Dulles, *John Foster Dulles: The Last Year* (New York: Harcourt, Brace & World, 1963), p. 31.

26. For a running account of the debates, see Congressional Quarterly, *Weekly Report* for February, March, and April 1978.

27. Thomas E. Cronin, *The State of the Presidency*, p. 13. Some of the thoughts in this section are from Chapter 1: "The Presidential Condition."

28. Johnson was quoted in Hugh Sidey, *A Very Personal Presidency* (New York: Atheneum, 1968), p. 260. Kennedy was quoted in Richard Rovere, "Letter from Washington," *New Yorker*, (November 30, 1963), p. 53.

29. *The Federalist*, No. 69.

30. Koenig, *The Chief Executive*, p. 215.

31. The five declared wars were the War of 1812, the Mexican War, the Spanish–American War, World War I, and World War II. There was no declaration of war during the naval war with France (1798–1800), the first Barbary War (1801–1805), the second Barbary War (1815), the Mexican–American clashes (1914–1917), the Korean War (1950–1953—presently in a status of truce), and the Vietnam War.

32. *Congressional Record*, vol. 115, no. 101 (Daily ed., June 19, 1969), p. 56830.

33. See John E. Mueller, *War, Presidents, and Public Opinion* (New York: Wiley, 1973).

34. *Hirabayashi v. United States*, 320 R.S. 81, (1943) and *Korematsu v. United States*, 323 U.S. 214 (1944).

35. *Youngstown Sheet & Tube Co. v. Sawyer*, 343 U.S. 579 (1952).

36. George E. Reedy, *The Twilight of the Presidency* (New York: The World Publishing Co., 1972), pp. 139–142. Also see Richard L. Strout, "The 22nd Amendment: A Second Look", *New York Times Magazine*, July 28, 1957. p. 5.

37. Clark Clifford, former Secretary of Defense under Johnson, quoted in Schlesinger, *The Imperial Presidency*, pp. 386–387. Alos see Reedy, *The Twilight of the Presidency*, pp. 135–139; and Cronin, "Putting the President Back Into Politics."

38. Twelve officials have been impeached and only four, all judges, have been convicted. President Nixon is not counted in the figure because his resignation headed off an impeachment vote in the House.

39. Schlesinger, *The Imperial Presidency*, p.

415. See pp. 414–419 for an interesting treatment of the Nixon case. Also see Raoul Berger, *Impeachment: The Constitutional Problem* (Cambridge: Harvard University Press, 1973).

40. Schlesinger, *The Imperial Presidency,* p. 415.

41. For text, see Congressional Quarterly, *Weekly Report,* 32 (September 14, 1974), p. 2455.

42. Quoted in Neustadt, *Presidential Power,* pp. 9–10.

43. "After Two Years—A Conversation with the President." Television and radio interview, December 17, 1962, in *Public Papers of the Presidents of the United States, John F. Kennedy,* *1962* (Washington, D.C.: U.S. Government Printing Office, 1963), pp. 889–904.

44. Hughes, *The Living Presidency,* p. 170.

45. Johnson, *The Vantage Point,* pp. 441–442.

46. Philippa Strum, *Presidential Power and American Democracy* (Pacific Palisades, Calif.: Goodyear Publishing Co., Inc., 1972), pp. 38–39.

47. Hughes, *The Living Presidency,* p. 287.

48. "Should We Abolish the Presidency," *New York Times,* February 13, 1973, p. 37.

49. Reedy, *The Twilight of the Presidency,* pp. 172–173.

50. Hughes, *The Living Presidency,* p. 287.

Suggested Readings

James David Barber, *The Presidential Character: Predicting Performance in the White House,* 2d ed. (Englewood Cliffs, N.J.: Prentice–Hall, 1977).

Raoul Berger, *Impeachment: The Constitutional Problem* (Cambridge: Harvard University Press, 1973).

Thomas E. Cronin, *The State of the Presidency,* 2d ed. (Boston: Little, Brown, 1980).

Louis Fisher, *President and Congress: Power and Policy* (New York: The Free Press, 1972).

Emmet John Hughes, *The Living Presidency* (New York: Coward, McCann & Geoghegan, 1973).

Robert F. Kennedy, *Thirteen Days* (New York: W.W. Norton, 1969).

John E. Mueller, *War, Presidents, and Public Opinion* (New York: Wiley, 1973).

Richard E. Neustadt, *Presidential Power: The Politics of Leadership* (New York: Wiley, 1976).

Arthur M. Schlesinger, Jr., *The Imperial Presidency* (Boston: Houghton Mifflin, 1973).

Philippa Strum, *Presidential Power and American Democracy,* 2d ed. (Pacific Palisades, Calif.: Goodyear Publishing, 1979).

CHAPTER 13

The Presidential Advisory System

The first impression that one gets of a ruler and of his brains is from seeing the men he has about him.

MACHIAVELLI
The Prince

The most important duty of the president is to make decisions. Although John F. Kennedy bemoaned the fact that "no one in the country is more assailed by divergent advice and clamorous counsel," he recognized that at the critical moment, presidents bear the heavy burden of acting alone.[1] The final decision and the ultimate responsibility belong to the chief executive.

The most dramatic and immediately visible decisions tend to fall into the area of foreign policy and war making. Yet a president usually has several alternatives to choose from, and often the evidence favoring one course of action over another is very slight.[2] Harry Truman had options other than using the atomic bomb against Japan in 1945, and President Johnson could have chosen a course different from retaliatory air strikes against North Vietnam in August 1964 after an alleged attack on the U.S.S. *Maddox* in the Gulf of Tonkin. In fact, the Pentagon Papers revealed that the Vietnam experience had offered a series of options and that the presidents were free to cite one form of evidence or another to justify the decisions that they made. More recently, President Carter had a range of options to choose from in reaction to the hostage crisis in Iran and the Soviet invasion of Afghanistan.

On the domestic front, the picture is the same. There was no irresistible logic forcing Richard Nixon to approve the creation of the "plumbers" unit to plug security leaks nor did he have to approve and become a participant in the Watergate cover-up. Ford's, Carter's, and Reagan's policy decisions concerning the energy and economic crises represented a choice of competing solutions. Almost all presidential decisions, great or small, are matters of perception.

To help him make decisions, an elabo-

★ ★

President Truman points out that presidential decision making is a very personal thing, and only the president understands all the "whys" of the decisions.

The Presidency of the United States carries with it a responsibility so personal as to be without parallel. . . . No one can make decisions for [the President]. No one can know all the processes and stages of his thinking. . . . Even those closest to him . . . never know all the reasons why he does certain things and why he comes to certain conclusions.

HARRY S. TRUMAN

Source: *Memoirs of Harry Truman*, Vol. I (Garden City, NY: Doubleday, 1955), p. ix.

rate bureaucracy has grown up around the president in the form of the Executive Office of the President (see Figure 13–1); it supplements the vice-presidency and Cabinet. The president can also rely on information and advice from the agencies of the permanent bureaucracy and the outside advisory system of innumerable individuals, boards, commissions, and committees that could be called "quasi-official agencies." The term **bureaucracy** usually is used to identify the executive branch. In this chapter we distinguish between the **presidential bureaucracy,** composed of the Cabinet and the Executive Office of the President, and the **permanent government,** composed of the departments, agencies, and bureaus staffed by career civil servants.

This chapter focuses on the nature and role of the presidential advisory system; however, we accept as an underlying assumption the idea that decision making is a very personal process and that the president must decide on problems that defy simple solutions. The president does not make all the decisions that come from the White House with his name on them. He may try to make only the

most significant decisions—and only on those issues which come to him. The "advisory" system may (1) screen certain matters from the president, and (2) actually make decisions rather than merely advise on them. One of President Johnson's press secretaries, George Reedy, said:

The real misery of the average presidential day is the haunting sense that decisions have been made on incomplete information and inadequate counsel. Tragically, the information must always be incomplete and the counsel always inadequate, for the arena of human activity in which a president operates is one in which there are no quantitative answers.[3]

What people the president listens to, and whose ideas influence his advisers, often determine policy outcomes. The decisions of the chief executive to cut back on certain programs, aid to urban areas for example, while increasing spending in another sector, such as defense, have serious economic and social implications, making losers of some individuals and groups and winners out of others. A cutback in federally financed jobs in the cities

President Ronald Reagan shares the Oval Office with two staff members on his first day as president.

hurts the chronically unemployed or under-employed—often minorities, who are the usual losers—while the increased dollars for defense aid the businesses that are awarded the contracts, their employees, and the communities in which they spend their money. Clearly, everyone has a considerable stake in the presidential advisers and the quality of advice they give.

The growth of the presidential bureaucracy has raised certain important questions that this chapter explores. Has the size of the advisory system made the president a prisoner of his own machinery, in the sense that he cannot exercise effective control over its operations? Was Watergate a logical outcome of the expanded presidential organization? What effective roles, if any, are played by the vice-president and the Cabinet? Do certain presidential styles encourage or discourage effective control? Has the presidential staff become the real operating arm of the government, replacing the agencies of the permanent bureaucracy? Finally, are our presidents isolated from political reality by the staff that serves them?

The Vice-Presidency

CONSTITUTIONAL DUTIES. The vice-presidency is one of the great paradoxes of American politics. The occupant of the office is a heartbeat away from the presidency, but John Adams, the first man to hold the post, described it as "the most insignificant office that ever the invention of man contrived or his imagination conceived."[4] Adams's disenchantment reflected the fact that the constitutional responsibilities of the vice-president are meager—to wait on the sidelines to take over in the case of the death, disability, or resignation of the president, and to serve as president of the Senate. In the latter capacity, he keeps parliamentary order and votes only in case of a tie. The Senate has never welcomed the presence of this "intruder" from the executive branch; and modern vice-presidents rarely sit in the Senate except on important issues when a close vote might require the vice-president to break a tie. Beyond these duties, the office has been what the presidents have made of it, and until the 1940s, vice-presidents did little more than what the Constitution assigned to them.

A second factor contributing to the low regard in which the office is held is the practice of choosing the vice-presidential candidate on the basis of "balancing the ticket" to add geographical strength or give representation to another ideological wing of the party or both. Historically, the evidence suggests that the candidates have not been selected on the basis of whether or not they were qualified, by experience and character, to be president. The key factor has been whether or not their being on the ticket would help the presidential nominee win the election. Although vice-presidents who have succeeded to the top office have performed competently, the assassination of Kennedy and the resignations from office of Vice-President Spiro T. Agnew in 1973 and President Nixon in 1974 provide strong arguments for a return to the "second-best man" theory of the pre–Twelfth Amendment days.

PROBLEMS OF SELECTION. In spite of contemporary events, the record of our major parties in making vice-presidential nominations remains spotty. Although Lyndon Johnson was paired in 1960 with the liberal Easterner John Kennedy in order to appeal to the more conservative southern, southwestern, and border states, Johnson was a presidential contender in his own right, and his running mate in 1964, Senator Hubert H. Humphrey of Minnesota, was also a man well-versed in national affairs. Senator Walter Mondale of Minnesota, Carter's running mate, had been a short-lived presidential contender in 1976 and was respected for his leadership in the Senate. In contrast, Barry Goldwater's partner in 1964 was William Miller, chosen because of his political contacts developed as chairman of the Republican National Committee, rather than his experience and stature in national politics. In 1968, Nixon's choice of Spiro T. Agnew, then governor of Maryland, was in response to the need to appeal to

southerners. When Ford chose Senator Robert Dole (R., Kan.) in 1976, critics complained that Dole's major talents were in the area of campaigning rather than policy formulation. On the other hand, Reagan's selection of George Bush of Texas, his leading challenger for the 1980 nomination and a man with considerable experience in elected and appointed office, was applauded widely.

Vice-President Agnew's resignation came while he was under investigation for alleged extortion, bribery, tax evasion, and conspiracy charges arising from misuse of his offices when he was a county official and then governor. Agnew pleaded "no contest" to the tax evasion charge, was fined, and placed on four years of probation. The Agnew case and the withdrawal of Thomas Eagleton from the 1972 Democratic ticket, after it was revealed that he had been treated for nervous disorders, suggest that candidates be subjected to greater scrutiny before selection. When Congress had to fill the vacancies created by Agnew and then Nixon, it subjected Ford and Rockefeller to an intense probe of their qualifications and political and personal backgrounds.

SUGGESTED REFORMS. A 1976 study by Harvard University's Institute of Politics recommended that presidential candidates make an early and public listing of prospective running mates, that party advisory committees play an active role in screening choices, and that the convention's nominee be given more time than the present half-day to decide on his choice for the number-two spot. At the time, both major parties had already created panels to look at the problem and both advocated an extended convention. Neither party took any further action.

Jimmy Carter may have set the example for future nominees who might have the good fortune to have the nomination sewn up far enough in advance of the convention to allow time for careful deliberation. Carter in-

Amidst calls for reform, one politician argues that the present method of selecting vice-presidential nominees is the proper one.

I basically don't think you should, or are we ever going to be able to change the system to any substantial degree. When you get all said and done, it is the [presidential] nominee's prerogative essentially.

Rep. WILLIAM A. STEIGER (R., Wis.)

Source: Congressional Quarterly, *Weekly Report* 34 (July 3, 1976), p. 1727.

vited a number of potential running mates to his Plains, Georgia home for consultation, and his staff undertook a thorough screening of the leading contenders. Of course, the exceptionally close Republican contest that year prevented Ford from adopting a similar strategy. Pressure from the very conservative Reagan forces in the party had led to Ford's "dumping" of Rockefeller from the ticket, and the "who-will-be-the-choice" game was an essential part of his plans to defeat Ronald Reagan, the favorite of the more conservative Republicans.

In a last-ditch effort to wrest the 1976 Republican nomination from President Ford, Reagan broke tradition and announced that the liberal Republican, Senator Richard A. Schweiker of Pennsylvania, would be his running mate. Reagan gambled on creating a coalition of conservatives and liberals, and he challenged Ford to name his running mate before the convention opened. The Reagan strategy failed.

In 1980, the nomination was in Reagan's grasp well before the convention. There is no public evidence pointing to the use of a Carter-like screening process. The GOP vice-presidential sweepstakes remained confused right up to the last moment. In fact, Reagan caused a stir at the convention when he became involved in negotiations with ex-President Ford which might have led to

Ford's joining the ticket as the vice-presidential nominee. It appears that reforming the vice-presidential selection procedure will not receive any official blessing from the parties.

THE REBIRTH OF THE VICE-PRESIDENCY

MODERN ROLES OF THE V.P. John Nance Garner, vice-president under Franklin Roosevelt from 1933 to 1941, said "the vice-presidency isn't worth a pitcher of warm spit." Harry Truman, Roosevelt's vice-president in 1945, called the office "as useful as a cow's fifth teat."[5] But, since 1949, vice-presidents have taken on many functions beyond the few prescribed by the Constitution. Alben Barkley, Truman's vice-president (1949–1953), took on many ceremonial functions and by law was a member of the National Security Council. Under Eisenhower, Richard Nixon went on highly publicized diplomatic missions and was often in the spotlight in his role as stand-in for the president in the time-consuming job of political fence-mender. It was Nixon's handling of the political leadership tasks for Eisenhower that made the vice-presidency of Johnson look less significant. In fact, he continued in the Nixon pattern by chairing a number of interdepartmental committees; and the vice-presidential role as chairman or mem-

Vice-President Walter Mondale arrives in Paris on an official visit during the Carter administration.

ber of various executive branch committees or councils is now firmly established.

The two "appointed" vice-presidents had different experiences. Gerald Ford kept a relatively low profile during Nixon's struggles with the Watergate scandal. When Nelson Rockefeller became Ford's vice-president, he was appointed vice-chairman of the Domestic Council, the White House agency that advised the president on major domestic policy questions. Rockefeller also headed the executive branch's probe of the Central Intelligence Agency. However, he was eventually frozen out of control of the Council and all other policy positions of any importance.

MONDALE: A NEW APPROACH?   President Carter made it clear when he chose Walter Mondale as his running mate that he expected him to play a larger role in his administration than previous vice-presidents had played, and that he would think of Mondale as his "top staff person." Mondale worked closely with Carter on the choice of Cabinet members, and in a break with precedent, Mondale occupied an office in the White House rather than in the Executive Office Building. The location of his office was more than symbolic, as Mondale was involved in many of the decisions made in the president's office.

Mondale had unlimited access to the president, sat on all advisory boards, was involved in both foreign and domestic policy functions, and served as a general adviser. He also acted as liaison with Congress, backing up the relatively inexperienced people offi-

Carter's V.P. discusses his role as a general adviser. His comments represent a departure from earlier administrations, when vice-presidents tended to have limited and specific duties and many were bored in the job.

I try to weigh in on the tough questions when I feel strongly about something, which is often. . . . But I don't do it publicly, I don't put out a score card. . . .

I'm going to try to take as many burdens off the president as I can.

If this is the last office I hold, if I do it in a way that doesn't humiliate my friends, I think that's not an insignificant opportunity for a man in public life.

WALTER F. MONDALE

Source: Quoted in Don Campbell, "Mondale Works at Being No. 2," *Rochester Times Union*, January 9, 1979, pp. 1, 19a. © Don Campbell, Gannett News Service.

cially assigned that role. And although vice-presidents must keep a fairly low profile and their victories go unnoticed by the general public, Mondale was influential. For example, insiders claimed that Mondale played a key role in convincing Carter to restore $2 billion for social programs to the 1980 budget. The roles of the office have expanded, but the importance of a particular vice-president as a part of the advisory system is a reflection of each president's attitude toward the office. And, the problem of selection remains with us.

Like his predecessor, George Bush is housed in the west wing of the White House, and the appointment of his top campaign aide, James A. Baker III, as Reagan's chief-of-staff was taken as a signal that Bush and Reagan would have a close working relationship. The vice-president's status was enhanced when the President designated him as the head of the "crisis management" team, taking advantage of Bush's foreign policy/intelligence background. Bush also provided a vital link to the more moderate elements within the Republican Party, and he speaks before many GOP groups.

The Cabinet

"Just what the hell good does a Cabinet do, anyway?" was a question asked of a close adviser by President-elect Kennedy shortly before his inauguration in 1961.[6] The answer depends upon the individual chief executive, and the Cabinet is best understood as a lengthened shadow of the president.

The existence of a **Cabinet** stems from custom; that is, it is not mentioned in the Constitution. However, it can be argued that the president's constitutional power to require the opinions of heads of executive departments is the basis for the Cabinet. Its members—the appointed heads of the executive departments—hold office solely at the pleasure of the chief executive; and the Cabinet meets only at his request. Of course, every Cabinet officer is also responsible for directing and coordinating the operations of his particular department "to promote the effective exercise of the President's authority and to help implement his ultimate responsibilities."[7] Beyond this, the impact of the Cabinet as an advisory group has varied from president to president. Presidents Truman and Eisenhower used it more often than did Presidents Roosevelt and Kennedy. President Johnson used the Cabinet more than his predecessor, but discussion of the Vietnam War was rarely on the agenda.

In recent administrations, the Cabinet has expanded with the addition to its regular membership of "Cabinet-level" appointees, such as the director of the Office of Management and Budget, the director of the Central Intelligence Agency, and individuals carrying

★ ★ ★ *Table 13-1* ★
The Cabinet departments

Department of State (1789)	Advises the president in the formulation and execution of foreign policy.
Department of the Treasury (1789)	The government's banker, responsible for production of currency, collection of revenues on imports, and tax collection through a major unit, the Internal Revenue Service.
Department of Defense (1949)	The modern descendant of the War Department (1789). DOD was a consolidation of the Department of the Army, Navy, and Air Force. Responsible for providing the military forces needed to protect the security of the nation.
Department of the Interior (1849)	National resource, wildlife, and public land management.
Department of Agriculture (1862)	Administers farm and food stamp programs and other assistance to farmers.
Department of Justice (1870)	Represents the U.S. in legal matters and its citizens in enforcing the law. The nation's law firm.
Department of Commerce (1913)	Originally part of the Department of Commerce and Labor (1903). Responsible for the census and programs to assist business by promoting economic development and technological advancement.
Department of Labor (1913)	Responsible for programs to foster, promote, and develop the welfare of wage earners in the U.S.
Department of Health and Human Services (1953)	Formerly known as Health, Education, and Welfare. Education was shifted in 1979. Responsible for health, welfare, and social security programs.
Department of Housing and Urban Development (1966)	Responsible for urban and housing programs.
Department of Transportation (1966)	Responsible for mass transportation and highway programs.
Department of Energy (1977)*	Created to coordinate and be responsible for energy policy and research.
Department of Education (1979)*	Responsible for education programs of the federal government.

*September 24, 1981, President Reagan proposed its elimination.

The Joint Chiefs of Staff pose with Texas Senator John Tower, Chairman of the Armed Services Committee.

the title of Counselor to the President. They usually participate in the Cabinet meetings, but unlike the department heads, they are part of the Executive Office of the President and serve only the chief executive.

When he took office, Richard Nixon said he would place more emphasis upon the Cabinet as part of his "open" administration. However, he met with it infrequently, and the highlight of the Nixon–Cabinet relationship was the 1970 firing of his Secretary of the Interior, Walter J. Hickel. Frustrated by the remoteness of the President, Hickel wrote a letter to Nixon suggesting more frequent contact with the Cabinet members. The letter led to strained relations, and Hickel's resignation was asked for and received.

By the end of 1975, Ford had made sweeping changes in the administration. He retained only three of the Cabinet members he inherited from Nixon. But, Ford's Cabinet was given little room for creativity, in part because the administration was preoccupied with its battles with Congress.

WHY CABINETS DO NOT ADVISE. A number of factors prevent the Cabinet as a body

from becoming part of the inner circle of intimate presidential advisers. First, not all appointees are chosen as a result of long association with the incumbent. In every Cabinet there are some whose selection is a reward for their having supported the president in his campaign for office. There are also a number of posts distributed on a regional basis; the Department of Interior, for example, is usually headed by a person from the Rocky Mountain or southwestern states. Most recent presidents have also attempted to have a religious, racial, and ethnic balance on the Cabinet. The appointees chosen for any of these reasons are usually competent administrators but many times not the "president's people" in the sense of being close political advisers. In addition, Cabinet members are often selected to reconcile party factions or to represent interests. For example, labor usually gets one of its own to head the Department of Labor, but this was not the case in the Reagan Cabinet.

Cabinet members are also subject to a conflict of loyalties. Although appointed by the president, they have a multiplicity of non-presidential and non-Cabinet relationships. As department heads they are pressured to meet the needs of their departments or their departments' clientele, such as agriculture, labor, business, etc. To do this, they must build good relationships with key members of Congress, who hold the fate of departmental programs and budgets in their hands. Because of this departmentalization, it is difficult for a Cabinet member to consider many issues without asking how it will affect the department. As a consequence, the Cabinet's effectiveness as an advisory or coordinating machine is reduced.

President Kennedy thought that Cabinet meetings were "a waste of time" because individual members might not have the breadth of perspective to discuss problems of a general rather than a departmental nature.[8] Of course, if the president does not want advice, the words of caution offered by Eisenhower's first Secretary of Defense, Charles Wilson, might be appropriate. He said: "Every Cabinet member should learn the lesson of the whale. The only time you get harpooned is when you're up on the surface spouting."[9]

CARTER'S GROUP APPROACH. Jimmy Carter's conception of Cabinet-making was to bring together a group of people committed to serving four years and who could, in fact, work together as a group. He wanted them to be judged, not merely as individuals, but as a council of presidential advisers who could tackle the large task of bringing the federal bureaucracy under control. Carter made much of this notion and considerable media attention was focussed on Cabinet activities prior to the major personnel changes made in 1979.

Carter's choice of Cabinet appointees disappointed some of his supporters, who anticipated the selection of more minority individuals and fresh, new faces that had not been previously associated with the Washington scene. This desire for "new" people was motivated by the assumption that the appointees would have the opportunity to help their backers win presidential support for particular policies that they felt had been neglected. However, five had extensive experience in previous administrations, and two others had been members of the House of Representatives. All of the appointees had held positions of influence in the public or private sectors, and none really were Washington "outsiders." Two women were appointed, Juanita M. Kreps (Commerce), who later resigned, and Patricia Roberts Harris (Housing and Urban Development, and later Health and Human Services). Mrs. Harris was the only black, but Carter chose black congressman Andrew Young (D., Ga.) as ambassador to the United Nations. The "new faces" and "minority" commitments received greater attention when filling sub-Cabinet rank positions.

Carter's selections reflected the need to have experienced individuals in Cabinet positions, particularly if the Cabinet was to be a meaningful instrument of advice and control. This was particularly true in the areas of foreign affairs and national security where Carter had little previous experience.

By the end of Carter's first year, the Cabinet was meeting less frequently, reflecting his view that the members were to be strong administrators of priorities set by the White House rather than independent operators. He had given back the responsibility for managing the departments to the Cabinet officers rather than trying to run them from the White House, as was characteristic of the Nixon years.

THE FAILURE OF CABINET GOVERNMENT. In July 1979, however, Carter shook up his Cabinet, and in a two-day period five Cabinet secretaries were fired or resigned. Two had planned to leave the government, but the other three left at the President's request. They were not regarded as "team players," and they had poor relations with key White

House staff members who made up the so-called "Georgia Mafia" in the White House Office.

Critics viewed the Cabinet purge as an indication that Carter valued loyalty above talent; however, much of the problem stemmed from the fact that giving the departments and agencies considerable freedom had led to too much infighting and a lack of coordination that made the administration look confused. Cabinet government Carter-style had not worked, and the "four-year" team had survived for only two-and-a-half years. However, the tenure of the average Cabinet member is approximately two years, and Carter's Cabinet had stayed intact longer than any other in the twentieth century.

REAGAN BUILDS A CABINET

With the exception of Secretary of State Alexander M. Haig, Jr., retired NATO commander and former White House chief of staff in the final months of Nixon's administration, and Secretary of Education Terrel H. Bell, Reagan's Cabinet choices were drawn from the top levels of the nation's law and business communities. The all-male Cabinet included one black, Samuel Riley Pierce, Jr., Secretary of Housing and Urban Development, and Reagan met his promises to appoint at least one woman and one Democrat by naming Jean J. Kirkpatrick, a political scientist whose conservative views on defense and foreign policy issues made her an attractive choice, to the Cabinet-level post of ambassador to the United Nations.

All of the appointees, with the exception of Kirkpatrick, were conservative mainstream Republicans with years of management expertise. They were loyal to Reagan's political philosophy and shared Reagan's expressed belief in Cabinet government. The choices pleased the business and legal worlds, but many were disappointments to far right

President Reagan quickly appointed former NATO Commander Alexander Haig as his Secretary of State.

groups that had supported Reagan and were anxious to see Cabinet and other top posts manned by ultra-conservatives.

Reagan made it clear that he intended to rely heavily on the Cabinet, and he envisioned his role as similar to the chairman of the board of a major corporation. The "board" functioned smoothly during the administration's first test, the budget battle, and the members worked well with Reagan's Executive Office staff.

THE INNER CIRCLE. Presidents have developed other avenues for employing close personal advisers, particularly by appointing them to positions in the White House Office. But individual members of the Cabinet often may be members of the inner circle, particularly those who hold the positions of attorney general, secretary of defense, state, and treasury. These posts deal with broad rather than parochial areas of concern. However, most of the president's inner circle is drawn from the advisers appointed to key posts in the Executive Office of the President, including some who hold Cabinet-level appointments.

The Executive Office of the President: Expanding Power

The president is at the top of a pyramid of approximately 2.8 million civilian employees who staff the components of the **Executive Office of the President,** the Cabinet departments, and the multitude of other agencies within the executive branch (see Figure 14–1). Another two million people are in the armed forces. However, this chapter focusses on the heart of the advisory network, the support staffs grouped under the Executive Office of the President (see Figure 13–1).

The growth of the Executive Office reflects the presidential need for expert advice on an increasing number of issues of public policy. Growth has also been a response to the enlargement of the rest of the federal bureaucracy and the chief executives' belief in the need to create a personal team to help them control the rest of the institution. But Howard E. McCurdy suggests that recent presidents have continued a trend of staff expansion that cannot be justified in terms of the growth of the entire bureaucracy. During World War II there were over 600,000 more employees working for the federal government

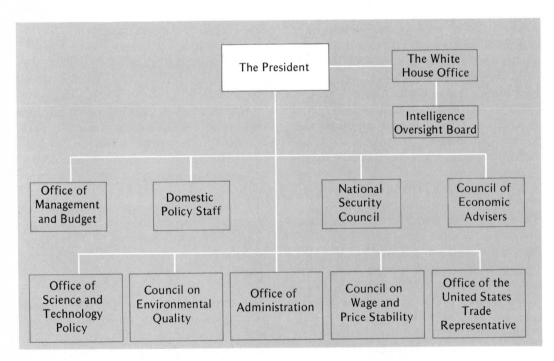

Figure 13–1 The Executive Office of the President. (Source: U.S. Government Manual.)

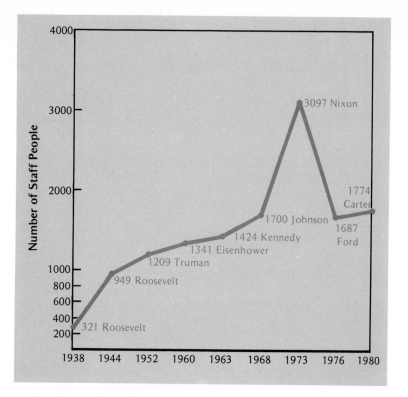

Figure 13–2 The growth of the Executive Office. (Sources: Howard E. McCurdy, "The Physical Manifestations of an Expanding Presidency"; Budget of the U.S. Government, Fiscal 1978; The Budget, Fiscal 1981.)

than there are today, and President Roosevelt managed them with an immediate staff of 48. While the size of the bureaucracy went down, the presidential staff enlarged, leveled off, and then took a huge jump under Richard Nixon. McCurdy states that Nixon simply exaggerated the staff-building tendencies of prior incumbents and, in doing so, added to his managerial problems.[10] There was considerable shrinkage under Ford, and Carter promised to further reduce the size of the presidential bureaucracy. However, as it turned out, there was an increase in the size of Carter's Executive Office.

Most of the components of the Executive Office have evolved since 1939, but the modern presidential establishment came into being during the incumbency of Harry Truman (1945–1953). Today's presidential establishment is a far cry from Thomas Jefferson's solitary messenger and secretary whom he paid out of his own pocket.

The development of the large presidential bureaucracy led to the use of the phrase "the institutionalization of the presidency." However, the phrase is misleading and, in a brilliant essay titled "Thoughts on the Presidency," Henry Fairlee claims that it is a myth that since World War II the presidency has become institutionalized. Rather, he argues, there is no high political office that, by his definition, is less institutionalized.[11] He defines an institution as an establishment with a corporate existence of its own: its func-

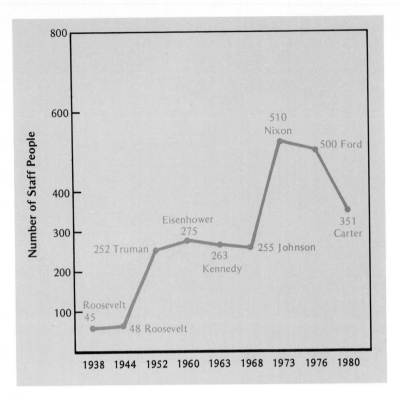

Figure 13–3 The growth of the White House staff. (Sources: Howard E. McCurdy, "The Physical Manifestations of an Expanding Presidency"; Budget of the U.S. Government, Fiscal 1979; The Budget, Fiscal 1981.)

tions, attitudes, and methods of procedure exist and remain much the same, irrespective of the people who staff the positions or the politicians to whom they are responsible; but, every study of the people around the president reveals that the relationship between the incumbent and the staffers is a very personal one and that the structure of the system and the assignment of responsibilities among the units also vary from president to president.

For example, Carter eliminated seven units that were part of Ford's last Executive Office structure and created one component, the Central Administrative Unit. The components of the Executive Office change as priorities change, and one cannot tell the players without an up-to-date scorecard. The ability to tailor the structure according to presiden-

tial desires provides a flexibility that cannot be duplicated in the Cabinet agencies whose creation, elimination, or major overhaul is subject to congressional control.

The elimination and creation of units is, in part, a reflection of the struggle of issues for the attention of the White House. The elimination of the once-prominent Office for Drug Abuse Prevention and the Office of Economic Opportunity represents a loss for those groups concerned with those areas. Such losses are usually reflected in a cutback, or at best no additions to resources allocated to these issues.

Among modern presidents, only Franklin Roosevelt operated with a small personal staff, and he regularly drew in people from the Cabinet departments to advise him

The adviser must walk a tightrope between reflecting presidential views and providing forthright and independent opinions.

He must serve with an absolute and undivided loyalty. He must represent no other constituency . . . nothing but the interests and needs of the president and his views and purposes. On the other hand . . . he must be willing at all times to tell the president, if need be, the kinds of facts that the Chief Executive least wants to hear. . . . He must know, in short, the terrible danger of isolation facing every president—a threat that the White House staff must not increase, but positively try to counter.

THEODORE H. SORENSON, Special Counsel to
Presidents Kennedy and Johnson

Source: Quoted in Emmet John Hughes, *The Living Presidency* (New York: Coward, McCann & Geoghegan, 1973), p. 366. Reprinted by permission of Coward, McCann & Geoghegan, Inc. Copyright © 1973 by Emmet John Hughes.

on issues of public policy. His style was to use the "competitive" model by building into his staff a wide diversity of opinions. He then had his staff and the department people thrash out their ideas while he listened; later he reached a decision. This approach was designed to ensure a full airing of competing ideas.

Roosevelt's successors have been served by a small personal army of counselors, consultants, assistants, special and deputy assistants, and a personal secretary, most of whom are a part of the White House Office (see Figure 13–3). As the Executive Office of the President has grown, the managerial styles of Roosevelt's successors have been most clearly reflected in their structuring and use of the White House Office.

THE WHITE HOUSE OFFICE

THE PRESIDENT'S MEN. Members of the staff are chosen for their "ability to serve the president's needs, and to talk the president's language."[12] Within the **White House Office**

are the people who are in charge of the vital tasks of coordinating domestic policy, foreign policy, and national security matters; providing liaison with the Congress, executive agencies, and departments, and the political party; scheduling the president's appointments and travel; writing speeches; and handling relations with the press and other forms of media.

PRESIDENTIAL ORGANIZATIONAL STYLES. President Kennedy's staff was organized like a wheel whose hub was the President. The Kennedy approach stressed close personal contact between the President and his staff; moreover, their roles were very fluid, combining fixed and general-purpose responsibilities. A major task of the Kennedy team was to serve as critics of the rest of the bureaucracy and to monitor departmental proposals in terms of their political and policy validity.[13]

Presidents Truman, Eisenhower, Johnson, and Nixon all adopted a more formal style, with themselves at the top of a pyramid and with the emphasis on procedure, order, and analysis rather than on compromise evolving out of conflicting views. Under Eisenhower, the White House staff had clearly defined areas of responsibility. All domestic matters had to be cleared through his chief of staff, Sherman Adams, who left the administration because of a scandal involving the acceptance of gifts from an industrialist for whom he had intervened before two federal agencies. There was no single gatekeeper of equivalent power in either the Truman or Johnson administrations, although information or individuals had to get past two or three powerful assistants before reaching Johnson. Like Roosevelt, Johnson used advisers outside the government, and he placed greater reliance upon the departments and their heads than did either Roosevelt or Kennedy. His personal staff was not as influential in developing policy as was Kennedy's. He preferred to employ them to ensure that the executive branch would work within the policy consensus that the president expected his staff to help develop in the bureaus, departments, agencies, etc.

NIXON'S CLOSED SHOP. President Nixon began his first term by attempting to avoid the Eisenhower and Johnson approach of having one or two people regulate the flow of information and the access of people to his office. By 1970, however, Nixon's desire for order and the privacy to work and think alone led him to put an end to his "open" administra-

Henry Kissinger (right) served President Nixon as National Security Affairs Adviser, where he overshadowed the Secretary of State in foreign policy influence. He later became Secretary of State.

H.R. Haldeman's comments suggest the danger of protecting the president from a wide variety of contacts. When opinions are given secondhand, the views naturally take on a different character because they are affected by the biases of the transmitter.

Ehrlichman, Kissinger, and I do our best to make sure all points of view are placed before the President. But we do act as a screen, because there is a real danger of some advocate of an idea rushing in to the President and actually managing to convince him in a burst of emotion or argument.

H.R. HALDEMAN

Source: Quoted in Allen Drury, *Courage and Hesitation* (Garden City, NY: Doubleday, 1971), p. 128.

tion and H.R. (Bob) Haldeman, a former advertising executive and part of the Nixon campaign team, became the chief gatekeeper and the most powerful man in the administration. He decided who would and would not see the president, and some called him the "abominable no-man." John D. Ehrlichman, the assistant for domestic affairs, and Henry Kissinger, National Security Affairs Adviser, were to serve as funnels, but not barriers, through which information and advice on domestic and foreign matters would flow. But it became clear that the funnels were acting more like the Berlin Wall, and Haldeman and Ehrlichman, in particular, isolated the president. When their involvement in Watergate forced their resignations in April 1973, the change in personnel did not open up the administration; it became more introverted as the scandal deepened. On January 1, 1975, Haldeman and Ehrlichman were convicted of perjury and obstructing justice and were sentenced to two-and-a-half to eight years in prison.[14]

In testimony before the House Judiciary Committee's impeachment proceedings, Alexander P. Butterfield, Nixon's chief of administration from 1969 to 1973, said that Haldeman was known in the White House as "the other President."[15] Butterfield drew up a schedule of a typical day for Nixon, and it revealed that of the approximately four hours a day the President spent with his White House staff, Haldeman was with him at least 53 percent of the time. Only three other staff members saw the President frequently, Ehrlichman (10%), Kissinger (10%), and Press Secretary Ronald Ziegler (5%).[16] An inner circle within the White House Office had the President's ear, controlled access to him, and made policy rather than coordinated the efforts of the executive departments. And, these key people were not publicly accountable.

FORD AND CARTER. President Ford kept about half the White House aides he inherited from his predecessor, but within six months it was clear that he had shifted 180 degrees from the highly centralized and tightly controlled system that Nixon employed. Although the structure remained formalistic, there was no equivalent gatekeeper(s); Cabinet members were more visible and vocal; and President

Ford encouraged a fairly open policy of access to the oval office. His style was to make his own contacts and talk every day to scores of people throughout the government. But, there was no reduction in the size of the bureaucracy surrounding the chief executive.

Not counting the national security adviser, Zbigniew Brzezinski, six of the seven top presidential assistants in Carter's White House (1977–1978) Office were young Georgians who had served him during his gubernatorial days and during the presidential campaign. Only one, Stuart M. Eizenstat, assistant for domestic affairs, had prior Washington experience. Like his predecessor, Carter surrounded himself with loyal, familiar people, but their inexperience, particularly in congressional relations, handicapped the administration.

As for style, Carter's approach was reminiscent of the Kennedy years, with the President at the hub of a wheel. There was no intention to have a "gatekeeper" or "no-man," and Carter attempted to keep personally involved in a wide range of activities. However, observers outside the White House, and some people in the inside, were critical of Carter's loosely structured staff organization, claiming that the President needed a chief of staff to protect him from too complete an immersion in details and to allow for better use of his time.

PROBLEMS OF AN "OPEN" ADMINISTRATION. In addition to the problem of organizing his time, Carter found that Cabinet members, people within the White House Office, and other officials were making public statements that often were contradictory and created the impression that confusion was the chief characteristic of the administration. Carter reorganized his staff and laid down the law at a Camp David, Maryland, meeting in April 1978. The key moves were to appoint Gerald Rafshoon as presidential assistant for communications and to make Hamilton Jordan his unofficial chief of staff, a title that became official after the Cabinet purge of 1979. Although born in New York and educated in Texas, Rafshoon had been an adviser to Carter since his first try for the Georgia governorship in 1966, and he ran a public relations firm in Atlanta. Rafshoon's job was to make sure that the administration spoke with one clear, authoritative voice and that the message was communicated to the people.

Rafshoon's appointment took some of the burdens off Jody Powell, the press secretary. And Tim Kraft, of New Mexico, became Jordan's assistant with the title of Assistant to the President for Political Affairs. This allowed Jordan to concentrate on his role as general adviser and political strategist, while Kraft handled political patronage and relations with the Democratic National Committee and state party leaders. In June 1980, Jordan took over the re-election campaign, and Jack Watson became chief of staff.

Carter had come to the overdue realization that he could not ignore politics and expect loyalty. He had let the Cabinet members appoint people that they wanted. When Kraft came in, his job was to fill top-level federal posts with people loyal to Jimmy Carter.

REAGAN'S WHITE HOUSE OFFICE. Unlike Carter's staff, Reagan's top nine appointees to the White House Office—eight men and one woman—were a blend of individuals with previous Washington experience (5) or whose ties with the President involved his campaigns and/or political service in his California administration (3). Interestingly, his chief of staff, James A. Baker III, a Texas lawyer, had been the campaign chairman for George Bush, Reagan's main rival for the nomination. All were in their forties or fifties, in contrast to the more youthful people from Georgia.

The composition of the Reagan staff indicated that the President placed more of a premium on experience and managerial skill, and less on surrounding himself with close

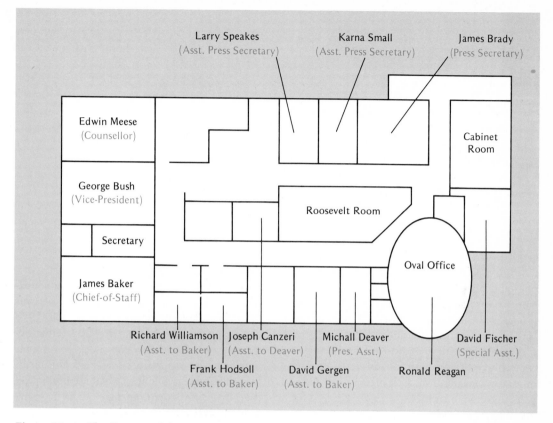

Figure 13–4 *The Reagan advisers.*

associates from the past. In contrast to Carter's appointee responsible for legislative affairs, Reagan's man, Max L. Friedersdorf, had been on the congressional liaison staff in the Nixon and Ford administrations.

The three advisers closest to the President were Baker, and two long time associates, Presidential Counsellor Edwin Meese and Presidential Assistant Michael Deaver. The general nature of their titles accurately reflected the fact that they advised the chief executive on a full range of domestic, foreign, and political strategy issues.

CONGRESSIONAL RELATIONS

An important subunit within the White House Office is the team of people re-sponsible for legislative liaison headed by the director of congressional relations. This staff is supposed to keep the president's finger on the pulse of the Congress (particularly the leadership of his own party), coordinate consultative efforts as the president formulates policy, and lobby for the passage of proposals once they have been placed in the hands of Congress.

In addition, each Cabinet department has a congressional relations staff, and the director attempts to coordinate their efforts.

PEOPLE EQUAL POLICY. What people the president places in what positions, how he uses the units of his staff, and who has his ear play a major role in determining political outcomes—who wins and who loses. Carter's re-

This quote from a prominent Republican legislator suggests that
Richard Nixon's problems with Congress stemmed from his attitude as
well as from the fact that he was a minority president.

*Nixon didn't like politicians, and that included congressmen. The result was
that these (congressional relations) people became second-class citizens
as far as the White House staff was concerned. Because they handled
dirty goods and had dirty hands, they were so treated.*

Rep. BARBER B. CONABLE, JR. (R., N.Y.)

Source: Congressional Quarterly, *Weekly Report* 33 (February 1, 1975), p. 226.

lationship with Congress was a very fragile one, and his critics claimed that he, and Director of Congressional Relations Frank Moore, who had no Capitol Hill experience, lacked a fundamental understanding of how to get along with Congress. The President came under attack both for failure to engage in steady consultation with members of Congress and failure to lobby strongly enough for his policies.

It is difficult to place the blame at a particular doorstep. Most of Moore's assistants, and those at the head of the departmental teams, had prior congressional staff experience, and we do not know if Moore listened to his people or if Carter listened to Moore or Vice-President Mondale who, as a twelve-year Senate veteran, assisted in congressional liaison. But the record of frustration included conflicts over the water projects, the B-1 bomber's development, energy, and a number of nominations that were not cleared with the appropriate legislators, to mention just a few examples. Effective legislative liaison should have been able to prevent many of Carter's conflicts with Congress.

Following the April 1978 shake up of the White House staff, there were indications that Carter and his legislative liaison team were learning more about how to play the game of dealing with Congress. Carter engaged in more extensive meetings and socializing with congressional leaders; there was more presidential involvement in the 1978 congressional campaigns than had been anticipated; and announcements of appointments or new programs were being made by members of Congress wishing to claim credit rather than from the federal agencies, who have no political IOUs outstanding against the administration. However, Carter's congressional relations never quite recovered from their rocky beginnings.

Clearly, the administration's generally poor record of dealing with Congress changed the odds on the President's ability to win legislative victories. Failure not only hurt his standing and future chances, but affected the people and agencies dependent upon presidential support. When the president wins, they win, when he loses, they lose.

In contrast, Reagan's legislative liaison team, headed by Max Friedersdorf, immediately earned the reputation of smooth professionals. They had the ability to sense when the mood of Congress required compromise, and they could identify the people with whom agreement could be reached. The staff paid close attention to details in the belief that if they took care of the little things—like arranging for personal thank-you notes from the President for legislators' support of a bill, securing an appointment favored by an important senator, or promptly returning phone calls—the big things will take care of themselves.

As we mentioned in Chapter 12, Friedersdorf and his aides received a large share of the credit for the Reagan budget victory, particularly on the House side where Democratic defections provided the margin of victory.

In recent years, from eleven to sixteen other councils or offices have made up the Executive Office of the President. A description of its major, and usually ongoing, components follows.

THE OFFICE OF MANAGEMENT AND BUDGET

The **Office of Management and Budget** (OMB) is the "president's agency," his major tool for attempting to plan and program the overall activities of the government and exercise some control over expenditures. The Bureau of the Budget was created by the Budget and Accounting Act of 1921, and in 1970 it was renamed the Office of Management and Budget and given an expanded role. Unlike the staffs of most of the components of the Executive Office, the bulk of the personnel of the OMB are permanent professionals who develop areas of expertise concerning the operations and budgetary needs of each of the components within the executive branch. Many of the staff have served under a number of administrations, but they are loyal to the values and responsive to the directives of each occupant of the White House. In recognition of the importance of the OMB, Congress enacted a bill in 1973 making the director and deputy director subject to senatorial confirmation.

A PRESIDENT'S RIGHT ARM. The main role of the OMB is to prepare the budget for the president to submit to the Congress. A budget represents more than the allocation of dollars; it is a statement of the nation's priorities and national purposes as envisioned by the president. The document submitted to Congress represents the OMB's attempt to reconcile the ideas and aspirations of agencies, bureaus, and departments, all of whom are competing for the limited resources available, and place them within the context of the president's program.[17] Agency heads may appeal the director's decisions concerning their requests for appropriations; however, the director has direct access to the president and is one of the chief executive's advisers on economic policy. In a real sense, the OMB decides how much should be spent on each program. Congressional action may result in different figures, but the president, on the advice of the OMB, can attempt to impound funds the Congress appropriates.

In 1981, the public became more aware of the OMB when thirty-four-year-old former Michigan congressman, David A. Stockman, was appointed as the director. Stockman, an advocate of massive federal budget reductions, was the key administration figure at congressional hearings on the Reagan budget.

BILL CLEARANCE. The OMB also serves as a central clearing house through which all bills drafted by departments and agencies are scrutinized to see if they fit into fiscal programs before they become a part of the president's legislative package. Bills passed by Congress are also reviewed by the OMB to determine whether or not they are within the bounds of the allocations made in the budget. Veto messages rejecting legislation for fiscal reasons are based on information provided by the OMB.

Along with the new name, the agency was given extensive management responsibilities, including monitoring the performance of

Cabinet officials and their departments and programs. This role includes the evaluation and coordination of federal programs, the development of new information and management systems, and the streamlining of the executive organization. As the president's principal managerial arm, OMB exercises a considerable power, and can be the most powerful agency of the presidential bureaucracy.

NATIONAL SECURITY COUNCIL

The **National Security Council** (NSC), created by the National Security Act of 1947, was a response to the United States' emergence as a world power. It has a top-level membership that includes the president, vice-president, and the secretaries of state and defense, and two advisers—the chairman of the Joint Chiefs of Staff and the Director of the Central Intelligence Agency. As its composition suggests, the NSC's fundamental purpose is to advise the president on national security matters and integrate and implement national security policy. Like other elements within the Executive Office, it is an extension of the president, and its organization and role have varied from administration to administration. It has largely replaced the Cabinet in matters of defense and foreign policy coordination.

The NSC was most prominent under Eisenhower, who put it at the top of a pyramid of agencies concerned with defense and security. President Kennedy rarely called the NSC, as such, into session. The NSC staff was placed under the special assistant for national security affairs, who, along with some of the

The National Security Council and other advisers were involved in President Nixon's decision to invade Cambodia.

NSC members, was a part of the informal group that Kennedy turned to for counsel. President Johnson made more frequent use of the NSC, but employed it more in the Kennedy, rather than the Eisenhower, fashion.

President Nixon referred to the NSC as "the principal forum for presidential consideration of foreign policy issues" and it met frequently.[18] Like the two previous incumbents, Nixon went beyond the NSC, consulting other White House aides before making controversial decisions, such as the invasion of Cambodia, which had serious domestic political implications. The NSC continued to play an important role in the Carter administration; however, Reagan indicated that he would reduce the role of the NSC, chaired by his National Security Adviser, Richard Allen.

DOMESTIC POLICY STAFF

In 1970 the Nixon administration felt the need to establish a domestic counterpart to the National Security Council. The Domestic Council's role was to evaluate domestic policy proposals from government agencies and develop its own recommendations for presidential consideration. The council was supported by a large staff whose first director was John Ehrlichman. Council members included the president, vice-president, the director of OMB, and all of the Cabinet members with the exception of the secretaries of defense and state.

President Ford continued the body, but Carter eliminated the council and retained the staff. Carter said that the old council was too large, had rarely functioned, its membership had been too diverse to make decisions efficiently, and its important functions had been performed by the staff. Under the Carter administration, the new **Domestic Policy Staff** was headed by his special assistant for domestic affairs. It was responsible for coordinating the making of domestic and most economic policy by working with Cabinet and agency heads to insure that their views are brought to the president before decisions are made. President Reagan gave early indications that the role of the Domestic Policy Staff would be reduced. But, his chief domestic adviser, Martie C. Anderson, was expected to play an important role.

COUNCIL OF ECONOMIC ADVISERS

The **Council of Economic Advisers** (CEA) was established by the Employment Act of 1946, which made the president responsible for overseeing the economy and giving to Congress an economic report shaped by the three-member council. Members are appointed by the president and subject to Senate confirmation. Walter W. Heller, President Kennedy's chairman of the council, said that "the unique function of Council . . . is to put at the president's disposal the best facts, appraisals, and forecasts that economic science, statistics, and surveys can produce."[19]

The CEA advises the president on such economically and politically significant matters as the government's use of wage and price controls, acceptable levels of unemployment, tax policy, and government spending as tools to control inflationary or recessionary trends. The council, unlike many other sources from which the president receives solicited or unsolicited economic advice, has no independent constituency. But the CEA operates in a political atmosphere and has been known to offer optimistic public predictions about the economy before elections when the statistics have suggested a less bright picture.

COUNCIL ON ENVIRONMENTAL QUALITY

In response to the growing awareness of environmental problems, the Nixon administration established the Council on Environ-

A president's policy to control inflation is likely to be influenced by the Council of Economic Advisers.

mental Quality (1970). The three-member council, appointed by the president and approved by the Senate, develops and recommends to the president national policies that promote environmental quality. It performs continuing analysis and assists in the preparation of the annual "Environmental Report." The actual carrying out of federal programs to control air and water pollution, solid waste disposal, and control of pesticides and radiation is the responsibility of the Environmental Protection Agency (1970). The problems of conflict and coordination between executive agencies operating in the same area was illustrated by the friction between the council, and its reduced environmental spending outlook,

and the EPA set up by Congress as an independent agency.

OTHER COMPONENTS OF THE EXECUTIVE OFFICE

Most of the remaining components of the Executive Office were created to coordinate activities in rather specialized areas such as wage and price stability, science and technology policy, and trade negotiations. Carter created a new entity, the Office of Administration, to provide administrative support services to the smaller units of the Executive Office. In the past, they depended on support received from the OMB and the White House Office, a system that the president viewed as inefficient. A number of these units may be short-lived, as the Executive Office changes with the incumbents and the particular priorities of the times. Carter eliminated five of the Executive Office units during his first year in office, including those that dealt with energy resources, drug abuse policy, federal property, telecommunications policy, and international economic policy.

The Executive Office is but one part of an advisory system that includes personnel of the thirteen line departments, the multitude of independent offices and establishments, and leaders of the Congress. All these people are part of this inside advisory network.

Each president uses his advisers differently. Nixon, for example, placed a very low priority on congressional liaison, a situation that Ford tried to remedy. Key groups are formed as situations require, and a look at a formal organization chart will not tell you who provides advice on what. The president may create a group drawn from the Executive Office of the President, Cabinet members, and people on loan from the agencies.

While the president can draw upon a tremendous talent pool within the government, he is free to seek advice from outside the official organs of government and to develop an outside advisory network.

The Outside Advisory Network

There is also an outside advisory network, composed of individuals, groups, and institutions, such as the Rand Corporation, not officially part of the national government. Its components are usually part-time and often temporary, called into existence to study a particular problem, such as President Nixon's Advisory Commission on the Creation of an All–Volunteer Army. Although every president has relied upon some individual non-governmental advisers, the growing number of task forces, advisory councils, commissions, conferences, and advisory corporations is a post–World War II phenomenon.[20] Some cynics claim that these bodies sometimes are created to give the appearance of action rather than to do anything substantive.

The United States Government Manual illustrates the size and breadth of the outside network in its listing of 120 selected boards, commissions, councils, and committees.[21] The listing includes only the major groups, and barely scratches the surface. When Carter took office he found approximately 1,300 advisory committees that had grown up in the shadows of federal agencies. While these committees are supposed to give citizens greater voice in helping to shape public policy, their more than 22,000 members provide little advice at the cost of many dollars, and Carter made major reductions in their number.

Most of the groups listed dealt with problems of a fairly permanent nature and were composed of people from outside the government; the list did not include the more temporary bodies, such as the Commission on the Creation of an All–Volunteer Army and other task forces, although these also are a part of the outside network. Examples drawn from the manual include the following: the National Academy of Science; the Advisory Commission on the Arts; the Council on Aging; and the Water Resources Council. The outside advisory network provides a valuable alternative to having most or all advice and information come from within the bureaucracy. Outside advisers may be more objective because they are unhindered by the vested interests that are a product of the institution in which the government official serves. But they are often understaffed, and the *ad hoc* bodies usually cease to exist after submitting their reports. The members are not in a position to influence the carrying out of their recommendations.

PROBLEMS OF OUTSIDE ADVICE. Presidents are occasionally embarrassed when a task force or commission focuses public attention on a problem and the chief executive is unwilling or unable to carry out its well-publicized recommendations. This was the case when the National Advisory Commission on the Causes and Prevention of Violence reported to President Nixon. It called for a reordering of national priorities to meet the grave internal threats facing the country that the report viewed as being more serious than any external dangers. The commission recognized that there were severe political problems in reordering priorities, particularly in view of the backlash among middle-class America, but concluded that "the majority of Americans have always responded constructively to national crises when they have been fully informed and responsibly led." In fact, the report challenged the president to lead; and it represented a fundamental difference of opinion with the President over how best to defend the country.[22] The report provided rallying points for the opponents and critics of administration policy. The Nixon administration was also less than happy with commission reports on pornography and "soft" drugs.

Like the inside network, the structure and employment of the outside network is a product of each chief executive's style. Despite the problems mentioned, recent incumbents have made extensive use of the system, and have often employed task forces operating behind the scenes whose reports can be considered carefully without the pressure of prior public announcement.

The Expanded Presidency: Control and Watergate

Writing in 1947, Edward S. Corwin warned that presidential power had become dangerously personal in two respects: first, leadership depends upon the accident of personality, against which the electoral system cannot guarantee safeguards; second, there is no governmental body with which the president is bound to consult that can be relied upon to give him independent advice. He advocated a new type of Cabinet, which he called a *joint legislative council,* composed of legislative leaders and department heads as the need arose. Corwin's remarks came ten years after the President's Committee on Administrative Management (the Brownlow Committee) had made the modest request that six administrative assistants be added to the president's staff, noting that more was needed than just secretarial help to coordinate the machinery of government. By 1957, Corwin noted approvingly that the expansion of the Executive Office of the President had probably reduced or removed the need for his original proposal.[23]

As early as 1960, Rexford Tugwell warned that the presidency had become more than any one man could handle, and he proposed that two incumbents were needed, one to make policy and one to handle administrative matters. He was also concerned that the president was being swallowed up by the bureaucracy.[24] While the proposal for a dual presidency has not received much attention, contemporary president-watchers are concerned that the presidential establishment has grown so large that the chief executive cannot exercise effective control over it.

A momentous task facing each occupant of the White House is to try to gain control of the existing bureaucracies. This goal is made more difficult by what appears to be the relentless growth of the executive branch and the development, by its units, of independent sources of support in Congress and among constituent groups (see Chapter 12).[25] The development of the Executive Office was envisioned as a means for the president to gain control of this "tiger."

Recent presidents, suspicious of the bureaucracies they have inherited and lacking confidence in them, have approached the task of control by creating new agencies or trans-

President Truman operated with a smaller staff than later presidents. But his successors have found that even a large staff does not relieve its chief executive of having to run a tight ship.

Within the first months I discovered that being a President is like riding a tiger. A man has to keep on riding or be swallowed. . . . A President is either constantly on top of events or . . . events will soon be on top of him. I never felt I could let up for a single moment.

HARRY S. TRUMAN

Source: *Memoirs of Harry Truman,* Vol. II (Garden City, NY: Doubleday, 1955), p. 1.

ferring more and more policy development and operational responsibilities into the Executive Office.[26] We can see this in the constantly shifting arrangements in the Executive Office as new problems take center stage and new councils or offices are established. While the job descriptions usually talk about "coordination" of policies and proposals coming up from the line departments and agencies, the reality is that policy formulation is the key role.

WHO CONTROLS WHOM? Ironically, there is considerable doubt about the ability of recent presidents to control or "manage" their own presidential establishment. Our presidents are usually trained and experienced politicians, but the only twentieth-century incumbents to come in with a background in political administration were Theodore and Franklin Roosevelt, Jimmy Carter and Ronald Reagan. And, as the presidential establishment expands, the lack of managerial skill is accentuated. Responsibility and authority are delegated to lieutenants, some of whom may be poor managers.

Howard McCurdy suggests that the record of the Nixon administration is, in part, a record of the success and failures of his aides as the president became isolated from the managerial function. He relied on Kissinger

for foreign affairs, John Ehrlichman to coordinate domestic matters, and John Mitchell and Charles Colson to run the 1972 campaign. And McCurdy calls Watergate "as much a consequence of the problems of managing the presidency as a question of misplaced morality."[27]

Mismanagement and the resultant lack of control may leave a president open to "Watergates." However, the record on Watergate made it clear that the chief executive sets the moral tone for those who serve him. This is particularly important in light of the fact that his subordinates, and those of other incumbents, tend to confuse the president with the presidency and his interests with the national interest. White House aides do not often do things they know their boss would not wish them to do.

Process and Policy: Winners and Losers

Presidents choose their own inner circle and adopt their own styles. The decision-making process developed by each occupant of the White House has a major impact on policy outcomes. The "open" or "closed" nature of the process will determine who has

Viewpoint:
Nixon's aides on the moral atmosphere
in the White House

These comments suggest that the president sets the tone for his staff. There is a real danger if the proposition, "What's good for the president, is good for the country," is accepted uncritically.

There was no independent sense of morality there. . . . If you worked for someone, he was God, and whatever the orders were, you did it. . . . It was all so narrow, so closed. . . . There emerged some kind of separate morality about things.

HUGH SLOAN

Because of a certain atmosphere that had developed in my working at the White House, I was not concerned about its illegality as I should have been.

JEB STUART MAGRUDER

The White House is another World. Expediency is everything.

JOHN DEAN

Source: Sloan quoted in *New York Times*, May 18, 1973, p. 20. Magruder quoted in *New York Times*, June 15, 1973, p. 18. Dean quoted in Mary McGrory, "A Talk with John Dean," *New York Post*, June 18, 1973.

access to the chief executive, what policies will receive consideration, and the eventual shape of the programs that the administration will support. Put differently, access and the receptivity of advisers to ideas often decides which groups win and lose in the struggle for government support of their objectives.

Obviously, an open system has advantages over a closed system, and the attitudes reflected by the key people around Nixon guaranteed that poverty and urban programs would be given a low priority. But the process had an orderliness to it. On the other hand, a very open process may be very time-consuming and create confusion. In either case, an intangible factor in any decision-making process is the amount of reliance a president places on particular advisers.

An insight into Carter's decision making was provided by the process used to formulate his urban program, announced in March 1978. The administration avoided the rush and the closed-door approach that led to problems with the energy package. An "urban policy group" was created and it undertook a year-long process that included bureaucratic struggles over policy turf, delays, false starts; on the positive side, it included massive involvement of numerous government agencies, the close evaluation of existing urban programs, and consultation with mayors, governors, legislators, and people on the delivery end of the programs.

Naturally, some of those consulted said that they were "told" what was planned rather than asked for their ideas. But the real flaw in the process may have been the delays that some attribute to Carter's lack of direct involvement until December, when he reportedly rejected the approach of giving him specific program choices to fund or not to fund. According to a number of aides, he wanted to decide what his urban policy was before approving particular programs. This meant that funding could not be included in his January budget message, and the decision led to a flurry of activity in order to meet congressional budget deadlines for fiscal year 1979.

Carter had forty-eight hours to decide on funding levels. Although administration sources denied it, he reportedly made massive cuts of billions of dollars and then restored many of the cuts only after last-minute persuasions from Stuart Eizenstat, assistant for domestic affairs, Vice-President Mondale, and political adviser Hamilton Jordan. The official version was that he made no cuts, but had asked for additional justifications before reaching his final decisions. "But by either account, the president in hours decided up or down on programs totaling billions of dollars and significantly altering the shape of his urban policy."[28]

The administration was pleased by the process, but many of the nation's mayors and leaders of urban minorities felt they were the "losers" because the program provided too little money to solve their problems.

★ Issue ★

Presidential Isolation

At the beginning of the chapter we called attention to George Reedy's view that decision making in the White House does not lend itself to step-by-step analysis. But there is general agreement that rational decision making involves acquiring knowledge, forming judgments, and executing decisions. Any factors that inhibit the president's getting the information necessary to make a well reasoned decision "isolate" him and can pose a threat to the nation, and perhaps the world. If this sounds a bit dramatic, we should remember that some decisions can be explained partly in terms of the president's being isolated from certain types of information and from political reality. These include the Bay of Pigs invasion in 1961, various aspects of our Southeast Asian Policy from the Eisenhower through the Nixon administrations, and Nixon's failure to anticipate or understand the reaction of segments of the public to the invasion of Cambodia in 1970.

WHY ARE PRESIDENTS ISOLATED?

Unfortunately, the benefits that may come from interacting with the people are largely denied to our presidents because of the extensive security precautions that surround their every public appearance. The assassination of President Kennedy, the generally tense atmosphere of the late sixties and early seventies, the two attempts on President Ford's life, and the wounding of President Reagan, have necessitated this form of isolation and increased the importance of the role of the presidential staff as the supposed conveyor of a wide range of ideas and attitudes.

Surrounded as he is by a large staff, and with his every action analyzed, supported, or criticized by the press, how can the president be isolated, and is there anything about the nature of the office that makes a president more susceptible to isolation than other politicians?

In *The Twilight of the Presidency,* Reedy argues that we have surrounded our chief executive with a large staff to serve his every need, and he is provided with private jets, helicopters, special automobiles, multiple residences, private entertainment facilities, etc., etc. There has been built into the presidency devices to remove the occupant of the oval office "from all of the forces which require most men to rub up against the harsh facts of life on a daily basis." The modern presidency has "taken on all the regalia of a monarchy except ermine robes, a scepter, and a crown."[29]

Added to the trappings of royalty is an atmosphere of deference in which the president works; this has been reinforced by a past tendency on the part of the public to assume that he and his staff have some special knowledge. For its part, the staff tends to identify "the prince" with "the state," or as H.R. Haldeman put it in an interview shown on CBS on March 23, 1975, he did not make a distinction between the president and the presidency. Clearly, a president can be seduced into viewing himself as something more than mortal.

Most other writers have not stressed the "trappings of royalty" thesis set forth by Reedy, but they have joined him in focussing upon the size, attitudes, and roles of presidential staff, particularly the White House Office, as the main sources of the problem of isolation.[30] The size factor, already discussed, makes it difficult for the president to stay on top of the workings of his people, and with size has come the tendency to rely on the Executive Office to provide the advice that traditionally came from the executive departments and agencies. The occupants of the White House have become isolated from the departments and more dependent on their own presidential establishment.

The question of attitude is more complex. Reedy, whose experience was with the Johnson administration, compares the White House Office with the seventeenth- and eighteenth-century courts of Western Europe noted for palace intrigue and continual struggles among advisers to have the King's, or Queen's, ear. He maintains that the goal of most staff members is to gain and maintain access to the president and enhance their own power or place in the pecking order by being the bearers of good news, rather than bad, or by telling their leader what they think he wants to hear.[31] Reedy's typical "court jester" shows little concern for objectivity. And in their book, *The Palace Guard,* Dan Rather and Gary Paul Gates suggest that Nixon's closest advisers chose to isolate him from reality either in an effort to build their own empires or out of mistaken loyalty.

LOYALTY. Mistaken or otherwise, loyalty appears a key element. In a special supplement to *The Living Presidency,* Emmet John Hughes presents the views of twelve men who worked intimately with one or more of the presidents from Franklin Roosevelt to and including Richard Nixon. All of them were agreed that a White House adviser should be completely loyal to his boss while at the same time trying to provide him with every important and essential shred of information on which a decision is to be based. But, Hughes was forced to conclude from his study that "the presidential staff has been prone to be, almost inevitably, less concerned with presidential conscience than with presidential comfort."[32]

Isolation may not be the result of either mistaken loyalty or less than honorable motives on the part of the staff. In *The Best and the Brightest,* David Halberstam describes the collection of the dynamic and talented people who served John Kennedy, and stayed in the Johnson administration in key positions of influence on foreign policy. Their

Perhaps because of their unquestioned loyalty, the president's family often serves as unofficial advisers: (Left) Nancy Reagan whispers a comment to her husband; (right) Amy Carter with her father.

isolation of the president was, in Halberstam's view, the product of their own self-deception.

. . . they had, for all their brilliance and hubris and sense of themselves, been unwilling to look to and learn from the past and they had been swept forward by their belief in the importance of anti-communism . . . and by the sense of power and glory . . . of America in this century. They were America, and they had been ready for what the world offered, the challenges posed.[33]

These were men of some differing views but who Halberstam said were not honest with themselves. They admired strength and toughness, and wanted to appear to have these qualities as they played their roles. And these were qualities admired by Kennedy and Johnson.

Because of combinations of factors that have varied from administration to adminis-

tration, presidents since F.D.R. have been isolated to varying degrees by their staffs. In the case of Gerald Ford, his time in office did not see the development of a Haldeman-like gatekeeper. Instead, it was an "open" administration, and Ford held periodic meetings with old friends whose role was to give him blunt advice and criticism about his policies and programs. His relations with Congress were friendly, if unproductive, and he took steps to move away from the image of the imperial presidency.

But the histories of past administrations provide many examples of presidents being told that their critics in the press or in other political positions were wrong, or instances of advisers who had serious reservations about going along with the series of "yes" responses to presidential questions that made it clear where the thinking of the boss was at that particular moment.

The staff of the White House thus has managed to be something of a paradox itself, alongside all other paradoxes of the presidency. Where it should be utterly invaluable, it may be nearly insidious. When it should make a president frown, it may prefer to make him laugh. And while its essential role is to keep a president awake and alert, the easier course, always, is to let him drowse.[34]

HOW CAN ISOLATION BE FOUGHT?

To fight isolation, the individual in the White House must keep both the gates and his mind open. The president sets the tone and the expectations for his staff, and students of the presidency are inclined to favor Roosevelt's "competitive" managerial style as the one best suited to overcoming the tendency toward isolation. Beyond that, they call for a reduction in the size of the presidential bureaucracy, a return to greater reliance on the executive departments and agencies and the Cabinet, and increased interaction with congressional leaders of both parties. Finally, George Reedy warns that the presidency must be made human again. "Somehow we must learn to govern our people from an office that is secular and not from a court that is sanctified."[35]

The first year of the Carter presidency placed a heavy emphasis on symbolic actions to demonstrate the abandonment of the pomp and ceremony of the office and the incumbent's intentions to stay close to the people (see Chapter 12). His intentions for his Cabinet, the vice-president, and the White House staff also pointed in the direction of an "open-minded" chief executive. But, as we pointed out earlier, openness can be carried too far, and in April 1978, Carter was forced to make changes that sacrificed some freedom of expression for administrative officials in an effort to achieve more coherence and coordination.

Whatever the staff arrangement may be, a president's own attitudes are a key element in decision-making. Carter indicated that he had some very set ideas and that he would move in certain areas—the international human rights issue for example—in spite of expert advice. And Carter exhibited a form of isolation when he made decisions and statements that took his staff, and friends and foes alike, by surprise. He resisted advice in handling the Lance case; his call for a homeland for the Palestinians was not checked out with the State Department, the Arabs, or the Israelis; and his energy and welfare programs were presented before an evaluation of congressional opposition was made.

Finally, staff is useful only if it is used and actions are not taken before the deliberative process can take place. An example of what appeared to be hasty action and an intolerance to opposition occurred in January 1979 and seriously strained relations between Carter and women's organizations.

There were indications that women's issues were not high in the administration's priorities when Midge Costanza, the Assistant for Special Interest Groups Relations, resigned in 1978. She had run into difficulties with the White House regarding her public opposition to some administration policies. She was replaced by Sarah Weddington, a Texan with Washington experience, who maintained a very low profile. But confrontation did not come until the first meeting of the President's National Advisory Committee for Women, a brainchild of Ms. Costanza that was created in 1977.

The first meeting of the group was scheduled for November 1978, but was cancelled because the president had allotted only fifteen minutes of his time for them. Before the January meeting, some members of the committee prepared a press release critical of Carter's austerity budget. Carter was angry and used the January meeting to tell the women that he sensed more confrontation than counsel among them. Bella Abzug, the outspoken former congresswoman from New York, replied hotly that the role of the committee was to register its views, not to serve as a rubber stamp for the administration. A few minutes later, Mrs. Abzug was called into Jordan's office and "fired." The general message appeared to be that public shows of dissatisfaction with Carter's policies, whether by administration officials or parts of the outside advisory network, would not be tolerated.

Within forty-eight hours of the dismissal of Mrs. Abzug, more than half of the forty-member committee had resigned in protest. Those who left included leaders of such major groups as the League of Women Voters, National Organization of Women, Democratic National Committee's Women's Caucus, American Indian Women's Caucus, Asian and Pacific Minority Women's Caucus, and the National Women's Political Caucus. They,

and the others, experienced disillusionment and a suspicion that women's issues were going to be ignored; they suggested that Carter could not take their support for granted in 1980. Gloria Steinem, a leading feminist, said:

It was such a politically dumb thing. The Committee was supposed to be a bridge to the Administration for women. Nothing was going over the bridge—and now Carter has burned it.[36]

We have used this incident as an example of isolation caused by having the gates of the mind closed. If a president isolates himself or allows himself to be isolated by his staff, he loses. But more important, if isolation hinders his ability to deal with our major ills, then we all lose.

History may record that one product of Richard Nixon's presidency was the subsequent de-sanctification of the Office and its staff. But this will not guarantee the "openness" of future administrations.

Summary

The expanded presidency provides the occupant of the White House with a large staff to assist him in decision making by providing information and policy alternatives, providing a mechanism for better management of the government, and making the arrangements for his daily schedule to allow for efficient allocation of his time. The quality of his advisers and the advice they give are key elements in determining which programs "win or lose" support and which elements in the society become "winners" or "losers."

The decision-making process itself and the use of staff defy any attempt at systematic explanation. They vary from president to president and situation to situation, and usually represent a choice of alternatives, none of which is the only "logical" choice. The presidency is a clear example of the impact of personality on politics: the individual shapes and is shaped by the office.

The vice-presidency and the Cabinet historically have not been major sources of influence on the chief executives, and their usefulness has depended upon the role that each president has assigned to them. Since 1947, presidents have been served by an ever-enlarging Executive Office, and most of the president's key advisers have been assigned to positions in the White House Office where they serve no other constituents.

Each incumbent has shaped the Executive Office to suit his own needs and managerial style, and there is evidence that the staff has become more a substitute for than a managerial tool to control and coordinate the executive departments and agencies. While there is no disagreement over the need for an expanded staff to help the president cope with his expanded responsibilities, the size of his personal bureaucracy has reached the point where it creates a problem of control for the man it serves. In addition, if the presidential bureaucracy is composed of too many people who think alike, and if it concerns itself too much with protecting the president from divergent opinions, it can do a disservice to the man and the nation by isolating the chief executive.

Terms to Remember

See the Glossary at the end of the book for definitions.

Bureaucracy

Cabinet

Council of Economic Advisers

Domestic Policy Staff

Executive Office of the President

National Security Council

Office of Management and Budget

Permanent government

Presidential bureaucracy

White House Office

Notes

1. Quoted in Theodore Sorenson, *Decision Making in the White House* (New York: Columbia University Press, 1963), pp. xi–xii.

2. Emmet John Hughes, *The Living Presidency* (New York: Coward, McCann & Geoghegan, 1973), p. 135. Chapter 5, "The Gates of the White House," provides an interesting analysis of decision making. Also see George E. Reedy, *The Twilight of the Presidency* (New York: The World Book Publishing Co., 1972), pp. 30–32.

3. Reedy, *The Twilight of the Presidency,* p. 26.

4. Quoted in Leonard White, *The Jacksonians: A Study in Administrative History, 1829–1861* (New York: Macmillan, 1954), p. 83.

5. Donald Young, *American Roulette: The History and Dilemma of the Vice Presidency* (New York: Holt, Rinehart and Winston, 1965), p. 5.

6. Hughes, *The Living Presidency,* p. 149.

7. Richard F. Fenno, Jr., *The President's Cabinet* (Cambridge: Harvard University Press, 1959), p. 5.

8. "Conversation between President Kennedy and NBC Correspondent Ray Scherer," broadcast on NBC–TV, April 11, 1961, Stenographic Transcript, p. 17.

9. Quoted by James Reston, *New York Times,* December 20, 1968, p. 46.

10. Howard E. McCurdy, "The Physical Manifestations of an Expanding Presidency," paper prepared for delivery at the 1974 Annual Meeting of the American Political Science Association, Chicago, Ill., August 29–September 2, 1974, p. 32.

11. *The Public Interest,* 9 (Fall 1967), pp. 28–48.

12. Sorenson, *Decision Making in the White House,* pp. 70–71.

13. Richard T. Johnson, *Managing the White House* (New York: Harper & Row, 1974).

14. John N. Mitchell, former attorney general and head of the 1972 Nixon re-election campaign, was convicted of the same crimes and received an identical sentence.

15. "Testimony of Alexander P. Butterfield," U.S. Congress House Committee on the Judiciary, *Testimony of Witnesses: Book I,* 93rd Congress, 2d Session, July 2, 1974, p. 66.

16. McCurdy, "The Physical Manifestations of an Expanding Presidency," pp. 14–15. McCurdy's figures are taken from the Butterfield testimony (see note 15).

17. See Aaron Wildavsky, *The Politics of the Budgetary Process* (Boston: Little, Brown, 1974). Also see Richard E. Neustadt, "Presidency and

Legislation: The Growth of Central Clearance," *American Political Science Review,* 48 (1954), pp. 64–72.

18. "State of the World" message, *New York Times,* February 19, 1970, pp. 17–25.

19. *New Dimensions of Political Economy* (Cambridge: Harvard University Press, 1966), p. 16.

20. Thomas E. Cronin and Sandford D. Greenberg, eds., *The Presidential Advisory System* (New York: Harper & Row, 1969), pp. 69–90.

21. *The United States Government Manual* (Washington, D.C.: U.S. Government Printing Office, 1976), pp. 657–663.

22. See the *Walker Report to the National Advisory Commission on the Causes and Prevention of Violence* (New York: Bantam Books, 1968). For highlights, see *New York Times,* December 13, 1969, pp. 1, 22.

23. Edward S. Corwin, *The President: Office and Powers,* 3rd ed. (New York: New York University Press, 1948), pp. 361–363, 372–373. His later remarks were contained in the 4th edition (1957). See pp. 312–313.

24. Rexford Tugwell, *The Enlargement of the Presidency* (New York: Doubleday, 1960).

25. Hughes, *The Living Presidency,* pp. 181–190.

26. Thomas E. Cronin, "President as Chief Executive," in Rexford Tugwell and Thomas E.

Cronin, eds., *The Presidency Reappraised* (New York: Praeger Publishers, 1974), pp. 234–265.

27. McCurdy, "The Physical Manifestations of an Expanding Presidency," p. 31.

28. For a review of the process, see Congressional Quarterly, *Weekly Report,* 36 (April 1, 1978), pp. 779–786.

29. Ibid., pp. 4, 9.

30. See Hughes, *The Living Presidency;* Arthur M. Schlesinger, Jr., *The Imperial Presidency,* (Boston: Houghton Mifflin, 1973); David Halberstam, *The Best and the Brightest* (New York: Random House, 1969); and Dan Rather and Gary Paul Gates, *The Palace Guard* (New York: Harper & Row, 1974).

31. Reedy, *The Twilight of the Presidency,* p. 88.

32. Hughes, *The Living Presidency,* p. 143.

33. Halberstam, *The Best and the Brightest,* p. 796. *Hubris* is insolence stemming from excessive pride.

34. Hughes, *The Living Presidency,* p. 145. Reprinted by permission of Coward, McCann & Geoghegan, Inc. Copyright © 1973 by Emmet John Hughes.

35. Reedy, *The Twilight of the Presidency,* p. 197.

36. Quoted in *Newsweek,* January 22, 1979, p. 27.

Suggested Readings

Thomas E. Cronin and Sandford D. Greenberg, eds., *The Presidential Advisory System* (New York: Harper & Row, 1969).

Richard F. Fenno, Jr., *The President's Cabinet* (Cambridge: Harvard University Press, 1959).

David Halberstam, *The Best and the Brightest* (New York: Random House, 1969).

Emmet John Hughes, *The Living Presidency* (New York: Coward, McCann & Geoghegan, 1973).

Richard T. Johnson, *Managing the White House* (New York: Harper & Row, 1974).

Dan Rather and Gary Paul Gates, *The Palace Guard* (New York: Harper & Row, 1974).

George E. Reedy, *The Twilight of the Presidency* (New York: The World Book Publishing Co., 1972).

Arthur M. Schlesinger, Jr., *The Imperial Presidency* (Boston: Houghton Mifflin, 1973).

Theodore Sorenson, *Decision-Making in the White House* (New York: Columbia University Press, 1963).

Donald Young, *American Roulette: The History and Dilemma of the Vice Presidency* (New York: Holt, Rinehart and Winston, 1965).

CHAPTER 14

The Permanent Government

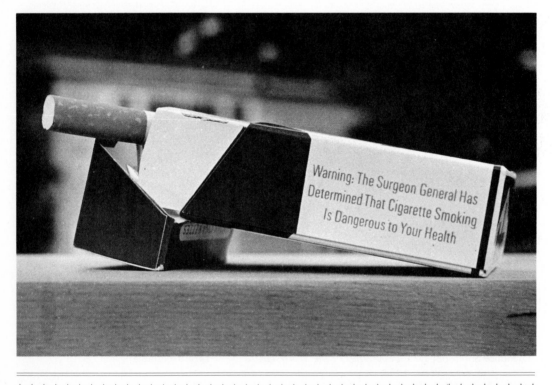

★ ★

[The federal bureaucracy] is not an orderly hierarchy with the President on top, but rather a complex and confusing collection of organizations supervised more or less closely with more or less success by successive Presidents.

JOHN W. DAVIS, JR.
The National Executive Branch

During the presidential campaign of 1976, President Gerald Ford and his challenger, Jimmy Carter, found a common villain to campaign against—the federal bureaucracy—a tactic also employed by Ronald Reagan in 1980. Carter boasted about reforms he made while governor of Georgia (1971–1974) and said that reorganization of the federal bureaucracy was one of his top priorities. He hoped to reduce the number of federal agencies from 1,900 to 200. Carter's press secretary admitted later that the figure 200 "seemed like a good number at the time." But, recommending changes in governmental structure is one thing; enacting them into law is quite another. Politicians, bureaucrats, journalists, and students of the political process raised their eyebrows and wondered if Carter wasn't a Don Quixote who would tilt in vain with the Washington windmills.

As we said in our discussion of the president as chief administrator, the chief executive inherits the bulk of the people in his executive branch as well as the existing structure. It is this inherited bureaucracy that sees presidents come and go; it comprises the civil servants who make up all but the tip of the bureaucratic iceberg. We call it the **permanent government,** distinguishing it from the **presidential bureaucracy** discussed in the previous chapter. And this permanent government, their clientele, and members of Congress can constitute a triple alliance that has vested interests in preventing radical change. An example of a **triple alliance** would be the Department of Agriculture, agricultural groups, legislators on the committees that handle the legislation dealing with agriculture, and other members of Congress with active agricultural groups in their districts.

At the end of this chapter we will return to the issue of reforming the bureaucracy

★ ★

and ask the question, can reform work? President Carter made some progress in restructuring the bureaucracy, but we can't resist including a quotation from the controversial columnist, Jack Anderson. He said:

Now out of the peanut pastures of southern Georgia, Carter is coming to Washington to reform the bureaucracy. He will find a vast civilian-suited army, soldiers of the swivel chair, bombarding one another with memos in septuplicate. At the end of each day, an estimated 100 tons of waste paper are picked up off the battlefield.[1]

(© 1976 United Feature Syndicate, Inc.)

A number of other important questions are raised in this chapter. How important is the bureaucracy in national politics? How are bureaucrats recruited, and does the merit system work? Can the president or Congress "control" the bureaucracy? Conversely, what restraints does the bureaucracy impose on the other branches of government? Does the bureaucracy often determine who wins and who loses?

The Rise of Bureaucracy

The words *bureaucracy* and *administration* often are used interchangeably, and we are using **bureaucracy** and **bureaucrats** to refer to the agencies of the executive branch of the federal government and the personnel who administer the government's programs and enforce the laws. Unfortunately, we often associate the terms with red tape, duplication of effort, and bungling, forgetting that all large organizations—governmental or private—are bureaucracies that share certain characteristics. These common traits are a division of labor along lines of specialized activities, fixed lines of command (hierarchy), and full-time career-oriented employees. An important product of these characteristics, particularly specialization, is the development of technical

expertise. It is this expertise which is the foundation of bureaucratic power in modern governments.

THE POWER OF EXPERTISE. The classic concept of bureaucracy was developed by the German sociologist Max Weber, who argued that political rulers cannot argue with the technical knowledge of the trained bureaucrat. "The absolute monarch is powerless opposite the superior knowledge of the bureaucratic expert."[2] While the president, Congress, and the courts have various means of exercising control over the bureaucracy—sometimes effective and sometimes not—they have neither the expertise nor the time to deal with the complexities of the issues facing the nation or the day-to-day implementation of government policies. Congress, as we have seen in previous chapters, can identify problems and pass broadly written legislation, but it must leave it to the experts in the departments and agencies to fill in the details and carry out the policies in accordance with the intent of the legislature. Programs passed by Congress and endorsed by the president represent good intentions that bureaucrats are supposed to turn into reality.

The growth of the permanent government has reflected the modern-day involvement of government in almost every facet of the nation's economic and social life, and non-elected officials make decisions that have great impact on the lives of the people concerned.

Most of us are directly affected by the Postal Service and the Internal Revenue Service, while different groups of people are concerned with the distribution of food stamps, the prompt receipt of Social Security benefits, the enforcement of laws supporting racial equality, or price-support payments for farmers. Less obvious, but also very important, are programs designed to guarantee a certain level of education and medical research, and attempts to guarantee a "clean" environment,

Price supports for farmers and selected industries are policies carried out by executive branch bureaucracies.

etc. Very few people realize how extensively their lives are governed by Washington.

POLITICS AND ADMINISTRATION. Finally, the classic theories of public administration suggest that "politics and administration are distinct" and that "politics in any 'bad' sense ought not to intrude upon administration."[3] This assumption was never valid, and today's students of government acknowledge that bureaucratic decisions involve political choices, who wins and who loses, and that effective bureaucrats build political alliances within the bureaucracy, with legislators, and with the groups in society that are affected by their jurisdiction. We will discuss the politics of bureaucratic decision-making later in the chapter.

Criticism of the Bureaucracy: The Price of Visibility

If all bureaucracies have common organizational characteristics, why is it that the government bureaucracies come in for so much criticism? Part of the answer is that government programs, such as the ones just mentioned, are very visible to the public. And we are used to judging efficiency in the private sector on a profit-and-loss basis. But few government services are sold in the market and there is usually no direct relationship between the income a government bureau receives and the services it provides. The separation of income from expenditures means that the bureaucrats employ yardsticks for decision-making different from those used in the private sector, and this leaves them more vulnerable to the charge of wasteful spending.[4]

The mistakes of government bureaucrats are also more obvious than their successes, and are called to our attention by the media. Interest groups opposed to certain actions use the media to point out the foibles and failings of the bureaucracy. Environmentalists criticize the Environmental Protection Agency for failure to enforce clean-air standards, while the automobile industry attacks the EPA for its attempt to force the car-makers to produce cleaner burning engines. And Detroit tells us that they will have to pass the costs on to us. Some groups use criticism as a tactic to obtain public exposure and pressure in order to influence or change decisions that affect them adversely.

A CASE STUDY IN CONFUSION. An example of an administrative foul-up that achieved nationwide publicity in 1976 was the case of Ramon Gonzales of Brooklyn, New York. He was forced to sue the federal government in an effort to break out of a tangle of rules that seemed to make him eligible for Social Security benefits when he was ineligible and ineli-

The following comment suggests both the growth of federal regulation and the idea that the passage of legislation is only a first step in the process.

Federal laws no longer are commands to the few so much as promises to the many, written by Congress, endorsed by Presidents, held constitutional by Supreme Courts, and handed to bureaucracies to fulfill.

LOUIS M. KOHLMEIER, JR.

Source: *The Regulators* (New York: Harper & Row, 1969), p. 3.

gible when he was eligible. In the fall of 1974, Mr. Gonzales was left crippled by an automobile accident and in November he applied for federal Supplemental Security Income benefits. While waiting for his application to be approved, he obtained home relief payments administered by New York City. His application took ten months to be approved, and in August 1975 he began receiving his SSI benefits of $218.55 per month. The Social Security Administration also sent him a check for $2,275 representing benefits retroactive to the time of his application.

At this point you may be thinking that the process was working well. But Mr. Gonzales made a "mistake." He put the check in the bank, and for the next ten months his bank balance exceeded the $1,500 limit on resources that supplemental income recipients may have and still be eligible for benefits. According to the rules, SSI payments are considered to be resources unless spent within three to six months. The SSI benefits were cut off, but Mr. Gonzales had spent enough of the remaining money to re-establish his eligibility. But the bureaucrats told him that since he had drawn benefits before they discovered his "ineligibility," they would cut him off for a number of months to make up for it.

Mr. Gonzales appealed the decision twice, and his appeals were rejected. Then he brought suit in 1976. Early in 1977 the Social Security Administration reversed itself, but it did not change its procedures which allow the same thing to happen to other people. Mr. Gonzales's mistake was putting the money in the bank rather than going on a spending spree.[5]

A PRIVATE–PUBLIC COMPARISON. The impact of the Gonzales story on many readers would be to create the impression that the Social Security Administration is inept. Of course, the agency's efficient handling of the bulk of its work does not receive any publicity; doing your job properly is not a newsworthy item.

Much of the criticism of government bureaucracies at all levels is due to organizational characteristics that are peculiar to governments. These characteristics underlie the problems of effectiveness, control, and reform that we will emphasize in this chapter. While reading the list of special characteristics, consider them in contrast to a major corporation such as the Eastman Kodak Company. There is stability of top management; the bureaucracy at Kodak does not compete with a separate, short-term presidential bureaucracy; Kodak serves a number of different types of customers, but it does not serve clients who are in direct competition for Kodak's resources; and, Kodak's basic policy and budgetary decisions are not made or ratified for the company by an outside agency with interests of its own.

Unlike Kodak, the federal bureaucracy (at the state and local level substitute legislature and governor or mayor for Congress and president) operates in an environment shaped by the following considerations:

1. The Constitution mandates an overlap of control of programs and funding by dividing powers between the president and Congress. These two centers of power compete with each other in setting program and dollar priorities that determine the nature of bureaucratic function.

2. The various units of the permanent bureaucracy compete with each other for control of programs and for available federal dollars. Many programs are divided among a number of agencies, creating overlap and confusion.

3. Each agency develops a constituency of its own among the private groups affected by the programs it administers and among members of Congress. These constituents support the agency in its battles with other agencies, the presidential bureaucracy, and other forces in Congress.

4. The bureaucracy is headed by an elected president and his top-level appointees who ordinarily survive no longer than the tenure of the president. While the top people are temporary, most of the bureaucrats are careerists. They have priorities different from those of the president and his appointees, and they do not feel the press of time imposed by a four- to eight-year term in office.

5. The bureaucrats do not simply carry out the programs established by Congress; they must interpret laws and make policy through rule making and the settlement of disputes between contenders for licenses, routes, and government contracts.

6. Many decisions made by the bureaucrats are subject to review by the federal courts.

Obviously, the environment we just described is not one designed to promote economy, efficiency, and effectiveness. But, as we said in previous chapters, politics and efficiency usually are not handmaidens.

The Bureaucracy: Personnel and Structure

WHO ARE THE BUREAUCRATS?

Almost one out of every thirty people employed in the United States, or 2.8 million, is employed by the federal government. Ninety-eight percent of these civilians are employed by the executive branch, our nation's largest buyer of goods and services and supplier of services. They staff the agencies that are responsible for an annual spending of over 600 billion dollars, and they make countless rules and semi-judicial decisions that affect almost every segment of our society. While the federal government is the single largest employer in the country, local governments employ 8.8 million individuals (including 3.6 million teachers) and state governments account for another 3.3 million.[6] By contrast, General Motors, the largest private employer, has only 750,000 employees. Federal employment has levelled off, while the rolls of state and local employees jumped by more than 60 percent between 1964 and 1976.

In 1805 there were only 130 clerks on the federal payroll, and the State Department was a five-man operation. In 1884, one year after the merit system was adopted, the U.S.

government had 131,000 civilian employees. By 1901, under Theodore Roosevelt, the number had doubled. The great expansion of governmental agencies and employees took place during the administration of Franklin Roosevelt (1933–1945), largely in response to the twin crises of economic depression and World War II.

A COMPLEX STRUCTURE. Figure 14–1 shows the major components of the executive branch and Figure 14–2 gives a view of the organizational structure of one department. In addition to the Executive Office of the President, Figure 14–1 lists the departments headed by Cabinet appointees and the major independent offices and establishments. It does not include the approximately 850 inter-agency committees, 700 citizen advisory groups, and 60 presidential committees, commissions, and task forces. In 1977, Jimmy Carter eliminated 500 generally forgettable advisory commissions. The funds for operating these other units—supplies, staff salaries, and payments to part-time members—come from the federal treasury.

Federal career civil servants are located throughout the nation, with only 10 to 12 percent working in the Washington, D.C. metropolitan area. More than 50,000 are posted overseas and nearly as many—300,000— work in California as serve in the Capitol. This decentralized work force is an important factor in the economy of many communities.

EMPLOYEES AND PRIORITIES. This distribution of employees within the bureaucracy is very uneven; approximately 38 percent of the full-time civilian employees work for the Department of Defense. This reflects the post–1940 preoccupation with defense and security matters and the large role defense spending plays in the economy. The Postal Service, with 22 percent, is the second largest employer. In contrast, approximately 10 percent are employed by what can be called the wel-

fare agencies, such as the Social Security Administration and the Rural Development Administration, and half of these are on the Veterans Administration staff. Given this division of manpower, it is not surprising that some agency heads complain of inadequate staffing.

In keeping with his campaign pledge, Ronald Reagan's budget called for a 32,900-person reduction in the federal payroll for fiscal 1981, and 63,100 in fiscal 1982. Additional civilian employees were added to the Defense Department, while most of the departments handling domestic programs (except Health and Human Services) were asked to make painful cuts. This reflected Reagan's policy and budget priorities.

Although the administration hoped that most of the cuts could be absorbed by people voluntarily leaving or retiring, this was little consolation to the 12,000 employees who lost their jobs or to those agencies who believed they were understaffed.

The employment figures can be misleading because they do not take into account the numerous people who are not directly employed by the federal government but who spend federal funds and implement federal policy. In this category are individuals involved in the contract activities of the Department of Defense and the "welfare" agencies that the agencies can use to evade employee ceilings. Also, a large number of state and local welfare employees actually are funded by such federal agencies as the Departments of Agriculture, Health and Human Services, Housing and Urban Development, and the Department of Labor.

It is worth mentioning again that an incoming president is usually dismayed to find that he has only 6,500 to 7,000 positions that he can fill by appointment. Of this number,

Figure 14–1 The government of the United States. (Source: U.S. Government Manual.)

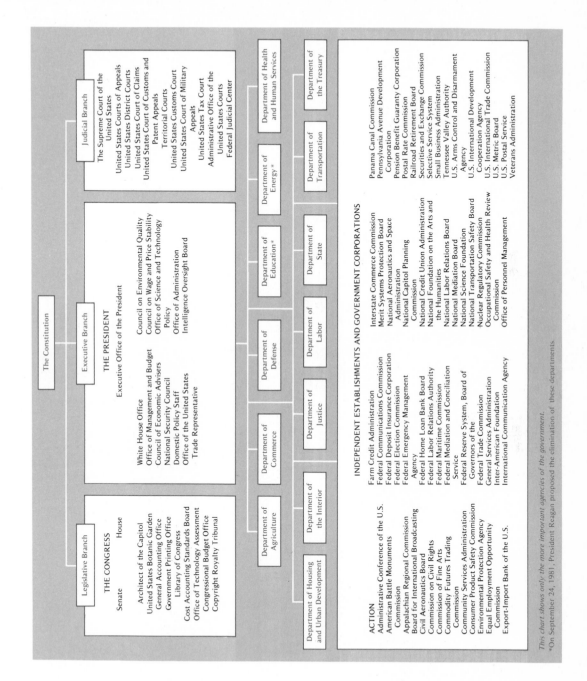

This chart shows only the more important agencies of the government.

On September 24, 1981, President Reagan proposed the elimination of these departments.

Secretary

Under Secretary

Deputy Under Secretaries

Executive Assistant to the Secretary/ Executive Secretary

Office of General Counsel

Office for Assistant Secretary for Planning and Evaluation

Office for Civil Rights

Office of Inspector General

Office of Assistant Secretary for Management and Budget

Office of Assistant Secretary for Legislation

Office of Assistant Secretary for Personnel Administration

Office of Assistant Secretary for Public Affairs

Social Security Administration

Office of Systems
Office of Governmental Affairs
Office of Family Assistance
Office of Hearings and Appeals
Office of Operational Policy and Procedures
Office of Assessment

Office of Child Support Enforcement

Health Care Financing Administration

Health Standards and Quality Bureau
Bureau of Quality Control
Bureau of Program Operations
Bureau of Program Policy
Bureau of Support Services

Public Health Service

Center for Disease Control
Food and Drug Administration
Health Resources Administration
Health Services Administration
National Institutes of Health
Alcohol, Drug Abuse, and Mental Health Administration

Office of Human Development Services

Administration for Children, Youth, and Families
Administration for Public Services
Administration for Native Americans
Administration on Aging

Principal Regional Officials

Region	Headquarters
I	Boston
II	New York
III	Philadelphia
IV	Atlanta
V	Chicago
VI	Dallas
VII	Kansas City
VIII	Denver
IX	San Francisco
X	Seattle

Viewpoint: The bureaucracy—It's the same in England

If you're pestered by critics and hounded by factions
To take some precipitate positive action,
The proper procedure, to take my advice, is
Appoint a commission and stave off the crisis.

GEOFFREY PARSONS

Source: "Royal Commission," *Punch,* August 24, 1955. © 1955 *Punch* (Rothco).

2,000 are considered to be key positions, including Cabinet and sub-Cabinet appointees, agency heads, aides and assistants with the Executive Office of the President, ambassadors, etc.

A REPRESENTATIVE BUREAUCRACY?

The theory of representative bureaucracy argues that if the attitudes of administrators are similar to the attitudes of the general public, decisions that they make will generally be responsive to the desires of the public. Since attitudes vary from group to group, the representativeness of the bureaucracy should share the characteristics (educational attainment, sex, race, family background in terms of parents' income and occupation, etc.) of the general population. While research indicates that the entire Civil Service is in general "representative" of the American population, and much more so than members of Congress or their staff or the Judiciary, it may be more important to look at one segment of the work force—the "supergrade" or "higher" Civil Service, GS–16 to GS–18 categories, which are the policy-making levels.

The supergrades are highly unrepresentative, drawn primarily and disproportionately from upper-middle class families. Less than 5 percent are non-white and less than 3 percent are women. They are a well-educated elite, with 11 out of 12 holding college degrees, as compared with the national average of 30 percent of high school graduates who complete college. Fifty-four percent of their fathers have been businessmen or professionals, as compared to 16 percent for the general population.[7]

But conclusions drawn from these facts may be misleading, as the research of Kenneth John Meier and Lloyd G. Nigro shows. They found that the supergrades held quite representative attitudes on a wide range of policy issues. This suggests that their social origins do not have much influence on their policy preferences. If this is so, why is there so much concern about a bureaucracy that is representative in terms of population characteristics? Meier and Nigro suggest that its value would be symbolic, inspiring more public confidence in administrators. "Political forms . . . come to symbolize what large masses of men need to believe about the state to reassure themselves."[8]

Figure 14–2 The Department of Health and Human Services. (*Source:* U.S. Government Manual.)

SO YOU WANT TO BE A BUREAUCRAT

During the years between Andrew Jackson's election in 1828 and the passage of

the Pendleton Act in 1883 setting up the Civil Service Commission (CSC), the appointment process was characterized by the slogan, "To the victor belongs the spoils." However, the test of competency was not ignored to any great extent until later administrations. Each shift in party control of the White House was the occasion for a mass turnover of federal government employees. The assassination of President James A. Garfield, by a rejected office-seeker in 1881 (four months after his inauguration), led to the creation of the Commission and the **merit system.** Although the Pendleton Act placed only a small percentage of employees under the new system, subsequent presidents expanded the coverage. The Ramspeck Act of 1940 allows the president to expand this protection to virtually all levels of the federal bureaucracy; and well over three-quarters of the civilian jobs are now covered by the merit system and approximately ninety

percent of the bureaucrats are under the system of job security.

OBSTACLES TO GETTING A JOB. On the surface it appears that the path to employment for the prospective bureaucrat is to take the appropriate oral and written tests administered throughout the country. Passage of the tests places the candidate's name on the appropriate list, and when a vacancy occurs or a new position is authorized, the Office of Personnel Management (one of the two agencies that replaced the CSC in 1978) sends the hiring agency the names and resumes of the top three people (according to exam scores) on the register. The administrator doing the hiring has discretion in choosing among the three people on the list. This is the theory behind the "merit" system. But a candidate for a professional-level job (GS–5 and above) should be aware of the following obstacles that he or she must overcome:

1. Very few of the people covered by some form of civil service protection are fired each year. It is difficult to fire an employee for cause. One of the few ways of losing one's job is to have the job abolished or the agency reduced in size.

2. Assuming that the candidate is a recent college graduate and is applying for a GS–5 to 7-level job covered by the Professional Administrative Career Examination (PACE), someone may get the job who receives a lower score on the exam because of a state quota that is considered, or because of veterans' preference.

3. Not all openings are listed in the job register. Many are filled from within. Because of personnel ceilings, few outsiders are being hired, and agencies are forced to promote or transfer from within.

4. Of the jobs listed, perhaps 35 to 40 percent will be filled by "name request." That is, an administrator will write a job description that a particular individual he or she knows or who has been brought to the administrator's attention by a friend or a member of Congress could qualify for. From the GS–9 level and above, most positions are filled from within and/or by name request.

5. Considering state quotas, promotion from within, and name requests, odds against getting the job are about 75 to 1.[9]

But if you want a civil service job, don't give up! Federal service can provide an interesting, financially rewarding career (see Table 14–1), and the government needs bright and dedicated people. Getting yourself "name-requested" for a post in the executive branch may not be as difficult as you may imagine. You can become a name request through your senator or congressman, particularly if you have helped in a campaign. Even if you have had no previous contact with a legislator, they are receptive to assisting young people from their states and districts. Of course, it won't hurt to have a friend of the congressman go to bat for you. And you may know a bureaucrat or someone with connections to a bureaucrat who can start the process that will lead to a name request. The name request, however, only ensures that your application will be considered. There is no guarantee of selection. Also, a name request may result from a visit to the agency personnel offices, or an on-campus interview and follow-up. In fact, most recent college graduates who are hired go this route.

An alternative to the bureaucracy would be a position on the staff of a member of Congress or a congressional committee, posts that are not covered by Civil Service. Whatever approach you take, it's our advice that you do more than take the exams and sit and wait. To win, you have to know how to play the game.

POLITICS OF HIRING AND FIRING. The low personnel turnover, promotion from within, and the dominance of Democratic administrations (1933–1953, 1961–1969, 1977–1981) since 1932 has meant that most of the people attracted to the bureaucracy have identified with the Democratic Party. This frustrated President Nixon, who wanted to clean out the Democratic–infested Civil Service, but disclosure of a manual designed to instruct top political appointees on how to accomplish this led to a Civil Service Commission inquiry, and the Civil Service Commission itself was accused by the General Services Administra-

★ ★ ★ *Table 14–1* ★
Bureaucratic salary levels

GS5–7	$12,266–19,747	GS13–15	$32,048–54,410
GS8–12	$16,826–35,033	GS16–18*	$52,247–71,734

*Congress has limited the Step 1 of GS16–18 to $50,112.50. This figure applied to the maximum rate payable to GS15 through 18 effective September 1980.

Source: "Policy and Supporting Positions" (Plum Book), U.S. House Comm. of Post Office and Civil Service, November 18, 1980, p. 155.

tion of participating in a "political patronage ring." After Nixon left office, President Ford did not try to carry on Nixon's effort.

One side of the coin is the politics of hiring; the other is the "politics of firing." President Carter faced the dilemma of how to have meaningful reorganization without firing anyone, as promised by the 1976 Democratic platform. There are very few "losers" in terms of jobs when it is difficult to remove employees who are marginal or incompetent. The "losers" are those who pay for these people, and receive inadequate return for their investment—the taxpayers. An example of the difficulty of removing a worker was the case of an employee of the Internal Revenue Service who frequently reported for work drunk. He was fired, but his union argued that the Internal Revenue Service had an obligation to establish programs to detect and treat alcoholism among its workers. The union won its case.[10] A dismissal can lead to a lengthy period of hearings and appeals, and the process discourages efforts to clean house. The more common approach is to transfer your problem to someone else's shop.

CIVIL SERVICE REORGANIZATION AND REFORM

In 1978, President Carter sent Congress a message outlining his proposal to revise the federal government's civil service system. Congress responded by giving the president most of what he sought. The Civil Service Commission was replaced by two bodies, an Office of Personnel Management and a Merit System Protection Board; the latter is the adjudicatory body that hears grievances and guarantees independent and impartial protection to employees. The president had described the federal workforce "as basically honest, competent, and dedicated," but he particularly criticized the lack of an incentive system and red tape and costly delays in the hiring and firing processes which detracted from the efficiency and responsiveness of the government (see insert).

To deal with the problems, a new Senior Executive Service, GS–16 and above, has been created. After five years, Congress can exercise a veto and eliminate the SES. At that level, salary adjustments would no longer be

Here the President repeats the oft-heard complaints about the inflexible system which makes it hard to hire, hard to fire, and robs employees of incentive.

The Civil Service [referring to the supergrades] treats top managers just like the . . . employees whose activities they direct. They are equally insulated from the risks of poor performance, and equally deprived of tangible rewards for excellence.

Managers are weakened in their ability to reward the best and most talented people—and to fire those few who are unwilling to work.

The sad fact is that it is easier to promote and transfer incompetent employees than to get rid of them. It can take up to three years to fire someone for just cause.

It has become a bureaucratic maze which neglects merit, tolerates poor performance, permits abuse of legitimate employee rights, and mires every personnel action in red tape, delay and confusion.

JIMMY CARTER

Source: Congressional Quarterly, *Weekly Report* 36 (March 11, 1978), pp. 658–660.

automatic and based on longevity. Instead, there are annual performance reviews and the opportunity to give annual performance bonuses (one-time payments) to up to fifty percent of the top administrators. Poor performance can mean demotion to GS–15, and transfers will be based on the government's need. Lower-level managers and supervisors (GS 13–15) receive only half of their annual automatic increases, but are eligible for bonuses of up to twelve percent of their annual salaries. Obviously, the incentive pay concept is aimed at the policy-making and supervisory levels only.

Carter called for a fairer and speedier disciplinary system, as well as better protection of employees' rights. This is to be the province of the Merit System Protection Board. In the area of hiring, promotion, and transfers, the plan allows the Office of Personnel Management to delegate personnel authority to departments and agencies in an attempt to avoid the six- to eight-month delays in filling important positions that often took place.

Reform often changes the rights or opportunities of individuals, creating winners and losers. The right of federal employees to organize and bargain collectively was guaranteed by law for the first time, but the unions were unhappy with Congress's failure to give them the right to strike, negotiate for pay or fringes, or require all employees to pay union dues (agency shop) whether they joined or not. And veterans' groups successfully lobbied against most of the president's proposals to restrict the preferential treatment given to veterans on the exams and job-cut protection. Carter had hoped that the change in veterans' preference would open up more opportunities to women, minorities, and other non-veteran candidates.

FORMAL STRUCTURE

Cabinet departments, independent executive agencies, government corporations, and independent regulatory commissions make up the major elements of the bureaucracy. Organization varies from unit to unit, but in general, the sub-units of the major components include one or more of the following: bureaus, offices, divisions, and regional or field offices. Most sub-units are not very visible to the public; a few, however, like the Federal Bureau of Investigation (Department of Justice), the Internal Revenue Service (Department of the Treasury), and the Social Security Administration (Department of Health and Human Services) are well known and many people probably do not associate them with their parent departments.

Departments are headed by secretaries (Justice is headed by the attorney general) appointed by the president and subject to confirmation by the Senate. The appointed department heads constitute the president's Cabinet. Each secretary is assisted by an appointed undersecretary or deputy secretary and one or more deputy under-secretaries and assistant secretaries (see Figure 14–2). These individuals conduct the staff functions (budgeting, personnel, program) of the organization and usually interact with other governmental agencies. Below this level we find the career bureaucrats who head and staff the various bureaus and smaller units that carry out

Career bureaucrats head various units within Cabinet-level departments that deal with people in need of services.

programs and deal with the people in the "real" world.

Those agencies that are not part of one of the Cabinet departments are grouped on the organization charts (see Figure 14–1) under the title of "Independent Offices and Establishments"; however, this is somewhat misleading, as there are significant differences between the "independence" of the independent executive agencies and the independent regulatory commissions.

Independent executive agencies, such as the Veterans Administration (the third-largest government agency), the Central Intelligence Agency, and the National Aeronautical and Space Administration, report directly to the president and the presidential appointees are subject to being dismissed by him.

The **independent regulatory commissions** (IRCs) have an unusual status as they are administratively independent of the three branches of government. They are independent in the sense that Congress has given them statutory independence from the executive branch. They are not supposed to be directly responsive to presidential directive, their responsibilities having been outlined by Congress; in most cases, their top administrators are appointed by the president but are not subject to removal by him without congressional authorization to do so. The Supreme Court, in *Humphrey's Executor* v. *United States* (1935) and *Wiener* v. *United States* (1948), upheld Congress's power over the removal of these appointees. Appointments are for terms of more than four years, overlapping presidential terms. The five to seven commissioners who head up each of the independent regulatory commissions (see Table 14–2) are appointed for five- to seven-year terms, and it would be very unusual for all of their terms to expire at the same time.

WHO CONTROLS THE IRCs? The term *independent* is somewhat misleading if it is assumed that it means that the agencies are free from political pressure from the White House, Congress, or their clientele. The independent regulatory agencies, for example, were established to supervise important aspects of the economy. They grant and withdraw licenses, award routes, approve or disapprove rate schedules, investigate complaints, and, in general, make decisions of tremendous financial consequence. The theory behind their status was that such bodies should be free from the normal political pressures that grow out of the president's appointment and removal power. In reality, most of the independent agencies were created after 1933, when Congress did not want to add to the growing power of the executive. But, Congress controls their funding and the guidelines within which the agencies exercise their power, as they do with non-independent departments. And they often are caught in a crossfire between the industry they are supposed to be regulating and the industry's advocates in Congress.

★ ★ ★ *Table 14–2* ★

The independent regulatory commissions

Civil Aeronautics Board (CAB)	National Labor Relations Board (NLRB)
Federal Communications Commission (FCC)	Securities Exchange Commission (SEC)
Federal Trade Commission (FTC)	Maritime Commission
Interstate Commerce Commission (ICC)	

Viewpoint:
What's in a name?

The following memo to the Federal Energy Administration from the Office of Management and Administration would be hilarious if it did not represent a waste of taxpayers' money. Think of all the letterhead that had to be changed.

MEMORANDUM FOR: FEA Senior Staff

SUBJECT: Executive Position Titles

In the past few weeks the number of titles available to important FEA personnel has been drastically reduced. It is also understood that OMB will shortly place a freeze on the proliferation of FEA titles. In the interest of maintaining staff morale, it has been decided to make the remaining titles available on a limited basis for the next two weeks. Written requests and justifications for the remaining titles should be filed with the Deputy Associate Assistant Administrator for Management Nomenclature.

Those titles currently in use are:

1. Administrator
2. Deputy Administrator
3. Assistant Administrator
4. Deputy Assistant Administrator
5. Associate Deputy Administrator
6. Associate Assistant Administrator
7. Deputy Associate Assistant Administrator *

Those titles available for selection during the next two weeks are:

1. Associate Administrator
2. Deputy Associate Administrator
3. Assistant Associate Administrator
4. Deputy Assistant Associate Administrator
5. Assistant Deputy Associate Administrator
6. Assistant Deputy Administrator
7. Assistant Associate Deputy Administrator
8. Associate Assistant Deputy Administrator
9. Associate Deputy Assistant Administrator

---

* Some offices have opted to call their Deputy Associate Assistant Administrators Office Directors. These persons, of course, are free to use the more formal title, Deputy Associate Assistant Administrator.

Although other titles are available, such as Deputy Associate Deputy Administrator, good form dictates avoidance of such redundancy. It is hoped that all desirous of titles will be satisfied with those listed above.

A memorandum describing titles available to the Office of General Counsel, Office of Congressional Affairs, Office of Communications and Public Affairs, Office of Private Grievances and Redress, and Office of Intergovernmental and Special Programs will be circulated within the next two weeks. The use of informal titles, such as Executive or Special Assistant, will remain flexible as in the past.

A recent example of a squeeze play came in 1980 when for one day, May 1, 1980, the Federal Trade Commission was "out of business." The FTC, the government's chief consumer cop, was created in 1914 to protect consumers from shady and illegal business practices. Critics say that the FTC has been too aggressive in regulating business and that the agency had not had a regular appropriation since 1976, operating on funds provided by stopgap bills. But on April 30, the money ran out.

President Carter signed an emergency appropriation bill putting the FTC back into business for thirty days. Congress then approved a compromise measure funding the agency for three years but curbing its power and giving Congress the right to veto future FTC rulings. For example, the bill eliminated the FTC authority over "unfair" advertising, leaving the agency authority only over "false or deceptive" advertising.

Finally, because they are charged with the supervision of highly complex and technical fields, the IRCs frequently turn to the industries being regulated as a source of trained people. A flow of personnel between the regulators and the regulated has developed that allows the industries to bring their philosophy into the IRCs and in a sense, capture them.

The losers are often the consumers of the services provided by the regulated industry, the very group that the IRCs were designed to protect. The industry being regulated replaces the consumer as the agency's constituency. "As nominally independent offshoots of the American institutional triad (trio), they languish in a never-never land of presidential, congressional, and private group pressures."[11]

GOVERNMENT CORPORATIONS. The Tennessee Valley Authority, a producer and seller of electric power, the Federal Deposit Insurance Corporation, which insures savings accounts, and the U.S. Postal Service are exam-

ples of another type of agency, **government corporations** or enterprises. Their status as corporations gives them more flexibility in lending, borrowing, personnel policies, buying and selling commodities, and the use of the revenues they generate. (Many of the corporations and enterprises are engaged in lending, financing, and insurance activities.) Although each is run by an independent board, they are subject to some of the fiscal controls of the Office of Management and Budget and the General Accounting Office. In recent years, Congress tightened control by requiring the corporations to get annual congressional appropriations, further blurring the distinction between the corporations and other agencies.

Most of the units of the bureaucracy include a **field service** that consists of a great number of regional, state, county, and local units. While policy making is usually controlled from Washington, operations are decentralized. This can be a mixed blessing. On the one hand, it may bring government "closer to the people," but it also opens up the delivery end of government to pressures from local interest groups who may wish to subvert federal standards. The other side of the coin is that decentralization can provide access for new citizens' groups whose previous participation in politics at the local level was slim or non-existent. For example, federal programs administered at the local level have encouraged the active involvement of community action groups in our cities.

Bureaucrats and Decision Making

Throughout our discussion we have suggested that bureaucrats make many important political decisions, from the authorship of much of the legislation introduced in Congress to the implementation of the programs. They are in a position to affect many decisions that determine who wins and who loses in the struggle for rewards or freedom from regulation. The old truism that politicians make policy and administrators simply carry out policy was always simplistic and ignored reality.

If policy making at the congressional level seems complicated, the tasks of interpreting, elaborating upon, and carrying out policy at the bureaucratic level can be worse. The bureaucrats operate within a broad framework of presidential directives and executive orders and the rather general wording of the laws passed by Congress. Some laws are not only general, but many are also ambiguous because legislators could not work out their differences in clear terms, leaving administrators to resolve the conflict. The result is that the bureaucrats often exercise a great deal of discretion in carrying out the government's programs.

ADMINISTRATIVE LEGISLATION

Bureaucratic policy making is the inevitable result of the ever-increasing complexity of the problems with which the government deals. Congress is composed of generalists who must legislate on almost every conceivable problem, while the real power of the agencies rests on their expertise or technological proficiency. In recognition of this, and the constraints of time, Congress writes its laws with broad brushstrokes, assigning the filling in of the details—administrative rules—to the agencies concerned. These rules, in turn, carry the full weight of law—subject to the scrutiny of the Congress and occasionally the courts—and we call the rules **administrative legislation** or the exercise of *quasi-legislative powers*.[12] Rule making is a constant activity of more than one hundred agencies, including the independent regulatory commissions such as the Securities and Exchange Commission (which has jurisdiction over the stock markets and investment business), and the Federal Communications Commission (whose authority covers radio, telephone, television, and telegraph). Some executive departments also exercise rule-making authority. For example, the Department of Agriculture prescribes the labeling requirements for pesticides, while the Department of Interior sets a standard of pesticide toxicity for fish and fowl.

It is no exaggeration to say that most of the federal law that affects most citizens is not found in the **Statutes at Large** (the annual product of Congress) or the **United States Code** (the collection of all statutes of the nation still in force); it is found in the rules, regulations, and directives compiled in the **Federal Register,** a daily publication whose annual volume staggers the imagination, and in **The Code of Federal Regulations** (the annual compilation of all effective regulations). If the impact of rule making does not jump up and grab you, consider the following examples:

1. When you take a trip on an airline your safety may depend on how well the Department of Transportation regulates the air traffic control system, pilot licensing, and safety requirements for the planes.

2. The effectiveness or safety of the drug prescribed by your doctor is the responsibility of the Food and Drug Administration, which should be diligent in demanding compliance with its rules.

3. The Federal Power Commission's rule making and enforcement may have contributed to the problems of 1976–77 when many parts of the U.S. suffered a worse winter than usual, and it can play a major role in preventing or minimizing future fuel shortfalls.

4. The fairness with which the Department of Defense applies rules that affect the bidding for government contracts may mean the difference between a job or no job for you if you are employed by a defense-related industry.

An agency must give notice through the *Federal Register* of a proposed new rule, in order to give interested parties an opportunity to be heard before the rule goes into effect. Hearings serve as a guide, but do not bind the agency. However, a rule can be, but rarely is, challenged in the courts to a limited extent, or the complaining party might seek change through Congress or higher executive officials including the president. Since the rules are made by specialists usually dealing with the implementation of complex policies, complaints of rule-making abuse are infrequent.

WHAT COST RULE MAKING?

Starting in 1977, almost everyone in Washington came out against regulation, blaming it for energy shortages, high transportation fares, poor service, and rising costs to consumers. And over the years, regulation has spread through the federal government like an oil spill. There is a serious question as to whether the costs of many of the regulations outweigh their benefits.

Obviously, some regulations are essential. For example, deregulation of the electric utility industry would leave customers hostage to potential rate gouging and also encourage a wasteful overlapping of facilities as companies tried to compete with each other to serve the same populations. On the other hand, the railroads blame many of their ills on regulation. One survey estimated that in 1980 industry spent $5 billion to comply with Occupational Safety and Health Administration rules that regulate everything from the shape of toilet seats to the presence of flammable liquids in retail stores. Figures from various studies estimate that in 1976 the federal government spent $3.2 billion on regulation,

while the cost of compliance paid by business and by consumers was a staggering $63 billion, including $25 billion for paperwork.[13]

The high cost of regulation is reflected in increased prices that stimulate inflation, and makes losers out of the affected businesses and the consuming public in general. Government regulation is having a direct affect on college students, as almost 450 federal agencies have some jurisdiction over higher education. Each new regulation drives up costs, some of which are passed on.

The Carter administration began applying cost-benefit concepts to regulation that may offer little or no social benefit in return for the costs. For example, Congress passed and the president signed an airline deregulation bill in 1978 that phases out federal controls of fares and routes over a seven-year period, culminating with the abolition of the Civil Aeronautics Board in 1984. The administration's next targets were the railroad industry, anxious for freedom from regulation, and the trucking industry, many of whose members do not want deregulation because they are enjoying high rates and the laws restrict entry of new companies into their markets. These two industries provide classic examples of attitudes toward regulation; they are often determined by whether the regulated wind up as winners or losers.

The Carter administration also ordered agencies to review their regulations, eliminate unnecessary ones, simplify the existing ones, and attempt to cut down on paperwork. Under the Paperwork Reduction Act of 1980 some progress was made, but the burden of filling out forms that is placed upon businesses, institutions, and individuals is staggering (see insert).

During his campaign, Ronald Reagan committed his administration to a major reduction of what the Republicans called excessive regulation that was stifling private initiative and the autonomy of state and local governments. The Republican platform called for a

Carrying out one of the government's regulatory functions are these meat inspectors for the U.S. Department of Agriculture.

temporary halt on all federal regulations that cut down on the supply of goods and services, and OSHA was a particular target.

ADMINISTRATIVE ADJUDICATION

Administrators also are involved in **administrative adjudication** (a quasi-judicial process), settling disputes between competing private interests or private interests and the government. In fact, under power delegated by Congress, the bureaucrats are transformed into judges acting in a court-like setting. Most of the adjudication takes place in the independent regulatory commissions, where the disputes may involve immensely valuable private economic rewards such as the awarding of airline routes, TV station licenses, the setting of public utility rates, or the privilege of offering stock for public sale on the stock markets. Many disputes are settled informally at lower levels of the agency. Others that would be brought to court are not for fear of the bad publicity that could result. For example, a stock brokerage firm that runs afoul of the SEC would probably accept whatever administrative sanction (penalty) is imposed rather than risk the potentially ruinous publicity that would go along with a challenge.

Adjudication is not confined to IRCs. The most frequent public involvement with bureaucrats as judges comes when a citizen

The cost, in dollars and man-hours, of filling out the more than 5,000 different kinds of government forms imposed upon Americans, is staggering.

In 1981, Americans were expected to spend 41.276 billion hours filling out government forms, or an average of five-and-a-half hours per man, woman, and child. Believe it or not, this figure represented a drop of 15 percent since 1977.

The principal demanders of paperwork are the Internal Revenue Service, which accounts for one-half of the time spent on forms, the Department of Transportation (20%), and the Department of Agriculture (10%).

Source: "41.276 Billion Hours of Paperwork." *Rochester Democrat and Chronicle,* January 18, 1981, p. 7F. © 1981 by the New York Times Company. Reprinted by permission.

has a federal income tax return audited and he or she is called in to defend the accuracy of the return. While the number of contacts that the average citizen will have with adjudications is very small, the decisions of the IRCs have a great impact upon all of us.

LESS BURDEN ON THE COURTS. The idea of administrators serving as judges of conflicts that often involve the rules and procedures of their own agency appears to be unfair. However, this process takes a tremendous burden off the courts, which are not prepared to deal with such technical issues as which airline is better qualified to service a new route. The courts have always had the power to review and overturn an agency's decisions on points of law—an absence of due process (fundamental fairness) in proceedings, actions in excess of powers granted, or misinterpretation of the law. The Administrative Procedures Act of 1946 expanded judicial review to allow the courts to review the evidence examined by the agency (questions of fact). Although the changes were made in response to complaints

about agency procedures, the courts have tended to avoid getting trapped in the thicket of technical evidence, preferring cases involving points of law, particularly the questions of due process.

Agencies are sometimes caught in the web of their own rules and time-consuming recourse to the courts available to contesting parties. For example, the Federal Trade Commission began to earn a reputation in the early 1970s of becoming a vigorous defender of consumer rights; however, its efforts have been characterized by long delays. The agency found that Geritol did not help "tired blood" or prevent "iron-deficiency anemia" and ordered the company to cease this type of advertising. The FTC eventually won its case, but it took thirteen years! In 1971 it started an inquiry to determine if eleven companies conspired to create a phony natural gas shortage in order to have the government decontrol prices. The companies dragged their feet, and refused to provide data. As time wore on, the FTC staff tired of the effort and shifted their attention to other issues. After all, the FTC was created to give "quick relief" to consumers. The balance between due process and effective regulation is difficult to find.

THE POLITICAL ENVIRONMENT OF DECISION MAKING

In addition to the entanglements of the rules and the legal process, bureaucratic decision making takes place in a political environment which finds administrators interacting with congressmen, interest groups, other agencies, the presidential bureaucracy, and private citizens. We have used the term *interacting* to avoid the impression that pressure is a one way street. Remember that bureaucrats develop "mutual assistance pacts" with individual congressmen, congressional commit-

tees, and clientele groups. Bureau chiefs, key operatives in the permanent government, have built up alliances over the years which often defy the attempts of presidential appointees to overcome these independent power bases of those they supposedly are supervising. While the organizational charts suggest an orderly chain of command, that is not consistent with the realities of politics. Francis E. Rourke observed: "In its most developed form, the relationship between an interest group and an administrative agency is so close that it is difficult to know where the group leaves off and the agency begins."[14]

Bureaucrats add to their advantage of expertise by mobilizing political support in Congress, among their clientele groups, and in the public at large. A 1970 estimate placed the number of people doing public relations

Public interest research groups (PIRGs) are organized attempts, based on a model initiated by Ralph Nader, to counteract bureaucratic power.

work in the executive branch at over 6,000, at a cost of more than $160 million a year.[15] The Pentagon's 1976 public relations costs were listed at $24.6 million. In any case, the official figures do not take into account some people engaged in public relations activities, and are probably low.

PUBLIC SUPPORT. The payoffs for public support can be substantial. The FBI and its long-time chief, J. Edgar Hoover, who died in 1972, achieved substantial independence from the president and Congress because of its public image. The Watergate scandal and subsequent revelations of illegal activities have resulted in increased control of the Bureau's activities.

The National Aeronautics and Space Administration (NASA) was able to use the public support generated by the Apollo moon missions to offset criticisms that massive funds were being wasted in space while more "earthly" problems were being neglected. With the end of the moon missions, NASA has had more difficulty in obtaining the funding it desires, but it got a boost from the successful 1981 space shuttle flight.

However, the FBI, NASA, and the Pentagon's image building are very visible examples that may obscure the fact that much of the most important mobilization of support is engaged in quietly. It involves agency-clientele relationships, such as the Department of Agriculture–farm group connection, which finds bureaucrats and clients cooperating on the formulation of proposals, lobbying in Congress for their passage, and formulating rules and procedures for implementation.

The message here builds on the discussion of executive branch lobbying, executive branch origination of many major bills considered by Congress, and congressional oversight of the administration (see Chapters 6 and 11). "Bureaucrats themselves have now become a central factor in the policy process: in the initiation of proposals, the weighing of

alternatives, and the resolution of conflict."[16] Their decisions can determine the allocation of resources—who wins and loses in the struggle for government services, contracts, and other benefits—as well as how much it will cost to comply with the overwhelming number of federal regulations controlling safety and health standards. Administrative decisions can have life-or-death consequences for business firms under their jurisdiction. For example, the FCC can grant or withhold a TV license, and new products cannot be marketed by drug firms without the approval of the Food and Drug Administration.

Controlling the Bureaucracy

The issue of bureaucratic control is a very complex one, involving the previously mentioned advantages of the bureaucrat and the potential power of control that is available to those officials primarily responsible: the president, his staff, and Congress. In addition, the courts, interest groups (including public interest groups), and the media can exert influence and some control. "The fundamental restriction under which bureaucrats operate is the fact that they share control with other elites in the political system."[17]

Obviously, program proposals require presidential endorsement before submission to Congress, and that body has the power of authorization and appropriation, as well as oversight of the administration. And, the breadth of the responsibility of Congress masks the fact that legislators specialize in a few areas, usually consistent with their committee assignments, and can develop a degree of expertise that rivals that of their administrative counterparts. But when bureaucratic and legislative experts cooperate with each other, they constitute a force that other political participants find difficult to resist. Of course, administrative decisions and practices are not beyond the reach of the courts.

The web of relations between interest groups and the bureaucracy has been explored, but these same groups, as well as organizations such as Common Cause, can attempt to counteract bureaucratic power through putting pressure on Congress, resorting to the courts, and attempting to bring problems to the media. The media, for its part, often acts independently to focus upon bureaucratic inefficiency, unresponsiveness, misdeeds, or occasional powerlessness at the hands of some politicians.

MEDIA IMPACT. A classic example of the media's impact upon both an agency and a member of Congress who used his power and expertise to dominate an area of its activity took place in February 1969. A series of television presentations called attention to the problems of hunger in America. Prior to this exposure, Rep. Jamie Whitten (D., Miss.), chairman of the Appropriation Committee's Subcommittee on Agriculture, was able to block effective expansion of the program. With his control of the purse strings, Whitten was known as the "permanent" Secretary of Agriculture.[18] But the publicity about hunger broke his grip on the issue. More recently, the networks have done specials on the Internal Revenue Service and the general paperwork overkill that ties up the government.

But, "bureaucratic power thrives on the inattention of other participants in the policy process."[19] This inattention may result from the secrecy often engaged in by executive agencies, the complexities of the issues of policy formation and/or implementation, or both.

The scope of the government's operation makes scrutiny almost impossible, and, the presidential bureaucracy usually does not have the time, information, or will to intervene in the process of policy making except with respect to high-priority situations. As for legislators, their preoccupation tends to be with the establishment of programs to serve their constituencies, not with performance. Often, too little is known about the impact and effectiveness of government programs. Are they doing what they are designed to do?

PRESIDENTIAL CONTROL PROBLEMS

We started this chapter with a quotation that suggested that presidents have difficulty controlling the permanent government. In *The State of the Presidency*, Thomas E. Cronin goes a step further and says that the president's key struggle is with the bureaucracy: "Presidential leadership has become less a matter of authority flowing downward and more a question of the extent to which loyalty extends upward."[20] The inherited bureaucracy, its size, the scope of the programs being administered, and the ability of career civil servants to develop other bases of support contribute to the loyalty problem and thus the control problem. In the absence of effective control, presidential initiatives face bureaucratic vetoes of inaction, delay, contrary interpretation, and the generally, if reluctantly, accepted fact that economy and efficiency are demonstrably not the purposes of public administration.[21] But recent chief executives have been contributors to their own dilemma.

PROBLEMS OF THE PRESIDENTIAL BUREAUCRACY. In 1969, President Nixon complained of a loss of public confidence in the federal government, laying most of the blame on the gap between the promise and performance of its programs.[22] Nixon was frustrated by the Democratic political leanings of most of his inherited bureaucracy and the Congress's predictable rejection of his imaginative reorganization plan. Part of his response was to swell the presidential bureaucracy (see Chapter 13) and to create a Domestic Council, in theory a counterpart to the National Security Council in the foreign affairs and defense areas. Unfortunately, the presidential bureaucracy became more a substitute for, than a means of controlling and using, the permanent government. The Domestic Council, under Nixon, and continued by Ford, became an "in-group" that existed in an environment of mutual hostility with the personnel of the agencies.[23] Both Nixon and Ford ignored the common-sense rule of not interposing a layer of bureaucracy between the president and those at the operating level.[24] The Carter administration pledged to pare down the presidential advisory corps and place more dependence upon the bureaucrats. The Domestic Council was eliminated but the staff was retained, and no major reduction in the presidential bureaucracy took place.

DOMINANCE OF FOREIGN POLICY. A second problem, one not completely within a president's control, has been presidential preoccupation with foreign policy and matters of security. Recent chief executives have spent one-half to two-thirds of their time dealing with these areas, where they find less resistance from Congress and the defense-foreign policy bureaucracy. And, foreign policy initiatives are rewarded in the opinion polls even if the president fails. Much of the remaining time is devoted to monetary and fiscal policy, the "bread and butter" issues, such as inflation, that affect the whole economy. This leaves little time or energy to be expended upon close supervision of specific social programs such as Social Security or food stamps.[25] Another barrier to presidential leadership has been our political system's modern tendency not to select people with considerable administrative experience to be president. Jimmy Carter was the first man since Franklin Roosevelt (1933–1945) to come to the White House having occupied a major governmental administrative post (governor of Georgia, 1971–1974). The other incumbents, with the exception of Dwight Eisenhower, earned their spurs as members of Congress before being

elected to the presidency or moving up from the vice-presidency. Reagan, of course, was governor of California from 1967 to 1975.

We are not suggesting that the president is powerless. He has considerable impact upon the bureaucracy through his budgetary priorities, his role as chief initiator of legislation, and the manner in which he shapes and uses his inner-circle bureaucracy. But the triple alliance of agencies, congressmen, and clientele groups may often resist presidential efforts, and no progress will be made unless the occupant of the White House makes an effort to infuse new spirit into, improve relations with, and bolster the self-image of the permanent government, particularly those who must implement the country's domestic policy or "quality-of-life" programs.

CONGRESSIONAL CONTROL

As we have seen, the president shares the responsibility of directing the bureaucracy with the Congress. Legislators can exercise control through appropriations, investigations, and the hearings that precede the passage of bills. The basic task of the agencies is to interpret, implement, and enforce the laws and programs created by Congress; where congressional intent and bureaucratic interpretations diverge, Congress can amend legislation to make its intent clear or appropriate members can make their wishes clear through more informal channels. Unfortunately, congressional control is hampered by the motivations of the overseers and the fact that as many as six committees may have oversight of a single department or agency. And Congress faces another formidable barrier: the amazing overlap and parceling out of jurisdiction over a subject area among a multitude of agencies and subunits. The *Government Organizational Manual* for 1976–77 listed thirty-three units housed in nine departments and a number of independent agencies as involved with one or more aspects of environmental protection. These obstacles not withstanding, bureaucrats are more sensitive to congressional concerns than those of a presidential bureaucracy are.

In 1976 Congress made two attempts, one unsuccessful, to exercise additional control over the executive branch. It passed, and the president signed, a "Government in the Sunshine" Act requiring most executive agencies, except the Cabinet departments, to conduct their business in regular public sessions. The law applies to boards, agencies, and commissions with more than one head or director. The law exempted agencies from having to discuss ten types of matters, such as personnel decisions, court proceedings, or security-related issues, in open meetings. However, transcripts or minutes of closed meetings must be kept.

LEGISLATIVE VETO. A more dramatic proposal that would have given Congress a veto power over any regulation made by the bureaucracy passed the Senate but fell two votes shy in the House. The bill would have required that all regulations be submitted to Congress, where either house would have sixty days to disapprove, unless overridden by the other, forcing the agency to reconsider its rule. The vote in the House came under a procedure (suspension of the rules) which required a two-thirds vote for passage.

A legislative veto does, however, exist on a bill-by-bill basis. Since 1932, the veto has been included in more than two hundred laws; more than half have been passed since 1957, including the War Powers and Federal Election Campaign Acts of 1974. And, the number of congressional veto provisions enacted into laws is multiplying rapidly in a congressional effort to exercise more control over executive branch actions. Presidents dislike the device, their major objections being a loss of administrative flexibility and the claim that the broad-based proposal would be an unconstitutional violation of the Separation of Powers Doctrine. President Carter said he would not feel bound by legislative vetoes. And some legislators are not keen about the prospect of reviewing the more than 10,000 regulations that are written each year.

CONGRESSIONAL INVESTIGATIONS. Occasionally, Congress uses its investigatory role to clean up a bureaucratic mess. In 1978, the Senate's Governmental Affairs Committee asked the General Accounting Office to investigate whether the General Services Administration was following proper procedures in making government purchases. The GSA spends over $5 billion a year to provide office space and supplies for the federal government.

The GAO uncovered a pattern of fraud that was costing the nation over $66 million a year and wasteful practices that used up another $34 million. A top GSA official suggested that the corruption exposed was only the beginning, the tip of the iceberg. The fraud included false claims for benefits and services, bribery of officials, and collusion among contractors. In addition, the GSA was cited for the lack of internal controls, lack of competitive bidding, irregular auditing practices, and weak management.

The investigation led to numerous criminal indictments, dismissals, and tightening of procedures. But the GAO warned that most federal agencies have made little systematic effort to identify or to combat fraud. The huge size of the government's operation when combined with presidential and congressional preoccupation with other matters, appears to create an environment in which corruption and inefficiency can breed and in which all citizens can lose the benefits that their tax dollars are supposed to provide.

CONGRESSIONAL–PRESIDENTIAL CONFLICT. Most reorganization of the executive branch by the president is subject to congressional approval (see "Issue" section); the case of the

Legislation often fails to provide specific guidelines for the bureaucrats who must seek a balance between the Congress and the regulated when implementing the law.

When the new law gets to the agency it must read all sorts of wondrous exceptions and hidden implications into that broad congressional language. The question is not who is breaking the law, but who is breaking the law worse.

Any sensible bureaucrat will pick his fights wisely. If he pushes the enforcement language to its fullest, he will be denounced as a "radical bureaucrat" who usurps congressional powers. If he proceeds timidly in certain areas, he will be exposed as a "captive" of the industry he is supposed to be regulating.

WILLIAM GREIDER

Source: "A Government Designed for Bargain Hunters," *The Washington Post,* January 20, 1977, p. 6 of special section, "The Carter Presidency." © *The Washington Post.*

Army Corps of Engineers provides a classic case of legislative obstructions.[26] The Corps, part of the Department of Defense, considers itself to be the consulting engineers to the Congress. It is responsible for evaluating requests for and carrying out projects relating to the navigability of rivers, lakes, and their usefulness for commerce. If a coastal congressman and his constituents want a harbor deepened, the Corps makes the decision on the appropriateness of the project. This gives the Corps considerable leverage with Congress, which it has used successfully in its fight with almost every president from FDR through Nixon, when each has attempted to take the functions of the Corps and place them under the Department of Interior. The Bureau of Reclamation of the Department engages in a running battle with the Corps over jurisdiction to build dams that serve the multiple purposes of land reclamation, recreation, and flood control. A merger would be a step toward a more rational water resources policy.

Congressional and presidential differ-ences over the political rights of bureaucrats came to a head in 1976 when President Ford vetoed a revision of the Hatch Acts of 1939 and 1940, which had placed major constraints on the political activity of federal employees. As passed by Congress, the revision would have allowed them to run for federal office, participate in partisan campaigns, and solicit and make campaign contributions except when on federal property.[27] The opponents of change, mainly Republicans, fear that the party in power might use the civil service to perpetuate itself in office and that pressure for contributions or campaign assistance would be brought to bear on the bureaucrats. Until recently it has been assumed that it is a virtue to isolate the civil service from political party battles.

The arguments for change are based upon the belief that public employees should not be denied the political freedoms enjoyed by other citizens. As to the constitutionality of the restrictions, the Supreme Court upheld the Hatch Acts in 1973 (*Civil Service Commission v. the Letter Carriers*).[28]

The FBI's fingerprint files are centralized at a location near Washington.

CONTROL OF INTELLIGENCE AGENCIES: A CASE STUDY

Congress's attempt to set up more effective oversight of the intelligence community—the Central Intelligence Agency, FBI, and parts of the Defense Department—provided a rare example of serious congressional efforts to control the bureaucracy. Both chambers established special intelligence investigations panels in 1975, but in January 1976, the House refused to publish its panel's final report. In contrast, the Senate group, headed by Frank Church (D., Idaho), went public and catalogued a long list of abuses by the agencies that spanned the administrations of presidents as far back as Franklin Roosevelt. The abuses included domestic spying ranging over a forty-year period, such as surveillance of

U.S. citizens, political spying, opening of U.S. mails, compiling lists of citizens calling the White House to protest our war policies, and efforts to disrupt protest groups. The Senate panel also noted the attempts of some presidents to misuse the Internal Revenue Service and concluded that the "Intelligence Agencies have served the political and personal objectives of presidents and other high officials."[29]

The Senate report also condemned U.S. involvement in assassination plots against foreign leaders, secret activities to topple governments such as the one led against President Salvador Allende of Chile (he was overthrown and killed in 1973), and "intelligence politics," in which the intelligence community distorted information to fit political needs.

President Ford issued executive orders banning assassination and plots, and attempting to spell out the missions of the various units. The Senate, in particular, was not satisfied, and acknowledged that Congress had failed to monitor the expenditures of the intelligence agencies or to provide the necessary statutory guidelines for their operations. Of course, budgets were difficult to control because funds were "hidden" under phony labels because of "security" reasons. In the absence of oversight, their activities had acquired a momentum of their own. The problem facing Congress was how the requirements of American democracy could be balanced in intelligence matters against the need for secrecy and security.

A 1974 law requires the president to notify the Senate Foreign Relations and House Foreign Affairs Committees before the CIA carries out covert (secret) operations abroad. Five other committees demanded and

Budgets are a guide to which groups and agencies are the winners and
losers in the struggle over the federal dollar.

*Human nature is never more evident than when men are struggling to gain a
larger share of funds to be appropriated among myriad claimants.
Budgeting deals with the purposes of men.*

AARON WILDAVSKY

Source: *The Politics of the Budgetary Process* (Boston: Little, Brown, 1964), p. 2.

received the same information. Of course, the intelligence community and the president argue that information that is that widely circulated can't be kept secret; however, there has been no evidence of "leaks" since 1974. The CIA also dislikes the requirement of prior presidential approval of all covert operations and having to provide the public with a limited range of information under the Freedom of Information Act.

In May 1976, the Senate established a permanent Select Committee on Intelligence with legislative and budgetary authority over the CIA and other federal intelligence agencies. This action came twenty years after the idea was first introduced. But even the debate over this issue was marred when the senators apparently put the jurisdiction of their own committees ahead of the national interest. The new committee has exclusive jurisdiction over the CIA, but shares oversight in the intelligence operations of the Department of Defense and the FBI with the Armed Services and Judiciary Committees respectively.

Partly in response to the 1979–80 crises in Iran and Afghanistan, President Carter and some members of Congress called for a comprehensive charter for intelligence agencies designed to prevent abuse while at the same time removing "unwarranted restraints" on their activities. The proposal did

not come up for a vote before the 96th Congress adjourned.

Before we elaborate on reorganization in the "Issue" section of the chapter, we will examine one very important facet of the operation of the bureaucracy, the budget process. It provides a view of the alliance-building and internal bureaucratic conflicts that affect the allocation of resources and the question of control.

The Bureaucratic Politics of the Budgetary Process

Spending by the national government accounts for approximately twenty percent of the **gross national product** (GNP). The GNP is best understood as the sum of spending by consumers, business, and government on goods and services produced in this country. This makes the national government the single largest determiner of the GNP and emphasizes the importance of the "how much" and "what for" decisions that determine the shape of the budget as presented by the president and acted upon by Congress. The budget is a blueprint for the future, "a series of goals with price tags attached."[30]

In Chapter 11 we discussed the new

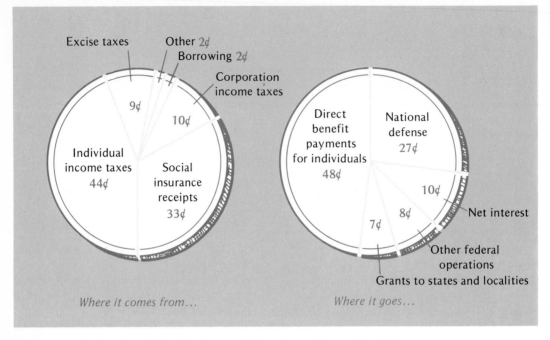

Excise taxes

Other 2¢

Borrowing 2¢

Corporation income taxes

9¢

10¢

Individual income taxes 44¢

Social insurance receipts 33¢

Direct benefit payments for individuals 48¢

National defense 27¢

10¢

8¢

7¢

Net interest

Other federal operations

Grants to states and localities

Where it comes from...

Where it goes...

Figure 14–3 The budget dollar: fiscal year 1982 estimate. (Source: Fiscal Year 1982 Budget Revisions.)

(since 1974) process by which Congress has attempted to gain more effective control over the power of the purse. But congressional action is a response to the president's budget message and accompanying appropriations requests. These documents are the result of at least ten months of negotiations and infighting in the executive branch which pit each agency against the president's right arm of budgetary control, the Office of Management and Budget, and involves agency efforts to bring outside pressure—from members of Congress and clientele groups—to bear on those who shape the budget. For, in the win-loss framework, the overriding goal of the bureaucrats are the expansion, or at least the survival, of their agencies.

An example of an ongoing struggle is the fight over how much of the budget should be allotted to national defense. The stakes are very high, with defense contracts on the line

and potential base closings providing just two examples. Conflict is inevitable, as the amount of defense spending (or the level for any other category of spending) affects what will be available for other programs.

Defense spending as a percentage of the total budget outlay had declined dramatically from a high of 43 percent in 1968 to 24 percent for 1981. President Reagan raised the total to 27 percent in his fiscal year 1982 budget and projected an increase to 32 percent by 1984. After 1972, the dollar outflow for defense spending actually rose even though the percentages dropped between 1968 and 1981 (see Figure 14–3).

During the Carter years, and continuing into the Reagan presidency, mayors and governors were unhappy with what they described as the relatively low spending proposed for urban programs, many of which directly affect black Americans. In Carter's

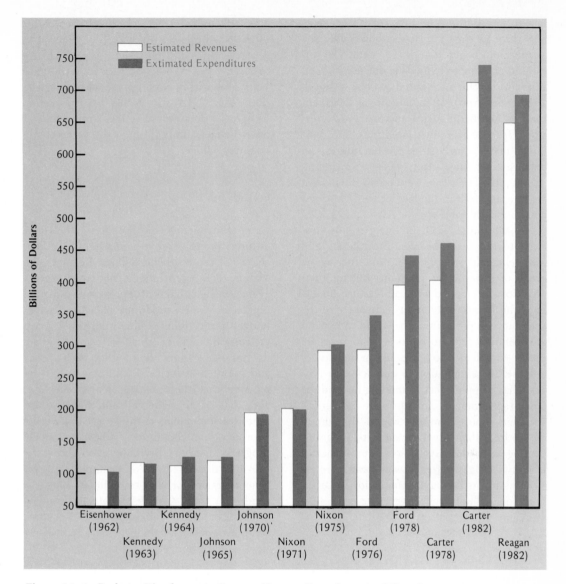

Figure 14–4   Budgets: Eisenhower to Reagan. (Source: Data from the Office of Management and Budget.)

attempt to fight inflation, cut the federal deficit, and provide a balanced budget, these and other social programs suffered. Although cost cutting cut a wide path through government programs, the poor and minorities, usual losers, found themselves less able to defend their piece of the federal pie in a period of rising public resentment against taxes and a demand for reduced spending.

The election in 1974 of a large number of liberal House freshmen sent a wave of fear through the defense establishment, the assumption being that there would be increased pressure to reduce the defense budget. But world events such as the collapse of South Vietnam in April, 1975, and Soviet intervention in southern Africa increased congressional fears of Moscow's intentions, and reinforced many already-strong vested interests in defense spending. And, defense spending equals jobs. The steam went out of the budget slashing in 1975 in the face of DOD and defense industry lobbying.

Of course, such lobbying is not confined to the sword-bearers. Bureaucrats and their clientele who benefit from the whole range of government programs defend their areas for all the good and bad reasons: honest belief in the necessity and effectiveness of the program; job protection; the desire to expand an operation (empire building) and translate increased dollars into power. As in the case of defense, the elimination or cutback of a program has a ripple effect, extending beyond the federal government. The "poverty-industrial" complex, those groups whose livelihood comes from their involvement with programs dealing with the psycho-social problems of poverty—social workers, mental health professionals—resists cuts and lobbies for increases with equal, if not as effective, rigor as does the Pentagon and its allies.[31]

BUDGET CYCLE

The budget cycle is a continuous process involving four overlapping phases, three of which are shown in Figure 14–5. At any one time an agency may be operating under one budget (execution phase), defending the next fiscal year's budget before the appropriations committees of Congress, and beginning to prepare estimates for a budget which will go into effect nineteen months later. For example, preparation of the budget for **fiscal year**

1982—October 1, 1981 through September 30, 1982—began in March 1979. The fourth phase, audit, takes place within each agency to ensure that transactions are in accordance with authorizing and appropriating legislation. The OMB also audits operations and Congress obtains selective, independent, after-the-fact audits through the General Accounting Office.

FORMULATION

Bureaucrats view the formulation stage as three rounds of a five-round fight for a "fair share" of the available dollars. Beginning in March, each organizational unit within every agency reviews current operations, program objectives, issues, and future plans, and makes budget projections. These individual plans are consolidated in each agency, and there are "winners and losers" both within each agency and between agencies. It is important to remember that these budget plans reflect, in part, the desires of clientele and the presumed attitudes of members of the House and Senate appropriations committees. They also reflect programs that have been approved during the previous fiscal years. For example, a three-year program for aid to colleges must be funded annually. Congressional and presidential appeals to build a nuclear carrier, or other weapons system, might become a part of the next defense budget.

At the same time, the president is receiving revenue estimates and economic projections from his primary sources of economic advice—the OMB, Treasury, and the Council of Economic Advisers. The information provided is the basis for the president's budget policy guidelines, which are transmitted by the OMB to the agencies.

AGENCIES VERSUS THE OMB. Round two finds each agency formulating detailed budgets that are scrutinized by the experienced

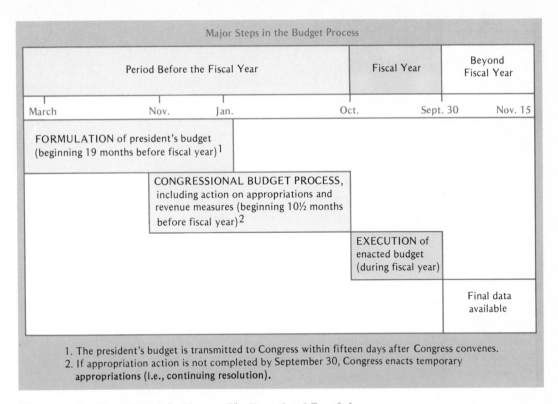

Figure 14–5 The budget cycle. (Source: The Executive Office of the
President/Office of Management and Budget.)

budget examiners of the OMB. The OMB holds hearings with agency representatives in an effort to resolve differences; agency requests usually come in on the high side, and are cut. In the fall, the director of the OMB makes his recommendations on programs and expenditures to the president and notifies the agencies of the Chief Executive's tentative decision.

Round three provides the agencies with the opportunity to appeal OMB recommendations to the president. After decisions are made final in December, the agencies make the necessary revisions, draft implementing legislation to be sponsored by members of Congress, and the OMB drafts the budget message for the president's revisions and approval.

The change in party control of the White House and the accompanying dramatic shift in economic philosophy embodied in Reagan's budget, injected a new element into the budget cycle of 1981–82. Agencies found themselves in a new struggle with an OMB directed by a conservative. In most instances, the battle was short, and the bureaucrats had to accept the downward revisions.

CONGRESSIONAL HEARINGS

AGENCIES VERSUS THE PRESIDENT. Rounds four and five provide the bureaucrats with a chance to undo the damage done by the OMB and the president by appealing to the members of the House and Senate appropriations

Viewpoint:
Senators Eagleton and Hatfield versus
Senator McClellan on priorities

From the Senate debate of August 2, 1976, when the Senate rejected
an amendment to cut $1 billion from the fiscal 1977 Defense
Department appropriation bill, three senators debate the concept of
"security."

*It is equally clear that the Pentagon, perceiving a fertile political environ-
ment, is asking for the moon and the stars. The cost we will all have to
pay is a reduction in the overall security of this nation—a reduction in
our capacity to protect ourselves from the internal threats of stagna-
tion, unemployment, and urban decay.*

THOMAS F. EAGLETON (D., Mo.)

*While the United States may be number one in the military strength . . . , we
lag behind other nations in literacy, health care, nutrition, per capita
income, and other indicators of our nation's strength.*

MARK O. HATFIELD (R., Ore.)

*Where is your safety in Social Security, where is your safety from any govern-
ment assistance, for any government program, unless the nation is safe
from its enemies?*

JOHN L. MCCLELLAN (D., Ark.)

Source: Quoted in Congressional Quarterly, *Weekly Report* 34 (August 7, 1976),
pp. 2121–22.

committees. There may be few better examples of the president's problem of controlling
his executive branch than to witness a parade
of bureaucrats seeking restoration of programs
and funds axed by the White House.

The agency spokespeople rehearse
prior to their appearances before the committee, attempting to foresee the questions that
will be asked. They also know the track record of the committees—how much the House
usually cuts and what the Senate puts back—a
situation which leads to a high degree of predictability, and also lends credibility to the
assumption that "the largest determining factor of the size and content of this year's
budget is last year's budget."[32]

The agencies cultivate a base of support among legislators and their constituents
who have vested interests in the programs
they propose and administer. It is at this point
in the budgetary process that the bureaucrats
try to call in the IOUs generated by this mutually beneficial relationship. This helps explain
the large number of appropriations measures
that go beyond the figures requested by the
president, in spite of the counter-lobbying
by the presidential bureaucracy, which lacks
the congressional ties of the members of the
permanent government.

These ties are a key element in congressional and bureaucratic resistance to reorganization.

★ Issue ★

Reorganizing the Bureaucracy: Will It Work?

Since the passage of the Reorganization Act of 1949, the president has been given the authority to submit reorganization plans to Congress. The plans become effective if neither the Senate nor the House rejects the proposal by majority vote within sixty days. This reorganization authority had been routinely granted for two-year periods to every incumbent since Truman until it was denied to Richard Nixon because of his ambitious reform proposals. Shortly after taking office, President Carter asked for and received a four-year reorganization license. However, this grant was opposed by some law-makers of Carter's party, who wanted to require the affirmative vote of each house before changes

could become operational. They feared an excess of presidential power and did not want to be overwhelmed by reform measures and have to act on them without sufficient consideration.

Carter's three major reorganizations during the 1977–80 period involved the creation of the Department of Energy, the restructuring of the Executive Office of the President, and the establishment of a separate Department of Education. Congress approved the first, and third, and did not block the second.

Internal reorganizations also took place in the Departments of Agriculture and Health and Human Services which should

Making human services bureaucracies more responsive to the people they are meant to serve is a challenge for every administration.

have major impact on the delivery of services. Carter also backed "sunset" legislation, which would require periodic review by Congress of all government agencies and programs. His 1978 Civil Service reform was a part of his reorganization plans, and deregulation efforts amount to a form of reorganization. But Carter did not follow through on campaign rhetoric which implied a major reorganization of the federal bureaucracy.

Perhaps his difficulties with Congress, and the past experiences of Nixon, suggested that the time was not ripe for any new grand design. But, Carter fared better than Nixon, whose imaginative plan for the overhaul of the bureaucracy was ignored by congressmen who did not wish to see their relationships with the bureaucrats disturbed or their committee jurisdictions affected. The bureaucrats, of course, were fearful of the new alignment, and interest groups with established contacts and patterns of behavior were unenthusiastic. Nixon's plan would have kept the Defense, Justice, Treasury, and State Departments intact, while reorganizing the remaining seven departments into four departments—Natural Resources, Human Resources, Economic Affairs, and Community Development.[33]

Jimmy Carter had the advantage of a friendly Congress and a growing disillusionment on the part of liberals as well as conservatives with big federal programs, many of which had turned out to be "turkeys." As early as 1975, former Senator Edmund Muskie (D., Maine), himself a liberal, said:

Why can't liberals start raising hell about a government so big, so complex, so expensive and so unresponsive that it's dragging down every good program we've worked for?[34]

Reagan's campaign rhetoric and his party's platform attacked two of Carter's creations, the Department of Education and the Department of Energy, as new villains in the story of expanded government, federal interference, and over-regulation. In September 1981, Reagan called for the abolition of the two departments as part of his effort to seek a second round of budget cuts for FY 1982 and a 75,000 person reduction in the federal workforce. He argued that fuctions that were essential could be shifted to other departments and agencies.

POLITICAL OBSTACLES. Unfortunately, the scope and effectiveness of reform is limited by a number of political realities that we have not previously mentioned. First, most people prefer known bureaucracies to the unknown consequences of reform. Second, any structural reform can be undone or thwarted by Congress, bit by bit. Finally, any major reduction in the federal work force is bitterly resisted by the public employees' unions.

Can reorganization lead to the hoped-for change in the widely held, if not entirely justified, view that the government is an inherently inefficient promoter of the general welfare? There is no simple answer to the question. Reorganization might promote effectiveness by eliminating duplication of effort by grouping related activities into cohesive units such as the new Department of Energy. And, plans that provide some decentralization of decision making may mean more opportunity for clientele groups—such as welfare service recipients—to influence the process. But reorganization itself cannot alter the behavior patterns of the bureaucrats or those responsible for administrative oversight.

Administrative units often fail to deal vigorously or imaginatively with problems that may be of real concern to the public. They can choose to ignore or not raise the issues they do not want to deal with. Agencies find it difficult to shift gears when old policies are no longer appropriate. As Francis Rourke puts it, ". . . executive agencies have an enormous capacity for non-decision."[35] And, the bureaucrats do not always give the president and his key people what they need—both the good news and the bad news; chief executives have often found that they could not have confidence in the accuracy of reports with the top people pleading ignorance about what their agencies were doing. Nixon went so far as to try to have Bob Haldeman infiltrate "spies" into the executive departments.

THE INFORMATION GAP. There is nothing sinister about the misinformation problem. Survival is the strongest human motivation, and bureaucrats of the permanent or presidential bureaucracy have a vested interest in their own survival, and that of the subunit and agency in which they work. Information flows up and rewards flow down in the form of paychecks, status, power, promotions, etc. It becomes important to protect your superiors. The "whistle-blowers" in government have tended to be squashed by the bureaucracy; it is too early to tell whether or not they will fare better in the future. This is another aspect of the "presidential isolation" issue we discussed in the last chapter.

A solution to the information problem was found by Sargent Shriver when he headed the Peace Corps. But the Peace Corps was unique in that Shriver had a rule that no employees would be with the agency more than two-and-one-half years, preferring the personnel to be "noble transients with no necks to protect." Shriver created an Office of Evaluation, an independent reporting unit that was outside the normal structure. Its members went out into the field to find what was going on and reported directly to Shriver. Their reports were made public within the agency and other members had a chance to react to the reports and confront the evaluators.[36] And, while a senator, Walter Mondale suggested that one-half to one percent of allocations for domestic programs be set aside to fund evaluation by evaluators from outside the government. The feasibility of this approach on a large scale remains to be seen.

President Carter's Civil Service reform, stressing an incentive system and more flexibility in personnel policies, could be a major factor in encouraging effectiveness, efficiency, and responsiveness. Agency heads—presidential appointees—would designate the recipients among the supergrades, and the Office of Personnel Management would prescribe the guidelines for the incentive pay of lower level managers and supervisors.

Perhaps most important to accomplishing the goals of reorganization is the willingness and commitment of other parts of the government, particularly Congress and the president, to exercise their oversight functions. If the president and his team cannot commit resources to this task, and if Congress generally neglects this role in favor of pursuits with a higher electoral payoff, then we will be able to say, once more, "everything changes, and everything remains the same."

Summary

The agencies of the government and the bureaucrats who staff them play very important roles in our political system. The career civil servants of the permanent government make policy through rule making, program development in cooperation with Congress and clientele groups, adjudication of the claims of contending parties, and their involvement in the budgetary process. Bureaucratic resistance to reorganization (and sometimes to programmatic change), and a decision-making environment that is often characterized by the absence of effective oversight by Congress or the presidential bureaucracy, can give administrators a veto over the initiatives of the other political actors.

The president inherits most of the bureaucracy, civil servants who, in theory, are recruited through the merit system. A major overhaul of the Civil Service system was undertaken in an effort to improve performance through an incentive system and more effective hiring and firing procedures.

Efforts to control the bureaucracy are spasmodic, with different presidents having more or less success. Key factors in the lack of oversight appear to be presidential preoccupation with the national security–foreign policy areas, and the vested interests of legislators more concerned with the creation rather than the carrying out of programs that will please their constituents. Devotion to oversight functions rarely pays off at the polls, and the overlapping programs of agencies and jurisdictions of congressional committees add to the problems of control already complicated by the constitutional separation of powers.

While some programs operate very effectively, we have seen that economy and efficiency are not dominating characteristics of the administrative process. Reorganization may or may not be the hoped-for means of achieving control, economy and efficiency. But to organize means to allocate power and responsibilities and to reorganize means to make shifts in power, in "winners" and "losers," and this does not come easily.

Terms to Remember

See the Glossary at the end of the book for definitions.

Administrative adjudication

Administrative legislation

Bureaucracy

Bureaucrats

The Code of Federal Regulations

Federal Register

Field service

Fiscal year

Government corporations

Gross National Product (GNP)

Independent executive agencies

Independent regulatory commissions

Merit system

Permanent government

Presidential bureaucracy

Statutes at Large

Triple alliance

United States Code

Notes

1. Jack Anderson, "Bureaucrats Ready for Carter Reform," *Rochester Democrat and Chronicle,* November 28, 1976, p. A16. © 1976 United Feature Syndicate, Inc.

2. Quoted in H.H. Gerth and C. Wright Mills, *Max Weber: Essays in Sociology* (New York: Oxford University Press, 1953), p. 234.

3. Dwight Waldo, "Public Administration," *Journal of Politics,* vol. 30, no. 2 (May 1968), p. 448.

4. Anthony Downs, *Inside Bureaucracy* (Boston: Little, Brown, 1967), p. 30.

5. Robert D. McFadden, "Welfare Catch–22 . . .", *The New York Times,* November 24, 1976, pp. 1, 38.

6. If we count the members of the armed forces as part of the executive branch, the total work force is close to 5.5 million people. U.S. Bureau of Census, *Statistical Abstract: 1977* (Washington, D.C.: Department of Commerce, 1977), p. 306.

7. Kenneth John Meier and Lloyd G. Nigro, "Representative Bureaucracy and Policy Preferences: A Study in the Attitudes of Federal Executives," *Public Administration Review,* 36 (July/August 1976), no. 4, pp. 458–469.

8. Murray Edelman, *The Symbolic Uses of Power* (Urbana: The University of Illinois Press, 1964), p. 3.

9. See Ann Pincus, "How To Get A Government Job," *The Washington Monthly,* (June 1976), p. 27.

10. Charles Peters, "A Kind Word for the Spoils System," *The Washington Monthly,* (September 1976), p. 27.

11. Charles E. Jacob, *Policy and Bureaucracy* (Princeton, N.J.: D. Van Nostrand, 1966), p. 100. Also see Marver Bernstein, *Regulating Business by Independent Commissions* (Princeton, N.J.: Princeton University Press, 1955); and Louis M. Kohlmeier, Jr., *The Regulators* (New York: Harper & Row, 1969).

12. One of the best discussions of the rule-making and administrative adjudication processes is found in Peter Woll, *American Bureaucracy* (New York: W.W. Norton, 1963).

13. Steven Rattner, "Regulation: Does Its Costs Outweigh Its Benefits?" *The New York Times,* June 18, 1978, p. E4. 1980 figures are from *The New York Times,* January 4, 1981, Sec. 3, p. 1.

14. Francis E. Rourke, *Bureaucracy, Politics, and Public Policy,* 2nd ed. (Boston: Little, Brown, 1976), p. 46.

15. David Wise, *The Politics of Lying: Government Deception, Secrecy and Power* (New York: Random House, 1973), pp. 200, 210.

16. Francis E. Rourke, *Bureaucratic Power in National Politics,* 1st ed. (Boston: Little, Brown, 1965), p. vii.

17. Rourke, *Bureaucracy, Politics, and Public Policy,* p. 167. For an excellent discussion, see Chapter 7, "Bureaucracy as a Power Elite," pp. 165–184.

18. The story of the policies of the Food Stamp Program is the subject of Nick Kotz's hard-hitting book, *Let Them Eat Promises* (New York: Anchor, 1971).

19. Rourke, *Bureaucracy, Politics, and Public Policy,* p. 183.

20. Thomas E. Cronin, *The State of the Presidency* (Boston: Little, Brown, 1975), p. 19.

21. Harold Seidman, *Politics, Position and Power* (New York: Oxford University Press, 1970), p. 27. Also see David Braybrooke and Charles E. Lindbloom, *A Strategy of Decision* (Glencoe, Ill.: The Free Press, 1963) for a discussion of the science of "muddling through" which the authors suggest is the only way for people to act if they are to operate in a sensible manner.

22. *Weekly Compilation of Presidential Documents,* (Washington, D.C.: U.S. Government Printing Office, October 13, 1969), p. 1399.

23. For the most complete discussion of the Domestic Council, see John H. Kessel, *The Domestic Presidency* (N. Scituate, Mass. Duxbury Press, 1975).

24. Cronin, *The State of the Presidency,* p. 129.

25. Cronin, *The State of the Presidency,* Chapter 1.

26. The Corps of Engineers should not be confused with the Combat Engineers, one of the traditional Army commands.

27. The activity of members of the Internal Revenue Service, CIA, and Justice Department, in "sensitive" positions would have been more restricted.

28. 413 U.S. 548 (1973).

29. For a review of the report, see the *Congressional Quarterly, Weekly Report,* (May 1, 1976), pp. 1019–1025. Data gathering is classified as an *intelligence* activity, and certain activities of the IRS can be classified as *intelligence.* The panel looked at the CIA, FBI, National Security Council, and the intelligence activities of the State Department.

30. Aaron Wildavsky, *The Politics of the Budgetary Process,* rev. ed. (Boston: Little, Brown, 1974), p. 2. This book provides one of the best accounts of the process.

31. Walter Shapiro, "The Intractables," *The Washington Monthly,* (May 1976), pp. 12–18.

32. Wildavsky, *The Politics of the Budgetary Process,* p. 13. For a discussion of the predictability of congressional committee action, see Richard F. Fenno, Jr., *The Power of the Purse* (Boston: Little, Brown, 1966).

33. Since World War II, all Cabinet-level reorganizations have been through legislation, not reorganization plans. Five departments (HEW, HUD,

Transportation, Energy, and Education) have been established; and the Post Office Department was changed into a public corporation.

34. Quoted in Shapiro, "The Intractables," p. 18.

35. Rourke, *Bureaucracy, Politics, and Public Policy*, 2d ed., p. 158.

36. Jack Gonzales and John Rothchild, "The Shriver Prescription: How the Government Can Find Out What It's Doing," *The Washington Monthly*, (November 1972), p. 37.

Suggested Readings

Anthony Downs, *Inside Bureaucracy* (Boston: Little, Brown, 1967).

Murray Edelman, *The Symbolic Uses of Power* (Urbana: University of Illinois Press, 1964).

Charles E. Jacob, *Policy and Bureaucracy* (Princeton, N.J.: D. Van Nostrand, 1966).

Louis M. Kohlmeier, Jr., *The Regulators* (New York: Harper & Row, 1969).

Nick Kotz, *Let Them Eat Promises* (New York: Anchor, 1971).

Francis E. Rourke, *Bureaucracy, Politics, and Public Policy*, 2d ed. (Boston: Little, Brown, 1976).

Francis E. Rourke, *Bureaucratic Power in National Politics*, 1st ed. (Boston: Little, Brown, 1968).

Harold Seidman, *Politics, Position, and Power* (New York: Oxford University Press, 1970).

Aaron Wildavsky, *The Politics of the Budgetary Process*, 3rd ed. (Boston: Little, Brown, 1979).

Peter Woll, *American Bureaucracy* (New York: W.W. Norton, 1963).

CHAPTER 15

Making Public Policy: The Case of Energy

For every complex problem, there's a simple answer, and it's wrong.

H.L. MENCKEN

The years 1977 through 1980 could be called the "energy years." While unemployment and inflation maintained their positions high on the list of the nation's ills, the attempt to develop a comprehensive energy policy appeared to be the number-one priority of the Carter administration and it occupied a considerable amount of Congress's time. As you read this chapter, our lawmakers are continuing to struggle with the exceptionally complex issues of energy that run the gamut from price controls and rationing to the question of the future of nuclear energy. And, the Reagan administration will have established priorities and directions that set it apart from some of Carter's policies.

In previous chapters we have looked at the legal framework, the institutions, patterns of political behavior, and political actors that make up the American political system. Our purpose here is to draw together all of these elements in a discussion of how they have interacted as the government has attempted to develop public policy on energy. We have exposed you to such variables as federalism and states' rights, the undisciplined nature of our political parties, shifting interest group alliances and public attitudes, the electoral connection, the limits of presidential power, and bureaucratic politics; many of these suggest that ours is a system structured for inaction. But, the first function of any political system is survival, and this whole chapter should be read as an "Issue"—the ability of the system to formulate and implement public policy, particularly in the face of a complex crisis.

The Energy "Crisis"

Events in the 1970s briefly aroused energy-rich Americans from a long dream of unlimited energy resources. The term *energy*

Representatives of two oil exporting countries confer about oil price policy in Algiers.

crisis burst upon the national consciousness in the fall of 1973, following the short but fierce war between Israel and a number of Arab states, Egypt and Syria in particular. Eleven Arab countries—members of the Organization of Petroleum Exporting Countries (OPEC)—announced a reduction in oil production and placed an embargo on the sale of oil to certain nations deemed friendly to Israel. The United States, of course, was one of the targets. The non–Arab members of OPEC—Bolivia, Indonesia, and Venezuela—didn't join the embargo, but raised their prices. The embargo was short-lived, but the world price of oil quadrupled, and Americans were angered by long lines at the gas stations during the winter of 1973–1974, lowered thermostats, and mid-winter closings of some schools and factories. OPEC had launched a new era, in which oil is an important instrument of national policy.

While foreign policy received some attention in our discussions of Congress, the presidency, and the "Concorde" issue in the chapter on interest groups, our focus and examples have concentrated on the domestic scene. The case of energy provides an opportunity to point out the interrelated nature of many aspects of domestic and foreign policy.

INTERACTION OF FOREIGN AND DOMESTIC POLICY. America's Middle East policy, reflected in the continued effort to seek an accommodation between Israel and her Arab neighbors, involves a delicate balancing act between our commitment to a sovereign Israel and the need for oil. In 1976, our oil imports exceeded domestic production for the first time, and the Arab oil-producing nations furnished the largest portion of these imports. By 1980, we were importing approximately 8.6 million barrels of oil per day, or forty-three

Former French President, Valery Giscard d'Estaing, tied America's
dependence on imported oil to the health of the world economy.

*At the present time, an important reduction in [U.S.] oil imports is the
precondition for an improvement in the world economy. . . . In my
view this is the most important single source of upheaval in the worldwide network of trade and payments.*

VALERY GISCARD d'ESTAING

Source: Quoted in Congressional Quarterly, *Weekly Report* XXXVI, 28 (July 15, 1978),
p. 1763.

percent of our consumption. Other Western
allies are even more heavily dependent on this
source and are thus affected by U.S.–Arab relations. (The U.S. was not as hard hit by the
1973 embargo as were Germany, the Nether-
lands, and Japan, all countries that are more
dependent than we are on Middle–East oil.)
And Saudi Arabia's control of over one-quar-
ter of the world's known oil reserves makes
that nation's attitudes potentially crucial. Any
U.S. program for energy independence must
consider our relations with other nations.

Our dependence upon imported oil
has had a negative effect on the value of the
American dollar in international money markets and this in turn affects inflation—the nation's public enemy number one. Our dramatic balance of payments deficit in the mid-
and late 1970s—we paid far more in dollars
for imported goods than we received in foreign currencies for exported goods—was increased by the fall in the dollar's value. The
Carter administration estimated that a fall of
one percent in the dollar's value abroad adds
.1 percent to the consumer price index, our
inflation barometer. And, foreign nations tied
confidence in the dollar and the U.S. economy to our willingness to tackle the energy
question. For, the rising cost of imported oil
was at the heart of our balance-of-payments
problem.

Obviously, the connection between

this aspect of the energy problem and domestic inflation gives most Americans a very direct stake in the outcome of energy politics.

THE WINTER OF 1976–77. Although President Nixon responded to the 1973–74 crisis
with a program we will discuss later, the embargo was lifted, we had relatively mild winters, and the preoccupation with Watergate in
1974 and inflation and unemployment in
1975 and 1976 muted any demand for a
meaningful energy program. However, a new
energy crisis hit the nation during the winter
of 1976–77. This one was not precipitated by
an oil shortage, but by severe cold weather
and a shortage of domestically produced natural gas, refueling a controversy that had en-
gulfed Congress for twenty-four or more years,
and almost scuttling Carter's energy program.

The economic impact of the fuel shortage of 1977 was tremendous. Every school in
Pennsylvania was closed for a time and
schools in parts of many northeastern and
midwestern states also closed their doors.
Over 400,000 workers were laid off in Ohio,
and the nationwide estimate was 2 million or
more layoffs. Eight states proclaimed states of
emergency, and the gross national product
(GNP) fell off approximately two percent during the last week in January and the first week
in February, a situation that, had it continued,

would have resulted in a $35 billion cut in the GNP.

Many students reading this may not realize that the events of 1977 and the costs of fuel probably have had a direct effect upon college calendars. Many schools extended the Christmas break into January 1977, and rising fuel bills since have led to decisions to stay closed during that month and to extend the semester later into the spring.

WHEN WILL THE OIL RUN OUT?

Oil supplies almost one-half of our energy needs. When will the oil run out? Estimates suggest that with new oil finds and maximum production and pumping, severe problems can be held off until the late 1980s or early 1990s. Through the 1980s at least, the U.S. and its friends will depend heavily on OPEC. Washington, and other world powers, must manage the intense and complex interactions between energy and foreign policy and prevent nations from colliding in the predicted mad scramble for the nonrenewable fuels that remain.[1]

Before we turn to the politics of energy policy, brief mention of the results of two 1977 studies may help to provide an understanding of the environment in which the energy game is being played. One was conducted by the Central Intelligence Agency and the other by the Massachusetts Institute of Technology (MIT).

THE CIA REPORT. The CIA's report was criticized by some people as overly gloomy and perhaps designed to bolster President Carter's position on energy. It predicted a worldwide crisis by 1985 unless conservation measures were implemented around the globe. By that date, domestic production of oil by the United States, Canada, Japan, and Western European nations would fall short of their needs by 34 million barrels of oil per

Rising gasoline costs has led many Americans to change their transportation habits.

day. The report also said that the Soviet Union's oil industry "was in trouble" and that by 1985 the Soviets would be competing for oil imports. The key to the situation, according to the report, is Saudi Arabia's willingness to meet the increased demand by doubling present production, an unlikely prospect, because it would deplete Saudi reserves and the nation does not really need the extra income from increased exports.[2]

THE MIT REPORT. The MIT report was based upon a two-and-one-half year study by a panel of thirty-five experts from the ranks of business, government, and academia of fifteen non-communist countries. In some respects, this report was grimmer than the CIA study, and added credence to the Agency's report.

The MIT panel predicted a worldwide shortage of oil before the year 2000, and perhaps as early as 1981 (remember, this is a 1977 study). The actual timing of the crisis depends upon Saudi Arabia, and the experts said that a doubling of Saudi production would hold off the crisis, delaying it to sometime between 1985 and 1995.

The report added that doubling of the non-communist world's coal production, multiplying nuclear power output 15 to 25 times, cutting the growth rate of oil consumption in half, and allowing oil prices to double will not eliminate the shortage. The panel urged conservation and a shift to other fuels, including a crash program to triple coal production and increased reliance on nuclear energy. They urged the development of renewable energy sources such as solar or thermal (underground steam) energy that could and must play a large role in the next century. In the absence of swift action, the panel predicted economic havoc and perhaps war.

The years up to 1985 are critical ones. We cannot afford to waste the years immediately ahead if we are to have any large scale energy options available before the end of the century. The time for decisive action is now.[3]

The Politics of Energy

If three presidents, Nixon, Ford, and Carter, appeared to recognize that a crisis exists, why was so little action taken between 1973 and 1976, and why did Carter's 1977 proposal fare so badly in Congress? Are government leaders shortsighted, or do they reflect the complacency and attitudes of the American public? Do we all share the blame for inaction? What conditions led to Carter's greater success with his second round of proposals, introduced in 1979? For part of the answer we can look at opinion polls taken between March 1973 and April 1977.

ENERGY POLICY 1973–1976: PUBLIC AWARENESS AND PARTISAN POLITICS

WHAT CRISIS? The energy concerns of the 1960s and early 1970s focussed on environmental issues rather than scarcity. Twice each year the Gallup organization asks its survey sample to identify the nation's top problems. In March 1973, energy was not listed as one of the responses. By September, just after the outbreak of armed conflict in the Middle East, eighty-three percent of the people said that they were aware of an energy crisis. But the October survey found only eight percent identifying energy as one of the top problems, placing it eighth on the list. The energy crisis did not move into the top spot, overtaking the "High Cost of Living"— the usual frontrunner—until the poll released in February 1974.[4] Its stay in first place was brief, with no more than seven percent of the survey sample mentioning energy in the second 1974 poll and the two taken in 1975. First Watergate, and then inflation and unemployment, dominated the public's concern. Another fuel shortage did not occur until January 1977, and energy was not mentioned often enough to be listed as a separate response on the three 1976 surveys.

The polls also provided decision-makers with other clues about public attitudes. Few people objected to such conservation measures as lowered thermostats, reduced speed limits, using less electricity, and using their cars less. But a majority disapproved of the idea of a ban on Sunday driving, prohibiting gas sales on Sunday, gas rationing, or closing schools for an extra week. And as far as assigning responsibility for the shortages, the public was divided. The oil companies came under criticism for their large profits after the 1973 embargo, and the largest group (25 percent) named them as the culprits, with the government in general, the administration, and consumers following in that order.

PUBLIC OPINION AND PUBLIC POLICY.
Public opinion rarely determines the details of
policy, but it can have a strong influence over
the general direction that policy takes. The
government's bandaid approach to energy
problems during the 1973–76 period reflected
public attitudes. And, public perceptions
handicapped Carter's energy initiatives. To
the general public, the energy planners were
like storm-wise householders on a cloudless
afternoon, nailing up windows and laying in
food against new storms approaching from
over the horizon, while passers-by looked on
with curious incomprehension.[5]

If the public dozed, why did Congress
wrestle so hard with the energy proposals of
three presidents? The answer, of course, is
that particular publics, the special interests,
had much to win or lose depending on the
shape of energy policy.

PARTISAN POLITICS. The best that can be
said about the results of the 1973–76
struggles between two Republican presidents
and the Democratic-dominated Congress is
that a hodgepodge of energy measures passed;
however, they added up to less than a policy.
There was a considerable expenditure of time
and effort, hundreds of proposals, and
thousands of words written and spoken, but
1977 found us even more vulnerable to
energy shortages.

What do you think went wrong? Give
yourself a *B* if you said that presidential
proposals reflected a traditional Republican
and southern Democratic alliance with the
views of industry, as opposed to most
Democrats' suspicion of industry's motives
and intentions—in this case the energy
industry—and their concern with the impact
of proposals upon the middle class and less
affluent members of society who make up the
bedrock of the party's support. If you added
that the issue was further complicated by
parochial attitudes based upon regional and
urban–rural differences about the effect of

one scheme or another upon particular constituencies, and that these divisions prevented
the congressional Democrats from formulating
an alternative policy, your answer rates a *A−*.
Finally, we would give you an *A* if you added
that at times it was hard to tell the interest
group line-ups without a scorecard. For example, the automobile industry (management)
and the United Automobile Workers were allied by their fear of the economic impact of
strict automobile emission controls and mileage standards. And, in the absence of a nationwide perception of the seriousness of the
crisis, the cards were stacked against the formulation of a real energy program.

REPUBLICAN PLANS. Before becoming preoccupied with Watergate, Nixon had announced
"Project Independence," a plan to make
America independent of foreign oil by 1980.
Most observers assumed that this was an unrealistic target, and about the only long-lasting
result of Nixon initiatives was the reduction of
the speed limit to 55 mph and the go-ahead
for construction of the more than 500-mile
Alaskan pipeline. President Ford's energy
proposals reflected the Republican view that
industry would work for energy independence
if it could be liberated from the constraints of
price controls, which make research and development unprofitable. Another assumption
was that if fuel prices were allowed to seek
their natural level, the public would conserve
energy.

THE "UNDISCIPLINED" DEMOCRATS. The
Democratic position was that industry was
driven almost exclusively by the profit motive,
and that decontrol of prices or the relaxation
of environmental standards would lead to
exploitation of the consumer and the environment. Beyond this plank, economic, philosophical, and regional differences divided the
party, and proved to be an insurmountable
barrier to the creation of an alternate plan. For
example, southern Democrats, in general,

Solar power applications resulting from the energy crisis include a McDonald's restaurant (top) and an experimental farm in Maryland.

took a conservative and pro-industry position, and the representatives of the energy producing states—Louisiana, Oklahoma, and Texas—joined Republicans in the defense of the oil and gas industries.

Congressional Democratic leaders felt the need to offer an alternate energy program rather than risk the charge that the majority party's approach was purely negative. In spite of the opinion polls, they decided upon a tax-based approach through a boosting of some fuel prices to encourage conservation. The House Ways and Means Committee put together a proposal in 1975, the key to which was an immediate three-cents-per-gallon increase for gasoline and a standby two-cents-per-gallon increase if gasoline consumption exceeded 1973 levels.

The gasoline tax proposal was overwhelmingly rejected by members of both parties in the House (345–72); the following year, a similar move in the Senate lost by a 65–21 margin. The message to the next administration should have been clear.

If we assume that the policy struggle over energy pitted the industry on one side, against environmentalists and relatively unorganized but well-represented (in Congress) consumer interests on the other, the scorecard for the period offers a confused picture of who won and who lost.

WHO WON, WHO LOST? The energy industry lobbied hard for deregulating the price of new natural gas sold in the interstate market, federal subsidy of research and development, decontrol of oil prices, and retention of the "oil depletion allowance." The allowance was a tax advantage, enjoyed since 1926, which allowed the oil and gas producers to reduce the amount of their income subject to federal income taxes by a percentage representing the extent to which their resources, oil and gas wells, were depleted each year by production. While the industry lost each of these battles, every decision did

not mean a victory for consumer interests. The maintenance of price controls certainly held down costs to the average person, but over the long run, the failure to provide incentives for research and development could make losers out of everyone.

Industry's victories included Ford's successful veto of a bill to provide minimum federal standards for the regulation of surface (strip) mining, and Congress's rejection of two bills, one to break up the major oil companies, and the other to require industry to share equally the cost of overruns on the nuclear breeder reactor project. Environmental interests were the clear losers in the strip mining veto.

STALEMATE. On balance, the energy industry did not fare badly during the 94th Congress (1975–76). With the exception of the oil depletion allowance, their wins and losses amounted to a retention of the system as it was—a status quo. The conservative coalition of Republicans and southern Democrats, reinforced by regional interests with a direct bearing on the "electoral connection," were able to protect industry. And, the stalemate in Congress was offset, in part, by executive branch action which allowed the average price of domestic crude oil to rise slowly, and a revised pricing system by the Federal Power Commission which saw the price of new natural gas rise in 1976 as much as 300 percent. This accounted for the increased cost to the consumer. The lesson here is that your wins or losses in one forum can be offset by decisions in another one.

THE BUREAUCRATIC HODGEPODGE. In the last chapter, we discussed the importance of the bureaucracy in the formulating and carrying out of public policy. The president relies on the expertise of the bureaucrats, but organizational problems can get in the way of coordinated advice.

Although an Energy Policy Office was

A powerful legislator expressed his frustrations with the failure of
Congress to produce energy policy.

*We have dabbled with oil and gas pricing. We have made more money availa-
ble for long-range research, for things like solar energy, that may help
us 30 or 40 years from now. But as for doing anything practical to
increase the supply of energy and reduce our dependence upon foreign
sources in the foreseeable future, we have done nothing.*

JIM WRIGHT (D., Texas)

Source: Quoted in Congressional Quarterly, *Weekly Report* 34 (October 16, 1976), pp.
2981–82.

established in 1973, during the entire period
in question, 1973–1976, the chief executive
was hampered by a crazy-quilt pattern of seventy or more offices, agencies, and committees
that had responsibilities relating to energy.
The establishment of the Energy Research
and Development Administration—a replacement for the Atomic Energy Commission—
eased the situation somewhat, but real reorganization did not take place until the creation
of the new Cabinet-level Department of Energy in 1977. Even so, the new Department
was not in place until four months after Carter
introduced his energy plan. Although he had
previously appointed James Schlesinger as
"Energy Czar" in an attempt to coordinate
policy formulation, our guess is that the administration's inexperience, and the dis-
jointed energy structure that Carter inherited,
hampered the creation of a program that could
be sold to Congress.

CARTER'S ENERGY POLICY
1977–1978: A PROGRAM
WITHOUT A CONSTITUENCY

During the 1976 election campaign,
President Ford and candidate Carter agreed
on the nation's fundamental energy needs:
less reliance on foreign oil; accelerated development of existing domestic energy and new
alternative sources; and more efficient use of
energy. However, they disagreed on the
means to these ends. But energy did not enjoy
the same campaign emphasis that Carter
placed on unemployment, inflation, and tax
welfare reform.

The new administration had no real
plan, but the natural gas crisis of the winter of
1976–77 forced Carter's hand, and in April
he sent Congress his program to meet the
crisis that he called "the greatest domestic
challenge that our nation will face in our lifetime." [6] Unfortunately, Carter erred in ordering
James Schlesinger—later to be the first secretary of energy—to come up with a plan
within ninety days. He, and a small group he
pulled together, hammered out the plan in
secret. They did not consult key members of
Congress from the committees that would
handle the legislation. And they did not consult with the available non-political energy
experts in the bureaucracy. These experts felt
left out, and were quick to point out the flaws
in the proposal after it was made public. The
administration had ignored the sensitivity of
the "permanent" government and paid the
price in terms of credibility.

The administration mobilized to sell its program to Congress and the people in anticipation of interest group and regional opposition. While the man in the White House had changed and Democrats controlled both ends of Pennsylvania Avenue for the first time in eight years, the old obstacles remained unaltered. The end of winter and the availability of fuel quickly drove the issue from the general public's mind. Regional differences about details of Carter's energy proposals cut across party lines. In addition, the questions of natural gas pricing created a coalition of pro-industry anti-regulation forces within both parties. The problems of presidential leadership of an "undisciplined" party were never more apparent. And Congress, irrespective of the party label worn by the chief executive, had no intention of giving up its post–1973 independence. Finally, Carter's early dealings with Congress over such matters as water projects had reinforced congressional backbones. It may not be an exaggeration to say that the new, inexperienced president could not have picked a worse subject as his first major test in the domestic policy arena.

Mr. Schlesinger's comment made during the struggle for passage of the plan identified the crux of the problem. He said:

The basic problem is that there is not constituency for an Energy Program: There are many constituencies opposed, but the basic constituency for the program is the future.[7]

THE CARTER PLAN. Table 15–1, an energy boxscore, outlines the key parts of the Carter program and the fate of the various proposals in the House and Senate. The "final action" column lists the elements of the compromise finally adopted.

The heart of this plan was "disincentives," or making energy cost more so that consumers would use less of it. To minimize the impact of the higher cost, Carter proposed to return much of the money to the consumers through tax credits. Almost the entire emphasis was placed on energy conservation as a short-run solution to the energy shortages. Incentives for increased production or research and development were not included.

IS ANYBODY HAPPY? In the great game of politics, as in almost all other endeavors, it is impossible to make everyone happy. But Carter's programs appeared to be designed to make no one happy. Where were the potential winners? Depending on high cost to force conservation has proven to be a high-risk gamble in the United States. Increased costs involve laying out money "up front," and both industry and the public are skeptical of tax credits that will put money back into their pockets. When you have to pay a bill now, the thought of a rebate in a year is little consolation. Increased prices for oil and gasoline were also suspect in that they have the greatest relative impact upon the less affluent members of society. One Federal Energy Administration official told of being at a town meeting in Kansas where an aged white-haired woman complained that her January 1977 home heating bill took $100 of her $160 month income. "And she looked at the panel," the official recalled, "and she said, 'What am I to do, heat or eat?'"[8]

Oil industry officials were dismayed by the lack of incentives for research and development, an oil tax from which they would not benefit, and Carter's plan to extend controls on natural gas to the interstate market. Spokesmen for the coal industry were skeptical of the program's insistence on environmental controls on both the mining and combustion of coal. They argued that these environmental concerns and the goal of doubling production were contradictory.

And, as you can guess, auto management and labor were vigorously opposed to the tax on gas "guzzlers." They feared that it would not encourage a switch to smaller cars,

CARTER ENERGY PROPOSAL	HOUSE ACTION	SENATE ACTION	CONFERENCE	FINAL ACTION
Tax credits for home insulation	Approved	Approved	Maximum $300 credit approved	Passed
Boost in gasoline tax	Rejected	Rejected by Finance Committee		
Tax on "gas guzzling" cars	Approved	Rejected; ban on their production approved instead	Approved	Passed
Rebate of "gas guzzler" tax to buyers of gas-saving cars	Rejected by Ways and Means Committee	Not considered		
Mandatory energy efficiency standards for home appliances	Approved	Approved	Approved	Passed
Extension of natural gas price controls with higher price ceiling	Approved	Rejected; approved ending federal price controls for new gas	Agreement to end federal price controls on new natural gas by 1985	Passed
Tax on crude oil	Approved	Rejected by Finance Committee	Killed by conference	
Tax on utility and industrial use of oil and natural gas	Approved, weaker than Carter plan	Approved, but weaker than House or Carter plan	Killed by conference	
Authority to force utility, industrial conversion from oil, gas to coal	Approved	Approved, but weaker than House version	Compromise reached Nov. 11, 1977; conference report filed July 14, 1978	Passed
Reform of electric utility rates	Approved	Rejected	Compromise reached	Passed

Source: Adapted from Congressional Quarterly, *Weekly Report* 36 (October 21, 1978).
p. 3040. Reprinted by permission.

but only make people hang on longer to their large cars, force layoff of workers, and damage the economy. The fact that foreign cars dominate the small-car market did nothing to encourage their support. Two years earlier, the UAW had supported a bill to impose strict mileage standards, but in 1977 the workers saw eye-to-eye with management. As for the consumers who would bear the burden of the tax, they did not approve of either the cost or the enforced change in lifestyle. The middle and lower income groups already found it difficult to purchase new cars, and how do you put a family of five or more in a compact car for a trip?

Even the environmentalists had mixed emotions. They approved of the delay in nuclear breeder reactors, but would have preferred delays or abandonment of plans for additional conventional nuclear plants. They feared the return to coal and were properly skeptical of the likelihood of Congress mandating tough standards.

THE LACK OF PUBLIC SUPPORT. President Carter addressed the nation on national TV three times in the spring of 1977 about the energy issue. He called the effort to deal with the problem the "moral equivalent of war" (see insert). He had anticipated the chorus of interest group dissent; the President hoped for grass-roots public support to counter-balance group lobbying in the House and Senate, but this support did not materialize. Gallup polls taken in February 1977, indicated widespread approval of Carter's handling of the cold-weather emergency, but this was two months before he unveiled his program. As had happened after the 1973 embargo, the public quickly forgot the problems of the winter of 1977.[9]

Following Carter's "declaration of

President Carter's words expressed an understanding of the seriousness of the situation. However, his program and public attitudes did not reflect the same depth of concern.

Tonight I want to have an unpleasant talk with you about a problem unprecedented in our history. With the exception of preventing war, this is the greatest challenge our country will face during our lifetime. The energy crisis has not yet overwhelmed us, but it will if we do not act quickly. . . . Our decision about energy will test the character of the American people and the ability of the president and Congress to govern this nation. This difficult effort will be the "moral equivalent of war"—except that we will be uniting our efforts to build and not to destroy.

JIMMY CARTER

Source: Television speech, April 18, 1977.

war," 44 percent of the public identified the energy situation as "very serious," a rise of three points from the pre-speech survey. Another 41 percent labeled it as "fairly serious." Successive 1977 and 1978 surveys found the figures for both categories fluctuating within a few points above or below 40 percent.[10] While this might suggest strong public backing, only 23 percent of the public identified the energy situation as our most important problem in April 1977, trailing inflation (58%) and unemployment (39%). In three following surveys, the energy score fell to 17.8 percent and then 4 percent, the last figure reflecting the public's view a month before the October 1978 passage of the compromise energy program.[11]

For their part, members of Congress were more attentive to the polls reporting that three out of four Americans travel to work by car, that one of three could not get to work without a car, and that 56 percent said that it would be "very difficult" or "fairly difficult" to decrease their dependence on automobiles.[12] And the President's confidence in

public opinion would have been badly damaged if he had known in April that a poll released in June would disclose the almost unbelievable fact that only about half of the American people understood that our country has to import oil to meet its energy needs.[13]

As we have argued in other chapters, Congress is a representative body, but certainly not a visionary one. In the absence of a perception by the public—or by the vocal segment of it—of a need for strong action, and the demand for such action, is it surprising that the partisan and regional differences over energy policy are extremely difficult to resolve? Unlike the environmental/conservation groups, no comparable organizations were warning us of the existence of an energy crisis, or pressuring Congress to deal with the issue as if our lives depended upon it.

THE RULES OF THE GAME. On August 5, 1977, following three months of relentless spurring from Speaker Thomas P. O'Neill, Jr. (D., Mass.), the House passed Carter's energy policy package. Although the gasoline tax was killed and natural gas regulation was made more digestible to the producing states by allowing a gradual price rise, Carter got most of what he wanted. What accounted for this relatively smooth trip through the House?

As we explained in an earlier chapter, the House is governed by a stricter set of rules than the Senate, and the leaders have more power than their counterparts in the upper chamber. Taking advantage of the strict rules, the Speaker insisted that the five committees considering various aspects of the package finish their deliberations within ten weeks and then used his influence to persuade the House to create an unprecedented *Ad Hoc* Committee on Energy to reconcile the versions of the energy bill coming from the five standing committees. It was a very unusual step, as committees are reluctant to give up any power over their particular policy turf. O'Neill handpicked the members of the *Ad Hoc* Committee, loading it with backers of the President's proposals.

The House Rules Committee sent the bill to the floor under a modified "closed" rule which minimized possible attacks on the legislation by limiting the sections that could be amended. And limited debate rules, unlike the unlimited debates allowed in the Senate, kept control of the debate in the hands of the leadership.

An attempt by most Republicans and southern Democrats to pass an amendment deregulating natural gas provided the greatest challenge to the package. After hours of debate, Speaker O'Neill made a rare speech from the floor, urging his colleagues to vote against "big oil" and its monumental lobbying effort. No doubt he exaggerated when he said that "America is watching this legislation more than it has watched any legislation in years," and he challenged the House to show that it could pull together an energy policy.[14]

The deregulation forces blamed their defeat on the compromise allowing price rises and the "electoral connection" membership concern with the 1978 elections. Unlike the gas pricing compromise of 1978, which found consumer and industry groups and pro- and anti-deregulation legislators joined against what they viewed as an unsatisfactory compromise, the package that the House passed in 1977 confined most of the Democratic defections to the South.

TROUBLES IN THE SENATE. If you ever doubted the old adage, "The rules of the game determine the outcome," the fate of the energy package in the Senate should erase any doubts. The distribution of power in the Senate is a barrier to the type of strong leadership that O'Neill exercised in the House, and Majority Leader Robert Byrd (D., W. Va.) could not control the situation. The Senate committees would not give up any powers, and there was no attempt to create an *Ad Hoc* Committee to pull together the work of the standing committees. Unlimited debate, the use of the filibuster, and the unavailability of a "closed" rule to restrict amendments guaranteed an open season on any controversial proposal when it reached the Senate floor.

The Senate Energy Committee gutted the non-tax provisions of Carter's plan, eliminating utility rate reform, weakening the coal conversion aspects, and deadlocking over natural gas regulation. Meanwhile, the Senate Finance Committee, chaired by Russell B. Long (D., La.) killed the crude oil and industrial user taxes, and substituted a series of very generous tax credits to industry for conservation and conversion.

The Senate divided the package into six separate bills and approved most of the changes made by its committees. Some of the president's tax proposals were restored, but the Senate voted in favor of deregulation of natural gas prices, a decision that was to delay final passage of the program for a year.

THE NATURAL GAS CONTROVERSY. Natural gas accounts for fully thirty percent of United

States energy consumption; it heats half of our homes and supplies fifty percent of industry's energy needs. It is a clean-burning, virtually pollution-free fuel, and it is a "bargain" as fuels go. Most of our natural gas comes from Texas, Louisiana, Oklahoma, offshore rigs in the Gulf of Mexico, and parts of California, Kansas, and New Mexico. It is usually found with oil, and its chief producers are the major oil companies, particularly Exxon, Gulf, Mobil, and Shell. They sell the gas to more than one hundred pipeline companies who own and operate the 200,000-plus miles of pipeline that serve the nation. The pipeline companies, in turn, sell to local distributors, who service the customers.

Government regulation has made natural gas a cheap fuel. The Natural Gas Act of 1938 gave the Federal Power Commission the authority to regulate the transport and wholesale price of natural gas moved in interstate commerce. In effect, this held down the price that the pipeline companies could charge to distributors. But gas sold intrastate—within Texas for example—has sold for as much as four times the price of interstate gas. Of course, it was more advantageous for producers to sell to intrastate pipeline companies, and producing states such as Texas capitalized on their energy abundance.

While the demand for natural gas has continued to rise, America's natural gas reserves decreased in the years between 1967 and 1977. The producers argued that the "artificially" low prices for interstate gas did not yield sufficient profit to provide incentives for exploration and development of new oil and gas fields. The lower prices for interstate gas discouraged producers from selling in that market and, as a result, the North and East have run dangerously low on gas during recent severe winters.

President Carter proposed that all natural gas—interstate and intrastate—be regulated, an idea that was hailed by consumer groups and many legislators from areas hard hit in 1977. Naturally, the producers and the legislators from the producer states argued for deregulation of all natural gas. The compromise that saved the energy bill was to control intrastate gas until 1985, while allowing a gradual rise in the price of gas in the interstate market until controls are removed on all natural gas in 1985. The politics behind this compromise made no one happy.

NATURAL GAS FILIBUSTER. The battle over natural gas deregulation culminated in an exhausting fourteen-day debate that included 128 roll-call votes and a nine-day "filibuster by amendment" by the anti-deregulation forces. The filibuster was ended by Vice-President Mondale, sitting in the chair, when he ruled that certain amendments were simply delaying tactics or out of order. The leaders of the filibuster felt they had been double-crossed by the White House, assuming that Mondale would not have ruled as he did if President Carter had not agreed to the tactic. Although conspiracy was denied, here was a case of the President's having to bow to the reality that a failure of the Senate to act would probably kill his whole program. He hoped that the next step, conference committee resolution of the differences between the House and Senate versions, would result in a compromise more to his liking.

The bill deregulating natural gas prices passed by a vote of 50 to 46 with Republicans dividing 34 to 3 and Democrats dividing 16 to 43. Eleven of the 16 Democrats voting in favor of the bill were from the South. The outcome illustrates that in our system of undisciplined parties, members of the minority party can often end up on the winning side.

THE CONFERENCE COMMITTEE STRUGGLE. Leaders of both houses appointed a conference committee drawn from the members of the committees that worked on the energy package and who represented the various viewpoints on the most controversial issues.

Senator Muskie describes the arguments on behalf of the natural gas compromise.

They don't talk about the merits of the bill. They tell you that the president needs a bill to pass to save face politically and that the country needs it for international prestige.

Senator EDMUND S. MUSKIE (D., Me.)

Source: Congressional Quarterly, *Weekly Report* 36 (September 6, 1978), p. 2452.

Agreement was reached rather quickly on the less controversial matters (see Table 15–1), but on natural gas, the confrontation was the climax of a twenty-five-year battle between oil states and consumer states.

It took the deeply divided Senate delegation four months to reach agreement on a compromise, but at that point, the House delegation refused to negotiate. It required direct presidential intervention, with Carter summoning both sides to the White House for intensive negotiations, to break the impasse. On May 24, 1978, the conferees approved the gas pricing compromise that temporarily controlled intrastate prices, allowed interstate prices to rise gradually, and lifted price controls on all natural gas in 1985. The vote was 23 to 19 with House conferees split 13 to 12 and Senate conferees dividing 10 to 7.

FINAL PASSAGE. President Carter praised the compromise as an "historic agreement" and predicted that it would cost the consumers no more than the inadequate system it was replacing. But consumer advocates took the opposite view, and Senator James Abourezk (D., S.D.) called it a "rip-off" and a "rape of the American consumer." He added that the sole beneficiaries would be the "titans of the oil and gas industry, whose lust for profits has been unmatched in the annals of American business."[15]

Perhaps a more accurate description of the bill was provided by Dale Bumpers (D., Ark.) who said that prices would go up whether the bill passed or was defeated. He added:

Depending on who one believes, the bill will either increase gas production, or slow it down; aid the dollar, or harm it; curb inflation, or fan it; encourage industry to use more gas, or prompt switches to coal; be easier to administer than current law, or spawn a regulatory nightmare.[16]

The Senate took up the bill in September, and the anti-regulation and some of the pro-regulation forces formed a strange coalition born out of mutual unhappiness with the compromise. To offset defections by his usual allies, Carter and the Democratic leaders in the Senate mounted an intense lobbying effort to get key industrial users of natural gas to support the compromise and bring pressure to bear on the senators. The main arguments were not about the merits of the bill but the alleged effect of its defeat on the health of the dollar, domestic inflation, and the prestige of the president.

Opponents of the compromise waged a ferocious battle in the Senate, but it passed on September 27, 1978 by a vote of 57 to 42, a margin that reflected the strength of the lobbying effort and the effectiveness of the loyalty-prestige appeals. Final passage found oil-producing state senators, some conservatives who wanted immediate deregulation, and some liberal pro-regulation senators linked in opposition.

LOSERS CAN BE WINNERS. The Congressional Quarterly's report of the scene that took place immediately after the vote provides an insight into the atmosphere that prevents the legislative process from breaking down. Senator Henry M. Jackson (D., Wash.), the chairman of the Energy Committee, had been a leader in the fight to break the conference deadlock and provide the President with an energy package. Among his staunchest opponents on the natural gas issue were Abourezk, Howard Metzenbaum (D., Ohio), and Clifford P. Hansen (R., Wyo.).

After the vote, Jackson turned to shake hands with his two top aides . . . then he reached across the aisle to Hansen, Metzenbaum came up to join them, grabbing elbow, shaking hands. Then Jackson moved along, greeting Abourezk with a big handshake. All were smiling.[17]

The losers were satisfied that they had waged the good fight, and for purposes of the electoral connection, they could campaign on the grounds that they did their best on behalf of consumer interests. As we discussed in an earlier chapter, it is more important, from an electoral point of view, to be on the right side rather than the winning side.

THE RULES AT WORK. While the House waited for Senate action, Speaker O'Neill was busy making preparations. The key to success hinged on his ability to get the House to vote to treat the energy program as one bill rather than take the Senate approach of dividing the package into six parts. Congress was in its final week of the session, and O'Neill was not confident that a separate compromise natural gas pricing bill would pass.

Friday, October 13, 1978, proved to be a lucky day for supporters of the package. By a one-vote margin, 207 to 206, the House defeated an attempt to split apart the eighteen-month-old energy plan. The coalition of Democrats and Republicans, conservatives and liberals, conceded defeat on the gas issue.

Congressional passage of a comprehensive energy program in 1978 was hailed by President Carter as an indication that those in government, particularly Congress, could courageously deal with an issue, and one that tests our national will and ability.

The words of praise probably represented Carter's relief at having salvaged something of the original energy proposal that he had sent to Congress in April 1977. The President had made energy his first major priority, and he was hungry for a legislative victory of sorts from a Congress that, although controlled by his own party, had given him few positive responses to his policy proposals.

WHO WON, WHO LOST? The energy package, in its final version, was far weaker than the measure the President sent to Capitol Hill. The crude oil tax, described by Carter as the centerpiece of the plan, was abandoned. And lifting price controls on natural gas by 1985 was contrary to the administration's desire to have long-standing controls on all natural gas. The tax disincentives designed to push industry to convert to coal and take other conservation steps became tax incentives to industry.

Carter won in the sense that the failure of Congress to enact the program would have been a blow to his standing as a legislative leader. But, when you ask whether the oil and automotive industries and the American public in general won or lost, the answers become less clear.

Why did the oil lobby fight the bill that would allow the price of newly produced gas to double by 1985? The answer to the question is that the industry was fighting for the whole pie, not half of the pie. Oil interests saw a chance to win a twenty-four-year battle for deregulation. Although a partial victory was won, the industry was and is worried that controls could be reinstated after 1985 (the law allows this for an 18-month period), or that future Congresses might undo the compromise and regulate all natural gas.

The automotive industry, management and labor, escaped a ban on the production of gas guzzlers. However, the bill provided a $200 to $500 tax on 1980 models getting less than 15 miles per gallon and raised to a maximum of $3,850 the tax on 1986 cars getting less than 12.5 mpg. This version provided less stringent minimums and a more gradual time-frame than Carter's original plan. And, it is our guess that the survival of the tax represented the automotive industry's confidence that it would have little difficulty in meeting the standards, a confidence that has been borne out since 1978.

People who insulate their homes were given a tax credit. But, these were the only bright spots for the consuming public, who are faced with steadily rising oil and natural gas prices and the spectre of uncontrolled natural gas prices after 1985. Whether or not the bill represented the "rape" of the American consumer, as opponents argued, awaits the judgment of history. Certainly, the legislation was a triumph of sorts for the special interests.

The Energy Bill of 1978 could hardly be considered an effective response to the crisis the world faces during the coming decades. Although one of the administration's advocates told industrial leaders prior to the bill's enactment that "it no longer makes a difference whether the bill is a *C* minus or an *A* plus. Certainly, it is better than zero, and it must pass;" over the long run, a program that is only better than zero represents a failure of public policy.[18]

Carter recognized the weaknesses in the compromise plan, and in 1979 he launched a second and more successful round of energy proposals.

ENERGY POLICY 1979–1980: A RESPONSE TO EVENTS

The energy policy enacted in 1978 had done little or nothing to extricate the U.S. from its dependence on foreign oil. Carter's proposal for taxes that would increase the cost of gas and oil and therefore reduce consumption had been rejected. Neither had the program addressed the need to develop alternate sources of energy. The attempt to force utilities to convert from gas and oil to coal had been watered down, and no real steps had been taken to redevelop the coal industry. Ironically, our coal reserves are estimated to be over 700 times greater than our current annual consumption of coal, but it ranks third behind oil and natural gas as a source of energy.

More than half the coal produced in the United States is used at electric generating plants; most of the rest is consumed at industrial plants or exported. The cost of conversion, environmental concerns such as pollution and the impact of strip mining, the need for expensive safety improvements in the mining industry, refurbishing of the railroad network that would have to move a greatly expanded coal tonnage, and the time and money needed for research and development of means to make coal "cleaner" or convert it economically to synthetic gas or oil, all suggest that coal, as an alternate source, will not provide a simple answer to our energy needs.

THE CARTER PROPOSALS. In 1979, under authority previously granted by the Congress, President Carter decided to gradually remove price controls on domestic oil, with all controls to be eliminated by October 1, 1981. This move to allow the prices to rise to world market levels was intended both to force consumers to conserve energy and to encourage oil companies to explore for new oil. At the heart of the plan was Carter's pledge to hold oil imports to 8.2 million barrels a day—the record 1977 level—in the short run and to cut imports to 4.5 million barrels a day by 1990.

In return for lifting controls, and in order to soften the political impact of increased prices, the President proposed a "windfall profits tax" on the oil companies to recover part of the difference between the decontrolled prices of oil and the controlled price. He wanted to use some of the revenue from the tax to aid the poor in meeting energy costs, improve mass transit, and develop synthetic fuels.

His second major proposal was the creation of a quasi-public synthetic fuel corporation to offer loans, price guarantees, and other incentive devices to promote private development of synthetic fuels. Actually, the plan had originated in Congress; the House had passed a version and the Senate was working on one of its own when Carter wisely moved to gain control of the issue.

The third proposal in Carter's energy "triple crown" called for the creation of an Energy Mobilization Board with authority to set aside state and local regulations that impede energy projects. Called "fast-track" legislation, it would have sped up the licensing of vital energy projects.

A windfall profits tax was passed by Congress in March 1980, and the synthetic fuels bill was enacted in June of that year. However, the Energy Mobilization Board legislation, surprisingly, was defeated in the House in June 1980.[19]

After rejecting a standby gasoline rationing plan in 1979, Congress did not block a 1980 Carter plan which would be imposed when oil supplies fall twenty percent below normal demand. However, the President's 1980 use of executive authority to impose an oil import fee that would have raised gasoline prices by 10 cents per gallon was blocked by Congress when it overwhelmingly overrode Carter's veto of a resolution killing the oil import fee.[20]

Although the President won some bat- tles, and lost others, he had much to be pleased about. After three years of effort, he and the Congress had finally agreed on a basic energy plan designed to move the nation toward greater energy self-sufficiency.

Why had 1980 proved to be a good year for energy? Had the President become more skillful or the Congress more visionary? Had the public been awakened from its energy apathy? Or had events provided the catalyst for change? Finally, what had happened to the controversy over nuclear energy?

PUBLIC AWARENESS AND SOARING PRICES. Public opinion became an ally of the President in 1979 as fuel prices for heating and at the gas pumps continued to rise. In March, the energy issue took over second place on the list of the nation's most important problems (33 percent to 57 percent for inflation) and remained there throughout the year.[21] And, after two-and-one-half years, the public seemed to be getting the administration's message. Forty-seven percent of Gallup interviewees said the energy problem was "very serious" and another 35 percent labelled it "fairly serious."[22] Almost half of the people blamed the domestic oil companies for the price rises, not the government or OPEC, but they remained opposed to rationing.[23]

OIL COMPANY PROFITS. The oil companies and their friends in Congress were vigorously opposed to a windfall profits tax, contending that it amounted to more government interference and a draining off of revenue needed for research and exploration. But, the October announcement by the companies of their third-quarter earnings enraged many citizens and undercut the industry's position. For example, Standard Oil of Ohio reported a 191 percent increase, while Conoco, Mobil, and Gulf had increased earnings of 134, 130, and 97 percent respectively over the same quarter in 1978.

The announcement prompted Carter

to point out that the "figures demonstrate the need for a major portion of unearned profits from the oil companies to go into the general service of the American people."[24]

THREE MILE ISLAND. Another major event that worked on behalf of the administration was the nuclear accident at the Three Mile Island plant near Harrisburg, Pennsylvania. Early on the morning of March 28, 1979, a pump that circulates cool water around rods that hold the uranium fuel pellets failed to operate. The nuclear reactor overheated, and automatically shut down, but a valve failed to close and radioactive water overflowed and flooded the floor of the containment structure. An operator mistakenly shut off the emer-

gency cooling system and radioactive steam was vented and released into the atmosphere. Ominously, a hydrogen gas bubble formed at the top of the reactor, raising the danger of an explosion or a fuel-rod meltdown that could have cracked the concrete containment walls.

Amidst considerable confusion and conflicting information, Governor Richard L. Thornburgh ordered the evacuation of young children and women living within a five-mile radius of the plant. The bubble dissipated, and by April 3rd, the situation was declared to be under control.

A SETBACK FOR NUCLEAR POWER. At the time of the accident, there were 72 nuclear generators in operation and they produced

The nuclear accident at the Three Mile Island power plant in Pennsylvania shook public confidence in safety standards maintained by the Nuclear Regulatory Commission and arroused opposition to nuclear plants.

12.5 percent of the nation's electricity or 3.5 percent of our total energy consumption. One hundred and twenty-five more were under construction or on order. For some states, such as Vermont (79%), Maine (65%), Connecticut (53%), Nebraska (50%), and South Carolina (44%), nuclear plants were, and are, a mainstay of electric power generation.[25]

The accident bolstered the efforts of the anti-nuclear power critics and such groups as the Clamshell Alliance, who repeatedly attempted to block construction of the plant at Seabrook, New Hampshire. Congress was forced to give serious consideration to its generally avid support of nuclear power. The accident raised serious questions about safety standards and emergency procedures.

President Carter asked for and received additional authority for the chairman of the Nuclear Regulatory Commission to act quickly in an emergency, and legislation requiring federal inspectors at each site was enacted. But both houses rejected bills that would have halted new reactor construction for six months. In January 1980, President Carter asked the NRC to resume licensing of new sites within six months.

NUCLEAR POWER AND ENERGY LEGISLATION. Three Mile Island did not kill the nuclear power industry. However, it caused a reassessment on the part of Congress and the public and shifted the emphasis to safety and the problems of nuclear waste disposal. During 1979 and 1980, Congress was bogged down over these complex issues, and many members were reluctant to take positions that could be labeled pro- or anti-nuclear in an election year. The fiscal year 1981 budget reflected a major policy shift by the administration by reducing nuclear energy funds by over twenty percent. The real cut came in long-term research on building reactors and future technologies, with a greater proportion of the funds devoted to waste management.

The "beneficiaries" of Three Mile Island were the proponents of the windfall profits and synthetic fuel legislation. The disenchantment, perhaps temporary, with nuclear power heightened awareness of the need for more oil independence and the development of alternate sources of energy. This awareness, and also a sense of urgency, was encouraged by developments in the Middle East.

IRAN AND AFGHANISTAN. America's potential energy vulnerability was dramatized by the revolution in Iran, the hostage seizure, and the subsequent invasion of Afghanistan. Although Iranian oil did not account for more than 6 percent of our imports, the greater threat was the unsettling influence of the Islamic revolution and the potential for its spread to other oil-producing nations in that area.

When the Soviet Union moved into Afghanistan in January 1980, there was widespread fear and speculation that this was only the initial thrust aimed at a takeover of the Middle-East oil fields. The administration was forced to admit that we did not have a "rapid deployment force" capable of moving into an area quickly to defend against a Soviet threat, perhaps only leaving us the option of nuclear conflict as a deterrent.

Rising fuel prices, excessive oil company profits, Three Mile Island, and international crisis combined to create an environment which made it impossible for the Congress to repeat its performance of 1977 and 1978. Election-year politics would have made it extremely risky to go home and face the voters empty handed. This did not mean, however, that the opponents of the windfall profits tax and of major government involvement with synthetic fuels were not able to wage a heated, and at least partially successful, rearguard action. And as we have pointed out in the chapters on Congress, even the losers can be winners. The representatives and senators from the oil-producing states, for example, are winners with their constituencies

Revolution and other instabilities in the Middle East helped create a public perception that the United States is a prisoner of international events in regard to oil policy.

for having fought the good fight, even if they were on the losing side.

THE WINDFALL PROFITS TAX. Carter's proposal was designed to recover for the government part of the extra $1 trillion consumers will pay for oil by 1990. The tax bite varies depending upon the type of oil company involved—major or independent—and when the oil was discovered. The administration wanted the tax to average out at approximately 60 percent, but the House-passed version came closer to 54 percent, or a recovery of $277 billion by 1990. However, industry advocates anticipated doing better in the Senate, where oil states are well represented on the Senate Finance Committee.

Their hopes were justified, and the weaker Senate version, passed after a filibuster by Republicans and oil state Democrats, amounted to an average 27 percent tax with a return of only $138 billion. The long struggle in the conference committee resulted in an anticipated $227 billion tax derived from taxes and rates of 30 to 70 percent, one of the largest transfers in history of money from private to public hands.

The President got less than he wanted, and in an example of institutional rivalry, Congress refused to link the tax to funding of the programs that Carter wanted, such as mass transit improvement, a trust fund for the poor, and synthetic fuels. The oil industry left the field of battle with controls lifted from domes-

Viewpoint:
A difference of opinion on windfall profits

President Carter's pleasure with the tax is in stark contrast with the views of an oil-state senator from his own party.

It's good news for the whole country, and I think also good news for the whole world.

JIMMY CARTER

The Tax is a tragic mistake. We will have more taxes and more government instead of more oil.

Senator DAVID L. BOREN (D., Okla.)

Source: Congressional Quarterly, *Weekly Report* 38 (March 29, 1980), p. 843.

tic oil and the anticipation of handsome profits, although not the whole loaf.

The tax amounted to the largest tax ever levied on an American industry. Although critics were offended by this imposition of government power over the private sector, and they claimed that the tax would hurt oil production (see insert), the record will probably show that the trade-off of decontrol for a tax that will be phased out between 1988 and 1991, will be a good one for the industry. The margin of victory for the legislation in both chambers, 66 to 31 in the Senate and 302 to 107 in the House, suggests that most legislators believed that both industry and national interests would be well served.

SYNTHETIC FUELS CORPORATION. The synthetic fuels legislation found a strange alliance of interest groups opposed to the creation of a quasi-governmental agency, the Synthetic Fuels Corporation, and the Carter proposal to spend $88 billion in order to produce 2.5 million barrels a day of synthetic fuels by 1990. The American Petroleum Institute—the industry's lobby—and the Chamber of Commerce claimed that the new corporation would put the government in direct competi-

tion with industry and was a clear threat to the future of private energy industry ownership. Environmentalist groups, such as the Sierra Club, feared that a crash program to extract oil from shale and gas from coal would ignore environmental concerns.

As previously mentioned, the President had been strategically wise to latch onto the Congress's concept of a synthetic fuels corporation as the House already had passed its own version calling for a two-million-barrel-per-day output. However, the program that was enacted drastically toned down Carter's proposal, providing $20 billion for the time being, with the promise that the remaining $68 billion would be provided if the program succeeds. The production goal was cut back to 500,000 barrels a day by 1987 and 2 million barrels a day by 1992, somewhat less of a crash program than first intended.

Actually, industry fared very well, once again demonstrating the power of concerted group effort. The money will be spent to nudge private industry into the synfuel business through federal price guarantees, purchase commitments, and loans. Only as a last resort, in the event that private industry failed to respond, could the Corporation hire contractors to build and operate up to three government-owned synfuel plants.

Congress added $5 billion to finance solar energy projects, and also ordered President Carter to begin filling our strategic petroleum reserve. The President had been reluctant to do this because of opposition from our leading oil supplier, Saudi Arabia.

ENERGY MOBILIZATION BOARD. The third major part of the Carter program was defeated in response to opposition from environmental groups and advocates of state and local authority, including the National Governors' Association, National League of Cities, and other state and local associations. The problem, as perceived by these groups and the coalition of Republicans and liberal Democrats who rejected a conference committee report by a lopsided 232-to-131 margin, was the proposed board's authority to waive, with congressional consent, any state and local laws that had been based upon authority in federal law. For example, most state and local clean air and water laws are based on federal statutes, and are of particular concern to environmentalists.

The bill would have provided a short-cut through bureaucratic red tape for the developers of pipelines, refineries, or synthetic fuels plants. If a state or local government was holding up a project, the Board would have had authority to step in and act in place of the local agency.

Proponents of the measure had not been overly enthusiastic, but argued that it was necessary to speed vital projects. One congressman said, "This is a bill not to be loved, but to be passed."[26]

The White House claimed that the proposal was a victim of Republican partisanship, as only 9 of 134 Republicans had supported it. But this ignored, at least in part, that the vote divided the Democrats down the middle.

OIL IMPORT FEE. Obviously, the impact of the synfuels and windfall profits tax approaches are long in range, and President Carter believed that it was essential to take action that would have an immediate impact upon oil consumption. In March 1980 he announced the imposition of an oil import fee that would have meant a dime-a-gallon fee at the gasoline pumps. A suit was brought by consumer groups, an independent gasoline dealers, association, an oil company, and five members of Congress to block the fee, and a federal judge ruled in their favor.

Members of Congress in general, and election-conscious Democrats in particular, wanted to be on record against what amounted to a new tax on gas that they said would further burden the consumer and conserve little energy. They tacked on a resolution blocking the fee to legislation extending the ceiling on the public debt. Carter vetoed the bill, but for the first time since 1952, a Democratic president's veto was overridden. The lopsided margins were 335 to 34 in the House and 68 to 10 in the Senate. It appears that the President never had any congressional support for the fee.

Representative Charles A. Vanik (D., Ohio), who had already announced his retirement, criticized his colleagues for playing election-year politics. He said:

I know what the American people want. They want unlimited supplies of gasoline at the 1972 prices. . . . They want no lines at the gas station, and they want to get free air and get the windshield washed. . . . Maybe more members of Congress should think about the next generation instead of the next election.[27]

ENERGY POLICY 1981 AND BEYOND

A combination of the prolonged hostage crisis (444 days) and the outbreak of armed conflict between Iraq and Iran in September 1980 again highlighted the danger of oil dependence. Our European allies and Japan were inconvenienced to a much greater extent than was the U.S. by their long break in relations with Iran and Iraq's major destruction of Iranian oil production and storage facilities. The latter created the unusual spectacle of Iran having to import oil to meet its needs.

Ronald Reagan was inaugurated on the day the hostage crisis ended, and he brought to the White House attitudes about energy that were substantially different from those of his predecessor. He placed his emphasis on production rather than on conservation, and the Republican platform even urged the abolition of the 55 mph speed limit. Reagan did not see any need to change the nation's energy habits, and in a theme heard during the Nixon and Ford years, he said that "the leading oil geologists will tell you that, with decontrol, we could be producing enough oil to be self-sufficient in five years." [28]

Reagan indicated that his administration would be less cautious than Carter's in developing nuclear power through speeding up the licensing process. And, he proposed that the development of solar energy and synthetic fuels should depend upon action from the private sector with less governmental support than the Democrats provided. It also appeared that the expiring Clean Air Act would be replaced by a weaker version, more in line with the views of industry, which claimed that stringent rules hampered development and production. Also, Reagan's tax bill repealed certain sections of the windfall profits tax and cut in half by 1986 the tax on newly discovered oil.

The administration moved swiftly, and one of Reagan's first tasks was to immediately end price controls on oil, scrapping the gradual phaseout process started by Carter. The result was a surge in the price of gasoline. He also sought to disband the Dept. of Energy.

Interior Secretary James Watt drew the fire of environmentalists when he proposed making more than three hundred million acres per year of off-shore land available for oil and gas exploration. This figure represents a colossal increase when one considers that only 19 million acres have been leased during the last twenty-five years. Watt also slashed federal controls on strip mining and ordered the Office of Surface Mining to relax its enforcement procedures, in effect, transfering most of the regulation to the states.

Summary

We began this chapter by stating that the "Issue" was the ability of our political system to formulate public policy, particularly in the face of a complex crisis. We chose the energy issue because of its paramount importance and public familiarity with it. However, many lessons of the politics of energy also apply to other complex and visible attempts to make public policy.

Perhaps the first lesson is that policy making can be a painfully slow process when it involves some or all of the following: huge financial stakes, clusters of competing special interests, federal-state relations, and the debate over the proper role of the federal government with relationship to the private sector. Delay is encouraged by the nature of the legislative process, with its two-house legislature and committee system providing a multitude of access points or forums where competing interests can argue for their views of proper policy. Viewed in this context, the four-year struggle to enact some meaningful energy program may not have been an unduly long one.

The ability of the government to respond with dispatch to complex situations is also hampered by the limits of presidential power. While it is considerably easier for the president to formulate and propose policy than it is for the Congress to do so, the undisciplined nature of our political parties, and the individual "electoral connections" that legislators respond to are key factors making presidential leadership difficult.

However, we are not making a judgment as to whether this situation is good or bad. An individual's view of presidential power is a product of one's beliefs about the president in the office and the particular public policies involved.

The energy issue also highlights the fact that events beyond the control of the politicians often determine the outcomes. The Middle–East situation, oil company profits, rising fuel costs, and the accident at Three Mile Island combined to create an environment in 1979 and 1980 that was much more conducive than that of 1977–1978 to putting the federal government more directly into moving the nation toward a greater degree of energy independence. Presidential proposals were shaped, in part, in response to the environment, legislators could not ignore the new energy awareness of their constituents, and special interests, particularly the oil industry, found the environment less favorable to defense of its position.

In other chapters we have argued that elections and public opinion surveys do not provide the lawmakers with public attitudes about policy details. But, the energy issue provides us with one of the clearest examples of the impact of public opinion—shaped by

events—on the formation of policy. With the public taking the energy crisis seriously in 1979 and 1980, and with public disenchantment with the oil companies, an election-year Congress was under considerable pressure to act. And public attitudes about rationing and increased prices for gasoline were major factors in the congressional modification of Carter's rationing plan and the rejection of the oil import fee. When the issue is a visible one, public opinion does count.

Throughout this book we have attempted to build on the theme of "winning and losing." The energy issue has provided a graphic example of the shifting interest-group and congressional alliances that changed from bill to bill. It has been difficult to tell who won and who lost. No interests were completely satisfied or totally unhappy with what was or was not enacted.

The oil industry and its congressional allies were able to convert Carter's initial proposals into a victory of sorts by achieving the long-sought elimination of price controls on natural gas, and by blocking a tax on utilities that used natural gas and oil. And consumers may have been the winners when Congress rejected the tax on crude oil and increased gasoline taxes. On the other hand, the windfall profits tax was passed over the rigorous opposition of the industry, but we are inclined to believe that in the long run, the industry won in the trade-off between the tax and decontrol of oil prices.

Obviously, all of us will have been winners if the energy program that has been enacted, and future modifications, give us a greater control over our energy destiny. And we may all have suffered by our unwillingness to attempt to mandate conservation through taxation that would create higher prices. History may provide the answer.

While we are not as clear as we would like to be about who won or who lost on what issues, it should be clear by now that "politics is the art of compromise."

1. "Dilemmas of World Energy: Options for a Fuel-Guzzling Superpower," in Foreign Policy Associates, *Great Decisions '78* (New York: Foreign Policy Association, 1978), pp. 36–47.
2. Cited in Congressional Quarterly, *Weekly Report*, 35 (April 23, 1977), p. 736.
3. Congressional Quarterly, *Weekly Report*, 35 (May 21, 1977), p. 963.
4. *Gallup Opinion Indexes*, no. 93, March 1973, p. 12; no. 100, September 1973, p. 11; no. 104, February 1974, p. 2.
5. "Dilemmas of World Energy," p. 36.
6. Speech to a joint session of Congress, April 20, 1977.
7. Congressional Quarterly, *Almanac*, 1977, p. 710.
8. *New York Times*, April 15, 1977. p. 136.
9. *Gallup Opinion Index*, no. 141, April 1977, p. 6.
10. For a summary, see *Gallup Opinion Index*, no. 170, September 1979, p. 16.
11. *Gallup Opinion Index*, no. 142, May 1977, p. 24. Also see numbers 137, 159, and 160.
12. *Gallup Opinion Index*, no. 140, March 1977, pp. 1–2.
13. *Gallup Opinion Index*, no. 143, June 1977, p. 17.
14. Congressional Quarterly, *Weekly Report*, 35 (August 6, 1977), p. 1627.
15. Congressional Quarterly, *Weekly Report*, 36 (May 27, 1978), p. 1291.
16. Congressional Quarterly, *Weekly Report*, 36 (September 16, 1978), p. 2451.
17. Ibid., p. 2453.
18. Robert S. Strauss, quoted in Congressional Quarterly, *Weekly Report*, 36 (September 6, 1978), p. 2452.
19. Congressional Quarterly, *Weekly Report*, 38 (March 29, 1980), p. 843 (windfall profits); 38 (June 28, 1980), p. 1790 (synfuels); and 38 (June 28, 1980), pp. 1790–91 (Energy Mobilization Board). For provisions of the windfall profits and synfuels bills, see 38 (March 8, 1980), pp. 668–669; and 38 (June 21, 1980), pp. 1691–95.
20. Congressional Quarterly, *Weekly Report*, 38 (June 7, 1980), pp. 1539–40.
21. *Gallup Opinion Indexes*, no. 164, March 1979, p. 4; and no. 172, November 1979, p. 17.
22. *Gallup Opinion Index*, no. 170, September 1979, p. 13.
23. *Gallup Opinion Index*, no. 167, June 1979, p. 23.
24. Congressional Quarterly, *Weekly Report*, 37 (October 27, 1979), p. 2415. Oil company profits are also listed on page 2415.
25. Congressional Quarterly, *Weekly Report*, 37 (April 7, 1979), p. 622.
26. Philip R. Sharp (D., Ind.), quoted in Congressional Quarterly, *Weekly Report*, 38 (June 28, 1980), p. 1790.
27. Congressional Quarterly, *Weekly Report*, 38 (June 7, 1980), p. 1540.
28. Congressional Quarterly, *Weekly Report*, 38 (October 4, 1980), pp. 2923–2925.

Suggested Readings

Congressional Quarterly, *Energy Policy* (Washington, D.C.: Congressional Quarterly, 1979).
Barbara S. Davies and Clarence J. Davies, *The Politics of Pollution*, 2d ed. (New York: Pegasus, 1975).
David H. Davis, *Energy Politics*, 2d ed. (New York: St. Martin's Press, 1977).
Robert Engler, *The Brotherhood of Oil: Energy Policy and the Public Interest* (Chicago: University of Chicago Press, 1977).
Richard Falk, *This Endangered Planet: Prospects and Proposals for Human Survival* (New York: Vintage, 1971).
Foreign Policy Associates, *Great Decisions '78* (New York: Foreign Policy Association, 1978).

Herman Kahn et al., *The Next 200 Years: A Scenario for America and the World* (New York: William Morrow, 1976).

William Ophuls, *Ecology and the Politics of Scarcity* (San Francisco: Freeman, 1977).

John C. Sawhill, ed., *Energy: Conservation and Public Policy* (New York: Spectrum, 1979).

Robert Stobaugh and Daniel Yergen, *Energy Future* (New York: Random House, 1979).

Appendix:
The Constitution
of the United States of America

PREAMBLE

We, the People of the United States, in Order to form a more perfect Union, establish Justice, insure domestic Tranquility, provide for the common defence, promote the general Welfare, and secure the Blessings of Liberty to ourselves and our Posterity, do ordain and establish this Constitution for the United States of America.

Article I

LEGISLATIVE DEPARTMENT

SECTION 1. *Two Houses*

All legislative powers herein granted shall be vested in a Congress of the United States, which shall consist of a Senate and House of Representatives.

SECTION 2. *House of Representatives*

1. The House of Representatives shall be composed of members chosen every second year by the people of the several States, and the electors in each State shall have the qualifications requisite for electors of the most numerous branch of the State legislature.

2. No person shall be a Representative who shall not have attained to the age of twenty-five years, and been seven years a citizen of the United States, and who shall not, when elected, be an inhabitant of that State in which he shall be chosen.

3. Representatives and direct taxes shall be apportioned among the several States which may be included within this Union, according to their respective numbers, [which shall be determined by adding to the whole number of free persons, including those bound to service for a term of years] and excluding Indians not taxed, [three-fifths of all other persons]. The actual enumeration shall be made within three years after the first meeting of the Congress of the United States, and within every subsequent term of ten years, in such manner as they shall by law direct. The number of Representatives shall not exceed one for every thirty thousand, but each State shall have at least one Representative; [and, until such enumeration shall be made, the State of New Hampshire shall be entitled to choose three, Massachusetts eight, Rhode Island and Providence Plantations one, Connecticut five, New York six, New Jersey four, Pennsylvania eight, Delaware one, Maryland six, Virginia ten, North Carolina five, South Carolina five, and Georgia three].

4. When vacancies happen in the representation from any State, the executive authority thereof shall issue writs of election to fill such vacancies.

5. The House of Representatives shall choose their Speaker and other officers; and shall have the sole power of impeachment.

SECTION 3. *Senate*

1. The Senate of the United States shall be composed of two Senators from each State [chosen by the legislature thereof] for six years; and each Senator shall have one vote.

2. Immediately after they shall be assembled in consequence of the first election, they shall be divided, as equally as may be, into three classes. The seats of the Senators of the first class shall be vacated at the expiration of the second year; of the second class, at the expiration of the fourth year; and of the third class, at the expiration of the sixth year; so that one-third may be chosen every second year; [and if vacancies happen by resignation, or otherwise, during the recess of the legislature of any State, the executive thereof may make temporary appointments until the next meeting of the legislature, which shall then fill such vacancies.]

3. No person shall be a Senator who shall not have attained to the age of thirty years, and been nine years a citizen of the United States, who shall not, when elected, be an inhabitant of that State for which he shall be chosen.

4. The Vice President of the United States shall be President of the Senate, but shall have no vote, unless they be equally divided.

5. The Senate shall choose their other officers, and also a President *pro tempore,* in the absence of the Vice President, or when he shall exercise the office of President of the United States.

6. The Senate shall have the sole power to try all impeachments. When sitting for that purpose, they shall be on oath or affirmation. When the President of the United States is tried, the Chief Justice shall preside; and no person shall be convicted without the concurrence of two-thirds of the members present.

7. Judgment in cases of impeachment shall not extend further than to removal from office, and disqualification to hold and enjoy any office of honor, trust, or profit under the United States; but the party convicted shall, nevertheless, be liable and subject to indictment, trial, judgment, and punishment, according to law.

SECTION 4. *Elections and Meetings of Congress*

1. The times, places, and manner of holding elections for Senators and Representatives, shall be prescribed in each State by the legislature thereof: but the Congress may at any time, by law, make or alter such regulations, except as to the places of choosing Senators.

2. The Congress shall assemble at least once in every year, [and such meeting shall be on the first Monday in December,] unless they shall by law appoint a different day.

SECTION 5. *Powers and Duties of the Houses*

1. Each House shall be the judge of the elections, returns, and qualifications of its own members, and a majority of each shall constitute a quorum to do business; but a smaller number may adjourn from day to day, and may be authorized to compel the attendance of absent members, in such manner, and under such penalties, as each House may provide.

2. Each House may determine the rules of its proceedings, punish its members for disorderly behavior, and, with the concurrence of two-thirds, expel a member.

3. Each House shall keep a journal of its proceedings, and from time to time, publish the same, excepting such parts as may, in their judgment, require secrecy; and the yeas and nays of the members of either House, on any question, shall, at the desire of one-fifth of those present, be entered on the journal.

4. Neither House, during the session of Congress, shall, without the consent of the other, adjourn for more than three days, nor to any other place than that in which the two Houses shall be sitting.

SECTION 6. *Privileges of and Prohibitions upon Members*

1. The Senators and Representatives shall receive a compensation for their services, to be ascertained by law, and paid out of the treasury of the United States. They shall, in all cases, except treason, felony, and breach of the peace, be privileged from arrest during their attendance at the session of their respective Houses, and in going to, and returning from, the same; and for any speech or debate in either House, they shall not be questioned in any other place.

2. No Senator or Representative shall, during the time for which he was elected, be appointed to any civil office under the authority of the United States, which shall have been created, or the emoluments whereof shall have been increased during such time; and no person, holding any office under the United States, shall be a member of either House during his continuance in office.

SECTION 7. *Revenue Bills, President's Veto*

1. All bills for raising revenue shall originate in the House of Representatives; but the Senate may propose or concur with amendments as on other bills.

2. Every bill which shall have passed the House of Representatives and the Senate, shall, before it become a law, be presented to the President of the United States; if he approve, he shall sign it, but if not, he shall return it, with his objections, to that House in which it shall have originated, who shall enter the objections

at large on their journal, and proceed to reconsider it. If, after such reconsideration, two-thirds of that House shall agree to pass the bill, it shall be sent, together with the objections, to the other House, by which it shall likewise be reconsidered, and, if approved by two-thirds of that House, it shall become a law. But in all such cases the votes of both Houses shall be determined by yeas and nays, and the names of the persons voting for and against the bill shall be entered on the journal of each House respectively. If any bill shall not be returned by the President within ten days (Sundays excepted) after it shall have been presented to him, the same shall be a law, in like manner as if he had signed it, unless the Congress, by their adjournment, prevent its return, in which case it shall not be a law.

3. Every order, resolution, or vote, to which the concurrence of the Senate and House of Representatives may be necessary (except on a question of adjournment), shall be presented to the President of the United States; and before the same shall take effect, shall be approved by him, or, being disapproved by him, shall be repassed by two-thirds of the Senate and House of Representatives, according to the rules and limitations prescribed in the case of a bill.

SECTION 8. *Legislative Powers of Congress*

The Congress shall have power:

1. To lay and collect taxes, duties, imposts, and excises, to pay the debts, and provide for the common defence and general welfare, of the United States; but all duties, imposts, and excises, shall be uniform throughout the United States;

2. To borrow money on the credit of the United States;

3. To regulate commerce with foreign nations, and among the several States, and with the Indian tribes;

4. To establish a uniform rule of naturalization, and uniform laws on the subject of bankruptcies, throughout the United States;

5. To coin money, regulate the value thereof, and of foreign coin, and fix the standard of weights and measures;

6. To provide for the punishment of counterfeiting the securities and current coin of the United States;

7. To establish post offices and post roads;

8. To promote the progress of science and useful arts, by securing, for limited times, to authors and inventors, the exclusive right to their respective writings and discoveries;

9. To constitute tribunals inferior to the Supreme Court;

10. To define and punish piracies and felonies, committed on the high seas, and offences against the law of nations;

11. To declare war, grant letters of marque and reprisal, and make rules concerning captures on land and water;

12. To raise and support armies; but no appropriation of money to that use shall be for a longer term than two years;

13. To provide and maintain a navy;

14. To make rules for the government and regulation of the land and naval forces;

15. To provide for calling forth the militia to execute the laws of the Union, suppress insurrections, and repel invasions;

16. To provide for organizing, arming, and disciplining the militia, and for governing such part of them as may be employed in the service of the United States, reserving to the States respectively the appointment of the officers, and the authority of training the militia, according to the discipline prescribed by Congress;

17. To exercise exclusive legislation in all cases whatsoever, over such district (not exceeding ten miles square) as may, by cession of particular States, and the acceptance of Congress, become the seat of the Government of the United States, and to exercise like authority over all places, purchased by the consent of the legislature of the State in which the same shall be, for the erection of forts, magazines, arsenals, dockyards, and other needful buildings;—And

18. To make all laws which shall be necessary and proper for carrying into execution the foregoing powers, and all other powers vested by this Constitution in the Government of the United States, or in any department or officer thereof.

SECTION 9. *Prohibitions upon the United States*

[1. The migration or importation of such persons as any of the States now existing shall think proper to admit, shall not be prohibited by the Congress prior to the year one thousand eight hundred and eight; but a tax or duty may be imposed on such importation, not exceeding ten dollars for each person.]

2. The privilege of the writ of *habeas corpus* shall not be suspended, unless when, in cases of rebellion or invasion, the public safety may require it.

3. No bill of attainder or *ex post facto* law shall be passed.

4. No capitation, or other direct tax, shall be laid, unless in proportion to the census or enumeration hereinbefore directed to be taken.

5. No tax or duty shall be laid on articles exported from any State.

6. No preference shall be given by any regulation of commerce or revenue to the ports of one State over those of another; nor shall vessels bound to, or from, one State, be obliged to enter, clear, or pay duties, in another.

7. No money shall be drawn from the treasury, but in consequence of appropriations made by law; and a regular statement and account of the receipts and expenditures of all public money shall be published from time to time.

8. No title of nobility shall be granted by the United States; and no person holding any office or profit or trust under them shall, without the consent of the Congress, accept of any present, emolument, office, or title, of any kind whatever, from any king, prince, or foreign state.

SECTION 10. *Prohibitions upon the States*

1. No State shall enter into any treaty, alliance, or confederation; grant letters of marque and reprisal; coin money; emit bills of credit; make anything but gold and silver coin a tender in payment of debts; pass any bill of attainder, *ex post facto* law, or law impairing the obligations of contracts, or grant any title of nobility.

2. No State shall, without the consent of the Congress, lay any imposts or duties on imports or exports, except what may be absolutely necessary for executing what may be necessary for executing its inspection laws; and the net produce of all duties and imposts, laid by any State on imports or exports, shall be for the use of the treasury of the United States; and all such laws shall be subject to the revision and control of the Congress.

3. No State shall, without the consent of Congress, lay any duty on tonnage, keep troops, or ships of war, in time of peace, enter into any agreement or compact with another State, or with a foreign power, or engage in war, unless actually invaded, or in such imminent danger as will not admit of delay.

Article II

EXECUTIVE DEPARTMENT

SECTION 1. *Term, Election, Qualifications, Salary, Oath of Office*

1. The executive power shall be vested in a President of the United States of America. He shall hold his office during the term of four years, and together with the Vice President, chosen for the same term, be elected as follows:

2. Each State shall appoint, in such manner as the legislature thereof may direct, a number of Electors, equal to the whole number of Senators and Representatives, to which the State may be entitled in the Congress; but no Senator or Representative, or person holding an office of trust or profit, under the United States, shall be appointed an Elector.

[3. The Electors shall meet in their respective States, and vote by ballot for two persons, of whom one, at least, shall not be an inhabitant of the same State with themselves. And they shall make a list of all the persons voted for, and of the number of votes for each; which list they shall sign and certify, and transmit, sealed, to the seat of the Government of the United States, directed to the President of the Senate. The President of the Senate shall, in the presence of the Senate and House of Representatives, open all the certificates, and the votes shall then be counted. The person having the greatest number of votes shall be the President, if such number be a majority of the whole number of Electors appointed; and if there be more than one, who have such majority, and have an equal number of votes, then, the House of Representatives shall immediately choose, by ballot, one of them for President; and if no person have a majority, then, from the five highest on the list, the said House shall, in like manner, choose the President. But in choosing the President, the votes shall be taken by States, the representation from each State having one vote; a quorum for this purpose shall consist of a member or members from two-thirds of the States, and a majority of all the States shall be necessary to a choice. In every case, after the choice of the President, the person having the greatest number of votes of the Electors shall be the Vice President. But if there should remain two or more who have equal votes, the Senate shall choose from them, by ballot, the Vice President.]

4. The Congress may determine the time of choosing the Electors, and the day on which they shall give their votes; which day shall be the same throughout the United States.

5. No person, except a natural-born citizen, or a citizen of the United States at the time of the adoption of this Constitution, shall be eligible to the office of President; neither shall any person be eligible to that office, who shall not have

attained to the age of thirty-five years, and been fourteen years a resident within the United States.

6. In case of the removal of the President from office, or of his death, resignation, or inability to discharge the powers and duties of the said office, the same shall devolve on the Vice President, and the Congress may by law provide for the case of removal, death, resignation or inability, both of the President and Vice President, declaring what officer shall then act as President, and such officer shall act accordingly, until the disability be removed, or a President shall be elected.

7. The President shall, at stated times, receive for his services a compensation, which shall neither be increased nor diminished during the period for which he shall have been elected, and he shall not receive, within that period, any other emolument from the United States, or any of them.

8. Before he enter on the execution of his office, he shall take the following oath or affirmation:

"I do solemnly swear (or affirm), that I will faithfully execute the office of President of the United States, and will, to the best of my ability, preserve, protect, and defend the Constitution of the United States."

SECTION 2. *President's Powers*

1. The President shall be Commander in Chief of the army and navy of the United States, and of the militia of the several States, when called into the actual service of the United States; he may require the opinion, in writing, of the principal officer in each of the executive departments upon any subject relating to the duties of their respective offices, and he shall have power to grant reprieves and pardons for offences against the United States, except in cases of impeachment.

2. He shall have power, by and with the advice and consent of the Senate, to make treaties, provided two-thirds of the Senators present concur; and he shall nominate, and, by and with the advice and consent of the Senate, shall appoint ambassadors, other public ministers, and consuls, judges of the Supreme Court, and all other officers of the United States whose appointments are not herein otherwise provided for, and which shall be established by law; but the Congress may by law vest the appointment of such inferior officers, as they think proper, in the President alone, in the courts of law, or in the heads of departments.

3. The President shall have power to fill up all vacancies that may happen during the recess of the Senate, by granting commissions which shall expire at the end of their next session.

SECTION 3. *President's Duties*

He shall, from time to time, give to the Congress information of the state of the Union, and recommend to their consideration such measures as he shall judge necessary and expedient; he may, on extraordinary occasions, convene both Houses, or either of them, and in case of disagreement between them, with respect to the time of adjournment, he may adjourn them to such time as he shall think proper; he shall receive ambassadors and other public ministers; he shall take care that the laws be faithfully executed, and shall commission all the officers of the United States.

SECTION 4. *Impeachment*

The President, Vice President, and all civil officers of the United States, shall be removed from office on impeachment for, and conviction of, treason, bribery, or other high crimes and misdemeanors.

Article III

JUDICIAL DEPARTMENT

SECTION 1. *Courts, Terms of Office*

The judicial power of the United States shall be vested in one Supreme Court, and in such inferior courts as the Congress may from time to time ordain and establish. The judges, both of the Supreme and inferior courts, shall hold their offices during good behavior, and shall, at stated times, receive for their services a compensation which shall not be diminished during their continuance in office.

SECTION 2. *Jurisdiction*

1. The judicial power shall extend to all cases, in law and equity, arising under this Constitution, the laws of the United States, and treaties made, or which shall be made, under their authority; to all cases affecting ambassadors, other public ministers, and consuls; to all cases of admiralty and maritime jurisdiction; to controversies to which the United States shall be a party; to controversies between two or more States, between a State and citizens of another State, between citizens of different States, between citizens of the same State claiming lands under grants of different States, and between a

State, or the citizens thereof, and foreign states, citizens, or subjects.

2. In all cases affecting ambassadors, other public ministers and consuls, and those in which a State shall be a party, the Supreme Court shall have original jurisdiction. In all the other cases before mentioned, the Supreme Court shall have appellate jurisdiction, both as to law and fact, with such exceptions and under such regulations as the Congress shall make.

3. The trial of all crimes, except in cases of impeachment, shall be by jury; and such trial shall be held in the State where the said crimes shall have been committed; but when not committed within any State the trial shall be at such place or places as the Congress may by law have directed.

SECTION 3. *Treason*

1. Treason against the United States shall consist only in levying war against them, or in adhering to their enemies, giving them aid and comfort. No person shall be convicted of treason unless on the testimony of two witnesses to the same overt act, or on confession in open court.

2. The Congress shall have power to declare the punishment of treason, but no attainder of treason shall work corruption of blood, or forfeiture except during the life of the person attainted.

3. No person held to service or labor in one State, under the laws thereof, escaping into another, shall, in consequence of any law or regulation therein, be discharged from such service or labor, but shall be delivered up on claim of the party to whom such service or labor may be due.

SECTION 3. *New States, Territories*

1. New States may be admitted by the Congress into this Union; but no new State shall be formed or erected within the jurisdiction of any other State, nor any State be formed by the junction of two or more States, or parts of States, without the consent of the legislatures of the States concerned as well as of the Congress.

2. The Congress shall have power to dispose of and make all needful rules and regulations respecting the territory or other property belonging to the United States; and nothing in this Constitution shall be so construed as to prejudice any claims of the United States, or of any particular State.

SECTION 4. *Protection Afforded to States by the Nation*

The United States shall guarantee to every State in this Union a republican form of government, and shall protect each of them against invasion; and on application of the legislature, or of the executive (when the legislature cannot be convened), against domestic violence.

Article IV

RELATIONS OF STATES

SECTION 1. *Full Faith and Credit*

Full faith and credit shall be given in each State to the public acts, records, and judicial proceedings of every other State. And the Congress may, by general laws, prescribe the manner in which such acts, records, and proceedings shall be proved, and the effect thereof.

SECTION 2. *Rights in One State of Citizens of Another*

1. The citizens of each State shall be entitled to all privileges and immunities of citizens in the several States.

2. A person charged in any State with treason, felony, or other crime, who shall flee from justice, and be found in another State, shall, on demand of the executive authority of the State from which he fled, be delivered up, to be removed to the State having jurisdiction of the crime.

Article V

PROVISIONS FOR AMENDMENT

The Congress, whenever two-thirds of both Houses shall deem it necessary, shall propose amendments to this Constitution, or, on the application of the legislatures of two-thirds of the several States, shall call a convention for proposing amendments, which, in either case, shall be valid, to all intents and purposes, as part of this Constitution, when ratified by the legislatures of three-fourths of the several States, or by conventions in three-fourths thereof, as the one or the other mode of ratification may be proposed by the Congress; [provided that no amendment which may be made prior to the year one thousand eight hundred and eight shall in any manner affect the first and fourth clauses in the ninth section of the first Article;] and that no State, without its consent, shall be deprived of its equal suffrage in the Senate.

Article VI

NATIONAL DEBTS, SUPREMACY OF NATIONAL LAW, OATH

SECTION 1. *Validity of Debts*

All debts contracted and engagements entered into, before the adoption of this Constitution, shall be as valid against the United States under this Constitution, as under the Confederation.

SECTION 2. *Supremacy of National Law*

This Constitution, and the laws of the United States which shall be made in pursuance thereof, and all treaties made, or which shall be made, under the authority of the United States, shall be the supreme law of the land; and the judges in every State shall be bound thereby, anything in the constitution or laws of any State to the contrary notwithstanding.

SECTION 3. *Oaths of Office*

The Senators and Representatives before mentioned, and the members of the several State legislatures, and all executive and judicial officers, both of the United States and of the several States, shall be bound, by oath or affirmation, to support this Constitution; but no religious test shall ever be required as a qualification to any office or public trust under the United States.

Article VII

ESTABLISHMENT OF CONSTITUTION

The ratification of the conventions of nine States shall be sufficient for the establishment of this Constitution between the States so ratifying the same.

Done in Convention, by the unanimous consent of the States present, the seventeenth day of September, in the year of our Lord one thousand seven hundred and eighty-seven, and of the Independence of the United States of America the twelfth. *In Witness* whereof, we have hereunto subscribed our names.

AMENDMENTS

1ST AMENDMENT. *Freedom of Religion, Speech, Press, Assembly, and Petition*

Congress shall make no law respecting an establishment of religion, or prohibiting the free exercise thereof; or abridging the freedom of speech, or of the press; or the right of the people peaceably to assemble, and to petition the government for a redress of grievances.

2ND AMENDMENT. *Right to Keep and Bear Arms*

A well-regulated militia being necessary to the security of a free state, the right of the people to keep and bear arms shall not be infringed.

3RD AMENDMENT. *Quartering of Troops*

No soldier shall, in time of peace, be quartered in any house, without the consent of the owner; nor, in time of war, but in a manner to be prescribed by law.

4TH AMENDMENT. *Searches and Seizures*

The right of the people to be secure in their persons, houses, papers, and effects, against unreasonable searches and seizures, shall not be violated; and no warrants shall issue, but upon probable cause, supported by oath or affirmation, and particularly describing the place to be searched and the persons or things to be seized.

5TH AMENDMENT. *Criminal Proceedings, Eminent Domain*

No person shall be held to answer for a capital, or otherwise infamous, crime, unless on a presentment of indictment of a grand jury, except in cases arising in the land or naval forces, or in the militia, when in actual service, in time of war, or public danger; nor shall any person be subject, for the same offence, to be twice put in jeopardy of life or limb; nor shall be compelled, in any criminal case, to be a witness against himself; nor be deprived of life, liberty, or property, without due process of law; nor shall private property be taken for public use, without just compensation.

6TH AMENDMENT. *Criminal Proceedings*

In all criminal prosecutions, the accused shall enjoy the right to a speedy and public trial, by an impartial jury of the state and district wherein the crime shall have been committed, which district shall have been previously ascertained by law; and to be informed of the nature and cause of the accusation; to be confronted with the witnesses against him; to have compulsory process for obtaining witnesses in his favor; and to have the assistance of counsel for his defence.

7TH AMENDMENT. *Jury Trial in Civil Cases*

In suits at common law, where the value in controversy shall exceed twenty dollars, the right of trial by jury shall be preserved; and no fact, tried by a jury, shall be otherwise re-examined in any court of the United States than according to the rules of the common law.

8TH AMENDMENT. *Excessive Punishments*

Excessive bail shall not be required, nor excessive fines imposed, nor cruel and unusual punishment inflicted.

9TH AMENDMENT. *Unenumerated Rights*

The enumeration in the Constitution of certain rights shall not be construed to deny or disparage others retained by the people.

10TH AMENDMENT. *Powers Reserved to the States*

The powers not delegated to the United States by the Constitution, nor prohibited by it to the States, are reserved to the States respectively, or to the people.

11TH AMENDMENT. *Suits against States*

The judicial power of the United States shall not be construed to extend to any suit in law or equity, commenced or prosecuted against one of the United States by citizens of another State or by citizens or subjects of any foreign state.

12TH AMENDMENT. *Presidential, Vice Presidential Elections*

The Electors shall meet in their respective States, and vote by ballot for President and Vice President, one of whom, at least, shall not be an inhabitant of the same State with themselves; they shall name in their ballots the person voted for as President, and in distinct ballots the person voted for as Vice President; and they shall make distinct lists of all persons voted for as President, and of all persons voted for as Vice President, and of the number of votes for each, which lists they shall sign, and certify, and transmit, sealed, to the seat of the Government of the United States, directed to the President of the Senate; the President of the Senate shall, in the presence of the Senate and the House of Representatives, open all the certificates, and the votes shall then be counted; the person having the greatest number of votes for President shall be the President, if such number be a majority of the whole number of Electors appointed; and if no person have such a majority, then, from the persons having the highest numbers, not exceeding three, on the list of those voted for as President, the House of Representatives shall choose immediately, by ballot, the President. But in choosing the President, the votes shall be taken by States, the representation from each State having one vote; a quorum for this purpose shall consist of a member or members from two-thirds of the States, and a majority of all the States shall be necessary to a choice. And if the House of Representatives shall not choose a President, whenever the right of choice shall devolve upon them, [before the fourth day of March next following,] then the Vice President shall act as President, as in case of death, or other constitutional disability, of the President. The person having the greatest number of votes as Vice President, shall be the Vice President, if such number be a majority of the whole number of Electors appointed; and if no person have a majority, then, from the two highest numbers on the list, the Senate shall choose the Vice President; a quorum for the purpose shall consist of two-thirds of the whole number of Senators; a majority of the whole number shall be necessary to a choice. But no person constitutionally ineligible to the office of President shall be eligible to that of Vice President of the United States.

13TH AMENDMENT. *Slavery, Involuntary Servitude*

Section 1. Neither slavery nor involuntary servitude, except as a punishment for crime, whereof the party shall have been duly convicted, shall exist within the United States, or any place subject to their jurisdiction.

Section 2. Congress shall have power to enforce this article by appropriate legislation.

14TH AMENDMENT. *Citizenship, Civil Rights, Apportionment, Political Disabilities, Debt*

Section 1. All persons born or naturalized in the United States, and subject to the jurisdiction thereof, are citizens of the United States and of the State wherein they reside. No State shall make or enforce any law which shall abridge the privileges or immunities of citizens of the United States; nor shall any State deprive any person of life, liberty, or property, without due process of law, nor deny to any person within its jurisdiction the equal protection of the laws.

Section 2. Representatives shall be apportioned among the several States according to their respective numbers, counting the whole number of persons in each State, excluding Indians not taxed. But when the right to vote at any election for the choice of electors for President and Vice President of the United States, Representatives in Congress, the executive and judicial officers of a State, or the members of the legislature thereof, is denied to any of the male inhabitants of such State, being twenty-one years of age, and citizens of the United States, or in any way abridged, except for participation in rebellion or other crime, the basis of representation therein shall be reduced in the proportion which the number of such male citizens shall bear to the whole number of male citizens twenty-one years of age in such State.

Section 3. No person shall be a Senator or Representative in Congress, or elector of President and Vice President, or hold any office, civil or military, under the United States, or under any State, who, having previously taken an oath, as a member of Congress, or as an officer of the United States, or as a member of any State legislature, or as an executive or judicial officer of any State, to support the Constitution of the United States, shall have engaged in insurrection or rebellion against the same, or given aid or comfort to the enemies thereof. But Congress may, by a vote of two-thirds of each House, remove such disability.

Section 4. The validity of the public debt of the United States, authorized by law, including debts incurred for payment of pensions and bounties for services in suppressing insurrection or rebellion, shall not be questioned. But neither the United States nor any State shall assume or pay any debt or obligation incurred in aid of insurrection or rebellion against the United States, or any claim for the loss or emancipation of any slave; but all such debts, obligations, and claims shall be held illegal and void.

Section 5. The Congress shall have power to enforce, by appropriate legislation, the provisions of this article.

15TH AMENDMENT. *Right to Vote*

Section 1. The right of citizens of the United States to vote shall not be denied or abridged by the United States or by any State on account of race, color, or previous condition of servitude.

Section 2. The Congress shall have power to enforce this article by appropriate legislation.

16TH AMENDMENT. *Income Tax*

The Congress shall have power to lay and collect taxes on incomes, from whatever source derived, without apportionment among the several States, and without regard to any census or enumeration.

17TH AMENDMENT. *Election of Senators*

The Senate of the United States shall be composed of two Senators from each State, elected by the people thereof, for six years; and each Senator shall have one vote. The electors in each State shall have the qualifications requisite for electors of the most numerous branch of the State legislatures.

When vacancies happen in the representation of any State in the Senate, the executive authority of such State shall issue writs of election to fill such vacancies: Provided, That the legislature of any State may empower the executive thereof to make temporary appointment until the people fill the vacancies by election as the legislature may direct.

This amendment shall not be so construed as to affect the election or term of any Senator chosen before it becomes valid as part of the Constitution.

18TH AMENDMENT. *Prohibition*

Section 1. After one year from the ratification of this article the manufacture, sale or transportation of intoxicating liquors within, the importation thereof into, or the exportation thereof from the United States and all territory subject to the jurisdiction thereof for beverage purposes is hereby prohibited.

Section 2. The Congress and the several States shall have concurrent power to enforce this article by appropriate legislation.

Section 3. This article shall be inoperative unless it shall have been ratified as an amendment to the Constitution by the legislatures of the several States, as provided in the Constitution, within seven years of the date of the submission hereof to the States by Congress.

19TH AMENDMENT. *Woman Suffrage*

The right of citizens of the United States to vote shall not be denied or abridged by the United States or by any State on account of sex.

Congress shall have power to enforce this article by appropriate legislation.

20TH AMENDMENT. *Presidential and Vice Presidential Terms, Interim Succession, Sessions of Congress*

Section 1. The terms of the President and Vice President shall end at noon on the 20th day of January, and the terms of Senators and Representatives at noon on the 3d day of January, of the years in which such terms would have ended if this article had not been ratified; and the terms of their successors shall then begin.

Section 2. The Congress shall assemble at least once in every year, and such meeting shall begin at noon on the 3d day of January, unless they shall by law appoint a different day.

Section 3. If, at the time fixed for the beginning of the term of the President, the President-elect shall have died, the Vice President-elect shall become President. If a President shall not have been chosen before the time fixed for the beginning of his term, or if the President-elect shall have failed to qualify, then the Vice President-elect shall act as President until a President shall have qualified; and the Congress may by law provide for the case wherein neither a President-elect nor a Vice President-elect shall have qualified, declaring who shall then act as President, or the manner in which one who is to act shall be selected, and such person shall act accordingly until a President or Vice President shall have qualified.

Section 4. The Congress may by law provide for the case of the death of any of the persons from whom the House of Representatives may choose a President whenever the right of choice shall have devolved upon them, and for the case of the death of any of the persons from whom the Senate may choose a Vice President whenever the right of choice shall have devolved upon them.

Section 5. Sections 1 and 2 shall take effect on the 15th day of October following the ratification of this article.

Section 6. This article shall be inoperative unless it shall have been ratified as an amendment to the Constitution by the legislatures of three-fourths of the several States within seven years from the date of its submission.

21ST AMENDMENT. *Repeal of 18th Amendment*

Section 1. The eighteenth article of amendment to the Constitution of the United States is hereby repealed.

Section 2. The transportation or importation into any State, Territory, or possession of the United States for delivery or use therein of intoxicating liquors, in violation of the laws thereof, is hereby prohibited.

Section 3. This article shall be inoperative unless it shall have been ratified as an amendment to the Constitution by conventions in the several States, as provided in the Constitution, within seven years from the date of the submission hereof to the States by the Congress.

22ND AMENDMENT. *Presidential Tenure*

Section 1. No person shall be elected to the office of the President more than twice, and no person who has held the office of President, or acted as President, for more than two years of a term to which some other person was elected President shall be elected to the office of the President more than once. But this Article shall not apply to any person holding the office of President when this Article was proposed by the Congress, and shall not prevent any person who may be holding the office of President, or acting as President, during the term within which this Article becomes operative from holding the office of President or acting as President during the remainder of such term.

Section 2. This article shall be inoperative unless it shall have been ratified as an amendment to the Constitution by the legislatures of three-fourths of the several States within seven years from the date of its submission to the State by the Congress.

23RD AMENDMENT. *Presidential Electors for the District of Columbia*

Section 1. The District constituting the seat of Government of the United States shall appoint in such manner as the Congress may direct:

A number of electors of President and Vice President equal to the whole number of Senators and Representatives in Congress to which the District would be entitled if it were a State, but in no event more than the least populous State; they shall be in addition to those appointed by the States, but they shall be considered, for the purposes of the election of President and Vice President, to be electors appointed by a State; and they shall meet in the District and perform such duties as provided by the twelfth article of amendment.

Section 2. The Congress shall have power to enforce this article by appropriate legislation.

24TH AMENDMENT. *Right to Vote*

Section 1. The right of citizens of the United States to vote in any primary or other election for President or Vice President, for electors for President or Vice President, or for Senator or Representative in Congress, shall not be denied or abridged by the United States or any State by reason of failure to pay any poll tax or other tax.

Section 2. The Congress shall have power to enforce this article by appropriate legislation.

25TH AMENDMENT. *Presidential Succession, Vice Presidential Vacancy, Presidential Inability*

Section 1. In case of the removal of the President from office or of his death or resignation, the Vice President shall become President.

Section 2. Whenever there is a vacancy in the office of the Vice President, the President shall nominate a Vice President who shall take office upon confirmation by majority vote of both Houses of Congress.

Section 3. Whenever the President transmits to

the President *pro tempore* of the Senate and the Speaker of the House of Representatives his written declaration that he is unable to discharge the powers and duties of his office, and until he transmits to them a written declaration to the contrary, such powers and duties shall be discharged by the Vice President as Acting President.

Section 4.   Whenever the Vice President and a majority of either the principal officers of the executive departments or of such other body as Congress may by law provide, transmit to the President *pro tempore* of the Senate and the Speaker of the House of Representatives their written declaration that the President is unable to discharge the powers and duties of his office, the Vice President shall immediately assume the powers and duties of the office of Acting President.

Thereafter, when the President transmits to the President *pro tempore* of the Senate and the Speaker of the House of Representatives his written declaration that no inability exists, he shall resume the powers and duties of his office unless the Vice President and a majority of either the principal officers of the executive departments or of such other body as Congress may by law provide, transmit within four days to the President *pro tempore* of the Senate and the Speaker of the House of Representatives their written declaration that the President is unable to discharge the powers and duties of his office. Thereupon Congress shall decide the issue, assembling within forty-eight hours for that purpose if not in session. If the Congress, within twenty-one days after receipt of the latter written declaration, or, if Congress is not in session, within twenty-one days after Congress is required to assemble, determines by two-thirds vote of both Houses that the President is unable to discharge the powers and duties of his office, the Vice President shall continue to discharge the same as Acting President; otherwise, the President shall resume the powers and duties of his office.

26TH AMENDMENT.   *18-year-old vote*

Section 1.   The right of citizens of the United States, who are eighteen years of age or older, to vote shall not be denied or abridged by the United States or by any State on account of age.

Section 2.   The Congress shall have power to enforce this article by appropriate legislation.

Glossary

Access to government   The ability to have decision-makers listen to one's interests and concerns.

Ad hoc **group**   A temporary organization that arises to affect one particular issue.

Administrative adjudication   The settling of disputes between competing private interests or private interests and the government. Most adjudication involves a court-like process and takes place in the independent regulatory commissions; they often involve issues such as the awarding of airline routes, TV station licenses, or public utility rates.

Administrative legislation   Rules made by the executive branch agencies that provide the details of legislation enacted by Congress. These rules carry the full weight of law.

Administrative oversight   A function of Congress; it involves evaluating the performance of the bureaucracy and seeing that the laws Congress has passed are administered as intended.

Affirmative action   A requirement or program in which employers take positive steps to ensure the hiring of women and minorities.

Amendment process   The formal means of changing the Constitution; an amendment must be both proposed and ratified.

Amicus curiae   Literally, "friend of the court;" it is a way for an interest group to bring pressure on the Supreme Court by showing that it is strongly concerned about a case.

Amicus curiae **brief**   A written argument filed by a so-called "friend of the court."

Appellate jurisdiction   The ability to hear cases on appeal from lower courts.

Appropriation   The actual allocation of funds through the passage of budget bills to provide the money to conduct authorized programs.

Associational interest group   A group whose members join so as to affect government decisions which are relevant to them.

Attentive public   Those who are relatively well-informed and provide a critical audience for opinion-makers.

Authorization   As used in Congress, the term refers to legislation that creates a program and, where appropriate, stipulates how much money may be expended.

Baker v. *Carr* (1962)   The Supreme Court case that required that the lower houses of state legislatures be apportioned on the basis of population. Hence, although apportionment was "political" in nature, the Supreme Court held implicitly that it was also justiciable.

Balanced budget   A budget which provides for an equal amount of income and expenditure.

Bandwagon effect   A presumed effect of surveys, in which people move to support an apparent winner, and vice-versa.

Bargaining   Vote trading and compromise that allows legislators to achieve some of their goals. Without this flexible approach, the diverse interests within Congress would cripple the legislative process.

Bill of attainder   A legislative act which violates the separation of powers principle by punishing an individual or several persons without a trial.

Bipartisan foreign policy   Close cooperation between the two major parties when dealing with foreign policy. In political terms, it has meant that foreign policy toward our real or potential enemies is immune from partisan criticism and debate.

Bipartisanship   The working with members of both major political parties.

Blanket primary   A type of primary, used in the state of Washington, in which the voter is given one ballot listing all of the candidates of all parties for all offices. A voter may choose a Democrat for one office and a Republican for another.

Brandeis brief   A brief which argues the consequences of a law or decision.

Briefs   Written summaries of the legal and constitutional issues involved in court cases.

Brown v. *Board of Education of Topeka* (1954)   The Supreme Court case that ruled that school segregation was unconstitutional.

Bureaucracy   The agencies and departments that make up the executive branch of the federal government, or that of state or local governments.

Bureaucrats The personnel of the agencies and departments who administer the government's program.

Cabinet An advising group chosen by the president; it is composed of the heads of the executive departments and other individuals that the president considers to be "Cabinet-level" appointees. The Cabinet is an informal group with no constitutional status.

Candidate orientation The extent to which one's vote is guided by an awareness of the candidate's personal qualities and/or what that candidate is likely to do if selected.

Casework A time-consuming but essential task of legislators; it consists of responding to the problems of constituents that arise as they deal with various parts of the government.

Categoric groups Unorganized groups with no formal membership by which we describe ourselves or are described, e.g., "the rich," "the working class," "women," etc.

Caucus A meeting of party members in one house of a legislative body in which decisions on leaders, committee assignments, or legislative business are made.

Caucus (delegate selection) District meetings held in non-primary states for the purpose of choosing convention delegates; they are open to all party members.

Censure A formal condemnation by majority vote of a legislator for some action judged to be improper.

Certiorari The main way by which cases reach the Supreme Court; it is an order to a lower court to forward the record of the case.

Checks and balances The limits placed on each branch of government by the other branches so that it cannot act entirely on its own.

Cherokee Indian case (1832) The case in which President Jackson refused to enforce a Supreme Court decision.

Citizens' lobbies Lobbying organizations formed on a basis other than economic interest, some of which are characterized by political amateurism.

Civil liberties Basic guaranteed freedoms.

Civil rights Equal treatment under the law.

Civil Rights Commission An investigative and publicizing agency dealing with civil rights, the findings of which may form the basis of legislation.

"Clear and present danger" doctrine A limit placed on freedom of speech, it suggested that speech may be limited in times of grave national crisis.

Closed primary The most common form of primary, in which voting is limited to party members.

Closed rule   A ruling by the House Rules Committee that some or all sections of a bill are exempted from amendment on the floor.

Cloture rule   The rule used to break a filibuster. Adoption of the rule requires the affirmative vote of three-fifths (sixty members) of the entire Senate.

Coalition   The development of alliances, normally between interest groups, in order to achieve their purposes.

Coattail effect   A term used to describe the situation in which a presidential (or gubernatorial or mayoral) candidate carries into office other candidates of his or her party largely on the strength of the head of the ticket's strong showing at the polls.

Code of Federal Regulations   The annual list of all effective regulations.

Cohens v. *Virginia* (1821)   The case in which the Supreme Court decided that it could review state court decisions in which the state was a party to the suit, if a federal question was involved.

Colegrove v. *Green* (1946)   The malapportionment case from Illinois in which the Supreme Court ruled that apportionment was a political question.

Committee of the whole   A parliamentary arrangement in the House which allows business to be conducted with a 100–member quorum. General floor debate is usually conducted using this rule.

Common Cause   A broad-based citizens' lobby that is primarily concerned with government reform.

Common law   The decisions or precedents from earlier cases, often called "judge-made law."

Compliance tradition   The tradition of accepting and complying with court decisions.

Concentration of media ownership   The relative absence of competition in the nation's media, especially in the press.

Concurrent powers   Those powers exercised by both national and state governments in areas for which both levels of government hold authority.

Confederation government   A form of government in which the central government has only those powers that the lower levels are willing to grant it.

Conference Committee   A committee comprised of members of both houses, appointed by the leadership, to work out major differences in the House and Senate versions of the same bill.

Conflict of interest   A situation in which an official's public actions are affected by the individual's personal—usually economic—interests.

Congressional interpretation   A device of informal change of the Constitution, in which the Congress interprets the document in its own way.

Congressional surveys   Usually inaccurate surveys taken by members of

Congress to determine their chances of re-election and how constituents feel about issues.

Congressional veto   A provision in a bill which allows Congress to disallow actions by the executive branch before they take effect.

Conservative coalition   A voting coalition of Republicans and southern Democrats that often appears in Congress when certain issues are voted upon.

Constituency   The geographic area, district, or state, represented by a legislator. A *constituent* is a resident of the district or state.

Contemporary community standards   The part of the Roth Doctrine that has caused a great deal of local variation in the judging of obscene materials.

Cooperative federalism   The arrival at joint or cooperative solutions to common problems by the national and state governments.

Coordinated spending   Money spent by the party for services requested by the candidates; the party has some say in how the money is spent.

Council of Economic Advisers   An agency within the Executive Office of the President; it consists of three leading economists who advise the president on issues vital to the nation's economy.

County committee   The real source of power in state politics; these committees are involved with patronage, candidate recruitment, and campaign management.

Court of Claims   A court established to hear suits against the government.

Court of Military Appeals   The highest level of the military justice system; it reviews decisions of courts-martial.

Courts of Appeals   Courts created in 1891 to hear appeals from district courts and certain executive agencies.

Decentralized party   Parties like those in the U.S.; they are loose coalitions in which organizational power exists mostly at the state and county level.

Delegate theory   A representational role that assumes that the decisions of legislators are made in response to the demands or beliefs of their constituents.

Delegate selection primary   A type of primary found in a few states; it provides only for the election of delegates to the national convention.

Democracy   A system of government in which the people participate in decision making through their choice of competing candidates for office.

Denied powers   The opposite of exclusive powers; powers which are denied to one level of government belong exclusively to the other.

Dennis v. *United States* (1951)   The case resulting in the conviction of Communist Party leaders of conspiracy to teach and advocate the overthrow of the government. The decision stated that the government does not have to wait until a crisis is imminent in order to limit speech.

Deviating election   An election in which prevailing patterns of party loyalty remain intact, but for some reason the majority party does not win.

Direct national primary   A reform proposal that would have party members vote in a closed presidential preference primary held on the same day throughout the nation.

Direction of attitudes   The taking of positions in favor of or against certain issues or personalities.

Disclosure rule   The requirement that members of Congress file an annual report listing their income, assets, and debts. Requirements for public disclosure are more stringent in the House than in the Senate.

Distributive policy   Legislation that gives funds, resources, or service to individuals or groups; agricultural subsidies, tax breaks, and defense contracts are examples of distributive policies.

Division of powers   The distribution of powers between the national (federal) and state governments.

Domestic Policy Staff   A unit within the Executive Office of the President whose members are responsible for coordinating the domestic policy of the executive branch.

Double jeopardy   The ability to be tried twice for the same offense by the same government.

Dred Scott decision (1857)   The case which held that blacks could not become citizens or hold the rights of citizenship.

Dual federalism   The orthodox interpretation of federalism; it holds that both state and national governments have exclusive powers, and that those belonging to the national government are only those delegated to it by the Constitution.

Due process   The right to fair treatment.

Elastic clause   An alternate term for the "necessary and proper" clause.

Electoral college   The device by which we elect presidents, under an essentially "winner-take-all" system within each state.

Electorate   The term is synonymous with *voters*. A senator's electorate are the voters within his or her state.

Enrolled voter   One who has indicated a choice of party and is

Equal Rights Amendment   An amendment sent to the states in 1972 which would have provided equality of rights regardless of sex. This proposal was the center of a major controversy, and best symbolized the struggle for women's rights.

Ex post facto law   A law which makes a certain action illegal after it has taken place; it is forbidden by the Constitution.

Exclusion   The refusal to administer the oath of office (seat) to a member of Congress because of the failure to meet the constitutionally mandated requirements of office or because of election fraud.

Exclusive powers   Powers which belong exclusively to either the national or state governments, but not to both.

Executive agreement   An agreement between the president and the head of state of another nation; it is not submitted to the Senate for approval or disapproval.

Executive lobbying   Attempts by the executive branch to lobby the Congress.

Executive Office of the President   The top staff agencies that assist and advise the president in carrying out his major policies and duties.

Executive privilege   The power of the president, or members of the executive branch under orders from the president, to withhold information from Congress and the courts.

Expulsion   The power of each house of Congress to expel, by two-thirds vote, a seated member as an extreme penalty for an illegal or unethical action.

Extra-constitutional   That which is neither unconstitutional or specifically provided for in the Constitution, such as political parties or the bureaucracy.

Federal Election Campaign Act of 1974   The most far-reaching campaign reform bill in our history; it imposed contribution limits on candidates, individuals, and organizations, and provided for partial public funding of presidential primaries and full public funding of the presidential general election.

Federal Election Commission   A bipartisan six-member commission established in 1974; it administers campaign finance laws and enforces compliance.

Federal government   A compromise between the unitary and confederation forms of government; it limits the authority of both the national and state governments, but allows each a certain amount of exclusive powers.

Federal Register   A publication issued every working day that contains proposed and adopted rules from the executive branch.

Federal Regulation of Lobbying Act of 1946   The means by which Congress regulates lobbies and their agents; it requires registration of and reporting by groups and individuals who attempt to influence legislation.

Federalism   The division of powers between national and state governments.

The Federalist A collection of essays written by Hamilton, Jay, and Madison designed to allay public fears regarding the proposed Constitution.

Field service Most executive branch agencies include a field service that consists of a large number of regional, state, county, and local units that administer that agency's programs.

Fifteenth Amendment The amendment that guaranteed the right to vote regardless of race, color, or previous condition of servitude.

Fifth Amendment protections The amendment that limits double jeopardy, and gives the right to remain silent and not testify against oneself and the right to due process.

Filibuster The use of the Senate's unlimited debate rule to prevent a measure from coming to a vote by talking it to death and holding up the other issues before the Senate.

First Amendment freedoms The "cornerstone of our society;" these include the guaranteed freedoms of religion, speech, press, peaceful assembly, and petition.

Fiscal year The budgetary year used by an organization. The fiscal year of the federal government runs from October 1 through September 30.

Folkways Norms or unwritten rules of behavior or procedure. The seniority system of Congress is a folkway.

Foreign Agents Registration Act Legislation requiring the registration of representatives of foreign governments (other than diplomats) who seek to influence Congress or the executive departments.

Fourteenth Amendment The amendment that overturned the *Dred Scott* decision; it is considered the source of many of our civil rights and liberties through its guarantees of "due process of law" and "equal protection of the laws."

Franking privilege The free use of the mails to allow members of Congress to communicate with their constituents. Congress has granted this privilege to other agencies and officials of the national government as well.

Functional representation The idea that citizens may be represented by someone other than their own representative or senator, and that this representation can be based upon occupational, ethnic, racial, religious, or other characteristics.

Furman v. *Georgia* (1972) The Supreme Court case that ruled that the death penalty was unconstitutional if there were other options available. Hence, this left open the possibility that mandatory death penalties might be acceptable (in the absence of other options).

Germane As used in Congress, the term refers to amendments to a bill that are related to the main subject of the bill.

Gerrymandering The practice of creating oddly shaped legislative districts in order to give one party an electoral advantage over another party or parties.

Gideon v. *Wainwright* (1963)   The Supreme Court case which established the requirement that states provide counsel in felony cases to those too poor to hire attorneys.

Government corporations   Agencies of the government that administer a business enterprise such as electric power distribution (Tennessee Valley Administration) or mail service (U.S. Postal Service).

"Grandfather clause"   A restrictive provision holding that one could vote only if one's grandfather had been eligible to vote before 1867.

Grants-in-aid   A major vehicle of cooperative federalism, in which the national government pays a major share of the costs of certain projects at the state or local level.

Griswold v. *Connecticut* (1965)   The Supreme Court ruling that married couples have a fundamental right to privacy; it cleared the way for distribution of birth control information.

Gross National Product (GNP)   The market value of the total output or production of a country's goods and services.

Habeas corpus   The constitutional requirement that prisoners cannot be held without being charged.

Hiring standards   The requirement that recipients of grants-in-aid use affirmative action and equal opportunity programs in the employment of minorities.

Honorarium   A fee paid to an individual for making speeches and writing articles.

Impeachment   The bringing of charges against an officer or judge of the United States before the House of Representatives. If an article of impeachment is voted by the House, the accused is tried in the Senate.

Implied powers   Authority held by the national government that is not specifically granted in the Constitution but can be inferred from a specific grant of power.

Impoundment   The president's power to refuse to spend money appropriated by Congress. Since 1974, this power has been subject to veto by either house of Congress.

Incumbent   The individual currently holding a public office.

Independent executive agencies   Agencies, such as the Central Intelligence Agency, that are not part of a Cabinet department, and that report directly to the president. Presidential appointees serving in these agencies can be dismissed by the president.

Independent regulatory commissions   Units, not attached to Cabinet departments, whose top administrators, although appointed by the president, can only be removed for cause. This "independence" was designed to keep them free from political control as they regulate areas such as the stock exchange, public utilities, airlines, and the communications industry.

Independent voter   A registered voter not enrolled in a party.

Inspired mail   Mail campaigns to government officials inspired by pressure groups in order to influence legislation.

Institutional interest groups   Groups formed for some purpose other than influencing public policy; they are sometimes present in the government itself.

Interstate commerce clause   The power given Congress by the Constitution to regulate interstate commerce; it has been a major vehicle for change as interpreted by the Supreme Court by applying the elastic clause.

Issue orientation   The extent to which one's vote is guided by the nature and substance of issues.

Joint committee   A committee consisting of members of both houses; its primary purpose is to study particular subjects and report its findings to the House and Senate.

Judicial activism   The taking of an active hand in governance by a court.

Judicial circuits   The twelve courts which hear appeals from federal district courts and from administrative courts.

Judicial discretion   The ability of a court to decide whether or not it will hear cases.

Judicial districts   Courts created by the Judiciary Act of 1789. They are the lowest layer of federal courts, having original jurisdiction in most cases involving constitutional questions.

Judicial interpretation   The opportunity for judges to interpret what the Constitution means.

Judicial restraint   The refusal by a court to hear a case or reverse previous decisions.

Judicial review   The power of the courts to accept and review certain types of cases.

Judiciary Act of 1789   The act that created most of our federal courts; it also set limits on their jurisdiction.

Justiciable   The availability of a legal remedy for a case.

Legitimate government   A government which exists by consent of the people.

Literacy tests   Tests designed to be difficult and which were often administered unfairly in order to restrict blacks from voting.

Literary Digest poll   The 1936 survey which demonstrated, through its inaccuracy, that the sheer size of sample cannot guarantee its accuracy.

Lobbying The process of pressuring lawmakers in order to influence government legislation or policy.

Maintaining elections Elections in which prevailing patterns of party loyalty persist.

Majority leader The leader elected by the majority party in each house; these individuals direct their party's legislative battles. In the Senate, the leader is the undisputed head of the party; in the House, the leader ranks second behind the Speaker of the House.

Marbury v. Madison (1803) The case which established judicial review of acts of Congress and the executive branch.

Margin of error A built-in allowance for sampling error in the analysis of survey results.

Martin v. Hunter's Lessee (1816) The case in which the Supreme Court decided that it could hear on appeal suits between private persons involving a federal or constitutional issue even if a state court had decided the case.

Mass public That group, on any given issue, which is indifferent or passive to the issue and hence unlikely to communicate with government decision-makers.

McCarran Act of 1950 A law that outlawed any conspiracy that attempts to establish foreign control over our government.

McCulloch v. Maryland (1819) The landmark case which established the usage of the "necessary and proper" or elastic clause, and established the nature of federal authority versus that of the states.

Merit system The system for hiring, retaining, and promoting government employees on the basis of demonstrated ability. Hiring is based upon competitive examinations.

Minority leader The leader elected by the minority party in each house of Congress; each is primarily concerned with directing the floor strategy of his party when attempting to defeat or amend the majority party's proposals.

Miranda decision The decision by the Supreme Court in 1966, that a person must be told of the right to counsel and the right to remain silent, even though the investigation is not necessarily focussed on that person.

Modified one-party system The system present in a state when one party dominates and the other party occasionally elects its candidates to state level offices.

National committee A party committee composed of one man and one woman from each state; it is directed by the national chairperson and engages in fund-raising, campaign assistance, publicity, and planning the national convention.

National Security Council An agency within the Executive Office of the President created in 1947 to advise the president on matters, domestic or foreign, that affect national security.

"Necessary and proper" clause That part of Article I, Section 8, which gives Congress the power "to make all Laws which shall be necessary and proper for carrying into Execution" the powers which had been specifically granted it.

Nineteenth Amendment The amendment that guaranteed the right of women to vote.

Ninth Amendment The reserved civil liberties amendment; it allows people to have rights, such as that of privacy, which are not specifically granted.

Non-germane amendment A device used in the Senate to attach a bill to another bill, even though the second measure is not related to the first one. This tactic may be used to avoid a hostile committee in one or both houses.

Office of Management and Budget An agency within the Executive Office of the President with primary responsibility for preparing the president's budget, administering it, and checking agency proposals and congressional actions for their consistency with the president's fiscal program.

Office-block ballot This form of ballot groups the candidates according to the position sought and requires the voter to make a separate mark or pull a separate lever for each office.

"One man, one vote" The principle, enunciated in the apportionment cases, that no one person's vote should be worth more or less than that of any other person.

One-party system The system present in a state when one party dominates the elections and the other party almost never has success at the polls.

Open primary A type of primary used in a few states, it permits any registered voter to vote in the primary of his or her choice without reference to party membership.

Open-seat races Elections in which the previous officeholder (incumbent) is not seeking re-election.

Opinion intensity The strength with which opinions are held.

Opinion-making public Those who shape opinions on one or many issues; it includes media personalities, public officials, and speakers for particular causes or groups, among others.

Opinion stability The extent to which opinions may or may not be changeable.

Original jurisdiction The right or authority of a court to first try or hear a case.

Oversight The responsibility of Congress to check on the executive branch's carrying out of congressional programs and policies.

Particularized benefits Actions that benefit specific individuals, groups, or geographical constituencies.

Party-column ballot A ballot that lists the names of candidates and offices in a vertical column under the party label; this form encourages straight-ticket voting.

Party identification The feeling held by an individual that a particular party best represents his or her attitudes about political issues. This may be a belief formed in early childhood and later reflected when the person enrolls in a party.

Party platform   The intentions, in terms of policies, that party candidates will attempt to implement if elected to office. Platforms serve primarily as campaign instruments.

Patronage   The practice of appointing party supporters to public jobs. Civil service reforms have limited this procedure at all levels of government.

Pentagon Papers   A top-secret study of our involvement in Vietnam; these papers led to a 1971 case in which the Supreme Court ruled that their publication could not be suppressed.

Performance standards   Minimum standards established by the national government which must be met by recipients of grants-in-aid.

Permanent government   The career civil servants who comprise most of the personnel of the departments and agencies of the executive branch.

Pigeonholing   A term used to refer to a committee's decision not to hold hearings on a bill, thereby killing the proposal.

Plessy v. *Ferguson* (1896)   The Supreme Court case that upheld a state law requiring segregation in public transportation, provided that "separate but equal" facilities were available. This case provided the legal basis for segregation in all matters of public accommodation.

Pluralism   The presence of conflicting societal interests.

Pocket veto   If Congress's final adjournment in the fall of even-numbered years (election years) takes place prior to the expiration of the ten-workday period that a president has to veto or accept a bill, the president's failure to sign results in the death of the bill. Having adjourned, the Congress has no opportunity to override the veto.

Police action   Armed conflicts between the United States and another nation for which Congress has made no formal declaration of war (Korea and Vietnam).

Police powers   The regulation of issues involving health, safety, welfare, and morals.

Policy constituency   That group particularly affected by or interested in a government proposal or action which may not be of major interest to other members of the general public.

Political Action committees   Groups, commonly formed by labor and business, to legally donate funds to candidates for various offices.

Political broker   A representational role in which legislators try to strike a balance between competing interests in their constituencies or between national and local needs.

Political party (U.S.-style)   Broad coalitions whose main purpose is to use the nomination and election processes to win public office and control the government.

Political question   An issue which involves the separation of powers between the three branches of the federal government.

Political socialization   The process by which we learn our basic orientation to the political system and how it functions.

"Political thicket"   Involvement of the Supreme Court in political questions.

Poll-tax   A tax formerly required in some states in order to vote; this tax was abolished by the Twenty-fourth Amendment in 1964.

Precinct   The basic unit for elections and party organization; each contains from 200 to 1,000 voters and one polling place, and is run by an elected or appointed precinct leader.

Preferments   Rewards made administratively by the party in control of the government, particularly at the state, county, and local level. Preferments include construction and printing contracts and the appointment of lawyers to handle estates.

Prerogative theory   A theory of presidential power attributed to Lincoln, who claimed that the president could take whatever action he deemed necessary to preserve and protect the nation, even if the action was "unconstitutional."

President *pro tempore*   The temporary presiding officer in the Senate, in the usual absence of the vice-president; this is a largely honorific position given to the eldest senator of the majority party.

Presidential bureaucracy   The elaborate bureaucracy built up around the president; it consists of the Cabinet and the units within the Executive Office of the President. These key advisers are presidential appointees who serve at the pleasure of the chief executive.

Presidential interpretation   A device of informal change of the Constitution, by which presidents daily interpret the Constitution and so change it through their activities.

Presidential lobbying   Activities by the president to influence the course of legislation.

Presidential preference primary   The type of primary, used in most states, in which the voters indicate their choice among candidates for the nominations as well as selecting delegates to the national convention.

Pressure group   An organization interested in affecting public policy to reflect the interests of its membership.

Prohibition   The Eighteenth Amendment, which prohibited the "manufacture, sale, or transportation of intoxicating liquors" in the United States.

Proposal   Two-thirds of both houses of Congress may either propose an amendment, or call a constitutional convention, after two-thirds of the state legislatures have requested the convention.

Public Interest Research Group (PIRG)   An organization in the Nader group which reviews the actions of governmental agencies and personnel.

Public opinion   That "which the government finds it prudent to heed."

Questionnaire   The instrument used by survey researchers to elicit desired information.

Raiding   A practice used in conjunction with open primaries, it refers to crossing over to vote in the opposition party's primary with the hope of selecting the weakest candidate to oppose your party's choice.

Random sampling   The drawing of a sample in such a manner that all persons have an equal chance of inclusion; it results in a sample that adequately reflects the most important characteristics of the population from which the sample is drawn.

Rank and file   The average party members, who are not party leaders or activists.

Ratification   Approval of a proposed amendment by three-fourths of either both houses of state legislatures, or state constitutional conventions called for the purpose within each state.

Realigning election   An election in which old loyalties are sufficiently disrupted to cause a shuffling of majority and minority party status.

Redistributive policy   Policies which usually affect large groups and involve a redistribution of resources such as money or power. For example, poverty and welfare programs involve a redistribution of federal dollars and means that less money is available for other purposes.

Re-election constituency   That part of a legislator's constituency which is most likely to have an effect, presumably positive, on that person's re-election chances.

Regents v. *Bakke* (1978)   The "reverse discrimination" case on medical school admissions. The Supreme Court held that racial quotas were unacceptable, but that race could be considered in admissions programs.

Registered voter   The act of registration places a qualified citizen on the voting rolls; a person may be registered but may choose not to enroll in a party.

Regulatory policy   A policy that usually affects a wide segment of the public and tends to limit one group for the benefit of others and/or reduce or expand the options of private citizens. Some examples are medicare, campaign finance regulation, or price controls applied to public utility rates.

Reinstating election An election in which the majority party regains control after a deviating election.

Relevant interests Those interests we have which are relevant to the functioning of government.

Relevant public Those persons for whom an issue is meaningful in a personal sense.

Repeal The Twenty-first Amendment, which repealed the Eighteenth Amendment which had banned the sale of liquor.

Representative government An alternative to direct democracy in which officeholders represent the wishes and interests of the people in a specific area (e.g., House by congressional districts; Senate by states; presidency, the nation).

Republic A representative government in which citizens choose their representatives.

Residency requirement Minimum period of residence required by most states in order to vote, now fixed at thirty days by the 1970 Voting Rights Act for voting in federal elections.

Residual powers Those powers which are reserved to the states.

"Responsible" party model Parties in nations outside the U.S.; they are disciplined, centralized, and are responsible in the sense that if they control a legislative body, they should be able to enact promised legislation.

Revenue sharing The provision of federal funds, with minimal strings attached, to be spent largely as states and local communities see fit; these funds are provided on a ratio of one-third to state governments, and two-thirds to the local governments within each state.

Reynolds v. *Sims* (1964) The Supreme Court case which held that upper houses of a state legislature must be apportioned on the basis of population.

Roth Doctrine An attempt by the Supreme Court to provide a standard of judging obscene materials. Criteria include whether they are "utterly without redeeming social importance," appeal to "prurient interest," and whether the average person could determine obscenity by "applying contemporary community standards."

Sample The selection of persons to be interviewed for a survey.

Senatorial courtesy The device by which a president normally defers to his party's senior senator from the state where an appointment is to be made.

Seniority Committee rank; it is based on years of consecutive service on a committee. The member of the majority party with the most uninterrupted service on the committee serves as committee chairman.

"Separate but equal" The principle embodied in *Plessy;* it formed the basis for enforced segregation.

Separation of powers The distribution of government powers among branches of government, each with distinct responsibilities. In the United States, and in most governments, these branches are the legislative, executive, and judicial.

Services-in-kind The provision of services of which the actual cost may be difficult to both compute and report.

Single-issue parties Parties that are formed to advocate a particular policy or set of policies such as the Right to Life Party or the Libertarian Party.

Single-issue politics The tendency of some to get involved in the political process out of a concern for the successful resolution of one single issue.

Single negative A term referring to the fact that legislation may be defeated at any single point in the legislative process, while passage requires achieving a majority vote at each point in the process.

Smith Act of 1940 The law that made it possible for the government to limit organizations that advocate the overthrow of the government by force.

Socio-economic characteristics Characteristics such as age, occupation, sex, place of residence, religion, race, ethnicity, and educational level.

Speaker of the House The presiding officer of the House; he or she is the leader of the majority party.

Special federal courts Courts created to handle special questions, such as military appeals and custom and patent appeals.

Special or select committee A committee created to study and investigate a particular problem; it is usually temporary and usually does not have the power to report out legislation.

Splinter parties Parties formed by individuals who temporarily desert from one of the major parties. The Dixiecrats who split away from the Democrats during the election of 1948 are an example.

Stability of attitudes The extent to which attitudes are likely to remain stable or to change.

Standing committee The fifteen Senate and twenty-two House permanent committees; each is assigned an area over which it has almost exclusive jurisdiction.

State committee The party committee headed by the state chairperson; it coordinates party efforts within the state, engages in fund raising, and assists with campaign management.

State of the Union Message An annual message from the president to the Congress; it is usually delivered in person, and in it are outlined desired legislative programs.

States' rights The assumption that states have certain exclusive rights in opposition to the power of the national government.

Statutes at Large The annual published by Congress that lists all new public laws.

Stewardship theory   The concept of presidential powers that assumes that the chief executive can do anything he believes is necessary for the interests of the nation as long as the action is not prevented by a direct constitutional or legislative prohibition.

Tenth Amendment   The amendment that grants residual powers to the states.

Test case   A case carefully selected by an interest group that embodies the crux of an argument it wishes to make or a principle it wishes to establish, and is likely to produce a favorable ruling.

Three-fifths compromise   The counting of five slaves as equal to three freemen for purposes of determining population of states for membership in the House of Representatives. It was used until 1865.

Three-way lobbying   Mutual pressure by congressional committees, executive departments and agencies, and pressure groups.

Triple alliance   An alliance between an executive branch agency, the agency's clientele, and key members of Congress, often in opposition to the president's point of view. An example would be the Department of Agriculture, farmers, and legislators from the agricultural committees.

Trustee theory   A representational role that suggests that legislators will represent the national interest according to their own best judgment, even if this conflicts with the opinion of their constituents.

Twenty-sixth Amendment   The amendment that gave the right to vote to eighteen-year-olds.

Two-party system   A system present in a state when both major parties regularly elect candidates to state-level offices.

Umbrella groups   Groups which are broad-ranging and diverse in their membership and seldom take positions on specific issues.

Undisciplined party   A term referring to the fact that party leaders cannot force party members in Congress to vote in support of the party's position.

Unearned income   As used in congressional codes of ethics and income limitations, it refers to dividends from stocks and bonds or income from a family-controlled business. Members are not limited to the amount of unearned income they can make.

Unit rule   An abandoned practice that required all of a state's delegation to the national convention to cast their votes for the candidate supported by a majority of the state's delegation.

Unitary government   A form of government in which all power is held by a central government. Lower levels of government may be delegated some of these powers, but the powers may be withdrawn at any time by the central government.

United States Code   The collection of all statutes (laws) of the federal government that are still in force.

U.S. v. *Nixon* (1974) The case in which the Supreme Court ruled that executive privilege could not be used to withhold evidence relevant to charges of a criminal nature unless there were overriding national security reasons to do so.

Voter turnout The extent to which the voting-age population actually votes, usually expressed in both absolute numbers and in percentage of eligibles participating.

Voting Rights Act of 1965 Sweeping legislation which suspended literacy tests and required the appointment of federal voting examiners to ensure registration where less than 25 percent of any race were registered. This act resulted in a great increase in southern black voter registration and the election of black public officials.

Ward committee In urban areas, large populations have required the creation of ward committees to serve as a link between the many precincts and the city committee.

Wesberry v. *Sanders* (1964) The Supreme Court case which required that the U.S. House of Representatives be apportioned within each state on the basis of population.

Whips The assistant majority or minority leader (elected, with the exception of the Democratic whip in the House) with major responsibility for communication with party members and getting out the vote.

White House Office The unit within the Executive Office of the President where the president's inner circle of eight to ten personal advisers are assigned. Its members include such people as the press secretary, the counsel to the president, and the assistant for legislative affairs.

White primary A party election, now outlawed, limited only to whites.

Witherspoon v. *Illinois* (1968) The Supreme Court case which established that one cannot be automatically excluded from sitting on a jury if one is opposed to the death penalty.

Yates v. *United States* (1957) The Supreme Court case which reversed *Dennis* substantially, holding that there is a difference between teaching what to believe and advocating action.

Youngstown Sheet and Tube Co. v. *Sawyer* (1952) The Supreme Court case in which President Truman, having lost in the Supreme Court, complied with the court order without dispute.

Author Index

Subject Index

Gann, Paul, 290
Gardner, John, 280
Garfield, James A., 484
Garner, John Nance, 443
Gasoline shortage. *See* Energy
General Accounting Office (GAO), 336, 491, 500
General Services Administration (GSA), 500
Gerrymandering, 276
Gibbons, Sam, 384
Gideon v. *Wainwright,* 138
Gilmore, Gary, 168–169
Glenn, John, 285
Godfrey v. *Georgia,* 148
Goldberg, Arthur, 97
Goldwater Barry, 219–220
Goodell, Charles, 183
Government corporations, 491
Grants-in-aid, 65–71
Grasso, Ella T., 261
Gregg v. *Georgia,* 148
Griswold v. *Connecticut,* 141
Gross National Product (GNP), 503, 519–520
Grovey v. *Townsend,* 147
Gulf Oil Corporation, 328
Gun control, 165, 266, 267
Gun Control Act (1968), 165

habeas corpus, 27, 101, 142
Haig, Alexander, 6, 416, 449
Haldeman, H.R., 455, 468, 511
Hamilton, Alexander, 35, 196, 421
Handicapped Americans, and discrimination, 127–128
Hanna, Richard T., 328–329
Hansen, Clifford, 533
Harding, Warren G., 169
Harris, Patricia Roberts, 448
Harrison, Benjamin, 45, 273
Hart, Gary, 327, 347
Hart, Peter D., 315
Hatch Acts (1939, 1940), 501
Hathaway, William D., 327
Hawkins, Paula, 324
Hayden, Carl, 426
Hayes, Rutherford B., 45
Hayes, Wayne L., 329
Haynsworth, Clement, 97, 98, 102, 375–376
Heller, Walter, 71–72, 461
Herrera, Omar Torrijos, 418–419
Hirabayashi v. *U.S.,* 148, 435
Hiring standards. *See* Federalism
Hispanic Americans, 7, 12, 121, 125, 127, 253, 255, 264, 303, 306, 323–324
Holmes, Oliver Wendell, 107, 131–132
Homosexuals, rights of, 129, 149
Hoover, Herbert, 198, 273, 497
Hostage crisis. *See* Iran
House of Representatives, 93, 116. *See also* Congress
   ad hoc Committee on Energy, 530
   clerk of, 173, 379
   committee assignments, 362–364
   Committee of the Whole, 382
   committee structure in, 43

   Ethics Committee, 319, 346
   floor debate in, 382
   leadership of, 358–361
   majority leader of, 359
   organization of, 358–369
   party committees in, 363
   speaker of the, 43, 358–359
   standing committees:
      agriculture, 162, 348
      appropriations, 319, 362, 369, 373, 506–508
      armed services, 373
      foreign affairs, 502–503
      judiciary, 102, 455
      public works, 334
      rules, 358–359, 362, 380, 530
      ways and means, 362, 369, 524
   turnover in, 309–310
   women in, 261–262
Hruska, Roman, 97
Humphrey, Hubert, 118, 202, 205, 209, 243, 258–259, 312
Humphrey's Executor v. *United States,* 435

Impeachment, 30–32, 101–102, 231, 378, 426–430
Impoundment, 371–372, 394, 414–415, 459
Independent executive agencies, 489
Independent regulatory commissions (IRCs), 489–491, 494–496
Intelligence agencies, 502–503. *See also* Central Intelligence Agency; Federal Bureau of Investigation
Interest groups, 7, 62–63, 151–186, 264–267. *See also* Single-issue politics
   academic, 167–168
   and access, 153, 163, 167
   ad hoc, 168–169
   agricultural, 161–162
   associational, 167
   and bipartisanship, 160, 163
   and the bureaucracy, 177–179
   business, 160–161, 353
   categoric, 156
   citizens' lobbies, 164–165, 182–183, 353–354, 537, 539
   and coalitions, 158–160
   conservative bias of, 180–182
   diversity of, 152, 155–169
   and energy policy, 528–529
   environmental, 158–159, 182, 537
   evaluation of, 180–182
   foreign, 165–166, 182–184
   functional, 180–181
   functions of, 193
   institutional, 166–167
   and the judiciary, 179–180
   Korean, 166
   labor, 162–163, 167, 291, 303, 308, 339–340
   and lobbying, 153, 159–160, 162
   and the media. *See* Media
   and political activity, 249
   and political parties, 191, 304, 312–313. *See also* Political action committees
   pluralism of, 156–163

Interest groups (continued)
  purposes of, 153–156
  and relevance to government, 153–169
  tactics of, 169–173, 244, 340
  three-way relationship, 178–179, 475, 496–503
Internal Revenue Service (IRS), 129–130, 177–178, 408,
    476, 488, 502
Iran, American hostages in, 3, 274, 377, 416, 417, 420,
    439, 503, 537–538
Italian Americans, and discrimination, 127

Jackson, Andrew, 99, 196, 398
Jackson, Henry, 532
Japanese Americans, and *habeas corpus,* 142
Javits, Jacob, 261, 362
Jaworski, Leon, 90, 408
Jay, John, 35
Jefferson, Thomas, 44, 116, 196, 397–398
Jehovah's Witnesses, and First Amendment, 130
Jenrette, John W., Jr., 337
Jews, voting behavior of, 260, 261, 263–264, 308
Johnson, Andrew, 378, 427
Johnson, Lyndon Baines, 71–72, 91, 98, 122–123, 125,
    439
  and abuse of power, 409
  and campaign finance, 284
  and Congress, 176–177, 386, 409–410
  and 1964 election, 220
  and 1968 eleciton, 209, 231–232, 243
  in the Senate, 359
  and Tonkin Gulf Resolution, 376–377, 422
Johnson v. *Zerbst,* 148
Jordan, Hamilton, 456, 467, 470
Judges, 7, 21, 101, 116. *See also* Judicial branch
Judicial branch, 21, 80–81, 85–113
  activism in, 94–95
  and appellate jurisdiction, 89–90, 101
  changing jurisdiction of, 101
  circuits, 87–88
  and compliance tradition, 99–100
  court discretion, 90–91
  Courts of Appeals, 86, 87–90
  and court structure, 85–89
  district courts, 86–87, 89–90
  districts, 86–88
  and judicial review, 103–105, 495–496
  legislative role of, 107–108
  original jurisdiction, 89
  and politics, 104–111
  restraint, 94
  reversing decisions of, 101
  selection of judges, 95–98, 108–111
  special courts, 88–89
Judiciary Act (1789), 104–105

Kaiser Aluminum v. *Weber,* 148
Kalmbach, Herbert W., 287
Kennedy, Edward, 169, 221, 224, 236–237, 291, 293,
    297–298, 395
Kennedy, John F., 43, 97, 109, 110, 258, 261, 300, 400,
    439
Kennedy, Robert F., 165, 209, 232, 409

King, Martin Luther, Jr., 165, 409
Kirbo, Charles, 153
Kirkpatrick, Jean J., 449
Kissinger, Henry A., 416, 417, 455
Korematsu v. *U.S.,* 148, 435
Kraft, Tim, 456
Kreps, Juanita M., 448
Krupsak, Mary Ann, 261

Landon, Alf, 240
League of Women Voters, 305–306
Lederer, Raymond F., 337
Legislative oversight, 358, 373–375
Legislative Reorganization Act (1946), 336, 361
Legislative Reorganization Act (1970), 367–368
Lincoln, Abraham, 142, 197, 398
Lobbying. *See* Interest groups
Long, Russell D., 313, 348, 530

MacArthur, Douglas, 265
McCarran Act (1950), 133
McCarthy, Eugene, 200, 232, 278
McCarthy, Joseph A., 338
McCollum v. *Board of Education,* 147
McCord, James W., Jr., 286
McCormick, John, 426
McCulloch v. *Maryland,* 56–57, 71
McGovern, George, 213, 220, 243, 259, 288, 298,
    303–304, 312
McLaurin v. *Oklahoma State Regents,* 50, 147
Madison, James, 35, 43, 55, 103
Mansfield, Mike, 359
Marbury v. *Madison,* 103–104
Marshall, John, 56–57, 59, 71, 94, 95, 99, 100, 103, 110,
    117–118
Marshall, Thurgood, 97, 110, 145
Martin v. *Hunter's Lessee,* 104
Mayaguez incident, 29, 77
Media, the. *See also* Public opinion
  and the bureaucracy, 498
  and election campaigns, 285, 298–299, 304, 305–306
  as interest group, 163–164
  objectivity of, 251–253
  as opinion source, 234–235, 243–244, 249–251
  ownership patterns of, 251
Medicare, 159–160, 178, 373
Meese, Edward, 457
Merit System Protection Board, 486–487
Metzenbaum, Howard, 285, 533
Meyers, Michael, 337
Meyers v. *United States,* 435
Migrant workers, 117, 340
Mikva, Abner, 194
Miller v. *California,* 148
Minorities. *See* Discrimination; Political parties; specific
    groups
Miranda v. *Arizona,* 138–139
Missouri ex rel. Gaines v. *Canada,* 50, 147
Mitchell, John, 465
Mondale, Walter, 302, 444–445, 458, 467, 511, 531
Moore, Frank, 458
Mormons, and First Amendment, 130

Mott, Stewart, 288
Moyers, Bill D., 251
Muskie, Edmund S., 298, 416

Nader, Ralph, 165, 353–354
National Anti-Saloon League, 40
National Association for the Advancement of Colored
  People (NAACP), 156, 180, 497
National Association of Manufacturers, 173, 353
National Conservative Political Action Committee
  (NCPAC), 291
National Farmers Union, 161, 172
National Grange, 161
National League of Cities v. *Usery,* 79, 82
National Organization of Women (NOW), 128, 249
National Rifle Association, 165
National Security Agency, 176
National Security Council, 401, 460–461
National Women's Political Caucus (NWPC), 262
Natural gas, 519, 530–534
Natural Gas Act (1938), 531
Near v. *Minnesota,* 148
Nelson, Gaylord, 285
New Deal, 100, 107, 197, 225, 260, 308
New York Times Co. v. *Sullivan,* 132
New York Times Co. v. *United States,* 148
Nineteenth Amendment, 123, 125–126
Ninth Amendment, 140–142
Nixon, Richard M. *See also* Watergate
  and abuse of power, 129–130
  and the bureaucracy, 498–499, 509–511
  and the Cabinet, 447
  and Congress, 176–177, 344, 354, 356, 402, 458
  and energy policy, 519, 522
  and 1968 election, 202, 258–259
  and 1972 election, 205, 206, 213, 243, 259, 285–288
  organizational style of, 454–455
  resignation and pardon of, 30–32, 42, 198, 427–430
  and revenue sharing, 71
  and the Supreme Court, 21, 97–98, 102, 109–110,
    375–376
  and Vietnam, 91
  and Watergate, 85, 90, 99, 163, 231–232, 246–247,
    251, 344, 374, 393–394, 408–409, 439
Nixon v. *Condon,* 147
Nixon v. *Herndon,* 147
North Atlantic Treaty Organization (NATO), 377–378,
  416, 418
Nuclear energy, 5, 536–538, 541

Obscenity, 134–136
Occupational Safety and Health Administration
  (OSHA), 493–494
O'Connor, Sandra Day, 95, 110
Office of Management and Budget (OMB), 371–373,
  446, 459–460, 491, 504–508, 511
Office of Personnel Management, 484, 486–487
Oil industry, 62–63, 161, 169, 526, 534–536, 538–539.
  See also Energy
O'Neill, Thomas P., Jr. (Tip), 344, 347, 353, 529–530,
  533
Oregon v. *Mitchell,* 126, 147

Organization of Petroleum Exporting Countries (OPEC),
  518, 520
Oriental Americans:
  as candidates for office, 264
  and *habeas corpus,* 142

Panama Canal treaties, 378, 416–417, 418–419
Paperwork Reduction Act (1980), 493
Park, Tongsun, 166, 328–329
Patrick, Luther, 332
Patronage. *See* Political parties
Peace Corps, 511
Pendleton Act (1883), 484
Pentagon Papers, 136–137, 163, 287, 394, 408, 439
Performance standards. *See* Federalism
Phillips, Cabell, 348
Pierce, Samuel Reilly, Jr., 449
Pike, Otis G., 347
Plessy v. *Ferguson,* 50, 118–119
Pluralism. *See* Interest groups
Poland, 6–7
Policy making, 383–384, 386, 388, 517–544
Polish Americans, voting behavior of, 261
Political action committees (PACs), 151, 169, 284,
  289–292
Political parties, 43, 189, 229
  as coalitions, 192, 198–199, 208, 225
  and competition, 204–205
  in Congress, 340–342, 358–369
  decentralized nature of, 192–194, 205–208
  differences between, 214–223
  and discipline, 192–194
  and energy policy, 522–541
  and federalism, 191, 206
  functions of, 191
  historical basis of, 195–198
  ideologies in, 217–221
  leaders of, 217–221
  local, 196, 209–212
  minor, 43, 194–195, 200–204
  national committees, 206–207, 209, 410
  national conventions, 300–303
  in office, 221–223
  and patronage, 209
  and personal politics, 207–209
  platforms, 217–218, 223, 301
  and presidential power, 206–207, 409–412
  and primaries, 278–280
  reform of, 224
  as responsible, 192–193, 223
  southern, 204–205
  state, 196, 204–206, 209–212
  structure of, 207–212
  and two-party system, 194–195
Political socialization, 245–249
Polk, James K., 202
Polls, 235–243, 259
Port of New York Authority, 182–183
Powell, Adam Clayton, 338–339
Powell, Jody, 456
Powell, Lewis, 98, 144–145
Powell v. *McCormack,* 338–339

Powers:
    concurrent, 57–59
    denied, 53–55
    exclusive, 33–34, 53–55, 63
    implied, 55–57
    reserved, 55
President, 393–434. *See also* specific presidents
    and abuse of power, 393–395, 408–409
    advisory system of, 403, 407, 439–473
    appointment power of, 20, 21, 30, 96–98, 108–111,
        375–376, 407
    behavior of, 400
    and the budget, 503–508
    and the Cabinet, 445–450
    as chief diplomat, 415–421
    as chief executive, 406–409
    as chief of state, 403–406
    as commander-in-chief, 376–377, 398–399, 401, 421–424
    and Congress, 319–323, 354–358, 406–408, 412–419,
        457–459, 500–501
    constitutional powers of, 395–397
    control of the bureaucracy, 464–465, 498–499
    and crises, 398–399, 401–402
    and decision making, 439–441
    discretion of, 42–43
    and domestic disorders, 423
    election of, 23, 43–48
    and executive agreements, 417–418
    Executive Office of the, 450–465, 509
    and executive privilege, 394, 408
    and foreign policy, 376–378, 432–433
    and foreign vs. domestic policy, 419–421
    frustrations of, 431–432
    implied powers of, 397–398
    and impoundment, 371–372, 394, 426–430
    isolation of, 454–455, 467–471
    as legislative leader, 412–415
    lobbying by, 176–177, 412–413
    as national representative, 401
    organizational styles of, 453–459
    pardoning power of, 42, 430
    as party chief, 409–412
    and policy making, 465–467
    powers of, 20, 400–402, 430–433
    and public opinion, 394–395
    roles of, 402–424
    and State of the Union Message, 33
    two-term limit of, 39, 109, 424–425
    types of, 396–397
    war powers of, 397–398
Presidential advisory system, 403, 407, 439–473, 498–499
    domestic policy staff, 461
    Executive Office of the President, 450–465
    and outside advice, 463–464
    White House Office, 453–459
Presidential bureaucracy. *See* Presidential advisory system
Presidential elections, 43–48, 273–315. *See also* specific years
Presidential Succession Act (1947), 43, 426
Presidential succession and disability, 39, 416, 425–426
Presidential Transition Act, 429–430
Pressure groups. *See* Interest groups; Single-issue politics
Price, Ray, 285

Primary elections, 278–280, 294–295
    and caucus, 297–299
    direct national, 300
    presidential, 294–300
    strategy in, 297–299
    types of, 279–280, 295–296
Privacy, right of, 141–142
Prohibition, 40
    repeal of, 39–40, 55
Protestants, voting behavior of, 260
Proxmire, William, 337
Public interest research groups (PIRGs), 165
Public opinion, 231–253. *See also* Polls; Interest groups;
        Voting behavior
    and Congress, 239–241, 243–245, 331
    definition of, 232–233
    and education, 247–248
    elements of, 235–239
    and energy, 521–522
    and families, 246–247
    non-survey measurement of, 243–245
    and the president, 394–395
    types of publics, 233–235
Public schools, prayer in, 100, 101
Public works programs, 10

Rafshoon, Gerald, 456
Ramspeck Act (1940), 484
Ray, Elizabeth, 329
Rayburn, Sam, 359
Reagan, Ronald:
    assassination attempt on, 3, 6, 243, 416,
        467
    and budget battle, 7, 39
    and the bureaucracy, 480, 493–494, 509–510
    and the Cabinet, 449–450
    and Congress, 409, 412, 458–459
    and domestic policy staff, 461
    and energy, 541
    and foreign policy, 377, 416–417
    and 1976 election, 46–47, 297, 299–300
    and 1980 election, 201, 221, 236, 258, 274, 293,
        298–299, 302, 305–306
    organizational style of, 446–447
    public image of, 406
    and vice-presidential selection, 442, 443
Reems, Harry, 135, 136
Regents of the University of California v. *Allan Bakke,* 143–146,
        148, 179
Rehnquist, William H., 99–100, 110
Reorganization Act (1949), 509
Republican Party. *See also* specific candidates and
        elections; Political parties
    national committee of, 206
    and 1980 platform, 274
    social characteristics of, 216–217
Revenue sharing, 39, 71–73
Reynolds v. *Sims,* 93–94, 101, 147
Richardson v. *Ramirez,* 147
Richmond, Fred D., 346
Rivers, L. Mendel, 176
Rockefeller, Nelson, 426, 442, 444

Chapter 4: p. 84, photo by Ellis Herwig/Stock, Boston; p. 86, photo by Wayne Miller/© Magnum Photos, Inc.; p. 90, photo © J.P. Laffont/Sygma; p. 95, photo by United Press International; p. 102, photo by United Press International; p. 105, photo © 1978 John J. Lopinot/Black Star; p. 108, photo by Arthur Grace/Stock, Boston.

Chapter 5: p. 114, photo © Peter Vilms/Jeroboam, Inc.; p. 119, photo © Cheryl A. Traendly/Jeroboam, Inc.; p. 121, photo by Michele Bogre/Sygma; p. 124, photo © Bettye Lane/Photo Researchers, Inc.; p. 128, © Suzanne Wu/Jeroboam, Inc.; p. 134, photo © Kent Reno 1978/Jeroboam, Inc.; p. 139, photo by United Press International; p. 140, photo by George W. Gardner.

Chapter 6: p. 150, photo by Nickelsberg/Liason Agency; p. 152, photo © Kay Lawson/Jeroboam, Inc.; p. 157, photo by United Press International; p. 162, photo © Lawrence Cameron/Jeroboam, Inc.; p. 164, photo by Mark Godfrey/© Magnum Photos, Inc.; p. 171, photo © 1978 Gil Kenney/Black Star; p. 178, photo by Burt Glinn/© Magnum Photos, Inc.; p. 181, photo © 1979 Jim Anderson/Black Star.

Chapter 7: p. 188, photo by Owen Franken/Stock, Boston; p. 191, photo by United Press International; p. 192, photo by United Press International; p. 192, photo © Alex Webb/Magnum Photos, Inc.; p. 197, photo © Richard Kalvar/Magnum Photos, Inc.; p. 198, photo © Charles Harbutt/Magnum Photos, Inc.; p. 200, photo by John Barr/Liason Agency; p. 211, photo © Rose Skytta/Jeroboam, Inc.; p. 214, photo by A. Maine/© Magnum Photos, Inc.; p. 220, photo by Arthur Grace/Sygma; p. 225, photo © Charles Harbutt/Magnum Photos, Inc.

Chapter 8: p. 230, photo by George W. Gardner; p. 233, photo by J.P. Laffont/Sygma; p. 235, photo by Paul S. Conklin; p. 237, Figure 8–1, Data from the *Gallup Opinion Index*, 183 (December 1980): 51. The Gallup Poll, Princeton, New Jersey 08540. By permission; p. 238, Figure 8–2, Data from the *Gallup Opinion Index*, 183 (December 1980): 13, 14. The Gallup Poll, Princeton, New Jersey 08540. By permission; p. 239, photo © Bohdan Hrynewych 1980/Stock, Boston; p. 245, photo by George W. Gardner; p. 246, photo by George W. Gardner; p. 250, photo by Elliott Erwitt/© Magnum Photos, Inc.; p. 254, Figure 8–3, For presidential election years 1824–1968, the data were compiled by Walter Dean Burnham, and may be found in the extension of remarks by Congressman Morris Udall, in the *Congressional Record* (December 11, 1970): E10313–14. Data for other elections are from U.S. Bureau of the Census, *Statistical Abstract of the United States, 1979*, Table 835, p. 513. For 1980, from Martin Plissner and Warren Mitofsky, "What if They Held an Election and Nobody Came?" *Public Opinion* 4 (February/March 1981): 50; p. 255, photo by George W. Gardner/Stock, Boston; p. 262, photo by United Press International.

Chapter 9: p. 272, photo by Mark Godfrey/© Magnum Photos, Inc.; p. 275, photo by United Press International; p. 284, photo by Wide World Photos; p. 290, Figure 9–3, *Election '80* (Washington, D.C.: Congressional Quarterly, Inc., 1980), p. 134. Reprinted with the permission of Congressional Quarterly, Inc. Data is from Federal Election Commission reports; p. 296, top left photo by Wide World Photos; p. 296, top middle photo © 1980 Roger Sandler/Black Star; p. 296, top right photo by Wide World Photos; p. 296, bottom left photo © 1980 Dennis Brack/Black Star; p. 296, bottom right photo by Michael Evans/Liason Agency; p. 298, photo by Jean-Louis Atlan/Sygma; p. 306, photo © 1980 Dennis Brack/Black Star.

Chapter 10: p. 318, photo by Hartmann/© Magnum Photos, Inc.; p. 321, photo by Ellis Herwig/Stock, Boston; p. 329, photo by United Press International; p. 333, photo © Sepp Seitz/Magnum Photos, Inc.; p. 536, photo by Jim Pozarik/Liason Agency; p. 343, photo by United Press International; p. 348, photo by United Press International.

Chapter 11: p. 352, photo by Alex Webb/© Magnum Photos, Inc.; p. 355, photo by United Press International; p. 367, photo © Dennis Brack 1980/Black Star; pp. 370–371, Figure 11–1, Adapted from David J. Vogler, *The Politics of Congress*, 2d ed. (Boston: Allyn and Bacon, Inc., 1977), pp. 193–195; p. 372, photo © Michael Rothstein/Jeroboam, Inc.; p. 375, photo by United Press International; p. 380, photo by Margaret Heckler; p. 387, photo by Cary Wolinsky/Stock, Boston.

Chapter 12: p. 392, photo by Wide World Photos; p. 393, Hughes quote, reprinted by permission of Coward, McCann & Geoghegau, Inc. from *The Living Presidency* by Emmet John Hughes. Copyright © 1973 by Emmet John Hughes; p. 399, photo by Peter Menzel/Stock, Boston; p. 404, photo by Wide World Photos; p. 411, top left photo by United Press International; p. 411, top right photo by United Press International; p. 411, bottom left photo by Wide World Photos; p. 411, bottom right photo by Tony Korody/Sygma; p. 418, photo © 1979 Sipa Press/Black Star; p. 420, photo by United Press International; p. 423, insert reprinted by permission of Coward, McCann & Geoghegau, Inc. from *The Living Presidency* by Emmet John Hughes. Copyright © 1973 by Emmet John Hughes; p. 429, photo by Jacques Tizion/Sygma; pp. 431, 432, and 433, Hughes quotes, reprinted by permission of Coward, McCann & Geoghegan, Inc. from *The Living Presidency* by Emmet John Hughes. Copyright © 1973 by Emmet John Hughes.

Chapter 13: p. 438, photo by Cornell Capa/© Magnum Photos, Inc.; p. 441, photo by Wide World Photos; p. 444, photo by J. Cunieres/Gamma-Liason; p. 447, photo by Wide World Photos; p. 449, photo © 1980 Dennis Brack/Black Star; p. 450, Figure 13-1, *U.S. Government Manual, 1980–81,* p. 98; p. 451, Figure 13-2, Roosevelt through Nixon, data from Howard E. McCurdy, "The Physical Manifestations of an Expanding Presidency," paper presented at the 1974 annual meeting of the American Political Science Association, Chicago, Illinois, August 29–September 2, 1974, p. 27. Data on Ford from the *Budget of the U.S. Government, Fiscal 1978,* pp. 811–812. Data on Carter from *The Budget, Fiscal 1981,* pp. 1006–1007; p. 452, Figure 13-3, Roosevelt through Nixon, data from Howard E. McCurdy, "The Physical Manifestations of an Expanding Presidency," paper presented at the 1974 annual meeting of the American Political Science Association, Chicago, Illinois, August 29–September 2, 1974, p. 7. Data on Ford from *The Budget of the U.S. Government, Fiscal Year 1978,* p. 811. Data on Carter from *The Budget, Fiscal Year 1981,* p. 1006; p. 453, insert reprinted by permission of Coward, McCann & Geoghegau, Inc. from *The Living Presidency* by Emmet John Hughes. Copyright © 1973 by Emmet John Hughes; p. 454, photo by United Press International; p. 460, photo by Jean-Claude Labbe/Gamma-Liason; p. 468, Hughes quote, reprinted by permission of Coward, McCann & Geoghegau, Inc. from *The Living Presidency* by Emmet John Hughes. Copyright © 1973 by Emmet John Hughes; p. 462, photo by Daniel S.

Brody/Stock, Boston; p. 469, photo on the left by Wide World Photos; p. 469, photo on the right by Owen Franken/Liason Agency; p. 470, Hughes quote, reprinted by permission of Coward, McCann & Geoghegau, Inc. from *The Living Presidency* by Emmet John Hughes. Copyright © 1973 by Emmet John Hughes.

Chapter 14: p. 474, photo by George W. Gardner; p. 477, photo by Paul S. Conklin; p. 481, Figure 14-1, *U.S. Government Manual, 1980–81,* p. 32; p. 482, Figure 14-2, *U.S. Government Manual, 1980–81,* p. 294; p. 484, photo by Patricia Hollander Gross/Stock, Boston; p. 488, photo © E. Budd Gray 1980/Jeroboam, Inc.; p. 494, photo by Cary Wolinsky/Stock, Boston; p. 496, photo by Donald Dietz/Stock, Boston; p. 502, photo by Art Seitz/Gamma-Liason; p. 504, Figure 14-3, *Fiscal Year 1982 Budget Revisions,* March 1981, pp. 122, 125; p. 505, Figure 14-4, Data from the Office of Management and Budget; p. 507, Figure 14-5, Executive Office of the President/Office of Management and Budget, January 1977; p. 509, photo by Leonard Freed/© Magnum Photos, Inc.

Chapter 15: p. 516, photo by George W. Gardner; p. 518, photo by Daniem Simon/Gamma-Liason; p. 520, photo by George W. Gardner; p. 523, top photo by Grumman/U.S. Department of Energy; p. 523, bottom photo by U.S. Department of Agriculture; p. 528, "The Summer of '73" a political cartoon by Paul Szep. Reprinted courtesy of the *Boston Globe;* p. 536, photo by Jean-Louis Atlan/Sygma; p. 538, photo by Abbas, Mingam, Artaut, Wildenberg/Gamma-Liason.